FIFTEENTH EDITION

Patterns for College Writing

A RHETORICAL READER AND GUIDE

Laurie G. Kirszner
University of the Sciences, Emeritus

Stephen R. Mandell
Drexel University

bedford/st.martin's
Macmillan Learning
Boston | New York

For Peter Phelps, 1936–1990, with thanks

For Bedford/St. Martin's
Vice President: Leasa Burton
Program Director: Stacey Purviance
Senior Program Manager: John E. Sullivan III
Director of Content Development: Jane Knetzger
Executive Development Manager: Susan McLaughlin
Senior Development Editor: Jesse Hassenger
Editorial Assistant: Samantha Storms
Director of Media Editorial: Adam Whitehurst
Associate Media Editor: Daniel Johnson
Marketing Manager: Amy Haines
Marketing Assistant: Cecilia McGuiness
Director, Content Management Enhancement: Tracey Kuehn
Senior Managing Editor: Lisa Kinne
Senior Content Project Manager: Edward Dionne
Senior Workflow Project Manager: Jennifer Wetzel
Production Supervisor: Brianna Lester
Director of Design, Content Management: Diana Blume
Interior Design: Richard Korab
Cover Design: William Boardman
Art Manager: Matthew McAdams
Director of Rights and Permissions: Hilary Newman
Text Permissions Researcher: Elaine Kosta, Lumina Datamatics, Inc.
Photo Permissions Editor: Angela Boehler
Photo Researcher: Krystyna Borgen, Lumina Datamatics, Inc.
Director of Digital Production: Keri deManigold
Media Project Manager: Allison Hart
Composition: Lumina Datamatics, Inc.
Cover Image: sbelov/Getty Images
Printing and Binding: LSC Communications

Library of Congress Control Number: 2020939174
ISBN 978-1-319-24379-1 (Student Edition)
ISBN 978-1-319-33026-2 (Loose-leaf Edition)

Printed in the United States of America.

1 2 3 4 5 6   25 24 23 22 21 20

Acknowledgments
Text acknowledgments and copyrights appear at the back of the book on pages 779–82, which constitute an extension of the copyright page. Art acknowledgments and copyrights appear on the same page as the art selections they cover.

At the time of publication all Internet URLs published in this text were found to accurately link to their intended website. If you do find a broken link, please forward the information to sherry.mooney@macmillan.com so that it can be corrected for the next printing.

For information, write: Bedford/St. Martin's, 75 Arlington Street, Boston, MA 02116

PREFACE

Since it was first published, *Patterns for College Writing* has been used by millions of students at colleges and universities across the United States. We are continually gratified by positive feedback from the many instructors who tell us that it is the most accessible and pedagogically sound rhetoric-reader they have used. For the fifteenth edition of *Patterns*, we have worked to retain everything that makes this book such a popular composition reader while updating it throughout to enhance its usefulness for both instructors and students, adding engaging new readings and visuals as well as coverage of additional topics, including working with sources.

What's New in This Edition

Engaging New Readings

More than two dozen new professional essays offer perspectives on a variety of topics that students will find meaningful. For example, Farhad Manjoo explains why he wants people to call "Call Me 'They,'" Mindy Kaling explores the tropes and formulas around "Flick Chicks: A Guide to Women in the Movies," and Ray Fisman and Michael Luca ask "Did Free Pens Cause the Opioid Crisis?" In all cases, readings have been carefully selected for their high-interest subject matter as well as for their diverse voices, accessible writing style, and effectiveness as teachable models for student writing.

More Visual Texts

Patterns for College Writing now boosts its already-strong coverage of visual texts with visual arguments added to both casebooks in Chapter 14, "Argumentation," providing students with more instruction on how to read and write about the kinds of images they are likely to encounter in their everyday lives. The visual texts throughout the rest of the book have also been updated, and alongside thought-provoking photographs, we offer engaging graphic art from acclaimed creators like Alison Bechdel, Matt Groening, and Marjane Satrapi.

New Student Essays

Two brand-new student essays, "Steps to the Dream" and "Food Insecurity on Campus," address two topics that resonate across college campuses: how students can secure a paid internship and how students in need can access enough food to remain healthy and productive. Additional student sample essays are also available in our Student Companion text.

Additional Coverage of Working with Sources

Chapter 16, "Working with Sources," now includes expanded coverage of doing research (both in the library and online) and evaluating sources. The chapter also includes a number of new tools that students can use to help them think critically about the sources they consult as they plan and write their essays.

Writing and Revision with Achieve

A new digital composition space paired with content you trust, Achieve with *Patterns for College Writing* helps you engage students in new ways and build an active writers' community in your class. Developed to support best practices in commenting on drafts — and co-designed with teachers and students from across the country — Achieve is a flexible, integrated suite of tools for designing and facilitating writing assignments, with actionable insights that make students' progress toward outcomes clear and measurable. It includes prebuilt, fully customizable assignments that support the book's approach; a peer review tool that helps students use feedback productively; reflection prompts to facilitate transfer of learning to other writing assignments; Source Check software that alerts writers to potential originality issues; and more.

What Instructors and Students Like about *Patterns for College Writing*

An Emphasis on Critical Reading

The Introduction, "How to Use This Book," and Chapter 1, "Reading to Write: Becoming a Critical Reader," prepare students to become analytical readers and writers by showing them how to apply critical reading strategies to a typical selection and by providing sample responses to the various kinds of writing prompts in the book. Not only does this material introduce students to the book's features, but it also prepares them to tackle reading and writing assignments in their other courses.

Extensive Coverage of the Writing Process

The remaining chapters in Part One, "The Writing Process," are a "mini-rhetoric," offering advice on drafting, writing, revising, and editing as they introduce students to activities such as freewriting, brainstorming, clustering, and journal writing. These chapters (Chapters 2 through 5) also include numerous writing exercises to give students opportunities for immediate practice.

Detailed Coverage of the Patterns of Development

In Part Two, "Readings for Writers," Chapters 6 through 15 explain and illustrate the patterns of development that students typically use in their college writing assignments: narration, description, exemplification, process, cause and effect, comparison and contrast, classification and division, definition, and argumentation. Each chapter begins with a comprehensive introduction that presents a definition and a paragraph-length example of the pattern to be discussed and then explains the particular writing strategies and applications associated with it. Next, each chapter analyzes one or two annotated student essays to show how the pattern can be used in particular college writing situations. Chapter 15, "Combining the Patterns," illustrates how the various patterns of development discussed in Chapters 6 through 14 can work together in an essay.

A Diverse and Popular Selection of Readings

Varied in subject, style, and cultural perspective, the sixty-eight professional selections engage students while providing them with outstanding models for writing. We have tried to achieve a balance between classic authors (such as George Orwell, Jessica Mitford, Martin Luther King Jr.) and newer voices (such as Trevor Noah and Mindy Kaling) so that instructors have a broad choice of readings.

More Student Essays Than Any Comparable Text

To provide students with realistic models for improving their own writing, we include eighteen sample student essays.

Helpful Coverage of Grammar Issues

Grammar in Context boxes in chapter introductions offer specific advice on how to identify and correct the grammar, mechanics, and punctuation problems that students are most likely to encounter when they work with particular patterns of development.

Apparatus Designed to Help Students Learn

Each professional essay in the text is followed by three types of questions. These questions are designed to help students assess their understanding of the essay's content and of the writer's purpose and audience, to recognize the stylistic and structural techniques used to shape the essay, and to become sensitive to the nuances of language. Each essay is also accompanied by a Journal Entry prompt, Writing Workshop topics (suggestions for full-length writing assignments), and Thematic Connections that identify related readings in the text. Also following each essay is a Combining the Patterns feature that focuses on different patterns of development used in the essay and possible alternatives to these patterns. Each chapter ends with a list of Writing Assignments and a Collaborative Activity. Many of these assignments and activities have been updated to reflect the most current topics and trends.

Extensive Cultural and Historical Background for All Readings

In addition to a biographical headnote, each reading is preceded by a headnote containing essential background information to help students make connections between the reading and the historical, social, and economic forces that shaped it.

An Introduction to Visual Texts

Every rhetorical chapter includes a visual text — such as a photograph, a piece of fine art, or panels from a graphic novel — that provides an accessible introduction to each rhetorical pattern, and Chapter 14, "Argumentation," now includes multiple visual texts. Apparatus that helps students discuss the pattern in its visual form follows each image.

Thorough Coverage of Working with Sources

Part Three, "Working with Sources," takes students through the process of writing a research paper and includes a model student paper in MLA style. (The Appendix addresses APA style and includes a model APA paper.)

Bedford/St. Martin's Puts You First

From day one, our goal has been simple: to provide inspiring resources that are grounded in best practices for teaching reading and writing. For more than forty years, Bedford/St. Martin's has partnered with the field, listening to teachers, scholars, and students about the support writers need. We are committed to helping every writing instructor make the most of our resources.

How Can We Help *You*?

- Our editors can align our resources to your outcomes through correlation and transition guides for your syllabus. Just ask us.
- Our sales representatives specialize in helping you find the right materials to support your course goals.
- Our learning solutions and product specialists help you make the most of the digital resources you choose for your course.
- Our *Bits* blog on the Bedford/St. Martin's English Community (**community.macmillan.com**) publishes fresh teaching ideas weekly. You will also find easily downloadable professional resources and links to author webinars on our community site.

Contact your Bedford/St. Martin's sales representative or visit **macmillanlearning.com** to learn more.

Print and Digital Options for *Patterns for College Writing*

Choose the format that works best for your course, and ask about our packaging options that offer savings for students.

Print

- *Paperback.* To order the paperback edition, use ISBN 978-1-319-24379-1. To order the paperback packaged with Achieve, use ISBN 978-1-319-39674-9.
- *Loose-leaf edition.* This format does not have a traditional binding; its pages are loose and hole punched to provide flexibility and a lower price to students. It can be packaged with Achieve for additional savings. To order the loose-leaf edition packaged with Achieve, use ISBN 978-1-319-39743-2.
- *Student Companion.* For students who need a little extra support, *A Student's Companion for Patterns for College Writing* reinforces the most foundational elements in academic writing. While recognizing and respecting students' abilities, this supplement breaks down the steps necessary to excel in college writing. The second edition of this companion volume has been updated to add what instructors have asked us for: more grammar coverage, more sample student papers, and more hands-on practice in the processes of writing and rewriting. To order the paperback packaged with the Student Companion, use ISBN 978-1-319-39742-5.

Digital

- *Achieve with Patterns for College Writing.* Achieve puts student writing at the center of your course and keeps revision at the core, with a dedicated composition space that guides students through drafting, peer review, source check, reflection, and revision. Developed to support best practices in commenting on student drafts, Achieve is a flexible, integrated suite of tools for designing and facilitating writing assignments paired with actionable insights that make students' progress toward outcomes clear and measurable. Fully editable prebuilt assignments support the book's approach, and an e-book is included. For details, visit **macmillanlearning.com/college/us/englishdigital**.
- *Popular e-book formats.* For details about our e-book partners, visit **macmillanlearning.com/ebooks**.
- *Inclusive Access.* Enable every student to receive course materials through your LMS on the first day of class. Macmillan Learning's Inclusive Access program is the easiest and most affordable way to ensure that all students have access to quality educational resources. Find out more at **macmillanlearning.com/inclusiveaccess**.

Your Course, Your Way

No two writing programs or classrooms are exactly alike. Our Curriculum Solutions team works with you to design custom options that provide the resources your students need. (Options below require enrollment minimums.)

- *ForeWords for English.* Customize any print resource to fit the focus of your course or program by choosing from a range of prepared topics, such as Sentence Guides for Academic Writers.

- *Macmillan Author Program (MAP).* Add excerpts or package acclaimed works from Macmillan's trade imprints to connect students with prominent authors and public conversations. A list of popular examples or academic themes is available upon request.

- *Mix and Match.* With our simplest solution, you can add up to 50 pages of curated content to your Bedford/St. Martin's text. Contact your sales representative for additional details.
- *Bedford Select.* Build your own print anthology from a database of more than 800 selections, or build a handbook and add your own materials to create your ideal text. Package with any Bedford/St. Martin's text for additional savings. Visit **macmillanlearning.com/bedfordselect**.

Instructor Resources

You have a lot to do in your course. We want to make it easy for you to find the support you need — and to get it quickly.

Resources for Instructors Using Patterns for College Writing is available as a PDF that can be downloaded from **macmillanlearning.com** and is also available in Achieve. In addition to chapter overviews and teaching tips, the instructor's manual includes sample syllabi, correlations to the Council of Writing Program Administrators' Outcomes Statement, classroom activities, and possible responses to every discussion question in the book.

Acknowledgments

As always, friends, colleagues, students, and family all helped this project along. Of particular value were the responses to the questionnaires sent to the following instructors, who provided frank and helpful advice: Melanie Abrams, Florida A&M University; Susan Achziger, Community College of Aurora; Stacey Berry, Dakota State University; Crystal Calhoun, West Georgia Technical College; Edward Dawley, Delaware State University; Betsy Delle-Bovi, Canisius College; Jennifer Elbe, Cleveland State Community College; Douglas Ford, State College of Florida; Julie Gibson, Greenville Technical College; Ken Haley, Paris Junior College; Amy Hankins, Gateway Technical

College; Marie Hendry, State College of Florida—Venice; Adella Irizarry, Palm Beach State College; Jay Johnson, Gateway Technical College; Leah Johnson, University of South Arkansas; Kristie Kemper, Georgia Highlands College; Kamisha Kirby, South Piedmont Community College; John Lusk, St. Clair County Community College; Amberyl Malkovich, Concord University; Erin McConomy, North Island College; Thomas McEahcin, Laredo College; Josh Miller, Cape Fear Community College; Theodore Rollins, Johnson County Community College; Bradlee Ross, Connors State College; Cheryl Saba, Cape Fear Community College; Anton Smith, Massachusetts Maritime Academy; Christopher Syrewicz, Arizona State University; Rachel Wall, Georgia Highlands College; Coreen Wees, Iowa Western Community College; Steve Werkmeister, Johnson County Community College; and Josephine Yu, Keiser University.

Special thanks go to Jeff Ousborne for his help with some of the apparatus and for revising the headnotes and the *Resources for Instructors*.

Through fifteen editions of *Patterns for College Writing*, we have enjoyed a wonderful working relationship with Bedford/St. Martin's. We have always found the editorial and production staff to be efficient, cooperative, and generous with their time and advice. During our work on this edition, we have benefited from our productive relationship with Karita dos Santos, senior program manager, who helped us make this edition of *Patterns* the best it could be. We are also grateful to Jesse Hassenger, senior development editor, and Edward Dionne, senior content project manager, for their work overseeing the production of this edition; William Boardman for the attractive new cover; and editorial assistant Samantha Storms for her invaluable help with tasks large and small. We are fortunate to have enjoyed our long and fulfilling collaboration; we know how rare a successful partnership like ours is. We also know how lucky we are to have our families to help keep us in touch with the things that really matter.

Laurie G. Kirszner
Stephen R. Mandell

CONTENTS

PART TWO: Readings for Writers 95

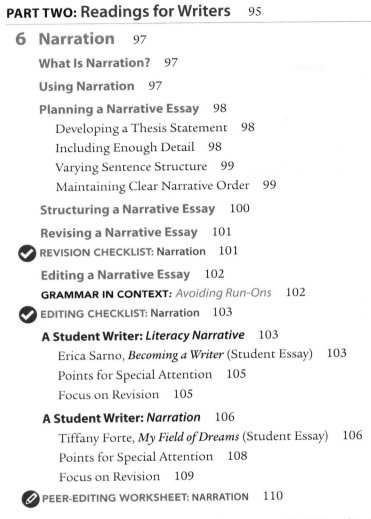
"The summer I was twelve, my family went away on a 'vacation' — one of my father's half-baked get-to-know-our-country-better-by-sleeping-in-the-van extravaganzas — and when we returned to Jersey, exhausted, battered, we found our front door unlocked. . . . The thieves had kept it simple; they'd snatched a portable radio, some of my Dungeons & Dragons hardcovers, and, of course, Mami's remittances."

"I knew the warnings from my father: Don't go on a run at night, don't reach into your pockets too quickly, be polite in front of them. And

I had seen the police make life difficult for other people in my home neighborhood, and yet I never learned to be afraid."

"From her wheelchair she canned pickles, baked bread, ironed clothes, wrote dozens of letters weekly to her friends and her 'half dozen or more kids,' and made three patchwork housecoats and one quilt."

"For more than half an hour thirty-eight respectable, law-abiding citizens in Queens watched a killer stalk and stab a woman in three separate attacks. . . . Not one person telephoned the police during the assault; one witness called after the woman was dead."

"But I did not want to shoot the elephant. I watched him beating his bunch of grass against his knees, with the preoccupied grandmotherly air that elephants have. It seemed to me that it would be murder to shoot him."

"But my friend Sergio and I, we solved junior high school. We would come home from school on the bus, put our books away, change shoes, and go across the street to the arroyo. It was the one place we were not supposed to go. So we did."

"We were running out of breath, as we ran out to meet ourselves."

"For me, a child of Vietnamese immigrants growing up in Michigan in the 1980s, Twinkies were a ticket to assimilation: the golden cake, more golden than the hair I wished I had, filled with sweet white cream. Back then, junk foods seemed to represent an ideal of American indulgence."

"For the millions of people who lived in Soweto there were no stores, no bars, no restaurants. There were no paved roads, minimal electricity, inadequate sewerage. But when you put one million people together in one place, they find a way to make a life for themselves."

"My car was not gross; it was occupied, cluttered, cramped. It became an extension of my bedroom, and thus an extension of myself."

"There's a reason landfills are tucked away, on the edge of town, in otherwise untraveled terrain, camouflaged by hydroseeded, neatly tiered slopes. If people saw what happened to their waste, lived with the stench, witnessed the scale of destruction, they might start asking difficult questions."

"We never paid for cable. The photographs weren't of my family. The carpet I vacuumed I only saw once a week, and the pastel shirts I folded I never wore. The house wasn't mine. My mother was only the cleaning lady, and I helped."

"Pity the poor software designers (and, undoubtedly, lawyers) who are trying to figure this out, because it can get much more complicated. What if a pedestrian acted recklessly, or even stepped out in front of the car with the intention of making it swerve, thereby killing the passenger? (Hollywood screenwriters, start your engines.)"

"[Y]ou can leave the island, master the English language, and travel as far as you can, but if you are a Latina, especially one like me who so obviously belongs to Rita Moreno's gene pool, the island travels with you."

"It was in the echo of that terrified woman's footfalls that I first began to know the unwieldy inheritance I'd come into — the ability to alter public space in ugly ways."

"So why does standard English impose a gender requirement on the third-person singular? And why do elite cultural institutions — universities, publishers, and media outlets like *The Times* — still encourage all this gendering?"

"And though emotions are themselves critical to making rational decisions, they were designed for a world in which dangers took the form of predators, not pollutants. Our emotions push us to make snap judgments that once were sensible — but may not be anymore."

"[T]his is how to bully a man; this is how a man bullies you; this is how to love a man, and if this doesn't work there are other ways, and if they don't work don't feel too bad about giving up. . . ."

"The most alarming of all man's assaults upon the environment is the contamination of air, earth, rivers, and sea with dangerous and even lethal materials. This pollution is for the most part irrecoverable; the chain of evil it initiates not only in the world that must support life but in living tissues is for the most part irreversible."

"For years now I have heard the word 'Wait!' It rings in the ear of every Negro with piercing familiarity. This 'Wait' has almost always meant 'Never.' We must come to see, with one of our distinguished jurists, that 'justice too long delayed is justice denied.'"

"If loan forgiveness becomes universal, students who made those smart financial decisions, ensuring they make their loan payments on time, will be given the same benefit as students who went to the most expensive university and have defaulted on their loan payments every month."

"In America today, 44 million people collectively carry $1.4 trillion in student debt. That giant pile of financial obligations isn't just a burden on individual borrowers, but on the nation's entire economy."

"Research on social behavior suggests lifestyle change can build momentum for systemic change. Humans are social animals, and we use social cues to recognize emergencies."

"These are people who, unlike the average individual, actually have the power to create the kinds of policy changes needed to avert the worst of climate change."

"Universities must educate our students to understand that academic freedom is not a law of nature. It is not something to be taken for granted.

It is, rather, a hard-won acquisition in a lengthy struggle for academic integrity."

"Racist hate speech has been linked to cigarette smoking, high blood pressure, anxiety, depression, and post-traumatic stress disorder, and requires complex coping strategies."

"Civic discourse in this country has become pretty ugly, so maybe it's not surprising that students are trying to create ways to have compassionate, civil dialogue."

"Even if they did work, how would we go about issuing them for all possible triggers? Different people have different triggers, which are based on personal experiences and may or may not be connected to what the average person considers disturbing or explicit."

"America doesn't have a monopoly on racism, sexism, other kinds of bigotry, mental illness, or violent video games. All of those things exist in countries across the world, many with much less gun violence. What is unique about the US is that it makes it so easy for people with any motive or problem to obtain a gun."

"The most effective way to tackle our national problem is to stop thinking of gun control as a political battle and instead see gun violence as a public-health issue."

"To shift the supply and demand dynamics of firearms in America, and thereby reduce gun violence, what if somebody acquired every handgun manufacturer in America? And what if that somebody were the federal government?"

"If all this sounds too horrifically familiar—an estranged loner, an AR-15, dozens dead in a matter of minutes—there is a remarkable twist to the story. In the wake of the Port Arthur massacre, Australian lawmakers did something about it."

15   Combining the Patterns   659

THEMATIC GUIDE TO THE CONTENTS

Business and Work

Race and Culture

Gender

Nature and the Environment

Media and Society

History and Politics

Ethics

Citizenship

Science and Health

Introduction: How to Use This Book

Patterns for College Writing is a book of readings, but it is also a book about writing. Every reading selection is followed by questions and exercises designed to help you become a thoughtful and proficient writer. The study questions that accompany the readings encourage you to think critically about writers' ideas. Although some of the questions (particularly those listed under **Comprehension**) call for fairly straightforward, factual responses, other questions (particularly the **Journal Entry** assignments) invite more complex responses that reflect your individual reaction to the selections.

The essay that begins on the following page, " 'What's in a Name?' " by Henry Louis Gates Jr., is typical of those that appear in this book. It is preceded by a **headnote** that gives readers information about the author's life and career. This headnote includes a **background** section that provides a social, historical, and cultural context for the essay.

HENRY LOUIS GATES JR.

"What's in a Name?"

Henry Louis Gates Jr. was born in 1950 in Keyser, West Virginia, and grew up in the small town of Piedmont. Currently Alphonse Fletcher University Professor and director of the Hutchins Center for African and African American Research at Harvard University, he has edited many collections of works by African American writers and published several volumes of literary criticism. He is probably best known as a social critic whose books and articles for a general audience explore a wide variety of issues and themes, often focusing on race and culture, and as the host of *Finding Your Roots*, a popular PBS television series. In the following essay, which originally appeared in the journal *Dissent*, Gates recalls a childhood experience that occurred during the mid-1950s.

Background on the civil rights movement In the mid-1950s, the first stirrings of the civil rights movement were under way, and in 1954 and 1955, the U.S. Supreme Court handed down decisions declaring racial segregation unconstitutional in public schools. Still, much of the United States — particularly the South — remained largely segregated until Congress passed the Civil Rights Act of 1964, which prohibited discrimination based on race, color, religion, or national origin in businesses (including restaurants and theaters) covered by interstate commerce laws and in employment. This legislation was followed by the Voting Rights Act of 1965, which guaranteed equal access to the polls, and the Civil Rights Act of 1968, which prohibited discrimination in housing and real estate. At the time of the experience Gates recalls here — before these laws were enacted — prejudice and discrimination against African Americans were the norm in many communities, including those outside the South.

The question of color takes up much space in these pages,
but the question of color, especially in this country, operates
to hide the graver questions of the self.

— JAMES BALDWIN, 1961

... blood, darky, Tar Baby, Kaffir, shine ... moor,
blackamoor, Jim Crow, spook ... quadroon, meriney,
red bone, high yellow ... Mammy, porch monkey, home,
homeboy, George ... spearchucker, schwarze, Leroy,
Smokey ... mouli, buck. Ethiopian, brother, sistah.

— TREY ELLIS, 1989

I had forgotten the incident completely, until I read Trey Ellis's essay 1
"Remember My Name" in a recent issue of the *Village Voice* (June 13, 1989). But there, in the middle of an extended italicized list of the bynames of "the race" ("the race" or "our people" being the terms my parents used in polite or

reverential discourse, "jigaboo" or "nigger" more commonly used in anger, jest, or pure disgust), it was: "George." Now the events of that very brief exchange return to mind so vividly that I wonder why I had forgotten it.

My father and I were walking home at dusk from his second job. He "moon- 2 lighted" as a janitor in the evenings for the telephone company. Every day but Saturday, he would come home at 3:30 from his regular job at the paper mill, wash up, eat supper, then at 4:30 head downtown to his second job. He used to make jokes frequently about a union official who moonlighted. I never got the joke, but he and his friends thought it was hilarious. All I knew was that my family always ate well, that my brother and I had new clothes to wear, and that all of the white people in Piedmont, West Virginia, treated my parents with an odd mixture of resentment and respect that even we understood at the time had something directly to do with a small but certain measure of financial security.

He had left a little early that evening because I was with him and I had to 3 be in bed early. I could not have been more than five or six, and we had stopped off at the Cut-Rate Drug Store (where no Black person in town but my father could sit down to eat, and eat off real plates with real silverware) so that I could buy some caramel ice cream, two scoops in a wafer cone, please, which I was busy licking when Mr. Wilson walked by.

Mr. Wilson was a very quiet man, whose stony, brooding, silent manner 4 seemed designed to scare off any overtures of friendship, even from white peo- ple. He was Irish, as was one-third of our village (another third being Italian), the more affluent among whom sent their children to "Catholic School" across the bridge in Maryland. He had white straight hair, like my Uncle Joe, whom he uncannily resembled, and he carried a black worn metal lunch pail, the kind that Riley* carried on the television show. My father always spoke to him, and for reasons that we never did understand, he always spoke to my father.

"Hello, Mr. Wilson," I heard my father say.　　5

"Hello, George."　　6

I stopped licking my ice cream cone, and asked my Dad in a loud voice why 7 Mr. Wilson had called him "George."

"Doesn't he know your name, Daddy? Why don't you tell him your name? Your name isn't George."

> "Doesn't he know your name, Daddy? Why don't you tell 9 him your name? Your name isn't George. . . ."

For a moment I tried to think of who Mr. Wilson was mixing Pop up with. But we didn't have any Georges among the colored people in Piedmont; nor were there colored Georges living in the neighboring towns and working at the mill.

"Tell him your name, Daddy."　　10

"He knows my name, boy," my father said after a long pause. "He calls all 11 colored people George."

---

* Eds. note — The lead character in the 1950s television program *The Life of Riley*, about a white working-class family and their neighbors.

A long silence ensued. It was "one of those things," as my Mom would put   12
it. Even then, that early, I knew when I was in the presence of "one of those
things," one of those things that provided a glimpse, through a rent curtain, at
another world that we could not affect but that affected us. There would be a
painful moment of silence, and you would wait for it to give way to a discussion of a Black superstar such as Sugar Ray or Jackie Robinson.

"Nobody hits better in a clutch than Jackie Robinson."   13

"That's right. Nobody."   14

I never again looked Mr. Wilson in the eye.   15

• • •

Responding to an Essay

The study questions that follow each essay will help you **think critically**
about what you are reading; they will help you formulate questions and draw
conclusions. (Critical thinking and reading are discussed in Chapter 1 of this
book.) Four types of questions follow each essay:

- *Comprehension* questions help you assess your understanding of what
  the writer is saying.
- *Purpose and Audience* questions ask you to consider why, and for whom,
  each selection was written and to examine the implications of the writer's choices in light of a particular purpose or intended audience.
- *Style and Structure* questions encourage you to examine the decisions
  the writer has made about elements such as arrangement of ideas,
  paragraphing, sentence structure, and imagery. One question in this
  category, designated **Vocabulary Project**, focuses on word choice and
  connotation.
- *Journal Entry* assignments ask you to write a short, informal response
  to what you read and to speculate freely about related ideas, perhaps
  by exploring ethical issues raised by the selection or by offering your
  opinions about the writer's statements. Briefer, less polished, and less
  structured than full-length essays, journal entries may suggest ideas
  for more formal kinds of writing.

Following these sets of questions are three additional features:

- *Writing Workshop* assignments ask you to write essays structured according to the pattern of development explained and illustrated in the chapter. Some of these assignments, designated **Working with Sources**, will
  ask you to refer to a particular essay in the book or to an outside source.
  In these cases, you will be reminded to include parenthetical documentation and a works-cited page that conform to MLA documentation style.
- *Combining the Patterns* questions focus on the various patterns of
  development — other than the essay's dominant pattern — that the
  writer uses. These questions ask why a writer uses particular patterns
  (narration, description, exemplification, process, cause and effect,

comparison and contrast, classification and division, definition, and argumentation), what each pattern contributes to the essay, and what other choices the writer might have had.

• *Thematic Connections* identify other readings in this book that explore similar themes. Reading these related works will enhance your understanding and appreciation of the original work and perhaps give you material to write about.

Following are some examples of study questions and possible responses, as well as a **Writing Workshop** assignment, a **Combining the Patterns** prompt, and a list of **Thematic Connections**, for " 'What's in a Name?' " (page 2). The numbers in parentheses after quotations refer to the paragraphs in which the quotations appear.

Comprehension

1. *In paragraph 1, Gates wonders why he forgot about the exchange between his father and Mr. Wilson. Why do you think he forgot about it?*

   Gates may have forgotten about the incident simply because it was something that happened a long time ago or because such incidents were commonplace when he was a child. Alternatively, he may *not* have forgotten the exchange between his father and Mr. Wilson but instead pushed it out of his mind because he found it so painful. (After all, he says he never again looked Mr. Wilson in the eye.)

2. *How is the social status of Gates's family different from that of other African American families in Piedmont, West Virginia? How does Gates account for this difference?*

   Gates's family is different from other African American families in town in that they are treated with "an odd mixture of resentment and respect" (2) by whites. Although other Black people are not permitted to eat at the drugstore, Mr. Gates is. Gates attributes this social status to his family's "small but certain measure of financial security" (2). Even so, when Mr. Wilson insults Mr. Gates, the privileged status of the Gates family is revealed as a sham.

3. *What does Gates mean when he says, "It was 'one of those things,' as my Mom would put it" (12)?*

   Gates's comment indicates that the family learned to see such mistreatment as routine. In context, the word *things* in paragraph 12 refers to the kind of incident that gives Gates and his family a glimpse of the way the white world operates.

4. *Why does Gates's family turn to a discussion of a "Black superstar" after a "painful moment of silence" (12) such as the one he describes?*

   Although Gates does not explain the family's behavior, we can infer that they speak of African American heroes like prizefighter Sugar Ray Robinson and baseball player Jackie Robinson to make themselves feel better. Such discussions are a way of balancing the negative images of African Americans created by incidents such as the one Gates describes and of bolstering the low self-esteem the family felt as a result. These heroes seem to have won the respect denied to the Gates family; to mention them is to participate vicariously in their glory.

5. *Why do you think Gates "never again looked Mr. Wilson in the eye" (15)?*

Gates may have felt that Mr. Wilson was somehow the enemy, not to be trusted, because he had insulted Gates's father. Or, he may have been ashamed to look Wilson in the eye because he believed his father should have insisted on being addressed properly.

Purpose and Audience

1. *Why do you think Gates introduces his narrative with the two quotations he selects? How do you suppose he expects his audience to react to these quotations? How do you react?*

Gates begins with two quotations, both by African American writers, written nearly thirty years apart. Baldwin's words seem to suggest that, in the United States, "the question of color" is a barrier to understanding "the graver questions of the self." That is, the labels *Black* and *white* may mask more fundamental characteristics or issues. Ellis's list of names (many pejorative) for African Americans illustrates that epithets can dehumanize people; they can, in effect, rob a person of his or her "self." This issue of the discrepancy between a name and what lies behind it is central to Gates's essay. In a sense, then, Gates begins with these two quotations because they are relevant to the issues he will discuss. More specifically, he is using the two quotations — particularly Ellis's shocking string of unpleasant names — to arouse interest in his topic and provide an intellectual and emotional context for his story. He may also be intending to make his white readers uncomfortable and his Black readers angry. How you react depends on your attitudes about race (and, perhaps, about language).

2. *What is the point of Gates's narrative? That is, why does he recount the incident?*

Certainly Gates wishes to make readers aware of the awkward, and potentially dangerous, position of his father (and, by extension, of other African Americans) in a small southern town in the 1950s. He also shows us how names help shape people's perceptions and actions: as long as Mr. Wilson can call all Black men "George," he can continue to see them as insignificant and treat them as inferiors. The title of the piece suggests that the writer's main focus is on how names shape perceptions.

3. *The title of this selection, which Gates places in quotation marks, is an allusion to act 2, scene 2, of Shakespeare's* Romeo and Juliet, *in which Juliet says, "What's in a name? That which we call a rose / By any other name would smell as sweet." Why do you think Gates chose this title? Does he expect his audience to recognize the quotation?*

Because his work was originally published in a journal read by a well-educated audience, Gates would have expected readers to recognize this **allusion** (and also to know a good deal about 1950s race relations). Although Gates could not have been certain that all members of this audience would recognize the reference to *Romeo and Juliet*, he could have been reasonably sure that if they did, it would enhance their understanding of the selection. In Shakespeare's play, the two lovers are kept apart essentially because of their names: she is a Capulet and he is a Montague, and the two families are involved in a bitter feud. In the speech from which Gates takes the title quotation, Juliet questions the logic of such a situation. In her view, what a person is called should not determine how he or she is regarded, which is Gates's point as well. Even if readers do not recognize the allusion, the title still foreshadows the selection's focus on names.

Style and Structure

1. *Does paragraph 1 add something vital to the narrative, or would Gates's story make sense without the introduction? Could another kind of introduction work as well?*

   Gates's first paragraph supplies the context in which the incident is to be read; that is, it makes clear that Mr. Wilson calling Mr. Gates "George" was not an isolated incident but part of a pattern of behavior that allowed those in positions of power to mistreat those they considered inferior. For this reason, it is an effective introduction. Although the narrative would make sense without paragraph 1, the story's full impact would probably not be as great. Still, Gates could have begun differently. For example, he could have started with the incident itself (paragraph 2) and interjected his comments about the significance of names later in the piece. He also could have begun with the exchange of dialogue in paragraphs 5 through 11 and then introduced the current paragraph 1 to supply the incident's context.

2. *What does the use of dialogue contribute to the narrative? Would the selection have a different impact without dialogue? Explain.*

   Gates was five or six years old when the incident occurred, and the dialogue helps establish the child's innocence as well as his father's quiet acceptance of the situation. In short, the dialogue is a valuable addition to the piece because it creates two characters, one innocent and one resigned to injustice, both of whom contrast with the voice of the adult narrator: wise, worldly, but also angry and perhaps ashamed, the voice of a man who has benefited from the sacrifices of men like Gates's father.

3. *Why do you think Gates supplies the specific details he chooses in paragraphs 2 and 3? In paragraph 4? Is all this information necessary?*

   The details Gates provides in paragraphs 2 and 3 help establish the status of his family in Piedmont; because readers have this information, the fact that the family was ultimately disregarded and discounted by some white people emerges as deeply ironic. The information in paragraph 4 also contributes to this **irony**. Here, we learn that Mr. Wilson was not liked by many white people, that he looked like Gates's Uncle Joe, and that he carried a lunch box — in other words, that he had no special status in the town apart from that conferred by race.

4. **Vocabulary Project.** *Consider the connotations of the words* colored *and* Black, *both used by Gates to refer to African Americans. What different associations does each word have? Why does Gates use both — for example,* colored *in paragraph 9 and* Black *in paragraph 12? What is your response to his father's use of the term* boy *in paragraph 11?*

In the 1950s, when the incident Gates describes took place, the term *colored*, along with *Negro*, was still widely used to designate Americans of African descent. In the 1960s, the terms *Afro-American* and *Black* replaced the earlier names, with *Black* emerging as the preferred term and remaining dominant through the 1980s. Today, *Black* is preferred by some and *African American* is used more and more often. Because the term *colored* is the oldest designation, it may seem old-fashioned and even racist today; *Black*, which connoted a certain degree of militancy in the 1960s, is probably now considered a neutral term by most people. Gates uses both words because he is speaking from two time periods. In paragraph 9, re-creating the thoughts and words of a child in a 1950s southern town, he uses the term *colored*; in paragraph 12, the adult Gates, commenting in 1989 on the incident, uses *Black*. The substitution of *African American* for the older terms might give the narrative a more contemporary flavor, but it might also seem awkward or forced — and, in paragraph 9, inappropriately formal. As far as the term *boy* is concerned, different readers are apt to have different responses. Although the father's use of the term can be seen as affectionate, it can also be seen as derisive in this context because it echoes the bigot's use of *boy* for all Black males, regardless of age or accomplishments.

Journal Entry

Do you think Gates's parents should have used experiences like the one in " 'What's in a Name?' " to educate him about the family's social status in the community? Why do you think they chose instead to dismiss such incidents as "one of those things" (12)?

Your responses to these questions will reflect your own opinions, based on your background and experiences as well as on your interpretation of the reading selection.

Writing Workshop

Write about a time when you, like Gates's father, could have spoken out in protest but chose not to. Would you make the same decision today?

By the time you approach the Writing Workshop assignments, you will have read a selection, responded to study questions about it, discussed it in class, and perhaps considered its relationship to other essays in the text. Often, your next step will be to write an essay in response to one of the Writing Workshop questions. (Chapters 2–4 follow Laura Bobnak, a first-year composition student, through the process of writing an essay in response to this Writing Workshop assignment.)

Combining the Patterns

*Although **narration** is the pattern of development that dominates " 'What's in a Name?' " and gives it its structure, Gates also uses **exemplification**, presenting an extended example to support his thesis. What is this example? What does it illustrate? Would several brief examples have been more convincing?*

The extended example is the story of the encounter between Gates's father and Mr. Wilson, which compellingly illustrates the kind of behavior African Americans were often forced to adopt in the 1950s. Because Gates's introduction focuses on "the incident" (1), one extended example is enough (although he alludes to other incidents in paragraph 12).

Thematic Connections

- "The Myth of the Latin Woman: I Just Met a Girl Named Maria" (page 224)
- " 'Girl' " (page 251)

As you read and think about the selections in this text, you should begin to see thematic links among them. Such parallels can add to your interest and understanding as well as give you ideas for class discussion and writing.

For example, one related work is Judith Ortiz Cofer's "The Myth of the Latin Woman: I Just Met a Girl Named Maria." Although Cofer is Latina, not African American, she too faces the stigma of being seen as a stereotype rather than as an individual; she is characterized as "Maria" just as Gates's father was characterized (and dismissed) as "George." Because Cofer's essay was written in 1993 and discusses more recent events than does Gates's essay, which explores an event that took place in the 1950s, it provides a more contemporary — and, perhaps, broader — context for discussing issues of race and class.

Jamaica Kincaid's short story " 'Girl,' " by an African American writer, also has some parallels with Gates's autobiographical essay. Like Gates's father, Kincaid's protagonist occupies a subservient position in a society whose rules she must obey. The lessons in life skills that are enumerated in the story are also similar to the lesson Gates learns from his father.

In the process of thinking about Gates's narrative, discussing it in class, or preparing to write an essay on a related topic (such as the one suggested under Writing Workshop on page 8), you might find it useful to read Cofer's essay and Kincaid's story.

Responding to Other Kinds of Texts

The first selection in Chapters 6 through 14 of this book is a visual text. It is followed by **Reading Images** questions, a **Journal Entry**, and a short list of **Thematic Connections** that will help you understand the image and shape your response to it.

The final selection in each chapter, a story or poem, is followed by **Reading Literature** questions, a **Journal Entry**, and **Thematic Connections**.

NOTE: At the end of each chapter, **Writing Assignments** offer additional practice in writing essays structured according to a particular pattern of development. Some of these assignments, designated **Working with Sources**, will ask you to refer to one or more of the essays in the chapter (or to outside sources). In these cases, you will be asked to include MLA parenthetical documentation and a works-cited page. Finally, a **Collaborative Activity** suggests an idea for a group project.

PART ONE

The Writing Process

Every reading selection in this book is the result of a struggle between a writer and his or her material. If a writer's struggle is successful, the finished work is welded together without a visible seam, and readers have no sense of the frustration the writer experienced while rearranging ideas or hunting for the right word. Writing is no easy task, even for a professional writer. Still, although there is no simple formula for good writing, some approaches are easier and more productive than others.

At this point, you may be asking yourself, "So what? What has this got to do with me? I'm not a professional writer." That's true enough, but during the next few years, you will be doing a good deal of writing. Throughout your college career, you will compose exams, reports, essays, and research projects. In your professional life, you may write progress reports, proposals, and memos. As diverse as these tasks are, they have something in common: they can be made easier if you are familiar with the stages of the **writing process** — a process that experienced writers follow when they write.

THE WRITING PROCESS

- **Invention** (also called **prewriting**) During invention, you decide what to write about and gather information to support or explain what you want to say.
- **Arrangement** During arrangement, you decide how you are going to organize your ideas.
- **Drafting and revising** During drafting and revising, you write several drafts as you reconsider your ideas and their organization and refine your style and structure.
- **Editing and proofreading** During editing, you focus on grammar and punctuation, sentence style, and word choice. During proofreading, you correct spelling, mechanical errors, and typos and check your essay's format.

Although the writing process is usually presented as a series of neatly defined steps, that model does not reflect the way people actually write. Ideas do not always flow easily, and the key ideas you set out to develop do not always wind up in the essay you ultimately write. In addition, writing often progresses in fits and starts, with ideas coming to you sporadically or not at all. Surprisingly, much good writing occurs when a writer gets stuck or confused but continues to work until ideas begin to take shape.

Because the writing process is so erratic, its stages overlap. Most writers engage in various steps simultaneously — finding ideas, considering possible methods of organization, looking for the right words, and correcting grammar and punctuation all at the same time. In fact, writing is such an idiosyncratic process that no two writers approach the writing process in exactly the same way. Some people outline; others do not. Some take elaborate notes during the invention stage; others keep track of everything in their heads.

The writing process discussed throughout this book reflects the many choices writers make at various stages of composition. Regardless of writers' different approaches, however, one thing is certain: the more you write, the better acquainted you will become with your personal writing process and the better you will learn how to modify it to suit various writing tasks.

Because much of your college writing will be done in response to texts you read, Chapter 1 of this book introduces you to critical reading; then, Chapters 2 through 5 discuss the individual stages of the writing process. These chapters will help you define your needs as a writer and understand your options as you approach writing tasks in college and beyond.

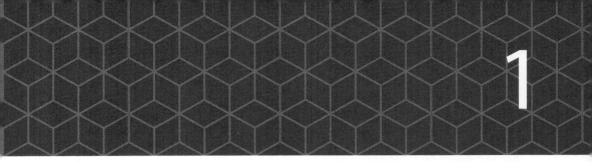

Reading to Write: Becoming a Critical Reader

On a purely practical level, you will read the selections in this book to answer study questions and to prepare for class discussions (and, often, for writing). More significantly, however, you will also read to evaluate the ideas of others, to form judgments, and to develop original viewpoints. In other words, you will engage in **critical reading**.

By introducing you to new ideas and new ways of thinking about familiar concepts, reading prepares you to respond critically to the ideas of others and to develop ideas of your own. When you read critically, you can form opinions, exchange insights with others, ask and answer questions, and discover ideas that can be further explored in writing. For all these reasons, critical reading is a vital part of your education.

Understanding Critical Reading

Reading is a two-way street. Readers are introduced to a writer's ideas, but they also bring their own ideas to what they read. After all, readers have different national, ethnic, cultural, and geographic backgrounds and different kinds of knowledge and experiences, so they may react differently to a particular essay or story. For example, readers from an economically homogeneous neighborhood may have difficulty understanding an essay about class conflict, but they may be more objective than readers who are struggling with such conflict in their own lives.

Readers may respond in different ways, but that does not mean that every interpretation is acceptable or that an essay (or story or poem) may mean whatever a reader wants it to mean. Readers must make sure they are not distorting a writer's words, overlooking (or ignoring) significant details, or seeing things in an essay or story that do not exist. It is not important for all readers to agree on a particular interpretation of a work. It *is* important, however, for each reader to develop an interpretation that the work itself supports.

When you read an essay in this book, or any text you expect to discuss in class, you should read it carefully, ideally more than once. If a text is accompanied by a headnote or other background material, as those in this book are, you should read this material as well because it will help you understand the text. Keep in mind that some of the texts you read may eventually be used as sources in your writing. In these cases, it is especially important that you understand what you are reading and can formulate a thoughtful response to the writer's ideas. (For information on how to evaluate the sources you read, see Chapter 16.)

To get the most out of your reading, you should use **active reading** strategies. In practical terms, that means actively participating in the reading process: first, approaching an assigned reading with a clear understanding of your prior knowledge and your purpose; and second, marking the text to help you understand what you are reading.

 REMINDER **NAMING YOUR FILES**

As you take notes about your sources and save each new draft as a separate file, it's important to give each file an accurate and descriptive title so that you can find it when you need it. Your file name should identify the class for which you're writing and the date you updated the file.

Comp-Plagiarism essay_9-25-17

Once you develop a system that works for you, you should use it consistently — for example, always listing elements (class, assignment, date) in the same order for each project. You can also create a separate folder for each class and then use subfolders for each assignment, gathering together all your notes and drafts for an assignment. A folder system will be particularly useful if you regularly use a remote storage site such as Dropbox or Google Drive, where files can easily become confused or be overwritten.

Assessing Your Prior Knowledge

Before you begin a reading assignment, you should assess your prior knowledge — that is, determine what you already know about the subject and what you still need (or want) to know about it. Assessing your prior knowledge will help you decide how much time you will need to read the material and how to approach it. For example, if you already know a good deal about charter schools (perhaps even having attended one), reading an essay about the pros and cons of this educational option may not be very challenging for you. If you have no personal experience with charter schools and have never read about or discussed them, however, you will probably have to spend more time reading an essay that compares charter schools with traditional public schools. (In fact, you may even have to look up a definition of *charter schools* before you begin reading.)

To assess your prior knowledge of a subject, begin by asking the questions in the following checklist.

> ✓ **CHECKLIST** **QUESTIONS FOR ASSESSING YOUR PRIOR KNOWLEDGE**
>
> ☐ What do you already know about the subject?
> ☐ How interested are you in this subject?
> ☐ How is the text similar to or different from other texts you have read?
> ☐ Is there anything in your background or experience that can help you connect to or understand the material?
> ☐ What do you hope to learn from your reading?

Determining Your Purpose

Before you begin to read, you should make sure you have a clear understanding of your **purpose** — why you are reading. The answers to the questions in the following checklist will help you figure out what kind of information you hope to get out of your reading and how you will use this information.

> ✓ **CHECKLIST** **QUESTIONS ABOUT YOUR PURPOSE**
>
> ☐ Will you be expected to discuss what you are reading? If so, will you discuss it in class? In a study group? In a conference with your instructor?
> ☐ Will you have to write about what you are reading? If so, will you be expected to write a brief informal response (for example, a journal entry) or a longer, more formal one (for example, an essay)?
> ☐ Will you be tested on the material?

Previewing

When you **preview**, you try to get a sense of the writer's main idea, key supporting points, and general emphasis. At this stage, you don't read every word; instead, you **skim** the text. You can begin by focusing on the title, the first paragraph (which often contains a purpose statement or overview), and the last paragraph (which may contain a summary of the writer's main idea). You should also look for clues to the writer's message in the passage's other **visual signals**.

Recognizing Visual Signals

- Look at the title.
- Look at the opening and closing paragraphs.
- Look at each paragraph's first sentence.
- Look for headings.

- Look for *italicized* and **boldfaced** words.
- Look for numbered lists.
- Look for bulleted lists (like this one).
- Look at any visuals (graphs, charts, tables, diagrams, photographs, and so on).
- Look at any information that is boxed.
- Look at any information that is in **color**.

When you have finished previewing the passage, you should have a general sense of what the writer wants to communicate.

As you read and reread, you will record your reactions in writing. These notes will help you understand the writer's ideas and your own thoughts about those ideas. Every reader develops a different system of recording responses, but many readers use a combination of *highlighting* and *annotating*.

Highlighting

When you **highlight**, you mark the text. You might, for example, underline (or double underline) important concepts, draw a box around key terms, number a series of related points, circle an unfamiliar word (or place a question mark beside it), draw a vertical line in the margin beside a particularly interesting passage, draw arrows to connect related points, or put a star next to discussions of the central issues or main idea.

At this stage, you continue to look for visual signals, but now, as you read more closely, you also begin to pay attention to the text's **verbal signals**.

Recognizing Verbal Signals

- Look for repeated words and phrases.
- Look for phrases that signal emphasis ("The *primary* reason"; "The *most important* idea").
- Look for words that signal addition (*also, in addition, furthermore*).
- Look for words that signal time sequence (*first, after, then, next, finally*).
- Look for words that identify causes and effects (*because, as a result, for this reason*).
- Look for words that introduce examples (*for example, for instance*).
- Look for words that signal comparison (*likewise, similarly*).
- Look for words that signal contrast (*unlike, although, in contrast*).
- Look for words that signal contradiction (*however, on the contrary*).
- Look for words that signal a narrowing of the writer's focus (*in fact, specifically, in other words*).
- Look for words that signal summaries or conclusions (*to sum up, in conclusion*).

The following pages reprint a column by journalist Brent Staples that focuses on the issue of plagiarism among college students. The column, "Cutting and Pasting: A Senior Thesis by (Insert Name)," and the accompanying headnote and background material have been highlighted by a student.

BRENT STAPLES

Cutting and Pasting: A Senior Thesis by (Insert Name)

Born in 1951 in Chester, Pennsylvania, Brent Staples is a writer and member of the editorial board of the *New York Times*. He often writes about culture, politics, race, and education. Staples has a B.A. in behavioral science from Widener University and a Ph.D. in psychology from the University of Chicago. Before joining the *New York Times*, he wrote for the *Chicago Sun-Times, Chicago Reader, Chicago Magazine,* and the jazz magazine *Down Beat*. His work has also appeared in publications such as *Ms.* and *Harper's*. Staples is the author of a memoir, *Parallel Time: Growing Up in Black and White* (1994), and winner of the 2019 Pulitzer Prize for Editorial Writing.

Background on prevalence of cheating and plagiarism in high school and college Studies suggest that high school and college students are increasingly likely to cheat or plagiarize. For example, one Duke University study conducted from 2002 to 2005 showed that 70 percent of the 50,000 undergraduate students surveyed admitted to cheating on occasion. A 2008 survey of high school students by the Center for Youth Ethics at the Josephson Institute showed that 82 percent had copied from another student's work, and 36 percent said that they had used the Internet to plagiarize an assignment. Moreover, students tend to view such academic dishonesty with indifference: according to surveys by the Center for Academic Integrity, only 29 percent of undergraduates believe that unattributed copying from the web rises to the level of "serious cheating."

Observers have proposed various reasons for the prevalence of plagiarism. Some point to new technologies that allow instant access to an apparently "common" store of unlimited information as sites like *Wikipedia* challenge traditional notions of singular authorship, originality, and intellectual property. Others see the problem as the result of declining personal morality and of a culture that rewards shady behavior. And many view plagiarism as the unavoidable consequence of the pressures many students feel.

Academic institutions have responded to the problem in a number of ways. Most colleges now use the Internet-based detection service Turnitin.com, which scans students' essays for plagiarism. A study by the National Bureau of Economic Research concluded that simply showing a web tutorial on the issue could reduce instances of plagiarism by two-thirds. Schools such as Duke University and Bowdoin College now require incoming students to complete this online instruction before they enroll. Additionally, the research of Rutgers professor Ronald McCabe, who founded the Center for Academic Integrity, indicates that honor codes — already in place at many colleges and universities — help create a campus culture of academic integrity.

A friend who teaches at a well-known eastern university told me recently that plagiarism was turning him into a cop. He begins the semester collecting evidence, in the form of an in-class essay that gives him a sense of how well students think and write. He looks back at the samples later when students turn in papers that feature their own, less-than-perfect prose alongside expertly written passages lifted verbatim from the .web.

"I have to assume that in every class, someone will do it," he said. "It doesn't stop them if you say, 'This is plagiarism. I won't accept it.' I have to tell them that it is a failing offense and could lead me to file a complaint with the university, which could lead to them being put on probation or being asked to leave."

Not everyone who gets caught knows enough about what they did to be remorseful. Recently, for example, a student who plagiarized a sizable chunk of a paper essentially told my friend to keep his shirt on, that what he'd done was no big deal. Beyond that, the student said, he would be ashamed to go home to the family with an F.

As my friend sees it: "This represents a shift away from the view of education as the process of intellectual engagement through which we learn to think critically and toward the view of education as mere training. In training, you are trying to find the right answer at any cost, not trying to improve your mind."

Like many other professors, he no longer sees traditional term papers as a valid index of student competence. To get an accurate, Internet-free reading of how much students have learned, he gives them written assignments in class—where they can be watched.

These kinds of precautions are no longer unusual in the college world. As Trip Gabriel pointed out in the *Times* recently, more than half the colleges in the country have retained services that check student papers for material lifted from the Internet and elsewhere. Many schools now require incoming students to take online tutorials that explain what plagiarism is and how to avoid it.

Nationally, discussions about plagiarism tend to focus on questions of ethics. But as David Pritchard, a physics professor at the Massachusetts Institute of Technology, told me recently: "The big sleeping dog here is not the moral issue. The problem is that kids don't learn if they don't do the work."

Prof. Pritchard and his colleagues illustrated the point in a study of cheating behavior by M.I.T. students who used an online system to complete homework. The students who were found to have copied the most answers from others started out with the same math and physics skills as their harder-working classmates. But by skipping the actual work in homework, they fell behind in understanding and became significantly more likely to fail.

✳✳   The Pritchard axiom — that repetitive cheating undermines learning — has ominous implications for a world in which even junior high school students cut and paste from the Internet instead of producing their own writing.   9

If we look closely at plagiarism as practiced by youngsters, we can see that they have a different relationship to the printed word than did the generations before them. When many young people think of writing, they don't think of fashioning original sentences into a sustained thought. They think of making something like a collage of found passages and ideas from the Internet.   10

✓ They become like rap musicians who construct what they describe as new works by "sampling" (which is to say, cutting and pasting) beats and refrains from the works of others.   11

This habit of mind is already pervasive in the culture and will be difficult to roll back. But parents, teachers, and policy makers need to understand that this is not just a matter of personal style or generational expression. It's a question of whether we can preserve the methods through which education at its best teaches people to think critically and originally.   12

·   ·   ·

The student who was assigned to read Staples's column and its headnote was preparing for a class discussion of a group of related articles on the problem of academic cheating. To prepare for class, she began by highlighting the essay to identify the writer's key ideas and mark points she might want to think further about. This highlighting laid the groundwork for the careful annotations she would make when she reread the article.

Exercise 1

Preview the following essay. Then, highlight it to identify the writer's main idea and key supporting points. (Previewing and highlighting the article's headnote, including the background material provided, can also help you understand the essay's ideas.) You might circle unfamiliar words, underline key terms or concepts, or draw lines or arrows to connect related ideas.

MOISÉS NAÍM

The YouTube Effect

A longtime journalist, professor, politician, and public intellectual, Moisés Naím is the author and editor of several books, including *Illicit: How Smugglers, Traffickers, and Copycats Are Hijacking the Global Economy* (2006) and *The End of Power: From Boardrooms to Battlefields and Churches to States, Why Being in Charge Isn't What It Used to Be* (2013). His writing has appeared in many magazines, journals, and newspapers. Educated at the Universidad Metropolitana in Venezuela and the Massachusetts Institute of Technology, he has served as the Venezuelan minister of trade and industry, the editor of *Foreign Policy* magazine, and a columnist for the Spanish newspaper *El Pais*. Naím is now a distinguished fellow at the Carnegie Endowment for International Peace and is a member of international organizations such as the Council in Foreign Relations and the World Economic Forum.

Background on YouTube In the following column from 2006, Moisés Naím writes, "YouTube has 34 million monthly visitors, and 65,000 new videos are posted every day." Today, on the video hosting and sharing site, founded in 2005, more than 500 hours of video content are uploaded every minute, and more than a billion hours of content are watched each day. Even as other social media platforms such as Twitter and Tumblr have arisen, YouTube remains an Internet fixture. It is available in seventy-six different languages and has distinctive localized versions in eighty-eight different countries. Moreover, its influence during the past decade — over everything from global politics to popular music to criminal justice — has been transformative. Although much of its content is notoriously frivolous, YouTube has changed our relationship to media (and, perhaps, to reality itself) since we no longer need to rely entirely on large news organizations to document current events. Instead, as the culture and technology critic Clay Shirky has observed, "we are increasingly becoming part of one another's [media] infrastructure."

A video shows a line of people trudging up a snow-covered footpath. A shot is heard; the first person in line falls. A voice-over says, "They are killing them like dogs." Another shot, and another body drops to the ground. A Chinese soldier fires his rifle again. Then a group of soldiers examines the bodies.

These images were captured in the Himalayas by a member of a mountaineering expedition who claims to have stumbled on the killing. The video first aired on Romanian television, but it only gained worldwide attention when it was posted on YouTube, the video-sharing website. (To view it, go to YouTube.com and type "Tibet, ProTV, China".) Human rights groups say the slain Tibetan refugees included monks, women, and children. The Chinese government had claimed the soldiers shot in self-defense after they were attacked by 70 refugees, but the video seems to render that explanation absurd. The U.S. ambassador to China lodged a complaint.

Welcome to the "YouTube effect." It is the phenomenon whereby video   3
clips, often produced by individuals acting on their own, are rapidly disseminated worldwide on websites such as YouTube and Google Video. YouTube has
34 million monthly visitors, and 65,000 new videos are posted every day. Most
are frivolous, produced by and for the teenagers who make up the majority of
the site's visitors. But some are serious. YouTube includes videos posted by terrorists, human rights groups, and U.S. soldiers in Iraq. Some are clips of incidents that have political consequences or document important trends, such as
global warming, illegal immigration, and corruption. Some videos reveal
truths. Others spread propaganda and outright lies.

Fifteen years ago, the world marveled at the "CNN effect" and believed   4
that the unblinking eyes of TV cameras, beyond the reach of censors, would
bring greater global accountability. These expectations were, to some degree,
fulfilled. Since the early 1990s, electoral frauds have been exposed, democratic
uprisings energized, famines contained, and wars started or stopped thanks to
the CNN effect. But the YouTube effect will be even more powerful. Although
international news operations employ thousands of professional journalists,
they will never be as omnipresent as millions of people carrying cellphones
that can record video. Thanks to the ubiquity of video technology, the world
was able to witness a shooting in a 19,000-foot-high mountain pass in Tibet.

This phenomenon is amplified by a double-echo chamber: One echo is   5
produced when content first posted on the Web is re-aired by mainstream
TV networks. The second echo occurs when television clips — until now
ephemeral — gain a permanent presence through websites such as YouTube.
Bloggers and activists everywhere are recognizing the power of citizen-pro-
duced and Web-distributed videos as the ultimate testimony. Witness.org arms
individuals in conflict zones with video cameras so they can record and expose
human rights abuses. Electoral watchdogs are taping elections. Even Al Qaeda
created a special media production unit called Al Sahab ("The Cloud").

YouTube is a mixed blessing: It is now harder to know what to believe.   6
How do we know that what we see in a video clip posted by a "citizen journalist" is not a manipulated montage? How do we know, for example, that the
YouTube video of terrorized American soldiers crying and praying while under
fire was filmed in Iraq and not staged somewhere else to manipulate public
opinion? The more than 86,000 people who viewed it in the first 10 days of its
posting will never know.

Governments are already feeling the heat of the YouTube effect — and   7
cracking down online. Almost a third of all reporters jailed this year were Internet journalists. The U.S. military recently ordered its soldiers to stop posting
videos online. Iran's government restricts connection speeds to limit its people's access to video streaming.

But these measures have not stopped the proliferation of Web videos shot   8
by U.S. soldiers in Iraq or kept savvy Iranians from viewing the images they
want to see. And although Beijing has been effective in censoring the content
its citizens can view, it has yet to figure out a way to prevent a growing number
of videos of peasant rebellions from being posted online. In the long run, Web

video censorship will fail because the same anonymity that makes videos difficult to authenticate also makes it harder to enforce governmental *diktats*.

The good news is that the YouTube effect is already creating a strong   9
demand for reliable guides — individuals, institutions, and technologies — that
we can trust to help us sort facts from lies online. The millions of bloggers who
are constantly watching, fact-checking, and exposing mistakes are a powerful
example of "the wisdom of crowds" being assisted by a technology that is as
open and omnipresent as we are.

·   ·   ·

REMINDER   **TAKING NOTES**

If you use your computer when you take notes
instead of writing annotations on the page, be
sure to label each note so that you remember
where it came from. (You will need this information for your essay's parenthetical references and
works-cited page.) Include the author's name
and the title of the reading selection as well as
the page on which the information you are citing
appears. Also note the page and paragraph number where you found the information so that you
will be able to find it again.

CLOSE   **VIEW**

Annotating

When you **annotate**, you
carry on a conversation with
the text. In marginal notes,
you can ask questions, suggest possible parallels with
other reading selections or
with your own ideas and
experiences, argue with the
writer's points, comment on
the writer's style or word
choice, or define unfamiliar
terms and concepts.

The questions below can
guide you as you read and
help you make useful annotations.

CHECKLIST   **QUESTIONS FOR CRITICAL READING**

- ☐ What is the writer's general subject?
- ☐ What is the writer's main idea? Is it stated directly or implied (suggested)?
- ☐ What are the writer's key supporting points?
- ☐ Does the writer seem to have a particular purpose in mind?
- ☐ What kind of audience is the writer addressing?
- ☐ What are the writer's assumptions about the audience? About the subject?
- ☐ Are the writer's ideas consistent with your own?
- ☐ Does the writer reveal any **bias**?
- ☐ Do you have any knowledge that challenges the writer's ideas?
- ☐ Is any information missing?
- ☐ Are any sequential or logical links missing?
- ☐ Can you identify themes or ideas that also appear in other works you have
  read?
- ☐ Can you identify parallels with your own experience?

The following pages reproduce the student's highlighting of "Cutting and Pasting: A Senior Thesis by (Insert Name)" from pages 17–19 and also include her annotations. (She annotated the headnote and background material as well, but those annotations are not shown here.)

Teachers as cops

A friend who teaches at a well-known eastern university told me recently that plagiarism was turning him into a cop. He begins the semester collecting evidence, in the form of an in-class essay that gives him a sense of how well students think and write. He looks back at the samples later when students turn in papers that feature their own, less-than-perfect prose alongside expertly written passages lifted verbatim from the Web.   1

Teachers resigned to situation

"I have to assume that in every class, someone will do it," he said. "It doesn't stop them if you say, 'This is plagiarism. I won't accept it.' I have to tell them that it is a failing offense and could lead me to file a complaint with the university, which could lead to them being put on probation or being asked to leave."   2

Not everyone who gets caught knows enough about what they did to be remorseful. Recently, for example, a student who plagiarized a sizable chunk of a paper essentially told my friend to keep his shirt on, that what he'd done was no big deal. Beyond that, the student said, he would be ashamed to go home to the family with an F.   3

Key problem —
Move from
"intellectual
engagement" and
critical thinking to
"mere training"

✱

As my friend sees it: "This represents a shift away from the view of education as the process of intellectual engagement through which we learn to think critically and toward the view of education as mere training. In training, you are trying to find the right answer at any cost, not trying to improve your mind."   4

Like many other professors, he no longer sees traditional term papers as a valid index of student competence. To get an accurate, Internet-free reading of how much students have learned, he gives them written assignments in class — where they can be watched.   5

Colleges as police states!

These kinds of precautions are no longer unusual in the college world. As Trip Gabriel pointed out in the *Times* recently, more than half the colleges in the country have retained services that check student papers for material lifted from the Internet and elsewhere. Many schools now require incoming students to take online tutorials that explain what plagiarism is and how to avoid it.   6

Nationally, discussions about plagiarism tend to focus on questions of ethics. But as David Pritchard, a physics   7

Problem isn't
just ethics

professor at the Massachusetts Institute of Technology, * told me recently: "The big sleeping dog here is not the moral issue. The problem is that kids don't learn if they don't do the work."

Prof. Pritchard and his colleagues illustrated the point   8 in a study of cheating behavior by M.I.T. students who used an online system to complete homework. The students who were found to have copied the most answers from others started out with the same math and physics skills as their harder-working classmates. But by skipping the actual work in homework, they fell behind in understanding and became significantly more likely to fail.

** The Pritchard axiom — that repetitive cheating   9 undermines learning— has ominous implications for a world in which even junior high school students cut and paste from the Internet instead of producing their own writing.

If we look closely at plagiarism as practiced by young-   10 sters, we can see that they have a different relationship to the printed word than did the generations before them.

True

When many young people think of writing, they don't think of fashioning original sentences into a sustained thought. They think of making something like a collage of found passages and ideas from the Internet.

"Cutting and
pasting" =
"sampling"

✓ They become like rap musicians who construct what   11 they describe as new works by "sampling" (which is to say, cutting and pasting) beats and refrains from the works of others.

This habit of mind is already pervasive in the culture   12 and will be difficult to roll back. But parents, teachers, and policy makers need to understand that this is not just a

What's the answer to
this question? (What
can schools do? Who
is responsible for
solving the problem?)

matter of personal style or generational expression. It's a question of whether we can preserve the methods through which education at its best teaches people to think critically and originally.

•   •   •

As illustrated above, the student who annotated Staples's column on plagiarism supplemented her highlighting with brief marginal summaries to help her understand key points. She also wrote down questions that she thought would help her focus her comments during class discussion.

SUMMARIZING KEY IDEAS

One strategy that can help you understand what you are reading is **summarizing** a writer's key ideas, as the student writer does in her marginal annotations of the Staples column on pages 23–24. Putting a writer's ideas into your own words can make an unfamiliar or complex concept more accessible and useful to you. For more on summarizing, see the section on this topic in Chapter 17 on page 718.

Exercise 2

Now, add annotations to the Naím essay and related material that you highlighted for Exercise 1. This time, focus on summarizing the writer's key points and on asking questions that will prepare you for discussing (and perhaps writing about) this essay.

Reading Visual Texts

The written texts you read often include **visuals** — graphs, charts, tables, infographics, maps, diagrams, photographs, cartoons, fine art, or advertisements — to enhance the appeal of the text and convey the writer's ideas. For example, a photograph of an overcrowded prison can make a news article about the inmates' plight more vivid, a diagram of the heart can supplement a biology text's explanation of the circulatory system, and a map can help readers understand an essay's discussion of seventeenth-century explorers' conquests. Sometimes a visual will stand alone, communicating its own message instead of enhancing the message of a written text. For example, an editorial cartoon or an advertisement can persuade readers to support a cause, take some type of social action, buy a product, or vote for a particular candidate.

The process you follow when you respond to a **visual text** — a photograph; an advertisement; a diagram, graph, or chart; an infographic; or a work of fine art, for example — is much the same as the one you follow when you respond to a written text. Here too your goal is to understand the text, and highlighting and annotating a visual text can help you interpret it.

With visual texts, however, instead of identifying elements such as words and ideas, you identify visual elements. These elements might include the use of color, the arrangement of shapes, the contrast between large and small or light and dark, and the particular images the visual includes.

Previewing a Visual

When you approach a visual, you should begin by looking for clues to its main idea, or message. Some visuals, particularly advertising images, include written text that conveys the main idea. Apart from words, however, the images themselves can help you understand the visual's purpose, its intended audience, and the argument (if any) that it is making.

When you preview a visual, considering the following questions will help you understand its content, purpose, and message.

✓ CHECKLIST   QUESTIONS FOR PREVIEWING

- ☐ For what purpose was the visual created?
- ☐ Who is the visual's target audience?
- ☐ How would you characterize the visual? For example, is it a work of fine art? A public service announcement? A technical diagram?
- ☐ What is the visual's main focal point — its most important or most striking image? What draws your eye to that image?
- ☐ What individual images appear in the visual?
- ☐ How close together (or far apart) are these images?
- ☐ How large is each image? Why are some larger than others?
- ☐ How is each image visually connected to the background?
- ☐ How is empty space used to emphasize — or de-emphasize — individual images?
- ☐ How are color and shading (for example, contrast between light and dark) used to emphasize — or de-emphasize — individual images?
- ☐ Does the visual include any special effects, such as blurring or nonrealistic images?
- ☐ Does the visual include images of people? If so, consider the people's activities, interaction, gestures, facial expressions, positions, body language, dress, and the like.
- ☐ How do the people interact with one another? With the objects depicted in the visual?
- ☐ Does the visual include any written text? If so, what purpose does it serve? Is it necessary? What is the relationship between the visual's words and its images?
- ☐ Are any two images juxtaposed to suggest an association between them — for example, an electric car and a meadow?

When you have considered the items listed above, you should have a sense of why a visual was created and what message it was designed to communicate. Now, look at the following visual.

This editorial cartoon by Nick Anderson was published in the *Houston Chronicle* on May 3, 2013, in response to a shocking industrial accident in Bangladesh when more than 1,100 workers were killed and some 2,500 injured, many seriously, in the collapse of a building that housed a clothing factory. This factory was located on the eight-story building's upper floors, which were not strong enough to bear the weight of the factory's heavy machinery. Cracks had been discovered in the building the day before the collapse, but the structure had been deemed safe, and the factory supervisor had ordered employees to return to work. Because the factory manufactured clothing for a number of U.S. companies, the creator of the cartoon could assume that its subject matter would be of interest to U.S. consumers.

The cartoon has three main visual elements: the message in the upper left corner directed to employers, the central scene of devastation, and the "factory death toll" sign in the lower right corner. These three elements work together to convey the cartoon's message: when clothing is produced under substandard conditions, workers pay a terrible price.

The first element sends an ironic (but supposedly positive) message to manufacturers; its bold black-on-white capital letters and its even rectangular shape stand in contrast to the random destruction shown in the central scene. The second element, the scene itself, conveys a highly negative message, showing a collapsed building surrounded by rubble and stretcher-bearers carrying bodies away. (Additional bodies can be seen lined up in rows in the lower left corner of the image.) Juxtaposed with the seemingly positive message in the upper left is the sign in the lower right. Unlike the optimistic invitation to employers, this sign conveys the ugly truth in straightforward language. Set beside the terrible central image of the collapsed building and the dead bodies, this sign makes the ironic point of the cartoon clear: manufacturing clothing under unsafe, potentially deadly, conditions can exact a heavy price.

Highlighting and Annotating a Visual

Once you have previewed a visual, you should **highlight** and **annotate** it, focusing your attention on images as well as words.

Begin by identifying key images—by starring, boxing, or circling them—and perhaps drawing lines or arrows to connect related images. Then, make annotations directly on the visual itself (or on sticky notes), commenting on the effectiveness of its individual images in communicating the message of the whole. As in the case of a written text, your annotations can be in the form of comments or questions.

The following visual, an ad for Discover the Forest, a public service advertising campaign aimed at reconnecting children and their families with nature, has been highlighted and annotated by a student.

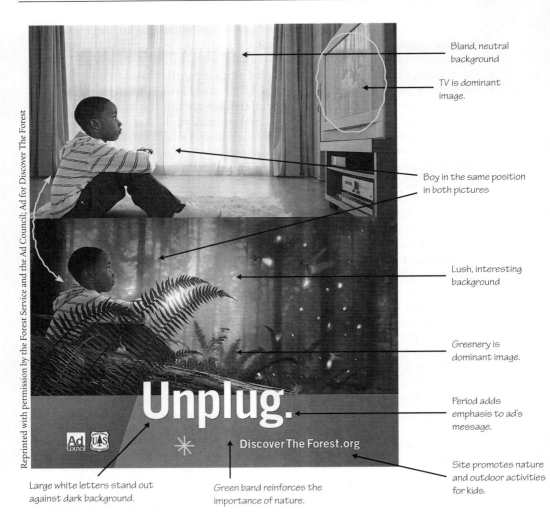

Reprinted with permission by the Forest Service and the Ad Council; Ad for Discover The Forest

Bland, neutral background

TV is dominant image.

Boy in the same position in both pictures

Lush, interesting background

Greenery is dominant image.

Period adds emphasis to ad's message.

Site promotes nature and outdoor activities for kids.

Large white letters stand out against dark background.

Green band reinforces the importance of nature.

Unplug.

Discover The Forest.org

Exercise 3

In this book, visuals are included in Chapters 6 through 14, where they are the first reading selection in each chapter, as well as in the debates and case-books in Chapter 14. Choose one of these visuals, and preview, highlight, and annotate it. When you have finished, write a sentence that sums up what you think the visual is trying to communicate. Then, consider how successful the visual is at accomplishing its goals.

2

Invention

Invention, or **prewriting**, is an important (and, frequently, the most neglected) part of the writing process. During invention, you discover what interests you about your subject and consider what ideas to develop in your essay.

When you are given a writing assignment, you may be tempted to start writing a first draft immediately. Before writing, however, you should be sure you understand your assignment and its limits, and you should think about what you want to say. Time spent on these issues now will pay off later when you draft your essay.

Understanding Your Assignment

Almost everything you write in college begins as an **assignment**. Some assignments are direct and easy to understand, but others are difficult and complex.

Before beginning to write, you need to understand exactly what your assignment is asking you to do. If the assignment is a question, read it carefully several times, and underline its keywords. If your instructor gives the assignment orally, be sure to write it down accurately. (A mistaken word — *analyze* for *compare*, for example — can make quite a difference.) If you are confused about anything, ask your instructor for clarification. Remember that no matter how well written an essay is, it will fall short if it does not address the assignment.

Setting Limits

Once you understand the assignment, you should consider its *length*, *purpose*, *audience*, and *occasion* and your own *knowledge* of the subject. Each of these factors helps you determine what you will say about your subject.

Length

Often, your instructor will specify the **length** of an assignment, and this word or page limit has a direct bearing on your essay's focus. For example, you would need a narrower topic for a two-page essay than for a ten-page one. Similarly, you could not discuss a question as thoroughly during an hour-long exam as you might in an essay written over several days.

If your instructor sets no page limit, consider how the nature of the assignment suggests an essay's length. A *summary* of a chapter or an article, for instance, should be much shorter than the original, whereas an *analysis* of a poem will most likely be longer than the poem itself. If you are uncertain about the appropriate length for your assignment, consult your instructor.

Purpose

Your **purpose** also limits what you say and how you say it. For example, if you were writing a job application letter, you would not emphasize the same elements of college life as you would in an email to a friend. In the first case, you would want to convince the reader to hire you, so you might include your grade point average, a list of the relevant courses you took, and perhaps a description of the work you did for a service-learning course. In the second case, you would want to inform and perhaps entertain, so you might share anecdotes about dorm life or describe one of your favorite instructors. In each case, your purpose would help you determine what information to include to evoke a particular response in a specific audience.

In general, you can classify your purposes for writing according to your relationship to the audience.

- In **expressive writing**, you convey personal feelings or impressions to readers. Expressive writing is used in diaries, personal emails, and journals, and often in narrative and descriptive essays as well.
- In **informative writing**, you inform readers about something. Informative writing is used in essay exams, lab reports, and expository essays, as well as in some research essays and personal web pages.
- In **persuasive writing**, you try to convince readers to act or think in a certain way. Persuasive writing is used in editorials, argumentative essays, proposals, research essays, and many types of electronic documents.

In addition to these general purposes, you might have a more specific purpose: to analyze, entertain, hypothesize, assess, summarize, question, report, recommend, suggest, evaluate, describe, recount, request, instruct, and so on. For example, suppose you wrote a report on homelessness in your community. Your general purpose might be to *inform* readers of the situation, but you might also want to *assess* the problem and *propose* ways to help those in need.

Audience

To be effective, your essay should be written with a particular **audience** in mind. An audience can be an *individual* (your instructor, for example), or it can be a *group* (like your classmates or coworkers). Your essay can address a *specialized* audience (such as a group of medical doctors or economists) or a *general* or *universal* audience whose members have little in common (such as the readers of a newspaper or magazine).

In college, your audience is usually your instructor, and your purpose in most cases is to demonstrate your mastery of the subject matter, your ability to think critically, and your competence as a writer. Other audiences may include classmates, professional colleagues, or members of your community. Considering the age and gender of your audience, its political and religious values, its social and educational level, and its interest in your subject may help you define it.

Often, you will find that your audience is just too diverse to be categorized. In such cases, many writers imagine a general (or universal) audience and make points that they think will appeal to a variety of readers. At other times, writers identify a common denominator, a role that characterizes the entire audience. For instance, when a report on the environmental dangers of disposable plastic bags asserts, "Now is the time for conservation-minded individuals to demand that single-use plastic bags be banned," it automatically casts its audience in the role of "conservation-minded individuals."

After you define your audience, you have to determine how much (or how little) its members know about your subject. This consideration helps you decide how much information your readers will need in order to understand the discussion. Are they highly informed? If so, you can present your points without much explanation. Are they relatively uninformed? If that is the case, you will have to include definitions of key terms, background information, and summaries of basic research.

Keep in mind that experts in one field will need background information in other fields. If, for example, you were writing an analysis of Joseph Conrad's novella *Heart of Darkness*, you could assume that the literature instructor who assigned the work would not need a plot summary. If you wrote an essay for your history instructor that used *Heart of Darkness* to illustrate the evils of European colonialism in nineteenth-century Africa, however, you would probably include a short plot summary. (Even though your history instructor would know a lot about colonialism in Africa, she might not be familiar with Conrad's work.)

Occasion

Occasion refers to the situation (or situations) that leads someone to write about a topic. In an academic writing situation, the occasion is almost always a specific assignment. The occasion suggests a specific audience—for example, a history instructor—as well as a specific purpose—for example, to discuss the major causes of World War I. In fact, even the format of an essay—whether you use (or do not use) headings or whether you present your response to an assignment as an essay, as a technical report, or as a Power-Point presentation—is determined by the occasion for your writing. For this reason, an essay suitable for a psychology or sociology class might not be suitable for a composition class.

Like college writing assignments, each writing task you do outside school requires an approach that suits the occasion. An email to coworkers, for instance, will be less formal than a report to a manager. In addition, the occasion suggests how much (or how little) information the piece of writing includes. Finally, your occasion suggests your purpose. For example, a message to members of an online discussion group might be strictly informational, whereas an email to a state senator about preserving a local landmark might be persuasive as well as informative.

Knowledge

What you know (and do not know) about a subject determines what you can say about it. Before writing about any subject, ask yourself what you know about the subject and what you need to find out.

Different writing situations require different kinds of knowledge. A personal essay will draw on your own experiences and observations; an argumentative essay often requires you to expand your frame of reference by doing research. In many cases, your page limit and the amount of time you have to do the assignment will help you decide how much information you need to gather before you can begin.

✓ **CHECKLIST**   **SETTING LIMITS**

Length
- ☐ Has your instructor specified a length?
- ☐ Does the nature of your assignment suggest a length?

Purpose
- ☐ Is your general purpose to express personal feelings? To inform? To persuade?
- ☐ In addition to your general purpose, do you have any more specific purposes?
- ☐ Does your assignment provide any guidelines about purpose?

Audience
- ☐ Is your audience a group or an individual?
- ☐ Are you going to address a specialized or a general audience?
- ☐ Should you take into consideration the audience's age, gender, education, biases, or political or social values?
- ☐ Should you cast your audience in a particular role?
- ☐ How much can you assume your audience knows about your subject?

Occasion
- ☐ Are you writing in class or at home?
- ☐ Are you addressing a situation outside the academic setting?
- ☐ What special approaches does your occasion for writing require?

Knowledge
- ☐ What do you know about your subject?
- ☐ What do you need to find out?

Exercise 1

Decide whether or not each of the following topics is appropriate for the stated limits, and then write a few sentences to explain why each topic is or is not acceptable.

1. *A two-to-three-page essay* A history of animal testing in medical research labs
2. *A two-hour final exam* The effectiveness of online courses
3. *A one-hour in-class essay* An interpretation of one of Andy Warhol's paintings of Campbell's soup cans
4. *An email to your college newspaper* A discussion of your school's policy on plagiarism

Exercise 2

Make a list of the different audiences to whom you speak or write in your daily life. (Consider all the different people you see regularly, such as family members, your roommate, instructors, your boss, and your friends.) Then, record your answers to the following questions:

1. Do you speak or write to each person in your life in the same way and about the same things? If not, how do your approaches to these people differ?
2. List some subjects that would interest some of these people but not others. How do you account for these differences?
3. Choose one of the following subjects, and describe how you would speak or write to different audiences about it.

   - A change that improved your life
   - Censoring Twitter or Instagram content
   - Taking a year off before college
   - Forgiving student-loan debt

Moving from Subject to Topic

Although many essays begin as specific assignments, some begin as broad areas of interest or concern. These **general subjects** always need to be narrowed to **specific topics** that can be discussed within the limits of the assignment. For example, a subject like fracking could be interesting, but it is too broad to write about. You need to limit such a subject to a topic that can be covered within the time and space available.

GENERAL SUBJECT	SPECIFIC TOPIC
Tablets	The benefits of using touchscreen tablets in elementary school classrooms
Herman Melville's *Billy Budd*	Billy Budd as a Christ figure
Social media	One unforeseen result of Twitter
Fracking	Should fracking be banned?

Two strategies can help you narrow a general subject to a specific topic: *questions for probing* and *freewriting*.

Questions for Probing

One way to move from a general subject to a specific topic is to examine your subject by asking a series of questions about it. These **questions for probing** are useful because they reflect how your mind operates — for example, by finding similarities and differences or by dividing a whole into its parts. By asking the questions on the following checklist, you can explore your subject systematically. Not all questions will work for every subject, but any single question may elicit many different answers, and each answer is a possible topic for your essay.

✔ **CHECKLIST** **QUESTIONS FOR PROBING**

☐ What happened?
☐ When did it happen?
☐ Where did it happen?
☐ Who did it?
☐ What does it look like?
☐ What are its characteristics?
☐ What impressions does it make?
☐ What are some typical cases or examples of it?
☐ How did it happen?
☐ What makes it work?
☐ How is it made?
☐ Why did it happen?
☐ What caused it?
☐ What are its effects?
☐ How is it like other things?
☐ How is it different from other things?
☐ What are its parts or types?
☐ How can its parts or types be separated or grouped?
☐ Do its parts or types fit into a logical order?
☐ Into what categories can its parts or types be arranged?
☐ On what basis can it be categorized?
☐ How can it be defined?
☐ How does it resemble other members of its class?
☐ How does it differ from other members of its class?

When applied to a subject, some of these questions can yield many workable topics, including some that you might never have considered had you not asked the questions. For example, by applying this approach to the general subject "the Brooklyn Bridge," you can generate more ideas and topics than you need:

> *What happened?* A short history of the Brooklyn Bridge
>
> *What does it look like?* A description of the Brooklyn Bridge
>
> *How is it made?* The construction of the Brooklyn Bridge
>
> *What are its effects?* The impact of the Brooklyn Bridge on American writers
>
> *How does it differ from other members of its class?* Innovations in the design of the Brooklyn Bridge

At this point in the writing process, you want to come up with possible topics, and the more ideas you have, the wider your choice. Begin by jotting down all the topics you think of. (You can repeat the process of probing several times to limit topics further.) Once you have a list of topics, eliminate those that do not interest you, are too complex, or do not fit your assignment. When you have discarded these less-promising topics, you should have several left. You can then select the topic that best suits your essay's length, purpose, audience, and occasion, as well as your interests and your knowledge of the subject.

REMINDER   QUESTIONS FOR PROBING

You can store the questions for probing listed on page 34 in a file that you can open whenever you have a new subject. Make sure you keep a record of your answers. If the topic you have chosen is too difficult or too narrow for the assignment, you can return to the questions-for-probing file and probe your subject again.

CLOSE   VIEW

Exercise 3

Indicate whether each of the following is a general subject or a specific topic that is narrow enough for a short essay.

1. An argument against fast-food ads that are aimed at young children
2. Home schooling
3. Texting and driving
4. Changes in U.S. immigration laws
5. Requiring college students to study a foreign language
6. The advantages of eTextbooks
7. A comparison of small-town and big-city living
8. A decision you regret
9. The advantages of service-learning courses
10. The drawbacks of self-driving cars

Exercise 4

In preparation for writing a 750-word essay, choose two of the following general subjects and generate three or four specific topics from each by using as many of the questions for probing as you can.

1. The writing center
2. Job interviews
3. Identity theft
4. Genetically modified food
5. Substance abuse
6. Voter ID laws
7. The minimum wage
8. Recreational marijuana
9. Cyberbullying
10. Virtual personal assistants
11. The person you admire most
12. Cell phones in the classroom
13. Online courses
14. Sensational trials
15. The widespread use of surveillance cameras

Freewriting

Another strategy for moving from subject to topic is **freewriting**. You can use freewriting at any stage of the writing process — for example, to generate supporting information or to find a thesis. However, freewriting is a particularly useful way to narrow a general subject or assignment.

When you freewrite, you write for a fixed period, perhaps five or ten minutes, without stopping and without paying attention to spelling, grammar, or punctuation. Your goal is to get your ideas down so that you can react to them and shape them. If you have nothing to say, write down anything until ideas begin to emerge — and in time they will. The secret is to *keep writing*. Try to focus on your subject, but don't worry if you wander off in other directions. The object of freewriting is to let your ideas flow. Often, your best ideas will come from the unexpected connections you make as you write.

> ⊗ **REMINDER**   **FREEWRITING**
>
> You may find yourself distracted when you try to freewrite on a computer. To avoid such distractions, turn off or disable the sound notifications for any messaging systems on your computer (iMessage, Facebook, Gmail, FaceTime, and so on). If you find yourself watching your computer's clock instead of working on your writing, hide the time on your toolbar by changing your computer's general settings.
>
> **CLOSE**   **VIEW**

After completing your freewriting, read what you have written, and look for ideas you can write about. Some writers underline or highlight ideas they think they might explore in their essays. Any of these ideas could become essay topics, or they could become subjects for other freewriting exercises. You might want to freewrite again, using a new idea as your focus. This process of writing more and more specific freewriting exercises — called **focused freewriting** or **looping** — can often yield a great deal of useful information and help you decide on a workable topic.

A STUDENT WRITER: Freewriting

After reading, highlighting, and annotating Henry Louis Gates Jr.'s "'What's in a Name?'" (page 2), Laura Bobnak, a student in a composition class, decided to write an essay in response to this Writing Workshop question.

> Write about a time when you, like Gates's father, could have spoken out in protest but chose not to. Would you make the same decision today?

In an attempt to narrow this assignment to a workable topic, Laura did the following freewriting exercise.

> Write for ten minutes . . . ten minutes . . . at 9 o'clock in the morning — Just what I want to do in the morning — If you can't think of something to say, just write about anything. Right! Time to get this over with — An experience — should have talked — I can think of plenty of times I should have kept quiet! I should have brought a bottle of water to class. I wonder what the people next to me are writing about. That reminds me. Next to me. Jeff Servin in chemistry. The time I saw him cheating. I was mad but I didn't do anything. I studied so hard and all he did was cheat. I was so mad. Nobody else seemed to care. What's the difference between now and then? It's only a year and a half. . . . Honor code? Maturity? A lot of people cheated in high school. I bet I could write about this — Before and after, etc. My attitude then and now.

After some initial thought, Laura discovered an idea that could be the basis for her essay. Although her discussion of the incident still had to be developed, Laura's freewriting helped her come up with a possible topic for her essay: a time she saw someone cheating and did not speak out.

Exercise 5

Do a five-minute freewriting exercise on one of the topics you generated in Exercise 4 (page 36).

Exercise 6

Read what you have just written, underline the most interesting ideas, and choose one idea as a topic you could write about in a short essay. Freewrite about this topic for another five minutes to narrow it further and to generate ideas for your essay. Underline the ideas that seem most useful.

Finding Something to Say

Once you have narrowed your subject to a workable topic, you need to find something to say about it. *Brainstorming* and *journal writing* are useful tools for generating ideas, and both can be helpful at this stage of the writing process (and whenever you need to find additional material).

Brainstorming

Brainstorming is a way of discovering ideas about your topic. You can brainstorm in a group, exchanging ideas with several students in your composition class. You can also brainstorm on your own, recording every fact, idea, or detail you can think of that relates to your topic. Your brainstorming can take the form of an orderly list, or it can be random notes. Your notes might include words, phrases, statements, questions, or even drawings or diagrams. Some items may be inspired by your class notes; others may be from your reading or from talking with friends; and still others may be ideas you have begun to wonder about, points you thought of while moving from subject to topic, or thoughts that occurred to you as you brainstormed.

A STUDENT WRITER: Brainstorming

Laura Bobnak made the brainstorming notes shown on page 39. After reading these notes several times, Laura decided to compare her current and earlier attitudes toward cheating. She knew that she could write a lot about this topic and relate it to the assignment, and she felt confident that her topic would be interesting both to her instructor and to the other students in the class.

 REMINDER   **BRAINSTORMING**

When you brainstorm on a computer, turn off Spelling and Grammar check so that you do not get distracted by the correction prompts. (You can address these technical issues at a later stage of the writing process.)

Journal Writing

Journal writing can be a useful source of ideas at any stage of the writing process. Many writers routinely keep journals, jotting down experiences and ideas they may want to use when they write. They write journal entries even when they have

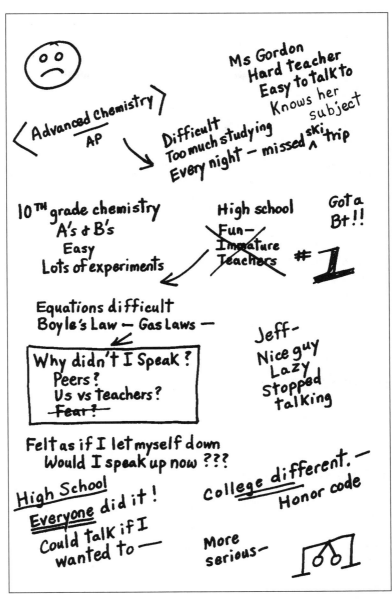

Laura's brainstorming notes

no particular writing projects in mind. Often, these entries are the kernels from which longer pieces of writing develop.

Your instructor may ask you to keep a writing journal, or you may decide to do so on your own. In either case, you will find your journal entries are likely to be more narrowly focused than freewriting or brainstorming, perhaps examining a small part of a reading selection or even one particular statement. Sometimes, you will write in your journal in response to specific questions, such as the Journal Entry assignments that appear throughout this book. Assignments like those can help you start thinking about a reading selection you may later discuss in class or write about.

A STUDENT WRITER: Journal Writing

In the following journal entry, Laura Bobnak explores one idea from her brainstorming notes: her thoughts about her college's honor code.

> At orientation, the dean of students talked about the college's honor code. She talked about how we were a community who were here for a common purpose — to take part in scholarly conversations. According to her, the purpose of the honor code is to make sure these conversations continue uninterrupted. This idea sounded dumb at orientation, but now it makes sense. If I saw someone cheating, I'd tell the instructor. First, though, I'd ask the *student* to go to the instructor. I don't see this as "telling" or "snitching." We're all here to get an education, and we should be able to assume everyone is being honest and fair. Besides, why should I go to all the trouble of studying while someone else does nothing and gets the same grade?

Even though Laura eventually included only a small part of this entry in her essay, writing in her journal helped her focus her ideas about her topic.

Grouping Ideas

Once you have generated material for your essay, you need to group ideas that belong together. *Clustering* and *outlining* can help you do that.

Clustering

Clustering or **mapping** is a way of visually arranging ideas so that you can tell at a glance where they belong and whether or not you need more information. Although you can use clustering at an earlier stage of the writing process, it is especially useful now for seeing how your ideas fit together. (Clustering can also help you narrow your essay's topic even further. If you find that your cluster diagram is too detailed, you can write about just one branch of the cluster.)

 REMINDER   **KEEPING A JOURNAL**

Keeping your journal in a computer file has some obvious advantages. Not only can you maintain a neat record of your ideas, but you can also easily locate and move entries from your journal into an essay without retyping. Word-processing software like Word or Pages also enables you to bold, italicize, underline, and add color to your journal entries. With these tools, you can easily differentiate your ideas from those of your sources. This is important because if you paste material from your sources directly into your essay without documenting it, you are committing plagiarism. (For information on avoiding plagiarism, see Chapter 17.)

Begin clustering by writing your topic in the center of a sheet of paper. After circling the topic, surround it with the words and phrases that identify the major points you intend to discuss. (You can get ideas from your brainstorming notes, from your journal, and from your freewriting.) Circle these words and phrases, and connect them to the topic in the center. Next, construct other clusters of ideas relating to each major point, and draw lines connecting them to the appropriate point. By dividing and subdividing your points, you get more specific as you move outward from the center. In the process, you identify the facts, details, examples, and opinions that illustrate and expand your main points.

A STUDENT WRITER: Clustering

Because Laura Bobnak was not very visually oriented, she chose not to use this method of grouping her ideas. If she had, however, her cluster diagram would have looked like the one below.

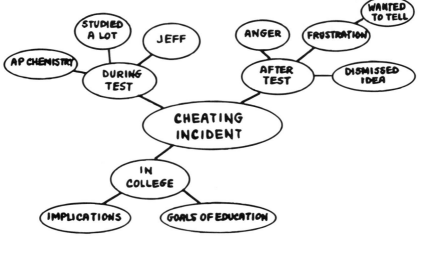

Making an Informal Outline

As an alternative or follow-up to clustering, you can organize your notes from brainstorming or other invention techniques into an **informal outline**. By providing an overview of your material, an informal outline can

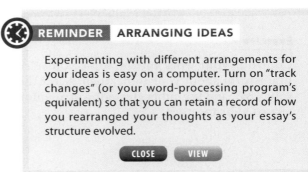

REMINDER   ARRANGING IDEAS

Experimenting with different arrangements for your ideas is easy on a computer. Turn on "track changes" (or your word-processing program's equivalent) so that you can retain a record of how you rearranged your thoughts as your essay's structure evolved.

CLOSE   VIEW

help you focus your thoughts and decide if you need more information.

REMINDER **MAKING AN INFORMAL OUTLINE**

You can easily arrange the notes you generated in your invention activities into an informal outline. You can construct an informal outline by typing words or phrases from your notes and rearranging them until the order makes sense. Later on, if you need to make a formal outline, you can use the categories from this informal outline to construct it (see page 61).

CLOSE   VIEW

Informal outlines do not include all the major divisions and subdivisions of your essay the way formal outlines do; they simply suggest the general shape of your emerging essay. Quite often, an informal outline is just a list of your major points presented in a tentative order. Sometimes, however, an informal outline will include supporting details or suggest a pattern of development.

A STUDENT WRITER: Making an Informal Outline

The following informal outline shows how Laura Bobnak grouped her ideas.

During test
　Found test hard
　Saw Jeff cheating
After test
　Got angry
　Wanted to tell
　Dismissed idea
In college
　Understand implications of cheating
　Understand goals of education

After looking at her informal outline, Laura decided that she could go on to decide on a thesis for her essay.

Exercise 7

Continue your work on the topic you selected in Exercise 6 (page 38). Brainstorm about your topic; then, select the ideas you plan to explore in your essay, and use either clustering or an informal outline to help you group related ideas together.

Developing a Thesis

Defining the Thesis Statement

Once you have grouped your ideas, you need to consider your essay's thesis. A **thesis** is the main point of your essay, its central idea. It is usually a single sentence (often placed at the end of your first paragraph) that tells readers what to expect from the rest of your discussion. Without this **thesis statement**, your essay would be just a collection of ideas with no focus or direction.

Your thesis statement should be more than a *title*, an *announcement of your intent*, or a *statement of fact*. Although a descriptive title orients your readers, it is not detailed enough to reveal your essay's purpose or direction. An announcement of your intent can reveal more, but it is stylistically distracting. Finally, a statement of fact — such as a historical fact or a statistic — is a dead end and therefore cannot be developed into an essay. For example, a statement like "Alaska became a state in 1959" or "Measles is highly contagious" or "The population of Greece is about eleven million" provides your essay with no direction. A judgment or opinion, however — for instance, "The continuing threat of a measles epidemic makes it necessary for all young children to be vaccinated" — *can* be an effective thesis.

Title	Self-Driving Cars: Pros and Cons
Announcement of intent	I will examine the pros and cons of self-driving cars.
Statement of fact	Self-driving cars have features that allow them to accelerate, brake, park, and steer with no driver interaction.
Thesis statement	Self-driving cars are safer than standard models because they operate more efficiently and eliminate accidents caused by human error.
Title	Orwell's "A Hanging"
Announcement of intent	This essay will discuss George Orwell's attitude toward the death penalty in his essay "A Hanging."
Statement of fact	In his essay, Orwell describes a hanging that he witnessed in Burma.
Thesis statement	In "A Hanging," George Orwell shows that capital punishment is not only brutal but also immoral.
Title	Speaking Out
Announcement of intent	This essay will discuss a time when I could have spoken out but did not.
Statement of fact	Once I saw someone cheating and did not speak out.
Thesis statement	As I look back at the cheating I witnessed, I wonder why I kept silent and what would have happened if I had acted.

WHAT A GOOD THESIS DOES

For writers
It helps writers plan an essay.
It helps writers organize ideas in an essay.
It helps writers unify all the ideas in an essay.

For readers
It identifies the main idea of an essay.
It guides readers through an essay.
It clarifies the subject and the focus of an essay.

Deciding on a Thesis

No rules determine when you draft your thesis; the decision depends on the scope of your assignment, your knowledge of the subject, and your method of writing. When you know a lot about a subject, you may come up with a thesis before doing any invention activities (freewriting or brainstorming, for example). At other times, you may have to review your notes and then think of a single statement that communicates your position on the topic. Occasionally, your assignment may specify a thesis by telling you to take a particular position on a topic. In any case, you should decide on a thesis statement before you begin to write your first draft.

As you write, you will continue to discover new ideas, and you will probably move in directions that you did not anticipate. For this reason, the thesis statement you develop at this stage of the writing process is only tentative. Still, because a tentative thesis helps you focus your ideas, it is essential at the initial stages of writing. As you draft your essay, review your thesis statement in light of the points you make, and revise it accordingly.

Stating Your Thesis

It is a good idea to include a one-sentence statement of your thesis early in your essay. An effective thesis statement has the following three characteristics.

1. *An effective thesis statement clearly expresses your essay's main idea.* It does more than state your topic; it indicates what you will say about your topic, and it signals how you will approach your material. The following thesis statement, from the essay "Grant and Lee: A Study in Contrasts" by the historian Bruce Catton, clearly communicates the writer's main idea.

> They [Grant and Lee] were two strong men, these oddly different generals, and they represented the strengths of two conflicting currents that, through them, had come into final collision.

This statement says that the essay will compare and contrast Grant and Lee. Specifically, it indicates that Catton will present the two Civil War generals as symbols of two opposing historical currents. If the statement had been less fully developed—for example, had Catton written, "Grant and Lee were quite different from each other"—it would have just echoed the essay's title.

2. *An effective thesis statement communicates your essay's purpose.* Whether your purpose is to evaluate or analyze or simply to describe or inform, your thesis statement should communicate that purpose to your readers. In general terms, your thesis can be **expressive**, conveying a mood or impression; it can be **informative**, perhaps listing the major points you will discuss or presenting an objective overview of the essay; or it can be **persuasive**, taking a strong stand or outlining the position you will argue.

Each of the following thesis statements communicates a different purpose.

To express feelings	The city's homeless families live in heartbreaking surroundings.
To inform	The plight of the homeless has become so serious that it is a major priority for many city governments.
To persuade	The best way to address the problems of the homeless is to renovate abandoned city buildings to create suitable housing for homeless families.

3. *An effective thesis statement is clearly worded.* To communicate your essay's main idea, an effective thesis statement should be clearly worded. (It should also speak for itself. It is not necessary to write, "My thesis is that . . ." or "The thesis of this essay is. . . .") The thesis statement should give a straightforward and accurate indication of what follows, and it should not mislead readers about the essay's direction, emphasis, scope, content, or viewpoint. Vague language, irrelevant details, and unnecessarily complex terminology have no place in a thesis statement. Keep in mind too that your thesis statement should not make promises that your essay is not going to keep. For example, if you are going to discuss just the *effects* of new immigration laws, your thesis statement should not just emphasize the *causes* that led to their passage.

Your thesis statement should not include every point you will discuss in your essay. Still, it should be specific enough to indicate your direction and scope. The sentence "Immigration laws have not been effective" is not an effective thesis statement because it does not give your essay much focus. The following sentence, however, *is* an effective thesis statement. It clearly indicates what the writer is going to discuss, and it establishes a specific direction for the essay.

Because they do not take into account the economic causes of immigration, current immigration laws do little to decrease the number of undocumented workers coming into the United States.

An Effective Thesis

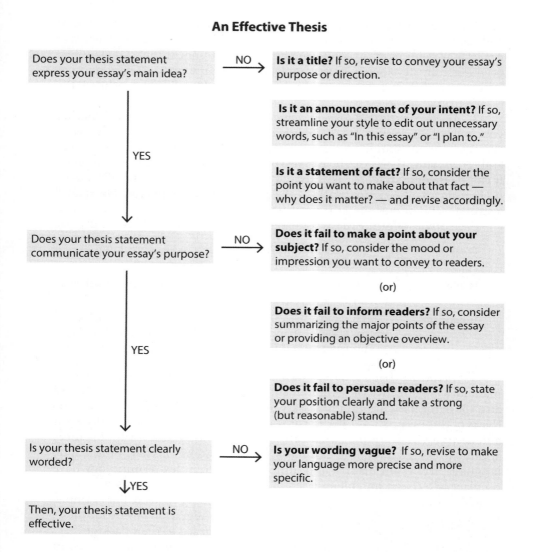

Does your thesis statement express your essay's main idea? ——**NO**→ **Is it a title?** If so, revise to convey your essay's purpose or direction.

Is it an announcement of your intent? If so, streamline your style to edit out unnecessary words, such as "In this essay" or "I plan to."

Is it a statement of fact? If so, consider the point you want to make about that fact — why does it matter? — and revise accordingly.

YES

Does your thesis statement communicate your essay's purpose? ——**NO**→ **Does it fail to make a point about your subject?** If so, consider the mood or impression you want to convey to readers.

(or)

Does it fail to inform readers? If so, consider summarizing the major points of the essay or providing an objective overview.

(or)

Does it fail to persuade readers? If so, state your position clearly and take a strong (but reasonable) stand.

YES

Is your thesis statement clearly worded? ——**NO**→ **Is your wording vague?** If so, revise to make your language more precise and more specific.

↓**YES**

Then, your thesis statement is effective.

Implying a Thesis

Like an explicitly stated thesis, an **implied thesis** conveys an essay's main focus, but it does not do so explicitly. Instead, the selection and arrangement of the essay's ideas suggest the focus. Professional writers sometimes prefer this option because an implied thesis is subtler than a stated thesis. (An implied thesis is especially useful in narratives, descriptions, and some arguments, where an explicit thesis would seem heavy-handed or arbitrary.) In most college writing, however, you should state your thesis to avoid any risk of being misunderstood or of wandering away from your topic.

A STUDENT WRITER: Developing a Thesis

After experimenting with different ways of arranging her ideas for her essay, Laura Bobnak summed them up in a tentative thesis statement.

> As I look back at the cheating I witnessed, I wonder why I kept silent and what would have happened if I had acted.

CHECKLIST   STATING YOUR THESIS

- ☐ Do you state your thesis in one complete, concise sentence?
- ☐ Does your thesis indicate your purpose?
- ☐ Is your thesis suited to the assignment?
- ☐ Does your thesis clearly convey the main idea you intend to support in your essay?
- ☐ Does your thesis suggest how you will organize your essay?

Exercise 8

Assess the strengths and weaknesses of the following as thesis statements.

1. My instructor has an attendance policy.
2. My instructor should change her attendance policy because it is bad.
3. My instructor should change her attendance policy because it is unreasonable, inflexible, and unfair.
4. For many students, a community college makes more sense than a four-year college or university.
5. Some children exhibit violent behavior.
6. Violence is a problem in our society.
7. Conflict-resolution courses should be taught to help prevent violence in U.S. schools.
8. Social networking sites such as Instagram can cause problems.
9. Instagram attracts many college students.
10. College students should be careful of what material they put on their Facebook pages because prospective employers routinely check them.

Exercise 9

Rewrite the following factual statements to make them effective thesis statements. Make sure each thesis statement is a clearly and specifically worded sentence.

1. Henry David Thoreau thought that we should get in touch with nature and lead more meaningful lives.
2. Several Supreme Court decisions have said that art containing explicit sexual images is not necessarily pornographic.

3. Many women earn less money than men do, in part because they drop out of the workforce during their child-rearing years.
4. People who watch more than five hours of television a day tend to think the world is more violent than do people who watch less than two hours of television daily.
5. In recent years, the suicide rate among teenagers — especially middle- and upper-middle-class teenagers — has risen dramatically.

Exercise 10

Read the following sentences from "The Argument Culture" by Deborah Tannen. Then, formulate a one-sentence thesis statement that summarizes the key points Tannen makes about the nature of argument in our culture.

- "More and more, our public interactions have become like arguing with a spouse."
- "Nearly everything is framed as a battle or game in which winning or losing is the main concern."
- "The argument culture pervades every aspect of our lives today."
- "Issues from global warming to abortion are depicted as two-sided arguments, when in fact most Americans' views lie somewhere in the middle."
- "What's wrong with the argument culture is the ubiquity, the knee-jerk nature of approaching any issue, problem, or public person in an adversarial way."
- "If you fight to win, the temptation is great to deny facts that support your opponent's views and say only what supports your side."
- "We must expand the notion of 'debate' to include more dialogue."
- "Perhaps it is time to re-examine the assumption that audiences always prefer a fight."
- "Instead of insisting on hearing 'both sides,' let's insist on hearing 'all sides.'"

Exercise 11

Going through as many steps as you need, draft an effective thesis statement for the essay you have been working on.

3

Arrangement

Each of the tasks discussed in Chapter 2 represents choices you have to make about your topic and your material. Now, before you begin to write, you have another choice to make: how to arrange your material into an essay.

Recognizing a Pattern

Deciding how to structure an essay is easy when your assignment specifies a particular pattern of development. That may be the case in a composition class, where the instructor may assign a descriptive or a narrative essay. Also, certain assignments or exam questions suggest how your material should be structured. For example, an instructor might ask you to tell about how something works, or an exam question might ask you to trace the circumstances leading up to an event. If you are perceptive, you will realize that your instructor is asking for a process essay and that the exam question is asking for either a narrative or a cause-and-effect response. The most important things are to recognize the clues that such assignments give (or those that you find in your topic or thesis statement) and to structure your essay accordingly.

One clue to structuring your essay can be found in the questions you asked when you probed your subject (see page 34). For example, if questions like "What happened?" and "When did it happen?" yielded the most useful information about your topic, you should consider structuring your essay as a narrative. The following chart connects various questions to the patterns of development that they suggest. Notice how the terms in the right-hand column — narration, description, and so on — identify patterns of development that can help you organize your ideas. Chapters 6 through 13 explain and illustrate each of these patterns.

CHECKLIST RECOGNIZING A PATTERN

What happened?
When did it happen?
Where did it happen?
Who did it?
⎫
⎬ Narration
⎭

What does it look like?
What are its characteristics?
What impressions does it make?
⎫
⎬ Description
⎭

What are some typical cases
    or examples of it?
⎫
⎬ Exemplification
⎭

How did it happen?
What makes it work?
How is it made?
⎫
⎬ Process
⎭

Why did it happen?
What caused it?
What does it cause?
What are its effects?
⎫
⎬ Cause and effect
⎭

How is it like other things?
How is it different from other
    things?
⎫
⎬ Comparison and contrast
⎭

What are its parts or types?
How can its parts or types be
    separated or grouped?
Do its parts or types fit into a
    logical order?
Into what categories can its
    parts or types be arranged?
On what basis can it be
    categorized?
⎫
⎬ Classification and division
⎭

How can it be defined?
How does it resemble other
    members of its class?
How does it differ from other
    members of its class?
⎫
⎬ Definition
⎭

Understanding the Parts of the Essay

No matter what pattern of development you use, your essay should consist of an **introduction** that presents your thesis statement, several **body paragraphs** that develop and support your thesis, and a **conclusion** that reinforces your thesis and provides closure. This **thesis and support** structure — stating your thesis and developing ideas that explain and expand it — is central to much college writing.

INTRODUCTORY PARAGRAPH

Thesis statement

BODY PARAGRAPH

Support for thesis

BODY PARAGRAPH

Support for thesis

BODY PARAGRAPH

Support for thesis

BODY PARAGRAPH

Support for thesis

CONCLUDING PARAGRAPH

Restatement of thesis or review of key points

The Introduction

Your **introduction**, usually one paragraph and rarely more than two, transports readers from their world into the world of your essay. A weak introduction will cause readers to lose interest in your essay. A strong introduction, however, will make them care about the issues you are discussing and want to read further. For this reason, an effective introduction usually identifies your subject, creates interest, and states your thesis.

Here are several effective strategies you can use to introduce an essay.

(Note that in each of these introductory paragraphs, the thesis is underlined.)

1. You can begin with *background information*. This approach works particularly well on exams, when there is no need (or time) for subtlety.

> The federal minimum wage was introduced by Franklin Delano Roosevelt in 1938. Since then, the minimum wage has been raised twenty-two times by twelve different presidents. (States can also set a minimum wage, as long as it does not fall below the federal level.) However, the Fair Labor Standards Act exempts certain categories of workers — for example, those who work for tips, some agricultural workers, home care aides, and employees of some small businesses — from the federal minimum wage requirements. As a result, many low-wage workers receive much less than the minimum wage. <u>Given the current economic situation, both federal and state governments should immediately reevaluate wage exemptions so that all American workers are treated fairly.</u>   (economics exam)

2. You can introduce an essay with your own original *definition* of a relevant term or concept. This technique is especially useful for research papers or exams, when the meaning of a specific term is crucial.

> Democracy is a form of government in which people choose leaders by voting. For democracy to work, elected representatives must have reasoned debates about important issues and be willing to compromise. Recently, however, both Republicans and Democrats have become more and more divided along party lines. As a result, hostility between the two parties is worse than it has been in decades. Sadly, a recent study suggests that these divisions are greatest among those who are most involved in the political process. The result is that partisan animosity has increased, and many people in government believe that the opposing party's policies threaten the well-being of the country. <u>Unless something is done to encourage bipartisan cooperation, we will soon become a nation divided, one that will be unable to agree on solutions to the nation's most pressing problems.</u>
>   (political science essay)

3. You can begin your essay with an *anecdote* or *story* that leads readers to your thesis.

> Three years ago, I went with my grandparents to my first auction. They live in a small town outside of Lancaster, Pennsylvania, where it is common for people to auction off the contents of a home when someone moves or dies. As I walked through the crowd, I smelled the funnel cakes frying in the food trucks, heard the hypnotic chanting of the auctioneer, and sensed the excitement of the crowd. <u>Two hours later, I walked off with an old trunk that I had bought for thirty dollars and a passion for auctions that I still have today.</u>
>   (composition essay)

4. You can begin with a *question*.

> What was it like to live through the Holocaust? The late Elie Wiesel, in *One Generation After*, answers this question by presenting a series of accounts about ordinary people who found themselves imprisoned in Nazi death

camps. As he does so, he challenges some of the assumptions we have about the Holocaust and those who survived.   (sociology book report)

5. You can begin with a *quotation*. If it arouses interest, it can encourage your audience to read further.

"The rich are different," F. Scott Fitzgerald wrote more than ninety years ago. Apparently, they still are. As an examination of the tax code shows, the wealthy receive many more benefits than the middle class or the poor do.
(accounting paper)

6. You can begin with a *surprising statement*. An unexpected statement catches readers' attention and makes them want to read more.

Believe it or not, many people who live in the suburbs are not white and rich. My family, for example, fits into neither of these categories. Ten years ago, my family and I came to the United States from Pakistan. My parents were poor then, and by some standards, they are still poor even though they both work two jobs. Still, they eventually saved enough to buy a small house in the suburbs of Chicago. Throughout the country, there are many suburban families like mine who are working hard to make ends meet so that their children can get a good education and go to college.
(composition essay)

7. You can begin with a *contradiction*. You can open your essay with an idea that most people believe is true and then get readers' attention by showing that it is inaccurate or ill-advised.

Many people think that after the Declaration of Independence was signed in 1776, the colonists defeated the British army in battle after battle. This commonly held belief is incorrect. The truth is that the colonial army lost most of its battles. The British were defeated not because the colonial army was stronger, but because George Washington refused to be lured into a costly winner-take-all battle and because the British government lost interest in pursuing an expensive war three thousand miles from home.
(history take-home exam)

8. You can begin with a *fact* or *statistic*.

Recently, the National Council on Teacher Quality released a report that said that of the 1,400 teacher-preparation programs in the United States, 1,100 are inadequate. According to this report, undergraduate teacher-preparation programs are not rigorous enough and do not include sufficient classroom-teaching experience. In addition, future educators are rarely required to major in the specific subject areas they are going to teach. Although many educators agree with this negative assessment, they do not agree on what should be done to remedy the situation. Instead of trying to modify existing programs, educators should look at new, more cost-effective ways of improving teacher training.   (education essay)

No matter which strategy you select, your introduction should be consistent in tone with the rest of your essay. If it is not, it can misrepresent your intentions and even damage your credibility. (For this reason, it is a good idea not to write your introduction until after you have finished your rough draft.)

A technical report, for instance, should have an introduction that reflects the formality and objectivity the occasion requires. The introduction to an auto-biographical essay, however, could have a more informal, subjective tone.

✓ **CHECKLIST**   **WHAT NOT TO DO IN AN INTRODUCTION**

- ☐ **Don't apologize.** Never use phrases such as "in my opinion" or "I may not be an expert, but. . . ." By doing so, you suggest that you don't really know your subject.
- ☐ **Don't begin with a dictionary definition.** Avoid beginning an essay with phrases like "According to Webster's Dictionary. . . ." This type of introduction is overused and trite. If you want to use a definition, develop your own.
- ☐ **Don't announce what you intend to do.** Don't begin with phrases such as "In this paper I will . . ." or "The purpose of this essay is to. . . ." Use your introduction to create interest in your topic, and let readers discover your intention when they get to your thesis statement.
- ☐ **Don't wander.** Your introduction should draw readers into your essay as soon as possible. Avoid irrelevant comments or annoying digressions that will distract or confuse readers.

Exercise 1

Look through magazine articles or the essays in this book, and find one example of each kind of introduction. Why do you think each introductory strategy was chosen? What other strategies might have worked?

The Body Paragraphs

The middle section, or **body**, of your essay develops your thesis. The body paragraphs present the **support** — examples, reasons, facts, and so on — that convinces your audience that your thesis is reasonable. To do so, each body paragraph should be *unified, coherent*, and *well developed*. It should also follow a particular pattern of development and should clearly support your thesis.

  • *Each body paragraph should be unified.*   A paragraph is **unified** when each sentence relates directly to the main idea of the paragraph. Frequently, the main idea of a paragraph is stated in a **topic sentence**. Like a thesis statement, a topic sentence acts as a guidepost, making it easy for readers to follow the paragraph's discussion. Although the placement of a topic sentence depends on a writer's purpose and subject, beginning writers often make it the first sentence of a paragraph.

Sometimes the main idea of a paragraph is not stated but **implied** by the sentences in the paragraph. Professional writers often use this technique because they believe that in some situations — especially narratives and descriptions — a topic sentence can seem forced or awkward. As a beginning writer, however, you will find it helpful to use topic sentences to keep your paragraphs focused.

Whether or not you include a topic sentence, remember that each sentence in a paragraph should develop the paragraph's main idea. If the sentences in a paragraph do not support the main idea, the paragraph will lack unity.

In the following excerpt from a student essay, notice how the topic sentence (underlined) unifies the paragraph by summarizing its main idea:

> Another problem with fast food is that it contains additives. Fast-food companies know that to keep their customers happy, they have to give them food that tastes good, and this is where the trouble starts. For example, to give fries flavor, McDonald's used to fry their potatoes in beef fat. Shockingly, their fries actually had more saturated fat than their hamburgers did. When the public found out how unhealthy their fries were, the company switched to vegetable oil. What most people don't know, however, is that McDonald's adds a chemical derived from animals to the vegetable oil to give it the taste of beef tallow.

The topic sentence, placed at the beginning of the paragraph, enables readers to grasp the writer's point immediately. The examples that follow all relate to that point, making the paragraph unified.

• *Each body paragraph should be coherent.*   A paragraph is **coherent** if its sentences are smoothly and logically connected to one another. Coherence can be strengthened in three ways. First, you can repeat **keywords** to carry concepts from one sentence to another and to echo important terms. Second, you can use **pronouns** to refer to key nouns in previous sentences. Finally, you can use **transitions**, words or expressions that show chronological sequence, cause and effect, and so on (see the list of transitions on page 56). These three strategies for connecting sentences — which you can also use to connect paragraphs within an essay — indicate for your readers the exact relationships among your ideas.

The following paragraph, from George Orwell's "Shooting an Elephant" (page 132), uses repeated keywords, pronouns, and transitions to achieve coherence.

> I got up. The Burmans were already racing past me across the mud. It was obvious that the elephant would never rise again, but he was not dead. He was breathing very rhythmically with long rattling gasps, his great mound of a side painfully rising and falling. His mouth was wide open — I could see far down into caverns of pale pink throat. I waited a long time for him to die, but his breathing did not weaken. Finally I fired my two remaining shots into the spot where I thought his heart must be. The thick blood welled out of him like red velvet, but still he did not die. His body did not even jerk when the shots hit him, the tortured breathing continued without a pause. He was dying, very slowly and in great agony, but in some world remote from me where not even a bullet could damage him further. I felt that I had got to put an end to that dreadful noise. It seemed dreadful to see the great beast lying there, powerless to move and yet powerless to die, and not even to be able to finish him. I sent back for my small rifle and poured shot after shot into his heart and down his throat. They seemed to make no impression. The tortured gasps continued as steadily as the ticking of a clock.

TRANSITIONS

SEQUENCE OR ADDITION

again	first, . . . second, . . . third	next
also	furthermore	one . . . another
and	in addition	still
besides	last	too
finally	moreover	

TIME

afterward	finally	simultaneously
as soon as	immediately	since
at first	in the meantime	soon
at the same time	later	subsequently
before	meanwhile	then
earlier	next	until
eventually	now	

COMPARISON

also	likewise
in comparison	similarly
in the same way	

CONTRAST

although	in contrast	on the one hand . . .
but	instead	on the other hand . . .
conversely	nevertheless	still
despite	nonetheless	whereas
even though	on the contrary	yet
however		

EXAMPLES

for example	specifically
for instance	that is
in fact	thus
namely	

CONCLUSIONS OR SUMMARIES

as a result	in summary
in conclusion	therefore
in short	thus

CAUSES OR EFFECTS

as a result	so
because	then
consequently	therefore
since	

Orwell keeps his narrative coherent by using transitional expressions (*already, finally, when the shots hit him*) to signal the passing of time. He uses pronouns (*he, his*) in nearly every sentence to refer back to the elephant, the topic of his paragraph. Finally, he repeats keywords like *shots* and *die* (and its variants *dead* and *dying*) to link the whole paragraph's sentences together.

• *Each body paragraph should be well developed.* A paragraph is **well developed** if it contains the support that readers need to understand its main idea. If a paragraph is not adequately developed, readers will think they have been given only a partial explanation of the subject.

If you decide you need more information in a paragraph, you can look back at your brainstorming notes. If that doesn't help, you can freewrite or brainstorm again, talk with friends and instructors, read more about your topic, or (with your instructor's permission) do some research. Your assignment and your topic will determine the kind and amount of information you need.

TYPES OF SUPPORT

- **Examples** Specific illustrations of a general idea or concept
- **Reasons** Underlying causes or explanations
- **Facts** Pieces of information that can be verified or proved
- **Statistics** Numerical data (for example, results of studies by reputable authorities or organizations)
- **Details** Parts or portions of a whole (for example, steps in a process)
- **Expert opinions** Statements by recognized authorities in a particular field
- **Personal experiences** Events that you lived through
- **Visuals** Diagrams, charts, graphs, or photographs

CHECKLIST EFFECTIVE SUPPORT

☐ **Support should be relevant.** Body paragraphs should clearly relate to your essay's thesis. Irrelevant material — material that does not pertain to the thesis — should be deleted.

☐ **Support should be specific.** Body paragraphs should contain support that is specific, not general or vague. Specific examples, clear reasons, and precise explanations engage readers and communicate your ideas to them.

☐ **Support should be adequate.** Body paragraphs should contain enough facts, reasons, and examples to support your thesis. How much support you need depends on your audience, your purpose, and the scope of your thesis.

☐ **Support should be representative.** Body paragraphs should present support that is typical, not atypical. For example, suppose you write an essay claiming that flu shots do not work. Your support for this claim is that your grandmother got the flu even though she was vaccinated. This example is not

representative because studies show that most people who get vaccinated do not get the flu.
- ☐ **Support should be documented.** Support that comes from research (print sources and the Internet, for example) should be documented. (For more information on using proper documentation, see Chapter 18 and the Appendix.) **Plagiarism** — failure to document the ideas and words of others — is not only unfair but is also dishonest. Always use proper documentation to acknowledge your debt to your sources, and keep in mind that words and ideas you borrow from the essays in this book must also be documented. (For more information on avoiding plagiarism, see Chapter 17.)

The following student paragraph uses two examples to support its topic sentence (underlined).

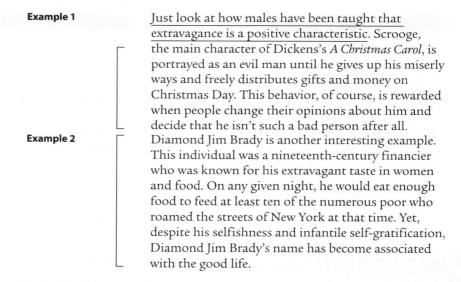

Example 1

<u>Just look at how males have been taught that extravagance is a positive characteristic.</u> Scrooge, the main character of Dickens's *A Christmas Carol*, is portrayed as an evil man until he gives up his miserly ways and freely distributes gifts and money on Christmas Day. This behavior, of course, is rewarded when people change their opinions about him and decide that he isn't such a bad person after all.

Example 2

Diamond Jim Brady is another interesting example. This individual was a nineteenth-century financier who was known for his extravagant taste in women and food. On any given night, he would eat enough food to feed at least ten of the numerous poor who roamed the streets of New York at that time. Yet, despite his selfishness and infantile self-gratification, Diamond Jim Brady's name has become associated with the good life.

- *Each body paragraph should follow a particular pattern of development.*   In addition to making sure your body paragraphs are unified, coherent, and well developed, you need to organize each paragraph according to a specific pattern of development. (Chapters 6 through 13 each begin with a paragraph-length example of the pattern discussed in the chapter.)

- *Each body paragraph should clearly support the thesis statement.*   No matter how many body paragraphs your essay has — three, four, five, or even more — each paragraph should introduce and develop an idea that clearly and convincingly supports the essay's thesis. Each paragraph's topic sentence should express one of these supporting points. The diagram that follows illustrates this thesis-and-support structure.

INTRODUCTORY PARAGRAPH

Thesis statement: Despite the emphasis by journalists on objective reporting, there are three reasons why television news is anything but objective.

BODY PARAGRAPH

Topic sentence: Television news is not objective because the people who gather and report the news are biased.

BODY PARAGRAPH

Topic sentence: In addition, television news is not objective because networks face pressure from sponsors.

BODY PARAGRAPH

Topic sentence: Finally, television news is not objective because networks focus on ratings rather than content.

CONCLUDING PARAGRAPH

Restatement of thesis: Even though television journalists claim they strive for objectivity, the truth is that this ideal has been impossible to achieve.

Exercise 2

Choose a body paragraph from one of the essays in this book. Using the criteria discussed on pages 54–59, decide whether the paragraph is unified, coherent, and well developed.

Exercise 3

Choose one essay in this book and underline its thesis statement. Then, determine how its body paragraphs support that thesis statement. (Note that in a long essay, several body paragraphs may develop a single supporting point, and some paragraphs may serve as transitions from one point to another.)

The Conclusion

Because readers re-member best what they read last, your **conclusion**

> (❂) **REMINDER**   **LABELING YOUR NOTES**
>
> You can use your word-processing program to insert comments into your notes and to label ideas that seem to suggest certain essay structures (narrative, cause and effect, process, and so on). This tip can be used along with the checklist on page 50 to get a sense of how to structure your essay.
>
>

is very important. It is your final word on your subject and your last chance to influence your readers, to demonstrate the importance of your ideas, and to suggest the broader implications of your thesis. For this reason, you should always end your essay in a way that reinforces your main point and gives a sense of closure.

Like your introduction, your conclusion is rarely longer than a paragraph. Regardless of its length, however, your conclusion should be consistent with the rest of your essay; that is, it should not introduce points you have not discussed earlier. Frequently, a conclusion will restate your essay's main idea or review your key points.

Here are several strategies you can use to conclude an essay:

1. You can conclude your essay by *reviewing your key points* or by *restating your thesis in different words*.

> Rotation of crops provided several benefits. It enriched soil by giving it a rest; it enabled farmers to vary their production; and it ended the cycle of "boom or bust" that had characterized the prewar South's economy when cotton was the primary crop. Of course, this innovation did not solve all the economic problems of the postwar South, but it did lay the groundwork for the healthy economy this region enjoys today.   (history exam)

2. You can end a discussion of a problem with a *recommendation of a course of action*.

> Not surprisingly, the population of students with disabilities attending American colleges and universities is growing each year. Even so, many of these students find that some campuses are not equipped to address the diverse range of needs that these students have. This situation exists even though students with disabilities are protected by local, state, and federal laws that guarantee them an equal level of access. For this reason, colleges must do more to make their campuses, classrooms, and social situations accessible to all students, regardless of their individual needs.   (public health essay)

3. You can conclude with a *prediction*. Be sure, however, that your prediction follows logically from the points you have made in the essay. Your conclusion is no place to make new points or to change direction.

> Despite recent advances in helmet technology, the number of head injuries in football remains unacceptably high. This is especially true for high school players, who face a higher risk of concussions than college players do. As current research has shown, there is limited evidence that current helmet design can eliminate, or even cut, the risk of concussions. As a result of repeated football-related head trauma, players experience a number of disturbing effects, including depression, suicide, and chronic traumatic encephalopathy. Unless this situation can be reversed, the future of football is in serious doubt. As they have done with boxing, fans will tune out and find other less dangerous sports to watch.   (composition essay)

4. You can end with a relevant *quotation*.

> In *Walden*, Henry David Thoreau says, "The mass of men lead lives of quiet desperation." This sentiment is reinforced by a drive through the Hill

District of our city. Perhaps the work of the men and women who run the clinic on Jefferson Street cannot totally change this situation, but it can give us hope to know that some people, at least, are working for the betterment of us all.   (social work essay)

✔ **CHECKLIST** **WHAT NOT TO DO IN A CONCLUSION**

- ☐ **Don't end by repeating the exact words of your thesis and listing your main points.** Avoid boring endings that tell readers what they already know.
- ☐ **Don't end with an empty phrase.** Avoid ending with a cliché like "This just goes to prove that you can never be too careful."
- ☐ **Don't introduce new points or go off in new directions.** Your conclusion should not introduce new points for discussion. It should reinforce the points you have already made in your essay.
- ☐ **Don't end with an unnecessary announcement.** Don't end by saying that you are ending — for example, "In conclusion, let me say. . . ." The tone of your conclusion should signal that the essay is drawing to a close.

Exercise 4

Look through magazine articles or the essays in this book, and find one example of each kind of conclusion. Why do you think each concluding strategy was chosen? What other strategies might have worked?

Constructing a Formal Outline

Before you begin to write, you may decide to construct a **formal outline** to guide you. Whereas informal outlines are preliminary lists that give you a general sense of which points to discuss, formal outlines are detailed, multi-level constructions that indicate the exact order in which you will present your key points and supporting details. The complexity of your assignment determines which type of outline you need. For a short essay, an informal outline like the one on page 42 is probably sufficient. For a longer, more complex essay, however, you will need a formal outline.

One way to construct a formal outline is to copy down the main headings from your informal outline. Then, arrange ideas from your brainstorming notes or cluster diagram as subheadings under the appropriate headings. As you work on your outline, make sure each idea you include supports your thesis. Ideas that don't fit should be reworded or discarded. As you revise your essay, continue to refer to your outline to make sure your thesis and support are clearly connected. The guidelines that follow will help you prepare a formal outline.

✓ CHECKLIST **CONSTRUCTING A FORMAL OUTLINE**

☐ Write your thesis statement at the top of the page.
☐ Group main headings under roman numerals (*I*, *II*, *III*, *IV*, and so on), and place them flush with the left-hand margin.
☐ Indent each subheading under the first word of the heading above it. Use capital letters (A, B, C, and so on) before major points, and use numbers before supporting details.
☐ Capitalize the first letter of the first word of each heading.
☐ Make your outline as simple as possible, avoiding overly complex divisions of ideas. (Try not to go beyond third-level headings — *1*, *2*, *3*, and so on.)
☐ Construct either a **topic outline**, with headings expressed as short phrases or single words ("Advantages and disadvantages"), or a **sentence outline**, with headings expressed as complete sentences ("The advantages of advanced placement chemistry outweigh the disadvantages"). *Never use both phrases and complete sentences in the same outline.*
☐ Express all headings at the same level in parallel terms. (If roman numeral *I* is a noun, *II*, *III*, and *IV* should also be nouns.)
☐ Make sure each heading contains at least two subdivisions. You cannot have a *1* without a *2* or an *A* without a *B*.
☐ Make sure your headings do not overlap.

A STUDENT WRITER: Constructing a Formal Outline

The topic outline Laura Bobnak constructed follows the guidelines discussed above. Notice that her outline focuses on the body of her paper and does not include the introduction or conclusion: these sections are usually developed after the body has been drafted. (Compare this formal outline with the informal outline on page 42, in which Laura simply grouped her brainstorming notes under three general headings.)

Thesis statement: As I look back at the cheating I witnessed, I wonder why I kept silent and what would have happened if I had acted.

I. The incident
   A. Test situation
   B. My observation
   C. My reactions
      1. Anger
      2. Silence
II. Reasons for keeping silent
   A. Other students' attitudes
   B. My fears
III. Current attitude toward cheating
   A. Effects of cheating on education
   B. Effects of cheating on students

This outline enabled Laura to arrange her points so that they supported her thesis. As she went on to draft her essay, the outline reminded her to emphasize the contrast between her present and former attitudes toward cheating.

Exercise 5

Read the thesis statement you developed in Chapter 2, Exercise 11 (on page 48), as well as all the notes you made for the essay you are planning. Then, make a topic outline that lists the points you will discuss in your essay. When you are finished, check to make sure your outline conforms to the guidelines on the checklist on page 62.

REMINDER   CONSTRUCTING A FORMAL OUTLINE

You can use your word-processing program to arrange and rearrange your headings until your outline is logical and complete. (Your word-processing program most likely has an outline function that automatically indents and numbers items.) If you saved your prewriting notes in computer files, you can refer to them while working on your outline and perhaps add or modify headings to reflect what you find.

CLOSE   **VIEW**

4

Drafting and Revising

After you decide on a thesis and an arrangement for your ideas, you can begin to draft and revise your essay. Keep in mind that even as you carry out these activities, you may have to generate more material or revise your thesis statement.

Writing Your First Draft

The purpose of your **first draft** is to get your ideas down on paper so that you can react to them. Experienced writers know that the first draft is nothing more than a work in progress; it exists to be revised. With this in mind, you should expect to cross out and extensively rearrange material. In addition, don't be surprised if you think of new ideas as you write. If a new idea comes to you, go with it. Some of the best writing comes from unexpected turns or accidents. The following guidelines will help you prepare your first draft.

✓ **CHECKLIST** **DRAFTING**

☐ **Begin with the body paragraphs.** Because your essay will probably be revised extensively, don't take the time at this stage to craft a complete introduction or conclusion. Let your thesis statement guide you as you draft the body paragraphs of your essay. Later, when you have finished, you can draft an appropriate introduction and conclusion.

☐ **Get your ideas down quickly.** Don't worry about grammar or word choice, and try not to interrupt the flow of your writing with concerns about style.

☐ **Take regular breaks as you write.** Don't write until you are so exhausted that you can't think straight. Many writers divide their writing into stages, perhaps completing one or two body paragraphs and then taking a short

> break. This strategy is more efficient than trying to write a complete first draft without stopping.
> ☐ **Leave yourself time to revise.** Remember, your first draft is a *rough draft*. All writing benefits from revision, so allow enough time to write two or more drafts.

A STUDENT WRITER: Writing a First Draft

Here is the first draft of Laura Bobnak's essay on the following topic: "Write about a time when you, like Henry Louis Gates Jr.'s father, could have spoken out but chose not to. Would you make the same decision today?"

When I was in high school, I had an experience like the one Henry Louis Gates   1
Jr. talks about in his essay. It was then that I saw a close friend cheat in chemistry class. As I look back at the cheating I witnessed, I wonder why I kept silent and what would have happened if I had acted.

The incident I am going to describe took place during the final exam for   2
my advanced placement chemistry class. I had studied hard for it, but even so, I found the test difficult. As I struggled to balance a particularly difficult equation, I noticed that my friend Jeff, who was sitting across from me, was acting strangely. I noticed that he was copying material from his cell phone. After watching him for a while, I dismissed the incident and got back to my test.

After the test was over, I began to think about what I had seen. The more I   3
thought about it the angrier I got. It seemed unfair that I had studied for weeks to memorize formulas and equations while all Jeff had done was to copy them onto his cell phone. For a moment I considered going to the teacher, but I quickly rejected this idea. After all, cheating was something everybody did. Besides, I was afraid if I told on Jeff, my friends would stop talking to me.

Now that I am in college I see the situation differently. I find it hard to believe   4
that I could ever have been so complacent about cheating. Cheating is certainly something that students should not take for granted. It undercuts the education process and is unfair to teachers and to the majority of students who spend their time studying.

If I could go back to high school and relive the experience, I now know that I   5
would have gone to the teacher. Naturally Jeff would have been angry at me, but at least I would have known I had the courage to do the right thing.

Exercise 1

Write a draft of the essay you have been working on in Chapters 2 and 3. Be sure to look back at all your notes as well as your outline.

Revising Your Essay

Revision is not something you do after your essay is finished. It is a continuing process during which you consider the logic and clarity of your ideas as well as how effectively they are presented.

Revision is not simply a matter of proofreading or editing, of crossing out one word and substituting another or correcting errors in spelling and punctuation; revision involves reseeing and rethinking what you have written. When you revise, you may find yourself adding and deleting extensively, reordering whole sentences or paragraphs as you reconsider what you want to communicate to your audience.

Revision can take a lot of time, so don't be discouraged if you have to go through three or four drafts before you think your essay is ready to submit. The following advice can help you when you revise your essay.

- *Give yourself a cooling-off period.*   Put your first draft aside for several hours or even a day or two if you can. This cooling-off period lets you distance yourself from your essay so that you can read it more objectively when you return to it. When you read it again, you will see things you missed the first time.
- *Revise on hard copy.*   Because a printed-out draft shows you all the pages of your paper and enables you to see your handwritten edits, revise on hard copy instead of directly on the computer screen. (Recent studies suggest that students who revise on printouts do a better job than students who revise on a computer screen.)
- *Read your draft aloud.*   Before you revise, read your draft aloud to help you spot choppy sentences, missing words, or phrases that do not sound right.
- *Take advantage of opportunities to get feedback.*   Your instructor may organize peer-editing groups, distribute a revision checklist, refer students to a writing center, or schedule one-on-one conferences. Make use of as many of these opportunities for feedback as you can; each offers you a different way of gaining information about what you have written. (See Strategies for Revising, page 71.)
- *Try not to get overwhelmed.*   It is easy to become overwhelmed by all the feedback you get about your draft. To avoid this, approach revision systematically. Don't automatically make all the changes people suggest; consider the validity of each change. Also ask yourself whether comments suggest larger issues. For example, does a comment about a series of choppy sentences suggest a need for you to add transitions, or does it mean you need to rethink your ideas?
- *Don't let your ego get in the way.*   Everyone likes praise, and receiving negative criticism is never pleasant. Experienced writers know, however, that they must get honest feedback if they are going to improve their work. Learn to see criticism — whether from an instructor or from your peers — as a necessary part of the revision process.
- *Revise in stages.*   Deal with the large elements (essay and paragraph structure) before moving on to the smaller elements (sentence structure and word choice).

How you revise—what specific strategies you decide to use—depends on your own preference, your instructor's instructions, and the time available. Like the rest of the writing process, revision varies from student to student and from assignment to assignment. Five useful revision strategies—*revising with an outline, revising with a checklist, revising with your instructor's written comments, revising in a conference, and revising in a peer-editing group*—are discussed in the pages that follow.

Revising with an Outline

When you begin the revision process, you can check your essay's structure by making a **review outline**. Either an informal outline or a formal one can show you whether you have left out any important points. An outline can also show you whether your essay follows a particular pattern of development. Finally, an outline can clarify the relationship between your thesis statement and your body paragraphs. (See pages 61–63 for guidelines for constructing an outline.)

Revising with a Checklist

If you have time, you can use a detailed **revision checklist**, like the one that follows, adapting it to your own writing needs.

✓ CHECKLIST   REVISING

☐ **Thesis statement** Is your thesis statement clear and specific? Does it indicate the direction your essay is taking? Is it consistent with the body of your essay? If you departed from your essay's original direction while you were writing, you may need to revise your thesis statement so that it accurately reflects the ideas and information now contained in the body.

☐ **Body paragraphs** Are the body paragraphs unified? Coherent? Well developed? If not, you might have to add more facts or examples or smoother transitions. Does each body paragraph follow a particular pattern of development? Do the points you make in these paragraphs support your thesis? If not, you may need to delete material that is unrelated to the thesis statement—or revise it so that it *is* relevant.

☐ **Introduction and conclusion** Are your introduction and your conclusion appropriate for your material, your audience, and your purpose? Are they interesting? Does your introduction include a thesis statement? Does your conclusion reinforce your thesis?

☐ **Sentences** Are your sentences effective? Interesting? Varied in length and structure? Should any sentences be deleted, combined, or moved?

☐ **Words** Do your words accurately express your ideas? Should you make any changes?

Revising with Your Instructor's Written Comments

Your **instructor's written comments** on a draft of your essay can suggest changes in content, arrangement, or style. These comments may question your logic, suggest a clearer thesis statement, ask for more explicit transitions, recommend that a paragraph be relocated, or even propose a new direction for your essay. They may also recommend stylistic changes or ask you to provide more support in one or more of your body paragraphs. You may decide to incorporate these suggestions into the next draft of your essay, or you may decide not to. Whatever the case, you should take your instructor's comments seriously and make reading and responding to them a part of your revision process.

Here is a paragraph from the first draft of Laura Bobnak's essay, which she submitted by email. Her instructor used Microsoft Word's *Comment* tool to insert comments onto her draft.

> Your tentative thesis statement is good—as far as it goes. It doesn't address the second half of the assignment—namely, would you make the same decision today?

When I was in high school, I had an experience like the one Henry Louis Gates Jr. talks about in his essay. It was then that I saw a close friend cheat in chemistry class. As I look back at the cheating I witnessed, I wonder why I kept silent and what would have happened if I had acted.

Revising in a Conference

A one-on-one **conference with your instructor** can also help you revise. If your instructor encourages (or requires) you to schedule a conference, make an appointment in advance, arrive on time, and be prepared. Before the conference, read all your drafts carefully, and bring a copy of your most recent draft as

> **REMINDER REVISING**
>
> It is not a good idea to revise an essay directly on the computer screen. Reading on a screen tends to encourage skimming, whereas revision requires careful close reading. Additionally, many screens (particularly on a phone or tablet) show only a portion of a page. That makes it difficult to move back and forth easily between pages and paragraphs to make sure that all your content supports your thesis. For these reasons, you should revise on hard copy. Once you have written out your corrections, you can type them into your essay.
>
>
> **CLOSE   VIEW**

well as a list of any questions you have. During the conference, ask your instructor to clarify marginal comments or to help you revise a particular section of your essay that is giving you trouble. Make sure you take notes during the conference so that you will have a record of what you and your instructor discussed. Remember that the more prepared for the conference you are, the more you will get out of it. (Some instructors use email, video links, or a chat room to answer questions and to give students feedback.)

If your instructor is not available or if you want another opinion about your work, a **conference with a writing tutor** at your campus writing center can be helpful. In the writing center, tutors meet with you on a one-on-one basis to address your concerns. Because writing tutors are collaborators, they will engage you in discussion to help you develop your own ideas. In addition, writing tutors can help you diagnose your writing problems, offer you feedback on drafts of your papers, suggest strategies to make your writing clearer and more effective, and identify grammatical or mechanical problems. (Many writing centers also have tutors who specialize in helping students whose first language is not English.) Keep in mind, however, that the writing center is a not a proofreading or editing service. The goal of the writing center is to make you a better writer, not to do your writing for you. For this reason, writing center tutors will not rewrite any part of an essay for you or insert their own words into your text.

Revising in a Peer-Editing Group

Another revision strategy involves getting feedback from other students. Sometimes this process is formal: an instructor may require students to exchange papers and evaluate their classmates' work according to certain standards, perhaps by completing a **peer-editing worksheet**. (See page 73 for an example.) Often, however, getting feedback from others is an informal process. Even if a friend is unfamiliar with your topic, he or she can still tell you whether you are getting your point across and maybe even advise you about how to communicate more effectively. (Remember, though, that your critic should be only your reader, not your ghostwriter.)

Getting feedback from others mirrors how people in the real world actually write. For example, businesspeople circulate reports to get feedback from coworkers; academics routinely collaborate when they write. (And, as you may have realized, this book is also the result of a collaboration.)

Your classmates can be helpful as you write the early drafts of your essay, providing suggestions that can guide you through the revision process. In addition, they can respond to questions you may have about your essay, such as whether your introduction works or whether one of your supporting points needs more explanation. When you are asked to critique another student's work, the following guidelines should help you.

 REMINDER   **REVISING**

When you revise, make sure you do not delete text that you may need later. Move this information to the end of the draft or to a separate file, track your changes with your word processor, or use a file storage service such as Google Drive. That way, if you change your mind about a deletion or if you find you need information you took out of a draft, you can recover it easily.

 CLOSE   VIEW

✓ **CHECKLIST**   **GUIDELINES FOR PEER EDITING**

☐ **Be positive.** Remember that your purpose is to help other students improve their essays.
☐ **Be tactful.** Be sure to emphasize the good points about the essay. Mention one or two things the writer has done particularly well before you offer your suggestions.
☐ **Be specific.** Offer concrete suggestions about what the writer could do better. Vague words like *good* or *bad* provide little help.
☐ **Be involved.** If you are doing a critique orally, make sure you interact with the writer. Ask questions, listen to responses, and explain your comments.
☐ **Look at the big picture.** Don't focus exclusively on issues such as spelling and punctuation. At this stage, the clarity of the thesis statement, the effectiveness of the support, and the organization of the writer's ideas are much more important.
☐ **Be thorough.** When possible, write down and explain your comments, either on a form your instructor provides or in the margins of the draft you are reviewing.

Strategies for Revising

Strategy	Advantages
Outlining Aaron Ontiveroz/Getty Images	• Enables you to see relationships between your ideas • Shows you whether your points support your thesis • Highlights topics and subtopics to show you whether you have covered everything • Shows you if you have put enough — but not too much — emphasis on each idea • Shows you whether any information is missing
Checklist Andrey_Popov/Shutterstock	• Enables you to revise in an orderly way • Enables you to learn to revise independently • Helps you focus on specific aspects of your writing

(continued)

Strategies for Revising (continued)

Strategy	Advantages
Instructor's Written Comments *(handwritten-marked paragraph sample)*	• Enables you to get specific feedback from your primary audience • Provides a road map for you to follow as you revise your essay • Helps you understand what your instructor is looking for and how to improve your writing throughout the course • Helps identify problem areas that you can continue to work on in the writing center
Instructor Conferences Monkey Business Images/ Shutterstock	• Enables you to meet your instructors in a relaxed atmosphere outside the classroom • Provides one-on-one feedback that can't be obtained in the classroom • Builds a student–teacher relationship • Enables you to collaborate with your instructors • Allows you to ask questions that you might not ask in a classroom setting
Writing Center Conferences Amir Ridhwan/Shutterstock	• Offers you a less formal, less stressful environment than a conference with your instructor • Enables you to get help from trained tutors (both students and professionals) • Gives you a perspective other than your instructor's • Offers specialized help if your first language is not English
Peer Editing antoniodiaz/Shutterstock	• Enables you and others working on the same assignment to share insights • Gives you the experience of writing for a real audience • Offers you several different readers' reactions to your work • Enables you to benefit from the ideas of your classmates

A STUDENT WRITER: Revising a First Draft

When she revised the first draft of her essay (page 66), Laura Bobnak followed some of the revision strategies discussed above. After writing her rough draft, she put it aside for a few hours and then reread it. Later, her instructor divided the class into pairs and had them read each other's essays and fill out **peer-editing worksheets**. After reading and discussing the following worksheet (filled out by one of her classmates), Laura focused on a number of areas she thought needed revision.

PEER-EDITING WORKSHEET

1. What is the essay's thesis? Is it clearly worded? Does it provide a focus for the essay?

   "As I look back at the cheating I witnessed, I wonder why I kept silent and what would have happened if I had acted." The thesis is clear and gives a good idea of what the essay is about.

2. Do the body paragraphs clearly support the essay's thesis? Should any of the topic sentences be revised? Which, if any, could be more clearly worded?

   The topic sentences seem fine — each one seems to tell what the paragraph is about.

3. How do the body paragraphs develop the essay's main idea? Where could the writer have used more detail?

   Each of the body paragraphs tells a part of the narrative. In paragraph 2, you could add more detail about how the exam room was set up — I really can't picture the scene.

4. Can you follow the writer's ideas? Does the essay need transitions?

   I have no problem following your ideas. Maybe you could have added some more transitions, but I think the essay moves OK.

5. Which points are especially clear? What questions do you have that are not answered in the essay?

   I think you clearly explained what you didn't like about Jeff's cheating. I'm not sure what AP chemistry is like, though. Do people cheat because it's so hard?

6. If this were your essay, what would you change before you handed it in?

   I'd add more detail and explain more about AP chemistry. Also, what were the other students doing while the cheating was going on?

7. Overall, do you think the paper is effective? Explain.

   Good paper; cheating is a big issue, and I think your essay really gets this across.

A peer-editing worksheet for each pattern of development appears at the end of the introductions for Chapters 6 through 15.

Points for Special Attention: First Draft

The Introduction

When she wrote her first draft (page 66), Laura knew she would have to expand her introduction. At this stage, though, she was more concerned with her thesis statement, which, as her instructor's comments pointed out, didn't address the second half of the assignment: to explain whether she would act differently today.

Keeping in mind the feedback she received, Laura rewrote her introduction. First, she created a context for her discussion by specifically linking her story to Gates's essay. Next, she decided to postpone mentioning her subject— cheating—until later in the essay, hoping this strategy would stimulate the curiosity of her readers and make them want to read further. Finally, she revised her thesis statement to reflect the specific wording of the assignment.

The Body Paragraphs

The students in her peer-editing group said Laura needed to expand her body paragraphs. Although she had expected most of her readers to be famil-iar with courses like advanced placement chemistry, she discovered some were not. In addition, some students in her group thought she should expand the paragraph in which she described her reaction to the cheating. They won-dered what the other students had thought about the incident. Did they know? Did they care? Laura's classmates were curious, and they thought other readers would be too.

Before revising the body paragraphs, Laura did some brainstorming for additional ideas. She decided to describe the difficulty of advanced placement chemistry and the pressure the students in the class had felt. She also decided to summarize discussions she had had with several of her classmates after the test. In addition, she wanted to explain in more detail her present views on cheating; she felt that the paragraph presenting these ideas did not contrast enough with the paragraphs dealing with her high school experiences.

To make sure her sentences led smoothly into one another, Laura added transitions and rewrote entire sentences when necessary, signaling the pro-gression of her thoughts by adding words and phrases such as *therefore, for this reason, for example*, and *as a result*. In addition, she repeated keywords so that important concepts would be reinforced.

The Conclusion

Laura's biggest concern as she revised was to make sure her readers would see the connection between her essay and the assignment. To make this con-nection clear, she decided to mention in her conclusion a specific effect the incident had on her: its impact on her friendship with Jeff. She also decided to link her reactions to those of Henry Louis Gates Jr. Like him, she had been upset by the actions of someone she knew. By employing this strategy, she was able to bring her essay full circle and develop an idea she had alluded to in her introduction. Thus, rewriting her conclusion helped Laura reinforce her thesis statement and provide closure to her essay.

A STUDENT WRITER: Revising a Second Draft

The following draft incorporates Laura's revisions as well as some preliminary editing of grammar and punctuation.

Speaking Out

In his essay "'What's in a Name?'" Henry Louis Gates Jr. recalls an incident from   1
his past in which his father did not speak up. Perhaps he kept silent because he was afraid or because he knew that nothing he said or did would change the situation in Piedmont, West Virginia. Although I have never encountered the kind of prejudice Gates describes, I did have an experience in high school where, like Gates's father, I could have spoken up but did not. As I now look back at the cheating I witnessed, I know I would not make the same decision today.

The incident I am going to describe took place during the final examination   2
in my advanced placement chemistry class. The course was very demanding and required hours of studying every night. Every day after school, I would meet with other students to outline chapters and answer homework questions. Sometimes we would even work on weekends. We would often ask ourselves whether we had gotten in over our heads. As the semester dragged on, it became clear to me, as well as to the other students in the class, that passing the course was not something we could take for granted. Test after test came back with grades that were well below the "As" and "Bs" I was used to getting in the regular chemistry course I took in tenth grade. By the time we were ready to take the final exam, most of us were worried that we would fail the course — despite the teacher's assurances that she would mark on a curve.

The final examination for advanced placement chemistry was given on a Friday   3
morning from nine to twelve o'clock. As I struggled to balance a particularly complex equation, I noticed that the person sitting across from me was acting strangely. I thought I was imagining things, but as I stared I saw Jeff, my friend and study partner, fumbling with his test booklet. I realized that he was copying material from his cell phone he had hidden under his test booklet. After watching him for a while, I dismissed the incident and finished my test.

Surprisingly, when I mentioned the incident to others in the class, they all   4
knew what Jeff had done. The more I thought about Jeff's actions, the angrier I got. It seemed unfair that I had studied for weeks to memorize formulas and equations while all Jeff had done was to copy them onto his cell phone. For a moment I considered going to the teacher, but I quickly rejected this idea. Cheating was nothing

new to me or to others in my school. Many of my classmates cheated at one time or another. Most of us saw school as a war between us and the teachers, and cheating was just another weapon in our arsenal. The worst crime I could commit would be to turn Jeff in. As far as I was concerned, I had no choice. I fell in line with the values of my high school classmates and dismissed the incident as "no big deal."

I find it hard to believe that I could ever have been so complacent about   5
cheating. The issues that were simple in high school now seem complex. I now ask questions that never would have occurred to me in high school. Interestingly, Jeff and I are no longer very close. Whenever I see him, I have the same reaction Henry Louis Gates Jr. had when he met Mr. Wilson after he had insulted his father.

Points for Special Attention: Second Draft

Laura could see that her second draft was stronger than her first, but she decided to schedule a conference with her instructor to help her improve her draft further.

The Introduction

Although Laura was satisfied with her introduction, her instructor identified a problem. Laura had assumed that everyone reading her essay would be familiar with Gates's essay, but her instructor pointed out that this might not be the case. To accommodate readers who didn't know about or remember Gates's comments, her instructor suggested that she add a brief explanation of the problems Gates's father had faced.

The Body Paragraphs

After rereading her first body paragraph, Laura thought she could sharpen its focus. Her instructor agreed, suggesting that she delete the first sentence of the paragraph, which seemed too conversational. She also decided she could delete the sentences that explained how difficult advanced placement chemistry was, even though she had added this material at the suggestion of a classmate. After all, cheating, not advanced placement chemistry, was the subject of her paper. She realized that if she included this kind of detail, she might distract readers from the real subject of her discussion.

Her instructor also pointed out that in the second body paragraph, the first and second sentences did not seem to be connected, so Laura decided to connect these ideas by adding a short discussion of her own reaction to the test. Her instructor also suggested that Laura add more transitional words and phrases to this paragraph to clarify the sequence of events she was describing. Phrases such as *at first* and *about a minute passed* would help readers follow her discussion.

Laura thought the third body paragraph was her best, but, even so, she thought she needed to add more material. She and her instructor decided that she should expand her discussion of the students' reactions to cheating. More information — perhaps some dialogue — would help Laura make the point that cheating was condoned by the students in her class.

The Conclusion

Laura's conclusion began by mentioning her present attitude toward cheating and then suddenly shifted to the effect that cheating had on her relationship with Jeff. Her instructor suggested that she take her discussion about her current view of cheating out of her conclusion and put it in a separate paragraph. By doing so, she could focus her conclusion on the effect that cheating had on both Jeff and her. This strategy enabled Laura to present her views about cheating in more detail and also helped her end her essay forcefully.

Working with Sources

Her instructor also suggested that Laura consider adding a quotation from Gates's essay to her conclusion to connect his experience to Laura's. He reminded her not to forget to document the quotation and to use correct MLA documentation format (as explained and illustrated in Chapter 18).

The Title

Laura's original title was only a working title, and now she wanted one that would create interest and draw readers into her essay. She knew, however, that a humorous, cute, or catchy title would undermine the seriousness of her essay. After she rejected a number of possibilities, she decided on "The Price of Silence." This title was thought-provoking and also descriptive, and it prepared readers for what was to follow in the essay.

CHOOSING A TITLE

Because it is the first thing in your essay that readers see, your title should create interest. Usually, single-word titles and cute ones do little to draw readers into your essay. To be effective, a title should reflect your purpose and your tone. The titles of some of the essays in this book illustrate the various kinds of titles you can use:

Statement of essay's focus: "How to Spot Fake News"

Question: "What Causes Cancer?"

Unusual angle: "Thirty-Seven Who Saw Murder Didn't Call the Police"

Controversy: "A Peaceful Woman Explains Why She Carries a Gun"

Provocative wording: "Did Free Pens Cause the Opioid Crisis?"

Humor: "Flick Chicks: A Guide to Women in Movies"

A STUDENT WRITER: Preparing a Final Draft

Based on the decisions she made during and after her conference, Laura revised and edited her draft and handed in this final version of her essay.

The Price of Silence

Introduction (provides background)

In his essay "'What's in a Name?'" Henry Louis Gates Jr. recalls an incident from his past in which his father encountered prejudice and did not speak up. Perhaps he kept silent because he was afraid or because he knew that nothing he said or did would change the racial situation in Piedmont, West Virginia. Although I have never encountered the kind of prejudice Gates describes, I did have an experience in high school where, like Gates's father, I could have *Thesis statement*   spoken out but did not. As I look back at the cheating incident that I witnessed, I realize that I have outgrown the immaturity and lack of confidence that made me keep silent.

1

Narrative begins

In my senior year in high school I, along with fifteen other students, took advanced placement chemistry. The course was very demanding and required hours of studying every night. As the semester dragged on, it became clear to me, as well as to the other students in the class, that passing the course was not something we could take for granted. Test after test came back with grades that were well below the As and Bs I was used to getting in the regular chemistry course I had taken in tenth grade. By the time we were ready to take the final exam, most of us were worried that we would fail the course — despite the teacher's assurances that she would mark on a curve.

2

Key incident occurs

The final examination for advanced placement chemistry was given on a Friday morning between nine o'clock and noon. I had studied all that week, but, even so, I found the test difficult. I knew the material, but I had a hard time answering the long questions that were asked. As I struggled to balance a particularly complex equation, I noticed that the person sitting across from me was acting strangely. At first I thought I was imagining things, but as I stared I saw Jeff, my friend and study partner, fumbling with his test booklet. About a minute passed before I realized that he was copying material from a cell phone he had hidden under his test booklet. After a short time, I stopped watching him and finished my test.

3

Narrative continues: reactions to the incident

It was not until after the test that I began thinking about what I had seen. Surprisingly, when I mentioned the incident to others in the class, they all knew what Jeff had done. Some

4

even thought that Jeff's actions were justified. "After all," one student said, "the test was hard." But the more I thought about Jeff's actions, the angrier I got. It seemed unfair that I had studied for weeks to memorize formulas and equations while all Jeff had done was copy them onto his cell phone. For a moment I considered going to the teacher, but I quickly rejected this idea. Cheating was nothing new to me or to others in my school. Many of my classmates cheated at one time or another. Most of us saw school as a war between us and the teachers, and cheating was just another weapon in our arsenal. The worst crime I could commit would be to turn Jeff in. As far as I was concerned, I had no choice. I fell in line with the values of my high school classmates and dismissed the incident as "no big deal."

Narrative ends

Now that I am in college, however, I see the situation   5
differently. I find it hard to believe that I could ever have been so complacent about cheating. The issues that were simple in high school now seem complex — especially in light of the honor code that I follow in college. I now ask questions that never would have occurred to me in high school. What, for example, are the implications of cheating? What would happen to the educational system if cheating became the norm? What are my obligations to all those who are involved in education? Aren't teachers and students interested in achieving a common goal? The answers to these questions give me a sense of the far-reaching effects of my failure to act. If confronted with the same situation today, I know I would speak out regardless of the consequences.

Analysis of key incident

Jeff is now a first-year student at the state university and,   6
like me, he was given credit for AP chemistry. I feel certain that by not turning him in, I failed not only myself but also Jeff. I gave in to peer pressure instead of doing what I knew to be right. The worst that would have happened to Jeff had I spoken up is that he would have had to repeat chemistry in summer school. By doing so, he would have proven to himself that he could, like the rest of us in the class, pass on his own. In the long run, this knowledge would have served him better than the knowledge that he could cheat whenever he faced a difficult situation.

Interestingly, Jeff and I are no longer very close. Whenever I   7
see him, I have the same reaction Henry Louis Gates Jr. had when he met Mr. Wilson after he had insulted his father: "'I never again looked [him] in the eye'" (4).

Conclusion (aftermath of incident)

Work Cited

Gates, Henry Louis, Jr. "'What's in a Name?'" *Patterns for College Writing*, 14th ed., edited by Laurie G. Kirszner and Stephen R. Mandell, Bedford/St. Martin's, 2021, pp. 2–4.

With each draft of her essay, Laura sharpened the focus of her discussion. In the process, she clarified her thoughts about her subject and reached some new and interesting conclusions. Although much of Laura's paper is a narrative, it also includes a contrast between her current ideas about cheating and the ideas she had in high school. Perhaps Laura could have explained the reasons behind her current ideas about cheating more fully. Even so, her paper gives a straightforward account of the incident and analyzes its significance without drifting off into clichés or simplistic moralizing. Especially effective is Laura's conclusion, in which she discusses the long-term effects of her experience and quotes Gates. By concluding in this way, she makes sure her readers will not lose sight of the implications of her experience. Finally, Laura documents the quotation she uses in her conclusion and includes a works-cited page at the end of her essay.

Exercise 2

Use the checklist on page 68 to help you revise your draft. If you prefer, outline your draft and use that outline to help you revise.

Exercise 3

Have another student read your second draft. Then, using the student's peer-critique checklist on page 71 as your guide, revise your draft.

Exercise 4

Using the essay on pages 78–80 as your guide, label the final draft of your own essay. In addition to identifying your introduction, conclusion, and thesis statement, you should also label the main points of your essay.

5

Editing and Proofreading

When you finish revising your essay, it is tempting to just submit it to your instructor and breathe a sigh of relief, but you should resist this temptation. You still have to edit and proofread your paper to fix any problems that may remain after you revise.

When you **edit**, you search for grammatical errors, check punctuation, and look over your sentence style and word choice one last time. When you **proofread**, you look for spelling errors, typos, incorrect spacing, or problems with your essay's format. The idea is to look carefully for any error, no matter how small, that might weaken your essay's message or undermine your credibility. Remember, this is your last chance to make sure your essay says exactly what you want it to say.

Editing for Grammar

As you edit, keep in mind that certain grammatical errors occur more frequently than others and even more frequently in particular kinds of writing. By focusing on these errors, as well as on those errors you yourself are most likely to make, you will learn to edit your essays quickly and efficiently.

Learning the rules that follow will help you to identify the most common errors. Later on, when you practice writing essays shaped by various patterns of development, the **Grammar in Context** section in each chapter can help you to recognize and correct these common errors.

Be Sure Subjects and Verbs Agree

Subjects and verbs must agree in number. A singular subject takes a singular verb.

Stephanie Ericsson discusses ten kinds of liars.

A plural subject takes a plural verb.

Chronic liars are different from occasional liars.

Liars and plagiarists have a lot in common.

For information on editing for subject–verb agreement with indefinite pronoun subjects, see the **Grammar in Context** section of Chapter 15 (pages 661–62).

Be Sure Verb Tenses Are Accurate and Consistent

Unintentional shifts in verb tense can be confusing to readers. Verb tenses in the same passage should be the same unless you are referring to two different time periods.

Single time period:	*past tense* When he was a child in El Paso, José Antonio *past tense* Burciaga ate tortillas every day.
Two different time periods:	As an adult, José Antonio Burciaga *present tense* has fond memories of the tortillas *past tense* that were such an important part of his childhood.

For more information on editing for consistent verb tenses, as well as to eliminate unwarranted shifts in voice, person, and mood, see the **Grammar in Context** section of Chapter 9 (pages 262–63).

Be Sure Pronoun References Are Clear

A pronoun is a word that takes the place of a noun in a sentence. Every pronoun should clearly refer to a specific **antecedent**, the word (a noun or pronoun) it replaces. Pronouns and antecedents must agree in number.

• Singular pronouns refer to singular antecedents.

When she was attacked, Kitty Genovese was on her way home from work.

• Plural pronouns refer to plural antecedents.

The people who watched the attack gave different reasons for their reluctance to call the police.

For information on editing for pronoun-antecedent agreement with indefinite pronouns, see the **Grammar in Context** section of Chapter 15 (pages 661–62).

Be Sure Sentences Are Complete

A **sentence** is a group of words that includes a subject and a verb and expresses a complete thought. A **fragment** is an incomplete sentence, one that is missing a subject, a verb, or both a subject and a verb or that has a subject and a verb but does not express a complete thought.

Sentence:	Although it was written in 1963, Martin Luther King Jr.'s "Letter from Birmingham Jail" remains just as powerful today as it was then.
Fragment (no subject):	Remains just as powerful today.
Fragment (no verb):	Martin Luther King Jr.'s "Letter from Birmingham Jail."
Fragment (no subject or verb):	Written in 1963.
Fragment (includes subject and verb but does not express a complete thought):	Although it was written in 1963.

To correct a fragment, you need to supply the missing part of the sentence (a subject, a verb, or both — or an entire independent clause). Often, you will find that the missing words appear in an adjacent sentence.

Be Careful Not to Run Sentences Together without Proper Punctuation

There are two kinds of **run-ons**: *comma splices* and *fused sentences.*

A **comma splice** is an error that occurs when two independent clauses are connected by just a comma.

Comma splice:	As Linda Hasselstrom points out, women who live alone need to learn how to protect themselves*;* sometimes that means carrying a gun.

A **fused sentence** is an error that occurs when two independent clauses are connected without any punctuation.

Fused sentence:	Residents of isolated rural areas may carry guns for protection *, but* sometimes these guns may be used against them.

For more information on editing run-ons, including additional options for correcting them, see the **Grammar in Context** section of Chapter 6 (page 102).

Be Careful to Avoid Misplaced and Dangling Modifiers

Modifiers are words and phrases that describe other words in a sentence. To avoid confusion, place modifiers as close as possible to the words they modify.

Limited by her circumstances, the protagonist of Jamaica Kincaid's "'Girl'" has a difficult life.

Working hard at seemingly endless repetitive tasks, she feels trapped.

A **misplaced modifier** appears to modify the wrong word because it is placed incorrectly in the sentence.

Misplaced modifier:	Judith Ortiz Cofer wonders why Latinas are so often stereotyped as either "hot tamales" or low-level workers in her essay "The Myth of the Latin Woman: I Just Met a Girl Named Maria." *(Does Cofer's essay stereotype Latinas?)*
Correct:	In her essay "The Myth of the Latin Woman: I Just Met a Girl Named Maria," Judith Ortiz Cofer wonders why Latinas are so often stereotyped as either "hot tamales" or low-level workers.

A **dangling modifier** "dangles" because it cannot logically describe any word in the sentence.

Dangling modifier:	Discussing the source of conspiracy theories, one suggestion is that they are rooted in people's feelings of powerlessness. *(Who was discussing this subject?)*
Correct:	Discussing the source of conspiracy theories, Maggie Koerth-Baker has suggested that they are rooted in people's feelings of powerlessness.

For more information on editing to correct misplaced and dangling modifiers, see the **Grammar in Context** section of Chapter 7 (pages 160–61).

Be Sure Sentence Elements Are Parallel

Parallelism is the use of matching grammatical elements (words, phrases, or clauses) to express similar ideas. Used effectively — for example, with paired items or items in a series — parallelism makes the links between related ideas clear and emphasizes connections.

Paired items:	As Deborah Tannen points out, men speak <u>more than women in public</u> but <u>less than women at home</u>.
Items in a series:	Amy Tan says, "I spend a great deal of my time thinking about the power of language — the way it can <u>evoke an emotion</u>, <u>a visual image</u>, <u>a complex idea</u>, or <u>a simple truth</u>" (456).

Faulty parallelism — the use of items that are not parallel in a context in which parallelism is expected — makes ideas difficult to follow and will likely confuse your readers.

Faulty parallelism:	As Deborah Tannen points out, men speak more than women in public, but at home less talking is done by them.
Correct:	As Deborah Tannen points out, men tend to speak more than women in public, but they tend to talk less at home.
Faulty parallelism:	Amy Tan says she often thinks about "the power of language" — for example, how it suggests images or emotions or complicated ideas can also be suggested or language can communicate a "simple truth" (456).
Correct:	Amy Tan says, "I spend a great deal of my time thinking about the power of language — the way it can evoke an emotion, a visual image, a complex idea, or a simple truth" (456).

For more information on using parallelism to strengthen your writing, see the **Grammar in Context** section of Chapter 11 (page 375).

✓ **CHECKLIST**   **EDITING FOR GRAMMAR**

☐ **Subject–verb agreement** Do all your verbs agree with their subjects? Remember that singular subjects take singular verbs and that plural subjects take plural verbs.

☐ **Verb tenses** Are all your verb tenses accurate and consistent? Have you avoided unnecessary shifts in tense?

☐ **Pronoun reference** Do pronouns clearly refer to their antecedents?

☐ **Fragments** Does each group of words punctuated as a sentence have both a subject and a verb and express a complete thought? If not, can you correct the fragment by adding the missing words or by attaching it to an adjacent sentence?

☐ **Run-ons** Have you been careful not to connect two independent clauses without the necessary punctuation? Have you avoided comma splices and fused sentences?

☐ **Modification** Does every modifier point clearly to the word it modifies? Have you avoided misplaced and dangling modifiers?

☐ **Parallelism** Have you used matching words, phrases, or clauses to express equivalent ideas? Have you avoided faulty parallelism?

Editing for Punctuation

Like grammatical errors, certain punctuation errors are more common than others, particularly in certain contexts. By understanding a few punctuation rules, you can learn to identify and correct these errors in your writing.

Learn When to Use Commas — and When Not to Use Them

Commas separate elements in a sentence. They are used most often in the following situations:

- To separate an introductory phrase or clause from the rest of the sentence

  In Janice Mirikitani's poem "Suicide Note," the speaker is a college student.

  According to the speaker, her parents have extremely high expectations for her.

  Although she has tried her best, she has disappointed them.

NOTE: Do not use a comma if a dependent clause *follows* an independent clause: She has disappointed them although she has tried her best.

- To separate two independent clauses that are joined by a coordinating conjunction

  The speaker in "Suicide Note" tried to please her parents, but they always expected more of her.

- To separate elements in a series

  Janice Mirikitani has studied creative writing, edited a literary magazine, and published several books of poetry.

For more information on using commas in a series, see the **Grammar in Context** section of Chapter 8 (pages 207–8).

- To separate a **nonrestrictive clause** (a clause that does not supply information that is essential to the sentence's meaning) from the rest of the sentence

  The poem's speaker, who is female, thinks her parents would like her to be a son.

NOTE: Do not use commas to set off a **restrictive clause** (a clause that supplies information that is essential to the sentence's meaning): The child who is overlooked is often the daughter.

Learn When to Use Semicolons

Semicolons, like commas, separate elements in a sentence. However, semicolons separate only grammatically equivalent elements — for example, two closely related independent clauses.

In Burma, George Orwell learned something about the nature of imperialism; it was not an easy lesson.

Shirley Jackson's "The Lottery" is fiction; however, many early readers thought it was a true story.

In most cases, use commas to separate items in a series. However, when one or more of the items in a series already include commas, separate the items with semicolons. This will make the series easier to follow.

Orwell set his works in <u>Paris, France</u>; <u>London, England</u>; and <u>Moulmein, Burma</u>.

Learn When to Use Apostrophes

Apostrophes have two uses: to indicate missing letters in contractions and to show possession or ownership.

- In contractions:

   Amy Chua notes, "<u>I've</u> thought long and hard about how Chinese parents can get away with <u>what they do</u>" (398).

- To show possession:

   <u>Chua's</u> essay identifies a number of things her daughters were never allowed to do, including <u>having a playdate</u>, <u>watching TV</u>, and <u>choosing their own extracurricular activities</u>.

NOTE: Be careful not to confuse contractions with similar-sounding possessive pronouns.

CONTRACTION	POSSESSIVE
they're (= they are)	their
it's (= it is, it has)	its
who's (= who is, who has)	whose
you're (= you are)	your

Learn When to Use Quotation Marks

Quotation marks are used to set off quoted speech or writing.

Early in her essay, Judy Brady asks, "Why do I want a wife?" (494).

NOTE: Quotation marks are *not* used in **indirect quotations**, which summarize what was said or written but do not quote it directly:

Early in her essay, Judy Brady asks readers to consider why she wants a wife.

Special rules govern the use of other punctuation marks with quotation marks:

- Commas and periods are always placed before quotation marks.
- Colons and semicolons are always placed after quotation marks.
- Question marks and exclamation points can go either before or after quotation marks, depending on whether or not they are part of the quoted material.

Quotation marks are also used to set off the titles of essays ("I Want a Wife"), stories ("The Lottery"), and poems ("Shall I compare thee to a summer's day?").

NOTE: Italics are used to set off titles of books, periodicals, and plays: *Life on the Mississippi, College English, Hamlet.*

For information on formatting quotations in research papers, see Chapter 17.

Learn When to Use Dashes

Dashes are occasionally used to set off and emphasize information within a sentence.

Jessica Mitford wrote a scathing critique of the funeral industry — and touched off an uproar. Her book *The American Way of Death* was widely read around the world.

Because this usage is somewhat informal, dashes should be used in moderation in your college writing.

Learn When to Use Colons

Colons are used to introduce lists, examples, and clarifications. A colon should always be preceded by a complete sentence.

Bich Minh Nguyen feels a sense of nostalgia for the snack cakes of her childhood: "Ho Hos, Ding Dongs, Sno Balls, Zingers, Donettes, Suzy Q's" (172).

For more information on using colons, see the **Grammar in Context** section of Chapter 12 (pages 435–36).

✓ **CHECKLIST**   **EDITING FOR PUNCTUATION**

☐ **Commas** Have you used commas when necessary — and only when necessary?

☐ **Semicolons** Have you used semicolons between only grammatically equivalent elements?

☐ **Apostrophes** Have you used apostrophes in contractions and possessive nouns and (when necessary) in possessive pronoun forms?

☐ **Quotation marks** Have you used quotation marks to set off quoted speech or writing and to set off titles of essays, stories, and poems? Have you used other punctuation correctly with quotation marks?

☐ **Dashes** Have you used dashes in moderation?

☐ **Colons** Is every colon that introduces a list, an example, or a clarification preceded by a complete sentence?

Exercise 1

Reread the essay you wrote in Chapters 2 through 4, and edit it for grammar and punctuation.

Exercise 2

Run a grammar check, and then make any additional corrections you think are necessary.

Editing for Sentence Style and Word Choice

As you edit your essay for grammar and punctuation, you should also be looking one last time at how you construct sentences and choose words. To make your essay as clear, readable, and convincing as possible, you should make sure that your

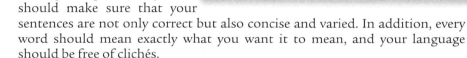

REMINDER   EDITING

Just as you do when you revise, you should edit on a hard copy of your essay. Seeing your work on the printed page makes it easy for you to spot surface-level errors in grammar and punctuation. You can also run a grammar check to help you find grammar and punctuation errors, but you should keep in mind that grammar checkers are far from perfect. They often miss errors (such as faulty modification), and they frequently highlight areas of text (such as a long sentence) that may not contain an error.

CLOSE   **VIEW**

sentences are not only correct but also concise and varied. In addition, every word should mean exactly what you want it to mean, and your language should be free of clichés.

Eliminate Awkward Phrasing

As you review your essay's sentences, check carefully for awkward phrasing, and do your best to smooth it out.

> **Awkward:**   The <u>reason</u> Thomas Jefferson drafted the Declaration of Independence <u>was because</u> he felt the king was a tyrant.

> **Correct:**   The <u>reason</u> Thomas Jefferson drafted the Declaration of Independence <u>was that</u> he felt the king was a tyrant.

For more information about this error, see the **Grammar in Context** section of Chapter 10 (page 324).

> **Awkward:**   *Patriotism* <u>is when</u> you feel love and support for your country.

> **Correct:**   *Patriotism* <u>is a feeling</u> of love and support for one's country.

For more information about this error, see the **Grammar in Context** section of Chapter 13 (pages 485–86).

Be Sure Your Sentences Are Concise

A **concise** sentence is efficient; it is not overloaded with extra words and complicated constructions. To make sentences concise, you need to eliminate repetition and redundancy, delete empty words and expressions, and cut everything that is not absolutely necessary.

Wordy: Brent Staples's essay "Just Walk On By" discusses his feelings, thoughts, and ideas about various events and experiences that were painful to him as a Black man living in a large metropolitan city.

Concise: Brent Staples's essay "Just Walk On By" discusses his painful experiences as a Black man living in a large city.

Be Sure Your Sentences Are Varied

To add interest to your paper, vary the length and structure of your sentences, and vary the way you open them.

- Mix long and short sentences.

  As time went on, and as he saw people's hostile reactions to him, Brent Staples grew more and more uneasy. Then, he had an idea.

- Combine some short sentences with *-ing* or *-ed* modifiers.

  Two short sentences: Staples took long walks every night. He whistled as he walked.

  Sentences combined with *-ing* modifier: Whistling as he walked, Staples took long walks every night.

  Two short sentences: Staples was concerned about his safety. He felt vulnerable.

  Sentences combined with *-ed* modifier: Concerned about his safety, Staples felt vulnerable.

- Mix simple, compound, and complex sentences.

  Simple sentence (*one independent clause*): Staples grew more and more uneasy.

  Compound sentence (*two independent clauses*): Staples grew more and more uneasy, but he stood his ground.

  Complex sentence (*dependent clause, independent clause*): Although Staples grew more and more uneasy, he continued to walk in the neighborhood.

For more information on how to form compound and complex sentences, see the **Grammar in Context** section of Chapter 14 (pages 539–40).

- Vary your sentence openings. Instead of beginning every sentence with the subject (particularly with a pronoun like *he* or *this*), begin some sentences with an introductory word, phrase, or clause that ties it to the preceding sentence.

Even though many of the details of the incident have been challenged, the 1964 murder of Kitty Genovese, discussed in Martin Gansberg's "Thirty-Seven Who Saw Murder Didn't Call the Police," remains relevant today. For one thing, urban crime remains a problem, particularly for women. Moreover, many people are still reluctant to intervene when they witness a crime. Although more than fifty years have gone by, the story of Kitty Genovese and the people who watched her die still stirs strong emotional responses.

Use Transitional Words and Phrases to Clarify Connections between Ideas

By linking sentences together smoothly, you can help readers follow your discussion and understand the causal and logical connections between ideas.

Sentences not linked by transitional word or phrase: As Moisés Naím sees it, YouTube is "a mixed blessing." It has disadvantages as well as advantages (page 21).

Sentences linked with a transitional word: As Moisés Naím sees it, YouTube is "a mixed blessing" because it has disadvantages as well as advantages (page 21).

For a list of commonly used transitional words and phrases, see page 56.

Choose Your Words Carefully

- **Use specific descriptive language**

  Vague: The rain beat upon the roof with a loud noise.

  Specific: "The rain beat upon the low, shingled roof with a force and clatter that threatened to break an entrance and deluge them there" (Chopin 195).

- **Use language that develops specific supporting examples and explanations**

  Vague: Melany Hunt was eager to change her appearance, but this decision turned out to be a bad thing.

  Specific: Melany Hunt was eager to change her appearance, but she eventually regretted this decision, concluding that the change was a mistake and that "some impulses should definitely be resisted" (page 269).

- Avoid **clichés**, overused expressions that rely on tired figures of speech.

  Clichés: We were as free as the birds.

  Revised: "We were free like comets in the heavens, and we did whatever our hearts wanted" (Truong 664).

- Be sure the word you choose has the connotation you need to convey your meaning.

Inaccurate: Judith Ortiz Cofer suggests it is important to be a <u>pushy</u> woman. (*Pushy* has a negative connotation.)

Accurate: Judith Ortiz Cofer suggests it is important to be an <u>assertive</u> woman. (*Assertive* has a positive connotation.)

✓ **CHECKLIST**   **EDITING FOR SENTENCE STYLE AND WORD CHOICE**

☐ **Awkward phrasing** Have you eliminated awkward constructions?
☐ **Concise sentences** Have you eliminated repetition, empty phrases, and excess words? Is every sentence as concise as it can be?
☐ **Varied sentences** Have you varied the length and structure of your sentences by combining some short sentences with modifiers? Have you varied your sentence openings?
☐ **Transitions** Have you connected ideas with transitional words and phrases?
☐ **Word choice** Have you selected specific words? Have you eliminated clichés? Does every word have the connotation you want it to have?

Exercise 3

Check your essay's sentence style and word choice.

Proofreading Your Essay

When you proofread, you check your essay for surface errors, such as commonly confused words, misspellings, faulty capitalization, and incorrect italic use; then, you check for typographical errors.

Check for Commonly Confused Words

Even if you have carefully considered your choice of words during the editing stage, you may have missed some errors. As you proofread, look carefully to see if you can spot any **commonly confused words**—*its* for *it's*, *there* for *their*, or *affect* for *effect*, for example—that a spell check will not catch.

For more information on how to distinguish between *affect* and *effect*, see the **Grammar in Context** section of Chapter 10 (page 325).

Check for Misspellings and Faulty Capitalization

It makes no sense to work hard on an essay and then undermine your credibility with spelling and mechanical errors. If you have any doubt about how a word is spelled or whether or not to capitalize it, check a dictionary site.

Check for Typos

The last step in the proofreading process is to read carefully and look for typos. Make sure you have spaced correctly between words and have not accidentally typed an extra letter, omitted a letter, or transposed two letters. Reading your essay *backward* — one sentence at a time — will help you focus on individual sentences, which in turn can help you see errors more clearly.

> ✔ **CHECKLIST** **PROOFREADING**
>
> ☐ **Commonly confused words** Have you proofread for errors involving words that are often confused with each other?
> ☐ **Misspelled words and faulty capitalization** Have you proofread for errors in spelling and capitalization? Have you run a spell check?
> ☐ **Typos** Have you checked carefully to eliminate any typing errors?

Exercise 4

Proofread your essay.

Checking Your Paper's Format

The final thing to consider is your paper's **format**: how your paragraphs, sentences, and words are arranged on the page. Your instructor will give you some general guidelines about format — telling you, for example, to type your last name and the page number at the top right of each page — and, of course, you should

> **REMINDER** **SPELL CHECKERS**
>
> You should certainly use the spell check to help you locate misspelled words and incorrect strings of letters caused by typos, but keep in mind that it will not discover every error. For example, it will not identify many misspelled proper nouns or foreign words, nor will it highlight words that are spelled correctly but used incorrectly — *work* for *word* or *form* for *from*, for example. For this reason, you must still proofread carefully — even after reviewing material highlighted by the spell check.
>
> **CLOSE** **VIEW**

follow these guidelines. Students writing in the humanities usually follow the format illustrated on page 94. (For information on MLA documentation format, see Chapter 18.)

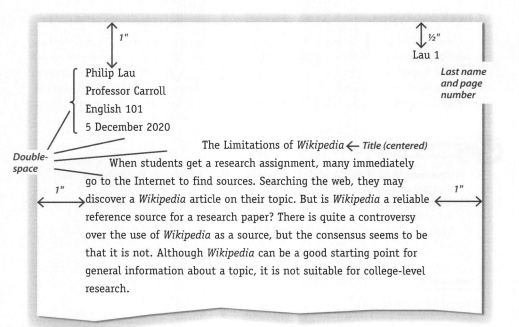

1"

½"

Lau 1

Philip Lau

Professor Carroll

English 101

5 December 2020

Last name and page number

The Limitations of *Wikipedia* ← *Title (centered)*

Double-space

When students get a research assignment, many immediately go to the Internet to find sources. Searching the web, they may discover a *Wikipedia* article on their topic. But is *Wikipedia* a reliable reference source for a research paper? There is quite a controversy over the use of *Wikipedia* as a source, but the consensus seems to be that it is not. Although *Wikipedia* can be a good starting point for general information about a topic, it is not suitable for college-level research.

1"

1"

✔ CHECKLIST   **CHECKING YOUR PAPER'S FORMAT**

☐ **Format** Have you followed your instructor's format guidelines?
☐ **Spacing** Have you double-spaced throughout?
☐ **Type size** Have you used ten- or twelve-point type?
☐ **Paragraphing** Have you indented the first line of every paragraph?
☐ **Visuals** If you used one or more visuals in your essay, did you insert each visual as close as possible to where it is discussed?
☐ **Documentation** Have you documented each source — and each visual — you used? Have you used the appropriate documentation format? Have you included a works-cited page?

Exercise 5

Make any necessary corrections to your essay's format, and then submit your final draft.

PART TWO

Readings for Writers

The relationship between reading and writing is a complex one. Sometimes you will write an essay based on your own experience; more often than not, however, you will respond in writing to something you have read. The essays in this book give you a chance to do both.

As you are probably aware, the fact that information has been published in print or online does not mean it should be taken at face value. Many of the books and articles you read will be reliable, but some — especially material found on many websites and blogs — will include contradictions, biased ideas, or even inaccurate or misleading information. For this reason, your goal should not be simply to understand what you read but to assess the credibility of the writers and judge the soundness of their ideas.

When you read the essays and other texts in this book, you should approach them critically. In other words, you should question (and sometimes challenge) the writers' ideas and, in the process, try to create new interpretations that you can explore in your writing. Approaching a text in this way is not easy, for it requires you to develop your own analytical and critical skills and your own set of standards to help you judge and interpret what you read. Still, you need to read and critically evaluate a text before you can begin to draw your ideas together and write about them.

Every reading selection in Chapters 6 through 15 is accompanied by a series of questions intended to guide you through the reading process. In many ways, these questions are a warm-up for the intellectual workout of writing an essay. The more time you devote to them, the more you will be practicing your analytical skills. In a real sense, then, these questions will help you develop the critical thinking skills you will need when you write. Moreover, becoming a proficient reader will also give you confidence in yourself as a writer.

Each reading selection in Chapters 6 through 14 is organized around one dominant pattern of development. In your outside reading, however, you will often find more than one pattern used in a single piece of writing (as in Chapter 15, Combining the Patterns, page 659). When you write, then, don't think you must follow these patterns blindly; instead, think of them as tools for making your writing more effective, and adapt them to your subject, your audience, and your purpose for writing.

The first selection in each chapter is a visual text such as a piece of fine art, an advertisement, or a photograph. By visually reinforcing the chapter's basic rhetorical concept, each visual text serves as a bridge to the chapter's essays. Following each visual is a set of questions designed to help you understand not just the image but also the rhetorical pattern that is the chapter's focus.

6

Narration

What Is Narration?

Narration tells a story by presenting events in an orderly, logical sequence. In the following paragraph from "The Stone Horse," essayist Barry Lopez recounts the history of the exploration of the California desert.

Topic sentence

Western man did not enter the California desert until the end of the eighteenth century, 250 years after Coronado brought his soldiers into the Zuni pueblos in a bewildered search for the cities of Cibola. The earliest appraisals of the land were cursory, hurried. People traveled *through* it, en route to Santa Fe or the California coastal settlements. Only miners tarried. In 1823 what had been Spain's became Mexico's, and in 1848 what had been Mexico's became America's; but the bare, jagged mountains and dry lake beds, the vast and uniform plains of creosote bush and yucca plants, remained as obscure as the northern Sudan until the end of the nineteenth century.

Narrative traces developments through the nineteenth century

Narration can be the dominant pattern in many kinds of writing (as well as in speech). Histories, biographies, and autobiographies have a narrative structure, as do diaries, journals, and some posts on blogs and social networking sites. Narration is the dominant pattern in many works of fiction and poetry, and it is an essential part of casual conversation. Narration also underlies folk and fairy tales and many news reports. In fact, anytime you tell what happened, you are using narration.

Using Narration

Narration can provide the structure for an entire essay, but narrative passages may also appear in essays that are not primarily narrative. For example, in an argumentative essay supporting stricter gun-safety legislation, you might devote one or two paragraphs to the story of a child accidentally killed by a handgun. In this chapter, however, we focus on narration as the dominant pattern of an essay.

Throughout your college career, many of your assignments will call for narration. In an English composition class, you may be asked to write about an experience that was important to your development as an adult; on a European history exam, you may need to summarize the events that led to Napoleon's defeat at the Battle of Waterloo; and in a technical writing class, you may be asked to write a report tracing a company's negligent actions. In each of these situations (as well as in many additional assignments), your writing will have a primarily narrative structure.

The skills you develop in narrative writing will also help you in other kinds of writing. A *process essay*, such as an explanation of a laboratory experiment, is like a narrative because it outlines a series of steps in chronological order; a *cause-and-effect essay*, such as your answer to an exam question that asks you to analyze the events that caused the Great Depression, also resembles a narrative in that it traces a sequence of events. Although a process essay explains how to do something and a cause-and-effect essay explains why events occur, writing both these kinds of essays will be easier after you master narration. (Process essays and cause-and-effect essays are discussed and illustrated in Chapters 9 and 10, respectively.)

Planning a Narrative Essay

Developing a Thesis Statement

Although the purpose of a narrative may be simply to recount events or to create a particular mood or impression, in college writing, a narrative essay is more likely to present a sequence of events for the purpose of supporting a thesis. For instance, in a narrative about your problems with credit card debt, your purpose may be to show your readers that college students should not have easy access to credit cards. Accordingly, you do not simply tell the story of your own unwise spending. Rather, you select and arrange details to show your readers why having a credit card encouraged you to spend money you didn't have. Although it is usually best to include an explicit **thesis statement** ("My negative experiences with credit have convinced me that college students should not have easy access to credit cards"), you may also **imply** (suggest) your thesis through your selection and arrangement of events. (See page 46 for more on using an implied thesis.)

Including Enough Detail

Narratives, like other types of writing, need to include rich, specific details if they are to be convincing. Each detail should help create a picture for the reader; even exact times, dates, and geographic locations can be helpful.

Look, for example, at the following paragraph from the essay "My Mother Never Worked" by Bonnie Smith-Yackel, which appears later in this chapter:

> In the winter she sewed night after night, endlessly, begging cast-off clothing from relatives, ripping apart coats, dresses, blouses, and trousers to remake them to fit her four daughters and son. Every morning and every evening she milked cows, fed pigs and calves, cared for chickens, picked eggs, cooked meals, washed dishes, scrubbed floors, and tended and loved her children. In the spring she planted a garden once more, dragging pails of water to nourish and sustain the vegetables for the family. In 1936 she lost a baby in her sixth month.

This list of details adds interest and authenticity to the narrative. The central figure in the narrative is a busy, productive woman, and readers know this because they are given an exhaustive catalog of her activities.

Varying Sentence Structure

When narratives present a long series of events, all the sentences can begin to sound alike: "She sewed dresses. She milked cows. She fed pigs. She fed calves. She cared for chickens." Such a string of sentences may become monotonous for your readers. You can eliminate this monotony by varying your sentence structure — for instance, by using a variety of sentence openings or by combining simple sentences as Smith-Yackel does in "My Mother Never Worked": "In the winter she sewed night after night, endlessly. . . . Every morning and every evening she milked cows, fed pigs and calves, cared for chickens. . . ."

Maintaining Clear Narrative Order

Many narratives present events in the exact order in which they occurred, moving from first event to last. Whether or not you follow a strict **chronological order** depends on the purpose of your narrative. If you are writing a straightforward account of a historical event or summarizing a record of poor management practices, you will probably want to move directly from beginning to end. In a personal-experience essay or a fictional narrative, however, you may want to engage your readers' interest by beginning with an event from the middle of your story, or even from the end, and then recounting the events that led up to it. You may also decide to begin in the present and then use one or more **flashbacks** (shifts into the past) to tell your story. To help readers follow the order of events in your narrative, it is very important to use correct verb tenses and clear transitional words and phrases.

Using Correct Verb Tenses

Verb tense is extremely important in writing that presents events in a fixed order because tenses indicate temporal (time) relationships. When you write a narrative, you should be careful to keep verb tenses consistent and accurate so that your readers can follow the sequence of events. Naturally, you need to shift tenses to reflect an actual time shift in your narrative. For instance, convention requires that you use present tense when discussing works of literature ("Hamlet *is* not happy about his mother's marriage to his uncle. . . ."), but a flashback to an earlier point in the story calls for a shift from present to past tense ("Before his mother's marriage, Hamlet *was* . . ."). Nevertheless, you should avoid unwarranted shifts in verb tense, which are likely to confuse your readers.

Using Transitions

Transitions — connecting words or phrases — help link events in time, enabling narratives to flow smoothly. Without transitional words and phrases, narratives would lack coherence, and readers would be unsure of the correct sequence of events. Transitions indicate the order of events, and they also signal shifts in time. In narrative writing, the transitions commonly used for these purposes include *first, second, next, then, later, at the same time, meanwhile, immediately, soon, before, earlier, after, afterward, now*, and *finally*. In addition to transitional words and phrases, specific time markers — such as *three years later, in 1927, after two hours*, and *on January 3* — indicate how much time has passed between events. (A more complete list of transitions appears on page 56.)

Structuring a Narrative Essay

Like other essays, a **narrative** essay has an introduction, a body, and a conclusion. If your essay's thesis is explicitly stated, it will, in most cases, appear in the **introduction**. The **body paragraphs** of your essay will recount the events that make up your narrative, following a clear and orderly plan. Finally, the **conclusion** will give your readers the sense that your narrative is complete, perhaps by restating your thesis in different words or by summarizing key points or events.

Suppose you are assigned to write a short history paper about the Battle of Waterloo. You plan to support the thesis that if Napoleon had kept more troops in reserve, he might have defeated the British troops serving under Wellington. Based on this thesis, you decide that the best way to organize your paper is to present the five major phases of the battle in chronological order. An informal outline of your essay might look like the one that follows.

SAMPLE OUTLINE: Narration

INTRODUCTION

Thesis statement: If Napoleon had kept more troops in reserve, he might have broken Wellington's line with another infantry attack and thus won the Battle of Waterloo.

FIRST EVENT

Phase 1 of the battle: Napoleon attacked the Château of Hougoumont.

SECOND EVENT

Phase 2 of the battle: The French infantry attacked the British lines.

THIRD EVENT

Phase 3 of the battle: The French cavalry staged a series of charges against the British lines that had not been attacked before; Napoleon committed his reserves.

FOURTH EVENT

Phase 4 of the battle: The French captured La Haye Sainte, their first success of the day but an advantage that Napoleon, having committed troops elsewhere, could not maintain without reserves.

FIFTH EVENT

Phase 5 of the battle: The French infantry was decisively defeated by the combined thrust of the British infantry and the remaining British cavalry.

CONCLUSION

Restatement of thesis (in different words) or review of key events.

By discussing the five phases of the battle in chronological order, you clearly support your thesis. As you expand your informal outline into a historical narrative, exact details, dates, times, and geographic locations will be extremely important. Without them, your statements will be open to question. In addition, to keep your readers aware of the order of events, you will need to select appropriate transitional words and phrases and pay careful attention to verb tenses.

Revising a Narrative Essay

When you revise a narrative essay, consider the items on Checklist: Revising on page 68. In addition, pay special attention to the items on the following checklist, which apply specifically to narrative essays.

✓ REVISION CHECKLIST NARRATION

- ☐ Does your assignment call for narration?
- ☐ Does your essay's thesis communicate the significance of the events you discuss?
- ☐ Have you included enough specific detail?
- ☐ Have you varied your sentence structure?
- ☐ Have you made the order of events clear to readers?
- ☐ Have you varied sentence openings and combined short sentences to avoid monotony?
- ☐ Do your transitions indicate the order of events and signal shifts in time?
- ☐ Does your narrative require any supporting documentation?

Editing a Narrative Essay

When you edit your narrative essay, follow the guidelines on the editing checklists on pages 85, 88, and 92. In addition, focus on the grammar, mechanics, and punctuation issues that are particularly relevant to narrative essays. A discussion of one of these issues — avoiding run-on sentences — follows.

GRAMMAR IN CONTEXT   AVOIDING RUN-ONS

When writing narrative essays, particularly personal narratives and essays that include dialogue, writers can easily lose sight of sentence boundaries and create **run-ons**. There are two kinds of run-ons: *fused sentences* and *comma splices*, and both should be avoided.

A **fused sentence** occurs when two sentences are incorrectly joined without punctuation.

CORRECT (TWO SENTENCES):	"The sun came out hot and bright, endlessly, day after day. The crops shriveled and died" (Smith-Yackel 123).
INCORRECT (FUSED SENTENCE):	The sun came out hot and bright, endlessly, day after day the crops shriveled and died.

A **comma splice** occurs when two sentences are incorrectly joined with just a comma.

INCORRECT (COMMA SPLICE):	The sun came out hot and bright, endlessly, day after day, the crops shriveled and died.

Five Ways to Correct These Errors

1. Use a period to create two separate sentences.
   The sun came out hot and bright, endlessly, day after day. The crops shriveled and died.

2. Join the sentences with a comma and a coordinating conjunction (*and, or, nor, for, so, but, yet*).
   The sun came out hot and bright, endlessly, day after day, and the crops shriveled and died.

3. Join the sentences with a semicolon.
   The sun came out hot and bright, endlessly, day after day; the crops shriveled and died.

4. Join the sentences with a semicolon and a transitional word or phrase (followed by a comma), such as *however, therefore,* or *for example*. (See page 56 for a list of transitional words and phrases.)
   The sun came out hot and bright, endlessly, day after day; eventually, the crops shriveled and died.

5. Create a complex sentence by adding a subordinating conjunction (*although, because, if,* and so on) or a relative pronoun (*who, which, that,* and so on) to one of the sentences.
   As the sun came out hot and bright, endlessly, day after day, the crops shriveled and died.

✔ **EDITING CHECKLIST**   **NARRATION**

☐ Have you avoided run-ons?
☐ Do your verb tenses clearly indicate time relationships between events?
☐ Have you avoided unnecessary tense shifts?
☐ If you use dialogue, have you punctuated correctly and capitalized where necessary?

A STUDENT WRITER: Literacy Narrative

In the following student essay, Erica Sarno traces her development as a writer. Her assignment was to write a **literacy narrative**, a personal account focusing on her experiences with reading and writing.

Becoming a Writer

Introduction

I used to think that writing was just about filling pages. Composing an essay for school meant getting the job done and checking it off my to-do list. During my last two years of high school, however, my attitude started to change. Several experiences helped me understand that writing is not a skill that some people are born with and others are not. I learned that if I wanted to write, I only needed a desire to express myself to others and a willing audience. *Thesis statement* Realizing that there was someone on the other side of the page, eager to listen, helped me develop into a more effective writer.   1

Narrative begins (junior year)

My first real lesson in my development as a writer took place in Mrs. Strickland's junior English class. Mrs. Strickland was hard to approach. She dressed as if she expected to be giving a press conference at the White House. She wore conservative suits and silk scarves, and she had a helmet of dyed blonde hair. We seemed to disappoint her just because we were high school students. Maybe I saw her lack of interest in us and our work as a challenge because, one day, I took a risk and wrote a very personal essay about losing my aunt to cancer. When I got the paper back, Mrs. Strickland had written only, "Did you read the instructions?" I could not believe it. For the first time, I had actually written about what was important to me rather than just filling the pages with words, and she had not even read past my introduction! Still, I knew that I had something to say. I just needed someone to listen.   2

Narrative continues (senior year)

The next year, I had Dr. Kelleher for senior English. My year with Dr. K profoundly changed the way I see myself as a writer (and as a reader). Finally, a teacher was paying attention to what   3

I had written. His only rule for writing was "Don't be boring!"
I rewrote sentences, hoping for an exclamation point or one of Dr. K's
other special marks in the margin. Dr. K had a whole list of codes and
abbreviations, like "BTH" ("Better than Hemingway") or "the knife"
(when the writer slayed the opponent in an argument). I also relied
on Dr. K to tell me when I was falling into my old habit of just filling
the page. He would write a funny comment like, "Come back! Log out
of Facebook!" Then, he would give me a chance to try again. Trusting
him to be a generous reader and an honest critic helped me develop
my voice and my confidence as a writer.

Narrative shifts to
focus on reading

    Meanwhile, I started to become a better reader, too. I could tell   4
when a writer was writing to me, wanting me to understand. I could
also tell when a writer was writing just to get the job done. Instead of
just skimming the assigned reading, I got in the habit of writing in the
margins and making notes about what I thought. I underlined ideas
that spoke to me, and I wrote "Really??" next to ideas that seemed
silly. Instead of assuming that an assigned reading would be boring,
I gave every assignment a chance. Whether I liked a book or not, I felt
that I could explain my reasons. I was finally seeing for myself that
writing is just another way for people to talk to each other.

Narrative moves
outside the
classroom

    Eventually, in the spring of my senior year, I experienced what   5
it feels like to connect with a broader audience. I suggested a series
of columns about "senioritis" to the school paper, and even though
I had never written for the public before, the editor loved my idea.
I knew what I wanted to say, and I knew I could collect plenty of
stories to help me illustrate my ideas. What I did not predict was how
much I would learn from the experience of writing those six columns.
Knowing that hundreds of people would be reading my pieces,
I revised them over and over again. When Dr. K read one of my last
columns aloud to our class, I got to see how my work affected people.
Watching the expressions on my classmates' faces and hearing them
laugh at the funny parts helped me understand the power of good
writing. In that moment, I truly connected with my audience.

Conclusion

    Although I still have a lot to learn, I now understand how   6
important the relationship between the writer and the reader is.
When I write, I am writing to be heard. When I read, I am reading
to understand. The communication may not be perfect, but I know
I am not alone in my task. And even though I am not in Dr. K's class
anymore, I still sometimes imagine that he will be reading what
I have written. Thinking about him reminds me that someone cares
about what I have to say.

Points for Special Attention

Assignment

Erica's assignment was to write a literacy narrative. At first, she considered writing about her favorite childhood books or about how she learned to read, but in the end she decided to focus on more recent experiences because she could remember them more clearly (and therefore could include more specific detail).

Thesis Statement

Because her focus was on her development as a writer, Erica was careful to include the words *develop* and *writer* in her thesis statement. Her thesis statement also clearly explains the key factor that encouraged her development—the presence of an interested reader.

Structure

In her essay's first two body paragraphs, Erica discusses her junior and senior English classes. Instead of just contrasting the two teachers, however, she explains how she herself reacted to their different approaches. In paragraph 4, she explains the connection between her reading and her writing, and in paragraph 5, she recounts her development into someone writing for a wider audience.

Topic Sentences

To move her narrative along, Erica was careful to include transitional words and phrases—*The next year, Meanwhile, Eventually*—in her topic sentences to show the movement from one stage of her development to the next.

Working with Sources

Erica's assignment made it clear that although other assignments in the course would be source-based, this narrative essay was to be based solely on her own memories and reflections.

Focus on Revision

When she reread an early draft of her essay, Erica immediately saw a problem: she had written a comparison-and-contrast essay instead of a narrative. Instead of focusing on her development as a writer, she had simply compared her junior- and senior-year English classes. This problem was revealed by her draft's thesis statement—"The difference between junior and senior year of high school was the difference between being ignored and being heard"—as well as by the topic sentences of her first two body paragraphs:

First body paragraph: Mrs. Strickland was an uninspiring teacher.

Second body paragraph: Unlike Mrs. Strickland, Dr. Kelleher encouraged me as a writer.

Erica also noticed that her draft focused on classroom style, further highlighting the contrast between her two teachers. Realizing that her development as a writer had also taken place outside the classroom, she condensed her discussion of the two English classes and added material about reading (paragraph 4) and about writing for her school paper (paragraph 5).

When she wrote her next draft, Erica was careful to include transitions and topic sentences that signaled her focus on her development over time, not on the differences between two classes or two teachers. Finally, as she reviewed her draft, she realized that her original summary statement — "Knowing that there was someone on the other side of the page made me a better writer" — could be expanded into an appropriate and effective thesis statement.

A STUDENT WRITER: Narration

The following essay is typical of the informal narrative writing many students are asked to do in English composition classes. It was written by Tiffany Forte in response to the assignment "Write an informal essay about a goal or dream you had when you were a child."

My Field of Dreams

Introduction   When I was young, I was told that when I grew up I could be   1
anything I wanted to be, and I always took for granted that this was true. I knew exactly what I was going to be, and I would spend hours

Thesis statement   dreaming about how wonderful my life would be when I grew up. One day, though, when I did grow up, I realized that things had not turned out the way I had always expected they would.

Narrative begins   When I was little, I never played with baby dolls or Barbies.   2
I was the only girl in the neighborhood where I lived, so I always played with boys. We would play army or football or (my favorite) baseball.

Almost every summer afternoon, all the boys in my neighborhood   3
and I would meet by the big oak tree to get a baseball game going. Surprisingly, I was always one of the first to be picked for a team. I was very fast, and (for my size) I could hit the ball far. I loved baseball more than anything, and I wouldn't miss a game for the world.

My dad played baseball too, and every Friday night I would go   4
to the field with my mother to watch him play. It was just like the big leagues, with lots of people, a snack bar, and lights that shone so high and bright you could see them a mile away. I loved my dad's games. When all the other kids would wander off and play, I would sit and cheer on my dad and his team. My attention was focused on the field, and my heart would jump with every pitch.

Even more exciting than my dad's games were the major league   5
games. The Phillies were my favorite team, and I always looked
forward to watching them on television. My dad would make popcorn,
and we would sit and watch in anticipation of a Phillies victory. We
would go wild, yelling and screaming at all the big plays. When the
Phillies would win, I would be so excited I couldn't sleep; when they
would lose, I would go to bed angry, just like my dad.

Key experience introduced (pars. 6–7)

It was when my dad took me to my first Phillies game that I   6
decided I wanted to be a major league baseball player. The excitement
began when we pulled into the parking lot of the old Veterans
Stadium. There were thousands of cars. As we walked from the car to
the stadium, my dad told me to hold on to his hand and not to let go
no matter what. When we gave the man our tickets and entered the
stadium, I understood why. There were mobs of people everywhere.
They were walking around the stadium and standing in long lines
for hot dogs, beer, and souvenirs. It was the most wonderful thing
I had ever seen. When we got to our seats, I looked down at the tiny
baseball diamond below and felt as if I were on top of the world.

The cheering of the crowd, the singing, and the chants were   7
almost more than I could stand. I was bursting with excitement.
Then, in the bottom of the eighth inning, with the score tied and
two outs, Mike Schmidt came up to bat and hit the game-winning
home run. The crowd went crazy. Everyone in the whole stadium
was standing, and I found myself yelling and screaming along with
everyone else. When Mike Schmidt came out of the dugout to receive
his standing ovation, I felt a lump in my throat and butterflies in my
stomach. He was everyone's hero that night, and I could only imagine
the pride he must have felt. I slept the whole way home and dreamed
of what it would be like to be the hero of the game.

Narrative continues

The next day, when I met with the boys at the oak tree, I told   8
them that when I grew up, I was going to be a major league baseball
player. They all laughed at me and said I could never be a baseball
player because I was a girl. I told them that they were all wrong and
that I would show them.

Analysis of childhood experiences

In the years to follow, I played girls' softball in a competitive   9
fast-pitch league, and I was very good. I always wanted to play
baseball with the boys, but there were no mixed leagues. After a few
years, I realized that the boys from the oak tree were right: I was
never going to be a major league baseball player. I realized that what
I had been told when I was younger wasn't the whole truth. What no

one had bothered to tell me was that I could be anything I wanted to be — as long as it was something that was appropriate for a girl to do.

Conclusion   In time, I would get over the loss of my dream. I found new   10
dreams, acceptable for a young woman, and I moved on to other things. Still, every time I watch a baseball game and someone hits a home run, I get those same butterflies in my stomach and think, for just a minute, about what might have been.

Points for Special Attention

Assignment

Tiffany's assignment was to write about a goal or dream she had when she was a child. As a nontraditional student, a good deal older than most of her classmates, Tiffany found this assignment challenging at first. She wondered if her childhood dreams would be different from those of her classmates, and she was somewhat hesitant to share her drafts with her peer-editing group. As it turned out, though, her childhood dreams were not very different from those of the other students in her class.

Introduction

Tiffany's introduction is straightforward, yet it arouses reader interest by setting up a contrast between what she expected and what actually happened. Her optimistic expectation — that she could be anything she wanted to be — is contradicted by her thesis statement, encouraging readers to read on to learn how things turned out and why.

Thesis Statement

Although the assignment called for a personal narrative, the instructor made it clear that the essay should have an explicitly stated thesis that made a point about a childhood goal or dream. Tiffany knew she wanted to write about her passion for baseball, but she also knew that just listing a series of events would not fulfill the assignment. Her thesis statement — "One day, though, when I did grow up, I realized that things had not turned out the way I had always expected they would" — puts her memories in context, suggesting that she will use them to support a general conclusion about the gap between dreams and reality.

Structure

The body of Tiffany's essay traces the chronology of her involvement with baseball — playing with the neighborhood boys, watching her father's games, watching baseball on television, and, finally, attending her first major league game. Each body paragraph introduces a different aspect of her experience with baseball, culminating in the vividly described Phillies game. The balance of the essay (paragraphs 8–10) summarizes the aftermath of that game, gives a brief overview of Tiffany's later years in baseball, and presents her conclusion.

Detail

Personal narratives like Tiffany's need a lot of detail because the writers want readers to see, hear, and feel what they did. To present an accurate picture, Tiffany includes all the significant sights and sounds she can remember: the big oak tree, the lights on the field, the popcorn, the excited cheers, the food and souvenir stands, the crowds, and so on. She also names Mike Schmidt ("everyone's hero"), his team, and the stadium where she saw him play. Despite all these details, though, she omits some important information — for example, how old she was at each stage of her essay.

Working with Sources

Tiffany's essay is very personal, and she supports her thesis with experiences and observations from her own childhood. Although she could have consulted sources to find specific information about team standings or players' stats — or even quoted her hero, Mike Schmidt — she decided that her own memories would provide enough convincing support for her thesis.

Verb Tense

Maintaining clear chronological order is very important in narrative writing, where unwarranted shifts in verb tenses can confuse readers. Knowing this, Tiffany was careful to avoid unnecessary tense shifts. In her conclusion, she shifts from past to present tense, but this shift is both necessary and clear. Elsewhere she uses *would* to identify events that recurred regularly. For example, in paragraph 5 she says, "My dad *would* make popcorn" rather than "My dad *made* popcorn," which would have suggested that he did so only once.

Transitions

Tiffany's skillful use of transitional words and expressions links her sentences and moves her readers smoothly through her essay. In addition to transitional words such as *when* and *then*, she uses specific time markers — "When I was little," "Almost every summer afternoon," "every Friday night," "As we walked," "The next day," "In the years to follow," and "After a few years" — to advance the narrative and carry her readers along.

Focus on Revision

In their responses to an earlier draft of Tiffany's essay, several students in her peer-editing group recommended that she revise one particularly monotonous paragraph. (As one student pointed out, all its sentences began with the subject, making the paragraph seem choppy and its ideas disconnected.) Here is the paragraph from her draft:

> My dad played baseball too. I went to the field with my mother every Friday night to watch him play. It was just like the big leagues. There were lots of people and a snack bar. The lights shone so high and bright you could see them a mile away. I loved my dad's games. All the other kids would wander off and play. I would sit and cheer on my dad and his team. My attention was focused on the field. My heart would jump with every pitch.

In the revised version of the paragraph (now paragraph 4 of her essay), Tiffany varies sentence length and opening strategies:

> My dad played baseball too, and every Friday night I would go to the field with my mother to watch him play. It was just like the big leagues, with lots of people, a snack bar, and lights that shone so high and bright you could see them a mile away. I loved my dad's games. When all the other kids would wander off and play, I would sit and cheer on my dad and his team. My attention was focused on the field, and my heart would jump with every pitch.

After reading Tiffany's revised draft, another student suggested that she might still polish her essay a bit. For instance, she could add some dialogue, quoting the boys' taunts and her own reply in paragraph 8. She could also revise to eliminate **clichés** (overused expressions), substituting fresher, more original language for phrases such as "I felt a lump in my throat and butterflies in my stomach" and "felt as if I were on top of the world." In the next draft of her essay, Tiffany followed up on these suggestions.

✏ PEER-EDITING WORKSHEET NARRATION

1. What point is the writer making about the essay's subject? Is this point explicitly stated in a thesis statement? If so, where? If the thesis is implied, can you state it in one sentence?

2. List some details that enrich the narrative. Where could more detail be added? What kind of detail? Be specific.

3. Does the writer vary sentence structure and avoid monotonous strings of similarly constructed sentences? Should any sentences be combined? If so, which ones? Can you suggest different openings for any sentences?

4. Should any transitions be added to clarify the order in which events occurred? If so, where?

5. Do verb tenses establish a clear chronological order? Identify any verb tenses you believe need to be changed.

6. Does the writer avoid run-on sentences? Point out any fused sentences or comma splices.

7. What could the writer *add* to this essay? What could the writer *delete* from this essay?

8. Evaluate the essay's introductory and concluding strategies. Should a different kind of introduction or conclusion be used?

9. What is the essay's greatest strength? Why?

10. What is the essay's greatest weakness? What steps should the writer take to improve the essay?

The selections that follow illustrate some of the many possibilities open to writers of narrative essays. The first selection, a visual text, is followed by questions designed to illustrate how narration can operate in visual form.

MARJANE SATRAPI

from *Persepolis II* (Graphic Fiction)*

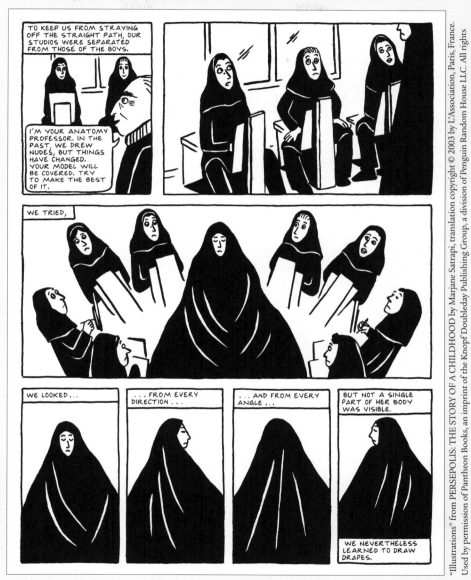

• • •

* These panels, from the graphic novel *Persepolis II*, tell part of a story about the changes in the life of a young girl during Iran's Islamic revolution. In 1979, the secular monarch was overthrown, and a government run by Islamic religious leaders instituted new rules, including extreme regulations restricting how women could dress.

Reading Images

1. Look carefully at the panels on page 111, and read the note that appears below them. Then, list the events depicted in the panels in the order in which they are shown.
2. What visual elements link each panel to the one that follows? Can you identify any words that serve as transitions? What additional transitional words and phrases might help move readers from one panel to the next?
3. What do you think happened right before (and right after) the events depicted here?

Journal Entry

Write a narrative paragraph summarizing the story told in these panels. Begin with a sentence that identifies the characters and the setting. Next, write a sentence that summarizes the events that might have preceded the first panel. Then, tell the story that the pictures tell. In your last sentence, bring the sequence of events to a logical close. Be sure to use present tense and to include all necessary transitions.

Thematic Connections

- "The Myth of the Latin Woman: I Just Met a Girl Named Maria" (page 224)
- "Photos That Change History" (page 354)
- "The Ways We Lie" (page 463)
- "I Want a Wife" (page 494)

JUNOT DÍAZ

The Money

Born in the Dominican Republic in 1968 and raised in New Jersey, Junot Díaz earned his bachelor's degree from Rutgers University and an M.F.A. in creative writing from Cornell University. He is the author of several works of fiction, including *Drown* (1996), *The Brief Wondrous Life of Oscar Wao* (2007), and *This Is How You Lose Her* (2012). The winner of many awards, including a Pulitzer Prize and MacArthur and Guggenheim Fellowships, Díaz is the fiction editor at *Boston Review* and the Rudge and Nancy Allen Professor of Writing at the Massachusetts Institute of Technology.

Background on Dominicans in the United States Dominicans living in the United States account for 3 percent of the U.S. Hispanic population; they numbered about 1.5 million when the Census Bureau made its American Community Survey in 2011. For many years, the Northeast has been home to the majority of Dominicans in the United States. Although historically almost half settled in New York City, in recent years they have established sizable populations in several other northeastern states, such as New Jersey, Massachusetts, and Pennsylvania. Dominicans living in the United States are significantly more likely to have been born outside the United States, as Díaz was, than the general Hispanic population. The Dominican population also has a slightly higher poverty rate compared to all Hispanics; however, it can also claim a higher level of education. Dominicans have had an impact on American food, music, and culture, and they are an integral part of social and commercial life in the United States, where they are teachers, bankers, lawyers, small business owners, entrepreneurs, and workers. With a long history of activism, Dominicans have also begun to wield political influence as elected officials in U.S. state, city, and local governments.

1   All the Dominicans I knew in those days sent money home. My mother didn't have a regular job besides caring for us five kids, so she scrimped the loot together from whatever came her way. My father was always losing his forklift jobs, so it wasn't like she ever had a steady flow. But my grandparents were alone in Santo Domingo, and those remittances, beyond material support, were a way, I suspect, for Mami to negotiate the absence, the distance, caused by our diaspora. She chipped dollars off the cash Papi gave her for our daily expenses, forced our already broke family to live even broker. That was how she built the nut — two, maybe three hundred dollars — that she sent home every six months or so.

2   We kids knew where the money was hidden, but we also knew that to touch it would have meant a violent punishment approaching death. I, who could take the change out of my mother's purse without thinking, couldn't have brought myself even to look at that forbidden stash.

So what happened? Exactly what you'd think. The summer I was twelve, my family went away on a "vacation"—one of my father's half-baked get-to-know-our-country-better-by-sleeping-in-the-van extravaganzas—and when we returned to Jersey, exhausted, battered, we found our front door unlocked. My parents' room, which was where the thieves had concentrated their search, looked as if it had been tornado-tossed. The thieves had kept it simple; they'd snatched a portable radio, some of my Dungeons & Dragons hardcovers, and, of course, Mami's remittances.

> **"Everybody got hit; no matter who you were, eventually it would be your turn."**

It's not as if the robbery came as a huge surprise. In our neighborhood, cars and apartments were always getting jacked, and the kid stupid enough to leave a bike unattended for more than a tenth of a second was the kid who was never going to see that bike again. Everybody got hit; no matter who you were, eventually it would be your turn.

And that summer it was ours.

Still, we took the burglary pretty hard. When you're a recent immigrant, it's easy to feel targeted. Like it wasn't just a couple of assholes that had it in for you but the whole neighborhood—hell, maybe the whole country.

No one took the robbery as hard as my mom, though. She cursed the neighborhood, she cursed the country, she cursed my father, and of course she cursed us kids, swore that we had run our gums to our idiot friends and they had done it.

And this is where the tale should end, right? Wasn't as if there was going to be any "C.S.I."-style investigation or anything. Except that a couple of days later I was moaning about the robbery to these guys I was hanging with at that time and they were cursing sympathetically, and out of nowhere it struck me. You know when you get one of those moments of mental clarity? When the nictitating membrane* obscuring the world suddenly lifts? That's what happened. I realized that these two dopes I called my friends had done it. They were shaking their heads, mouthing all the right words, but I could see the way they looked at each other, the Raskolnikov glances. I *knew*.

Now, it wasn't like I could publicly denounce these dolts or go to the police. That would have been about as useless as crying. Here's what I did: I asked the main dope to let me use his bathroom (we were in front of his apartment) and while I pretended to piss I unlatched the window. Then we all headed to the park as usual, but I pretended that I'd forgotten something back home. Ran to the dope's apartment, slid open the bathroom window, and in broad daylight wriggled my skinny ass in.

Where the hell did I get these ideas? I have not a clue. I guess I was reading way too much Encyclopedia Brown and the Three Investigators in those days. And if mine had been a normal neighborhood this is when the cops would have been called and my ass would have been caught *burglarizing*.

---

* Eds. note—Transparent inner eyelid found in birds, reptiles, and some mammals.

The dolt and his family had been in the U.S. all their lives and they had a   11
ton of stuff, a TV in every room, but I didn't have to do much searching.
I popped up the dolt's mattress and underneath I found my D.&D. books and
most of my mother's money. He had thoughtfully kept it in the same envelope.

And that was how I solved the Case of the Stupid Morons. My one and   12
only case.

The next day at the park, the dolt announced that someone had broken   13
into *his* apartment and stolen all his savings. This place is full of thieves, he
complained bitterly, and I was, like, No kidding.

It took me two days to return the money to my mother. The truth was I   14
was seriously considering keeping it. But in the end the guilt got to me. I guess
I was expecting my mother to run around with joy, to crown me her favorite
son, to cook me my favorite meal. Nada. I'd wanted a party or at least to see her
happy, but there was nothing. Just two hundred and some dollars and fifteen
hundred or so miles — that's all there was.

· · ·

Comprehension

1. Díaz grew up poor. How does he communicate this fact to readers?
2. According to Díaz, why is the money in his mother's "forbidden stash"
   (2) different from the money in her purse? Do you think this distinction
   makes sense?
3. How did Díaz solve "the Case of the Stupid Morons" (12)?
4. What does Díaz mean when he says, "Just two hundred and some dollars
   and fifteen hundred or so miles — that's all there was" (14)?
5. In paragraph 6, Díaz says, "When you're a recent immigrant, it's easy to feel
   targeted"; in paragraph 9, he states matter-of-factly that going to the police
   was not an option for him. What relationship, if any, do you see between
   these two statements?

Purpose and Audience

1. Even though Díaz uses a very informal style, full of slang expressions, he
   also uses words like *diaspora* (1) and expressions like "Raskolnikov glances" (8).
   What does the use of such language tell you about him — and about how he
   sees his audience?
2. This essay does not have a stated thesis. What is Díaz's main idea? Write a
   sentence that could serve as a thesis statement. Where in the essay could this
   sentence be added? *Should* such a sentence be added? Why or why not?
3. Does this essay have a persuasive purpose, or is Díaz just trying to share his
   memories with readers? Explain.

Style and Structure

1. Identify the one- and two-sentence paragraphs in this essay. Are these
   very brief paragraphs effective as they are, or should they be expanded or
   combined with other paragraphs? Explain.

2. This is a personal, informal essay, and it uses first person pronouns (*I*, *we*) and contractions. It also includes a number of fragments. Identify a few fragments, and try to turn each one into a complete sentence. Then, explain why you think Díaz used each fragment.
3. In paragraphs 3, 8, and 10, Díaz asks **rhetorical questions**. How would you answer these questions?
4. **Vocabulary Project.** What words, besides *morons*, does Díaz use to describe the thieves? Which word seems most appropriate to you? Why?
5. Like a crime story, Díaz's narrative moves readers through events from the crime itself to its effect to its final outcome. Identify each of these sections of the narrative.

Journal Entry

Do you think Díaz feels angrier at the "morons" or at himself? Does he also feel frustrated? Disappointed? If so, with whom (or what)?

Writing Workshop

1. Díaz mentions Encyclopedia Brown and the Three Investigators, fictional young detectives whose adventures he followed. When you were young, what was as important to you as these fictional characters were to Díaz? In a narrative essay, trace the development of your fascination with a particular fictional character, pastime, or hobby.
2. When he returns the money to his mother, Díaz expects "a party or at least to see her happy" (14), but that isn't the reaction he gets. Write a narrative essay about a time when you expected a particular reaction or outcome but were disappointed or surprised.
3. **Working with Sources.** Consult several dictionaries to find out what the term *diaspora* has meant throughout history. Then, write a narrative essay tracing your own family's diaspora, focusing on your family's movement from one country, region, or neighborhood to another. Include a definition from one of the dictionaries you consult, and be sure to include parenthetical documentation for the definition and a works-cited page. (See Chapter 18 for information on MLA documentation.)

Combining the Patterns

Díaz discusses both his family's life in a Dominican neighborhood in New Jersey and his relatives' lives back in Santo Domingo. If he wanted to write a **comparison-and-contrast** paragraph comparing his life to his relatives', what details might he include? Do you think he should add such a paragraph? If so, why — and where?

Thematic Connections

- "The Secret Lion" (page 140)
- "The Ways We Lie" (page 463)
- "Tortillas" (page 498)

HANIF ABDURRAQIB

My First Police Stop

Poet, cultural critic, and essayist Hanif Abdurraqib (b. 1983) was born in Columbus, Ohio. His first full-length book of poetry, *The Crown Ain't Worth Much*, was published in 2016 and was named a finalist for the Eric Hoffer Book Prize and a nominee for a Hurston-Wright Legacy Award. His second poetry collection, *A Fortune for Your Disaster*, followed in 2019. Abdurraqib also published the essay collection *They Can't Kill Us Until They Kill Us* in 2017 and *Go Ahead in the Rain: Notes to a Tribe Called Quest* in 2019. His writing has appeared in the *New York Times*, *The Fader*, *Pitchfork*, MTV News, and *Muzzle*, among many others.

Background on police reform Hanif Abdurraqib's story is about something that happened to him in 2001, but it still feels contemporary because the systemic problems of U.S. police forces remain a major issue in the lives of citizens, particularly people of color. Police reforms under the Lyndon Johnson presidential administration and Supreme Court decisions during the 1960s led to the standardization of rules regarding unreasonable search and seizure, informing criminal suspects of their rights, and treatment of juvenile offenders. However, these protections are not always effective if the suspects are unfairly targeted for police harassment — or if officers violently escalate a situation based on racial profiling. This form of offense has received more attention over the past decade, which has seen a series of police shootings involving unarmed individuals. One of the most famous such incidents was the shooting of Michael Brown, shot and killed in 2014 in Ferguson, Missouri. After the officer in question was not charged, protests against the Ferguson police continued for over a week and sparked a national conversation about how to prevent further violence. Debates continue over whether improved community policing, mandatory implementation of body cameras on police officers, or more rigorous bias training might result in less police violence.

My father went with me to the used-car lot on a summer day before my senior year in high school. We paid $1,995, from savings left to me after my mother's death, for a 1994 Nissan Maxima. 1

It was an odd shade of brown, with a thin gold stripe painted along the body, and it had a small exhaust leak, which made the engine loud. Still, it was mine. 2

Almost immediately, the car had issues. The alarm went off whenever you unlocked the driver's door because of an electrical problem that, I was told, would cost almost as much to fix as I had paid for the car. 3

This resulted in two solutions: Either I had to unlock the driver's door and quickly start the engine (to stop the blaring horn and flashing lights), or I would have to unlock the passenger-side door (which did not trigger the alarm) and climb toward the driver's seat. 4

It was a typical high school car. It was imperfect, a bit of a wreck and I 5
loved it.

During the school year, Capital University, in Bexley, Ohio, recruited me to 6
play soccer. At 17, with an offer from a college a few miles from my father's
house, I didn't really consider what it would be like to exist as Black in a community that had managed to keep itself white.

So in the late summer of 2001, before the start of my freshman year in 7
college, I stepped onto the field for a preseason practice session as the first
American-born player of color in the soccer program's history.

By that time I had learned to deal with the Nissan's quirks; I decided 8
whether or not to endure the burst of the car's alarm depending on the area I
was in. If I found myself in a place where my existence might raise suspicion, I
chose the safer but more difficult route of going in through the passenger
door.

On a September night, eager to escape a house imprisoned by a thick cloud 9
of body heat and drink, I skipped out of a college party and rushed to my car. I
slid the key into the driver's door. But before turning it, I checked the street:
the towering and expensive homes, the paved sidewalks, the darkness and
silence.

I opted for what my father would say was the smarter choice: I went in 10
through the passenger-side door. The engine let out a rumble that cut through
the suburban night. As I pulled away from the curb, I saw the flashing lights of
a police car.

I spend a lot of time trying to pinpoint how fear is learned. Or, rather, how 11
we decide that fear is a necessary animal that grows out of our expectation to
survive at all costs, and how I have been afraid and feared at the same time.

When I reflect, I think the fact that I had gone 17 years without having 12
developed a direct fear of the police meant that I was lucky.

I knew the warnings from my father: Don't go on a run at night, don't 13
reach into your pockets too quickly, be polite in front of them. And I had seen
the police make life difficult for other people in my home neighborhood, and
yet I never learned to be afraid.

Until this early fall night in 2001, with its unseasonable cold, the Midwest 14
wind like daggers.

Bexley sits on the east side of Columbus. A small and flourishing mostly 15
white suburb, it is sandwiched by two significantly poorer, mostly Black neighborhoods. One of these is where I grew up.

When you are asked to step out of a car that you own, your body no longer 16
belongs to you, but instead to the lights drowning it. There are two sides of the
night that you can end up on: one where you see the sunrise again and one
where you do not. You may not consider this in the moment.

That particular night, the police officers — first two, and then three 17
more — were responding to a call of suspicious behavior. I was asked to exit my
car before I was asked for ID. When I mentioned that this was my own vehicle,
I was silenced and held by two officers while the others huddled around a
squad car.

When I was finally asked to produce ID, I reached into a pocket, only to   18
remember that it was in the book bag I had left in the trunk. I moved to get it.
That's when I was grabbed and forcefully held down in the grass.

People who had been watching out of windows now emerged from their   19
homes. I wondered which one of them had called the police. I thought about
my pants, a pair of new Old Navy jeans purchased with money I had gotten as a
graduation gift, now stained with grass, and I thought about how much they
had cost me.

I thought about how much the car had cost me. How much it had cost me   20
to get here, to Bexley, just five miles away from a neighborhood that no one
from the nearby homes would venture to. But mostly I thought about how
I perhaps owned nothing. Not even my hands, now pressed behind my back.

I was eventually pulled up from the grass after what felt like hours, but   21
must have been about five minutes. My car ransacked, my book bag's contents
scattered across the otherwise empty street.

A police officer stared at my face, stared at my ID, and he mumbled: 22
"Interesting name. Sorry for the trouble."

After the officers were gone, I sat on the curb and watched my hands shake.   23
No one who lived in the nearby homes offered to help or asked if I was O.K.

I didn't hate the police that night. Even today, while being critical of the   24
institution of police and systems of policing, I feel no hatred toward the men
and women themselves.

I have had many interactions with police officers since then, some better, a   25
few just as bad. But I go into each one expecting to fear and to be feared. And
when I see the news of another unarmed person's death, I wonder how their
stories began.

If they began something like mine.   26

· · ·

Comprehension

1. In what respects is the writer's car a "typical high school car" (5)?
2. What key problems does the car have? Why doesn't Abdurraqib get them
   fixed? Why are these quirks a significant element of his narrative?
3. Why do the police officers stop Abdurraqib? Do you think their actions
   were justified?
4. Why do the police suddenly become more violent, grabbing Abdurraqib and
   holding him down in the grass? How does he react to this escalation?
5. Do you think the police who stopped Abdurraqib were white or Black? Why
   do you think he doesn't specify their race?
6. Abdurraqib says that over the years he has been "afraid and feared at the
   same time" (11) and that he now expects "to fear and to be feared" (25).
   How does his narrative illustrate this **paradox**?

Purpose and Audience

1. This essay does not have an explicitly stated thesis. In one sentence, paraphrase the essay's main idea.
2. In addition to recounting his experience for readers, what other purpose (if any) does Abdurraqib have? For example, does he have a persuasive purpose? If so, what is it?
3. Why does Abdurraqib begin his essay with information about his car? Do you think this is an effective opening strategy? Why or why not?
4. Why does Abdurraqib mention that he was "the first American-born player of color in the [college] soccer program's history" (7)? Is this paragraph a digression, or does it provide important information?

Style and Structure

1. List some of the transitional words and phrases Abdurraqib uses to move readers from sentence to sentence and from paragraph to paragraph. Does he supply enough transitions to move his narrative smoothly along? Does he need to add any chronological links? If so, where?
2. What is implied by the word *first* in the essay's title? Where does the writer provide information that explains why this word is appropriate?
3. What adjectives does Abdurraqib use to describe his car? To describe the neighborhood in which he is stopped? How are the dominant impressions he conveys through these descriptions different?
4. **Vocabulary Project.** Abdurraqib recounts the events in paragraphs 17 and 18 in a tone that is quite matter of fact, using expressions like "*exit* my car" and "*produce* ID." Why doesn't he use more emotional—or even angry—language? Do you think he made the right choice?
5. Two stylistic techniques that Abdurraqib uses are following a long sentence with a short one, as in paragraph 2, and isolating a sentence in a single paragraph, as in paragraph 12. Find some other examples of these two techniques, and explain their effect.
6. What is the use of the word *managed* (6) intended to convey? What does this word suggest about the community in which the incident occurs?

Journal Entry

Despite his status as a young African American male, and despite his father's cautions, Abdurraqib says that before the incident he describes, he "never learned to be afraid" (13). Do you think he (and other young men of color) should learn to be afraid? Why or why not?

Writing Workshop

1. Write a narrative report of this incident from the point of view of one of the responding police officers.
2. **Working with Sources.** Research the Black Lives Matter movement, which began in 2013. What are the goals of this movement? How do you think the incident Abdurraqib describes is related to these goals? For example,

might the movement's eventual success make incidents like this one less frequent? Write a narrative essay in which you answer these questions, taking care to cite your sources and to include a works-cited page. (See Chapter 18 for information on MLA documentation.)

3. For Abdurraqib, this incident was a **rite of passage**, an experience that served as an important milestone in his life. Write a narrative essay that recounts a rite of passage in your own life, explaining what happened, how the incident changed you, and how you view it now.

Combining the Patterns

In this narrative essay, the police officers who stop the writer are mentioned but not described. Why do you suppose the essay does not include any description of the officers? How might adding passages of description change the essay?

Thematic Connections

- " 'What's in a Name?' " (page 2)
- "Stability in Motion" (page 179)
- "Just Walk On By: A Black Man Ponders His Power to Alter Public Space" (page 231)
- "Emmett Till and Tamir Rice, Sons of the Great Migration" (page 414)

BONNIE SMITH-YACKEL

My Mother Never Worked

Bonnie Smith-Yackel was born into a farm family in Willmar, Minnesota, in 1937. She began writing as a young homemaker in the early 1960s and for the next fourteen years published short stories, essays, and book reviews in such publications as *Catholic Digest, Minnesota Monthly*, and *Ms.* magazine, as well as in several local newspapers. As Smith-Yackel explained, "The catalyst for writing the [following] essay shortly after my mother's death was recounting my telephone conversation with Social Security to the lawyer who was helping me settle my mother's estate. When I told him what the SS woman had said, he responded: 'Well, that's right. Your mother didn't work, you know.' At which point I stood and said, 'She worked harder throughout her life than you or a hundred men like you!' and stomped out of his office, drove home, sat down and wrote the essay in one sitting." Although this narrative essay, first published in *Women: A Journal of Liberation* in 1975, is based on personal experience, it also makes a broader statement about how society values "women's work."

Background on Social Security benefits Social Security is a federal insurance program that requires workers to contribute a percentage of their wages to a fund from which they may draw benefits if they become unemployed due to disability. After retirement, workers can receive a monthly income from this fund, which also provides a modest death benefit to survivors. The contribution is generally deducted directly from a worker's paycheck, and employers must contribute a matching amount. According to federal law, a woman who is a homemaker, who has never been a wage earner, is eligible for Social Security benefits only through the earnings of her deceased husband. (The same would be true for a man if the roles were reversed.) Therefore, a homemaker's survivors would not be eligible for the death benefit. Although the law has been challenged in the courts, the survivors of a homemaker who has never been a wage earner are still not entitled to a Social Security death benefit.

"Social Security Office." (The voice answering the telephone sounds very self-assured.)   1

"I'm calling about . . . my mother just died . . . I was told to call you and see about a . . . death-benefit check, I think they call it. . . ."   2

"I see. Was your mother on Social Security? How old was she?"   3

"Yes . . . she was seventy-eight. . . ."   4

"Do you know her number?"   5

"No . . . I, ah . . . don't you have a record?"   6

"Certainly. I'll look it up. Her name?"   7

"Smith. Martha Smith. Or maybe she used Martha Ruth Smith? . . . Sometimes she used her maiden name . . . Martha Jerabek Smith?"   8

"If you'd care to hold on, I'll check our records—it'll be a few minutes."   9

"Yes. . . ."   10

Her love letters — to and from Daddy — were in an old box, tied with   11
ribbons and stiff, rigid-with-age leather thongs: 1918 through 1920; hers written on stationery from the general store she had worked in full-time and managed, single-handed, after her graduation from high school in 1913; and his, at
first, on YMCA or Soldiers and Sailors Club stationery dispensed to the fighting men of World War I. He wooed her thoroughly and persistently by mail,
and though she reciprocated all his feelings for her, she dreaded marriage. . . .

"It's so hard for me to decide when to have my wedding day — that's all I've   12
thought about these last two days. I have told you dozens of times that I won't
be afraid of married life, but when it comes down to setting the date and then
picturing myself a married woman with half a dozen or more kids to look after,
it just makes me sick. . . . I am weeping right now — I hope that some day I can
look back and say how foolish I was to dread it all."

They married in February, 1921, and began farming. Their first baby, a   13
daughter, was born in January, 1922, when my mother was twenty-six years
old. The second baby, a son, was born in March, 1923. They were renting farms;
my father, besides working his own fields, also was a hired man for two other
farmers. They had no capital initially, and had to gain it slowly, working from
dawn until midnight every day. My town-bred mother learned to set hens and
raise chickens, feed pigs, milk cows, plant and harvest a garden, and can every
fruit and vegetable she could scrounge. She carried water nearly a quarter of a
mile from the well to fill her wash boilers in order to do her laundry on a scrub
board. She learned to shuck grain, feed threshers, shock and husk corn, feed
corn pickers. In September, 1925, the third baby came, and in June, 1927, the
fourth child — both daughters. In 1930, my parents had enough money to buy
their own farm, and that March they moved all their livestock and belongings
themselves, fifty-five miles over rutted, muddy roads.

In the summer of 1930 my mother and her two eldest children reclaimed a   14
forty-acre field from Canadian thistles, by chopping them all out with a hoe. In
the other fields, when the oats and flax began to head out, the green and blue
of the crops were hidden by the bright yellow of wild mustard. My mother
walked the fields day after day, pulling each mustard plant. She raised a new
flock of baby chicks — five hundred — and she spaded up, planted, hoed, and
harvested a half-acre garden.

During the next spring their hogs caught cholera and died. No cash that   15
fall.

And in the next year the drought hit. My mother and father trudged from   16
the well to the chickens, the well to the calf pasture, the well to the barn, and
from the well to the garden. The sun came out hot and bright, endlessly, day
after day. The crops shriveled and died. They harvested half the corn, and
ground the other half, stalks and all, and fed it to the cattle as fodder. With the
price at four cents a bushel for the harvested crop, they couldn't afford to haul
it into town. They burned it in the furnace for fuel that winter.

In 1934, in February, when the dust was still so thick in the Minnesota air   17
that my parents couldn't always see from the house to the barn, their fifth
child — a fourth daughter — was born. My father hunted rabbits daily, and my
mother stewed them, fried them, canned them, and wished out loud that she

could taste hamburger once more. In the fall the shotgun brought prairie chickens, ducks, pheasant, and grouse. My mother plucked each bird, carefully reserving the breast feathers for pillows.

In the winter she sewed night after night, endlessly, begging cast-off cloth- 18 ing from relatives, ripping apart coats, dresses, blouses, and trousers to remake them to fit her four daughters and son. Every morning and every evening she milked cows, fed pigs and calves, cared for chickens, picked eggs, cooked meals, washed dishes, scrubbed floors, and tended and loved her children. In the spring she planted a garden once more, dragging pails of water to nourish and sustain the vegetables for the family. In 1936 she lost a baby in her sixth month.

In 1937 her fifth daughter was born. She was forty-two years old. In 1939 a 19 second son, and in 1941 her eighth child — and third son.

But the war had come, and prosperity of a sort. The herd of cattle had 20 grown to thirty head; she still milked morning and evening. Her garden was more than a half acre — the rains had come, and by now the Rural Electricity Administration and indoor plumbing. Still she sewed — dresses and jackets for the children, housedresses and aprons for herself, weekly patching of jeans, overalls, and denim shirts. She still made pillows, using feathers she had plucked, and quilts every year — intricate patterns as well as patchwork, stitched as well as tied — all necessary bedding for her family. Every scrap of cloth too small to be used in quilts was carefully saved and painstakingly sewed together in strips to make rugs. She still went out in the fields to help with the haying whenever there was a threat of rain.

In 1959 my mother's last child graduated from high school. A year later 21 the cows were sold. She still raised chickens and ducks, plucked feathers, made pillows, baked her own bread, and every year made a new quilt — now for a married child or for a grandchild. And her garden, that huge, undying symbol of sustenance, was as large and cared for as in all the years before. The canning, and now freezing, continued.

In 1969, on a June afternoon, mother and father started out for town so 22 that she could buy sugar to make rhubarb jam for a daughter who lived in Texas. The car crashed into a ditch. She was paralyzed from the waist down.

In 1970 her husband, my father, died. My mother struggled to regain some 23 competence and dignity and order in her life. At the rehabilitation institute, where they gave her physical therapy and trained her to live usefully in a wheelchair, the therapist told me: "She did fifteen pushups today — fifteen! She's almost seventy-five years old! I've never known a woman so strong!"

> "Well, you see — your mother never worked."

From her wheelchair she canned pickles, 24 baked bread, ironed clothes, wrote dozens of letters weekly to her friends and her "half dozen or more kids," and made three patchwork housecoats and one quilt. She made balls and balls of carpet rags — enough for five rugs. And kept all her love letters.

"I think I've found your mother's records — Martha Ruth Smith; married 25 to Ben F. Smith?"

"Yes, that's right." 26

"Well, I see that she was getting a widow's pension. . . ."   27
"Yes, that's right."   28
"Well, your mother isn't entitled to our $255 death benefit."   29
"Not entitled! But why?"   30
The voice on the telephone explains patiently: 31
"Well, you see—your mother never worked."   32

• • •

Comprehension

1. What kind of work did Martha Smith do while her children were growing up? List some of the chores she performed.
2. Why aren't Martha Smith's survivors entitled to a death benefit when their mother dies?
3. How does the federal government define *work*?

Purpose and Audience

1. What point is the writer trying to make? Why do you suppose her thesis is never explicitly stated?
2. This essay appeared in *Ms.* magazine and other publications whose audiences are sympathetic to feminist goals. Could it have appeared in a magazine whose audience had a more traditional view of gender roles? Why or why not?
3. Smith-Yackel says very little about her father in this essay. Why do you think she does not tell readers more about him? Should she have added material about him?
4. This essay was first published in 1975. Do you think it is dated, or do you think the issues it raises are still relevant today?

Style and Structure

1. Is the essay's title effective? If so, why? If not, what alternate title can you suggest?
2. Smith-Yackel could have outlined her mother's life without framing it with the telephone conversation. Why do you think she decided to include this frame? Was this a good decision?
3. What strategies does Smith-Yackel use to indicate the passing of time in her narrative?
4. This narrative piles details one on top of another. Why does the writer include so many details? Do you think she includes *too many* details?
5. In paragraphs 20 and 21, what is accomplished by the repetition of the word *still*?
6. **Vocabulary Project.** Try substituting equivalent words for those italicized in this sentence:
   He *wooed* her *thoroughly* and *persistently* by mail, and though she *reciprocated* all his feelings for her, she *dreaded* marriage . . . (11).
   How do your substitutions change the sentence's meaning?

Journal Entry

Do you believe that a homemaker who has never been a wage earner should be entitled to a Social Security death benefit for her survivors? Explain your reasoning.

Writing Workshop

1. **Working with Sources.** Interview one of your parents or grandparents (or another person you know who reminds you of Smith-Yackel's mother) about his or her work history, and write a chronological narrative based on what you learn. Include a thesis statement that your narrative can support, and quote your subject's responses when possible. Be sure to include parenthetical documentation for these quotations and a works-cited page. (See Chapter 18 for information on MLA documentation.)

2. Write Martha Smith's obituary as it might have appeared in her hometown newspaper. (If you are not familiar with the form of an obituary, read a few in your local paper or online at Legacy.com or Obituaries.com.)

3. Write a narrative account of a typical day at the worst job you ever had. Include a thesis statement that conveys your negative impression.

Combining the Patterns

Because of the repetitive nature of the farm chores that Smith-Yackel describes in her narrative, some passages come very close to explaining a **process**, a series of repeated steps that always occur in a predictable order. Identify several such passages. If Smith-Yackel's essay were written entirely as a process explanation, what, if anything, would have to be added? What material would have to be left out? How would these omissions change the essay?

Thematic Connections

- "'Girl'" (page 251)
- "Patterns" (page 473)
- "I Want a Wife" (page 494)

MARTIN GANSBERG

Thirty-Seven Who Saw Murder Didn't Call the Police

Martin Gansberg (1920–1995), a native of Brooklyn, New York, was a reporter and editor for the *New York Times* for forty-three years. The following article, written for the *Times* two weeks after the 1964 murder it recounts, earned Gansberg an award for excellence from the Newspaper Reporters Association of New York. Gansberg's thesis, although not explicitly stated, still retains its power.

Background on the Kitty Genovese murder case The events reported here took place on March 14, 1964, as contemporary American culture was undergoing a complex transition. The relatively placid years of the 1950s were giving way to more troubling times: the civil rights movement was leading to social unrest in the South and in northern inner cities, the escalating war in Vietnam was creating angry political divisions, President John F. Kennedy had been assassinated just four months earlier, violent imagery was increasing in television and film, crime rates were rising, and a growing drug culture was becoming apparent. The brutal, senseless murder of Kitty Genovese — and, more important, her neighbors' failure to respond immediately to her cries for help — became a nationwide, and even worldwide, symbol for what was perceived as an evolving culture of violence and indifference.

In recent years, some of the details Gansberg mentions have been challenged. For example, as the *New York Times* now acknowledges, there were only two attacks on Ms. Genovese, not three; the first attack may have been shorter than initially reported; the second attack may have occurred in the apartment house foyer, where neighbors would not have been able to see Genovese; and some witnesses may, in fact, actually *have* called the police. In April 2016, the murderer of Kitty Genovese died in prison, bringing the case back to national attention, and in June of that same year, Kitty Genovese's brother Bill Genovese and director James Solomon released *The Witness*, a documentary tracing Bill's search for the truth about his sister's murder. The film comes to the conclusion that the incident did not occur just as Gansberg had reported it. At the time, however, the world was shocked by the incident, and even today social scientists around the world debate the causes of "the Genovese syndrome."

1   For more than half an hour thirty-eight respectable, law-abiding citizens in Queens watched a killer stalk and stab a woman in three separate attacks in Kew Gardens.

2   Twice their chatter and the sudden glow of their bedroom lights interrupted him and frightened him off. Each time he returned, sought her out, and stabbed her again. Not one person telephoned the police during the assault; one witness called after the woman was dead.

That was two weeks ago today.   3

Still shocked is Assistant Chief Inspector Frederick M. Lussen, in charge   4
of the borough's detectives and a veteran of twenty-five years of homicide
investigations. He can give a matter-of-fact recitation on many murders. But
the Kew Gardens slaying baffles him — not because it is a murder, but because
the "good people" failed to call the police.

> **"Not one person telephoned the police during the assault; one witness called after the woman was dead."**

"As we have reconstructed the crime," he   5
said, "the assailant had three chances to kill
this woman during a thirty-five-minute period.
He returned twice to complete the job. If we
had been called when he first attacked, the
woman might not be dead now."

This is what the police say happened begin-   6
ning at 3:20 A.M. in the staid, middle-class, tree-
lined Austin Street area:

Twenty-eight-year-old Catherine Genovese,   7
who was called Kitty by almost everyone in the neighborhood, was returning home
from her job as manager of a bar in Hollis. She parked her red Fiat in a lot adjacent
to the Kew Gardens Long Island Rail Road Station, facing Mowbray Place. Like
many residents of the neighborhood, she had parked there day after day since
her arrival from Connecticut a year ago, although the railroad frowns on the
practice.

She turned off the lights of her car, locked the door, and started to walk   8
the one hundred feet to the entrance of her apartment at 82-70 Austin Street,
which is in a Tudor building, with stores in the first floor and apartments on
the second.

The entrance to the apartment is in the rear of the building because the   9
front is rented to retail stores. At night the quiet neighborhood is shrouded in
the slumbering darkness that marks most residential areas.

Miss Genovese noticed a man at the far end of the lot, near a seven-story   10
apartment house at 82-40 Austin Street. She halted. Then, nervously, she
headed up Austin Street toward Lefferts Boulevard, where there is a call box to
the 102nd Police Precinct in nearby Richmond Hill.

She got as far as a street light in front of a bookstore before the man   11
grabbed her. She screamed. Lights went on in the ten-story apartment house at
82-67 Austin Street, which faces the bookstore. Windows slid open and voices
punctuated the early-morning stillness.

Miss Genovese screamed: "Oh, my God, he stabbed me! Please help me!   12
Please help me!"

From one of the upper windows in the apartment house, a man called   13
down: "Let that girl alone!"

The assailant looked up at him, shrugged, and walked down Austin Street   14
toward a white sedan parked a short distance away. Miss Genovese struggled to
her feet.

Lights went out. The killer returned to Miss Genovese, now trying to make   15
her way around the side of the building by the parking lot to get to her
apartment. The assailant stabbed her again.

"I'm dying!" she shrieked. "I'm dying!"   16

Windows were opened again, and lights went on in many apartments. The   17
assailant got into his car and drove away. Miss Genovese staggered to her feet.
A city bus, 0–10, the Lefferts Boulevard line to Kennedy International Airport,
passed. It was 3:35 A.M.

The assailant returned. By then, Miss Genovese had crawled to the back of   18
the building, where the freshly painted brown doors to the apartment house
held out hope for safety. The killer tried the first door; she wasn't there. At the
second door, 82-62 Austin Street, he saw her slumped on the floor at the foot
of the stairs. He stabbed her a third time—fatally.

It was 3:50 by the time the police received their first call, from a man who   19
was a neighbor of Miss Genovese. In two minutes they were at the scene. The
neighbor, a seventy-year-old woman, and another woman were the only
persons on the street. Nobody else came forward.

The man explained that he had called the police after much deliberation.   20
He had phoned a friend in Nassau County for advice, and then he had crossed
the roof of the building to the apartment of the elderly woman to get her to
make the call.

"I didn't want to get involved," he sheepishly told police.   21

Six days later, the police arrested Winston Moseley, a twenty-nine-year-old   22
business machine operator, and charged him with homicide. Moseley had no
previous record. He is married, has two children, and owns a home at 133-19
Sutter Avenue, South Ozone Park, Queens. On Wednesday, a court committed
him to Kings County Hospital for psychiatric observation.

When questioned by the police, Moseley also said that he had slain Mrs.   23
Annie May Johnson, twenty-four, of 146-12 133d Avenue, Jamaica, on Feb. 29
and Barbara Kralik, fifteen, of 174-17 140th Avenue, Springfield Gardens, last
July. In the Kralik case, the police are holding Alvin L. Mitchell, who is said to
have confessed to that slaying.

The police stressed how simple it would have been to have gotten in touch   24
with them. "A phone call," said one of the detectives, "would have done it." The
police may be reached by dialing "0" for operator or SPring 7-3100.

Today witnesses from the neighborhood, which is made up of one-family   25
homes in the $35,000 to $60,000 range with the exception of the two apartment houses near the railroad station, find it difficult to explain why they
didn't call the police.

A housewife, knowingly if quite casually, said, "We thought it was a lovers'   26
quarrel." A husband and wife both said, "Frankly, we were afraid." They seemed
aware of the fact that events might have been different. A distraught woman,
wiping her hands in her apron, said, "I didn't want my husband to get
involved."

One couple, now willing to talk about that night, said they heard the first   27
screams. The husband looked thoughtfully at the bookstore where the killer
first grabbed Miss Genovese.

"We went to the window to see what was happening," he said, "but the   28
light from our bedroom made it difficult to see the street." The wife, still appre-
hensive, added: "I put out the light and we were able to see better."

Asked why they hadn't called the police, she shrugged and replied: "I don't   29
know."

A man peeked out from a slight opening in the doorway to his apartment   30
and rattled off an account of the killer's second attack. Why hadn't he called the
police at the time? "I was tired," he said without emotion. "I went back to bed."

It was 4:25 A.M. when the ambulance arrived to take the body of Miss   31
Genovese. It drove off. "Then," a solemn police detective said, "the people
came out."

· · ·

Comprehension

1. According to Gansberg, how much time elapsed between the first stabbing
   of Kitty Genovese and the time when the people finally came out?
2. What excuses do the neighbors make for not coming to Kitty Genovese's aid?

Purpose and Audience

1. This article appeared in 1964, just two weeks after the incident. What effect
   was it intended to have on its audience? Do you think it has the same
   impact today, or has its impact changed or diminished?
2. What is the article's main point? Why does Gansberg imply his thesis rather
   than state it explicitly?
3. What is Gansberg's purpose in describing the Austin Street area as "staid,
   middle-class, tree-lined" (6)?
4. Why do you suppose Gansberg provides the police department's phone
   number in his article? (Note that New York City did not have 911 emergency
   service in 1964.)

Style and Structure

1. Gansberg is very precise in this article, especially in his references to time,
   addresses, and ages. Why?
2. The objective newspaper style is dominant in this article, but the writer's
   anger shows through. Point to words and phrases that reveal his attitude
   toward his material.
3. Because this article was originally set in the narrow columns of a newspaper,
   it has many short paragraphs. Would the narrative be more effective if some
   of these brief paragraphs were combined? If so, why? If not, why not? Give
   examples to support your answer.
4. **Vocabulary Project.** The word *assailant* appears frequently in this article.
   Why is it used so often? What effect is this repetition likely to have on
   readers? What other words could have been used?
5. Review the dialogue quoted in this article. Does it strengthen Gansberg's
   narrative? Would the article be more compelling with additional dialogue?
   Without dialogue? Explain.
6. This article does not have a formal conclusion; nevertheless, the last paragraph sums up the writer's attitude. How?

Journal Entry

Because they provide easy access to 911 service — and because many also have the ability to record video — cell phones have dramatically changed the way people respond to crimes they witness or are victim to. How might the availability of cell phones have changed Kitty Genovese's story?

Writing Workshop

1. In your own words, write a ten-sentence **summary** (see page 718) of this newspaper article. Try to reflect Gansberg's order and emphasis as well as his ideas, and be sure to include all necessary transitions.
2. Rewrite this article as if it were a blog post written by one of the thirty-eight people who watched the murder. Summarize what you saw, and explain why you decided not to call for help. (You may invent details that Gansberg does not include.)
3. **Working with Sources.** If you have ever been involved in or witnessed a situation in which someone was in trouble, write a narrative essay about the incident. If people failed to help the person in trouble, explain why you think no one acted. If people did act, tell how. Be sure to account for your own actions. In your essay's introduction, refer to Gansberg's account of Kitty Genovese's murder. If you quote Gansberg, be sure to include documentation and a works-cited page. (See Chapter 18 for information on MLA documentation.)

Combining the Patterns

Because the purpose of this newspaper article is to give basic factual information, it has no extended descriptions of the victim, the witnesses, or the crime scene. It also does not explain *why* those who watched did not act. Where might passages of **description** or **cause and effect** be added? How might such additions change the article's impact on readers? Do you think they would strengthen the article?

Thematic Connections

- "Shooting an Elephant" (page 132)
- "How to Spot Fake News" (page 289)
- "The Lottery" (page 303)
- "Photos That Change History" (page 354)

GEORGE ORWELL

Shooting an Elephant

George Orwell (1903–1950) was born Eric Blair in Bengal, India, where his father was a British civil servant. Rather than attend university, Orwell joined the Imperial Police in neighboring Burma (now renamed Myanmar), where he served from 1922 to 1927. Finding himself increasingly opposed to British colonial rule, Orwell left Burma to live and write in Paris and London. A political liberal and a fierce moralist, Orwell is best known today for his novels *Animal Farm* (1945) and *1984* (1949), which portray the dangers of totalitarianism. In "Shooting an Elephant," written in 1936, he recalls an incident from his days in Burma that clarified his thinking about British colonial rule.

Background on British imperialism The British had gradually taken over Burma through a succession of wars beginning in 1824; by 1885, the domination was complete. Like a number of other European countries, Britain had forcibly established colonial rule in countries throughout the world during the eighteenth and nineteenth centuries, primarily to exploit their natural resources. This empire building, known as *imperialism*, was justified by the belief that European culture was superior to the cultures of the indigenous peoples, particularly in Asia and Africa. Therefore, imperialist nations claimed, it was "the white man's burden" to bring civilization to these "heathen" lands. In most cases, such control could be achieved only through force. Anti-imperialist sentiment began to grow in the early twentieth century, but colonial rule continued until the mid-twentieth century in much of the less-developed world. Not until the late 1940s did many European colonies begin to gain independence. The British ceded home rule to Burma in 1947.

In Moulmein, in Lower Burma, I was hated by large numbers of people — the only time in my life that I have been important enough for this to happen to me. I was sub-divisional police officer of the town, and in an aimless, petty kind of way anti-European feeling was very bitter. No one had the guts to raise a riot, but if a European woman went through the bazaars alone somebody would probably spit betel juice over her dress. As a police officer I was an obvious target and was baited whenever it seemed safe to do so. When a nimble Burman tripped me up on the football field and the referee (another Burman) looked the other way, the crowd yelled with hideous laughter. This happened more than once. In the end the sneering yellow faces of young men that met me everywhere, the insults hooted after me when I was at a safe distance, got badly on my nerves. The young Buddhist priests were the worst of all. There were several thousands of them in the town and none of them seemed to have anything to do except stand on street corners and jeer at Europeans.

All this was perplexing and upsetting. For at that time I had already made up my mind that imperialism was an evil thing and the sooner I chucked up my job and got out of it the better. Theoretically — and secretly, of course — I was all for the Burmese and all against their oppressors, the British. As for the job I was doing, I hated it more bitterly than I can perhaps make clear. In a job like that you see the dirty work of Empire at close quarters. The wretched prisoners huddling in the stinking cages of the lockups, the grey, cowed faces of the long-term convicts, the scarred buttocks of the men who had been flogged with bamboos — all these oppressed me with an intolerable sense of guilt. But I could get nothing into perspective. I was young and ill-educated and I had had to think out my problems in the utter silence that is imposed on every Englishman in the East. I did not even know that the British Empire is dying, still less did I know that it is a great deal better than the younger empires that are going to supplant it.* All I knew was that I was stuck between my hatred of the empire I served and my rage against the evil-spirited little beasts who tried to make my job impossible. With one part of my mind I thought of the British Raj** as an unbreakable tyranny, as something clamped down, in *saecula saeculorum*,*** upon the will of prostrate peoples; with another part I thought that the greatest joy in the world would be to drive a bayonet into a Buddhist priest's guts. Feelings like these are the normal by-products of imperialism; ask any Anglo-Indian official, if you can catch him off duty.

> **"**It was a tiny incident in itself, but it gave me a better glimpse than I had had before of the real nature of imperialism. . . .**"**

One day something happened which in a roundabout way was enlightening. It was a tiny incident in itself, but it gave me a better glimpse than I had had before of the real nature of imperialism — the real motives for which despotic governments act. Early one morning the sub-inspector at a police station the other end of the town rang me up on the phone and said that an elephant was ravaging the bazaar. Would I please come and do something about it? I did not know what I could do, but I wanted to see what was happening and I got on to a pony and started out. I took my rifle, an old .44 Winchester and much too small to kill an elephant, but I thought the noise might be useful *in terrorem*.† Various Burmans stopped me on the way and told me about the elephant's doings. It was not, of course, a wild elephant, but a tame one which had gone "must."‡ It had been chained up, as tame elephants always are when their attack of "must" is due, but on the previous night it had broken its chain and escaped. Its mahout,' the only person who could manage it when it was in that state, had set out in pursuit, but had taken the wrong direction and was

3

---

* Eds. note — Orwell was writing in 1936, when Hitler and Stalin were in power and World War II was only three years away.
** Eds. note — The former British rule of the Indian subcontinent.
*** Eds. note — From time immemorial.
† Eds. note — For the purpose of frightening.
‡ Eds. note — Was in heat, a condition likely to wear off.
' Eds. note — A keeper and driver of an elephant.

now twelve hours' journey away, and in the morning the elephant had suddenly reappeared in the town. The Burmese population had no weapons and were quite helpless against it. It had already destroyed somebody's bamboo hut, killed a cow, and raided some fruit-stalls and devoured the stock; also it had met the municipal rubbish van and, when the driver jumped out and took to his heels, had turned the van over and inflicted violences upon it.

The Burmese sub-inspector and some Indian constables were waiting for   4
me in the quarter where the elephant had been seen. It was a very poor quarter, a labyrinth of squalid bamboo huts, thatched with palm-leaf, winding all over a steep hillside. I remember that it was a cloudy, stuffy morning at the beginning of the rains. We began questioning people as to where the elephant had gone, and, as usual, failed to get any definite information. That is invariably the case in the East; a story always sounds clear enough at a distance, but the nearer you get to the scene of events the vaguer it becomes. Some of the people said that the elephant had gone in one direction, some said that he had gone in another, some professed not even to have heard of an elephant. I had almost made up my mind that the whole story was a pack of lies, when we heard yells a little distance away. There was a loud, scandalized cry of "Go away, child! Go away this instant!" and an old woman with a switch in her hand came round the corner of a hut, violently shooing away a crowd of naked children. Some more women followed, clicking their tongues and exclaiming; evidently there was something that the children ought not to have seen. I rounded the hut and saw a man's dead body sprawling in the mud. He was an Indian, a Black Dravidian coolie,* almost naked, and he could not have been dead many minutes. The people said that the elephant had come suddenly upon him round the corner of the hut, caught him with its trunk, put its foot on his back, and ground him into the earth. This was the rainy season and the ground was soft, and his face had scored a trench a foot deep and a couple of yards long. He was lying on his belly with arms crucified and head sharply twisted to one side. His face was coated with mud, the eyes wide open, the teeth bared and grinning with an expression of unendurable agony. (Never tell me, by the way, that the dead look peaceful. Most of the corpses I have seen looked devilish.) The friction of the great beast's foot had stripped the skin from his back as neatly as one skins a rabbit. As soon as I saw the dead man I sent an orderly to a friend's house nearby to borrow an elephant rifle. I had already sent back the pony, not wanting it to go mad with fright and throw me if it smelled the elephant.

The orderly came back in a few minutes with a rifle and five cartridges, and   5
meanwhile some Burmans had arrived and told us that the elephant was in the paddy** fields below, only a few hundred yards away. As I started forward practically the whole population of the quarter flocked out of the houses and followed me. They had seen the rifle and were all shouting excitedly that I was going to shoot the elephant. They had not shown much interest in the elephant when he was merely ravaging their homes, but it was different now that he was going to be shot. It was a bit of fun to them, as it would be to an English

---

* Eds. note — An unskilled laborer.
** Eds. note — Wet land for growing rice.

crowd; besides they wanted the meat. It made me vaguely uneasy. I had no intention of shooting the elephant—I had merely sent for the rifle to defend myself if necessary—and it is always unnerving to have a crowd following you. I marched down the hill, looking and feeling a fool, with the rifle over my shoulder and an ever-growing army of people jostling at my heels. At the bottom, when you got away from the huts, there was a metalled road and beyond that a miry waste of paddy fields a thousand yards across, not yet ploughed but soggy from the first rains and dotted with coarse grass. The elephant was standing eight yards from the road, his left side towards us. He took not the slightest notice of the crowd's approach. He was tearing up bunches of grass, beating them against his knees to clean them and stuffing them into his mouth.

I had halted on the road. As soon as I saw the elephant I knew with perfect   6 certainty that I ought not to shoot him. It is a serious matter to shoot a working elephant—it is comparable to destroying a huge and costly piece of machinery—and obviously one ought not to do it if it can possibly be avoided. And at that distance, peacefully eating, the elephant looked no more dangerous than a cow. I thought then and I think now that his attack of "must" was already passing off; in which case he would merely wander harmlessly about until the mahout came back and caught him. Moreover, I did not in the least want to shoot him. I decided that I would watch him for a little while to make sure that he did not turn savage again, and then go home.

But at that moment I glanced round at the crowd that had followed me. It   7 was an immense crowd, two thousand at the least and growing every minute. It blocked the road for a long distance on either side. I looked at the sea of yellow faces above the garish clothes—faces all happy and excited over this bit of fun, all certain that the elephant was going to be shot. They were watching me as they would watch a conjurer about to perform a trick. They did not like me, but with the magical rifle in my hands I was momentarily worth watching. And suddenly I realized that I should have to shoot the elephant after all. The people expected it of me and I had got to do it; I could feel their two thousand wills pressing me forward, irresistibly. And it was at this moment, as I stood there with the rifle in my hands, that I first grasped the hollowness, the futility of the white man's dominion in the East. Here was I, the white man with his gun, standing in front of the unarmed native crowd—seemingly the leading actor of the piece; but in reality I was only an absurd puppet pushed to and fro by the will of those yellow faces behind. I perceived in this moment that when the white man turns tyrant it is his own freedom that he destroys. He becomes a sort of hollow, posing dummy, the conventionalized figure of a sahib.* For it is the condition of his rule that he shall spend his life in trying to impress the "natives," and so in every crisis he has got to do what the "natives" expect of him. He wears a mask, and his face grows to fit it. I had got to shoot the elephant. I had committed myself to doing it when I sent for the rifle. A sahib has got to act like a sahib; he has got to appear resolute, to know his own mind and

---

* Eds. note—An official. The term was used among Hindus and Muslims in colonial India.

do definite things. To come all that way, rifle in hand, with two thousand people marching at my heels, and then to trail feebly away, having done nothing—no, that was impossible. The crowd would laugh at me. And my whole life, every white man's life in the East, was one long struggle not to be laughed at.

But I did not want to shoot the elephant. I watched him beating his bunch of grass against his knees, with the preoccupied grandmotherly air that elephants have. It seemed to me that it would be murder to shoot him. At that age I was not squeamish about killing animals, but I had never shot an elephant and never wanted to. (Somehow it always seems worse to kill a *large* animal.) Besides, there was the beast's owner to be considered. Alive, the elephant was worth at least a hundred pounds; dead, he would only be worth the value of his tusks, five pounds, possibly. But I had got to act quickly. I turned to some experienced-looking Burmans who had been there when we arrived, and asked them how the elephant had been behaving. They all said the same thing: he took no notice of you if you left him alone, but he might charge if you went too close to him.   8

It was perfectly clear to me what I ought to do. I ought to walk up to within, say, twenty-five yards of the elephant and test his behavior. If he charged I could shoot, if he took no notice of me it would be safe to leave him until the mahout came back. But also I knew that I was going to do no such thing. I was a poor shot with a rifle and the ground was soft mud into which one would sink at every step. If the elephant charged and I missed him, I should have about as much chance as a toad under a steamroller. But even then I was not thinking particularly of my own skin, only of the watchful yellow faces behind. For at that moment, with the crowd watching me, I was not afraid in the ordinary sense, as I would have been if I had been alone. A white man mustn't be frightened in front of "natives"; and so, in general, he isn't frightened. The sole thought in my mind was that if anything went wrong those two thousand Burmans would see me pursued, caught, trampled on, and reduced to a grinning corpse like that Indian up the hill. And if that happened it was quite probable that some of them would laugh. That would never do. There was only one alternative. I shoved the cartridges into the magazine and lay down on the road to get a better aim.   9

The crowd grew very still, and a deep, low, happy sigh, as of people who see the theatre curtain go up at last, breathed from innumerable throats. They were going to have their bit of fun after all. The rifle was a beautiful German thing with cross-hair sights. I did not then know that in shooting an elephant one would shoot to cut an imaginary bar running from ear-hole to ear-hole. I ought, therefore, as the elephant was sideways on, to have aimed straight at his ear-hole; actually I aimed several inches in front of this, thinking the brain would be further forward.   10

When I pulled the trigger I did not hear the bang or feel the kick—one never does when a shot goes home—but I heard the devilish roar of glee that went up from the crowd. In that instant, in too short a time, one would have thought, even for the bullet to get there, a mysterious, terrible change had come over the elephant. He neither stirred nor fell, but every line on his body   11 had altered. He looked suddenly stricken, shrunken, immensely old, as though the frightful impact of the bullet had paralyzed him without knocking him down. At last, after what seemed a long time — it might have been five seconds, I dare say — he sagged flabbily to his knees. His mouth slobbered. An enormous senility seemed to have settled upon him. One could have imagined him thousands of years old. I fired again into the same spot. At the second shot he did not collapse but climbed with desperate slowness to his feet and stood weakly upright, with legs sagging and head drooping. I fired a third time. That was the shot that did for him. You could see the agony of it jolt his whole body and knock the last remnant of strength from his legs. But in falling he seemed for a moment to rise, for as his hind legs collapsed beneath him he seemed to tower upwards like a huge rock toppling, his trunk reaching skywards like a tree. He trumpeted, for the first and only time. And then down he came, his belly towards me, with a crash that seemed to shake the ground even where I lay.

I got up. The Burmans were already racing past me across the mud. It was 12 obvious that the elephant would never rise again, but he was not dead. He was breathing very rhythmically with long rattling gasps, his great mound of a side painfully rising and falling. His mouth was wide open — I could see far down into caverns of pale pink throat. I waited a long time for him to die, but his breathing did not weaken. Finally I fired my two remaining shots into the spot where I thought his heart must be. The thick blood welled out of him like red velvet, but still he did not die. His body did not even jerk when the shots hit him, the tortured breathing continued without a pause. He was dying, very slowly and in great agony, but in some world remote from me where not even a bullet could damage him further. I felt that I had got to put an end to that dreadful noise. It seemed dreadful to see the great beast lying there, powerless to move and yet powerless to die, and not even to be able to finish him. I sent back for my small rifle and poured shot after shot into his heart and down his throat. They seemed to make no impression. The tortured gasps continued as steadily as the ticking of a clock.

In the end I could not stand it any longer and went away. I heard later that 13 it took him half an hour to die. Burmans were bringing dahs* and baskets even before I left, and I was told they had stripped his body almost to the bones by the afternoon.

Afterwards, of course, there were endless discussions about the shooting of 14 the elephant. The owner was furious, but he was only an Indian and could do nothing. Besides, legally I had done the right thing, for a mad elephant has to be killed, like a mad dog, if its owner fails to control it. Among the Europeans opinion was divided. The older men said I was right, the younger men said it was a damn shame to shoot an elephant for killing a coolie, because an elephant was worth more than any damn Coringhee coolie. And afterwards I was very glad that the coolie had been killed; it put me legally in the right and it gave me a sufficient pretext for shooting the elephant. I often wondered whether any of the others grasped that I had done it solely to avoid looking a fool.

· · ·

* Eds. note — Heavy knives.

Comprehension

1. Why is Orwell "hated by large numbers of people" (1) in Burma? Why does he have mixed feelings toward the Burmese people?
2. Why do the local officials want something done about the elephant? Why does the crowd want Orwell to shoot the elephant?
3. Why does Orwell finally decide to kill the elephant? What makes him hesitate at first?
4. Why does Orwell say at the end that he was glad the coolie had been killed?

Purpose and Audience

1. One of Orwell's purposes in telling his story is to show how it gave him a glimpse of "the real nature of imperialism" (3). What does he mean? How does his essay illustrate this purpose?
2. Do you think Orwell wrote this essay to inform or to persuade his audience? How did Orwell expect his audience to react to his ideas? How can you tell?
3. What is the essay's thesis?

Style and Structure

1. What does Orwell's first paragraph accomplish? Where does the introduction end and the narrative itself begin?
2. The essay includes almost no dialogue. Why do you think Orwell's voice as narrator is the only one readers hear? Is the absence of dialogue a strength or a weakness? Explain.
3. Why do you think Orwell devotes so much attention to the elephant's misery (11–12)? Do you think this passage should come with a "trigger warning"? (See Casebook: Is Free Speech on Campus in Peril? on pages 600–1 for background on trigger warnings.)
4. Orwell's essay includes a number of editorial comments, which appear within parentheses or dashes. How would you characterize these comments? Why are they set off from the text?
5. **Vocabulary Project.** Because Orwell is British, he frequently uses words or expressions that an American writer would not likely use. Substitute a contemporary American word or phrase for each of the following, making sure it is appropriate in Orwell's context.

raise a riot (1)	rubbish van (3)	a bit of fun (5)
rang me up (3)	inflicted violences (3)	I dare say (11)

   What other expressions in Orwell's essay might need to be "translated" for a contemporary American audience?
6. Consider the following statements: "Some of the people said that the elephant had gone in one direction, some said that he had gone in another" (4); "Among the Europeans opinion was divided. The older men said I was right, the younger men said it was a damn shame to shoot an elephant" (14). How do these comments reinforce the idea expressed in paragraph 2 ("All I knew was that I was stuck between my hatred of the empire I served and my rage against the evil-spirited little beasts")? What other comments reinforce this idea?

Journal Entry

Do you think Orwell is a coward? Do you think he is a racist? Explain your conclusions.

Writing Workshop

1. **Working with Sources.** Orwell says that even though he hated British imperialism and sympathized with the Burmese people, he found himself a puppet of the system. Write a narrative essay about a time when you had to do something that went against your beliefs or convictions. Begin by summarizing Orwell's situation in Burma, and go on to show how your situation was similar to his. If you quote Orwell, be sure to include documentation and a works-cited page. (See Chapter 18 for information on MLA documentation.)
2. Orwell's experience taught him something not only about himself but also about something beyond himself — the way British imperialism worked. Write a narrative essay that reveals how an incident in your life taught you something about some larger social or political force as well as about yourself.
3. Write an objective, factual newspaper article recounting the events Orwell describes.

Combining the Patterns

Implicit in this narrative essay is an extended **comparison and contrast** that highlights the differences between Orwell and the Burmese people. Review the essay, and list the most obvious differences Orwell perceives between himself and them. Do you think his perceptions are accurate? If all the differences were set forth in a single paragraph, how might such a paragraph change your perception of Orwell's dilemma? Of his character?

Thematic Connections

- "Thirty-Seven Who Saw Murder Didn't Call the Police" (page 127)
- "Should Driverless Cars Kill Their Own Passengers to Save a Pedestrian?" (page 219)
- "Just Walk On By: A Black Man Ponders His Power to Alter Public Space" (page 231)
- "The Untouchable" (page 487)

ALBERTO ÁLVARO RÍOS

The Secret Lion (Fiction)

Poet and fiction writer Alberto Álvaro Ríos was born in 1952 in Nogales, Arizona, where he spent his childhood. His father was Mexican, and his mother was originally from Lancashire, England. As he strongly resembled his mother, Ríos's dual background shaped his identity from an early age: "I was in this dilemma: physical appearance versus cultural context," he wrote. He received both his undergraduate degree and his M.F.A. in creative writing from the University of Arizona. Since 1994, he has been Regents Professor of English at Arizona State University. Ríos's works include *Whispering to Fool the Wind* (1982), *The Theater of Night* (2005), and *A Small Story about the Sky* (2015). He is the recipient of many awards and honors, including a Guggenheim Foundation Fellowship, a National Endowment for the Arts Fellowship, and a Walt Whitman Award.

The border town of Nogales Writing about Ríos's work, poet Mary Logue once noted its connection to his childhood in Nogales, Arizona, a place "where one is neither in this country nor the other." Indeed, Nogales, Arizona, and Nogales, Sonora, Mexico, are twin cities — referred to as Ambos Nogales (Both Nogales) in Spanish — separated by national borders. Prior to the arrival of European explorers, the settlement was a crossroads on a migratory path and trade route. Later, it was a Spanish colony and a Mexican territory before it became part of the United States in the 1853 Gadsden Purchase. In the 1880s, an ambitious San Francisco merchant built a trading post in Nogales, Arizona; within three years, the town was connected to the Santa Fe Railway, and trade between the United States and Mexico boomed. In the years since, Nogales has remained (as many of its residents see it) one city in two countries. It has also remained a bilingual center for international commerce — and a border town, both literally and figuratively. As Ríos writes in his poem "The Border: A Double Sonnet": "The border used to be an actual place, / but now, it is the act of a thousand imaginations."

> **"Everything changed."**

I was twelve and in junior high school and 1
something happened that we didn't have a
name for, but it was there nonetheless like a
lion, and roaring, roaring that way the biggest
things do. Everything changed. Just like that. Like the rug, the one that gets pulled — or better, like the tablecloth those magicians pull where the stuff on the table stays the same but the gasp! from the audience makes the staying-the-same part not matter. Like that.

What happened was there were teachers now, not just one teacher, 2
teach-erz, and we felt personally abandoned somehow. When a person had all these teachers now, he didn't get taken care of the same way, even though six was more than one. Arithmetic went out the door when we walked in. And we saw girls now, but they weren't the same girls that we used to know because we

couldn't talk to them anymore, not the same way we used to, certainly not to Sandy, even though she was my neighbor too. Not even to her. She just played the piano all the time. And there were words, oh there were words in junior high school, and we wanted to know what they were, and how a person did them—that's what school was supposed to be for. Only, in junior high school, school wasn't school, everything was backwardlike. If you went up to a teacher and said the word to try and find out what it meant you got in trouble for saying it. So we didn't. And we figured it must have been that way about other stuff, too, so we never said anything about anything—we weren't stupid.

But my friend Sergio and I, we solved junior high school. We would come   3
home from school on the bus, put our books away, change shoes, and go across the street to the arroyo. It was the one place we were not supposed to go. So we did. That was, after all, what junior high had at least shown us. It was our river, though, our personal Mississippi, our friend from long back, and it was full of stories and all the branch forts we had built in it when we were still the Vikings of America, with our own symbol, which had been carved everywhere, even in the sand, which let the water take it. That was good, we had decided; whoever was at the end of the river would know about us.

At the very top of our growing lungs, what we would do down there was   4
shout every dirty word that we could think of, in every combination we could come up with, and we would yell about girls, and all the things we wanted to do with them, as loud as we could—we didn't know what we wanted to do with them, just things—and we would yell about teachers and how we loved some of them, like Miss Crevelone, and how we wanted to dissect some of them, making signs of the cross, like priests, and we would yell this stuff over and over because it felt good, we couldn't explain why, it just felt good and for the first time in our lives there was nobody to tell us we couldn't. So we did.

One Thursday we were walking along shouting this way, and the railroad,   5
the Southern Pacific, which ran above and along the far side of the arroyo, had dropped a grinding ball down there, which was, we found out later, a cannonball thing used in mining. A bunch of them were put in a big vat which turned around and crushed ore. One had been dropped, or thrown—what do those caboose men do when they get bored—but it got down there regardless and as we were walking along yelling about one girl or another, a particular Claudia, we found it, one of those things, looked at it, picked it up, and got very very excited, and held it and passed it back and forth, and we were saying, "Guythisis, this is, geeGuythis . . .": we had this perception about nature then, that nature is imperfect and that round things are perfect: we said, "GuyGod this is perfect, thisisthis is perfect, it's round, round and heavy, it'sit's the best thing we've everseen. Whatisit?" We didn't know. We just knew it was great. We just, whatever, we played with it, held it some more.

And then we had to decide what to do with it. We knew, because of a lot of   6
things, that if we were going to take this and show it to anybody, this discovery, this best thing, was going to be taken away from us. That's the way it works with little kids, like all the polished quartz, the tons of it we had collected piece by piece over the years. Junior high kids too. If we took it home, my mother,

we knew, was going to look at it and say, "Throw that dirty thing in the, get rid of it." Simple like, like that. "But ma it's the best thing I" "Getridofit." Simple.

So we didn't. Take it home. Instead we came up with the answer. We dug a hole and we buried it. And we marked it secretly. Lots of secret signs. And we came back the next week to dig it up and, we didn't know, pass it around some more or something, but we didn't find it. We dug up the whole bank, and we never found it again. We tried.   7

Sergio and I talked about that ball or whatever it was when we couldn't find it. All we used were small words, neat, good. Kid words. What we were really saying, but didn't know the words, was how much that ball was like that place, the whole arroyo: couldn't tell anybody about it, didn't understand what it was, didn't have a name for it. It just felt good. It was just perfect in the way it was that place, that whole going to that place, that whole junior high school lion. It was iron-heavy, it had no name, it felt good or not, we couldn't take it home to show our mothers, and once we buried it, it was gone forever.   8

The ball was gone, like the first reasons we had come to the arroyo years earlier, like the first time we had seen the arroyo, it was gone like everything else that had been taken away. This was not our first lesson. We stopped going to the arroyo after not finding the thing, the same way that we had stopped going there years earlier and headed for the mountains. Nature seemed to keep pushing us around one way or another, teaching us the same thing every place we ended up. Nature's gang was tough that way, teaching us stuff.   9

· · ·

When we were young we moved away from town, me and my family. Sergio's was already out there. Out in the wilds. Or at least the new place seemed like the wilds since everything looks bigger the smaller a man is. I was five, I guess, and we moved three miles north of Nogales, where we had lived, three miles north of the Mexican border. We looked across the highway in one direction and there was the arroyo; hills stood up in the other direction. Mountains, for a small man.   10

When the first summer came the very first place we went to was of course the one place we weren't supposed to go, the arroyo. We went down there and found water running, summer rainwater mostly, and we went swimming. But every third or fourth or fifth day, the sewage treatment plant that was, we found out, upstream, would release whatever it was that it released, and we would never know exactly what that day was, and a person couldn't tell right away by looking at the water, not every time, not so a person could get out in time. So, we went swimming that summer and some days we had a lot of fun. Some days we didn't. We found a thousand ways to explain what happened on those other days, constructing elaborate stories about neighborhood dogs, and hadn't she, my mother, miscalculated her step before, too? But she knew something was up because we'd come running into the house those days, wanting to take a shower, even—if this can be imagined—in the middle of the day.   11

That was the first time we stopped going to the arroyo. It taught us to look the other way. We decided, as the second side of summer came, we wanted to   12 go into the mountains. They were still mountains then. We came running in one summer Thursday morning, my friend Sergio and I, into my mother's kitchen, and said, well, what'zin, what'zin those hills over there—we used her word so she'd understand us—and she said nothingdon'tworryaboutit. So we went out, and we weren't dumb, we thought with our eyes to each other, ohhoshe'stryingtokeep somethingfromus. We knew adults.

We had read books, after all; we knew about bridges and castles and   13
wildtreacherouseaging alligatormouth rivers. We wanted them. So we were going out to get them. We went back that morning into the kitchen and said, "We're going out there, we're going into the hills, we're going for three days, don't worry." She said, "All right."

"You know," I told Sergio, "if we're going to go away for three days, well we   14
ought to at least pack a lunch."

But we were two young boys with no patience for what we thought at the   15
time was mom-stuff: making sa-and-wiches. My mother didn't offer. So we got out our little kid knapsacks that my mother had sewn for us, and into them we put the jar of mustard. A loaf of bread. Kniveforksplates, bottles of Coke, a can opener. This was lunch for the two of us. And we were weighed down, humped over to be strong enough to carry this stuff. But we started walking, anyway, into the hills. We were going to eat berries and stuff otherwise. "Goodbye." My mom said that.

After the first hill we were dead. But we walked. My mother could still see   16
us. And we kept walking. We walked until we got to where the sun is straight overhead, noon. That place. There that it doesn't matter; it's time to eat. The truth is we weren't anywhere close to that place. We just agreed that the sun was overhead and that it was time to eat, and by tilting our heads a little we could make that the truth.

"We really ought to start looking for a place to eat."   17

"Yeah, let's look for a place to eat." We went back and forth saying that for   18
fifteen minutes, making it lunch time because that's what we always said back and forth before lunch times at home. "Yeah, I'm hungry all right." I nodded my head. "Yeah, I'm hungry all right too. I'm hungry." He nodded his head. I nodded my head back. After a good deal more nodding, we were ready, just as we came over a little hill.

And on the other side of this hill we found heaven.   19

It was just as we thought it would be.   20

Perfect. Heaven was green, like nothing else in Arizona. And it wasn't a   21
cemetery or like that because we had seen cemeteries and they had gravestones and stuff and this didn't. This was perfect, had trees, lots of trees, had birds, like we had never seen before. It was like The Wizard of Oz, like when they got to Oz and everything was so green, so emerald, they had to wear those glasses, and we just ran like them, laughing, laughing that way we did at that moment, and we were running down to this clearing in it all, hitting each other that good way that we did.

We got down there, we were laughing, we kept hitting each other, we   22
unpacked our stuff and we were acting "rich." We knew all about how to do that. Like blowing on our nails, then rubbing them on our chests for a shine.

We made our sandwiches, opened our Cokes, got out the rest of the stuff, the salt and pepper shakers. I found this particular hole and I put my Coke right into it, a perfect fit, and I called it my Coke-holder. I got down next to it on my back, because everyone knows that rich people eat lying down, and I got my sandwich in one hand and I put my other arm around the Coke in its holder. When I wanted a drink, I lifted my neck a little, put out my lips, and tipped my Coke a little with the crook of my elbow. Ah.

23   We were there, lying down, eating our sandwiches, laughing, throwing bread at each other and out for the birds. This was heaven. We were laughing and we couldn't believe it. My mother was keeping something from us, ah ha, but we had found her out. We even found water over at the side of the clearing to wash our plates with—we had brought plates. Sergio started washing his plates when he was done, and I was being rich with my Coke, and this day in summer was right.

24   When suddenly these two men came, from around a corner of trees and the tallest grass we had ever seen. They had bags on their backs, leather bags, bags with sticks.

25   We didn't know what clubs were, but I learned later, like I learned about grinding balls. The two men yelled at us. Most specifically, one wanted me to take my Coke out of my Coke-holder so he could sink his golf ball into it.

26   Something got taken away from us that moment. Heaven. We grew up a little bit, and couldn't go backward. We learned. No one had ever told us about golf. They had told us about heaven. And it went away. We got golf in exchange.

27   We went back to the arroyo for the rest of the summer, and tried to have fun the best that we could. We learned to be ready for finding the grinding ball. We loved it, and when we buried it we knew what would happen. The truth is, we didn't look so hard for it. We were two boys and twelve summers then, and not stupid. Things get taken away.

28   We buried it because it was perfect. We didn't tell my mother, but together it was all we talked about, til we forgot. It was the lion.

• • •

Reading Literature

1. Identify some of the transitional words and phrases that connect events in this story. How much time passes during the course of these events? How do you know?

2. Beyond their literal meaning, what might each of the following items suggest to the narrator and his friend Sergio?

   - The lion
   - The arroyo
   - The grinding ball
   - The mountains
   - The golf course

3. In the story's first paragraph, the narrator says, "Everything changed." What exactly changes during the course of this story?

Journal Entry
What is the secret lion? Write a few paragraphs exploring the possible meanings of the story's title.

Thematic Connections
* "How the Other Half Lives" (page 190)
* "Tortillas" (page 498)
* "The Park" (page 663)
* "Long Live the Albatross" (page 683)

JOY HARJO

An American Sunrise (Poetry)

For Joy Harjo (b. 1951), the role of the poet has been inseparable from her role as an activist, feminist, and Native American advocate. As she once said, "I feel strongly that I have a responsibility to . . . all past and future ancestors, to my home country, to all places that I touch down on and that are myself, to all voices, all women, all of my tribe, all people, all earth." A native of Tulsa, Oklahoma, Harjo is a member of the Muscogee Nation. She received a B.A. from the University of New Mexico and an M.F.A. from the Iowa Writers' Workshop. Her many books of poetry include *She Had Some Horses* (1983), *In Mad Love and War* (1990), and *A Map to the Next World: Poems and Tales* (2000). Her 2012 memoir, *Crazy Brave*, won the American Book Award and the 2013 PEN Center USA prize for creative nonfiction. In addition to her writing career, Harjo is also a skilled musician. She is currently the U.S. Poet Laureate.

History of the Crow Nation Harjo's poem is, among other things, a fierce lyric of Native American alienation and persistence in modern America. Perhaps no tribe is more emblematic of this experience than the Crow Nation, a nomadic tribe that migrated from the Lake Winnipeg region of Canada to the Bighorn and Yellowstone River basins of present-day Montana and Wyoming before Europeans arrived in America. In their own language, they called themselves *Apsaalooke* or *Absaroka*, which means "children of the large-beaked bird." The term was misunderstood and simplified by early European trappers and settlers, who called them the Crows. As with other Native Americans, the Crow faced radical changes and hardships as the United States developed, from smallpox and the destruction of the bison (a staple of their diet and their trading) to wars with other tribes, failed treaties with the U.S. government, and ultimately confinement to a reservation. Their overall population dwindled to 1,625 in the 1930s. Today, around 7,000 members of the tribe live on the Crow Indian Reservation, a region covering roughly 2.3 million acres in south-central Montana.

We were running out of breath, as we ran out to meet ourselves. We
were surfacing the edge of our ancestors' fights, and ready to strike.
It was difficult to lose days in the Indian bar if you were straight.
Easy if you played pool and drank to remember to forget. We
made plans to be professional — and did. And some of us could sing   5
so we drummed a fire-lit pathway up to those starry stars. Sin
was invented by the Christians, as was the Devil, we sang. We
were the heathens, but needed to be saved from them — thin
chance. We knew we were all related in this story, a little gin
will clarify the dark and make us all feel like dancing. We   10
had something to do with the origins of blues and jazz
I argued with a Pueblo as I filled the jukebox with dimes in June,
forty years later and we still want justice. We are still America. We

know the rumors of our demise. We spit them out. They die
soon.   15

                                    .   .   .

Reading Literature

1. Who is the "we" in this poem? Who are "they"? Explain.
2. What do you think the speaker means by "We are still America" (line 13) and
   by "We know the rumors of our demise" (13–14)?
3. How are this poem's style, structure, and subject matter different from
   those of other poems with which you are familiar? Why do you think Harjo
   chose to use these unconventional elements?

Journal Entry

In your own words, retell the "story" this poem tells. Begin by establishing the
setting and characters, and then trace the events that unfold.

Thematic Connections

- from *Persepolis II* (page 111)
- "The Money" (page 113)
- "The Untouchable" (page 487)
- The Declaration of Independence (page 548)

Writing Assignments for Narration

1. Trace the path you expect to follow to establish yourself in your chosen profession, considering possible obstacles you may face and how you expect to deal with them. Include a thesis statement that conveys the importance of your goals. If you like, you may refer to an essay in this book that focuses on work, such as "My Mother Never Worked" (page 122).

2. Write a personal narrative looking back from some point in the far future on your own life as you hope others will see it. Use the third person if you like, and write your own obituary, or use first person, assessing your life in a letter to your great-grandchildren.

3. Write a news article recounting in objective terms the events described in an essay that appears anywhere in this text, such as "The Twin Revolutions of Lincoln and Darwin" (page 420) or "Emmett Till and Tamir Rice, Sons of the Great Migration" (page 414). Include a descriptive headline.

4. Write the introductory narrative for the home page of your family's (or community's) website. In this historical narrative, trace the roots of your family or your hometown or community. Be sure to include specific detail, dialogue, and descriptions of people and places. (You may also include visuals if you like.)

5. Write an account of one of these "firsts": your first serious argument with your parents, your first experience with physical violence or danger, your first extended stay away from home, your first encounter with someone whose culture was very different from your own, or your first experience with the serious illness or death of a close friend or relative. Make sure your essay includes a thesis statement your narrative can support.

6. **Working with Sources.** Both George Orwell and Martin Gansberg deal with the consequences of failing to act. Write an essay or story recounting what would have happened if Orwell had *not* shot the elephant or if one of the eyewitnesses *had* called the police right away. Be sure to document references to Orwell or Gansberg and to include a works-cited page. (See Chapter 18 for information on MLA documentation.)

7. **Working with Sources.** Write a narrative about a time when you were an outsider, isolated because of social, intellectual, or ethnic differences between you and others. Did you resolve the problems your isolation created? Explain. If you like, you may refer to the Orwell's essay in this chapter or to "Just Walk On By" (page 231), taking care to include parenthetical documentation and a works-cited page. (See Chapter 18 for information on MLA documentation.)

8. Imagine a meeting between any two people (real or fictional) who appear in this chapter's reading selections. Using dialogue and narrative, write an account of this meeting.

9. Write the story of your own education.
10. List the five books you have read that most influenced you at important stages of your life. Then, write your literary autobiography, tracing your personal development through these books. (Or write your wardrobe autobiography — discussing what you wore at different times of your life — or your film or music autobiography.)

Collaborative Activity for Narration

Working with a group of students who are about your own age, write a history of your television-viewing habits. Start by working individually to list all your most-watched television shows in chronological order, beginning as far back as you can remember. Then, compile a single list that reflects a consensus of the group's preferences, perhaps choosing one or two representative programs for each stage of your lives (preschool, elementary school, and so on). Have a different student write a paragraph on each stage, describing the chosen programs in as much detail as possible and using "we" as the subject. Finally, combine the individual paragraphs to create a narrative essay that traces the group's changing tastes in television shows (and changing habits in television watching). Be sure to discuss changes in how you accessed programs as well as the changing content of the shows you watched and the increased or decreased significance of television in your lives over time, as other media competed for your attention. The essay's thesis statement should express what your group's television preferences reveal about your generation's development.

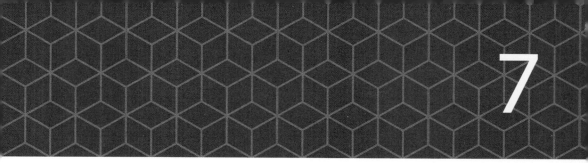

Description

What Is Description?

You use **description** to tell readers about the physical characteristics of a person, place, or thing. Description relies on the five senses: sight, hearing, taste, touch, and smell. In the following paragraph from "Knoxville: Summer 1915," James Agee uses sight, touch, and sound to re-create a summer's evening for his audience.

Topic sentence

Description using sight

Description using touch

Description using sound

It is not of games children play in the evening that I want to speak now, it is of a contemporaneous atmosphere that has little to do with them; that of fathers and families, each in his space of lawn, his shirt fishlike pale in the unnatural light and his face nearly anonymous, hosing their lawns. The hoses were attached to spigots that stood out of the brick foundations of the houses. The nozzles were variously set but usually so there was a long sweet stream of spray, the nozzle wet in the hand, the water trickling the right forearm and the peeled-back cuff, and the water whishing out a long loose and low-curved cone, and so gentle a sound. First an insane noise of violence in the nozzle, then the still irregular sound of adjustment, then the smoothing into steadiness and a pitch as accurately tuned to the size and style of stream as any violin. So many qualities of sound out of one hose: so many choral differences out of those several hoses that were in earshot. Out of any one hose, the almost dead silence of the release, and the short still arch of the separate big drops, silent as a held breath, and the only noise the flattering noise on leaves and the slapped grass at the fall of each big drop. That, and the intense hiss with the intense stream; that, and the same intensity not growing less but growing more quiet and delicate with the turn of the nozzle, up to that extreme tender whisper when the water was just a wide bell of film.

A descriptive essay tells what something looks like or what it feels like, sounds like, smells like, or tastes like. However, description often goes beyond personal sense impressions: novelists can create imaginary landscapes, historians can paint word pictures of historical figures or events, and scientists can describe physical phenomena they have never actually seen. When you write description, you use language to create a vivid impression for your readers.

Using Description

In your college writing, you use description in many different kinds of assignments. In a comparison-and-contrast essay, for example, you may describe the designs of two proposed buildings to show that one is more energy efficient than the other. In an argumentative essay, you may describe a fish kill in a local river to make the point that industrial waste dumping is a problem. Through description, you communicate your view of the world to your readers. If your readers come to understand or share your view, they are likely to accept your observations, your judgments, and, eventually, your conclusions. Therefore, in almost every essay you write, knowing how to write effective description is important.

Understanding Objective Description

Description can be *objective* or *subjective*. **Objective description** focuses on the object itself rather than on your personal reactions to it. Your purpose is to present a precise, literal picture of your subject. Many writing situations require exact descriptions of apparatus or conditions, and in these cases, your goal is to construct an accurate picture for your audience. A biologist describing what he sees through an electron microscope and a historian describing a Civil War battlefield would both write objectively. The biologist would not, for instance, say how exciting his observations were, nor would the historian say how disappointed she was at the outcome of the battle. Many newspaper reporters also try to achieve this level of objectivity, as do writers of technical reports, scientific papers, and certain types of business correspondence. Still, objectivity is an ideal that writers strive for but never fully achieve. In fact, by selecting some details and leaving out others, writers are making subjective decisions.

In the following descriptive passage, Shakespearean scholar Thomas Marc Parrott aims for objectivity by giving his readers the factual information they need to visualize Shakespeare's theater:

The main or outer stage [of Shakespeare's theater] was a large platform, which projected out into the audience. Sections of the floor could
be removed to make such things as the grave in the grave digger's scene
in *Hamlet*, or they could be transformed into trapdoors through which
characters could disappear, as in *The Tempest*. The players referred to the
space beneath the platform as the Hell. At the rear of the platform and at
the same level was the smaller, inner stage, or alcove. . . . Above the alcove at
the level of the second story, there was another curtained stage, the chamber. . . . The action of the play would move from one scene to another, using
one, two, or all of them. Above the chamber was the music gallery; . . . and
above this were the windows, "The Huts," where characters and lookouts
could appear.

Note that Parrott is not interested in responding to or evaluating the theater he describes. Instead, he chooses words that convey sizes and directions,
such as *large* and *above*.

Artist's rendering of the Globe Theatre, London.

Objective descriptions are sometimes accompanied by **visuals**, such as diagrams, drawings, or photographs. A well-chosen visual can enhance a description by enabling writers to avoid tedious passages of description that might confuse readers. For example, the illustration that accompanies Parrott's description of Shakespeare's theater on page 153 makes the passage easier to understand, helping readers visualize the multiple stages on which Shakespeare's plays were performed.

✔ **CHECKLIST**   **USING VISUALS EFFECTIVELY**

If you use visuals in your descriptive essay, ask the following questions to make sure you have used them responsibly and effectively.

- ☐ **Is your visual directly related to your discussion?** To be effective, a visual should clearly illustrate what is being discussed and not introduce new material.
- ☐ **Does your visual add something to your essay?** For example, you could use a diagram to help explain a process, a chart or graph to clarify statistics, or a photograph to show an unusual structure.
- ☐ **Is your visual located as close as possible to where it is discussed in the essay?** This placement will establish the context for the visual and ensure that readers understand why you have included it.
- ☐ **Have you documented your visual?** Like all material you borrow from a source, visuals must be documented. (For more on documentation, see Chapter 18.)

Understanding Subjective Description

In contrast to objective description, **subjective description** conveys your personal response to your subject. Here your perspective is not necessarily stated explicitly; often it is revealed indirectly, through your choice of words and phrasing. If a first-year composition assignment asks you to describe a place that has special meaning to you, you could give a subjective reaction to your topic by selecting and emphasizing details that show your feelings about the place. For example, you could write a subjective description of your room by focusing on particular objects—your desk, your window, and your bookshelves—and explaining the meanings these things

REMINDER   **FINDING VISUALS**

You can find visuals on the Internet, in clip-art compilations, or from Google Images. You can also scan pictures you find in print sources or download pictures you take with your phone or with a digital camera. Once the visual is downloaded onto your computer as a file, you can cut and paste it into your essay. Remember, however, that all visual material you get from a source — whether print or Internet — must be documented.

have for you. Thus, your desk could be a "warm brown rectangle of wood whose surface reveals the scratched impressions of a thousand school assignments."

A subjective description should convey not just a literal record of sights and sounds but also their significance. For example, if you objectively described a fire that destroyed a house in your neighborhood, you might include the fire's temperature, duration, and scope. In addition, you might describe, as accurately as possible, the fire's movement and intensity. If you subjectively described the fire, however, you would try to re-create for your audience a sense of how the fire made you feel — your reactions to the noise, to the dense smoke, to the destruction.

In the following passage, notice how Mark Twain subjectively describes a sunset on the Mississippi River:

> I still kept in mind a certain wonderful sunset which I witnessed when steamboating was new to me. A broad expanse of the river was turned to blood; in the middle distance the red hue brightened into gold, through which a solitary log came floating, black and conspicuous; in one place a long, slanting mark lay sparkling upon the water; in another the surface was broken by boiling, tumbling rings, that were as many-tinted as an opal.

In this passage, Twain conveys his strong emotional reaction to the sunset by using vivid, powerful images, such as the river "turned to blood," the "solitary log . . . black and conspicuous," and the "boiling, tumbling rings." He also chooses words that suggest great value, such as *gold* and *opal.*

Neither objective nor subjective description exists independently. Objective descriptions usually include some subjective elements, and subjective descriptions need some objective elements to convey a sense of reality. The skillful writer adjusts the balance between objectivity and subjectivity to suit the topic, thesis, audience, and purpose as well as occasion for writing.

Using Objective and Subjective Language

As the passages by Parrott and Twain illustrate, both objective and subjective descriptions rely on language that appeals to readers' senses. But these two types of description use language differently. Objective descriptions rely on precise, factual language that presents a writer's observations without conveying his or her attitude toward the subject. Subjective descriptions, however, often use richer and more suggestive language than objective descriptions do. They are more likely to rely on the **connotations** of words, their emotional associations, than on their **denotations**, or more literal meanings (such as those found in a dictionary). In addition, they may deliberately provoke the reader's imagination with striking phrases or vivid language, including **figures of speech** (also called **figurative language**) such as *simile, metaphor, personification,* and *allusion.*

- A **simile** uses *like* or *as* to compare two dissimilar things. These comparisons occur frequently in everyday speech — for example, when someone claims to be "happy as a clam," "free as a bird," or "hungry as a bear." As a rule, however, you should avoid overused expressions like

these in your writing. Effective writers constantly strive to create original similes. In his classic essay "Once More to the Lake," for instance,
E. B. White uses a striking simile to describe the annoying sound of
boats on a lake when he says that in the evening, "they whined about
one's ears *like mosquitoes.*"

- A **metaphor** compares two dissimilar things without using *like* or *as*.
  Instead of saying that something is *like* something else, a metaphor
  says it *is* something else. Mark Twain uses a metaphor when he says,
  "A broad expanse of the river was turned to blood."
- **Personification** speaks of concepts or objects as if they had life or
  human characteristics. If you say that the wind whispered or that an
  engine died, you are using personification.
- An **allusion** is a reference to a person, place, event, or quotation that
  the writer assumes readers will recognize. In "Letter from Birmingham
  Jail" (page 562), for example, Martin Luther King Jr. enriches his argument by alluding to biblical passages and proverbs that he expects his
  audience of clergy to recognize.

Your purpose and audience determine whether you should use objective
or subjective description. An assignment that specifically asks for reactions
calls for a subjective description. Legal, medical, technical, business, and scientific writing assignments, however, require objective descriptions because
their primary purpose is to convey factual information. Even in these areas,
though, figures of speech are often used to describe an unfamiliar object or
concept. For example, in their pioneering article on the structure of DNA,
scientists James Watson and Francis Crick use a simile when they describe
a molecule of DNA as looking like two spiral staircases winding around
each other.

Selecting Details

Sometimes inexperienced writers pack their descriptions with bland,
overused words such as *nice, great, terrific,* or *awful,* substituting their own general reactions to an object for the qualities of the object itself. To produce an
effective description, however, you must do more than just *say* something is
wonderful; you must also use language that evokes this response in your readers, as Twain does with the sunset. (Twain does use the word *wonderful* at the
beginning of his description, but he then goes on to supply many specific
details that make the scene he describes vivid and specific.)

All good descriptive writing, whether objective or subjective, relies on
specific details. Your aim is not simply to *tell* readers what something looks
like but to *show* them. Every person, place, or thing has its special characteristics, and you should use your powers of observation to detect them. Then, you
need to select the specific details that will enable your readers to imagine what
you describe. Don't be satisfied with "He looked angry" when you can say,
"His face flushed, and one corner of his mouth twitched as he tried to control
his anger." What's the difference? In the first case, you simply identify the

man's emotional state. In the second, you provide enough detail so that readers can tell not only that he was angry but also how he revealed the intensity of his anger.

You could have provided even more detail by describing the man's beard, his wrinkles, or any number of other features. Keep in mind, however, that not all details are useful or desirable. You should include only those that contribute to the **dominant impression** — the mood or quality emphasized in the piece of writing — you wish to create. Thus, in describing a man's face to show how angry he was, you would probably not include the shape of his nose or the color of his hair. (After all, a person's hair color does not change when he or she gets angry.) In fact, the number of particulars you use is less important than their quality and appropriateness. You should select and use only those details relevant to your purpose.

Factors such as the level, background, and knowledge of your audience also influence the kinds of details you include. For example, a description of a DNA molecule written for high school students would contain more basic descriptive details than a description written for college biology majors. In addition, the more advanced description would contain details — the sequence of amino acid groups, for instance — that might be inappropriate for high school students.

Planning a Descriptive Essay

Developing a Thesis Statement

Writers of descriptive essays often use an **implied thesis** when they describe a person, place, or thing. This technique allows them to suggest the essay's main idea through the selection and arrangement of details. When they use description to support a particular point, however, many writers prefer to use an **explicitly stated thesis**. This strategy lets readers see immediately what point the writer is making; an example is "The sculptures that adorn Philadelphia's City Hall are a catalog of nineteenth-century artistic styles."

Whether you state or imply your thesis, the details of your descriptive essay must work together to create a single dominant impression. In many cases, your thesis may be just a statement of the dominant impression; sometimes, however, your thesis may go further and make a point about that dominant impression.

Organizing Details

When you plan a descriptive essay, you usually begin by writing down descriptive details in no particular order. You then arrange these details in a way that supports your thesis and communicates your dominant impression. As you consider how to arrange your details, keep in mind that you have a number of options. For example, you can move from a specific description of an object to a general description of other things around it. Or you can reverse this order, beginning with the general and proceeding to the specific. You can also progress from the least important feature to the most important one, from the smallest to the largest item, from the least unusual to the most unusual detail, or from left to right, right to left, top to bottom, or bottom to top. Another option is to combine approaches, using different organizing schemes in different parts of the essay. The strategy you choose depends on the dominant impression you want to convey, your thesis, and your purpose and audience.

Using Transitions

Be sure to include all the transitional words and phrases readers need to follow your description. Without them, readers will have difficulty understanding the relationship of one detail to another. Throughout your description, especially in the topic sentences of your body paragraphs, use words or phrases indicating the spatial arrangement of details. In descriptive essays, the transitions commonly used include *above, adjacent to, at the bottom, at the top, behind, below, beyond, in front of, in the middle, next to, over, under, through,* and *within.* (A more complete list of transitions appears on page 56.)

Structuring a Descriptive Essay

Descriptive essays begin with an **introduction** that presents the **thesis** or establishes the dominant impression that the rest of the essay will develop. Each **body paragraph** includes details that support the thesis or convey the dominant impression. The **conclusion** reinforces the thesis or dominant impression, perhaps echoing an idea stated in the introduction or using a particularly effective simile or metaphor.

Suppose your first-year composition instructor has asked you to write a short essay describing a person, place, or thing. After thinking about the assignment for a day or two, you decide to write an objective description of the National Air and Space Museum in Washington, DC, because you have visited it recently and many details are fresh in your mind. The museum is large and has many exhibits, so you know you cannot describe them all. Therefore, you decide to concentrate on one, the heavier-than-air flight exhibit, and you choose as your topic the display you remember most vividly: *The Spirit of St. Louis,* the airplane Charles Lindbergh flew solo across the Atlantic in 1927. You begin by brainstorming to recall all the details you can. When you read over your notes, you realize you could present the details of the airplane in the order in which you saw them, from front to rear. The dominant impression you wish to create is how small and fragile *The Spirit of St. Louis* appears, and your thesis statement communicates this impression. An informal outline for your essay might look like the one that follows.

SAMPLE OUTLINE: Descriptive Essay

INTRODUCTION

Thesis statement: It is startling that a plane as small as *The Spirit of St. Louis* could fly across the Atlantic.

FIRST GROUP OF DETAILS

Front of plane: Single engine, tiny cockpit

SECOND GROUP OF DETAILS

Middle of plane: Short wingspan, extra gas tanks

THIRD GROUP OF DETAILS

Rear of plane: Limited cargo space filled with more gas tanks

CONCLUSION

Restatement of thesis (in different words) or review of key details

Revising a Descriptive Essay

When you revise a descriptive essay, consider the items on Checklist: Revising on page 68. In addition, pay special attention to the items on the following checklist, which apply specifically to descriptive essays.

REVISION CHECKLIST **DESCRIPTION**

- ☐ Does your assignment call for description?
- ☐ Does your descriptive essay clearly communicate its thesis or dominant impression?
- ☐ Is your description primarily objective or subjective?
- ☐ If your description is primarily objective, have you used precise, factual language? Would your essay be enriched by a visual?
- ☐ If your description is primarily subjective, have you used figures of speech as well as words that convey your feelings and emotions?
- ☐ Have you included enough specific details?
- ☐ Have you arranged your details in a way that supports your thesis and communicates your dominant impression?
- ☐ Have you used the transitional words and phrases that readers need to follow your description?

Editing a Descriptive Essay

When you edit your descriptive essay, follow the guidelines on the editing checklists on pages 85, 88, and 92. In addition, focus on the grammar, mechanics, and punctuation issues that are particularly relevant to descriptive essays. One of these issues — avoiding misplaced and dangling modifiers — is discussed below.

GRAMMAR IN CONTEXT   AVOIDING MISPLACED AND DANGLING MODIFIERS

When writing descriptive essays, you use **modifying words** and **phrases** to describe people, places, and objects. Because these modifiers are important in descriptive essays, you need to place them correctly to ensure they clearly refer to the words they describe.

Avoiding Misplaced Modifiers

A **misplaced modifier** appears to modify the wrong word because it is placed incorrectly in the sentence. Sentences that contain misplaced modifiers are always illogical and frequently humorous.

> **MISPLACED:** Marina Keegan drove her grandmother's 1990 Toyota Camry, wearing a sweatshirt and running shoes. (*Was the Toyota wearing a sweatshirt and running shoes?*)

> **MISPLACED:** Filled with hydrogenated oils and high-fructose corn syrup, America was symbolized by Hostess Twinkies. (*Was America filled with hydrogenated oils and high-fructose corn syrup?*)

In these sentences, the phrases *wearing a sweatshirt and running shoes* and *filled with hydrogenated oils and high-fructose corn syrup* appear to modify words that they cannot logically modify. You can correct this problem by rearranging the sentences so that the phrases refer to the words they should modify.

> **CORRECT:** Wearing a sweatshirt and running shoes, Marina Keegan drove her grandmother's 1990 Toyota Camry.

> **CORRECT:** Filled with hydrogenated oils and high-fructose corn syrup, Hostess Twinkies symbolized America.

Avoiding Dangling Modifiers

A modifier "dangles" when it cannot logically modify any word that appears in the sentence. Often, these **dangling modifiers** come at the beginning of sentences (as present or past participle phrases), where they illogically seem to modify the words that come immediately after them.

DANGLING: Determined to prepare for the approaching storm, the windows and doors of the house were closed. (*Who was determined to prepare for the approaching storm?*)

DANGLING: Standing at the edge of the landfill, large trailers dump tons of paper, rotting food, and hazardous materials into the trench. (*Who was standing at the edge of the landfill?*)

In the preceding sentences, the phrases *determined to prepare for the approaching storm* and *standing at the edge of the landfill* seem to modify *windows and doors* and *large trailers*, respectively. However, how can windows and doors prepare for a storm? How can large trailers stand at the edge of a landfill? These sentences make no sense because they do not contain the words that the modifying phrases can logically describe. In each case, you can correct this problem by supplying the missing word and rewriting the sentence accordingly.

CORRECT: Determined to prepare for the approaching storm, Calixta closed the windows and doors of the house.

CORRECT: Standing at the edge of the landfill, you can see large trailers dump tons of paper, rotting food, and hazardous materials into the trench.

EDITING CHECKLIST   DESCRIPTION

- ☐ Have you avoided misplaced modifiers?
- ☐ Have you avoided dangling modifiers?
- ☐ Have you used figures of speech effectively?
- ☐ Have you avoided general words such as *nice*, *great*, and *terrific*?

A STUDENT WRITER: Objective Description

The following essay, an objective description of a globe from 1939, was written by Mallory Cogan for a composition class. The assignment was to write a description of an object that has special meaning for her.

My Grandfather's Globe

Introduction   Each afternoon, sunlight slants through the windows of my   1
grandfather's bedroom. Slowly, slowly, it sweeps over the bookshelves. Late in the day, just before the light disappears altogether, it rests sleepily on a globe in the corner. My great-grandfather bought this

Thesis statement   globe in 1939, just before World War II. The world has changed since then, and the globe is a record of what it looked like at that time.

Description
of Western
Hemisphere

Turning the globe left, I begin my world tour with the Western   2
Hemisphere. The blue of the Pacific Ocean gives way to the faded
pinks, browns, and oranges of North and South America. In the north
is a large area dotted with lakes and bays. This is the Dominion of
Canada, now simply Canada. In the far north, the Canadian mainland
breaks into islands that extend into the Arctic Ocean. Below it is the
multicolored United States. To the north, Canada sprawls and breaks
apart; to the south, Mexico narrows, then curves east, extended by
the uneven strip of land that is Central America. This strip of land
is connected to the northernmost part of South America. South
America, in the same colors as the United States, looks like a face in
profile looking east, with a nose extending into the Atlantic Ocean
and a long neck that narrows as it reaches toward Antarctica at the
South Pole.

Description
of Africa

As I trace the equator east across the Atlantic Ocean, I come   3
to French Equatorial Africa. The huge African continent, like a fat
boomerang, is labeled with names of European countries. A large,
kidney-shaped purple area to the northwest is called French West
Africa. To the east, about halfway down the continent, is the Belgian
Congo, a substantial orange splotch that straddles the equator. On the
eastern coast just above the equator is a somewhat smaller, almost
heart-shaped yellow area called Italian East Africa. These regions, once
European colonies, are now divided into dozens of independent nations.

Description
of Europe

Moving north, I follow the thick blue ribbon of the   4
Mediterranean Sea until I reach Western Europe. I pause on yellow,
boot-shaped Italy and glance to the west and southwest at purple
France and orange Spain. The northwestern coasts of both countries
extend slightly into the Atlantic. To the northwest of France, the pink
clusters of the British Isles droop like bunches of grapes.

Description
of Europe
and changes
since 1939

Looking eastward, I see a water stain on Germany. It extends   5
down through Italy and across the Mediterranean, ending in the
Sahara Desert on the African continent. Following the stain back
into Europe, I look north, where Norway, Sweden, and Finland
reach toward the rest of Europe. Returning to Germany, I move
east, through Poland. On a modern globe, I would find Belarus and
Ukraine on Poland's eastern border. On this globe, however, my finger
passes directly into a vast area called the Union of Soviet Socialist
Republics. The U.S.S.R. (today called the Russian Federation) cuts a
wide swath across the northern part of the Asian continent; there
is plenty of room for its long name to be displayed horizontally

across the country's light-brown surface. Still in the southern half of the country, I travel east, crossing the landlocked Caspian Sea into a region of the U.S.S.R. called Turkistan, now the country of Turkmenistan. To the southeast, green Afghanistan sits between light-purple Iran to the west and pink India to the east. India is cone shaped, but with a pointed top, and green rectangular Nepal sits atop its western border.

Description of China and additional changes

Looking north again, I continue moving east. In Tibet, there   6
is a small tear in the globe. I continue into China's vast interior. Just as the U.S.S.R. blankets the northern part of the Asian continent, China spreads over much of the southeast. I notice that China's borders on this globe are different from what they are today. China includes Mongolia but not a purple region to the northwest labeled Manchoukuo, also known as Manchuria. Following Manchoukuo to its southern border, I see a strip of land that extends into the sea, surrounded by water on three sides. The area is small, so its name — Chosen — has been printed in the Sea of Japan to the east. Today, it is called Korea.

Description of Southeast Asia

Backtracking west and dropping south, past China's southern   7
border, I see Siam, now called Thailand. Siam is a three-leaf clover with a stem that hangs down. Wrapped along its eastern border, bordering two of its "leaves," is a purple country called French Indo-China. Today, this region is divided into the countries of Cambodia, Laos, and Vietnam. Bordering Siam on the west is the larger country of Burma, in pink. Like Siam, Burma is top-heavy, like a flower or a clover with a thin stem.

Description of Indonesia and Australia

Tracing that stem south, I come to the numerous islands of   8
Indonesia, splashes of yellow spreading east-west along, above, and below the equator. I do not need to travel much farther before I arrive at a large landmass: Australia. This country is pink and shaped like half of a very thick doughnut. On Australia's eastern coast is the Pacific; on its western coast is the Indian Ocean.

Conclusion

Of course, it is not surprising that I would end where I started,   9
with the ocean, since water covers seventy percent of the Earth. Still, countries — not oceans — are what interest me most about this globe. The shifting names and borders of countries that no longer exist remind me that although the world seems fixed, just as it did to the people of 1939, it is always changing. The change happens slowly, like the sun crossing my grandfather's room. Caught at any single moment, the world, like the afternoon light, appears still and mysterious.

Points for Special Attention

Objective Description

Because her essay is primarily an objective description, Mallory uses concrete language and concentrates on the shapes, colors, and surroundings of the countries she describes.

This objective description does include a few subjective elements. For example, in her introduction, Mallory says that the sunlight rests "sleepily" on her grandfather's globe. In her conclusion, she observes that the world represented by her grandfather's globe is "still and mysterious." (Her instructor had told the class that they could include a few subjective comments to convey the special meaning that the items they describe have for them.)

Figurative Language

To give readers a clear sense of what the countries on the globe look like, Mallory uses figurative language. For example, she uses similes when she describes South America as "like a face in profile" and Africa as looking "like a fat boomerang." She also uses metaphor when she says that the Mediterranean Sea is a "thick blue ribbon" and Siam is "a three-leaf clover with a stem that hangs down." Finally, Mallory uses personification when she says that the Belgian Congo "straddles the equator." By using these figures of speech, Mallory creates a vivid and striking picture of her grandfather's globe.

Structure

Mallory structures her description by moving from north to south as she moves east around the globe. She begins by describing the colors of North America, and then she describes South America. She directs her readers' attention to specific areas — for example, Central America. She then moves east, to Africa, and repeats the process of describing the regions in the north (Western Europe) and then in the south (Africa). As she does so, she notes that some countries, such as the U.S.S.R., have changed names since the globe was made in 1939. She repeats the pattern of moving east, north, and south and ends by describing Australia. Mallory frames her description of the globe with a description of her grandfather's bedroom. In her conclusion, she connects the sunlight in her grandfather's room to the world pictured on the globe by observing that both seem "still and mysterious."

Selection of Detail

Mallory's instructor defined her audience as people who know about the world today but have never seen her grandfather's globe and do not know much about the world in 1939. For this reason, Mallory includes details such as the tear in Tibet and the water stain that runs through Germany and Italy. In addition, she explains how some countries' names and borders differ from those that exist today.

Working with Sources

Before she wrote her essay, Mallory thought about looking at old atlases or history books. She decided that because her assignment called for a description of an object—not an analysis of how the world changed due to war or to the decline of colonialism—she did not have to consult these sources. She did, however, look up a few facts, such as the current name of Manchoukuo, but since facts are considered common knowledge, she did not have to document her sources for this information.

Focus on Revision

During a conference, Mallory's instructor suggested three possible changes. First, he thought that Mallory should consider including descriptions of additional countries, such as Japan in Asia and Chile, Argentina, and Brazil in South America. He thought that without these descriptions, readers might not fully appreciate how much information the globe contained. Next, he suggested that Mallory add more detail about the globe itself, such as its size, whether it was on a table or on a floor stand, and the materials from which it was constructed. Finally, he suggested that Mallory should consider including a picture of the globe in her essay. He thought that it would give students a clearer idea of what the globe looked like and would eliminate the need to add more description.

Mallory decided that it made sense to add a photograph of the globe. She thought that a picture she could take with her phone would be much more effective than another paragraph of description. She also decided that she had discussed enough countries in her essay and that more examples would cause her readers to lose interest.

A STUDENT WRITER: Subjective Description

The essay that follows, a subjective description of an area in Burma (officially known as Myanmar since a military coup in 1989), was written by Mary Lim for her composition class. Her assignment was to write an essay about a place that had a profound effect on her. Mary's essay uses **subjective description** so that readers can share, as well as understand, her experience.

The Valley of Windmills

Introduction

In my native country of Burma, strange happenings and exotic   1 scenery are not unusual, for Burma is a mysterious land that in some areas seems to have been ignored by time. Mountains stand jutting their rocky peaks into the clouds as they have for thousands of years. Jungles are so dense with exotic vegetation that human beings or

Description (identifying the scene)

large animals cannot even enter. But one of the most fascinating areas in Burma is the Valley of Windmills, nestled between the tall mountains near the beautiful city of Taungaleik. In this fertile valley there is beautiful and breathtaking scenery, but there are also old, massive, and gloomy structures that can disturb a person deeply.

*Description
(moving toward
the valley)*

The road to Taungaleik twists out of the coastal flatlands into   2
those heaps of slag, shale, and limestone that are the Tenasserim
Mountains in the southern part of Burma. The air grows rarer
and cooler, and stones become grayer, the highway a little more
precarious at its edges, until, ahead, standing in ghostly sentinel

*Description
(immediate view)*

across the lip of a pass, is a line of squat forms. They straddle the
road and stand at intervals up hillsides on either side. Are they
boulders? Are they fortifications? Are they broken wooden crosses on
graves in an abandoned cemetery?

These dark figures are windmills standing in the misty   3
atmosphere. They are immensely old and distinctly evil, some
merely turrets, some with remnants of arms hanging derelict from
their snouts, and most of them covered with dark green moss. Their
decayed but still massive forms seem to turn and sneer at visitors.

*Description (more
distant view)*

Down the pass on the other side is a circular green plateau that lies
like an arena below, where there are still more windmills. Massed in
the plain behind them, as far as the eye can see, in every field, above
every hut, stand ten thousand iron windmills, silent and sailless. They
seem to await only a call from a watchman to clank, whirr, flap, and
groan into action. Visitors suddenly feel cold. Perhaps it is a sense of
loneliness, the cool air, the desolation, or the weirdness of the arcane
windmills — but something chills them.

Conclusion

As you stand at the lip of the valley, contrasts rush in to   4
overwhelm you. Beyond, glittering on the mountainside like a solitary

*Description
(windmills
contrasted with city)*
Thesis statement

jewel, is Taungaleik in the territory once occupied by the Portuguese.
Below, on rolling hillsides, are the dark windmills, still enveloped
in morning mist. These ancient windmills can remind a person of
the impermanence of life and the mystery that still surrounds these
hills. In a strange way, the scene in the valley can be disturbing, but
it also can offer insight into the contradictions that define life here
in Burma.

Points for Special Attention

Subjective Description

One of the first things her classmates noticed when they read Mary's essay
was her use of vivid details. The road to Taungaleik is described in specific
terms: it twists "out of the coastal flatlands" into the mountains, which are
"heaps of slag, shale, and limestone." The iron windmills are decayed and
stand "silent and sailless" on a green plateau that "lies like an arena." Through
her use of detail, Mary creates her dominant impression of the Valley of

Windmills as dark, mysterious, and disquieting. The point of her essay — the thesis — is stated in the last paragraph: the Valley of Windmills embodies the contrasts that characterize life in Burma.

Subjective Language

By describing the windmills, Mary conveys her sense of foreboding. When she first introduces them, she questions whether these "squat forms" are "boulders," "fortifications," or "broken wooden crosses," each of which has a menacing connotation. After telling readers what they are, she uses personification, describing the windmills as dark, evil, sneering figures with "arms hanging derelict." She sees them as ghostly sentinels awaiting "a call from a watchman" to spring into action. With this figure of speech, Mary skillfully re-creates the unearthly quality of the scene.

Structure

Mary's purpose in this essay was to give her readers the experience of being in the Valley of Windmills. She uses an organizing scheme that takes readers along the road to Taungaleik, up into the Tenasserim Mountains, and finally to the pass where the windmills wait. From her perspective on the lip of the valley, she describes the details closest to her and then those farther away, as if following the movement of her eyes. She ends by bringing her readers back to the lip of the valley, contrasting Taungaleik "glittering on the mountainside" with the windmills "enveloped in morning mist." With her description, Mary builds up to her thesis about the nature of life in her country. She withholds the explicit statement of her main point until her last paragraph, when readers are fully prepared for it.

Focus on Revision

Mary's peer-editing group suggested that she make two changes. One student thought that Mary's thesis about life in Burma needed additional support. The student pointed out that although Mary's description is quite powerful, it does not fully convey the contrasts she alludes to in her conclusion.

Mary decided that adding another paragraph discussing something about her life (perhaps her reasons for visiting the windmills) could help supply this missing information. She could, for example, tell her readers that right after her return from the valley, she found out that a friend had been accidentally shot by border guards and that it was this event that had caused her to characterize the windmills as she did. Such information would help explain the passage's somber mood and underscore the ideas presented in the conclusion.

Working with Sources

Another student suggested that Mary add some information about the political situation in Burma. He pointed out that few, if any, students in the class knew much about that country, not knowing, for example, that after a coup in 1989, the military threw out the civilian government and changed the name of Burma to Myanmar. In addition, he said that he had no idea how repressive the current government of Burma was. For this reason, the student thought readers would benefit from a paragraph that gave a short history of the country. Mary considered this option but decided that such information would distract readers from the main point of her description. (A sample peer-editing worksheet for description appears below.)

 PEER-EDITING WORKSHEET: **DESCRIPTION**

1. What is the essay's dominant impression or thesis?

2. What points does the writer emphasize in the introduction? Should any other points be included? If so, which ones?

3. Would you characterize the essay as primarily an objective or subjective description? What leads you to your conclusion?

4. Point out some examples of figures of speech. Could the writer use figures of speech in other places? If so, where?

5. What specific details does the writer use to help readers visualize what is being described? Where could the writer have used more details? Would a visual have helped readers understand what is being described?

6. Are all the details necessary? Can you identify any that seem excessive or redundant? Where could the writer have provided more details to support the thesis or convey the dominant impression?

7. How are the details in the essay arranged? What other arrangement could the writer have used?

8. List some transitional words and phrases the writer uses to help readers follow the discussion. Which sentences need transitional words or phrases to link them to other sentences?

9. Do any sentences contain misplaced or dangling modifiers? If so, which ones?

10. How effective is the essay's conclusion? Does the conclusion reinforce the dominant impression?

The following selections illustrate various ways description can shape an essay. As you read them, pay particular attention to the differences between objective and subjective description. The first selection, a visual text, is followed by questions designed to illustrate how description can operate in visual form.

ANSEL ADAMS

Jackson Lake (Photo)

National Archives Catalog, Ansel Adams photograph, 1941–42.

• • •

Reading Images

1. This photograph, "Jackson Lake," was taken by the well-known photographer and environmentalist Ansel Adams. Describe what you see in the picture, starting with the image of the driftwood and then moving away toward the mountains.
2. Think of a few similes or metaphors that might be used to describe the lake. How would these figures of speech help someone who has not seen the picture visualize the lake and its surroundings?
3. What dominant impression do you think the photographer wanted to create? How do the details in the picture communicate this dominant impression?

Journal Entry

Go to Google Images and find other photographs by Ansel Adams. Choose one, and decide what dominant impression you think Adams was trying to create. Is it different from or similar to the dominant impression created by Adams in the photograph reproduced here?

Thematic Connections

- "An American Sunrise" (page 146)
- "Photos That Change History" (page 354)
- *The Kiss* (page 387)
- "Tortillas" (page 498)

BICH MINH NGUYEN

Goodbye to My Twinkie Days

Writer Bich Minh Nguyen was born in 1974 in the Vietnamese city of Saigon, now known as Ho Chi Minh City. In 1975, she and her family fled to the United States, where they settled in Grand Rapids, Michigan. Nguyen holds an M.F.A. in creative writing from the University of Michigan and teaches at the University of San Francisco, where she serves as program director of the M.F.A. in Writing program. Her books include a memoir, *Stealing Buddha's Dinner* (2007), which won a PEN/Jerard Award from the PEN American Center, and the novels *Short Girls* (2009) and *Pioneer Girl* (2014).

Background on the snack cake Individually wrapped, inexpensive, accessible, and unpretentious, the American snack cake is a democratic and egalitarian representation of mass-produced efficiency. Moreover, these processed products are also a guilty pleasure, even in today's health-conscious era. Although the Twinkie is perhaps the most iconic American snack cake, it is part of a larger history of mass-produced baked goods stretching back to the late nineteenth and early twentieth centuries. Although the Twinkie remains one of the best-selling snack cakes in history, it was not the first one. In 1888, Norman Drake established Drake Brothers, a commercial bakery in Brooklyn, New York, that sold individual slices of "Drake's Cakes" pound cake. Eventually, the company became better known for treats such as Yodels and Ring Dings. In the South, the first Moon Pie was sold by the Chattanooga Baking Company in 1917. Exactly who sold the first mass-produced snack cake remains a subject of dispute, however. For example, the Philadelphia company Tastykake claims that its individually packaged Junior layer cakes and chocolate cupcakes appeared in 1914 and 1915, predating Hostess products and the Moon Pie by several years. Regardless, no one disagrees that the first Twinkie appeared in 1930, created by baker James Dewar. The Hostess brand filed for bankruptcy in 2011, fueling fears that the Twinkie would disappear forever, yet the snack cake returned to store shelves—with the help of a new parent corporation—in 2013.

When I heard this week that the Hostess cake company was going out of business, I decided to pay my respects: I went out and bought a ten-pack box of Twinkies. 1

Though the more immediate cause of the company's trouble is a labor dispute with members of the Bakery, Confectionery, Tobacco Workers and Grain Millers International Union, its demise has been a long time coming. After all, we're not supposed to eat like this anymore. The partially hydrogenated oils, artificial flavors, high fructose corn syrup—Michael Pollan would not approve. Mr. Pollan, I swear that I have not tasted a Twinkie in years. I would not feed them to my kids. 2

But I can't stop the nostalgia, rising even now in the recitation of names: 3
Ho Hos, Ding Dongs, Sno Balls, Zingers, Donettes, Suzy Q's. Generations of
us carried these Hostess treats in our lunchboxes, traded them, saved bites of
frosting and cream for last. Soon, unless another company buys the brands,
they'll be nothing but liquidated assets.

"Junk food" is a phrase at once grotesque and appealing. We know it's bad,   4
and that's why we want it. The Twinkie, introduced in 1930, was a best-selling
treat of the Depression and is still one of the company's top items. The inventor got the idea after seeing baking equipment for strawberry cakes go unused
when the fruit was out of season. (It seems incredible now that mass-
production of food once shifted with the seasons.) We have Hostess largely to
thank for the very concept of the "snack cake," lifting sweets from dessert time
to anytime. Of the company's many products—the chocolate CupCakes with
the white squiggle across the top, Fruit Pies, Dolly Madison cakes, even Wonder Bread—the Twinkie, fresh from the package or deep-fried at a county fair,
has been its most enduring icon.

> **" 'Junk food' is a phrase at once grotesque and appealing. "**

For me, a child of Vietnamese immigrants   5
growing up in Michigan in the 1980s,
Twinkies were a ticket to assimilation: the
golden cake, more golden than the hair I
wished I had, filled with sweet white cream.
Back then, junk foods seemed to represent an
ideal of American indulgence.

They've since become a joke, a stereotype of shallow suburbia. For   6
Asian-Americans, to be a twinkie is to be a sellout: yellow on the outside, white
on the inside. Even the name "Hostess" seems quaintly outdated, like
"stewardess" or "butler." On the box of Twinkies I bought there's a cartoon of a
Twinkie as a cowboy; his sidekick is a short, swarthy chocolate cupcake.
Whether Hostess meant to evoke the Lone Ranger and Tonto or was simply
trying to recapture a glory-days notion of sweet-toothed kids playing dress-up,
the company seems determined to be retro.

Yet maybe that's exactly why the Twinkie has continued to fascinate: it is   7
already a relic. When I opened one, the smell of sugary, fake, buttery-ish vanilla
took me back to my elementary school and the basketball lines on the floor of
the gym that doubled as our lunchroom. The underside of the cake had the
same three white dots where the cream filling had been punched in, and it
tasted like what it was, a blend of shortening and corn syrup, coating the
tongue. I didn't think the Twinkie would thrill the way it used to, and it didn't.
But it tasted like memory.

We might bake our own cakes now, eat whole grain bread, and try to follow   8
those grocery store Food Rules, but who among us can forget being
sugar-shocked by processed goods? What will it mean if Twinkies and Zingers
become footnotes, gone the way of Uneeda Biscuit and Magic Middles? There's
nothing like junk foods, emblems of our shared pop culture, to create a conversation and establish common ground. Losing the Twinkie will mean losing a
connection to our shared past; it will be another part of the long goodbye to
our youth. As Hostess goes under, we become older.

According to popular myth, Twinkies are so stuffed with chemicals and   9
preservatives that they will last for decades. Hostess insists that the shelf life is
more like twenty-five days. I decided to store the rest of mine in the cupboard
above my refrigerator, out of reach but available, just in case. I may never eat
them, but I like knowing that they exist, that I can still taste my way back to the
childhood living room where I watched episodes of *Silver Spoons* and dreamed
of all the possibilities yet to be consumed.

· · ·

Comprehension

1. Despite saying that she has not eaten a Twinkie in years and that she would
   not give one to her children, Nguyen buys a ten-pack. Why?
2. According to Nguyen, what is the significance of a "snack cake"?
3. In paragraph 5, Nguyen says, "Twinkies were a ticket to assimilation."
   What does she mean? In what sense is junk food particularly American?
4. What special meaning do Hostess Twinkies have for Asian Americans?
5. What significance would losing Twinkies have for Nguyen? For all
   Americans?

Purpose and Audience

1. How much does Nguyen assume her readers know about Twinkies? How
   can you tell?
2. What is Nguyen's purpose? Is she writing about how much she will miss
   Twinkies, or is she writing about something else? Explain.
3. Does this essay have an explicitly stated thesis, or is the thesis implied?
   What dominant impression does Nguyen want to convey?

Style and Structure

1. Nguyen begins her essay with a one-sentence paragraph. How effective is
   this opening strategy? How else could she have begun her essay?
2. In paragraph 2, Nguyen refers to Michael Pollan, who writes about culture
   and food — especially about how industrial food production has lost touch
   with nature. Why does Nguyen mention Pollan?
3. In paragraph 6, Nguyen includes one sentence that contains a colon and
   another that contains a semicolon. Instead of the colon, why doesn't
   Nguyen use a comma? Instead of the semicolon, why doesn't she use a
   period?
4. **Vocabulary Project.** In paragraph 4, Nguyen discusses junk food. What do
   you think she means by this term? Is your definition of junk food different
   from Nguyen's? If so, how?
5. In paragraph 6, Nguyen describes the box that contains the Twinkies.
   Then, in paragraph 7, she describes a Twinkie. Are these two descriptions
   primarily objective or subjective? What specific words lead you to your
   conclusion?

Journal Entry

What snack food do you most associate with your childhood? Is this association positive or negative? Why?

Writing Workshop

1. **Working with Sources.** Write an essay in which you describe a food that is as meaningful to you as Twinkies are to Nguyen. Make sure your essay has a clear thesis and includes at least one reference to Nguyen's essay. Be sure to document all material that you borrow from Nguyen's essay and to include a works-cited page. (See Chapter 18 for information on MLA documentation.)

2. Write an email to someone in another country in which you describe the foods that you traditionally eat on a particular holiday. Assume the person is not familiar with the foods you describe. Be sure your description conveys a clear dominant impression.

3. Write an essay in which you describe a parent or grandparent (or any other older person) who has had a great influence on you. Make sure you include basic biographical information as well as a detailed physical description.

Combining the Patterns

In addition to describing Nguyen's fascination for Twinkies, this essay examines **causes and effects** (in paragraph 2). What purpose does this cause-and-effect paragraph serve?

Thematic Connections

- "My Field of Dreams" (page 106)
- "Why Chinese Mothers Are Superior" (page 396)
- "Tortillas" (page 498)

TREVOR NOAH

Soweto

Writer, producer, comedian, and television host Trevor Noah was born in 1984 in Johannesburg, South Africa. Noah's mother was Black, and his father was white. Under South Africa's system of apartheid, his birth was illegal because interracial marriages and sexual relationships were forbidden by law. As Noah writes, "Where most children are proof of their parents' love, I was the proof of their criminality." While his mother Patricia maintained a secret relationship with Noah's father, she raised Noah in Soweto, a Black municipal township that is now part of Johannesburg. In his late teens, Noah acted in the South African soap opera *Isidingo*, and in his twenties, moved to stand-up comedy. Noah achieved international recognition with his 2009 one-man comedy show, *The Daywalker*. He began working as a correspondent for Comedy Central's *The Daily Show* in 2014 before succeeding Jon Stewart as host of the program in 2015. He has also produced several comedy specials. His memoir, *Born a Crime: Stories from a South African Childhood*, was published in 2016.

Background on Apartheid South Africa was colonized by the Dutch and English in the seventeenth century. They were drawn to the region by its abundant natural resources, especially diamonds and gold. In 1910, South Africa became a self-governing territory of the British Empire. This political arrangement allowed the white minority of the country to segregate, disenfranchise, and dominate the Black population. In 1948, the Afrikaner Nation Party came to power running on a platform of *apartheid*, an Afrikaner word meaning *separate*. As a result, white supremacy and racial segregation were codified into law. South Africans were classified into four racial groups, and all citizens over the age of sixteen were required to carry identity cards to verify their race. Interracial marriages and sexual relations between different racial groups were prohibited. This system led to several decades of violent political struggles, including the 1976 Soweto Youth Uprising in which many young Black students were killed or injured. As a result, many countries — including the United States and Great Britain — imposed economic sanctions on South Africa, severely damaging its economy. The government began loosening restrictions in the 1980s, and the remaining apartheid laws were repealed in 1991. In 1990, activist Nelson Mandela was released after twenty-seven years in prison, and in 1994, he became the first Black president of South Africa.

There is something magical about Soweto. Yes, it was a prison designed by our oppressors, but it also gave us a sense of self-determination and control. Soweto was ours. It had an aspirational quality that you don't find elsewhere. In America the dream is to make it out of the ghetto. In Soweto, because there was no leaving the ghetto, the dream was to transform the ghetto.

> **❝**For millions of people who lived in Soweto there were no stores, no bars, no restaurants.**❞**

For the millions of people who lived in 2 Soweto there were no stores, no bars, no restaurants. There were no paved roads, minimal electricity, inadequate sewerage. But when you put one million people together in one place, they find a way to make a life for themselves. A black-market economy rose up, with every type of business being run out of someone's house: auto mechanics, day care, guys selling refurbished tires.

The most common were the *spaza* shops and the shebeens. The *spaza* 3 shops were informal grocery stores. People would build a kiosk in their garage, buy wholesale bread and eggs, and then resell them piecemeal. Everyone in the township bought things in minute quantities because nobody had any money. You couldn't afford to buy a dozen eggs at a time, but you could buy two eggs because that's all you needed that morning. You could buy a quarter loaf of bread, a cup of sugar. The shebeens were unlawful bars in the back of someone's house. They'd put chairs in their backyard and hang out an awning and run a speakeasy. The shebeens were where men would go to drink after work and during prayer meetings and most any other time of day as well.

People built homes the way they bought eggs: a little at a time. Every family in the township was allocated a piece of land by the government. You'd first build a shanty on your plot, a makeshift structure of plywood and corrugated iron. Over time, you'd save up money and build a brick wall. One wall. Then you'd save up and build another wall. Then, years later, a third wall and eventually a fourth. Now you had a room, one room for everyone in your family to sleep, eat, do everything. Then you'd save up for a roof. Then windows. Then you'd plaster the thing. Then your daughter would start a family. There was nowhere for them to go, so they'd move in with you. You'd add another corrugated-iron structure onto your brick room and slowly, over years, turn that into a proper room for them as well. Now your house had two rooms. Then three. Maybe four. Slowly, over generations, you'd keep trying to get to the point where you had a home.

My grandmother lived in Orlando East. She had a two-room house. Not a 5 two-bedroom house. A two-room house. There was a bedroom, and then there was basically a living room/kitchen, everything-else room. Some might say we lived like poor people. I prefer "open plan."

My mom and I would stay there during school holidays. My aunt and 6 cousins would be there whenever she was on the outs with Dinky. We all slept on the floor in one room, my mom and me, my aunt and my cousins, my uncle and my grandmother and my great-grandmother. The adults each had their own foam mattresses, and there was one big one that we'd roll out into the middle, and the kids slept on that.

We had two shanties in the backyard that my grandmother would rent 7 out to migrants and seasonal workers. We had a small peach tree in a tiny patch on one side of the house and on the other side my grandmother had a driveway. I never understood why my grandmother had a driveway. She didn't have a car. She didn't know how to drive. Yet she had a driveway. All of our neighbors had driveways, some with fancy, cast-iron gates. None of them had cars, either. There was no future in which most of these families would ever have cars. There was maybe one car for every thousand people, yet almost everyone had a driveway. It was almost like building the driveway was a way of willing the car to happen. The story of Soweto is the story of the driveways. It's a hopeful place.

• • •

Comprehension

1. According to Noah, what is "magical" about Soweto (1)?
2. In paragraph 1, Noah says that Soweto "had an aspirational quality that you don't find elsewhere." What does he mean?
3. What are *spaza* shops and shebeens? What is their function in Soweto?
4. What does Noah mean in paragraph 4 when he says, "People built homes the way they bought eggs"?
5. What was the significance of the driveway at Noah's grandmother's house? Why, according to Noah, is the story of Soweto "the story of the driveways" (7)?

Purpose and Audience

1. What is the thesis of this essay? Is it stated or implied?
2. What attitude toward Soweto does Noah assume his readers have? How do you know?
3. What is Noah's purpose in writing this description?

Style and Structure

1. Noah begins his essay by saying, "There is something magical about Soweto" (1). He goes on to concede that Soweto was "a prison designed by our oppressors." In what sense are these two sentences **ironic**? How does this use of irony help Noah introduce his description?
2. What specific features of Soweto does Noah identify in his description? What dominant impression do these details help convey?
3. Much of this essay focuses on the hardships of living in Soweto. Would you say that Noah's childhood memories of Soweto are positive or negative? Explain.
4. How does Noah's conclusion echo the first paragraph of his essay?
5. **Vocabulary Project.** Look up the word *ghetto*. In what sense is Soweto a ghetto? How is it different from your understanding of what a racial ghetto is?

Journal Entry

What place is "something magical" for you?

Writing Workshop

1. Write a description of a place you remember from your childhood. In your essay, explain what significance this place has for you as an adult.

2. **Working with Sources.** Assume you are a travel agent. Stressing both the physical features and historical significance of Soweto, write a descriptive travel brochure designed to bring tourists to this area. (Before writing this essay, do some research on Soweto.) Be sure to include parenthetical documentation for information you borrow from sources and to include a works-cited page. (See Chapter 18 for information on MLA documentation.)

3. **Working with Sources.** Look at pictures of Soweto on Google Images. Then, write an objective description of one of the pictures. Make sure your description has a thesis statement that conveys your essay's dominant impression. Be sure to include parenthetical documentation for references to Noah's essay and to include a works-cited page. (See Chapter 18 for information on MLA documentation.)

Combining the Patterns

In paragraph 3, Noah **defines** *spaza* shops and shebeens. Why does he include this paragraph of definition? Does he need to define any additional terms?

Thematic Connections

- " 'Girl' " (page 251)
- "Tortillas" (page 498)
- "Letter from Birmingham Jail" (page 562)

MARINA KEEGAN

Stability in Motion

Author and playwright Marina Keegan (1989–2012) was raised in Wayland, Massachusetts, and attended Yale University, where she majored in English. While at Yale, she was an intern at the *New Yorker* magazine and the *Paris Review*. Her work was read on National Public Radio and was published in the *New York Times* as well as the *New Yorker*. She also organized a campus protest, Occupy Morgan Stanley, which opposed on-campus corporate recruiting by the financial industry. That issue informed her writing as well: in 2012, she wrote "Even Artichokes Have Doubts" for the *Yale Daily News*, a widely discussed article that explored why so many Yale graduates chose to work in consulting or finance. Ironically, given the subject of "Stability in Motion," Keegan was killed at the age of twenty-two in a car crash on Cape Cod.

Background on the automobile in the twentieth century Although he did not invent the automobile, Henry Ford built the first mass-produced car that was both reliable and affordable. Consequently, the automobile moved from being a toy of the rich to a necessity of everyday life and profoundly changed people's employment patterns, social interactions, and living conditions. In the post–World War II boom of the 1950s and 1960s, cars came to represent freedom and individuality for America's teenagers. Drive-in movie theaters and fast-food restaurants became staples of everyday life, and hit songs like "409" by the Beach Boys and "Mustang Sally" by Wilson Pickett romanticized the joys of driving a fast car. By the time Marina Keegan got her first car in the 1990s, concerns about pollution, safety, and urban congestion had begun to dampen Americans' romance with the car. Today, because of rising tuition and student-loan debt, many millennials cannot afford cars, and as a result are turning to less expensive means of transportation.

My 1990 Camry's DNA was designed inside the metallic walls of the Toyota Multinational Corporation's headquarters in Tokyo, Japan; transported via blueprint to the North American Manufacturing nerve center in Hebron, Kentucky; grown organ by organ in four major assembly plants in Alabama, New Jersey, Texas, and New York; trucked to 149 Arsenal Street in Watertown, Massachusetts; and steered home by my grandmother on September 4, 1990. It featured a 200 hp, 3.0 L V6 engine, a four-speed automatic, and an adaptive Variable Suspension System. She deemed the car too "high tech." In 1990 this meant a cassette player, a cup holder, and a manually operated moon roof.

During its youth, the car traveled little. In fifteen years my grandmother accumulated a meager twenty-five thousand miles, mostly to and from the market, my family's house, and the Greek jewelry store downtown. The black exterior remained glossy and spotless, the beige interior crisp and pristine. Tissues were disposed of, seats vacuumed, and food prohibited. My grandmother's old-fashioned cleanliness was an endearing virtue—one that I evidently did not inherit.

I acquired the old Camry through an awkward transaction. Ten days 3 before my sixteenth birthday, my grandfather died. He was eighty-six and it had been long expected, yet I still felt a guilty unease when I heard the now surplus car would soon belong to me. For my grandmother, it was a symbolic goodbye. She needed to see only *one* car in her garage — needed to comprehend her loss more tangibly. Grandpa's car was the "nicer" of the two, so that one she would keep. Three weeks after the funeral, my grandmother and I went to the bank, I signed a check for exactly one dollar, and the car was legally mine. That was that. When I drove her home that evening, I manually opened the moon roof and put on a tape of Frank Sinatra. My grandma smiled for the first time in weeks.

Throughout the next three years, the car evolved. When I first parked the 4 Toyota in my driveway, it was spotless, full of gas, and equipped with my grandmother's version of survival necessities. The glove compartment had a magnifying glass, three pens, and the registration in a little Ziploc bag. The trunk had two matching black umbrellas, a first aid kit, and a miniature sewing box for emergency repairs. Like my grandmother's wrists, everything smelled of Opium perfume.

For a while, I maintained this immaculate condition. Yet one Wrigley's 5 wrapper led to two and soon enough my car underwent a radical transformation — the vehicular equivalent of a midlife crisis. Born and raised in proper formality, the car saw me as *that* friend from school, the bad example who washes away naïveté and corrupts the clean and innocent. We were the same age, after all — both eighteen. The Toyota was born again, crammed with clutter, and exposed to decibel levels it had never fathomed. I filled it with giggling friends and emotional phone calls, borrowed skirts and bottled drinks.

The messiness crept up on me. Parts of my life began falling off, forming 6 an eclectic debris that dribbled gradually into every corner. Empty sushi containers, Diet Coke cans, half-full packs of gum, sweaters, sweatshirts, socks, my running shoes. My clutter was nondiscriminatory. I had every variety of newspaper, scratched-up English paper, biology review sheet, and Spanish flash card discarded on the seats after I'd sufficiently studied on my way to school. The left door pocket was filled with tiny tinfoil balls, crumpled after consuming my morning English muffin. By Friday, I had the entire house's supply of portable coffee mugs. By Sunday, someone always complained about their absence and I would rush out, grab them all, and surreptitiously place them in the dishwasher.

My car was not gross; it was occupied, cluttered, cramped. It became an 7 extension of my bedroom, and thus an extension of myself. I had two bumper stickers on the back: REPUBLICANS FOR VOLDEMORT and the symbol for the Equal Rights Campaign. On the back side windows were OBAMA '08 signs that my parents made me take down because they "dangerously blocked my sight lines." The trunk housed my guitar but was also the library, filled with textbooks and novels, the giant tattered copy of *The Complete Works of William Shakespeare* and all one hundred chapters of *Harry Potter* on tape. A few stray cassettes littered the corners, their little brown insides ripped out, tangled and mutilated. They were the casualties of the trunk trenches, sprawled out forgotten next to the headband I never gave back to Meghan.

On average, I spent two hours a day driving. It was nearly an hour each way 8
to school, and the old-fashioned Toyota — regarded with lighthearted amusement by my classmates — came to be a place of comfort and solitude amid the chaos of my daily routine. My mind was free to wander, my muscles to relax. No one was watching or keeping score. Sometimes I let the deep baritone of NPR's Tom Ashbrook lecture me on oil shortages. Other times I played repetitive mix tapes with titles like *Pancake Breakfast*, *Tie-Dye and Granola*, and *Songs for the Highway When It's Snowing*.

Ravaging my car, I often found more than just physical relics. For two 9
months I could hardly open the side door without reliving the first time he kissed me. His dimpled smile was barely visible in the darkness, but it nevertheless made me stumble backward when I found my way blushingly back into the car. On the backseat there was the June 3 issue of the *New York Times* that I couldn't bear to throw out. When we drove home together from the camping trip, he read it cover to cover while I played Simon and Garfunkel — hoping he'd realize all the songs were about us. We didn't talk much during that ride. We didn't need to. He slid his hand into mine for the first time when we got off the highway; it was only after I made my exit that I realized I should have missed it. Above this newspaper are the fingernail marks I dug into the leather of my steering wheel on the night we decided to *just be friends*. My car listened to me cry for all twenty-two-and-a-half miles home.

The physical manifestations of my memories soon crowded the car. My 10
right back speaker was broken from the time my older brother and I pulled an all-nighter singing shamelessly during our rainy drive home from the wedding. I remember the sheer energy of the storm, the lights, the music — moving through us, transcending the car's steel shell, and tracing the city. There was the folder left behind from the day I drove my dad to an interview the month after he lost his job. It was coincidental that *his* car was in the shop, but I knew he felt more pathetic that it was he, not his daughter, in the passenger seat. I kept my eyes on the road, feeling the confused sadness of a child who catches a parent crying.

I talked a lot in my car. Thousands of words and songs and swears are 11
absorbed in its fabric, just like the orange juice I spilled on my way to the dentist. It knows what happened when Allie went to Puerto Rico, understands the difference between the way I look at Nick and the way I look at Adam, and remembers the first time I experimented with talking to myself. I've practiced for auditions, college interviews, Spanish oral presentations, and debates. There's something novel about swearing alone in the car. Yet with the pressures of APs and SATs and the other acronyms that haunt high school, the act became more frequent and less refreshing.

> **"**Thousands of words and songs and swears are absorbed in its fabric, just like the orange juice I spilled on my way to the dentist.**"**

My car has seen three drive-in movies. 12
During *The Dark Knight*, its battery died and, giggling ferociously, we had to ask the overweight family in the next row to jump it. The smell of popcorn permeated every crevice of the sedan, and all rides for the next week were like a

trip to the movies. There was a variety of smells in the Camry. At first it smelled like my grandmother — perfume, mint, and mothballs. I went through a chai-tea phase during which my car smelled incessantly of Indian herbs. Some mornings it would smell slightly of tobacco and I would know immediately that my older brother had kidnapped it the night before. For exactly three days it reeked of marijuana. Dan had removed the shabbily rolled joint from behind his ear and our fingers had trembled as the five of us apprehensively inhaled. Nothing happened. Only the seats seemed to absorb the plant and get high. Mostly, however, it smelled like nothing to me. Yet when I drove my friends, they always said it had a distinct aroma. I believe this functioned in the same way as not being able to taste your own saliva or smell your own odor — the car and I were pleasantly immune to each other.

In the Buckingham Browne & Nichols High School yearbook I was voted worst driver, but on most days I will refute this superlative. My car's love for parking tickets made me an easy target, but I rarely received other violations. My mistakes mostly harmed me, not others — locking my keys in the car or parking on the wrong side of the road. Once, last winter, I needed to refill my windshield wiper fluid and in a rushed frenzy poured an entire bottle of similarly blue antifreeze inside. Antifreeze, as it turns out, burns out engines if used in excess. I spent the next two hours driving circles around my block in a snowstorm, urgently expelling the antifreeze squirt by thick blue squirt. I played no music during this vigil. I couldn't find a playlist called *Poisoning Your Car.* 13

It may have been awkward-looking and muddled, but I was attached to my car. It was a portable home that heated my seat in winter and carried me home at night. I had no diary and rarely took pictures. That old Toyota Camry was an odd documentation of my adolescence. When I was seventeen, the car was seventeen. My younger brother entered high school last September and I passed my ownership on to him. In the weeks before I left for college, my parents made me clean it out for his sake. I spread six trash bags over the driveway, filling them with my car's contents as the August sun heated their black plastic. The task was strange, like deconstructing a scrapbook, unpeeling all the pictures and whiting out the captions. 14

Just like for my grandmother, it was a symbolic good-bye. Standing outside my newly vacuumed car, I wondered, if I tried hard enough, whether I could smell the Opium perfume again, or if I searched long enough, whether I'd find the matching umbrellas and the tiny sewing kit. My brother laughed at my nostalgia, reminding me that I could still drive the car when I came home. He didn't understand that it wasn't just the driving I'd miss. That it was the tinfoil balls, the *New York Times*, and the broken speaker; the fingernail marks, the stray cassettes, and the smell of chai. Alone that night and parked in my driveway, I listened to Frank Sinatra with the moon roof slid back. 15

·   ·   ·

Comprehension

1. How does Keegan acquire her grandmother's car? Why does she call this transaction "awkward" (3)?
2. In paragraph 4, Keegan says that her car "evolved," and in paragraph 5, she says that her car was "born again." In each case, what does she mean?
3. Keegan observes that her car was not "gross." Instead, she says, "it was occupied, cluttered, cramped" (7). Why do you think she makes this distinction? Does it make sense?
4. How are Keegan and her grandmother different? How are they alike?
5. What are the "physical manifestations of her memories" that Keegan refers to in paragraph 10? How do they "crowd" her car?

Purpose and Audience

1. Does "Stability in Motion" have an explicitly stated thesis? If so, where? If not, suggest a one-sentence thesis statement for this essay.
2. What dominant impression is Keegan trying to create? Is she successful? Why or why not?
3. Is "Stability in Motion" primarily an objective or subjective description? What words and phrases lead you to your conclusion?

Style and Structure

1. What is the significance of the essay's title? In what sense is it a **paradox**?
2. Why does Keegan begin her essay with the details of her car's manufacture? How does this information help set up the rest of her discussion?
3. An **elegy** is a poem that is written to express praise and sorrow for someone who is dead. In what sense is this essay elegiac?
4. To which of the five senses does Keegan appeal as she describes her car? Find examples of each type.
5. Keegan concludes by repeating an image that she uses at the beginning of her essay. What is this image? Do you think this concluding strategy is effective? Why or why not?
6. **Vocabulary Project.** Throughout her essay, Keegan uses similes, metaphors, personification, and allusion. Find examples of this **figurative language**. What does Keegan accomplish by using this kind of language?

Journal Entry

Based on the things Keegan kept in her car, how would you describe her? What was (and was not) important to her?

Writing Workshop

1. Go through your own car (or room), and list ten things you find there. Then, write an essay in which you describe some of these items, and, like Keegan, tell why they are important.
2. What possession — like Keegan's Toyota — has a special meaning to you? Write an essay in which you describe the item, and be sure to discuss the qualities that give the item you describe significance.
3. **Writing with Sources.** Find a picture of a 1990 Toyota Camry. Then, write an objective description of the car, pointing out any differences you see between the car in the picture and the car Keegan describes. In your essay, make specific references to "Stability in Motion." Be sure to document all references to Keegan's essay and to include a works-cited page. (See Chapter 18 for information on MLA documentation.)

Combining the Patterns

At several points in her essay, Keegan uses **comparison** — for example, when she compares her treatment of the car to her grandmother's treatment of it. What do these comparisons add to Keegan's essay?

Thematic Connections

- "My Grandfather's Globe" (page 161)
- "Goodbye to My Twinkie Days" (page 171)
- "Photos That Change History" (page 354)
- "Mother Tongue" (page 456)

HEATHER ROGERS

The Hidden Life of Garbage

Journalist Heather Rogers (b. 1970) has written articles on the environmental effects of mass production and consumption for the *New York Times Magazine*, the *Utne Reader, Architecture*, and a variety of other publications. Her 2002 documentary film, *Gone Tomorrow: The Hidden Life of Garbage*, has been screened at festivals around the world and served as the basis for a book of the same title. Named an Editor's Choice by the *New York Times* and the *Guardian*, the book, published in 2005, traces the history and politics of household garbage in the United States, drawing connections between modern industrial production, consumer culture, and our contemporary throwaway lifestyle. In the following excerpt from that book, Rogers provides a detailed description of a giant landfill in central Pennsylvania and asks readers to think about the ramifications of accumulating so much trash. Her most recent book is *Green Gone Wrong: How Our Economy Is Undermining the Environmental Revolution* (2010).

Background on waste disposal Human beings have always faced the question of how to dispose of garbage. The first city dump was established in ancient Athens, and the government of Rome had begun the collection of municipal trash by 200 C.E. Even as late as the 1800s, garbage was, at worst, simply thrown out into the streets of U.S. cities or dumped into rivers and ditches; in more enlightened communities, it might have been carted to foul-smelling open dumps or burned in incinerators, creating clouds of dense smoke. Experiments with systematically covering the garbage in dumps began as early as the 1920s, and the first true "sanitary landfill," as it was called, was created in Fresno, California, in 1937. Today, more than 60 percent of the solid waste in the United States ends up in landfills, and the amount of waste seems to keep growing. According to the Environmental Protection Agency, Americans produce about 4.4 pounds of garbage a day, 29 pounds a week, and an astounding 1,600 pounds a year. These figures do not include industrial waste and commercial trash.

In the dark chill of early morning, heavy steel garbage trucks chug and creep along neighborhood collection routes. A worker empties the contents of each household's waste bin into the truck's rear compaction unit. Hydraulic compressors scoop up and crush the dross, cramming it into the enclosed hull. When the rig is full, the collector heads to a garbage depot called a "transfer station" to unload. From there the rejectamenta is taken to a recycling center, an incinerator, or, most often, to what's called a "sanitary landfill."

Land dumping has long been the favored disposal method in the U.S. thanks to the relative low cost of burial and North America's abundant supply of unused acreage. Although the great majority of our castoffs go to landfills, they are places the public is not meant to see. Today's garbage graveyards are sequestered, guarded, veiled. They are also high-tech, and, increasingly, located in rural areas that receive much of their rubbish from urban centers that no longer bury their own wastes.

There's a reason landfills are tucked away, on the edge of town, in otherwise   3
untraveled terrain, camouflaged by hydroseeded, neatly tiered slopes. If people
saw what happened to their waste, lived with the stench, witnessed the scale of
destruction, they might start asking difficult questions. Waste Management
Inc., the largest rubbish handling corporation in the world, operates its Geolog-
ical Reclamation Operations and Waste Systems (GROWS) landfill just outside
Morrisville, Pennsylvania—in the docile river valley near where Washington
momentously crossed the Delaware leading his troops into Trenton in 1776.
Sitting atop the landfill's 300-foot-high butte composed entirely of garbage,
the logic of our society's unrestrained consuming and wasting quickly unravels.

Up here is where the dumping takes place; it is referred to as the fill's   4
"working face." Clusters of trailer trucks, yellow earthmovers, compacting
machines, steamrollers, and water tankers populate this bizarre, thirty-acre
nightmare. Churning in slow motion through the surreal landscape, these
machines are remaking the earth in the image of garbage. Scores of seagulls
hover overhead then suddenly drop into the rotting piles. The ground underfoot is torn from the metal treads of the equipment. Potato chip wrappers, tattered plastic bags, and old shoes poke through the dirt as if floating to the
surface. The smell is sickly and sour.

The aptly named GROWS landfill is part of Waste Management Inc.'s (WMI)   5
6,000-acre garbage treatment complex, which includes a second landfill, an incinerator, and a state-mandated leaf composting lot. GROWS is one of a new breed
of waste burial sites referred to as "mega-fills." These high-tech, high-capacity
dumps are comprised of a series of earth-covered "cells" that can be ten to one
hundred acres across and up to hundreds of feet deep—or tall, as is the case at
GROWS. (One Virginia whopper has disposal capacity equivalent to the length of
one thousand football fields and the height of the Washington Monument.) As
of 2002, GROWS was the single largest recipient of New York City's garbage in
Pennsylvania, a state that is the country's biggest depository for exported waste.

WMI's Delaware-side operation sits on land that has long served the inter-   6
ests of industry. Overlooking a rambling, mostly decommissioned US Steel factory, WMI now occupies the former grounds of the Warner Company. In the
previous century, Warner surface mined the area for gravel and sand, much of
which was shipped to its cement factory in Philadelphia. The area has since been
converted into a reverse mine of sorts; instead of extraction, workers dump, pack,
and fill the earth with almost forty million pounds of municipal wastes daily.

Back on top of the GROWS landfill, twenty-ton dump trucks gather at the   7
low end of the working face, where they discharge their fetid cargo. Several feet
up a dirt bank, a string of large trailers are being detached from semi trucks. In
rapid succession each container is tipped almost vertical by a giant hydraulic
lift and, within seconds, twenty-four tons of putrescence cascades down into
the day's menacing valley of trash. In the middle of the dumping is a "landfill
compactor"—which looks like a bulldozer on steroids with mammoth metal
spiked wheels—that pitches back and forth, its fifty tons crushing the detritus
into the earth. A smaller vehicle called a "track loader" maneuvers on tank
treads, channeling the castoffs from kitchens and offices into the compactor's
path. The place runs like a well-oiled machine, with only a handful of workers
orchestrating the burial.

Get a few hundred yards from the landfill's working face and it's hard to   8
smell the rot or see the debris. The place is kept tidy with the help of thirty-five-
foot-tall fencing made of "litter netting" that surrounds the perimeter of the
site's two landfills. As a backup measure, teams of "paper pickers" constantly
patrol the area retrieving discards carried off by the wind. Small misting machines
dot fence tops, roads, and hillsides, spraying a fine, invisible chemical-water
mixture into the air, which binds with odor molecules and pulls them to the
ground.

In new state-of-the-art landfills, the cells that contain the trash are built   9
on top of what is called a "liner." The liner is a giant underground bladder
intended to prevent contamination of groundwater by collecting leachate —
liquid wastes and the rainwater that seeps through buried trash — and channeling it to nearby water treatment facilities. WMI's two Morrisville landfills
leach on average 100,000 gallons daily. If this toxic stew contaminated the
site's groundwater it would be devastating.

Once a cell is filled, which might take years, it is closed off or "capped." The   10
capping process entails covering the garbage with several feet of dirt, which gets
graded, then packed by steamrollers. After that, layers of clay-embedded fabric,
synthetic mesh, and plastic sheeting are draped across the top of the cell and
joined with the bottom liner (which is made of the same materials) to encapsu-
late all those outmoded appliances, dirty diapers, and discarded wrappers.

Today's landfill regulations, ranging from liner construction to postcapping   11
oversight, mean that disposal areas like WMI's GROWS are potentially less dangerous than the dumps of previous generations. But the fact remains that these
systems are short-term solutions to the garbage problem. While they may not
seem toxic now, all those underground cells packed with plastics, solvents, paints,
batteries, and other hazardous materials will someday have to be treated since the
liners won't last forever. Most liners are expected to last somewhere between
thirty and fifty years. That time frame just happens to coincide with the postclo-
sure liability private landfill operators are subject to: thirty years after a site is
shuttered, its owner is no longer responsible for contamination, the public is.

There is a palpable tension at waste treatment facilities, as though at any   12
minute the visitor will uncover some illegal activity. But what's most striking
at these places isn't what they might be hiding; it's what's in plain view. The
lavish resources dedicated to destroying
used commodities and making that obliter-
ation acceptable, even "green," is what's so
astounding. Each landfill (not to mention
garbage collection systems, transfer sta-
tions, recycling centers, and incinerators) is
an expensive, complex operation that uses
the latest methods developed and perfected
at laboratories, universities, and corporate
campuses across the globe.

> "But what's most striking at these places isn't what they might be hiding; it's what's in plain view."

The more state-of-the-art, the more "environmentally responsible" the   13
operation, the more the repressed question pushes to the surface: what if we
didn't have so much trash to get rid of?

∙ ∙ ∙

Comprehension

1. According to Rogers, why are landfills "tucked away, on the edge of town, in otherwise untraveled terrain" (3)?
2. What is the landfill's "working face" (4)? How does it compare with other parts of the landfill?
3. Why does Rogers think the GROWS landfill is "aptly named" (5)? What **connotations** do you think Waste Management Inc. intended the name GROWS to have? What connotations does Rogers think the name has?
4. What are the dangers of the "new state-of-the-art landfills" (9)? What point does Rogers make about liners being "expected to last somewhere between thirty and fifty years" (11)?
5. According to Rogers, what is the "repressed question" (13) that is not being asked?

Purpose and Audience

1. At what point in the essay does Rogers state her thesis? Why do you think she places the thesis where she does?
2. What dominant impression does Rogers try to create in her description? Is she successful?
3. What is Rogers's attitude toward waste disposal in general and toward disposal companies like Waste Management Inc. in particular? Do you share her feelings?

Style and Structure

1. Rogers begins her essay with a description of garbage trucks collecting trash. What specific things does she describe? How does this description establish the context for the rest of the essay?
2. What determines the order in which details are arranged in Rogers's essay?
3. Is this essay a subjective or objective description of the landfill? Explain.
4. In paragraph 13, why does Rogers put the phrase *environmentally responsible* in quotation marks? What impression is she trying to convey?
5. Rogers never offers a solution to the problems she writes about. Should she have? Is her failure to offer a solution a shortcoming of the essay?
6. **Vocabulary Project.** Some critics of waste disposal methods accuse both municipalities and waste disposal companies of "environmental racism." Research this term on the web. Do you think the methods described by Rogers are examples of environmental racism? Explain.

Journal Entry

What do you think you and your family could do to reduce the amount of garbage you produce? How realistic are your suggestions?

Writing Workshop

1. Write an essay in which you describe the waste that you see generated at your school, home, or job. Like Rogers, write your description in a way that will motivate people to do something about the problem.
2. **Working with Sources.** In 1986, the city of Philadelphia hired a company to dispose of waste from a city incinerator. More than thirteen thousand tons of waste — some of which was hazardous — was loaded onto a ship called the *Khian Sea*, which unsuccessfully tried to dispose of it. After two years, the cargo mysteriously disappeared. Go to Google Images, and find several pictures of the *Khian Sea*. Then, write a description of the ship and its cargo. Make sure the thesis statement of your description clearly conveys your dominant impression. If you wish, you may insert one of the images you found into your essay. Be sure to document the image and to include a works-cited page. (See Chapter 18 for information on MLA documentation.)
3. Describe a place that has played an important role in your life. Include a narrative passage that conveys the place's significance to you.

Combining the Patterns

In paragraphs 9 and 10, Rogers includes a **definition** as well as a **process** description. Explain how these paragraphs help Rogers develop her description.

Thematic Connections

- "The Irish Famine, 1845–1849" (page 326)
- "The Obligation to Endure" (page 554)
- "Reducing Your Carbon Footprint Still Matters" (page 589)
- "On Dumpster Diving" (page 668)

JONATHAN ABABIY

How the Other Half Lives

The son of Moldovan refugees, Jonathan Ababiy grew up in Blaine, Minnesota, where he graduated from Blaine High School in 2017, when this essay was published. He currently attends the University of Minnesota. Ababiy is an opinion columnist for the *Minnesota Daily*.

Background on *How the Other Half Lives* The title of Ababiy's essay is an allusion to social reformer and photojournalist Jacob Riis's 1890 book *How the Other Half Lives: Studies among the Tenements of New York*. In the book, Riis used flash photography, a newly developed technology, to dramatically convey the squalid and often wretched lives of the urban poor, many of whom were immigrants living in crammed, run-down buildings with no running water, indoor plumbing, lighting, or ventilation. In such conditions, diseases such as cholera, tuberculosis, and typhus spread quickly. According to Riis, these tenements were the "nurseries of pauperism and crime that fill our jails and police courts; that throw off a scum of forty thousand human wrecks to the island asylums and workhouses . . . [and that] touch the family life with deadly moral contagion." Riis's book shocked the American public and led to many reforms that improved the lives of the poor. In March 1901, Theodore Roosevelt, then vice president, called Riis the "most useful citizen of New York."

At age six, I remember the light filled openness of the house, how the whir of my mother's vacuum floated from room to room. At nine, I remember how I used to lounge on the couch and watch Disney cartoons on the sideways refrigerator of a TV implanted in a small cave in the wall. At twelve, I remember family photographs of the Spanish countryside hanging in every room. At fourteen, I remember vacuuming each foot of carpet in the massive house and folding pastel shirts fresh out of the dryer.

I loved the house. I loved the way the windows soaked the house with light, a sort of bleach against any gloom. I loved how I could always find a book or magazine on any flat surface.

But the vacuum my mother used wasn't ours. We never paid for cable. The photographs weren't of my family. The carpet I vacuumed I only saw once a week, and the pastel shirts I folded I never wore. The house wasn't mine. My mother was only the cleaning lady, and I helped.

My mother and father had come as refugees almost twenty years ago from the country of Moldova. My mother worked numerous odd jobs, but once I was born she decided she needed to do something different. She put an ad in the paper advertising house cleaning, and a couple, both professors, answered.

Jonathan Ababiy, "How the Other Half Lives: The Professor's Home Was a Telescope to How the Other (More Affluent) Half Lived," *The New York Times*, May 12, 2017. Copyright © 2017 by The New York Times. All rights reserved. Used under license.

They became her first client, and their house became the bedrock of our suste-nance. Economic recessions came and went, but my mother returned every Monday, Friday, and occasional Sunday.

She spends her days in teal latex gloves, guiding a blue Hoover vacuum over what seems like miles of carpet. All the mirrors she's cleaned could prob-ably stack up to be a minor Philip Johnson skyscraper. This isn't new for her. The vacuums and the gloves might be, but the work isn't. In Moldova, her family grew gherkins and tomatoes. She spent countless hours kneeling in the dirt, growing her vegetables with the care that professors advise their protégés, with kindness and proactivity. Today, the fruits of her labor have been replaced with the suction of her vacuum.

The professors' home was a telescope to how the other (more affluent) half lived. They were rarely ever home, so I saw their remnants: the lightly crinkled *New York Times* sprawled on the kitchen table, the overturned, half-opened books in their overflowing personal library, the TV consistently left on the National Geographic channel. I took these remnants as a celebrity-endorsed path to prosperity. I began to check out books from the school library and started reading the news religiously.

Their home was a sanctuary for my dreams. It was there I, as a glasses-wearing computer nerd, read about a mythical place called Silicon Valley in *Bloomberg Business-week* magazines. It was there, as a son of immigrants, that I read about a young sen-ator named Barack Obama, the child of an immigrant, aspiring to be the president of the United States. The life that I saw through their home showed me that an immigrant could succeed in America, too. Work could be done with one's hands and with one's mind. It impressed on me a sort of social capital that I knew could be used in America. The professors left me the elements to their own success, and all my life I've been trying to make my own reaction.

> "Their home was a sanctuary for my dreams."

Ultimately, the suction of the vacuum is what sustains my family. The squeal of her vacuum reminds me why I have the opportunity to drive my squealing car to school. I am where I am today because my mom put an enor-mous amount of labor into the formula of the American Dream. It's her blue Hoover vacuums that hold up the framework of my life. Someday, I hope my diploma can hold up the framework of hers.

· · ·

Comprehension

1. Why does Ababiy love the house his mother cleaned? What do the details he mentions reveal about the house's owner? About Ababiy?
2. In what sense did the professors' home become the "bedrock" (4) of his family's subsistence?
3. In paragraph 4, Ababiy says that his parents came to the United States as refugees from Moldavia. Why does he mention this fact?

4. What lessons does Ababiy learn as a child in the professors' house? How do these lessons help him in his later life?
5. Does Ababiy think that his experiences at the professors' house were positive or negative? Explain.

Purpose and Audience

1. Does Ababiy state or imply his thesis? Why do you think he made the decision he did? State Ababiy's thesis in your own words.
2. What is Ababiy's purpose in writing his essay?
3. What assumptions does Ababiy make about his readers' ideas about immigrants? About success in the United States? How can you tell?

Style and Structure

1. Ababiy begins his essay by recounting a series of memories. What do these memories show about him? Why does he introduce his essay this way?
2. In paragraphs 1 through 4, Ababiy uses the past tense. Then, in paragraph 5, he shifts to the present tense, and in paragraph 6, he moves back to the past tense. Why?
3. What figures of speech does Ababiy use in each of the following sentences?
   - I loved the way the windows soaked the house with light, a sort of bleach against my gloom. (2)
   - The professors' home was a telescope to how the other (more affluent) half lived. (6)
   - Their home was a sanctuary for my dreams. (7)
   What does his use of figurative language accomplish in each case?
4. How does Ababiy organize the details in his essay? What are the advantages and disadvantages of this organizational scheme?
5. Why does Ababiy end his essay by discussing the vacuum his mother used to clean the professors' house? What impression does he hope to leave readers with? Is he successful?
6. Is Ababiy's essay primarily an objective or a subjective description? Explain.
7. **Vocabulary Project.** In paragraph 5, Ababiy says that all the mirrors his mother cleaned "could probably stack up to be a minor Philip Johnson skyscraper." After looking up Philip Johnson, explain Ababiy's use of **hyperbole here**. Do you think it is effective? Why or why not?

Journal Entry

Ababiy's essay was originally written as a college application essay. For a college application essay to be successful, it has to stand out from the rest and have a distinctive voice. In addition, it has to be clear and logical and leave readers with a lasting impression. Do you think Ababiy has written a successful college application essay? What are its specific strengths? What, if anything, could Ababiy do to improve it?

Writing Workshop

1. Write a description of a place you remember from your childhood, as Ababiy does. Make sure your description conveys a clear dominant impression.
2. Write a subjective description of a scene you remember from you childhood. In your thesis statement and in your conclusion, explain how your adult impressions differ from those of your childhood.
3. **Working with Sources.** Locate images of Philip Johnson's skyscrapers online. Choose one, and then, after reading about it, write an essay in which you describe the building. (You may want to include a picture of the building in your essay.) Include an explicit thesis statement, and use descriptive details to convey your impression of the building. Be sure to document any information that you borrow from your sources and to include a works-cited page. (See Chapter 18 for information on MLA documentation.)

Combining the Patterns

In addition to containing a great deal of description, this essay also uses **narration**. Find two or three examples of narration, and explain what they add to the essay. Would Ababiy have been able to support his thesis without these passages? Explain.

Thematic Connections
- "My Mother Never Worked" (page 122)
- "Goodbye to My Twinkie Days" (page 171)
- "'Girl'" (page 251)
- "Tortillas" (page 498)

KATE CHOPIN

The Storm (Fiction)

Kate Chopin (1851–1904) was born Catherine O'Flaherty in St. Louis, Missouri. In 1870, she married Oscar Chopin and moved with him to New Orleans. After suffering business reversals, Chopin relocated to Cloutierville, Louisiana, to be closer to his extended Creole family. Oscar Chopin died suddenly in 1882, and Kate Chopin, left with six children to raise, returned to St. Louis. There she began writing short stories, many set in the colorful Creole country of central Louisiana. Her first collection, *Bayou Folk*, was published in 1894, followed by *A Night in Arcadie* in 1897. Her literary success was cut short, however, with the publication of her first novel, *The Awakening* (1899), a story of adultery that outraged many of her critics and readers because it was told sympathetically from a woman's perspective. Her work languished until the middle of the twentieth century, when it was rediscovered, largely by feminist literary scholars.

Background on Creole culture The following story was probably written about the same time as *The Awakening*, but Chopin never attempted to publish it. Its frank sexuality — franker than that depicted in her controversial novel — and its focus on an adulterous liaison between two lovers (Calixta and Alcée) would have been too scandalous for middle-class readers of the day. Even within the more liberal Creole culture in which the story is set, Calixta's actions would have been outrageous. While Creole men were expected to have mistresses, Creole wives were expected to remain true to their wedding vows. The Creoles themselves were descendants of the early Spanish and French settlers in Louisiana, and they lived lives quite separate from — and, they believed, superior to — those whose ancestors were British. Their language became a mix of French and English, as did their mode of dress and cuisine. A strong Creole influence can still be found in New Orleans and the surrounding Louisiana countryside; Mardi Gras, for example, is a Creole tradition.

I

The leaves were so still that even Bibi thought it was going to rain. Bobinôt, 1
who was accustomed to converse on terms of perfect equality with his little
son, called the child's attention to certain sombre clouds that were rolling with
sinister intention from the west, accompanied by a sullen, threatening roar.
They were at Friedheimer's store and decided to remain there till the storm had
passed. They sat within the door on two empty kegs. Bibi was four years old
and looked very wise.

"Mama'll be 'fraid, yes," he suggested with blinking eyes. 2

"She'll shut the house. Maybe she got Sylvie helpin' her this evenin'," 3
Bobinôt responded reassuringly.

"No; she ent got Sylvie. Sylvie was helpin' her yistiday," piped Bibi. 4

Bobinôt arose and going across to the counter purchased a can of shrimps,   5
of which Calixta was very fond. Then he returned to his perch on the keg and
sat stolidly holding the can of shrimps while the storm burst. It shook the
wooden store and seemed to be ripping great furrows in the distant field. Bibi
laid his little hand on his father's knee and was not afraid.

II

Calixta, at home, felt no uneasiness for their safety. She sat at a side win-   6
dow sewing furiously on a sewing machine. She was greatly occupied and did
not notice the approaching storm. But she felt very warm and often stopped to
mop her face on which the perspiration gathered in beads. She unfastened her
white sacque at the throat. It began to grow dark, and suddenly realizing the
situation she got up hurriedly and went about closing windows and doors.

Out on the small front gallery she had hung Bobinôt's Sunday clothes to   7
air and she hastened out to gather them before the rain fell. As she stepped
outside, Alcée Laballière rode in at the gate. She had not seen him very often
since her marriage, and never alone. She stood there with Bobinôt's coat in her
hands, and the big rain drops began to fall. Alcée rode his horse under the shelter of a side projection where the chickens had huddled and there were plows
and a harrow piled up in the corner.

"May I come and wait on your gallery till the storm is over, Calixta?" he   8
asked.

"Come 'long in, M'sieur Alcée."   9

His voice and her own startled her as if from a trance, and she seized   10
Bobinôt's vest. Alcée, mounting to the porch, grabbed the trousers and
snatched Bibi's braided jacket that was about to be carried away by a sudden
gust of wind. He expressed an intention to remain outside, but it was soon
apparent that he might as well have been out in the open: the water beat in
upon the boards in driving sheets, and he went inside, closing the door after
him. It was even necessary to put something beneath the door to keep the
water out.

"My! what a rain! It's good two years since it rain' like that," exclaimed   11
Calixta as she rolled up a piece of bagging and Alcée helped her to thrust it
beneath the crack.

She was a little fuller of figure than five years before when she married; but   12
she had lost nothing of her vivacity. Her blue eyes still retained their melting
quality; and her yellow hair, dishevelled by the wind and rain, kinked more
stubbornly than ever about her ears and temples.

The rain beat upon the low, shingled roof with a force and clatter that   13
threatened to break an entrance and deluge them there. They were in the din-
ing room — the sitting room — the general utility room. Adjoining was her bed
room, with Bibi's couch along side her own. The door stood open, and the
room with its white, monumental bed, its closed shutters, looked dim and
mysterious.

Alcée flung himself into a rocker and Calixta nervously began to gather up   14
from the floor the lengths of a cotton sheet which she had been sewing.

"If this keeps up, *Dieu sait** if the levees goin' to stan' it!" she exclaimed.   15

"What have you got to do with the levees?"   16

"I got enough to do! An' there's Bobinôt with Bibi out in that storm—if he   17
only didn't left Friedheimer's!"

"Let us hope, Calixta, that Bobinôt's got sense enough to come in out of a   18
cyclone."

She went and stood at the window with a greatly disturbed look on her   19
face. She wiped the frame that was clouded with moisture. It was stiflingly hot.
Alcée got up and joined her at the window, looking over her shoulder. The rain
was coming down in sheets obscuring the view of far-off cabins and enveloping
the distant wood in a gray mist. The playing of the lightning was incessant. A
bolt struck a tall chinaberry tree at the edge of the field. It filled all visible space
with a blinding glare and the crash seemed to invade the very boards they stood
upon.

Calixta put her hands to her eyes, and with a cry, staggered backward.   20
Alcée's arm encircled her, and for an instant he drew her close and spasmodi-
cally to him.

"Bonté!"** she cried, releasing herself from his encircling arm and retreat-   21
ing from the window, "the house'll go next! If I only knew w'ere Bibi was!" She
would not compose herself; she would not be seated. Alcée clasped her shoulders and looked into her face. The contact of her warm, palpitating body when
he had unthinkingly drawn her into his arms, had aroused all the old-time
infatuation and desire for her flesh.

> **"**Calixta put her
> hands to her eyes, and
> with a cry, staggered
> backward.**"**

"Calixta," he said, "don't be frightened.   22
Nothing can happen. The house is too low
to be struck, with so many tall trees standing about. There! aren't you going to be
quiet? say, aren't you?" He pushed her hair
back from her face that was warm and
steaming. Her lips were as red and moist as
pomegranate seed. Her white neck and a
glimpse of her full, firm bosom disturbed him powerfully. As she glanced up
at him the fear in her liquid blue eyes had given place to a drowsy gleam that
unconsciously betrayed a sensuous desire. He looked down into her eyes and
there was nothing for him to do but to gather her lips in a kiss. It reminded
him of Assumption.***

"Do you remember—in Assumption, Calixta?" he asked in a low voice bro-   23
ken by passion. Oh! she remembered; for in Assumption he had kissed her and
kissed and kissed her; until his senses would well nigh fail, and to save her he
would resort to a desperate flight. If she was not an immaculate dove in those
days, she was still inviolate; a passionate creature whose very defenselessness had

---

* Eds. note—God knows.
** Eds. note—Goodness!
*** Eds. note—A parish near New Orleans.

made her defense, against which his honor forbade him to prevail. Now—well, now—her lips seemed in a manner free to be tasted, as well as her round, white throat and her whiter breasts.

They did not heed the crashing torrents, and the roar of the elements made 24 her laugh as she lay in his arms. She was a revelation in that dim, mysterious chamber; as white as the couch she lay upon. Her firm, elastic flesh that was knowing for the first time its birthright, was like a creamy lily that the sun invites to contribute its breath and perfume to the undying life of the world.

The generous abundance of her passion, without guile or trickery, was like 25 a white flame which penetrated and found response in depths of his own sensuous nature that had never yet been reached.

When he touched her breasts they gave themselves up in quivering ecstasy, 26 inviting his lips. Her mouth was a fountain of delight. And when he possessed her, they seemed to swoon together at the very borderland of life's mystery.

He stayed cushioned upon her, breathless, dazed, enervated, with his heart 27 beating like a hammer upon her. With one hand she clasped his head, her lips lightly touching his forehead. The other hand stroked with a soothing rhythm his muscular shoulders.

The growl of the thunder was distant and passing away. The rain beat softly 28 upon the shingles, inviting them to drowsiness and sleep. But they dared not yield.

The rain was over; and the sun was turning the glistening green world into 29 a palace of gems. Calixta, on the gallery, watched Alcée ride away. He turned and smiled at her with a beaming face; and she lifted her pretty chin in the air and laughed aloud.

III

Bobinôt and Bibi, trudging home, stopped without at the cistern to make 30 themselves presentable.

"My! Bibi, w'at will yo' mama say! You ought to be asham'. You oughtn' 31 put on those good pants. Look at 'em! An' that mud on yo' collar! How you got that mud on yo' collar, Bibi? I never saw such a boy!" Bibi was the picture of pathetic resignation. Bobinôt was the embodiment of serious solicitude as he strove to remove from his own person and his son's the signs of their tramp over heavy roads and through wet fields. He scraped the mud off Bibi's bare legs and feet with a stick and carefully removed all traces from his heavy brogans. Then, prepared for the worst—the meeting with an over-scrupulous housewife, they entered cautiously at the back door.

Calixta was preparing supper. She had set the table and was dripping 32 coffee at the hearth. She sprang up as they came in.

"Oh, Bobinôt! You back! My! but I was uneasy. W'ere you been during the 33 rain? An' Bibi? he ain't wet? he ain't hurt?" She had clasped Bibi and was kissing him effusively. Bobinôt's explanations and apologies which he had been composing all along the way, died on his lips as Calixta felt him to see if he were dry, and seemed to express nothing but satisfaction at their safe return.

"I brought you some shrimps, Calixta," offered Bobinôt, hauling the can 34 from his ample side pocket and laying it on the table.

"Shrimps! Oh, Bobinôt! you too good fo' anything!" and she gave him a   35
smacking kiss on the cheek that resounded. "*J'vous réponds,** we'll have a feas'
tonight! umph-umph!"

Bobinôt and Bibi began to relax and enjoy themselves, and when the three   36
sated themselves at table they laughed much and so loud that anyone might
have heard them as far away as Laballière's.

IV

Alcée Laballière wrote to his wife, Clarisse, that night. It was a loving letter,   37
full of tender solicitude. He told her not to hurry back, but if she and the babies
liked it at Biloxi, to stay a month longer. He was getting on nicely; and though
he missed them, he was willing to bear the separation a while longer — realizing
that their health and pleasure were the first things to be considered.

V

As for Clarisse, she was charmed upon receiving her husband's letter. She   38
and the babies were doing well. The society was agreeable; many of her old
friends and acquaintances were at the bay. And the first free breath since her
marriage seemed to restore the pleasant liberty of her maiden days. Devoted as
she was to her husband, their intimate conjugal life was something which she
was more than willing to forego for a while.

So the storm passed and everyone was happy.   39

· · ·

Reading Literature

1. How does the storm help set in motion the action of the story? List the
   events caused by the storm.
2. Is the last line of the story to be taken literally, or is it meant to be **ironic**
   (that is, does it actually suggest the opposite meaning)? Explain.
3. What do the story's specific descriptive details tell us about Calixta?

Journal Entry

On one level, the story's title refers to the storm that takes place through much
of the story. To what else could the story's title refer?

Thematic Connections

- " 'Girl' " (page 251)
- *The Kiss* and *LOVE* (pages 387–88)
- "Sex, Lies, and Conversation" (page 408)
- "The Ways We Lie" (page 463)

---

* Eds. note — I tell you.

Writing Assignments for Description

1. Choose a character from a book, movie, or video game who you think is interesting. Write a descriptive essay conveying what makes this character so special.

2. Several of the essays in this chapter deal with places and how they affect the writers who describe them. For example, Trevor Noah describes Soweto, the Black township of Johannesburg where he lived as a child under a system of enforced racial segregation. In "The Hidden Life of Garbage," a visit to a landfill outside Morrisville, Pennsylvania, enables Heather Rogers to grasp the enormity of the task of disposing of garbage in the United States. Write an essay describing a place that has special significance for you. In addition to describing the place, make sure you explain how it has taught you something about yourself.

3. Locate some photographs of your relatives. Describe three of these pictures, including details that provide insight into the lives of the people you discuss. Use your descriptive passages to support a thesis about your family.

4. **Working with Sources.** Visit an art museum (or go to a museum site on the web), and select a painting that interests you. Study it carefully, and then write an essay-length description of it. Before you write, decide how you will organize your details and whether you will write a subjective or objective description. If possible, include a photograph of the painting in your essay. Be sure to document the photograph and to include a works-cited page. (See Chapter 18 for information on MLA documentation.)

5. Select an object you are familiar with, and write an objective description of it. Include a diagram.

6. Assume you are writing an email to someone in another country who knows little about life in the United States. Describe to this person something you consider typically American — for example, a state fair or a food court in a shopping mall.

7. Visit your college library, and write a brochure in which you describe the reference area. Be specific, and select an organizing scheme before you begin your description. Your purpose is to acquaint students with some of the reference materials they will use. If possible, include a diagram that will help orient students to this section of the library.

8. Describe your neighborhood to a visitor who knows nothing about it. Include as much specific detail as you can.

9. After reading "Soweto," write a description of a sight or scene that fascinated, surprised, or shocked you. Your description should explain why you were so deeply affected by what you saw.

10. Write an essay describing an especially frightening horror film. What specific sights and sounds make this film so horrifying? Include a thesis statement assessing the film's success as a horror film. (Be careful not to simply summarize the plot of the film.)

Collaborative Activity for Description

Working in groups of three or four students, go to Google Maps, Street View, and select a city you would like to visit. Then, as a group, write a description of a street, a building, or even a block in that city, making sure to include as much physical detail as possible.

Exemplification

What Is Exemplification?

Exemplification uses one or more particular cases, or **examples**, to illustrate or explain a general point or an abstract concept. In the following paragraph from *Sexism and Language*, Alleen Pace Nilsen uses a series of well-chosen examples to illustrate her statement that the armed forces use words that have positive masculine connotations to encourage recruitment.

Topic sentence

The armed forces, particularly the Marines, use the positive masculine connotation as part of their recruitment psychology. They promote the idea that to join the Marines (or the Army, Navy, or Air Force) guarantees that you will become a man. But this brings up a problem, because much of the work that is necessary to keep a large organization running is what is traditionally thought of as *woman's work*. Now, how can the Marines ask someone who has signed up for a *man-sized job* to do *woman's work*? Since they can't, they euphemize and give the jobs titles that are more prestigious or, at least, don't make people think of females. Waitresses are called *orderlies*, secretaries are called *clerk-typists*, nurses are called *medics*, assistants are called *adjutants*, and cleaning up an area is called *policing* the area. The same kind of word glorification is used in civilian life to bolster a man's ego when he is doing such tasks as cooking and sewing. For example, a *chef* has higher prestige than a *cook* and a *tailor* has higher prestige than a *seamstress*.

Series of related examples

Using Exemplification

When watching interviews on television (or on YouTube or other online sites) or listening to classroom discussions, you have probably noticed that the most effective exchanges occur when participants support their points with specific examples. Sweeping generalizations and vague statements are not nearly as effective as specific observations, anecdotes, details, and opinions. It is one thing to say, "The mayor is corrupt and should not be reelected" and another to illustrate your point by saying, "The mayor should not be reelected because he has fired two city workers who refused to contribute to his campaign fund, has put his family and friends on the city payroll, and has used public employees to make improvements to his home." The same principle applies to writing: many of the most effective essays use examples extensively. Exemplification is used in every kind of writing situation to *explain and clarify*, to *add interest*, and to *persuade*.

Using Examples to Explain and Clarify

Writers often use examples to explain and clarify their ideas. For instance, on a midterm exam in a film course, you might write, "Even though horror movies seem modern, they really aren't." You may think your statement is perfectly clear, but if that is all you say about horror movies, you should not be surprised if your exam comes back with a question mark in the margin next to this sentence. After all, you have only made a general statement about your subject. It is not specific, nor does it anticipate readers' questions about how horror movies are not modern. To be certain your audience knows exactly what you mean, state your point precisely: "Even though horror movies seem modern, two of the most memorable ones are adaptations of nineteenth-century Gothic novels." Then, use examples to ensure clarity and avoid ambiguity. For example, you could illustrate your point by discussing two films—*Frankenstein*, directed by James Whale, and *Dracula*, directed by Todd Browning—and linking them to the nineteenth-century novels on which they are based. With the benefit of these specific examples, readers would know what you mean: that the literary roots of such movies are in the past, not that their cinematic techniques or production methods are dated. Moreover, readers would know exactly which horror movies you are discussing.

Using Examples to Add Interest

Writers also use well-chosen examples to add interest. Brent Staples does this in his essay "Just Walk On By," which appears later in this chapter. In itself, the claim that during his time away from home Staples became "thoroughly familiar with the language of fear" is not very interesting. This statement becomes compelling, however, when Staples illustrates it with specific examples—experiences he had while walking the streets at night. For example, his presence apparently inspired so much fear in people that they locked their car doors as he walked past or crossed to the other side of the street when they saw him approaching.

When you use exemplification, choose examples that are interesting as well as pertinent. Test the effectiveness of your examples by putting yourself in your readers' place. If you don't find your essay lively and absorbing, chances are your readers won't either. If this is the case, try to add more thought-provoking and spirited examples. After all, your goal is to communicate ideas to your readers, and imaginative examples can make the difference between an engrossing essay and one that is a chore to read.

Using Examples to Persuade

Although you can use examples to explain or to add interest, examples are also an effective way of persuading people that what you are saying is reasonable and worth considering. A few well-chosen examples can provide effective support for otherwise unconvincing general statements. For instance, a broad statement that school districts across the country cannot cope with the numerous students with limited English skills is one that needs support. If you make such a statement in an essay, you need to back it up with appropriate examples. For instance, in the United States there are currently more than five million English-language learners in public schools, and they represent almost 10 percent of all public-school students. In California alone, the more than 1.3 million students who lack proficiency in English make up more than 21 percent of the state's public elementary and secondary school enrollment. Similarly, a statement in a biology essay that DDT should continue to be banned is unconvincing without persuasive examples such as these to support it:

- Although DDT has been banned since December 31, 1972, scientists are finding traces of it in the eggs of various fish and waterfowl.
- Certain lakes and streams cannot be used for sport and recreation because DDT levels are dangerously high, presumably because of farmland runoff.
- Because of its stability as a compound, DDT does not degrade quickly; therefore, existing residues will threaten the environment well into the twenty-first century.

Planning an Exemplification Essay

Developing a Thesis Statement

The **thesis statement** of an exemplification essay makes a point that the rest of the essay will support with examples. This statement usually identifies your topic as well as the main point you want to make about it.

The examples you gather during the invention stage of the writing process can help you develop your thesis. By doing so, they can help you test your ideas as well as the ideas of others. For instance, suppose you plan to write an essay for a composition class about students' writing skills. Your tentative thesis is that writing well is an inborn talent and that teachers can do little to help people write better. But is that really true? Has it been true in your own life? To test your point, you brainstorm about the various teachers you have had who tried to help you improve your writing.

As you assemble your list, you remember a teacher you had in high school. She was strict, required lots of writing, and seemed to accept nothing less than perfection. At the time, neither you nor your classmates liked her, but looking back, you recall her one-on-one conferences, her organized lessons, her insightful comments on your essays, and her timely replies to your emails. You realize that after completing her class, you felt much more comfortable writing. When examining some essays you saved, you are surprised to see how much your writing actually improved during that year. These examples lead you to reevaluate your ideas and to revise your thesis:

> Even though some people seem to have a natural flair for writing, a good teacher can make a difference.

Providing Enough Examples

Unfortunately, no general rule exists to tell you when you have enough examples. The number you need depends on your thesis statement. If, for instance, your thesis is that an educational institution, like a business, needs careful financial management, a single detailed examination of one college or university could provide all the examples you need to support your point.

If, however, your thesis is that conflict between sons and fathers is a major theme in Franz Kafka's writing, more than one example would be necessary. A single example would show only that the theme is present in *one* of Kafka's works. In this case, the more examples you include, the more effectively you support your point.

For some thesis statements, however, even several examples would not be enough. Examples alone, for instance, could not demonstrate convincingly that children from small families are more successful than children from large families. This thesis would have to be supported with a **statistical study** — that is, by collecting and interpreting numerical data representing a great many examples.

Choosing a Fair Range of Examples

Selecting a sufficient **range of examples** is just as important as choosing an appropriate number. If you want to persuade readers that Steve Jobs was a visionary innovator, you should choose examples from several stages of his career. Likewise, if you want to convince readers that outdoor advertising is dangerous because it distracts drivers, you should discuss an area larger than your immediate neighborhood. Your objective in each case is to choose a cross section of examples to represent the full range of your topic.

Similarly, if you want to argue for a ban on smoking in all public spaces, you should not limit your examples to sports stadiums. To be convincing, you should include examples involving many public places, such as parks, beaches, and sidewalks. For the same reason, one person's experience is not enough to support a general conclusion involving many people unless you can clearly establish that the experience is typical.

If you decide you cannot cite a fair range of examples that support your thesis, reexamine it. Rather than switching to a new topic, try to narrow your thesis. After all, the only way your essay will be convincing is if your readers believe that your thesis is adequately supported by your examples and that your examples fairly represent the scope of your topic.

To be convincing, you must not only *choose* examples effectively but also *use* them effectively. You should keep your thesis statement in mind as you write, taking care not to get so involved with one example that you digress from your main point. No matter how carefully developed, no matter how specific and lively, your examples accomplish nothing if they do not support your essay's main idea.

Using Transitions

Be sure to use transitional words and phrases to introduce your examples. Without them, readers will have difficulty seeing the connection between an example and the general statement it is illustrating. In some cases, transitions will help you connect examples to your thesis statement (*"Another* successful program for the homeless provides telephone answering services for job seekers"). In other cases, transitions will link examples to topic sentences (*"For instance*, I have written articles for my college newspaper"). In exemplification essays, the most frequently used transitions include *for example, for instance, in fact, namely, specifically, that is,* and *thus.* (A more complete list of transitions appears on page 56.)

Structuring an Exemplification Essay

Exemplification essays usually begin with an **introduction** that includes the *thesis statement*, which is supported by examples in the body of the essay. Each **body paragraph** may develop a separate example, present a point illustrated by several brief examples, or explore one part of a single extended example that is developed throughout the essay. The **conclusion** reinforces the essay's main idea, perhaps restating the thesis. At times, however, variations of this basic pattern are advisable and even necessary. For instance, beginning your essay with a striking example might stimulate your reader's interest and curiosity; ending with one might vividly reinforce your thesis.

Exemplification presents one special organizational problem. If you do not select your examples carefully and arrange them effectively, your essay can become a thesis statement followed by a list or by ten or fifteen brief, choppy paragraphs. One way to avoid this problem is to develop your best examples fully in separate paragraphs and then discard the others. Another effective strategy is to group related examples together in one paragraph.

Within each paragraph, you can arrange examples **chronologically**, beginning with those that occurred first and moving to those that occurred later. You can also arrange examples **in order of increasing complexity**, beginning with the simplest and moving to the most difficult or complex. Finally, you can arrange examples **in order of importance**, beginning with those that are less significant and moving to those that are most significant or persuasive.

The following informal outline for an essay evaluating the nursing care at a hospital illustrates one way to arrange examples. Notice how the writer presents examples in order of increasing importance under three general headings: *patient rooms*, *emergency room*, and *clinics*.

SAMPLE OUTLINE: Exemplification

INTRODUCTION

Thesis statement: Because of its focus on the patient, the nursing care at Montgomery Hospital can serve as a model for other medical facilities.

FIRST GROUP OF EXAMPLES: CARE IN PATIENT ROOMS

- Being responsive
- Establishing rapport
- Delivering bedside care

SECOND GROUP OF EXAMPLES: CARE IN EMERGENCY ROOM

- Staffing treatment rooms
- Circulating among patients in the waiting room
- Maintaining good working relationships with physicians

THIRD GROUP OF EXAMPLES: CARE IN CLINICS

- Preparing patients
- Assisting during treatment
- Instructing patients after treatment

CONCLUSION

Restatement of thesis (in different words) or review of key examples

Revising an Exemplification Essay

When you revise an exemplification essay, consider the items on Checklist: Revising on page 68. In addition, pay special attention to the items on the following checklist, which apply specifically to exemplification essays.

✔ **REVISION CHECKLIST** **EXEMPLIFICATION**

☐ Does your assignment call for exemplification?
☐ Does your essay have a clear thesis statement that identifies the point you will illustrate?
☐ Do your examples explain and clarify your thesis statement?
☐ Have you provided enough examples?
☐ Have you used a range of examples?
☐ Are your examples persuasive?
☐ Do your examples add interest?
☐ Have you used transitional words and phrases that reinforce the connection between your examples and your thesis statement?
☐ Do your examples require sources and documentation for support?

Editing an Exemplification Essay

When you edit your exemplification essay, follow the guidelines on the editing checklists on pages 85, 88, and 92. In addition, focus on the grammar, mechanics, and punctuation issues that are most relevant to exemplification essays. One of these issues — using commas in a series — is discussed here.

🔍 **GRAMMAR IN CONTEXT** **USING COMMAS IN A SERIES**

When you write an exemplification essay, you often use a **series of examples** to support a statement or to illustrate a point. When you use a series of three or more examples in a sentence, you should separate them with commas.

- Always use commas to separate three or more items — words, phrases, or clauses — in a series.

  In "Just Walk On By," Brent Staples says, "I was <u>surprised</u>, <u>embarrassed</u>, and <u>dismayed</u> all at once" (232).

  In "Just Walk On By," Staples observes that the woman thought she was being stalked <u>by a mugger</u>, <u>by a rapist</u>, or <u>by something worse</u> (232).

  <u>"Waitresses are called *orderlies*, secretaries are called *clerk-typists*, nurses are called *medics*, assistants are called *adjutants*, and cleaning up an area is called *policing* the area</u>" (Nilsen 201).

NOTE: Although newspaper and magazine writers routinely leave out the comma before the last item in a series of three or more items, you should always include this comma in your college writing.

- Do not use a comma after the final element in a series of three or more items.

INCORRECT:	Staples was <u>shocked, horrified</u>, and <u>disillusioned</u>, to be taken for a mugger.
CORRECT:	Staples was <u>shocked, horrified</u>, and <u>disillusioned</u> to be taken for a mugger.

- Do not use commas if all the elements in a series of three or more items are separated by coordinating conjunctions (*and, or, but*, and so on).

In her essay, Judith Ortiz Cofer mentions the three ways that Hispanic women are stereotyped in the United States: they are seen <u>as exotics</u> or <u>as sexual firebrands</u> or <u>as housemaids</u>. (*no commas*)

✔ **EDITING CHECKLIST** **EXEMPLIFICATION**

☐ Have you used commas to separate three or more items in a series?
☐ Have you made sure not to use a comma after the last element in a series?
☐ Have you made sure not to use a comma in a series with items separated by coordinating conjunctions?
☐ Are all the elements in a series stated in **parallel** terms (see page 375)?

A STUDENT WRITER: Exemplification

Exemplification is frequently used in nonacademic writing situations, such as business reports, memos, and proposals. One of the most important situations for using exemplification is in a letter you write to apply for a job.* Kristy Bredin's letter of application to a prospective employer follows.

---

* Eds. note — In business letters, paragraphs are not indented and extra space is added between paragraphs.

1028 Geissinger Street
Bethlehem, PA 18018
September 8, 2020

Kim Goldstein, Internship Coordinator
Rolling Stone
1290 Avenue of the Americas
New York, NY 10104-0298

Dear Ms. Goldstein:

Introduction

I am writing to apply for the paid internship that   1
you posted on RollingStone.com. I believe that my education and

Thesis statement

my experience in publishing qualify me for the position you
advertised.

Examples

I am currently a senior at Moravian College, where I am majoring   2
in English (with a concentration in creative writing) and music.
Throughout my college career, I have maintained a 3.6 average. After
I graduate in May, I would like to find a full-time job in publishing.
For this reason, I am very interested in your internship. It would not
only give me additional editorial and administrative experience, but it
would also give me insight into a large-scale publishing operation. An
internship at RollingStone.com would also enable to me to read, edit,
and possibly write articles about popular music — a subject I know a
lot about.

Examples

Throughout college, I have been involved in writing and editing. I   3
have served as both secretary and president of the Literary Society
and have written, edited, and published its annual newsletter. I have
also worked as a tutor in Moravian's Writing Center; as a literature
editor for the *Manuscript*, Moravian's literary magazine; and as a
features editor for the *Comeneian*, the student newspaper. In these
jobs I have gained a good deal of practical experience in publishing
as well as insight into dealing with people. In addition, I acquired
professional editing experience as well as experience posting across
platforms this past semester, when I worked as an intern for Taylor
and Francis Group (Routledge) Publishing in New York.

Conclusion   I believe that my education and my publishing experience make me   4
a good candidate for your position. As your ad requested, I have
enclosed my résumé, information on Moravian College, and several
writing samples for your consideration. You can contact me by phone
at (484) 625-6731 or by email at stkab@moravian.edu. I will be available for an interview anytime after September 23. I look forward to
meeting with you to discuss my qualifications.

Sincerely,

Kristy Bredin

Kristy Bredin

Points for Special Attention

Organization

Exemplification is ideally suited for letters of application. The best way
Kristy Bredin can support her claims about her qualifications for the internship at RollingStone.com is to give examples of her educational and professional qualifications. For this reason, the body of her letter is divided into two
categories — her educational record and her editorial experience.

Each of the body paragraphs has a clear purpose and function. The second paragraph contains two examples pertaining to Kristy's educational
record. The third paragraph contains examples of her editorial experience.
These examples tell the prospective employer what qualifies Kristy for the
internship. Within these two body paragraphs, she arranges her examples in
order of increasing importance. Because her practical experience as an editor
relates directly to the position she is applying for, Kristy considers this her
strongest point and presents it last.

Kristy ends her letter on a strong note, expressing her willingness to be
interviewed and giving the first date she will be available for an interview.
Because people remember best what they read last, a strong conclusion is
essential here, just as it is in other writing situations.

Persuasive Examples

To support a thesis convincingly, examples should convey specific information, not generalizations. Saying "I am a good student who is not afraid of
responsibility" means very little. It is far better to say, as Kristy does, "Throughout my college career, I have maintained a 3.6 average" and "I have served as
both secretary and president of the Literary Society." A letter of application

should specifically show a prospective employer how your strengths and background correspond to the employer's needs; well-chosen examples can help you accomplish this goal.

Focus on Revision

After reading her letter, the students in Kristy's peer-editing group identified several areas they thought needed work.

One student said Kristy should have mentioned that she had taken a desktop publishing course as an elective and worked with publishing and graphics software when she was the features editor of the student newspaper. Kristy agreed that this expertise would make her a more attractive candidate for the job and thought she could work these examples into her third paragraph.

Another student asked Kristy to explain how her experience as secretary and president of the Literary Society relates to the job she is applying for. If her purpose is to show that she can assume responsibility, she should say so; if it is to illustrate that she can supervise others, she should make that point clear.

A third student suggested that Kristy expand the discussion of her internship with Taylor and Francis Publishing in New York. Specific examples of her duties there would be persuasive because they would give her prospective employer a clear idea of her experience. (A peer-editing worksheet for exemplification can be found on page 216.)

Working with Sources

Kristy's instructor recommended that Kristy specifically refer to the ad to which she was responding. He said that this strategy would help Kristy's readers — potential employers — see that she was tailoring her letter to the specific job at RollingStone.com. Kristy considered this suggestion and decided to quote the language of the ad in her letter.

A STUDENT WRITER: Exemplification

The following essay, by Zoe Goldfarb, was written for a composition class in response to the following assignment: "Write an essay about a problem that would be of interest to college students. If you can, use two or three outside sources to help you support your points. Be sure to include documentation as well as a works-cited page."

Food Insecurity on Campus

There have always been jokes about college students' unhealthy eating habits, from undergrads living on cheap ramen noodles to first-year students gaining the "freshman fifteen." However, beyond the jokes lies an ugly truth: a large number of college students experience food insecurity. In other words, they do not have

1

consistent access to enough food to pursue their studies and to lead active, healthy lives. At first glance, it would seem that this should be a problem that only occurs in developing countries, but a 2016 study found that up to "48 percent of [college] students faced food insecurity in the previous month" (Williams). That is nearly half of the student population. Thankfully, many colleges and universities are aware of this situation and have begun implementing strategies that will help those students who are experiencing food insecurity.

The first question is how did this situation come about? Recently, the *New York Times* collected stories of students facing food insecurity for an article entitled "Tuition or Dinner? Nearly Half of College Students Surveyed in a New Report Are Going Hungry." The article describes an undergraduate student who "has been so delirious from hunger, he's caught himself walking down the street not realizing where he's going" and another student who often "decides to go to sleep rather than deal with her hunger pangs" (Latermen). How is such a situation possible? According to Joseph P. Williams at *U.S. News*, a college education costs more than the financial aid that federal and state grants provide, and the cost just keeps rising. For this reason, many students—especially low-income students—are forced to spend so much money on tuition, books, and living expenses that they have little left over for food and other essentials.

The most common solution to the problem of food insecurity has been for universities to create food panties. For example, Columbia University recently partnered with the national organization Swipe Out Hunger to open a food pantry on campus. Columbia is located in Manhattan, one of the most expensive cities in which to live in the United States, especially when the high price of food is considered. In its mission statement, the Columbia University food pantry says that it "envisions a campus in which every student, regardless of their affiliation or socioeconomic status, has sufficient access to nutritious food" ("About Us"). To accomplish this end, the pantry has instituted a point system that allows students with different needs (for example, those with families) to take different amounts of food from the pantry, insuring a fair and easy system for everyone who needs help. Many other colleges—for example, the University of Maryland and Michigan State University—have also started food panties. In fact, currently over 300 colleges are members of the College and University Food Bank Alliance (Williams).

Colleges are also addressing food insecurity by encouraging students to sign up for the Supplemental Nutrition Assistance Program (SNAP). SNAP, formerly known as food stamps, is a federal program that offers food benefits to low-income individuals and families. As such, it enables eligible people to obtain food items at their local grocery stores. The City University of New York (CUNY) began connecting students to SNAP in 2009, and since then, over 122,000 CUNY students have been assisted, "each of whom have received about $3,000 worth of benefits each year" (Laterman). The SNAP program is particularly useful for nontraditional students, especially those that have children or other dependents. The one drawback of SNAP, however, is that in many states people have to work a certain number of hours to receive benefits. This can be a problem for students carrying a full course load.

Another way colleges are dealing with food insecurity is to partner with   5
local farms and community gardens. In 2018, for example, CUNY partnered with local farms, one of which "produced 3000 pounds of food that was handed out to over 1,000 students" (Laterman). This program is a healthy and convenient alternative to handing out money to be spent at grocery stores of varying quality, where sometimes the items that cost the least can also be the most unhealthy. Many colleges across the country are developing ambitious initiatives to source food locally. Not only do these programs help small farmers but they also enable students to get the freshest possible products at the lowest cost.

Although food insecurity is a growing problem all across the United States,   6
many colleges are aware of the problem and are trying a variety of solutions. From food banks to food distribution programs to partnering with local farms, schools are trying to meet the food needs of their students. Perhaps in time food insecurity will no longer be so widespread, but for now, there is a pressing need to combat this hardship. It is clear that when students are hungry, their academic achievement suffers, and in the long run, so does the rest of society by being deprived of the potential these students represent.

Works Cited

"About Us." *The Food Pantry at Columbia*. 14 Oct. 2019, thefoodpantry.studentgroups
    .columbia.edu/content/about-us.

Laterman, Kaya. "Tuition or Dinner? Nearly Half of College Students Surveyed in a
    New Report Are Going Hungry." *New York Times*, 2 May 2019, www.nytimes
    .com/2019/05/02/nyregion/hunger-college-food-insecurity.html.

Williams, Joseph P. "Fighting Food Insecurity on College Campuses." *US News & World
    Report*, www.usnews.com/news/healtiest-communities/articles/2019-02-04/a-fight
    -against-food-insecurity-hunger-on-college-campuses.

Points for Special Attention

Organization

Zoe Goldfarb begins her introduction by acknowledging the preconceived ideas that people have about college students and food. She then
introduces the issue of food insecurity by saying that beyond the jokes is a
serious problem. She realizes that some of her readers may not be familiar
with her topic, so she provides background information about the issue. Her
opening paragraph prepares reader for her thesis that many colleges are aware
of the situation and are addressing it in several ways.

In her first body paragraph, Zoe examines how food insecurity on college campuses has come about. She begins by describing the experiences of
two students who are experiencing food insecurity. She then gives the reasons
why food insecurity has become such a problem, especially for low-income
students.

In paragraphs 3, 4, and 5, Zoe uses examples to illustrate the different
ways that colleges are addressing food insecurity. In paragraph 3, she explains
the most common approach — food pantries. She then presents one example,
the food pantry at Columbia University, to illustrate this approach. She ends
the paragraph with a statistic that indicates how many colleges have established food pantries. In paragraph 4, Zoe examines SNAP, the Supplemental
Nutrition Assistance Program. She explains how the City University of New
York encourages students who are experiencing food insecurity to sign up for
this program. Finally, in paragraph 5, she talks about how CUNY and other
colleges are partnering with local farmers to provide fresh, low-cost food to
students.

Zoe concludes her essay by restating the ways that colleges are addressing
food insecurity. She ends by making a point that she hopes will stay with her
readers after they have finished the essay.

Working with Sources

Because the assignment asked students to use two or three outside
sources, Zoe looked for essays online that had to do with food insecurity. Her
Google search using the key words "food insecurity" yielded a number of
useful results. She narrowed her search by looking specifically at recent articles, which led her to the three essays she used as sources. Once Zoe decided
on her sources, she took notes and was careful to integrate this material
smoothly into her essay. She also made sure she documented her sources and
did not unintentionally commit plagiarism. Finally, she included bibliographic information for the essay in a works-cited page at the end of her essay.
(See Chapter 18 for information on MLA documentation.)

Enough Examples

No single example, no matter how graphic, could support this essay's thesis. To establish the scope of the problem, Zoe includes a statistic in her first

body paragraph. She then goes on to discuss the ways that various colleges are addressing the issue of food insecurity. Throughout the rest of her essay, Zoe uses a number of examples to support her points. Although additional examples would have added to the essay, the ones she uses are compelling enough to support her thesis that students who experience food insecurity face hardship and that many colleges are trying to solve this problem.

Range of Examples

In her essay, Zoe considers the most widely used ways of addressing the food insecurity of students and uses examples to explain each method. She selects examples that illustrate the full range of her subject and is careful not to include atypical examples that apply to just a single school or locality. She also assumes that her readers do not know much about food insecurity. For this reason, she uses examples that will help her make her points and enable readers to understand the problem.

Effective Examples

All Zoe's examples support her thesis statement. As she develops these examples, she never loses sight of her main idea; consequently, she does not get sidetracked with irrelevant discussions. She also avoids the temptation to preach to her readers about the injustice of food insecurity. By allowing her examples to speak for themselves, Zoe gives readers a clear idea of the problem and what colleges are doing to solve it.

Focus on Revision

After reading this draft, a classmate suggested that Zoe go into more detail about how food insecurity became such a big problem for college students. For example, what is the average cost of tuition? What expenses do grants and loans cover? How much money is needed to pay for the expenses that they do they not cover?

Zoe thought she could add more examples of colleges that encourage students to enroll in SNAP. In addition, she thought she should give more information about the work requirements necessary to qualify for this program. How many hours would a student have to work to get benefits? Is there any possibility of having these requirements lessened or waived for college students?

In paragraph 5, Zoe thought she could be more specific about the number of colleges that partner with local farmers. She also thought she should explore the difficulties of implementing this type of program.

Finally, Zoe decided to follow the advice of another student to include one or two comments by students who were benefiting from the programs she described. She already had this information in her notes but originally had decided against including it.

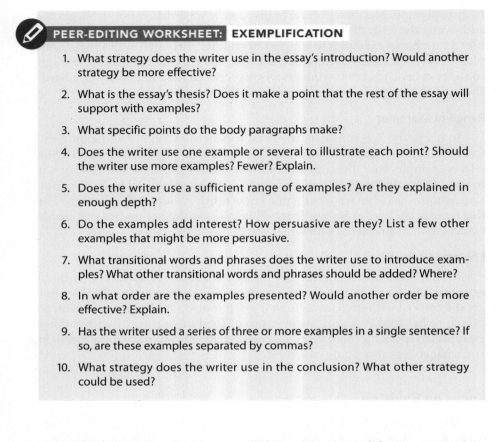

PEER-EDITING WORKSHEET: EXEMPLIFICATION

1. What strategy does the writer use in the essay's introduction? Would another strategy be more effective?

2. What is the essay's thesis? Does it make a point that the rest of the essay will support with examples?

3. What specific points do the body paragraphs make?

4. Does the writer use one example or several to illustrate each point? Should the writer use more examples? Fewer? Explain.

5. Does the writer use a sufficient range of examples? Are they explained in enough depth?

6. Do the examples add interest? How persuasive are they? List a few other examples that might be more persuasive.

7. What transitional words and phrases does the writer use to introduce examples? What other transitional words and phrases should be added? Where?

8. In what order are the examples presented? Would another order be more effective? Explain.

9. Has the writer used a series of three or more examples in a single sentence? If so, are these examples separated by commas?

10. What strategy does the writer use in the conclusion? What other strategy could be used?

The selections in this chapter all depend on exemplification to explain and clarify, to add interest, or to persuade. The first selection, a visual text, is followed by questions designed to illustrate how exemplification can operate in visual form.

Four Inventions (Photographs)

Bettmann/Getty Images

Found Image Holdings Inc/Corbis Historical/
Getty Images

H. Armstrong Roberts/Retrofile/Getty Images

Mark Madeo/Future Publishing/Getty Images

Although they don't look much like the versions we know today, these early versions of the telephone, phonograph, television set, and home computer were world-changing inventions.

• • •

Reading Images

1. How would you describe each of the four inventions pictured on the previous page? List the prominent features of each, and then write two or three sentences that describe each invention.
2. After studying the four pictures (and reviewing your answer to question 1), write a one-sentence general statement that sums up your ideas about these inventions. For example, how have these inventions changed people's lives? Were these changes good, bad, or both? What would the world be like without each one of them?
3. List several more examples that support the general statement you made in question 2.

Journal Entry

What current inventions have changed your life? Write a paragraph answering this question. Use your answers to support the main idea in your topic sentence.

Thematic Connections

- "Stability in Motion" (page 179)
- "Should Driverless Cars Kill Their Own Passengers to Save a Pedestrian?" (page 219)
- "I'm Your Teacher, Not Your Internet Service Provider" (page 402)
- "Reducing Your Carbon Footprint Still Matters" (page 589)

OLIVIA GOLDHILL

Should Driverless Cars Kill Their Own Passengers to Save a Pedestrian?

Brooklyn-based journalist Olivia Goldhill writes about data, artificial intelligence, philosophy, and brain sciences for *Quartz*, a business media company and publication. Previously, she was a reporter and features writer for the *Daily Telegraph*. Goldhill grew up in England, attended Harvard University, and earned a master's degree in newspaper journalism from the City University of London.

Background on self-driving cars The self-driving car has long been a staple of science fiction. The first driverless automobile, a radio-controlled vehicle designed by electrical engineer Francis Houdina, debuted in 1925 when the "American Wonder" impressed New York City spectators on Broadway and Fifth Avenue before crashing into another car. In the years since, many large companies and institutions — including Japan's Tsukuba Mechanical Engineering Laboratory, Carnegie Mellon University, Mercedes-Benz, Google, and Tesla — have sought to create a safe self-driving automobile. The benefits of these cars are clear: they would eliminate driver error, help decrease traffic, free passengers to do other things while commuting, and reduce the need for parking. But they also raise important questions. For example, who would be liable if a self-driving car were in an accident — the driver or the manufacturer? These cars would likely contain hackable technologies that could create risks for both passengers and manufacturers. It is also unclear how these vehicles would function in situations where circumstances on the road change — for example, when they encounter roadblocks, work crews, crossing guards, or inclement weather.

1   Imagine you're in a self-driving car, heading towards a collision with a group of pedestrians. The only other option is to drive off a cliff. What should the car do?

2   Philosophers have been debating a similar moral conundrum for years, but the discussion has a new practical application with the advent of self-driving cars, which are expected to be commonplace on the road in the coming years.

3   Specifically, self-driving cars from Google, Tesla, and others will need to address a much-debated thought experiment called the Trolley Problem. In the original set-up, a trolley is headed towards five people. You can pull a lever to switch to a different track, where just one person will be in the trolley's path. Should you kill the one to save five?

4   Many people believe they should, but this moral instinct is complicated by other scenarios. For example: You're standing on a footbridge above the track and can see a trolley hurtling towards five people. There's a fat man standing next to you, and you know that his weight would be enough to stop the trolley. Is it moral to push him off the bridge to save five people?

Go Off the Cliff

When non-philosophers were asked how driverless cars should handle a situation where the death of either passenger or pedestrian is inevitable, most believed that cars should be programmed to avoid hurting bystanders, according to a paper uploaded to the scientific research site Arxiv.

> "Imagine you're in a self-driving car, heading towards a collision with a group of pedestrians." 5

The researchers, led by psychologist Jean-François Bonnefon from the Toulouse School of Economics, presented a series of collision scenarios to around 900 participants in total. They found that 75 percent of people thought the car should always swerve and kill the passenger, even to save just one pedestrian. 6

Among the philosophers debating moral theory, this solution is complicated by various arguments that appeal to our moral intuitions but point to different answers. The Trolley Problem is fiercely debated precisely because it is a clear example of the tension between our moral duty not to cause harm, and our moral duty not to do bad things. 7

The former school of thought argues that the moral action is that which causes the maximum happiness to the maximum number of people, a theory known as utilitarianism. Based on this reasoning, a driverless car should take whatever action would save the most number of people, regardless of whether they are passenger or pedestrian. If five people inside the car would be killed in a collision with the wall, then the driverless car should continue on even if it means hitting an innocent pedestrian. The reasoning may sound simplistic, but the details of Utilitarian theory, as set out by John Stuart Mill, are difficult to dispute. 8

Who Is Responsible?

However, other philosophers who have weighed in on the Trolley Problem argue that utilitarianism is a crude approach, and that the correct moral action doesn't just evaluate the consequences of the action, but also considers who is morally responsible. 9

Helen Frowe, a professor of practical philosophy at Stockholm University, who has given a series of lectures on the Trolley Problem, says self-driving car manufacturers should program vehicles to protect innocent bystanders, as those in the car have more responsibility for any danger. 10

"We have pretty stringent obligations not to kill people," she tells Quartz. "If you decided to get into a self-driving car, then that's imposing the risk." 11

The ethics are particularly complicated when Frowe's argument points to a different moral action than utilitarian theory. For example, a self-driving car could contain four passengers, or perhaps two children in the backseat. How does the moral calculus change? 12

If the car's passengers are all adults, Frowe believes that they should die to avoid hitting one pedestrian, because the adults have chosen to be in the car and so have more moral responsibility. 13

Although Frowe believes that children are not morally responsible, she still argues that it's not morally permissible to kill one person in order to save the lives of two children. 14

"As you increase the number of children, it will be easier to justify killing   15
the one. But in cases where there are just adults in the car, you'd need to be able
to save a lot of them — more than ten, maybe a busload — to make it moral to
kill one."

It's Better to Do Nothing

Pity the poor software designers (and, undoubtedly, lawyers) who are   16
trying to figure this out, because it can get much more complicated. What if a
pedestrian acted recklessly, or even stepped out in front of the car with the
intention of making it swerve, thereby killing the passenger? (Hollywood
screenwriters, start your engines.) Since driverless cars cannot judge pedestrians' intentions, this ethical wrinkle is practically very difficult to take into
account.

Philosophers are far from a solution despite the scores of papers that   17
debate every tiny ethical detail. For example, is it more immoral to actively
swerve the car into a lone pedestrian than to simply do nothing and allow the
vehicle to hit someone? Former UCLA philosophy professor Warren Quinn
explicitly rejected the utilitarian idea that morality should maximize happiness. Instead, he argued that humans have a duty to respect other persons
(pdf), and so an action that directly and intentionally causes harm is ethically
worse than an indirect action that happens to lead to harm.

Of course, cars will very rarely be in a situation where there are only two   18
courses of action, and the car can compute, with 100 percent certainty, that
either decision will lead to death. But with enough driverless cars on the road,
it's far from implausible that software will someday have to make such a choice
between causing harm to a pedestrian or passenger. Any safe driverless car
should be able to recognize and balance these risks.

Self-driving car manufacturers have yet to reveal their stance on the issue.   19
But, given the lack of philosophical unanimity, it seems unlikely they'll find a
universally acceptable solution. As for philosophers, time will tell if they enjoy
having their theories tested in a very real way.

•   •   •

Comprehension

1. What is the trolley problem? How does it apply to driverless cars?
2. According to Goldhill, how do nonphilosophers address the trolley
   problem? How do their responses differ from those of philosophers?
3. What is utilitarianism? Why do some philosophers consider it "a crude
   approach" (9)?
4. According to Helen Frowe, a professor of philosophy quoted by Goldhill, why should manufacturers of driverless cars be more concerned with
   protecting bystanders than passengers? How does the presence of children
   in a driverless car complicate this situation?
5. Why, according to Goldhill, should we pity the software designers and
   lawyers who are trying to address the trolley problem?
6. Does Goldhill think that the trolley problem can ever be solved? Explain.

Purpose and Audience

1. How does Goldhill expect her readers to react to her essay? How do you know?
2. Is this essay primarily about driverless cars, or is it about something else? Explain.
3. Does Goldhill state her thesis? If so, where? If not, what do you think her thesis is?
4. What does Goldhill hope to accomplish with her essay? Does she want to change people's minds? Inform them? Move them to action? Something else?

Style and Structure

1. This essay begins with a brief three-sentence introduction. Why do you think Goldhill begins this way? Is it an effective opening?
2. Throughout her essay, Goldhill includes headings. What information do these headings provide? Are they helpful, or do they simply get in the way?
3. Does Goldhill provide enough examples? Does she provide a sufficient range of examples? Explain.
4. What determines how Goldhill presents her examples? Are they presented in order of importance? In order of complexity? According to some other organizing principle?
5. **Vocabulary Project.** In paragraph 8, Goldhill mentions "Utilitarian theory." Research this term online. Do you agree with Goldhill when she says that the details of this theory "are difficult to dispute"?
6. What ideas does Goldhill emphasize in her conclusion? Is it an effective strategy? How else could she have ended her essay?

Journal Entry

How would you address the trolley problem? Is it as complicated as Goldhill and other philosophers say it is? Explain.

Writing Workshop

1. Write an email to the CEOs of Tesla and Google in which you discuss how they should address the trolley problem when they design their self-driving cars. Be sure to include specific examples to support your thesis.
2. Write an essay in which you discuss the advantages of self-driving cars. (For example, they would give the elderly and the disabled new mobility.) Be sure to present a sufficient number of examples and a fair range of examples to support your points.
3. **Working with Sources.** In addition to the ethical issues presented by self-driving cars, there are also some practical problems. After researching these problems, write an essay in which you make the case for or against

these vehicles, using specific examples to illustrate your points. Be sure to document all material that you borrow from your sources and to include a works-cited page. (See Chapter 18 for information on MLA documentation.)

Combining the Patterns
Goldhill includes a section of **comparison and contrast** in which she compares nonphilosophers to philosophers. How does this comparison help Goldhill support her thesis?

Thematic Connections
- "Shooting an Elephant" (page 132)
- "Stability in Motion" (page 179)
- "Ten Ways We Get the Odds Wrong" (page 242)
- "What Causes Cancer? It's Complicated" (page 344)

JUDITH ORTIZ COFER

The Myth of the Latin Woman: I Just Met a Girl Named Maria

Judith Ortiz Cofer (1952–2016) was born in Puerto Rico and moved to New Jersey with her family when she was four. She was the Emeritus Regents' and Franklin Professor of English and Creative Writing at the University of Georgia. Widely anthologized, Cofer published essays, poetry, novels, and the short-story collection *An Island Like You: Stories of the Barrio* (1995). In one interview, she commented on her early writing: "Poetry allowed me to become intimate with English. And it allowed me to master the one skill that I try to teach my students — and if that's the only thing I accomplish, I consider it a success — and that is succinctness: economy and concentration of language. Why use fifteen words when one clear, elegant sentence will do it?"

Background on images of Hispanic women in film During the era of silent film, Hispanic performers found a niche with the popularity of the stereotypical "Latin lover." Although Hispanic actors enjoyed success, only a handful of Hispanic actresses, such as Myrtle Gonzalez and Beatriz Michelena, played in leading roles that did not always cast them as Latina. For example, Mexican-born Dolores del Rio, the only Hispanic actress to achieve international stardom during the period, played characters named Evelyn Iffield and Jeanne Lamont as well as Carlotta de Silva and Carmelita de Granados. In the late 1920s, however, the advent of sound brought many fewer movie roles for Hispanic actresses. Some who found success during the 1930s and 1940s conformed to broad stereotypes — for example, "Mexican Spitfire" Lupe Vélez, Carmen "the Lady in the Tutti-Frutti Hat" Miranda, and Maria Montez's hot-blooded seductresses. Others concealed their Hispanic identities on-screen (as was the case for Margarita Carmen Cansino, whose hair was dyed, eyebrows heavily plucked, and skin lightened to make her into the movie star Rita Hayworth). In the 1950s and 1960s, actresses such as Katy Jurado and Rita Moreno (who won a supporting actress Academy Award for her performance in *West Side Story*) rarely played leads. The 1960s saw the stardom of Raquel Welch (born Jo Raquel Tejada), who, like Hayworth, played down her Hispanic roots, but it was not until the 1990s that young performers such as Jessica Alba, Jennifer Lopez, Penelope Cruz, and Salma Hayek came into their own, playing Latinas who are more than stereotypes or characters whose ethnicity completely defines them.

On a bus trip to London from Oxford University where I was earning some graduate credits one summer, a young man, obviously fresh from a pub, spotted me and as if struck by inspiration went down on his knees in the aisle. With both hands over his heart he broke into an Irish tenor's rendition of

1

"Maria" from *West Side Story*.* My politely amused fellow passengers gave his lovely voice the round of gentle applause it deserved. Though I was not quite as amused, I managed my version of an English smile: no show of teeth, no extreme contortions of the facial muscles — I was at this time of my life practicing reserve and cool. Oh, that British control, how I coveted it. But "Maria" had followed me to London, reminding me of a prime fact of my life: you can leave the island, master the English language, and travel as far as you can, but if you are a Latina, especially one like me who so obviously belongs to Rita Moreno's** gene pool, the island travels with you.

This is sometimes a very good thing — it may win you that extra minute of someone's attention. But with some people, the same things can make *you* an island — not a tropical paradise but an Alcatraz, a place nobody wants to visit. As a Puerto Rican girl living in the United States*** and wanting like most children to "belong," I resented the stereotype that my Hispanic appearance called forth from many people I met.

Growing up in a large urban center in New Jersey during the 1960s, I suffered from what I think of as "cultural schizophrenia." Our life was designed by my parents as a microcosm of their *casas*† on the island. We spoke in Spanish, ate Puerto Rican food bought at the *bodega*,‡ and practiced strict Catholicism at a church that allotted us a one-hour slot each week for mass, performed in Spanish by a Chinese priest trained as a missionary for Latin America.

As a girl I was kept under strict surveillance by my parents, since my virtue and modesty were, by their cultural equation, the same as their honor. As a teenager I was lectured constantly on how to behave as a proper *senorita*. But it was a conflicting message I received, since the Puerto Rican mothers also encouraged their daughters to look and act like women and to dress in clothes our Anglo friends and their mothers found too "mature" and flashy. The difference was, and is, cultural; yet I often felt humiliated when I appeared at an American friend's party wearing a dress more suitable to a semi-formal than to a playroom birthday celebration. At Puerto Rican festivities, neither the music nor the colors we wore could be too loud.

I remember Career Day in our high school, when teachers told us to come dressed as if for a job interview. It quickly became obvious that to the Puerto Rican girls "dressing up" meant wearing their mother's ornate jewelry and clothing, more appropriate (by mainstream standards) for the company Christmas party than as daily office attire. That morning I had agonized in front of my closet, trying to figure out what a "career girl" would wear. I knew how to dress for school (at the Catholic school I attended, we all wore uniforms),

---

* Eds. note — A Broadway musical, based on *Romeo and Juliet*, about two rival New York street gangs, one Anglo and one Puerto Rican.
** Eds. note — Puerto Rico–born actress who won an Oscar for her role in the 1961 movie version of *West Side Story*.
*** Eds. note — Although it is an island, Puerto Rico is part of the United States.
† Eds. note — Homes.
‡ Eds. note — Small grocery store.

I knew how to dress for Sunday mass, and I knew what dresses to wear for parties at my relatives' homes. Though I do not recall the precise details of my Career Day outfit, it must have been a composite of these choices. But I remember a comment my friend (an Italian American) made in later years that coalesced my impressions of that day. She said that at the business school she was attending, the Puerto Rican girls always stood out for wearing "everything at once." She meant, of course, too much jewelry, too many accessories. On that day at school we were simply made the negative models by the nuns, who were themselves not credible fashion experts to any of us. But it was painfully obvious to me that to the others, in their tailored skirts and silk blouses, we must have seemed "hopeless" and "vulgar." Though I now know that most adolescents feel out of step much of the time, I also know that for the Puerto Rican girls of my generation that sense was intensified. The way our teachers and classmates looked at us that day in school was just a taste of the cultural clash that awaited us in the real world, where prospective employers and men on the street would often misinterpret our tight skirts and jingling bracelets as a "come-on."

Mixed cultural signals have perpetuated certain stereotypes — for example, that of the Hispanic woman as the "hot tamale" or sexual firebrand. It is a one-dimensional view that the media have found easy to promote. In their special vocabulary, advertisers have designated "sizzling" and "smoldering" as the adjectives of choice for describing not only the foods but also the women of Latin America. From conversations in my house I recall hearing about the harassment that Puerto Rican women endured in factories where the "boss-men" talked to them as if sexual innuendo was all they understood, and worse, often gave them the choice of submitting to their advances or being fired.

> "Mixed cultural signals have perpetuated certain stereotypes — for example, that of the Hispanic woman as the 'hot tamale' or sexual firebrand."

6

It is custom, however, not chromosomes, that leads us to choose scarlet over pale pink. As young girls, it was our mothers who influenced our decisions about clothes and colors — mothers who had grown up on a tropical island where the natural environment was a riot of primary colors, where showing your skin was one way to keep cool as well as to look sexy. Most important of all, on the island, women perhaps felt freer to dress and move more provocatively since, in most cases, they were protected by the traditions, mores, and laws of a Spanish/Catholic system of morality and machismo whose main rule was: *You may look at my sister, but if you touch her I will kill you.* The extended family and church structure could provide a young woman with a circle of safety in her small pueblo on the island; if a man "wronged" a girl, everyone would close in to save her family honor.

7

My mother has told me about dressing in her best party clothes on Saturday nights and going to the town's plaza to promenade with her girlfriends in front of the boys they liked. The males were thus given an opportunity to admire the women and to express their admiration in the form of *piropos*: erotically charged

8

street poems they composed on the spot. (I have myself been subjected to a few *piropos* while visiting the island, and they can be outrageous, although custom dictates that they must never cross into obscenity.) This ritual, as I understand it, also entails a show of studied indifference on the woman's part; if she is "decent," she must not acknowledge the man's impassioned words. So I do understand how things can be lost in translation. When a Puerto Rican girl dressed in her idea of what is attractive meets a man from the mainstream culture who has been trained to react to certain types of clothing as a sexual signal, a clash is likely to take place. I remember the boy who took me to my first formal dance leaning over to plant a sloppy, over-eager kiss painfully on my mouth; when I didn't respond with sufficient passion, he remarked resentfully: "I thought you Latin girls were supposed to mature early," as if I were expected to *ripen* like a fruit or vegetable, not just grow into womanhood like other girls.

It is surprising to my professional friends that even today some people,   9
including those who should know better, still put others "in their place." It happened to me most recently during a stay at a classy metropolitan hotel favored by young professional couples for weddings. Late one evening after the theater, as I walked toward my room with a colleague (a woman with whom I was coordinating an arts program), a middle-aged man in a tuxedo, with a young girl in satin and lace on his arm, stepped directly into our path. With his champagne glass extended toward me, he exclaimed "Evita!"*

Our way blocked, my companion and I listened as the man half-recited,   10
half-bellowed "Don't Cry for Me, Argentina." When he finished, the young girl said: "How about a round of applause for my daddy?" We complied, hoping this would bring the silly spectacle to a close. I was becoming aware that our little group was attracting the attention of the other guests. "Daddy" must have perceived this too, and he once more barred the way as we tried to walk past him. He began to shout-sing a ditty to the tune of "La Bamba" — except the lyrics were about a girl named Maria whose exploits rhymed with her name and gonorrhea. The girl kept saying "Oh, Daddy" and looking at me with pleading eyes. She wanted me to laugh along with the others. My companion and I stood silently waiting for the man to end his offensive song. When he finished, I looked not at him but at his daughter. I advised her calmly never to ask her father what he had done in the army. Then I walked between them and to my room. My friend complimented me on my cool handling of the situation, but I confessed that I had really wanted to push the jerk into the swimming pool. This same man — probably a corporate executive, well-educated, even worldly by most standards — would not have been likely to regale an Anglo woman with a dirty song in public. He might have checked his impulse by assuming that she could be somebody's wife or mother, or at least *somebody* who might take offense. But, to him, I was just an Evita or a Maria: merely a character in his cartoon-populated universe.

Another facet of the myth of the Latin woman in the United States is the   11
menial, the domestic — Maria the housemaid or countergirl. It's true that work

---

* Eds. note — A Broadway musical about Eva Duarte de Perón, the former first lady of Argentina.

as domestics, as waitresses, and in factories is all that's available to women with little English and few skills. But the myth of the Hispanic menial — the funny maid, mispronouncing words and cooking up a spicy storm in a shiny California kitchen — has been perpetuated by the media in the same way that "Mammy" from *Gone with the Wind* became America's idea of the Black woman for generations. Since I do not wear my diplomas around my neck for all to see, I have on occasion been sent to that "kitchen" where some think I obviously belong.

One incident has stayed with me, though I recognize it as a minor offense.   12
My first public poetry reading took place in Miami, at a restaurant where a luncheon was being held before the event. I was nervous and excited as I walked in with notebook in hand. An older woman motioned me to her table, and thinking (foolish me) that she wanted me to autograph a copy of my newly published slender volume of verse, I went over. She ordered a cup of coffee from me, assuming that I was the waitress. (Easy enough to mistake my poems for menus, I suppose.) I know it wasn't an intentional act of cruelty. Yet of all the good things that happened later, I remember that scene most clearly, because it reminded me of what I had to overcome before anyone would take me seriously. In retrospect I understand that my anger gave my reading fire. In fact, I have almost always taken any doubt in my abilities as a challenge, the result most often being the satisfaction of winning a convert, of seeing the cold, appraising eyes warm to my words, the body language change, the smile that indicates I have opened some avenue for communication. So that day as I read, I looked directly at that woman. Her lowered eyes told me she was embarrassed at her faux pas, and when I willed her to look up at me, she graciously allowed me to punish her with my full attention. We shook hands at the end of the reading and I never saw her again. She has probably forgotten the entire incident, but maybe not.

Yet I am one of the lucky ones. There are thousands of Latinas without the   13
privilege of an education or the entrees into society that I have. For them life is a constant struggle against the misconceptions perpetuated by the myth of the Latina. My goal is to try to replace the old stereotypes with a much more interesting set of realities. Every time I give a reading, I hope the stories I tell, the dreams and fears I examine in my work, can achieve some universal truth that will get my audience past the particulars of my skin color, my accent, or my clothes.

I once wrote a poem in which I called all Latinas "God's brown daughters."   14
This poem is really a prayer of sorts, offered upward, but also, through the human-to-human channel of art, outward. It is a prayer for communication and for respect. In it, Latin women pray "in Spanish to an Anglo God/with a Jewish heritage," and they are "fervently hoping/that if not omnipotent,/at least He be bilingual."

· · ·

Comprehension

1. What does Cofer mean by "cultural schizophrenia" (3)?
2. What "conflicting message" (4) did Cofer receive from her family?

3. What points does Cofer make by including each of the following in her essay?
   - The story about the young man in Oxford (1)
   - The story about Career Day (5)
   - The story about the poetry reading (12)
4. According to Cofer, what stereotypes are commonly applied to Latinas?
5. How does Cofer explain why she and other Puerto Rican women like to dress as they do? Why do outsiders think they dress this way?
6. What exactly is "the myth of the Latin woman" (11)?
7. How does Cofer hope to help people see beyond the stereotypes she describes? Is she successful?

Purpose and Audience

1. Which of the following do you think is Cofer's thesis? Why?
   - "[I]f you are a Latina, especially one like me who so obviously belongs to Rita Moreno's gene pool, the island travels with you" (1).
   - "As a Puerto Rican girl living in the United States . . . I resented the stereotype that my Hispanic appearance called forth from many people I met" (2).
   - "My goal is to try to replace the old stereotypes with a much more interesting set of realities" (13).
2. Why does Cofer begin paragraph 13 with "Yet I am one of the lucky ones"? How do you think she expects her audience to react to this statement?
3. Despite its use of Spanish words, this essay is directed at an Anglo audience. How can you tell?

Style and Structure

1. Cofer opens her essay with a story about an incident in her life. Considering her subject matter and her audience, is this an effective opening strategy? Why or why not?
2. What do you think Cofer means to suggest with these expressions in paragraph 8?
   - "erotically charged"
   - "studied indifference"
   - "lost in translation"
   - "mainstream culture"
3. Cofer does not introduce the image of the Latina as "the menial, the domestic" until paragraph 11, when she devotes two paragraphs to this part of the stereotype. Why does she wait so long? Should this discussion have appeared earlier? Should it have been deleted altogether? Explain your reasoning.
4. Cofer uses exemplification to support her thesis. Does she provide enough examples? Are they the right kinds of examples?
5. How do you interpret the lines of poetry that Cofer quotes in her conclusion? Is this an effective concluding strategy? Why or why not?
6. **Vocabulary Project.** Cofer uses Spanish words throughout this essay, and she does not define them. Find definitions of these words online. Would the English equivalents be just as effective as — or even more effective than — the Spanish words?

Journal Entry

On the basis of what she writes here, it seems as if Cofer does not confront the people who stereotype her and does not show anger, even in the incident described in paragraphs 9 and 10. Do you think she should have acted differently, or do you admire her restraint?

Writing Workshop

1. What stereotypes are applied by outsiders to your racial or ethnic group (or to people of your gender, intended profession, or geographic region)? Write an exemplification essay in which you argue that these stereotypes are untrue and potentially harmful. Support your thesis with specific narrative examples.

2. Think of some books, films, advertisements, or TV shows that feature characters of your own racial or ethnic group. Write a classification essay in which you discuss the different ways in which these characters are portrayed. Use exemplification and description to explain your categories. In your thesis, evaluate the accuracy of these characterizations.

3. **Working with Sources.** In paragraph 1 of her essay, Cofer says that "you can leave the island, master the English language, and travel as far as you can, but if you are a Latina, especially one like me who so obviously belongs to Rita Moreno's gene pool, the island travels with you." Editing this statement to suit your own "gene pool," use it as the thesis of an essay about the problems you have fitting in to some larger segment of society. Be sure to acknowledge Cofer as your source, including parenthetical documentation for references to her essay, and to include a works-cited page. (See Chapter 18 for information on MLA documentation.)

Combining the Patterns

The examples Cofer uses are personal narratives — stories of her own experience. What are the advantages and disadvantages of using **narration** here? Would other kinds of examples be more effective? Explain.

Thematic Connections

- " 'What's in a Name?' " (page 2)
- "An American Sunrise" (page 146)
- "Just Walk On By: A Black Man Ponders His Power to Alter Public Space" (page 231)
- "Emmett Till and Tamir Rice, Sons of the Great Migration" (page 414)

BRENT STAPLES

Just Walk On By: A Black Man Ponders His Power to Alter Public Space

Born in Chester, Pennsylvania, in 1951, Brent Staples joined the staff of the *New York Times* in 1985, writing on culture and politics, and he became a member of its editorial board in 1990. His columns appear regularly on the paper's op-ed pages. Staples has also written a memoir, *Parallel Time: Growing Up in Black and White* (1994), about his escape from the poverty and violence of his childhood.

Background on racial profiling "Just Walk On By" can be read in the light of controversies surrounding racial profiling of criminal suspects, which occurs, according to the American Civil Liberties Union, "when the police target someone for investigation on the basis of that person's race, national origin, or ethnicity. Examples of profiling are the use of race to determine which drivers to stop for minor traffic violations ('driving while Black') and the use of race to determine which motorists or pedestrians to search for contraband." Although law enforcement officials have often denied that they profile criminals solely on the basis of race, studies have shown a high prevalence of police profiling directed primarily at Black and Latinx Americans. A number of states have enacted laws barring racial profiling, and some people have won court settlements when they objected to being interrogated by police solely because of their race. Since the terrorist attacks of September 11, 2001, people of Arab descent have also been targets of heightened interest at airports and elsewhere. In addition, the campaign and subsequent presidential rhetoric of Donald Trump, who has repeatedly made anti-immigrant statements in support of building a border wall between the United States and Mexico, caused many Latinx people to fear that they would be singled out for scrutiny solely on the basis of race. Clearly, these events, as well as incidents that sparked the current Black Lives Matter movement, have added to the continuing controversy surrounding the association of criminal behavior with particular ethnic groups.

My first victim was a woman — white, well dressed, probably in her early   1
twenties. I came upon her late one evening on a deserted street in Hyde Park, a relatively affluent neighborhood in an otherwise mean, impoverished section of Chicago. As I swung onto the avenue behind her, there seemed to be a discreet, uninflammatory distance between us. Not so. She cast back a worried glance. To her, the youngish Black man — a broad six feet two inches with a beard and billowing hair, both hands shoved into the pockets of a bulky military jacket — seemed menacingly close. After a few more quick glimpses, she picked up her pace and was soon running in earnest. Within seconds she disappeared into a cross street.

That was more than a decade ago. I was twenty-two years old, a graduate student newly arrived at the University of Chicago. It was in the echo of that terrified woman's footfalls that I first began to know the unwieldy inheritance I'd come into—the ability to alter public space in ugly ways. It was clear that she thought herself the quarry of a mugger, rapist, or worse. Suffering a bout of insomnia, however, I was stalking sleep, not defenseless wayfarers. As a softy who is scarcely able to take a knife to a raw

> **"**It was in the echo of that terrified woman's footfalls that I first began to know the unwieldy inheritance I'd come into—the ability to alter public space in ugly ways.**"**

2

chicken—let alone hold it to a person's throat—I was surprised, embarrassed, and dismayed all at once. Her flight made me feel like an accomplice in tyranny. It also made it clear that I was indistinguishable from the muggers who occasionally seeped into the area from the surrounding ghetto. That first encounter, and those that followed, signified that a vast, unnerving gulf lay between nighttime pedestrians—particularly women—and me. And I soon gathered that being perceived as dangerous is a hazard in itself. I only needed to turn a corner into a dicey situation, or crowd some frightened, armed person in a foyer somewhere, or make an errant move after being pulled over by a policeman. Where fear and weapons meet—and they often do in urban America—there is always the possibility of death.

In that first year, my first away from my hometown, I was to become thoroughly familiar with the language of fear. At dark, shadowy intersections in Chicago, I could cross in front of a car stopped at a traffic light and elicit the *thunk, thunk, thunk, thunk* of the driver—Black, white, male, or female—hammering down the door locks. On less traveled streets after dark, I grew accustomed to but never comfortable with people who crossed to the other side of the street rather than pass me. Then there were the standard unpleasantries with police, doormen, bouncers, cab drivers, and others whose business it is to screen out troublesome individuals *before* there is any nastiness.

I moved to New York nearly two years ago and I have remained an avid night walker. In central Manhattan, the near-constant crowd cover minimizes tense one-on-one street encounters. Elsewhere—visiting friends in SoHo, where sidewalks are narrow and tightly spaced buildings shut out the sky—things can get very taut indeed.

Black men have a firm place in New York mugging literature. Norman Podhoretz in his famed (or infamous) 1963 essay, "My Negro Problem—and Ours," recalls growing up in terror of Black males; they "were tougher than we were, more ruthless," he writes—and as an adult on the Upper West Side of Manhattan, he continues, he cannot constrain his nervousness when he meets Black men on certain streets. Similarly, a decade later, the essayist and novelist Edward Hoagland extols a New York where once "Negro bitterness bore down mainly on other Negroes." Where some see mere panhandlers, Hoagland sees "a mugger who is clearly screwing up his nerve to do more than just *ask* for money." But Hoagland has "the New Yorker's quick-hunch posture for broken-field maneuvering," and the bad guy swerves away.

I often witness that "hunch posture," from women after dark on the   6
warrenlike streets of Brooklyn where I live. They seem to set their faces on neutral and, with their purse straps strung across their chests bandolier style, they forge ahead as though bracing themselves against being tackled. I understand, of course, that the danger they perceive is not a hallucination. Women are particularly vulnerable to street violence, and young Black males are drastically overrepresented among the perpetrators of that violence. Yet these truths are no solace against the kind of alienation that comes of being ever the suspect, against being set apart, a fearsome entity with whom pedestrians avoid making eye contact.

It is not altogether clear to me how I reached the ripe old age of twenty-two   7
without being conscious of the lethality nighttime pedestrians attributed to me. Perhaps it was because in Chester, Pennsylvania, the small, angry industrial town where I came of age in the 1960s, I was scarcely noticeable against a backdrop of gang warfare, street knifings, and murders. I grew up one of the good boys, had perhaps a half-dozen fist fights. In retrospect, my shyness of combat has clear sources.

Many things go into the making of a young thug. One of those things is   8
the consummation of the male romance with the power to intimidate. An infant discovers that random flailings send the baby bottle flying out of the crib and crashing to the floor. Delighted, the joyful babe repeats those motions again and again, seeking to duplicate the feat. Just so, I recall the points at which some of my boyhood friends were finally seduced by the perception of themselves as tough guys. When a mark cowered and surrendered his money without resistance, myth and reality merged — and paid off. It is, after all, only manly to embrace the power to frighten and intimidate. We, as men, are not supposed to give an inch of our lane on the highway; we are to seize the fighter's edge in work and in play and even in love; we are to be valiant in the face of hostile forces.

Unfortunately, poor and powerless young men seem to take all this non-   9
sense literally. As a boy, I saw countless tough guys locked away; I have since buried several, too. They were babies, really — a teenage cousin, a brother of twenty-two, a childhood friend in his mid-twenties — all gone down in episodes of bravado played out in the streets. I came to doubt the virtues of intimidation early on. I chose, perhaps even unconsciously, to remain a shadow — timid, but a survivor.

The fearsomeness mistakenly attributed to me in public places often has a   10
perilous flavor. The most frightening of these confusions occurred in the late 1970s and early 1980s when I worked as a journalist in Chicago. One day, rushing into the office of a magazine I was writing for with a deadline story in hand, I was mistaken for a burglar. The office manager called security and, with an ad hoc posse, pursued me through the labyrinthine halls, nearly to my editor's door. I had no way of proving who I was. I could only move briskly toward the company of someone who knew me.

Another time I was on assignment for a local paper and killing time before   11
an interview. I entered a jewelry store on the city's affluent Near North Side.
The proprietor excused herself and returned with an enormous red Doberman
pinscher straining at the end of a leash. She stood, the dog extended toward
me, silent to my questions, her eyes bulging nearly out of her head. I took a
cursory look around, nodded, and bade her good night. Relatively speaking,
however, I never fared as badly as another Black male journalist. He went to
nearby Waukegan, Illinois, a couple of summers ago to work on a story about a
murderer who was born there. Mistaking the reporter for the killer, police
hauled him from his car at gunpoint and but for his press credentials would
probably have tried to book him. Such episodes are not uncommon. Black
men trade tales like this all the time.

In "My Negro Problem — and Ours," Podhoretz writes that the hatred he   12
feels for Blacks makes itself known to him through a variety of avenues — one
being his discomfort with that "special brand of paranoid touchiness" to
which he says Blacks are prone. No doubt he is speaking here of Black men. In
time, I learned to smother the rage I felt at so often being taken for a criminal.
Not to do so would surely have led to madness — via that special "paranoid
touchiness" that so annoyed Podhoretz at the time he wrote the essay.

I began to take precautions to make myself less threatening. I move about   13
with care, particularly late in the evening. I give a wide berth to nervous people
on subway platforms during the wee hours, particularly when I have exchanged
business clothes for jeans. If I happen to be entering a building behind some
people who appear skittish, I may walk by, letting them clear the lobby before I
return, so as not to seem to be following them. I have been calm and extremely
congenial on those rare occasions when I've been pulled over by the police.

And on late-evening constitutionals along streets less traveled by, I employ   14
what has proved to be an excellent tension-reducing measure: I whistle melo-
dies from Beethoven and Vivaldi and the more popular classical composers.
Even steely New Yorkers hunching toward nighttime destinations seem to
relax, and occasionally they even join in the tune. Virtually everybody seems to
sense that a mugger wouldn't be warbling bright, sunny selections from Vivaldi's *Four Seasons*. It is my equivalent of the cowbell that hikers wear when they
know they are in bear country.

· · ·

Comprehension

1. Why does Staples characterize the woman he encounters in paragraph 1 as a
   "victim"?
2. What does Staples mean when he says he has the power to "alter public
   space" (2)?
3. Why does Staples walk the streets at night?
4. What things, in Staples's opinion, contribute to "the making of a young
   thug" (8)? According to Staples, why are young, poor, and powerless men
   especially likely to become thugs?
5. How does Staples attempt to make himself less threatening?

Purpose and Audience

1. What is Staples's thesis? Does he state it or imply it?
2. Does Staples use logic, emotion, or a combination of the two to appeal to his readers? How appropriate is his strategy?
3. What preconceptions about race does Staples assume his audience has? How does he challenge these preconceptions?
4. What is Staples trying to accomplish with his first sentence? Do you think he succeeds? Why or why not?

Style and Structure

1. Why does Staples mention Norman Podhoretz? Could he make the same points without referring to Podhoretz's essay?
2. Staples begins his essay with an anecdote. How effective is this strategy? Do you think another opening strategy would be more effective? Explain.
3. Does Staples present enough examples to support his thesis? Are they representative? Would other types of examples be more convincing? Explain.
4. In what order does Staples present his examples? Would another order be more effective? Explain.
5. **Vocabulary Project.** In paragraph 8, Staples uses the word *thug*. List as many synonyms as you can for this word. Do all these words convey the same idea, or do they differ in their connotations? Explain. (If you like, consult an online thesaurus.)

Journal Entry

Have you ever been in a situation such as the ones Staples describes, where you perceived someone (or someone perceived you) as threatening? How did you react? After reading Staples's essay, do you think you would react the same way now?

Writing Workshop

1. Use your journal entry to help you write an essay using a single long example to support this statement: "When walking alone at night, you can (or cannot) be too careful."
2. **Working with Sources.** Relying on examples from your own experience and from Staples's essay, write an essay discussing what part you think race plays in people's reactions to Staples. (If you wish, you can go online and consult some articles about racial profiling.) Do you think Staples's perceptions are accurate? Be sure to document any references to your sources and to include a works-cited page. (See Chapter 18 for information on MLA documentation.)
3. How accurate is Staples's observation concerning the "male romance with the power to intimidate" (8)? What does he mean by this statement? What examples from your own experience support (or do not support) the idea that this "romance" is an element of male upbringing in our society?

Combining the Patterns

In paragraph 8, Staples uses **cause and effect** to demonstrate what goes "into the making of a young thug." Would several **examples** have better explained how a youth becomes a thug?

Thematic Connections

FARHAD MANJOO

Call Me "They"

As Farhad Manjoo notes in the following essay, they prefer to be referred to by the pronouns *they* and *them*, instead of *he* and *him*: "So: If you write about me, interview me, tweet about me, or if you are a Fox News producer working on a rant about my extreme politics, I would prefer if you left my gender out of it. Call me 'they' or 'them.'" Manjoo was born in South Africa in 1978 to a family of Indian descent and moved to Southern California in 1986. Manjoo graduated from Cornell University and wrote for *Wired News*, *Salon*, *Slate*, and the *Wall Street Journal* before joining the *New York Times* in 2014. Manjoo is also a regular contributor to National Public Radio and is author of the book *True Enough: Learning to Live in a Post-Fact Society* (2008).

Background on changing pronoun use The use of *they* and *them* as singular pronouns may seem new to English, but examples of this usage can be found in Chaucer, Shakespeare, and Austen. From about the eighteenth century onward, however, third-person personal pronouns reflected a binary gender choice: *she/her* for females, *he/him* for males. Moreover, lexicographers and grammarians advised people to use *he* as a default for singular nouns of unknown gender — for example, *anyone* and *anybody*. To many, this usage reflects a patriarchal social and linguistic history that privileges the male and the masculine. The need for nonbinary English pronouns was recognized in the nineteenth century: the obscure terms *heesh*, *ne*, *nis*, and *nim* date from the second half of the nineteen hundreds. Currently, discussions of sex, gender, and inclusivity have dominated mainstream culture, and as a result, the old rules on pronoun usage are changing. For example, both the American Psychological Association's style guide and *Merriam-Webster's Dictionary* have adopted the use of *they* as a singular personal pronoun and designated it their word of the year for 2019.

Note: We use Manjoo's preferred pronoun *they* in this headnote and in the questions that follow the essay.

I am your stereotypical, cisgender, middle-aged suburban dad. I dabble in woodworking, I take out the garbage, and I covet my neighbor's Porsche. Though I do think men should wear makeup (it looks nice!), my tepid masculinity apparently rings loudly enough online and in person that most people guess that I go by "he" and "him." And that's fine; I will not be offended if you refer to me by those traditional, uselessly gendered pronouns.

But "he" is not what you *should* call me. If we lived in a just, rational, inclusive universe — one in which we were not all so irredeemably obsessed by the particulars of the parts dangling between our fellow humans' legs, nor the ridiculous expectations signified by those parts about how we should act and speak and dress and feel — there would be no requirement for you to have to assume my gender just to refer to me in the common tongue.

There are, after all, few obvious linguistic advantages to the requirement. 3 When I refer to myself, I don't have to announce my gender and all the baggage it carries. Instead I use the gender-nonspecific "I." Nor do I have to bother with gender when I'm speaking directly to someone or when I'm talking about a group of people. I just say "you" or "they."

So why does standard English impose a gender requirement on the third-person singular? And why do elite cultural institutions — universities, publishers, and media outlets like *The Times* — still encourage all this gendering? To get to my particular beef: When I refer to an individual whose gender I don't know here in *The Times*, why do I usually have to choose either "he" or "she" or, in the clunkiest phrase ever cooked up by small-minded grammarians, "he or she"? 4

> "So why does standard English impose a gender requirement on the third-person singular?"

The truth is, I shouldn't have to. It's time for the singular "they." Indeed, 5 it's well past time — and I'd like to do my part in pushing "they" along.

So: If you write about me, interview me, tweet about me, or if you are a Fox 6 News producer working on a rant about my extreme politics, I would prefer if you left my gender out of it. Call me "they" or "them," as in: "Did you read Farhad's latest column — they've really gone off the deep end this time!" And — unless you feel strongly about your specific pronouns, which I respect — I would hope to call you "they" too, because the world will be slightly better off if we abandoned unnecessary gender signifiers as a matter of routine communication. Be a "him" or "her" or anything else in the sheets, but consider also being a "they" and "them" in the streets.

I suspect my call will be dismissed as useless virtue-signaling, but there are 7 several clear advantages, both linguistic and cultural, to the singular "they." One of the main ones is that it's ubiquitous. According to linguists who study gender and pronouns, "they" and "them" are increasingly and widely seen as legitimate ways to refer to an individual, both generically and specifically, whether you know their gender or not — as I just did right in this sentence.

"In our latest study, 90 percent of the time when people refer to a hypo- 8 thetical person, they use 'they,'" said Evan Bradley, who studies language and gender at Penn State.

But "they" is also used so commonly to refer to specific individuals that it 9 doesn't trip people up. The same thing isn't true when you add a new, neutral pronoun to the language — something like "ze," which in Bradley's research was not recognized by many people, and when it was used, it was often taken to refer specifically to gender-nonconforming people.

By contrast, "they" is universal and purely neutral, Bradley told me. When 10 people encounter it, they infer nothing about gender. This makes singular "they" a perfect pronoun — it's flexible, inclusive, unobtrusive and obviates the risk of inadvertent misgendering. And in most circumstances, it creates perfectly coherent sentences that people don't have to strain to understand.

That's probably why the singular, gender-neutral "they" is common not just   11
in transgender and nonbinary communities, for whom it is necessary, but also in mainstream usage, where it is rapidly becoming a standard way we refer to all people. If you watch closely, you'll see the usage in marketing copy, on social media, in app interfaces and just about everywhere else you look. For instance, when Uber or Lyft wants to tell you that your driver has arrived, they send you a notification that says something like: "Juan is almost here. Meet them outside."

Other than plainly intolerant people, there's only one group that harbors   12
doubts about the singular "they": grammarians. If you're one of those people David Foster Wallace called a "snoot," Lyft's use of "them" to refer to one specific Juan rings grammatically icky to you. The singular, gender nonspecific "they" has been common in English as long as people have spoken English, but since the 18th century, grammar stylists have discouraged it on the grounds that "they" has to be plural. That's why institutions that cater to snoots generally discourage it. *The Times*, whose stylebook allows the singular "they" when the person being referred to prefers it, warns against its widespread usage: "Take particular care to avoid confusion if using they for an individual" the stylebook counsels.

I think that's too cautious; we should use "they" more freely, because lan-   13
guage should not default to the gender binary. One truth I've come to understand too late in life is how thoroughly and insidiously our lives are shaped by gender norms. These expectations are felt most acutely and tragically by those who don't conform to the standard gender binary — people who are transgender or nonbinary, most obviously.

But even for people who do mainly fit within the binary, the very idea that   14
there is a binary is invisibly stifling. Every boy and girl feels this in small and large ways growing up; you unwittingly brush up against preferences that don't fit within your gender expectations, and then you must learn to fight those expectations or strain to live within them.

But it was only when I had a son and a daughter of my own that I recog-   15
nized how powerfully gendered constructs shape our development. From their very earliest days, my kids, fed by marketing and entertainment and (surely) their parents' modeling, seemed to hem themselves into silly gender norms. They gravitated to boy toys and girl toys, boy colors and girl colors, boy TV shows and girl TV shows. This was all so sad to me: I see them limiting their thoughts and their ambitions, their preferences and their identity, their very liberty, only to satisfy some collective abstraction. And there's little prospect for escape: Gender is a ubiquitous prison for the mind, reinforced everywhere, by everyone, and only rarely questioned.

We're a long way from eradicating these expectations in society. But we   16
don't have to be wary about eradicating them in language.

"Part of introducing the concept of gender-neutral pronouns to people is   17
to get them to ask, 'Why does this part of society need to be gendered in the first place?'" said Jay Wu, director of communications at the National Center for Transgender Equality. They continued: "Part of how we fix that is more and

more people noticing that things are so gendered and being like, why does it have to be that way? What benefit does it bring us?"

None, I say, other than confusion, anxiety, and grief. Call me "they," and   18
I'll call you "them." I won't mind, and I hope you won't, either.

*   *   *

Comprehension

1. According to Manjoo, what constitutes a "just, rational, inclusive universe" (2)?
2. What is the singular "they"? Why does Manjoo think "it's well past time" for the singular "they" (5)?
3. Why, according to Evan Bradley, is "singular 'they' a perfect pronoun" (10)?
4. Why do grammarians have doubts about the singular "they"? Why does Manjoo think they are being "too cautious" (13)?
5. What does Manjoo mean when they say that our lives are "insidiously . . . shaped by gender norms" (13)?
6. According to Jay Wu, director of communications at the National Center for Transgender Equality, what is the point of introducing the idea of gender-neutral pronouns into the language? Do you agree?

Purpose and Audience

1. Does Manjoo assume that their readers are aware of the issue they discuss? How can you tell?
2. What preconceived attitudes about nongendered pronouns does Manjoo assume that their readers have? Is Manjoo respectful of those who disagree with this opinion? Explain.
3. Where does Manjoo state their thesis? Why do they state it where they do?
4. Is Manjoo's purpose to inform their readers or to persuade them? How do you know?

Style and Structure

1. Manjoo begins this essay by identifying as "your stereotypical, cisgender, middle-aged suburban dad" (1). What does Manjoo hope to accomplish by beginning this way? What are the advantages and the disadvantages of this strategy?
2. Paragraph 4 contains three **rhetorical questions**. Why does Manjoo ask these questions?
3. What examples does Manjoo present to illustrate their points? Does Manjoo present enough examples? Are their examples convincing? Explain.
4. Where does Manjoo address opposing points of view? How effectively does Manjoo deal with these objections?

5. **Vocabulary Project.** In paragraph 7, Manjoo says that they are afraid their ideas will be dismissed as "virtue-signaling." What does this term mean? What other word (or words) could Manjoo have used?

Journal Entry

Do you agree with Manjoo that it is time for the singular "they?"

Writing Workshop

1. Does Manjoo make a convincing case? Write an email to Manjoo in which you agree or disagree with their position. Use examples from your own experience to support your thesis.
2. Write an exemplification essay that shows how Manjoo's ideas would affect a school, business, or organization that you know well.
3. **Working with Sources.** In a response to Manjoo's essay, one reader made the following point.

> I appreciate the need to be sensitive to some, but come on. I don't want to be referred to as "they" unless it makes sense grammatically. Let's drop the idea that we're stifling the vast majority of us. It's not language that is defining gender roles, it's how people behave and their willingness to be exposed to different ideas and individuals.

Write an essay in which you use examples from your own experience and from Manjoo's essay to support or challenge this statement. Be sure to document all references to Manjoo and to include a works-cited page. (See Chapter 18 for information on MLA documentation.)

Combining the Patterns

In paragraph 15, Manjoo uses **cause and effect**. How does this discussion help Manjoo to conclude the essay?

Thematic Connections
- "The Myth of the Latin Woman: I Just Met a Girl Named Maria" (page 224)
- "Sex, Lies, and Conversation" (page 408)
- "Flick Chicks" (page 444)
- "The Case for Restricting Hate Speech" (page 610)

MAIA SZALAVITZ

Ten Ways We Get the Odds Wrong

Maia Szalavitz (b. 1965), a journalist who writes about science, health, addiction, and public policy, has published articles in the *New York Times*, the *Washington Post*, *New Scientist*, *Time*, and many other publications. She is the author of *Help at Any Cost: How the Troubled-Teen Industry Cons Parents and Hurts Kids* (2006) and is coauthor, with Bruce D. Perry, of *The Boy Who Was Raised as a Dog* (2006) and *Born for Love: Why Empathy Is Essential — and Endangered* (2010). Her most recent book, *Unbroken Brain: A Revolutionary New Way of Understanding Addiction* (2016), explores the possibility that addictions are actually a form of learning disorder.

Background on odds and risks Odds making is most often associated with sports and casino gambling, although people can place bets on nearly everything from presidential races to celebrity deaths and the weather. For sporting events (such as NFL games), professional oddsmakers are generally less interested in predicting the winner than in setting an appropriate line for "spread-betting," creating a situation that will attract an equal number of bettors on both sides. The result is that the oddsmakers reduce their risks and make money regardless of the outcome. Odds making and risk assessment are not just confined to sports betting, however. The first stirrings of the modern insurance industry in the seventeenth and eighteenth centuries coincided with advancements in mathematics and probability theory. As a result of advances in both statistics and technology, the actuarial sciences — the use of mathematics and statistics to assess risk — now flourish not only in the insurance sector but also in finance, global economics, medicine, and public policy. The management of risk has become so central to our social and economic lives that the German sociologist Ulrich Beck famously coined the term *risk society* to define the modern world.

Is your gym locker room crawling with drug-resistant bacteria? Is the guy with the bulging backpack a suicide bomber? And what about that innocent-looking arugula: Will pesticide residue cause cancer, or do the leaves themselves harbor *E. coli*? But wait! Not eating enough vegetables is also potentially deadly. 1

These days, it seems like everything is risky, and worry itself is bad for your health. The more we learn, the less we seem to know — and if anything makes us anxious, it's uncertainty. At the same time, we're living longer, healthier lives. So why does it feel like even the lettuce is out to get us? 2

The human brain is exquisitely adapted to respond to risk — uncertainty about the outcome of actions. Faced with a precipice or a predator, the brain is biased to make certain decisions. Our biases reflect the choices that kept our ancestors alive. But we have yet to evolve similarly effective responses to statistics, media coverage, and fear-mongering politicians. For most of human existence twenty-four-hour news channels didn't exist, so we don't have cognitive shortcuts to deal with novel uncertainties. 3

Still, uncertainty unbalances us, pitching us into anxiety and producing an array
of cognitive distortions. Even minor dilemmas like deciding whether to get a cell
phone (brain cancer vs. dying on the road
because you can't call for help?) can be
intolerable for some people. And though
emotions are themselves critical to making
rational decisions, they were designed for a world in which dangers took the
form of predators, not pollutants. Our emotions push us to make snap
judgments that once were sensible—but may not be anymore.

> "Our emotions push us to make snap judgments that once were sensible—but may not be anymore." 4

I. We Fear Snakes, Not Cars

Risk and emotion are inseparable.

Fear feels like anything but a cool and detached computation of the odds. 5
But that's precisely what it is, a lightning-fast risk assessment performed by
your reptilian brain, which is ever on the lookout for danger. The amygdala
flags perceptions, sends out an alarm message, and—before you have a chance
to think—your system gets flooded with adrenaline. "This is the way our
ancestors evaluated risk before we had statistics," says Paul Slovic, president of
Decision Research. Emotions are decision-making shortcuts.

As a result of these evolved emotional algorithms, ancient threats like spi- 6
ders and snakes cause fear out of proportion to the real danger they pose, while
experiences that should frighten us—like fast driving—don't. Dangers like
speedy motorized vehicles are newcomers on the landscape of life. The instinctive response to being approached rapidly is to freeze. In the ancestral environment, this reduced a predator's ability to see you—but that doesn't help when
what's speeding toward you is a car.

II. We Fear Spectacular, Unlikely Events

Fear skews risk analysis in predictable ways.

Fear hits primitive brain areas to produce reflexive reactions before the sit- 7
uation is even consciously perceived. Because fear strengthens memory,
catastrophes such as earthquakes, plane crashes, and terrorist incidents completely capture our attention. As a result, we overestimate the odds of dreadful
but infrequent events and underestimate how risky ordinary events are. The
drama and excitement of improbable events make them appear to be more
common. The effect is amplified by the fact that media tend to cover what's
dramatic and exciting, Slovic notes. The more we see something, the more
common we think it is, even if we are watching the same footage over and over.

After 9/11, 1.4 million people changed their holiday travel plans to avoid 8
flying. The vast majority chose to drive instead. But driving is far more dangerous than flying, and the decision to switch caused roughly 1,000 additional
auto fatalities, according to two separate analyses comparing traffic patterns
in late 2001 to those the year before. In other words, 1,000 people who chose to
drive wouldn't have died had they flown instead.

III. We Fear Cancer but Not Heart Disease

We underestimate threats that creep up on us.

Humans are ill-prepared to deal with risks that don't produce immediate negative consequences, like eating a cupcake or smoking cigarettes. As a result, we are less frightened of heart disease than we should be. Heart disease is the end result of actions that one at a time (one cigarette or one french fry) aren't especially dangerous. But repeated over the years, those actions have deadly consequences. "Things that build up slowly are very hard for us to see," says Kimberly Thompson, a professor of risk analysis at the Harvard School of Public Health. Obesity and global warming are in that category. "We focus on the short-term even if we know the long-term risk."

Our difficulty in understanding how small risks add up accounts for many unplanned pregnancies. At most points during the menstrual cycle, the odds of pregnancy are low, but after a year of unprotected sex, 85 percent of couples experience it.

IV. No Pesticide in My Backyard — Unless I Put It There

We prefer that which (we think) we can control.

If we feel we can control an outcome, or if we choose to take a risk voluntarily, it seems less dangerous, says David Ropeik, a risk consultant. "Many people report that when they move from the driver's seat to the passenger's seat, the car in front of them looks closer and their foot goes to the imaginary brake. You're likely to be less scared with the steering wheel in your hand, because you can do something about your circumstances, and that's reassuring." Could explain why your mother always criticizes your driving.

The false calm a sense of control confers, and the tendency to worry about dangers we can't control, explains why when we see other drivers talking on cell phones we get nervous but we feel perfectly fine chatting away ourselves. Similarly, because homeowners themselves benefit if they kill off bugs that are destroying their lawns, people fear insecticide less if they are using it in their own backyard than if a neighbor uses the same chemical in the same concentration, equally close to them. The benefits to us reduce the level of fear. "Equity is very important," says Slovic, and research shows that if people who bear the risk also get the benefit, they tend to be less concerned about it.

V. We Speed Up When We Put Our Seat Belts On

We substitute one risk for another.

Insurers in the United Kingdom used to offer discounts to drivers who purchased cars with safer brakes. "They don't anymore," says John Adams, a risk analyst and emeritus professor of geography at University College. "There weren't fewer accidents, just different accidents."

Why? For the same reason that the vehicles most likely to go out of control in snowy conditions are those with four-wheel drive. Buoyed by a false sense of safety that comes with the increased control, drivers of four-wheel-drive vehicles take more risks. "These vehicles are bigger and heavier, which should keep them on the road," says Ropeik. "But police report that these drivers go faster, even when roads are slippery."

Both are cases of risk compensation: People have a preferred level of risk, and they modulate their behavior to keep risk at that constant level. Features designed to increase safety — four-wheel drive, seat belts, or air bags — wind up making people drive faster. The safety features may reduce risks associated with weather, but they don't cut overall risk. "If I drink a diet soda with dinner," quips Slovic, "I have ice cream for dessert."

15

VI. Teens May Think Too Much about Risk — and Not Feel Enough
Why using your cortex isn't always smart.

Parents worry endlessly that their teens will drive, get pregnant, or overdose on drugs; they think youth feel immortal and don't consider negative consequences. Curiously, however, teens are actually less likely than adults to fall into the trap of thinking, "It won't happen to me." In fact, teens massively overestimate the odds of things like contracting HIV or syphilis if they have sex. One study found that teens thought a sexually active girl had a 60 percent chance of getting AIDS. So why do they do it anyway?

16

Teens may not be irrational about risk but too rational, argues Valerie Reyna, a psychologist at Cornell University. Adults asked to consider absurd propositions like "Is it a good idea to drink Drano?" immediately and intuitively say no. Adolescents, however, take more than twice as long to think about it. Brain-scan research shows that when teens contemplate things like playing Russian roulette or drinking and driving, they primarily use rational regions of the brain — certain regions of cortex — while adults use emotional regions like the insula.

17

When risky decisions are weighed in a rational calculus, benefits like fitting in and feeling good now can outweigh real risks. As a result, teaching reasoned decision-making to teens backfires, argues Reyna. Instead, she says, we should teach kids to rule out risks based on emotional responses — for example, by considering the worst-case scenario, as adults do. But research suggests there may be no way to speed up the development of mature decision-making. Repetition and practice are critical to emotional judgment — which means that it takes time to learn this skill.

18

VII. Why Young Men Will Never Get Good Rates on Car Insurance
The "risk thermostat" varies widely.

People tend to maintain a steady level of risk, sensing what range of odds is comfortable for them and staying within it. "We all have some propensity to take risk," says Adams. "That's the setting on the 'risk thermostat.'" Some people have a very high tolerance for risk, while others are more cautious.

19

Forget the idea of a risk-taking personality. If there's a daredevil gene that globally affects risk-taking, researchers haven't found it. Genes do influence impulsivity, which certainly affects the risks people take. And testosterone

20

inclines males to take more risks than females. But age and situation matter as much as gender. Men fifteen to twenty-five are very risk-prone compared to same-age women and older people.

More importantly, one person's risk thermostat may have different set-   21
tings for different types of risk. "Somebody who has their whole portfolio in junk bonds is not necessarily also a mountain climber," explains Baruch Fischhoff, a professor of psychology at Carnegie Mellon University.

VIII. We Worry about Teen Marijuana Use, but Not about Teen Sports
Risk arguments cannot be divorced from values.

If the risks of smoking marijuana are coldly compared to those of playing   22
high-school football, parents should be less concerned about pot smoking. Death by marijuana overdose has never been reported, while thirteen teen players died of football-related injuries in 2006 alone. And marijuana impairs driving far less than the number one drug used by teens: alcohol. Alcohol and tobacco are also more likely to beget addiction, give rise to cancer, and lead to harder drug use.

If the comparison feels absurd, it's because judgments of risk are insepa-   23
rable from value judgments. We value physical fitness and the lessons teens learn from sports, but disapprove of unearned pleasure from recreational drugs. So we're willing to accept the higher level of risk of socially preferred activities — and we mentally magnify risks associated with activities society rejects, which leads us to do things like arresting marijuana smokers.

"Risk decisions are not about risks alone," says Slovic. "People usually take   24
risks to get a benefit." The value placed on that benefit is inherently subjective, so decisions about them cannot be made purely "on the science."

IX. We Love Sunlight but Fear Nuclear Power
Why "natural" risks are easier to accept.

The word radiation stirs thoughts of nuclear power, X-rays, and danger, so   25
we shudder at the thought of erecting nuclear power plants in our neighborhoods. But every day we're bathed in radiation that has killed many more people than nuclear reactors: sunlight. It's hard for us to grasp the danger because sunlight feels so familiar and natural.

Our built-in bias for the natural led a California town to choose a toxic   26
poison made from chrysanthemums over a milder artificial chemical to fight mosquitoes: People felt more comfortable with a plant-based product. We see what's "natural" as safe — and regard the new and "unnatural" as frightening.

Any sort of novelty — including new and unpronounceable chemicals —   27
evokes a low-level stress response, says Bruce Perry, a child psychiatrist at Child Trauma Academy. When a case report suggested that lavender and tea-tree oil products caused abnormal breast development in boys, the media shrugged and activists were silent. If these had been artificial chemicals, there

likely would have been calls for a ban, but because they are natural plant products, no outrage resulted. "Nature has a good reputation," says Slovic. "We think of natural as benign and safe. But malaria's natural and so are deadly mushrooms."

X. We Should Fear Fear Itself

Why worrying about risk is itself risky.

Though the odds of dying in a terror attack like 9/11 or contracting Ebola are infinitesimal, the effects of chronic stress caused by constant fear are significant. Studies have found that the more people were exposed to media portrayals of the 2001 attacks, the more anxious and depressed they were. Chronically elevated stress harms our physiology, says Ropeik. "It interferes with the formation of bone, lowers immune response, increases the likelihood of clinical depression and diabetes, impairs our memory and our fertility, and contributes to long-term cardiovascular damage and high blood pressure."   28

The physiological consequences of overestimating the dangers in the world—and revving our anxiety into overdrive—are another reason risk perception matters. It's impossible to live a risk-free life: Everything we do increases some risks while lowering others. But if we understand our innate biases in the way we manage risks, we can adjust for them and genuinely stay safer—without freaking out over every leaf of lettuce.   29

•   •   •

Comprehension

1. What does Szalavitz mean in paragraph 3 when she says, "The human brain is exquisitely adapted to respond to risk"?
2. Why, according to Szalavitz, have human beings been unable to develop effective responses to risks posed by "statistics, media coverage, and fear-mongering politicians" (3)?
3. How does Szalavitz explain the following in her essay?
   - We fear snakes but not cars.
   - We fear spectacular, unlikely events.
   - We fear cancer but not heart disease.
   - We fear pesticides in our neighbor's yard but not in our own yard.
   - We speed up when we put on seat belts.
   - We fear nuclear power but not sunlight.
4. What is a "risk thermostat" (21)? What does Szalavitz mean when she says that "one person's risk thermostat may have different settings for different types of risk"?
5. According to Szalavitz, what are the consequences of overestimating the dangers of the world? How does understanding our "innate biases" (29) help us manage the way we respond to risk?

Purpose and Audience

1. Szalavitz states her thesis at the end of paragraph 4. What information does she present in her first four paragraphs? Would readers be able to understand her thesis without this information? Explain.

2. What preconceived ideas does Szalavitz assume her readers have about risk? How can you tell?

3. What is Szalavitz's purpose in writing this essay? To inform readers? To persuade them? Or does she have some other purpose in mind?

4. Szalavitz's essay appeared in *Psychology Today,* a publication aimed at readers who are interested in psychology. How would Szalavitz have to revise this essay to make it appeal to readers with more general interests?

Style and Structure

1. Szalavitz uses headings and subheadings to introduce the sections of her essay. Why? Would her essay be as effective without these headings and subheadings?

2. Szalavitz presents ten examples to support her thesis. Does she present enough examples? Does she include a fair range of examples? Are all her examples necessary? Are they equally appropriate and convincing?

3. Szalavitz draws some of her examples from research sources. Would the essay have been more or less convincing if all Szalavitz's examples were drawn from her own experience? Explain.

4. Does Szalavitz arrange her examples in any particular order — for example, from least important to most important? Explain.

5. **Vocabulary Project.** At several points in her essay, Szalavitz defines some basic terms — for example, *risk* (3), *fear* (5), and *emotions* (5). Why does she think she has to define these terms for readers?

Journal Entry

Do you agree with Szalavitz when she says our emotions cause us to make snap decisions? Could she be accused of overstating her case?

Writing Workshop

1. Choose one of the ten types of risks Szalavitz discusses. Then, write an essay in which you use several examples from your own experience to illustrate Szalavitz's point about this risk.

2. Do you consider yourself to be risk averse or risk inclined? Write an essay in which you use at least four examples to support your thesis.

3. **Working with Sources.** The following quiz appeared along with Szalavitz's essay. Take the quiz, and then, on the basis of your score, write an essay in which you agree or disagree with Szalavitz's thesis. In your essay, use examples from the quiz as well as from Szalavitz's essay. Be sure to include parenthetical documentation and a works-cited page. (See Chapter 18 for information on MLA documentation.)

How good is your grasp of risk?

1. What's more common in the United States, (a) suicide or (b) homicide?
2. What's the more frequent cause of death in the United States, (a) pool drowning or (b) falling out of bed?
3. What are the top five causes of accidental death in America, following motor-vehicle accidents, and which is the biggest one?
4. Of the top two causes of nonaccidental death in America, (a) cancer and (b) heart disease, which kills more women?
5. What are the next three causes of nonaccidental death in the United States?
6. Which has killed more Americans, (a) bird flu or (b) mad cow disease?
7. How many Americans die from AIDS every year, (a) 12,995, (b) 129,950, or (c) 1,299,500?
8. How many Americans die from diabetes every year, (a) 72,820, (b) 728,200, or (c) 7,282,000?
9. Which kills more Americans, (a) appendicitis or (b) salmonella?
10. Which kills more Americans, (a) pregnancy and childbirth or (b) malnutrition?

ANSWERS (all refer to number of Americans per year, on average):

1. a
2. a
3. In order: drug overdose, fire, choking, falling down stairs, bicycle accidents
4. b
5. In order: stroke, respiratory disease, diabetes
6. No American has died from either one
7. a
8. a
9. a
10. b

Sources:

• Centers for Disease Control and Prevention (Division of Vital Statistics)
• National Transportation Safety Board

Combining the Patterns

Although this essay is primarily an exemplification, it contains several **cause-and-effect** paragraphs—for example, paragraphs 6 and 10. Read these two paragraphs, and determine what they contribute to the essay.

Thematic Connections
- "Should Driverless Cars Kill Their Own Passengers to Save a Pedestrian?" (page 219)
- "How to Spot Fake News" (page 289)
- "Why Rational People Buy into Conspiracy Theories" (page 338)
- "The Ways We Lie" (page 463)

JAMAICA KINCAID

"Girl" (Fiction)

Jamaica Kincaid's novels, short stories, and nonfiction frequently reflect on race, colonialism, adolescence, gender, and the weight of family relationships and personal history. Born Elaine Potter Richardson in St. John's, Antigua, in 1949, she changed her name to Jamaica Kincaid in 1973 partly to avoid a negative response from her family, who disapproved of her writing. She moved to New York City at seventeen and worked as a nanny. She began college but dropped out to write for *Ingenue*, a teen magazine, as well as the *Village Voice*. In 1985, she became a staff writer for the *New Yorker*, where she worked until 1996. Her first published work of fiction, "Girl," appeared in that magazine in 1978. Kincaid credits *New Yorker* editor William Shawn for "show[ing] me what my voice was. . . . He made me feel that what I thought, my inner life, my thoughts as I organized them, were important." The author of *Annie John* (1985), *My Brother* (1997), *Among Flowers: A Walk in the Himalaya* (2005), and many other books, Kincaid is a professor of African and African American Studies in Residence at Harvard University.

Background on slavery and colonialism in the West Indies   Europeans brought Africans to the Caribbean islands in the sixteenth and seventeenth centuries to work as slaves, primarily on sugar plantations. In her nonfiction book *A Small Place*, Kincaid writes searingly of her native island's dark colonial history, the "large ships filled up with human cargo." The human beings, she says, were "forced to work under conditions that were cruel and inhuman, they were beaten, they were murdered, they were sold, their children were taken from them and these separations lasted forever." Although the British outlawed slavery in the 1830s, Blacks remained the largest percentage of the population in the British Caribbean colonies. Antigua remained a British colony until 1981. After independence, economic conditions on the island declined, with many of the descendants of the original slaves living in poverty, some in abject poverty. Currently, the economy of Antigua is weak, relying mostly on tourism and government-service industries. The area was also heavily impacted by Hurricane Irma, which made landfall in Antigua in autumn 2017.

Wash the white clothes on Monday and put them on the stone heap; wash the color clothes on Tuesday and put them on the clothesline to dry; don't walk barehead in the hot sun; cook pumpkin fritters in very hot sweet oil; soak your little cloths right after you take them off; when buying cotton to make yourself a nice blouse, be sure that it doesn't have gum on it, because that way it won't hold up well after a wash; soak salt fish overnight before you cook it; is it true that you sing benna* in Sunday school?; always eat your food in such a way that it won't turn someone else's stomach; on Sundays try to walk like a lady

1

---

* Eds. note — Form of popular music.

and not like the slut you are so bent on becoming; don't sing benna in Sunday school; you mustn't speak to wharf-rat boys, not even to give directions; don't eat fruits on the street — flies will follow you; *but I don't sing benna on Sundays at all and never in Sunday school;* this is how to sew on a button; this is how to make a button-hole for the button you have just sewed on; this is how to hem a dress when you see the hem coming down and so to prevent yourself from looking like the slut I know you are so bent on becoming; this is how you iron your father's khaki shirt so that it doesn't have a crease; this is how you iron your father's khaki pants so that they don't have a crease; this is how you grow okra — far from the house, because okra tree harbors red ants; when you are growing dasheen, make sure it gets plenty of water or else it makes your throat itch when you are eating it; this is how you sweep a corner; this is how you sweep a whole house; this is how you sweep a yard; this is how you smile to someone you don't like too much; this is how you smile to someone you don't like at all; this is how you smile to someone you like completely; this is how you set a table for tea; this is how you set a table for dinner; this is how you set a table for dinner with an important guest; this is how you set a table for lunch; this is how you set a table for breakfast; this is how to behave in the presence of men who don't know you very well, and this way they won't recognize immediately the slut I have warned you against becoming; be sure to wash every day, even if it is with your own spit; don't squat down to play marbles — you are not a boy, you know; don't pick people's flowers — you might catch something; don't throw stones at blackbirds, because it might not be a blackbird at all; this is how to make a bread pudding; this is how to make doukona;* this is how to make pepper pot; this is how to make a good medicine for a cold; this is how to make a good medicine to throw away a child before it even becomes a child; this is how to catch a fish; this is how to throw back a fish you don't like, and that way something bad won't fall on you; this is how to bully a man; this is how a man bullies you; this is how to love a man, and if this doesn't work there are other ways, and if they don't work don't feel too bad about giving up; this is how to spit up in the air if you feel like it, and this is how to move quick so that it doesn't fall on you; this is how to make ends meet; always squeeze bread to make sure it's fresh; *but what if the baker won't let me feel the bread?;* you mean to say that after all you are really going to be the kind of woman who the baker won't let near the bread?

> "[T]his is how you set a table for lunch; this is how you set a table for breakfast. . . . "

·   ·   ·

---

* Eds. note — A spiced pudding.

Reading Literature

1. Who is the speaker in the story? To whom is she speaking?
2. What do the speaker's remarks suggest about being female? Do the speaker's ideas correspond to your own ideas about being female? Explain.
3. Do you think this story has political or social implications? For example, what does the speaker's list suggest about the status of working-class women who live in poverty in the West Indies?

Journal Entry

Write a journal entry in which you record the duties of a woman (or a man) in your family.

Thematic Connections

- " 'What's in a Name?' " (page 2)
- "My Mother Never Worked" (page 122)
- "I Want a Wife" (page 494)

Writing Assignments for Exemplification

1. Write a humorous essay about a ritual, ceremony, or celebration you experienced and the types of people who participated in it. Make a point about the event, and use the participants as examples to support your point.
2. Write an essay establishing that you are an optimistic (or pessimistic) person. Use examples to support your case.
3. If you could change three or four things at your school, what would they be? Use examples from your own experience to support your recommendations, and tie your recommendations together in your thesis statement.
4. **Working with Sources.** Write an essay discussing two or three of the greatest challenges facing the United States today. Refer to essays in this chapter, such as "Just Walk On By" (page 231), or to essays elsewhere in this book, such as "The Hidden Life of Garbage" (page 185), "On Dumpster Diving" (page 668), or "Did Free Pens Cause the Opioid Crisis?" (page 332). Be sure to document any references to your sources and to include a works-cited page. (See Chapter 18 for information on MLA documentation.)
5. Using your family and friends as examples, write an essay suggesting some of the positive or negative characteristics of Americans.
6. Write an essay presenting your formula for achieving success in college. You may, if you wish, talk about things such as scheduling time, maintaining a high energy level, and learning how to relax. Use examples from your own experience to make your point.
7. Write an exemplification essay discussing how cooperation has helped you achieve some important goal. Support your thesis with a single well-developed example.
8. Choose an event you believe illustrates a less-than-admirable moment in your life. Then, write an essay explaining your feelings about it.
9. Americans have always had a long-standing infatuation with music icons. Choose several pop groups or stars, old and new — such as Elvis Presley, the Beatles, Michael Jackson, Alicia Keys, Adele, Beyoncé Knowles, Drake, and Taylor Swift, to name only a few — and use them to illustrate the characteristics that you think make pop stars so appealing.

Collaborative Activity for Exemplification

The following passage appeared in a handbook given to parents of entering students at a midwestern university:

The freshman experience is like no other — at once challenging, exhilarating, and fun. Students face academic challenges as they are exposed to many new ideas. They also face personal challenges as they meet many new people from diverse backgrounds. It is a time to mature and grow. It is an opportunity to explore new subjects and familiar ones. There may be no more challenging and exciting time of personal growth than the first year of university study.

Working in groups of four, brainstorm to identify examples that support or refute the idea that there "may be no more challenging and exciting time of personal growth" than the first year of college. Then, choose one person from each group to tell the class the position the group took and explain the examples you collected. Finally, work together to write an essay that presents your group's position. Have one student write the first draft, two others revise this draft, and the last student edit and proofread the revised draft.

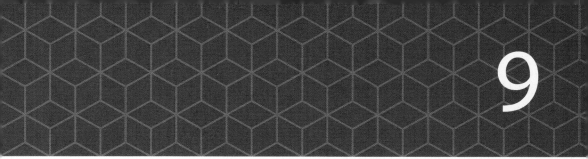

Process

What Is Process?

A **process** essay explains how to do something or how something occurs. It presents a sequence of steps and shows how those steps lead to a particular result. In the following paragraph from the college biology textbook *What Is Life? A Guide to Biology*, writer Jay Phelan explains a scientific process.

Process presents series of steps in chronological order

Topic sentence

Researchers have developed a way to make the bacteria of interest identify themselves. First, a chemical is added to the entire population of bacterial cells, separating the double-stranded DNA into single strands. Next, a short sequence of single-stranded DNA is washed over the bacteria. Called a DNA probe, this DNA contains part of the sequence of the gene of interest and has also been modified so that it is radioactive. Bacteria with the gene of interest bind to this probe and glow with radioactivity. <u>These cells can then be separated out and grown in large numbers—for example, vats of *E. coli* that produce human growth hormone.</u>

Process, like narration, generally presents events in chronological order. Unlike a narrative, however, a process essay typically presents a particular series of events that produce the same outcome whenever it is duplicated. Because these events form a sequence with a fixed order, clarity is extremely important. Whether your readers will actually perform the process or are simply trying to understand how it occurs, your essay should make clear not only the order of the individual steps but also their relationships to one another and to the process as a whole. This means that you need to provide logical transitions between the steps in a process and that you need to present the steps in chronological order—that is, in the order in which they occur or are to be performed.

Depending on its purpose, a process essay can be either a set of *instructions* or a *process explanation*.

Understanding Instructions

The purpose of **instructions** is to enable readers to perform a process —
for example, how to use a library's online databases or how to register for
classes on a school's website. Recipes are structured as instructions, as are
GPS directions and guidelines for assembling furniture or setting up a new
computer. Instructions use the present tense and, like commands, they use
the imperative mood, speaking directly to readers: "*Disconnect* the system, and
check the electrical source."

Understanding Process Explanations

The purpose of a **process explanation** is not to enable readers to perform a
process but rather to help them understand how it is carried out. Such essays may
examine anything from how silkworms spin their cocoons to how Michelangelo
and Leonardo da Vinci painted their masterpieces on plaster walls and ceilings.

A process explanation may use the first person (*I*, *we*) or the third (*he, she, it,
they,* and so on), the past tense or the present. Because its readers need to understand the process, not perform it, a process explanation does not use the second
person (*you*) or the imperative mood (commands). The style of a process explanation varies, depending on whether a writer is explaining a process that takes
place regularly or one that occurred in the past, and also depending on whether
the writer or someone else carries out the steps. The following chart suggests
the stylistic options available to writers of process explanations.

	First Person	*Third Person*
Present tense	"Before I begin writing my draft, I take some time to plan." *(habitual process performed by the writer)*	"Before he begins writing his draft, he takes some time to plan." *(habitual process performed by someone other than the writer)*
Past tense	"Before I began writing my draft, I took some time to plan." *(process performed in the past by the writer)*	"Before he began writing his draft, he took some time to plan." *(process performed in the past by someone other than the writer)*

Using Process

College writing frequently calls for instructions or process explanations.
In a biology essay on genetic testing, you might devote a paragraph to an
explanation of the process of amniocentesis; in an editorial about the negative side of fraternity life, you might include a brief account of the process of
pledging. You can also organize an entire essay around a process pattern. For
example, in a literature essay, you might trace the steps in a fictional
character's progress toward some new insight; on a finance midterm, you
might explain the procedure for approving a commercial loan.

Planning a Process Essay

As you plan a process essay, remember that your primary goal is to explain the process accurately. This means that you need to distinguish between what usually or always happens and what occasionally or rarely happens as well as between necessary steps and optional ones. You should also mentally test all the steps in sequence to make sure the process really works as you say it does, checking carefully for omitted steps or incorrect information. If you are writing about a process you observed, try to test the accuracy of your explanation by observing the process again.

Accommodating Your Audience

As you write, remember to keep your readers' needs in mind. When necessary, explain the reasons for performing each step, describe unfamiliar materials or equipment, define terms, and warn readers about possible problems that may occur during the process. (Sometimes you may want to include illustrations to clarify one or more steps.) Besides complete information, your readers need a clear and consistent discussion, without ambiguities or digressions. For this reason, you should avoid unnecessary shifts in tense, person, voice, and mood. You should also be careful not to omit articles (*a, an,* and *the*); if you want your discussion to flow smoothly, you need to avoid the kind of choppy sentences often found in cookbooks.

Developing a Thesis Statement

Both instructions and process explanations can be written either to persuade or simply to present information. If its purpose is persuasive, a process essay may take a strong stand in a **thesis statement**, such as "Applying for food stamps is a needlessly complex process that discourages many qualified recipients" or "The process of slaughtering baby seals is inhumane and sadistic." Many process essays, however, communicate nothing more debatable than the standard procedure for blood typing. Even in such a case, though, the essay should have a clear thesis statement that identifies the process and perhaps tells why it is performed: "Typing their own blood can familiarize students with some basic laboratory procedures."

Using Transitions

Throughout your essay, use transitional words and phrases to make sure each step, each stage, and each paragraph lead logically to the next. Transitions such as *first, second, meanwhile, after this, next, then, at the same time, when you have finished,* and *finally* help establish sequential and chronological relationships so that readers can follow the process. (A more complete list of transitions appears on page 56.)

Structuring a Process Essay

Like other essays, a process essay generally consists of three sections. The **introduction** identifies the process and indicates why and under what circumstances it is performed. This section may include information about necessary materials or preliminary preparations, or it may present an overview of the process, perhaps even listing its major stages. The essay's thesis is also usually stated in the introduction.

Each paragraph in the **body** of the essay typically treats one major stage of the process. Each stage may group several steps, depending on the nature and complexity of the process. These steps are presented in chronological order, interrupted only for essential definitions, explanations, or cautions.

A short process essay may not need a formal **conclusion**. If an essay does have a conclusion, however, it will often briefly review the procedure's major stages. Such an ending is especially useful if the essay has outlined a technical procedure that may seem complicated to general readers. The conclusion may also reinforce the thesis by summarizing the results of the process or explaining its significance.

Suppose you are taking a midterm exam in a course in childhood and adolescent behavior. One essay question calls for a process explanation: "Trace the stages that children go through in acquiring language." After thinking about the question, you draft the following thesis statement: "Although individual cases may differ, most children acquire language in a predictable series of stages." You then plan your essay and develop an informal outline, which might look like the one below.

SAMPLE OUTLINE: Process

INTRODUCTION

Thesis statement: Although individual cases may differ, most children acquire language in a predictable series of stages.

FIRST STAGE

Two to twelve months: Prelinguistic behavior, including "babbling" and appropriate responses to nonverbal cues

SECOND STAGE

End of first year: Single words as commands or requests; infant catalogs his or her environment

THIRD STAGE

Beginning of second year: Expressive jargon (flow of sounds that imitates adult speech); real words along with jargon

FOURTH AND FINAL STAGE

Middle of second year to beginning of third year: Two-word phrases; longer strings; missing parts of speech

CONCLUSION

Restatement of thesis (in different words) or review of major stages of process

Your essay, when completed, will show not only what the stages of the process are but also how they relate to one another. In addition, it will support the thesis that children learn language through a well-defined process.

Revising a Process Essay

When you revise a set of instructions or a process explanation, consider the items on Checklist: Revising on page 68. In addition, pay special attention to the items on the following checklist, which apply specifically to revising process essays.

✓ REVISION CHECKLIST **PROCESS**

- ☐ Does your assignment call for a set of instructions or a process explanation?
- ☐ Is your essay's style appropriate for the kind of process essay (instructions or process explanation) you are writing?
- ☐ Does your essay have a clearly stated thesis that identifies the process and perhaps tells why it is (or was) performed?
- ☐ Have you included all necessary steps?
- ☐ Are the steps presented in chronological order?
- ☐ Do transitions clearly indicate where one step ends and the next begins?
- ☐ Have you included all necessary reminders and cautions?
- ☐ Do your steps require supporting sources and documentation?

Editing a Process Essay

When you edit your process essay, follow the guidelines on the editing checklists on pages 85, 88, and 92. In addition, focus on the grammar, mechanics, and punctuation issues that are particularly relevant to process essays. One of these issues — avoiding unnecessary shifts in tense, person, voice, and mood — is discussed on pages 262–63.

🔍 GRAMMAR IN CONTEXT AVOIDING UNNECESSARY SHIFTS

To explain a process to readers, you need to use consistent verb **tense** (past or present), **person** (first, second, or third), **voice** (active or passive), and **mood** (statements or commands). Unnecessary shifts in tense, person, voice, or mood can confuse readers and make it difficult for them to follow your process.

Avoiding Shifts in Tense Use present tense for a process that is performed regularly.

"The body <u>is</u> first laid out in the undertaker's morgue — or rather, Mr. Jones <u>is</u> reposing in the preparation room — to be readied to bid the world farewell" (Mitford 297).

Use past tense for a process that was performed in the past.

"Soon the men <u>began</u> to gather, surveying their own children, speaking of planting and rain, tractors and taxes" (Jackson 304).

Shift from present to past tense only when you need to indicate a change in time: *Usually, I <u>study</u> several days before a test, but this time I <u>studied</u> the night before.*

Avoiding Shifts in Person In process explanations, use first or third person.

FIRST PERSON (*I*):	"<u>I</u> reached for the box of Medium Ash Brown hair color just as my friend Veronica grabbed the box labeled Sparkling Sherry" (Hunt 269).
FIRST PERSON (*WE*):	"<u>We</u> decided to use my bathroom to color our hair" (Hunt 269).
THIRD PERSON (*HE*):	"The embalmer, having allowed an appropriate interval to elapse, returns to the attack, but now <u>he</u> brings into play the skill and equipment of sculptor and cosmetician" (Mitford 299).

In instructions, use second person.

SECOND PERSON (*YOU*):	"For the waste pie chart, <u>you</u> only need to collect one bag of waste" (Spranz 281).

When you give instructions, be careful not to shift from third to second person.

INCORRECT:	<u>Everyone</u> needs to pick up every nonorganic piece of waste <u>you</u> come across. (shift from third to second person)

CORRECT: "<u>You</u> need to pick up every non-organic piece of waste <u>you</u> come across" (Spranz 282). (second person used consistently)

Avoiding Shifts in Voice Use active voice when you want to emphasize the person performing the action.

"Fake news <u>is</u> nothing new" (Kiely and Robertson 289).

Use passive voice to emphasize the action itself rather than the person performing it.

"The patching and filling completed, Mr. Jones <u>is</u> now <u>shaved</u>, <u>washed</u>, and <u>dressed</u>" (Mitford 300).

Do not shift between the active and the passive voice, especially within a sentence, unless your intent is to change your emphasis.

INCORRECT: Once you <u>know</u> how many items you <u>have</u> in each group, they can <u>be added</u> up to get your total number of waste items. (shift from active to passive voice)

CORRECT: "Once you <u>know</u> how many items you <u>have</u> in each category, <u>add</u> them up to get your total number of waste items" (Spranz 282). (active voice used consistently)

Avoiding Shifts in Mood Use the indicative mood (statements) for process explanations.

"The children <u>assembled</u> first, of course" (Jackson 303).

Use the imperative mood (commands) only in instructions.

"<u>Check</u> your biases" (Kiely and Robertson 293).

Be careful not to shift from the imperative mood to the indicative mood.

INCORRECT: When you leave the room, <u>do not yell</u> at the medical student who has a question. When you get home, <u>you should not yell</u> at your husband. (shift from imperative to indicative mood)

CORRECT: "When you leave the room, <u>do not yell</u> at the medical student who has a question. When you get home, <u>do not yell</u> at your husband" (Rosenberg 277). (imperative mood used consistently)

CORRECT: When you leave the room<u>, you should not</u> yell at the medical student who has a question. When you get home<u>, you should not</u> yell at your husband. (indicative mood used consistently)

✓ **EDITING CHECKLIST** **PROCESS**

☐ Have you used commas correctly in a series of three or more steps, including a comma before the *and*?
☐ Have you used parallel structure for items in a series?
☐ Have you avoided unnecessary shifts in tense?
☐ Have you avoided unnecessary shifts in person?
☐ Have you avoided unnecessary shifts in voice?
☐ Have you avoided unnecessary shifts in mood?

A STUDENT WRITER: Instructions

The following essay, by Mya Nunnally, gives readers instructions for how to find a paid internship. It was written for a composition class in response to this assignment: "Write an essay giving practical instructions for doing something that people you know might need to do at one time or another. Be sure to acknowledge any sources you use."

Steps to the Dream

Introduction

My dream for my last summer in college was to live in New York   1
City. For years, I'd wanted to spend a summer in the city, surrounded by art, opportunities, and an endlessly interesting population. The only problem was that I didn't come from a wealthy background. While some of my peers could afford to work at unpaid internships and still survive in one of the most expensive places in the world, that simply wasn't an option for me. Instead, I needed to secure a paid position for the summer. Though it was tough, I eventually succeeded. Obtaining a rewarding paid internship was challenging as

Thesis statement

well as time consuming, but I learned that if I followed a few crucial steps, I could do it.

First step in process: Plan your search

If you want to find a paid internship, you'll want to start early   2
because many companies begin their hiring process several months before the start date of the position. For example, if you want to work in the summer, you shouldn't wait to start looking until March or April; you should really begin as early as December of the previous year. Before you even begin looking anywhere, you need to decide what your parameters for the internship will be. Where do you want to work, and how far are you willing to commute every day? How many hours are you looking to commit to per week? And, perhaps most important: what do you even want to do?

Second step: Explore your school's resources

Once you have set your internal goals, it's time to check out   3
your school's resources. Most colleges and universities have an office
set up specifically for helping students find jobs and internships.
There, specialists can do anything from helping you to create a
resume to conducting practice interviews. The career-services office
also might have resources like a list of alumni who are willing to
meet informally with students to advise them on opportunities in
their fields—or even help students find a position where they work.
This office is sure to be helpful, so make sure to stop there instead of
beginning your search all on your own.

Third step: Prepare application materials

The next step is to fine-tune your application materials.   4
Update your resume, and go through it with a fine-tooth comb to
ensure it is flawless, free from grammar mistakes or resume faux pas
(like including a picture of yourself). Any glaring mistakes on your
resume will immediately stop potential employers from seeing you as
a viable candidate, and into the trash pile you will go. Finally, limit
your resume to one page. According to *TIME* magazine's business blog,
recruiters spend an average of *six seconds* on each individual resume
that crosses their desk (Sanburn). This means that a long resume is
not likely to be read.

Fourth step: Search online resources

Now, it's time to start your search. Though a Google search might   5
yield some results, better, more focused results can be found through
specific search engines, such as internships.com, internmatch.com, and
LinkedIn. There are also some engines specific to the field you might
be looking in. For example, I was looking for jobs in the publishing
industry, so I explored bookjobs.com and mediabistro.com. In addition,
your school might have its own search engine for positions; Handshake
is one example. Whatever search tool you use, be sure to narrow down
your search by using filters for location, field, and experience level so
that you get a manageable number of results.

You also might want to go directly to the company websites of   6
places you know you're interested in. For example, many well-known
publishers have career opportunity pages, and I found many positions
listed there. Because you're only looking for *paid* experiences, make
sure you are only applying to openings that explicitly say they pay
their interns. If a position mentions paying in "college credit" or
"experience," that should be a red flag.

Fifth step: Apply for specific positions

Once you're ready to apply for a position, it's important to read   7
the job description carefully so you can play to the specific strengths
that the company is looking for. If they are looking for someone who

can multitask, for instance, the cover letter you write for them should highlight your experience juggling multiple projects. You should always include a cover letter that is at least a little personalized and tailored to the internship you're applying for.

Sixth step: Prepare for interviews

Finally, when you get calls for interviews, remember to practice   8 interview etiquette. Dress neatly and conservatively, assume strong body posture, and *always* send a follow-up email thanking your interviewer. Many hiring managers will not consider candidates who don't follow these guidelines. If all goes well, you'll be deciding among several job offers in no time.

Conclusion (paragraphs 9–11)

The process of looking for a paid internship can be draining,   9 and rejections can pile up quickly because so many people apply for each opening. But the secret is to not give up. My internship offers came only after months of non-stop applying, and only at the tail end of the process! If I had given up after a few weeks, I wouldn't have had any options at all.

My paid internship allowed me to gain valuable workplace   10 experience while living in the greatest city in the world. As SUNY's blog explains, "Learning is one thing, but taking those skills into the workforce and applying them is a great way to explore different career paths and specializations that suit individual interests" (Maio). I also had the opportunity to dip my toes gently into the life of full-time work before jumping in completely after college. I am probably most grateful for one particular aspect of my internship: it helped me to understand what I do and don't want to do once I graduate this coming year. This knowledge will allow me to decide which full-time positions to apply for once I'm out in the real world.

Though this process might seem daunting and arduous, it   11 doesn't have to be if you start early and take your time. And trust me, when you're getting paid while accumulating priceless months of experience, you'll know it was worth it.

Works Cited

Maio, Julie. "10 Reasons Why an Internship Is Important to All Students." *Blog of the State University of New York*, 29 June 2018, blog.suny .edu/2018/06/10-reasons-why-an-internship-is-important-to -all-students/

Sanburn, Josh. "How to Make Your Resume Last Longer Than 6 Seconds." *TIME*, 13 April 2012, business.time.com/2012/04/13 /how-to-make-your-resume-last-longer-than-6-seconds/

Points for Special Attention

Introduction

Mya Nunnally begins her essay by giving readers some background about her own experiences looking for a paid internship. This strategy enables her to engage her readers right away and also gives her some credibility, establishing her as an "expert" who is qualified to explain the process. She ends her introduction with a thesis statement that tells readers that following the process she will outline, although challenging, can help them achieve their goal.

Structure

As she planned her essay, Mya made sure to order the process chronologically because she believed that readers would need to follow the steps in this order to have a successful outcome. In the paragraph that follows the introduction, Mya explains what to consider before the search gets under way. Then, in paragraphs 3 through 8, she explains how to go about the actual search for an internship. Finally, her conclusion (paragraphs 9–11) reinforces her thesis and then returns to her own experiences to reassure readers that a positive outcome is possible and worth the struggle.

Purpose and Style

Because Mya's assignment asked her to write instructions, she knew she had to write about a process readers could actually be expected to perform. Therefore, she uses the second person ("If *you* want to find a paid internship . . .") and the present tense, with many of her verbs in the form of commands ("*Dress neatly and conservatively . . .*").

Because she knew how difficult finding an internship could be and how threatening the process might be to students' self-esteem, she tried to use a positive tone throughout. She hoped that reading an essay that was honest about how difficult the process could be but also hopeful about the potential outcome could help students in the same position she was in.

Transitions

To make her essay clear and easy to follow, Mya includes transitions that indicate the order in which the steps in the process should be performed ("Now," "The next step," "Finally," and so on). She also includes transitional sentences to move her essay from one step in the process to the next:

- "If you want to find a paid internship, you'll want to start early" (2)
- "Once you have set your internal goals . . ." (3)
- "The next step is to fine-tune your application materials." (4)
- "Now, it's time to start your search." (5)
- "Once you're ready to apply for a position . . ." (6)
- "Finally, when you get calls for interviews . . ." (8)

Focus on Revision

When they reviewed her essay, the students in Mya's peer-editing group questioned the appropriateness of her use of contractions. Although their instructor had explained that this essay was to be informal and had approved the use of first-person pronouns for this assignment, the group agreed that the contractions made the essay's voice seem less authoritative. When Mya tried editing out a few contractions, she saw at once that her substitutions made her discussion more convincing, and she planned to continue to replace contractions when she revised.

When the discussion turned to paragraphing, various students had comments to make. One thought that paragraph 8 needed further development; another thought paragraph 6's topic sentence wasn't strong enough. In both cases, Mya thought she might be able to address their criticisms by combining these two paragraphs with others. For example, paragraph 6 could be combined with paragraph 5 because both focus on online searching. Also, she considered relocating paragraph 9 to the beginning of her essay's last paragraph. With a little editing, this adjustment might solve another problem: a student's objection that the current three-paragraph conclusion was too long.

Finally, Mya's fellow students, all of whom had different majors, wanted her to provide more information on the kinds of internships available in fields other than publishing. That seemed like a good idea to Mya, and she decided to add a few brief references to other fields in paragraphs 5 and 6. Students in her group also thought she could add more information about what she actually did in her publishing internship, but Mya decided not to do that. In fact, she had originally included a paragraph devoted to her own internship, including some anecdotes, but she had deleted that paragraph because she thought it strayed from the true topic of her essay, which was about *finding* an internship, not experiencing one.

Working with Sources

Mya's classmates thought that the two sources she used strengthened her essay, but they had two suggestions. First, one student suggested that Mya move the quotation from the SUNY blog from paragraph 10 to the introduction, where it would help establish a motivation for seeking an internship. Mya liked this idea, particularly because moving the quotation would help shorten her long conclusion. In addition, the peer-reviewers agreed that adding quotations from students who had benefited from internships—particularly those in fields other than publishing—would broaden the essay's appeal. That suggestion made sense to Mya, who decided to try to create a new paragraph immediately after the introduction to include these viewpoints.

All in all, Mya's meeting with her peer-editing group gave her a lot to think about, but she would still have to decide which of their suggestions to follow. (A sample peer-editing worksheet appears on page 272.)

A STUDENT WRITER: Process Explanation

The essay that follows, by Melany Hunt, is a **process explanation**. It was written for a composition class in response to the assignment "Write an essay explaining a process that changed your appearance in some way."

Medium Ash Brown

Introduction

The beautiful chestnut-haired woman pictured on the box   1
seemed to beckon to me. I reached for the box of Medium Ash Brown hair color just as my friend Veronica grabbed the box labeled Sparkling Sherry. I can't remember our reasons for wanting to change our hair color, but they seemed to make sense at the time. Maybe we were just bored. I do remember that the idea of transforming our appearance came up unexpectedly. Impulsively, we decided to change

Thesis statement

our hair color — and, we hoped, ourselves — that very evening. The process that followed taught me that some impulses should definitely be resisted.

Materials assembled

We decided to use my bathroom to color our hair. Inside   2
each box of hair color, we found two little bottles and a small tube wrapped in a page of instructions. Attached to the instruction page itself were two very large, one-size-fits-all plastic gloves, which looked and felt like plastic sandwich bags. The directions recommended having some old towels around to soak up any spills or drips that might occur. Under the sink we found some old, frayed towels that I figured my mom had forgotten about, and we spread

First stage of process: Preparing the color

them around the bathtub. After we put our gloves on, we began the actual coloring process. First we poured the first bottle into the second, which was half-full of some odd-smelling liquid. The smell was not much better after we combined the two bottles. The directions advised us to cut off a small section of hair to use as a sample. For some reason, we decided to skip this step.

Second stage of process: Applying the color

At this point, Veronica and I took turns leaning over the tub   3
to wet our hair for the color. The directions said to leave the color on the hair for fifteen to twenty minutes, so we found a little timer and set it for fifteen minutes. Next, we applied the color to our hair. Again, we took turns, squeezing the bottle in order to cover all our hair. We then wrapped the old towels around our sour-smelling hair and went outside to get some fresh air.

Third stage of process: Rinsing

After the fifteen minutes were up, we rinsed our hair.   4
According to the directions, we were to add a little water and scrub as

if we were shampooing our hair. The color lathered up, and we rinsed our hair until the water ran clear. So far, so good.

Last stage of process: Applying conditioner

The last part of the process involved applying the small tube   5 of conditioner to our hair (because colored hair becomes brittle and easily damaged). We used the conditioner as directed, and then we dried our hair so that we could see the actual color. Even before I looked in the mirror, I heard Veronica's gasp.

Outcome of process

"Nice try," I said, assuming she was just trying to make me   6 nervous, "but you're not funny."

"Mel," she said, "look in the mirror." Slowly, I turned around.   7 My stomach turned into a lead ball when I saw my reflection. My hair was the putrid greenish-brown color of a winter lawn, dying in patches yet still a nice green in the shade.

The next day in school, I wore my hair tied back under a   8 baseball cap. I told only my close friends what I had done. After they were finished laughing, they offered their deepest, most heartfelt condolences. They also offered many suggestions — none very helpful — on what to do to get my old hair color back.

Conclusion

It is now three months later, and I still have no idea what   9 prompted me to color my hair. My only consolation is that I resisted my first impulse: to use a wild color, like blue or fuchsia. Still, as I wait for my hair to grow out, and as I assemble a larger and larger collection of baseball caps, it is small consolation indeed.

Points for Special Attention

Structure

In Melany's opening paragraph, her thesis statement makes it very clear that the experience she describes is not one she would recommend to others. The temptation she describes in her introduction's first few sentences lures readers into her essay, just as the picture on the box lured her. Her second paragraph lists the contents of the box and explains how she and her friend assembled the other necessary materials. Then, she explains the first stage in the process: preparing the color. Paragraphs 3 through 5 describe the other stages in the process in chronological order, and paragraphs 6 through 8 record Melany's and her friend Veronica's reactions to their experiment. In paragraph 9, Melany sums up the impact of her experience and once again expresses her annoyance with herself for her impulsive act.

Purpose and Style

Melany's purpose is not to enable others to duplicate the process she explains; on the contrary, she wants to discourage readers from doing what she did. Consequently, she presents her process not as a set of instructions but as a process explanation, using first person and past tense to explain her and her friend's experiences. She also largely eliminates cautions and reminders that her readers, who are not likely to undertake the process, will not need to know.

Detail

Melany's essay includes vivid descriptive detail that gives readers a clear sense of the process and its outcome. Throughout, her emphasis is on the negative aspects of the process — the "odd-smelling liquid" and the "putrid greenish-brown color" of her hair, for instance — and this emphasis is consistent with her essay's purpose.

Transitions

To move readers smoothly through the process, Melany includes clear transitions ("First," "At this point," "Next," "then") and clearly identifies the beginning of the process ("After we put our gloves on, we began the actual coloring process") as well as the end ("The last part of the process").

Focus on Revision

The writing center tutor who read Melany's draft thought it was clearly written and structured and that its ironic, self-mocking tone was well suited to her audience and purpose. He thought, however, that some minor revisions would make her essay even more effective. Specifically, he thought that paragraph 2 began too abruptly: paragraph 1 recorded the purchase of the hair color, and paragraph 2 opened with the sentence "We decided to use my bathroom to color our hair," leaving readers wondering how much time had passed between purchase and application. Because the thesis rests on the idea of the foolishness of an impulsive gesture, it is important for readers to understand that the girls presumably went immediately from the store to Melany's house.

After thinking about this criticism, Melany decided to write a clearer opening for paragraph 2: "As soon as we paid for the color, we returned to my house, where, eager to begin our transformation, we locked ourselves in my bathroom. Inside each box. . . ." She also decided to divide paragraph 2 into two paragraphs, one describing the materials and another beginning with "After we put our gloves on," which introduces the first step in the process.

Another possible revision Melany considered was developing Veronica's character further. Although both girls purchase and apply hair color, readers never learn what happens to Veronica. Melany knew she could easily add a brief paragraph after paragraph 7, describing Veronica's "Sparkling Sherry" hair in humorous terms. Her writing center tutor agreed that it would be a good addition, and Melany planned to add this material in her essay's final draft.

Working with Sources

Melany's tutor suggested that she might refer in her essay to Judith Ortiz Cofer's "The Myth of the Latin Woman: I Just Met a Girl Named Maria" (p. 224), which also examines the idea of changing one's outward appearance.

(In fact, the class's assignment—"Write an essay explaining a process that changed your appearance in some way"—was inspired by their discussion of Cofer's essay.) Melany considered this suggestion but decided not to add a reference to Cofer. After all, Cofer is critical of outside pressure to change the way she looks (in her case, to bury her ethnic identity and blend into the dominant culture). Melany, on the other hand, gives in to social pressure, hoping to look more glamorous—more like the woman on the hair-color box. More important, Melany thought Cofer's serious discussion of her self-image would not be a good fit for her own lighthearted essay. In fact, she was concerned that adding such a reference might seem to trivialize the important issues Cofer discusses.

PEER-EDITING WORKSHEET: PROCESS

1. What process does this essay describe?

2. Does the writer include all the information the audience needs? Is any vital step or piece of information missing? Is any step or piece of information irrelevant? Is any necessary definition, explanation, or caution missing or incomplete?

3. Is the essay a set of instructions or a process explanation? How can you tell? Why do you think the writer chose this strategy rather than the alternative? Do you think it was the right choice?

4. Does the writer consistently follow the stylistic conventions for the strategy—instructions or process explanation—he or she has chosen?

5. Are the steps presented in a clear, logical order? Are they grouped logically into paragraphs? Should any steps be combined or relocated? If so, which ones?

6. Does the writer use enough transitions to move readers through the process? Should any transitions be added? If so, where?

7. Does the writer need to revise to correct confusing shifts in tense, person, voice, or mood? If so, where?

8. Is the essay interesting? What descriptive details would add interest to the essay? Would a visual be helpful?

9. How would you characterize the writer's opening strategy? Is it appropriate for the essay's purpose and audience? What alternative strategy might be more effective?

10. How would you characterize the writer's closing strategy? Is it appropriate for the essay's purpose and audience? What alternative strategy might be more effective?

The reading selections that follow illustrate how varied the uses of process writing can be. The first selection, a visual text, is followed by questions designed to illustrate how process can operate in visual form.

Yellowstone Fires, Past and Future (Illustration)

Serotinous cone

Lodgepole pine

Mountain bluebird

Elk

Lupine

Aspen seedling

Heartleaf arnica

Ross's sedge

Fireweed

Lodgepole pine

SOON AFTER A FIRE
Roots of perennial flowers and grasses can survive large fires. Heat triggers lodgepole pines' serotinous cones to release seeds; those that survive take hold in newly mineral-rich soil that's open to sunlight.

1 YEAR AFTER
Aspen and lodgepole pine seedlings start small but establish quickly. Studies of the 1988 fires show that most pine seedlings germinated from seeds released from cones on fire-killed trees.

2 YEARS AFTER
Flowering plants and wildflowers take hold. Elk and foraging mammals return to burned areas, as some of their food sources, such as aspen seedlings, grow larger.

25 YEARS AFTER
Most burned trunks have fallen, and new lodgepole pines have grown to be 10 to 15 feet tall. The ecosystem has shown it can adapt well to severe fires—when they happen only every few centuries.

Matthew Twombly/National Geographic Creative

Reading Images

1. What process do these four images illustrate? Could the images communicate this process on their own, without the text?
2. Study the four images closely. What specific changes do you observe from one image to the next?
3. What message do these images convey? Is this message positive or negative? Explain.

Journal Entry

Write a short paragraph that explains the process illustrated in these four images.

Thematic Connections

- "How Do Hurricanes Form: A Step-by-Step Guide" (page 285)
- "Photos That Change History" (page 354)
- "The Obligation to Endure" (page 554)

NAOMI ROSENBERG

How to Tell a Mother Her Child Is Dead

Naomi Rosenberg attended medical school at the University of Pennsylvania, graduating in 2013. In 2010, while working toward her degree, Rosenberg took a year off to help provide medical care to victims of the Haitian earthquake. As part of this work, she helped start a group home where these refugees could continue their treatment and receive support for getting back on their feet. After graduation, Rosenberg accepted a residency at Temple University Hospital in Philadelphia. She has remained there as an assistant professor of clinical emergency medicine while practicing for Temple Health. She participated in a nonfiction writing workshop through the Narrative Medicine program at Temple University and wrote the following essay in response to the prompt "Tell someone how to do something that you know how to do."

Background on emergency rooms Although early hospitals in the United States had dedicated "accident rooms" or "accident wards" for those suffering from sudden injuries, they were typically staffed by teams of registered nurses and hospital interns, most of whom had no specific training in handling trauma. Doctors saw their patients in offices and spent little or no time serving in the unglamorous accident rooms. Injured patients were usually brought in by police patrol wagons or by family or friends, because ambulances were rare and typically found only in major urban centers such as New York or Chicago. Even when an ambulance was available to transport a patient, there were no emergency medical technicians (EMTs) trained to begin medical care en route to the hospital. Instead, ambulance services were often managed by the directors of funeral homes, who had vehicles already designed for transporting people who were lying down.

Things changed rapidly in the 1960s, however, when an increasing number of medical professionals were choosing to specialize in emergency medicine. This created an opportunity for doctors to acquire the sort of expertise that was lacking in the accident rooms that currently existed. The first formal emergency departments appeared in the United States in 1961, when independent groups of physicians in Virginia and Michigan recognized the need for urgent care that would be available around the clock and opened dedicated emergency medicine practices. Around the same time, a standardized curriculum was created for EMTs, who were — and are — able to serve as important first responders. In the years that followed, emergency medicine became a formal field of academic study and the number of emergency rooms rapidly expanded. Today there are well over five thousand emergency rooms across the United States, with more than 145 million visits per year.

First you get your coat. I don't care if you don't remember where you left it, you find it. If there was a lot of blood you ask someone to go quickly to the basement to get you a new set of scrubs. You put on your coat and you go into the bathroom. You look in the mirror and you say it. You use the mother's name and you use her child's name. You may not adjust this part in any way.

I will show you: If it were my mother you would say, "Mrs. Rosenberg. I have terrible, terrible news. Naomi died today." You say it out loud until you can say it clearly and loudly. How loudly? Loudly enough. If it takes you fewer than five tries you are rushing it and you will not do it right. You take your time.

After the bathroom you do nothing before you go to her. You don't make a phone call, you do not talk to the medical student, you do not put in an order. You never make her wait. She is his mother.

> " You never make her wait. She is his mother. "

When you get inside the room you will know who the mother is. Yes, I'm very sure. Shake her hand and tell her who you are. If there is time you shake everyone's hand. Yes, you will know if there is time. You never stand. If there are no seats left, the couches have arms on them.

You will have to make a decision about whether you will ask what she already knows. If you were the one to call her and tell her that her son had been shot then you have already done part of it, but you have not done it yet. You are about to do it now. You never make her wait. She is his mother. Now you explode the world. Yes, you have to. You say something like: "Mrs. Booker. I have terrible, terrible news. Ernest died today."

Then you wait.

You will not stand up. You may leave yourself in the heaviness of your breath or the racing of your pulse or the sight of your shoelaces on your shoe, but you will not stand up. You are here for her. She is his mother.

If the mother has another son with her and he has punched the wall or broken the chair, do not be worried. The one that punched the wall or broke the chair will be better than the one who looks down and refuses to cry. The one who punched the wall or broke the chair will be much easier than the sister who looks up and closes her eyes as they fill.

Security is already outside the room and when they hear the first loud noise they will know to come in. No, you will not have to tell them. They know about the family room in the emergency department in summer in North Philadelphia. It is all right. They will be kind. If the chair cannot be sat in again that is all right. We have money for new chairs every summer. If he does not break your chair you stay in your chair. If he does you find a new place to sit. You are here for the mother and you have more to do.

If she asks you, you will tell her what you know. You do not lie. But do not say he was murdered or he was killed. Yes, I know that he was, but that is not what you say. You say that he died; that is the part that you saw and that you know. When she asks if he felt any pain, you must be very careful. If he did not, you assure her quickly. If he did, you do not lie. But his pain is over now. Do not ever say he was lucky that he did not feel pain. He was not lucky. She is not lucky. Don't make that face. The depth of the stupidity of the things you will say sometimes is unimaginable.

Before you leave you break her heart one more time. "No, I'm so sorry, but you cannot see him. There are strict rules when a person dies this way and the police have to take him first. We cannot let you in. I'm so sorry." You do not ever say "the body." It is not a body. It is her son. You want to tell her that you know that he was hers. But she knows that and she does not need for you to tell her. Instead you tell her you will give her time and come back in case she has questions. More questions, or questions for the first time. If she has no questions you do not give her the answers to the questions she has not asked. 11

When you leave the room, do not yell at the medical student who has a question. When you get home, do not yell at your husband. If he left his socks on the floor again today, it is all right. 12

· · ·

Comprehension

1. Why is it Rosenberg's responsibility to tell the mother about the death of her child? Why doesn't she ask someone else to break the difficult news?
2. Why does Rosenberg recommend practicing in front of a mirror before breaking the news to the mother? Why is this better than practicing in front of her fellow doctors?
3. Why does Rosenberg warn readers to "never stand" (4)?
4. Why does Rosenberg say not to worry if members of the family begin breaking the furniture? Why does she seem to think this is a healthy response?
5. Why does Rosenberg say that readers must break the mother's heart "one more time" (11)?
6. In paragraph 11, Rosenberg cautions readers not to give the mother "the answers to the questions she has not asked." What does she mean? Why is such a caution necessary?

Purpose and Audience

1. When she wrote this essay, Rosenberg was a resident physician at a large urban hospital. How did this position qualify her to write this essay?
2. At what point in the process does Rosenberg begin her essay? Why might she have chosen this moment as her starting point?
3. In paragraph 9, Rosenberg explains that security knows about "the family room in the emergency department in summer in North Philadelphia." What does security know? Why do you think Rosenberg includes this comment?
4. What is this essay's thesis? Is it stated or implied? Explain.
5. What does Rosenberg hope to achieve in this essay? For example, does she simply intend to present information about her experiences, or does she hope to change her readers' attitudes? What evidence in the essay supports your answer?

6. Rosenberg spends a great deal of time explaining what *not* to do. Why do you think she does this?

7. Why does Rosenberg include paragraph 11? How would the essay be different without this paragraph?

Style and Structure

1. How is the style of this essay different from that of this chapter's other process essays?

2. What stylistic clues indicate that this essay is a set of instructions rather than a process explanation?

3. List the steps in the process Rosenberg describes. Would you include any other steps? If so, where would you add them? Are there any steps that you would delete?

4. Do you think the steps in this process will always occur in the same order? Why or why not?

5. Rosenberg does not expect most of her readers to carry out the process she describes. Why, then, does she write a series of instructions rather than just explaining the process?

6. Identify some of the transitional words Rosenberg uses to move readers from one step to the next. Does she need to include additional transitions? If so, where?

7. Note the frequent use of "you" in this essay. To whom does it refer? Is "you" the same person as the audience for the essay?

8. Rosenberg repeats the phrase "She is his mother" numerous times throughout the first half of the essay. What point does this repetition make?

9. In paragraph 2, Rosenberg says, "You take your time." In paragraph 5, however, she says you should "never make her wait." Is this advice contradictory? Explain.

10. **Vocabulary Project.** In paragraph 11, Rosenberg says, "It is not a body. It is her son." Why does she make this distinction? Identify other places in the essay where she makes suggestions about the words a doctor should and should not use. What other words would you suggest that a doctor use or avoid in this situation?

11. Throughout her essay, Rosenberg addresses possible responses to her instructions (for instance, "Don't make that face. The depth of the stupidity of the things you will say sometimes is unimaginable" in paragraph 10). Why does she include these responses? Do you think they are likely responses?

12. Why does Rosenberg conclude her essay with instructions for how to behave after leaving the hospital? What do these instructions tell you about the impact of completing the process she describes?

Journal Entry

Do you think this essay's headnote should include a "trigger warning" advising readers that the subject matter may be upsetting, or do you believe such a warning is unnecessary — or might even seem condescending?

Writing Workshop

1. Write a set of instructions for how to complete a task that is emotionally difficult, such as breaking up with a longtime partner or consoling someone who is grieving. Be specific, including advice about the best setting for the conversation, the importance of word choice, and cautions against taking certain actions.

2. **Working with Sources.** Write a set of guidelines for the security team at a hospital like the one in which Rosenberg works. Advise them on how to "know to come in," how to "be kind" while making sure that everyone is safe, and how to make allowances for the grief of families (10). Consider doing some additional research into the psychology of grief to help support your guidelines, and be sure to include parenthetical documentation and a works-cited page for any material you incorporate. (See Chapter 18 for information on MLA documentation.)

3. Assume that you are one of the family members whom Rosenberg addressed in the family room. Write an essay in which you give Rosenberg instructions for how to address grieving families. Make sure you tell her which of her assumptions were correct and which were misguided. You may also want to address aspects of the situation that Rosenberg did not cover.

Combining the Patterns

What does Rosenberg gain by structuring her essay as instructions rather than as a **narrative**? What, if anything, does she lose?

Thematic Connections

- "Did Free Pens Cause the Opioid Crisis?" (page 332)
- "Emmett Till and Tamir Rice, Sons of the Great Migration" (page 414)
- " 'Hope' is the thing with feathers" (page 514)
- Casebook: "How Can We Stem the Tide of Gun Violence?" (page 626)

ROGER SPRANZ

How to Make a Waste Pie Chart

Roger Spranz is an economist, cultural anthropologist, and environmentalist. He has graduate degrees from the University of Freiburg and a Ph.D. from the Leibniz Centre for Tropical Marine Research in Bremen, Germany. Spranz's research and environmental work have focused on marine litter. His Ph.D. dissertation addressed this problem in Indonesia, one of the largest contributors of plastic waste to the oceans. In 2018, Spranz won an innovation prize from the United Nations Environment Program. He is a cofounder of the nonprofit organization Making Oceans Plastic Free.

Background on the Great Pacific Garbage Patch The Great Pacific Garbage Patch, also known as the Pacific Trash Vortex, is essentially a giant floating landfill made up of marine debris. Actually, it is *two* floating landfills: the Western Garbage Patch, located near Japan, and the Eastern Garbage Patch, located between Hawaii and California. Some researchers estimate that the vortex has a surface area roughly the size of the contiguous United States. It likely contains more than 1.8 trillion pieces of trash and weighs around 88,000 tons. This debris — along with other marine waste — is devastating to wildlife such as birds and turtles. Likewise, small sea creatures consume microplastics, which means that these compounds work their way into the food chain of larger fish and ultimately human beings. Many individuals and organizations have sought to clean up — or at least reduce the size of — these patches, including the young Boyan Slat, a Dutch inventor who created the Ocean Cleanup project. His system of filtering and gathering nets is currently being tested in the Pacific.

Our real waste pie chart has been a great success at the launch of the [1] United Nations Environment Programme's #cleanseas campaign at the World Ocean Summit, and with the help of Bye Bye Plastic Bags it has already been shared on Facebook more than 500 times. Find out what kind of waste is most common at your next beach clean up event! We show you here how to do it yourself!

How to Make a Waste Pie Chart

1. **Draw a circle into the sand:** [2]

   You can use your finger, or a stick.

   Tip: You make it more perfect when you use a rope! Your friend holds the rope in the middle, and you — holding the rope on the other hand — walk around him while your finger is drawing the line into the sand.

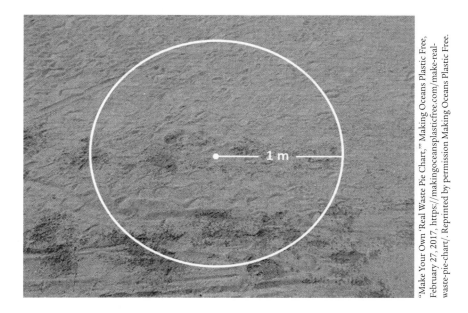

2. **Cut it like a pie — in 10 pieces:**   3

   Draw straight lines into the sand, to create 10 equal sections. Use this image for orientation for where to draw the lines.

3. **Collect, Sort, and Count:**   4
   (a) **Collect**. For the waste pie chart you only need to collect one bag of waste. Make sure you are the one walking across the beach before the

others of your group. You need to pick up every non-organic piece of waste you come across. You can stop when the bag is full.

(b) **Sort**. You may want to sort them differently (check Ocean Conservancy — oceanconservancy.org — for standards), but we used following categories: Straws, Plastic Bottles and Cups, Plastic Bags, Food Wrappings, Other Plastic Items, Shoes/Sandals, Glass Pieces/Bottles, Cigarette Ends, Cans.

(c) **Count the items in each category**.

4. **Calculate (it's easy) and fill the chart**:   5
   (a) **Total**. Once you know how many items you have in each category, add them up to get your total number of waste items.
   (b) **Divide each category by the total**. To get the percentage and know how to fill the pie you need to do this: You calculate e.g. # of Straws/total # of waste items. You can use the calculator on your phone: You will get a number like 0.1521, which means 15% of the waste you collected is straws. Do this calculation for each category.
   (c) **Put waste into the pie slices**. Once you have the percentage of each category, you can start filling the pie with waste. Each of your 10 pie slices is 10%. So, if you have 15% straws, you will fill one slice and another 1/2 slice with straws. You continue like this with all waste categories.

"Make Your Own 'Real Waste Pie Chart,'" Making Oceans Plastic Free, February 27, 2017, https://makingoceansplasticfree.com/make-real-waste-pie-chart/. Reprinted by permission Making Oceans Plastic Free.

Congratulations, your waste pie chart is done! You may want to edit the photo into an info-graphic and add percentages for each category. #MakeOceansPlasticFree and post it on Instagram or Facebook so we can gather different waste pie charts and learn what others have found.   6

· · ·

Comprehension

1. What is a pie chart? In what respects is it an appropriate graphic representation of different kinds of waste?
2. Are the images that accompany this essay essential, or would the process be clearer without them? Explain.
3. Why do you think the "real waste pie chart" Spranz describes was "a great success" (1) at the World Ocean Summit?

Purpose and Audience

1. Why does Spranz advise readers to create their own waste pie charts? What does he expect them to get out of this process?
2. What do Spranz's references to Facebook in the introductory paragraph and to Instagram and Facebook in the concluding paragraphs suggest about his purpose?
3. In one sentence, summarize this essay's thesis. Is it stated anywhere in the essay? If not, should it be?

Style and Structure

1. Is this essay an explanation of a process or a set of instructions? What stylistic features identify it as one or the other? Why did Spranz choose this strategy?
2. Where does Spranz include the cautions and reminders that are often found in process essays? Does he need more? Why or why not?
3. Should Spranz add any transitional words or phrases? If so, where?
4. What is your reaction to the exclamation points Spranz uses in paragraph 1 and in his essay's last sentence? Do you think he should have used periods instead? Why or why not?
5. Spranz includes a numbered boldfaced heading to identify each step in the process. Are these headings effective? How else could he have distinguished the steps from one another?
6. **Vocabulary Project.** Would rewording the essay's headings make the process more appealing? Suggest some possible alternative language for each heading.

Journal Entry

What kinds of discarded waste do you typically see on the streets of your neighborhood? What, if anything, do you do in your daily life to reduce such waste? Do you think you should do more? Explain.

Writing Workshop

1. Draw a pie chart for the various items on your desk or in your car, listing related items in each section of the chart. Then, write a process essay explaining how you assembled and sorted the items. Be sure to give each section of the chart an appropriate name, and describe the contents of each section in detail. Include a thesis statement that explains the value of this exercise.

2. Write an essay explaining how you would create a pie chart to represent the kinds of items you would want to pass down to your children and grandchildren. Steps in the process might include choosing categories, naming each category, and deciding what percentage of the pie to assign to each category.

3. **Working with Sources.** This essay's pie chart was assembled on a beach in Bali, Indonesia, by an environmental group. Explore the United Nations Environmental Programme's website and similar sites to learn more about ocean pollution in Bali and elsewhere, and then write a process essay that tells readers what steps they can take to reduce this type of pollution. (You can include making a waste pie chart as one of the steps in the process.) Be sure to cite the outside source(s) you use, as well as Spranz, and to include a works-cited page. (See Chapter 18 for information on MLA documentation.)

Combining the Patterns

Do you think Spranz should have added passages of **description** to this process essay? If so, where? What might such passages accomplish?

Thematic Connections

- "Jackson Lake" (page 169)
- "The Obligation to Endure" (page 554)
- Debate: "Can Individuals Do Anything to Resolve the Climate Crisis?" (page 587)
- "On Dumpster Diving" (page 668)

BRAD PLUMER AND RUAIRI ARRIETA-KENNA

How Do Hurricanes Form?
A Step-by-Step Guide

Reporter Brad Plumer (b. 1982) covers climate change, energy policy, and other environmental issues for the *New York Times*. Plumer, a former senior editor at Vox.com, reporter at the *Washington Post*, and blogger for the *New Republic*, graduated from Dartmouth College. Ruairi Arrieta-Kenna (b. 1996) is a graduate of Stanford University. Currently, he is an assistant editor at *Politico*. Previously, he interned at *Vox*.

Background on recent hurricanes As a force of nature, devastating hurricanes are not new. For example, the Galveston hurricane of 1900 remains the deadliest natural disaster in U.S. history, killing at least eight thousand and perhaps as many as twelve thousand people. But the consistency and power of these storms over the last decade or two has led many to connect them to the effects of climate change. Only thirty-five Category Five hurricanes have emerged in the Atlantic since record keeping began in the mid-nineteenth century. Five of those catastrophic storms have occurred since 2015. Indeed, although the total number of hurricanes per season has stayed the same, they do seem more likely to intensify into more severe Category 4 and Category 5 storms. Some research suggests that the number of tropical storms that ultimately become hurricanes has tripled since 1990. Climate change could well be a factor, particularly because it is causing sea levels to rise and ocean temperatures to warm. It is also creating a wider, warmer tropical band in which hurricanes can form. To alert people to these changing conditions, some climatologists have proposed adding a new, stronger category designation: a Category 6 hurricane.

1 Whenever hurricane season arrives in the Atlantic Ocean — typically between June and November — a bunch of meteorological terms get hurled around. Tropical storm. Tropical depression. Category 3 hurricanes. Category 4 hurricanes.

2 So what's the difference between all these types of weather events? One way to understand this is to walk through the different stages of a hurricane, step by step. We'll use Hurricane Irma, which started out as a wave off the African coast and went on to pound several Caribbean islands before it hit Florida as a Category 4 storm in 2017, as an example:

3 **1) Tropical disturbance:** A hurricane in the Atlantic Ocean typically begins life as a lowly "tropical disturbance" — defined as organized thunderstorm activity that stretches at least 100 miles across and maintains its identity for more than 24 hours.

4 During the summer, these disturbances often start as storms moving westward off the coast of Africa in what are known as "tropical waves."

5 If meteorologists think a tropical disturbance may develop further, they'll designate it as an "investigative area," or invest. Irma became a disturbance off the Cape Verde Islands in late August, with forecasters keeping close watch as it headed west.

> "Tropical storms can intensify quickly . . ."

2) Tropical depression or cyclone: Under the right conditions, a tropical disturbance can develop further and start to spin around a low-pressure center. Once that happens, it's classified as a "tropical cyclone" or "tropical depression": 6

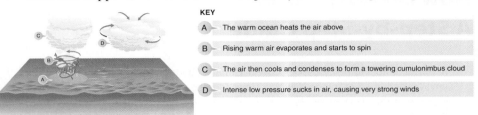

KEY

A → The warm ocean heats the air above

B → Rising warm air evaporates and starts to spin

C → The air then cools and condenses to form a towering cumulonimbus cloud

D → Intense low pressure sucks in air, causing very strong winds

For a tropical depression to form, conditions have to be just right: The water has to be warm enough to fuel the system, with temperatures of 80°F or hotter. There needs to be enough moisture in the lower and middle part of the atmosphere. Local winds also have to be arranged so that they allow the depression to spin — too much wind shear can tear an aspiring tropical cyclone apart. 7

3) Tropical storm: This is the next stage. When the pressure in the center of the tropical depression drops, air rushes in, creating strong winds. If the system strengthens and wind speeds rise past 39 mph, the system is dubbed a "tropical storm" and is given a name. That's what happened to Irma on August 30 [2017], as it picked up speed in the far Eastern Atlantic and intensified. 8

The US National Hurricane Center makes the call for when a tropical depression officially becomes a tropical storm. It relies on data from islands and buoys as well as from reconnaissance aircrafts that fly into the storms to measure wind speed. 9

4) Hurricane: Tropical storms can intensify quickly if they pass over a region of especially warm water and don't face much wind shear. As that happens, the pressure in the center drops even further and the winds *really* pick up. The system gets rounder and often forms a clearly defined "eye." 10

When the winds reach sustained speeds of 74 mph or more, the storm system is classified as a hurricane. Hurricanes are categorized according to the Saffir-Simpson Scale based on their wind speed and propensity for damage. 11

Saffir-Simpson Hurricane Wind Scale (1 = least extreme; 5 = most extreme)

Category 1	Category 2	Category 3
· Winds range from **74 to 95 mph**	· Winds range from **96 to 110 mph**	· Winds range from **111 to 130 mph**
· Minor damage to property (roof damage)	· Significant property damage, flooding	· Mobile and frame homes destroyed, extensive flooding
· Injuries to humans are isolated	· Increased threat to humans due to falling debris	· Evacuation necessary for human safety
· Short-term power outages	· Extensive, multi-day power outages	· Electricity, water unavailable for up to several weeks

Category 4	Category 5
· Winds range from **131 to 155 mph** · Houses, shopping centers irreparably damaged · Humans at serious risk of death in certain areas · Long-term power outages, water shortages	· Winds of **155 mph+** · Complete destruction of homes, shopping centers · Trees uprooted, extreme flooding · Power and water potentially out for months

Source: National Hurricane Center

Irma was a Category 5 as of September 5 with wind speeds of 185 miles per   12
hour. That's serious — major hurricanes can do structural damage to buildings, take down trees, and cause widespread flooding.

Side note: The fact that you need especially warm water here explains why   13
hurricanes only form in the Atlantic during the late summer months. (It also helps explain why global warming may lead to stronger hurricanes, although this gets complicated, since climate change can also affect wind shear that suppresses hurricanes.)

5) Back down to tropical storm: Hurricanes can also weaken, however, as   14
they move over land (or cooler water) and no longer have warm, moist air to fuel them. Once wind speeds drop below 75 miles per hour, the hurricane gets downgraded to a tropical storm — and, later on, a "post-tropical cyclone" as it degrades further.

For example, Hurricane Hermine in 2016 was downgraded to a tropical   15
storm not long after it made landfall in Florida in September. But then Hermine moved *back* over the Atlantic Ocean and hit record-warm ocean temperatures there, gathering to hurricane strength again.

It's worth emphasizing that even tropical cyclones that *aren't* hurricanes   16
can still do a great deal of damage by bringing torrential rain, dangerous surf, beach erosion, high winds, and flooding. In 2012, "superstorm" Sandy was technically no longer a hurricane when it hit the East Coast, but it still proved devastating to the New York and New Jersey coasts.

· · ·

Comprehension

1. List the individual steps in this "step-by-step guide." Is there any indication that the steps can occur in a different order? That any step can sometimes be skipped?
2. What is an "invest" (5)? Why are invests significant to meteorologists?
3. Do the illustrations just reinforce the essay's content, or do they provide important supplementary information? Explain.

Purpose and Audience

1. Is this essay written for meteorologists or for the general public? How can you tell?

2. Why do Plumer and Arrieta-Kenna trace this process step by step? What point are they trying to communicate to readers by explaining this process?
3. Paragraph 13 presents a "side note" to readers. Why do you think the writers include this note? Is it intrusive? Does it need further development? Should it be deleted? Explain.

Style and Structure

1. **Vocabulary Project.** This is a scientific essay, and it uses technical language. Give some examples of this language. Where do the writers define technical terms? Should any additional terms be defined?
2. Is this essay's style too informal for its subject matter? For example, is the use of expressions such as "a bunch of" (1) and the use of contractions such as "they'll" (5) appropriate here? Why or why not?
3. In addition to the headings, what language indicates the introduction of each new stage of the process? Do the writers need more of these linguistic signals, or are the headings sufficient?
4. Do Plumer and Arrieta-Kenna provide enough transitional words and phrases? Where might additional transitions between stages be helpful?
5. Does this essay end too abruptly, or is the ending effective as it stands? If you think an additional concluding paragraph is called for, what should it accomplish?

Journal Entry

Write a process paragraph that briefly traces the development of a significant weather event that you witnessed—for example, a severe rainstorm or snowstorm, a flood, or a heat wave.

Writing Workshop

1. **Working with Sources.** The writers use 2017's Hurricane Irma as a point of reference in this essay. Locate several accounts of 2005's devastating Hurricane Katrina, and write a process essay tracing that storm's development as it intensified. You may include events associated with the storm—for example, efforts to rescue and evacuate residents of the storm area and steps taken by the Federal Emergency Management Agency and other local and national government agencies to manage the situation. Be sure to document information (including quoted statements and statistics) from your sources and to include a works-cited page. (See Chapter 18 for information on MLA documentation.)
2. Expand your journal entry into a process essay, including as much detail as you can. Be sure to clearly identify each stage of the process.

Combining the Patterns

Where in this essay do the writers use **cause and effect**? Should they have spent more time exploring the causes or the effects of hurricanes?

Thematic Connections

- "The Storm" (page 194)
- "Yellowstone Fires, Past and Present" (page 273)

EUGENE KIELY AND LORI ROBERTSON

How to Spot Fake News

Journalist Eugene Kiely is director of FactCheck.org, a nonprofit organization that evaluates the "factual accuracy of what is said by major U.S. political players in the form of TV ads, debates, speeches, interviews and news releases." Previously, Kiely held reporting and editorial positions at *USA Today*, the *Philadelphia Inquirer*, and New Jersey's *The Record*. He graduated from Rutgers University. Lori Robertson is the managing editor of FactCheck.org. Before joining FactCheck.org, Robertson was a writer and editor at *American Journalism Review*, where she won a Bart Richards Award for Media Criticism. She graduated from Duquesne University.

Background on fake news Although the term "fake news" has taken on fresh connotations since the 2016 U.S. presidential election, the broader concept has a long media history — from the *New York Sun*'s "Great Moon Hoax" of 1835, when the paper reported that a complex civilization on the moon had been discovered, to Orson Welles's famous *War of the Worlds* radio broadcast in 1938 to today's scurrilous political rumors on Facebook and Twitter. The motives behind fake news and hoaxes vary. In some cases, such sensational stories are designed to attract viewers and readers for commercial benefit; in other cases, as with parody news sites such as The Onion, the purpose is to entertain. These motivations have taken on a more sinister cast, however. Misleading political propaganda has existed for a long time, but during the 2016 political campaigns, fake news became a more sophisticated, elusive, and influential phenomenon in the United States: deliberately contrived "news" stories about the pope endorsing Donald Trump and about Hillary Clinton running a child-abuse ring were just two of the false stories disseminated across social media. These stories, sometimes spread by automated Twitter "bots," confirmed biases and played into political polarization. In a liberal democracy, citizens need accurate information to make reasonable and well-informed decisions. Ultimately, it is up to individuals to exercise their judgment and critical thinking skills. In addition, sites like FactCheck.org can help filter fake news and other forms of misinformation.

Fake news is nothing new. But bogus stories can reach more people more quickly via social media than what good old-fashioned viral emails could accomplish in years past. 1

> **"Fake news is nothing new."**

Concern about the phenomenon led Facebook and Google to announce that they'll crack down on fake news sites, restricting their ability to garner ad revenue. Perhaps that could dissipate the amount of malarkey online, though news consumers themselves are the best defense against the spread of misinformation. 2

Not all of the misinformation being passed along online is complete fiction, though some of it is. Snopes.com has been exposing false viral claims 3 since the mid 1990s, whether that's fabricated messages, distortions containing bits of truth and everything in between. Founder David Mikkelson warned in a Nov. 17 article [2016] not to lump everything into the "fake news" category. "The fictions and fabrications that comprise fake news are but a subset of the larger *bad news* phenomenon, which also encompasses many forms of shoddy, unresearched, error-filled, and deliberately misleading reporting that do a disservice to everyone," he wrote.

A lot of these viral claims aren't "news" at all, but fiction, satire, and efforts to fool readers into thinking they're for real.   4

We've long encouraged readers to be skeptical of viral claims, and make   5
good use of the delete key when a chain email hits their inboxes. In December 2007, we launched our Ask FactCheck feature, where we answer readers' questions, the vast majority of which concern viral emails, social media memes and the like. Our first story was about a made-up email that claimed then-House Speaker Nancy Pelosi wanted to put a "windfall" tax on all stock profits of 100 percent and give the money to, the email claimed, "the 12 Million Illegal Immigrants and other unemployed minorities." We called it "a malicious fabrication"—that's "fake news" in today's parlance.

In 2008, we tried to get readers to rid their inboxes of this kind of garbage.   6
We described a list of red flags—we called them Key Characteristics of Bogusness—that were clear tip-offs that a chain email wasn't legitimate. Among them: an anonymous author; excessive exclamation points, capital letters, and misspellings; entreaties that "This is NOT a hoax!"; and links to sourcing that does not support or completely contradicts the claims being made.

Those all still hold true, but fake stories—as in, completely made-up   7
"news"—have grown more sophisticated, often presented on a site designed to look (sort of) like a legitimate news organization. Still, we find it's easy to figure out what's real and what's imaginary if you're armed with some critical thinking and fact-checking tools of the trade.

Here's our advice on how to spot a fake: 8

Consider the source. In recent months, we've fact-checked fake news   9
from abcnews.com.co (not the actual URL for ABC News), WTOE 5 News (whose "about" page says it's "a fantasy news website"), and the Boston Tribune (whose "contact us" page lists only a gmail address). Earlier this year, we debunked the claim that the Obamas were buying a vacation home in Dubai, a made-up missive that came from WhatDoesItMean.com, which describes itself as "One Of The Top Ranked Websites In The World For New World Order, Conspiracy Theories and Alternative News" and further says on its site that most of what it publishes is fiction.

Clearly, some of these sites do provide a "fantasy news" or satire warning,   10
like WTOE 5, which published the bogus headline, "Pope Francis Shocks World, Endorses Donald Trump for President, Releases Statement." Others aren't so upfront, like the Boston Tribune, which doesn't provide any information on its mission, staff members, or physical location—further signs that maybe this site isn't a legitimate news organization. The site, in fact, changed

its name from Associated Media Coverage, after its work had been debunked by fact-checking organizations.

Snopes.com, which has been writing about viral claims and online rumors since the mid-1990s, maintains a list of known fake news websites, several of which have emerged in the past two years. 11

Read beyond the headline. If a provocative headline drew your attention, read a little further before you decide to pass along the shocking information. Even in legitimate news stories, the headline doesn't always tell the whole story. But fake news, particularly efforts to be satirical, can include several revealing signs in the text. That abcnews.com.co story that we checked, headlined "Obama Signs Executive Order Banning The Pledge Of Allegiance In Schools Nationwide," went on to quote "Fappy the Anti-Masturbation Dolphin." We have to assume that the many readers who asked us whether this viral rumor was true hadn't read the full story. 12

Check the author. Another tell-tale sign of a fake story is often the byline. The pledge of allegiance story on abcnews.com.co was supposedly written by "Jimmy Rustling." Who is he? Well, his author page claims he is a "doctor" who won "fourteen Peabody awards and a handful of Pulitzer Prizes." Pretty impressive, if true. But it's not. No one by the name of "Rustling" has won a Pulitzer or Peabody award. The photo accompanying Rustling's bio is also displayed on another bogus story on a different site, but this time under the byline "Darius Rubics." The Dubai story was written by "Sorcha Faal, and as reported to her Western Subscribers." The Pope Francis story has no byline at all. 13

What's the support? Many times these bogus stories will cite official — or official-sounding — sources, but once you look into it, the source doesn't back up the claim. For instance, the Boston Tribune site wrongly claimed that President Obama's mother-in-law was going to get a lifetime government pension for having babysat her granddaughters in the White House, citing "the Civil Service Retirement Act" and providing a link. But the link to a government benefits website doesn't support the claim at all. 14

The banning-the-pledge story cites the number of an actual executive order — you can look it up. It doesn't have anything to do with the Pledge of Allegiance. 15

Another viral claim we checked a year ago was a graphic purporting to show crime statistics on the percentage of whites killed by Blacks and other murder statistics by race. Then-presidential candidate Donald Trump retweeted it, telling Fox News commentator Bill O'Reilly that it came "from sources that are very credible." But almost every figure in the image was wrong — FBI crime data is publicly available — and the supposed source given for the data, "Crime Statistics Bureau – San Francisco," doesn't exist. 16

Recently, we've received several questions about a fake news story on the admittedly satirical site Nevada County Scooper, which wrote that Vice President–elect Mike Pence, in a "surprise announcement," credited gay conversion therapy for saving his marriage. Clearly such a "surprise announcement" would garner media coverage beyond a website you've never heard of. In 17 fact, if you Google this, the first link that comes up is a Snopes.com article revealing that this is fake news.

Check the date. Some false stories aren't completely fake, but rather distortions of real events. These mendacious claims can take a legitimate news story and twist what it says — or even claim that something that happened long ago is related to current events.

Since Trump was elected president, we've received many inquiries from readers wanting to know whether Ford had moved car production from Mexico to Ohio, because of Trump's election. Readers cited various blog items that quoted from and linked to a CNN Money article titled "Ford shifts truck production from Mexico to Ohio." But that story is from August 2015, clearly not evidence of Ford making any move due to the outcome of the election. (A reminder again to check the support for these claims.)

One deceptive website didn't credit CNN, but instead took CNN's 2015 story and slapped a new headline and publication date on it, claiming, "Since Donald Trump Won The Presidency . . . Ford Shifts Truck Production From Mexico To Ohio." Not only is that a bogus headline, but the deception involves copyright infringement.

If this Ford story sounds familiar, that's because the CNN article has been distorted before.

In October 2015, Trump wrongly boasted that Ford had changed its plans to build new plants in Mexico, and instead would build a plant in Ohio. Trump took credit for Ford's alleged change of heart and tweeted a link to a story on a blog called Prntly.com, which cited the CNN Money story. But Ford hadn't changed its plans at all, and Trump deserved no credit.

In fact, the CNN article was about the transfer of some pickup assembly work from Mexico to Ohio, a move that was announced by Ford in March 2014. The plans for new plants in Mexico were still on, Ford said. "Ford has not spoken with Mr. Trump, nor have we made any changes to our plans," Ford said in a statement.

Is this some kind of joke? Remember, there is such thing as satire. Normally, it's clearly labeled as such, and sometimes it's even funny. Andy Borowitz has been writing a satirical news column, the Borowitz Report, since 2001, and it has appeared in the *New Yorker* since 2012. But not everyone gets the jokes. We've fielded several questions on whether Borowitz's work is true.

Among the headlines our readers have flagged: "Putin Appears with Trump in Flurry of Swing-State Rallies" and "Trump Threatens to Skip Remaining Debates If Hillary Is There." When we told readers these were satirical columns, some indicated that they suspected the details were far-fetched but wanted to be sure.

And then there's the more debatable forms of satire, designed to pull one over on the reader. That "Fappy the Anti-Masturbation Dolphin" story? That's the work of online hoaxer Paul Horner, whose "greatest coup," as described by the *Washington Post* in 2014, was when Fox News mentioned, as fact, a fake piece titled, "Obama uses own money to open Muslim museum amid government shutdown." Horner told the *Post* after the election that he was concerned his hoaxes aimed at Trump supporters may have helped the campaign.

The posts by Horner and others — whether termed satire or simply "fake 27 news" — are designed to encourage clicks, and generate money for the creator through ad revenue. Horner told the *Washington Post* he makes a living off his posts. Asked why his material gets so many views, Horner responded, "They just keep passing stuff around. Nobody fact-checks anything anymore."

Check your biases. We know this is difficult. Confirmation bias leads 28 people to put more stock in information that confirms their beliefs and discount information that doesn't. But the next time you're automatically appalled at some Facebook post concerning, say, a politician you oppose, take a moment to check it out.

Try this simple test: What other stories have been posted to the "news" 29 website that is the source of the story that just popped up in your Facebook feed? You may be predisposed to believe that Obama bought a house in Dubai, but how about a story on the same site that carries this headline: "Antarctica 'Guardians' Retaliate Against America With Massive New Zealand Earthquake." That, too, was written by the prolific "Sorcha Faal, and as reported to her Western Subscribers."

We're encouraged by some of the responses we get from readers, who — like 30 the ones uncertain of Borowitz's columns — express doubt in the outrageous, and just want to be sure their skepticism is justified. But we are equally discouraged when we see debunked claims gain new life.

We've seen the resurgence of a fake quote from Donald Trump since the 31 election — a viral image that circulated last year claims Trump told *People* magazine in 1998: "If I were to run, I'd run as a Republican. They're the dumbest group of voters in the country. They believe anything on Fox News. I could lie and they'd still eat it up. I bet my numbers would be terrific." We found no such quote in *People*'s archives from 1998, or any other year. And a public relations representative for the magazine confirmed that. *People*'s Julie Farin told us in an email last year: "We combed through every Trump story in our archive. We couldn't find anything remotely like this quote — and no interview at all in 1998."

Comedian Amy Schumer may have contributed to the revival of this fake 32 meme. She put it on Instagram, adding at the end of a lengthy message, "Yes this quote is fake but it doesn't matter."

Consult the experts. We know you're busy, and some of this debunking takes 33 time. But we get paid to do this kind of work. Between FactCheck.org, Snopes .com, the *Washington Post* Fact Checker, and PolitiFact.com, it's likely at least one has already fact-checked the latest viral claim to pop up in your news feed.

FactCheck.org was among a network of independent fact-checkers who 34 signed an open letter to Facebook's Mark Zuckerberg suggesting that Facebook "start an open conversation on the principles that could underpin a more accurate news ecosystem on its News Feed." We hope that conversation happens, but news readers themselves remain the first line of defense against fake news.

On our Viral Spiral page, we list some of the claims we get asked about the 35 most; all of our Ask FactChecks can be found here. And if you encounter a new claim you'd like us to investigate, email us at editor@factcheck.org.

• • •

Comprehension

1. Does this essay define the term *fake news*, or does it assume that readers already know what it means?
2. Why do Kiely and Robertson see fake news as more of a problem now than it was in the past? Do you agree with them?
3. What specific steps should readers take to help them identify fake news?
4. Why is it important to take the source of a news report into account?
5. Why is the date of a news story important?
6. When evaluating a news story, why is it important for readers to consider their own biases?

Purpose and Audience

1. What determines the order in which the steps are presented in this essay? Are the steps meant to be performed in a fixed order? Would you change the order of these steps? If so, how?
2. Does this essay have a stated thesis? If so, where does it appear? If not, write an appropriate one-sentence thesis statement.
3. Do the writers have a persuasive purpose? If so, what is it? Or, is their goal simply to share useful information with readers?

Style and Structure

1. As its headings indicate, this essay presents a set of instructions. How is it different from a typical set of instructions? How can you account for these differences?
2. Most of the headings that identify the steps in the process are stated in the form of commands — "Consider the source," "Read beyond the headlines," and so on. However, "What's the support?" and "Is this some kind of joke?" are not stated as commands. Rewrite these two headings to make them consistent with the others.
3. **Vocabulary Project.** What connotations does the term *fake news* have? Does the term always have a negative meaning?
4. After a few introductory paragraphs, the process itself is introduced by a one-sentence paragraph: "Here's our advice on how to spot a fake" (8). How could you expand this sentence into a longer paragraph that conveys the importance and value of the steps that follow? Do you think such an expanded paragraph would improve the essay? Why or why not?

Journal Entry

Locate several definitions of *fake news* online, and then write your own comprehensive one-paragraph definition of the term, including at least one example.

Writing Workshop

1. Rewrite this essay as a set of instructions aimed at middle-school students. Include all the steps enumerated here, but simplify the language, add definitions and explanations where necessary, and clearly explain why fake news is a problem. (Your essay will be much shorter than this one, and it will include fewer and briefer examples.)

2. Write a satirical essay that gives instructions for creating a fake news story, posting it on the Internet, and making it go viral.

3. **Working with Sources.** Go to a website you visit often and locate a political article there that interests you. Then, follow the process discussed by Kiely and Robertson to help you evaluate the article. Does the article present any information that you consider to be fake news? Write a process essay in which you explain the steps you took to evaluate the information. (You can use the criteria listed by Kiely and Robertson, but if so, be sure to cite their essay as well as the article you evaluated and to include a works-cited page. (See Chapter 18 for information on MLA documentation.)

Combining the Patterns

Exemplification is very important in this essay, which depends on a wide variety of examples to illustrate the steps it enumerates and convey their importance. Do any steps need more examples? Fewer examples? Different examples?

Thematic Connections

- "Cutting and Pasting: A Senior Thesis by (Insert Name)" (page 17)
- "The YouTube Effect" (page 20)
- "Why Rational People Buy into Conspiracy Theories" (page 338)
- "The Ways We Lie" (page 463)

JESSICA MITFORD

The Embalming of Mr. Jones

Jessica Mitford (1917–1996) was born in Batsford Mansion, England, to a wealthy, aristocratic family. Rebelling against her sheltered upbringing, she became involved in left-wing politics and eventually immigrated to the United States. Mitford wrote two volumes of autobiography: *Daughters and Rebels* (1960), about her eccentric family, and *A Fine Old Conflict* (1977). In the 1950s, she began a career in investigative journalism, which produced the books *The American Way of Death* (1963), about abuses in the funeral business; *Kind and Usual Punishment* (1973), about the U.S. prison system; and *The American Way of Birth* (1992), about the crisis in American obstetrical care.

Background on the funeral industry "The Embalming of Mr. Jones" is excerpted from *The American Way of Death*, a scathing critique of the funeral industry in the United States. The book prompted angry responses from morticians, but also led to increased governmental regulation, culminating in a 1984 Federal Trade Commission ruling requiring funeral homes to disclose in writing the prices for all goods and services, as well as certain consumer rights; barring funeral homes from forcing consumers to purchase more than they really want; and forbidding funeral directors from misleading consumers regarding state laws governing the disposal of bodies. Still, industry critics charge that many abuses continue. Although funeral services can be purchased for less than a thousand dollars, the standard rate is between two and four thousand dollars — and it can go much higher. The difference in cost is based largely on the price of a casket, and grieving family members are often strongly pressured into buying the most expensive caskets, which may be marked up as much as 500 percent. Advocates for reform suggest consumers choose cremation over burial (currently, about half of Americans who died are cremated rather than buried) and that they hold memorial services in churches or other settings, where costs are much lower than in funeral homes.

Embalming is indeed a most extraordinary procedure, and one must wonder at the docility of Americans who each year pay hundreds of millions of dollars for its perpetuation, blissfully ignorant of what it is all about, what is done, how it is done. Not one in ten thousand has any idea of what actually takes place. Books on the subject are extremely hard to come by. They are not to be found in most libraries or bookshops.

In an era when huge television audiences watch surgical operations in the comfort of their living rooms, when, thanks to the animated cartoon, the geography of the digestive system has become familiar territory even to the nursery school set, in a land where the satisfaction of curiosity about almost all matters is a national pastime, the secrecy surrounding embalming can, surely, hardly be attributed to the inherent gruesomeness of the subject. Custom in this regard has within this century suffered a complete reversal. In the early days of

American embalming, when it was performed in the home of the deceased, it was almost mandatory for some relative to stay by the embalmer's side and witness the procedure. Today, family members who might wish to be in attendance would certainly be dissuaded by the funeral director. All others, except apprentices, are excluded by law from the preparation room.

A close look at what does actually take place may explain in large measure the undertaker's intractable reticence concerning a procedure that has become his major *raison d'être.** Is it possible he fears that public information about embalming might lead patrons to wonder if they really want this service? If the funeral men are loath to

> **"For those who have the stomach for it, let us part the formaldehyde curtain."**

discuss the subject outside the trade, the reader may, understandably, be equally loath to go on reading at this point. For those who have the stomach for it, let us part the formaldehyde curtain. . . .

The body is first laid out in the undertaker's morgue — or rather, Mr. Jones is reposing in the preparation room — to be readied to bid the world farewell.

The preparation room in any of the better funeral establishments has the tiled and sterile look of a surgery, and indeed the embalmer-restorative artist who does his chores there is beginning to adopt the term "dermasurgeon" (appropriately corrupted by some mortician-writers as "demisurgeon") to describe his calling. His equipment, consisting of scalpels, scissors, augers, forceps, clamps, needles, pumps, tubes, bowls, and basin, is crudely imitative of the surgeon's, as is his technique, acquired in a nine- or twelve-month post-high-school course in an embalming school. He is supplied by an advanced chemical industry with a bewildering array of fluids, sprays, pastes, oils, powders, creams, to fix or soften tissue, shrink or distend it as needed, dry it here, restore the moisture there. There are cosmetics, waxes, and paints to fill and cover features, even plaster of Paris to replace entire limbs. There are ingenious aids to prop and stabilize the cadaver: a Vari-Pose Head Rest, the Edwards Arm and Hand Positioner, the Repose Block (to support the shoulders during the embalming), and the Throop Foot Positioner, which resembles an old-fashioned stocks.

Mr. John H. Eckels, president of the Eckels College of Mortuary Science, thus describes the first part of the embalming procedure: "In the hands of a skilled practitioner, this work may be done in a comparatively short time and without mutilating the body other than by slight incision — so slight that it scarcely would cause serious inconvenience if made upon a living person. It is necessary to remove all the blood, and doing this not only helps in the disinfecting, but removes the principal cause of disfigurements due to discoloration."

Another textbook discusses the all-important time element: "The earlier this is done, the better, for every hour that elapses between death and embalming will add to the problems and complications encountered. . . ." Just

---

* Eds. note — Reason for being (French).

how soon should one get going on the embalming? The author tells us, "On the basis of such scanty information made available to this profession through its rudimentary and haphazard system of technical research, we must conclude that the best results are to be obtained if the subject is embalmed before life is completely extinct—that is, before cellular death has occurred. In the average case, this would mean within an hour after somatic death." For those who feel that there is something a little rudimentary, not to say haphazard, about this advice, a comforting thought is offered by another writer. Speaking of fears entertained in early days of premature burial, he points out, "One of the effects of embalming by chemical injection, however, has been to dispel fears of live burial." How true; once the blood is removed, chances of live burial are indeed remote.

8   To return to Mr. Jones, the blood is drained out through the veins and replaced by embalming fluid pumped in through the arteries. As noted in *The Principles and Practices of Embalming*, "every operator has a favorite injection and drainage point—a fact which becomes a handicap only if he fails or refuses to forsake his favorites when conditions demand it." Typical favorites are the carotid artery, femoral artery, jugular vein, subclavian vein. There are various choices of embalming fluid. If Flextone is used, it will produce a "mild, flexible rigidity. The skin retains a velvety softness, the tissues are rubbery and pliable. Ideal for women and children." It may be blended with B. and G. Products Company's Lyf-Lyk tint, which is guaranteed to reproduce "nature's own skin texture . . . the velvety appearance of living tissue." Suntone comes in three separate tints: Suntan; Special Cosmetic Tint, a pink shade "especially indicated for young female subjects"; and Regular Cosmetic Tint, moderately pink.

9   About three to six gallons of a dyed and perfumed solution of formaldehyde, glycerin, borax, phenol, alcohol, and water is soon circulating through Mr. Jones, whose mouth has been sewn together with a "needle directed upward between the upper lip and gum and brought out through the left nostril," with the corners raised slightly "for a more pleasant expression." If he should be buck-toothed, his teeth are cleaned with Bon Ami and coated with colorless nail polish. His eyes, meanwhile, are closed with flesh-tinted eye caps and eye cement.

10   The next step is to have at Mr. Jones with a thing called a trocar. This is a long, hollow needle attached to a tube. It is jabbed into the abdomen, poked around the entrails and chest cavity, the contents of which are pumped out and replaced with "cavity fluid." This done, and the hole in the abdomen sewed up, Mr. Jones's face is heavily creamed (to protect the skin from burns which may be caused by leakage of the chemicals), and he is covered with a sheet and left unmolested for a while. But not for long—there is more, much more, in store for him. He has been embalmed, but not yet restored, and the best time to start restorative work is eight to ten hours after embalming, when the tissues have become firm and dry.

11   The object of all this attention to the corpse, it must be remembered, is to make it presentable for viewing in an attitude of healthy repose. "Our customs require the presentation of our dead in the semblance of normality . . . unmarred by the ravages of illness, disease, or mutilation," says Mr. J. Sheridan

Mayer in his *Restorative Art*. This is rather a large order since few people die in the full bloom of health, unravaged by illness and unmarked by some disfigurement. The funeral industry is equal to the challenge: "In some cases the gruesome appearance of a mutilated or disease-ridden subject may be quite discouraging. The task of restoration may seem impossible and shake the confidence of the embalmer. This is the time for intestinal fortitude and determination. Once the formative work is begun and affected tissues are cleaned or removed, all doubts of success vanish. It is surprising and gratifying to discover the results which may be obtained."

The embalmer, having allowed an appropriate interval to elapse, returns to   12
the attack, but now he brings into play the skill and equipment of sculptor and cosmetician. Is a hand missing? Casting one in plaster of Paris is a simple matter. "For replacement purposes, only a cast of the back of the hand is necessary; this is within the ability of the average operator and is quite adequate." If a lip or two, a nose, or an ear should be missing, the embalmer has at hand a variety of restorative waxes with which to model replacements. Pores and skin texture are simulated by stippling with a little brush, and over this cosmetics are laid on. Head off? Decapitation cases are rather routinely handled. Ragged edges are trimmed, and head joined to torso with a series of splints, wires, and sutures. It is a good idea to have a little something at the neck—a scarf or high collar—when time for viewing comes. Swollen mouth? Cut out tissue as needed from inside the lips. If too much is removed, the surface contour can easily be restored by padding with cotton. Swollen necks and cheeks are reduced by removing tissue through vertical incisions made down each side of the neck. "When the deceased is casketed, the pillow will hide the suture incisions . . . as an extra precaution against leakage, the suture may be painted with liquid sealer."

The opposite condition is more likely to present itself—that of emacia-   13
tion. His hypodermic syringe now loaded with massage cream, the embalmer seeks out and fills the hollowed and sunken areas by injection. In this procedure the backs of the hands and fingers and the underchin area should not be neglected.

Positioning the lips is a problem that recurrently challenges the ingenuity   14
of the embalmer. Closed too tightly, they tend to give a stern, even disapproving expression. Ideally, embalmers feel, the lips should give the impression of being ever so slightly parted, the upper lip protruding slightly for a more youthful appearance. This takes some engineering, however, as the lips tend to drift apart. Lip drift can sometimes be remedied by pushing one or two straight pins through the inner margin of the lower lip and then inserting them between the two front upper teeth. If Mr. Jones happens to have no teeth, the pins can just as easily be anchored in his Armstrong Face Former and Denture Replacer. Another method to maintain lip closure is to dislocate the lower jaw, which is then held in its new position by a wire run through holes which have been drilled through the upper jaws at the midline. As the French are fond of saying, *il faut souffrir pour être belle.**

---

* Eds. note—It is necessary to suffer in order to be beautiful.

If Mr. Jones has died of jaundice, the embalming fluid will very likely turn   15
him green. Does this deter the embalmer? Not if he has intestinal fortitude.
Masking pastes and cosmetics are heavily laid on, burial garments and casket
interiors are color-correlated with particular care, and Jones is displayed
beneath rose-colored lights. Friends will say, "How *well* he looks." Death by
carbon monoxide, on the other hand, can be rather a good thing from an
embalmer's viewpoint: "One advantage is the fact that this type of discoloration is an exaggerated form of a natural pink coloration." This is nice because
the healthy glow is already present and needs but little attention.

The patching and filling completed, Mr. Jones is now shaved, washed,   16
and dressed. Cream-based cosmetic, available in pink, flesh, suntan, brunette,
and blonde, is applied to his hands and face, his hair is shampooed and
combed (and, in the case of Mrs. Jones, set), his hands manicured. For the
horny-handed son of toil special care must be taken; cream should be applied
to remove ingrained grime, and the nails cleaned. "If he were not in the habit
of having them manicured in life, trimming and shaping is advised for better
appearance — never questioned by kin."

Jones is now ready for casketing (this is the present participle of the verb "to   17
casket"). In this operation his right shoulder should be depressed slightly
"to turn the body a bit to the right and soften the appearance of lying flat on the
back." Positioning the hands is a matter of importance, and special rubber positioning blocks may be used. The hands should be cupped slightly for a more
lifelike, relaxed appearance. Proper placement of the body requires a delicate
sense of balance. It should lie as high as possible in the casket, yet not so high
that the lid, when lowered, will hit the nose. On the other hand, we are cautioned,
placing the body too low "creates the impression that the body is in a box."

Jones is next wheeled into the appointed slumber room where a few last   18
touches may be added — his favorite pipe placed in his hand or, if he was a great
reader, a book propped into position. (In the case of little Master Jones a Teddy
bear may be clutched.) Here he will hold open house for a few days, visiting
hours 10 A.M. to 9 P.M.

· · ·

Comprehension

1. How, according to Mitford, has the public's knowledge of embalming
   changed? How does she explain this change?
2. To what other professionals does Mitford compare the embalmer? Are these
   analogies flattering or critical? Explain.
3. List the major stages in the process of embalming and restoration.

Purpose and Audience

1. Mitford's purpose in this essay is to convince her audience of something.
   What is her thesis?
2. Do you think Mitford expects her audience to agree with her thesis? How
   can you tell?

3. In one of her books, Mitford refers to herself as a *muckraker*, one who informs the public of misconduct. Does she achieve this status here? Cite specific examples.
4. Mitford's tone in this essay is subjective, even judgmental. What effect does her tone have on you? Does it encourage you to trust her? Should she have presented her facts in a more objective way? Explain.

Style and Structure

1. Identify the stylistic features that distinguish this process explanation from a set of instructions.
2. In this selection, as in many process essays, a list of necessary materials is provided before the start of the procedure. What additional details does Mitford include along with the list in paragraph 5? What effect do these details have on you?
3. Locate Mitford's remarks about the language of embalming. How do her comments about euphemisms, newly coined words, and other aspects of language help support her thesis?
4. **Vocabulary Project.** Reread paragraphs 5 through 9 carefully. Then, list all the words in this section of the essay that suggest surgical techniques and all the words that suggest cosmetic artistry. What do your lists tell you about Mitford's intent in these paragraphs?
5. Throughout the essay, Mitford quotes various experts. How does she use their remarks to support her thesis?
6. Give examples of transitional phrases that link the various stages of Mitford's process.
7. Mitford uses a good deal of sarcasm and biased language in this essay. Identify some examples. Do you think her use of this kind of language strengthens or weakens her essay? Why?

Journal Entry

What are your thoughts about how your religion or culture deals with death and dying? What practices, if any, make you uncomfortable? Why?

Writing Workshop

1. Use the information in this process explanation to help you prepare a two-page set of instructions for undertakers. Unlike Mitford, keep your essay objective.
2. **Working with Sources.** In the role of a funeral director, write a blog post taking issue with Mitford's essay. As you explain the process of embalming, paraphrase or quote two or three of Mitford's statements and argue against them, making sure to identify the source of these quotations. Your objective is to defend the practice of embalming as necessary and practical. Be sure to include parenthetical documentation citing Mitford as your source and to include a works-cited page. (See Chapter 18 for information on MLA documentation.)

3. Write an explanation of a process you personally find disgusting—or delightful. Make your attitude clear in your thesis statement and in your choice of words.

Combining the Patterns

Although Mitford structures this essay as a process, many passages rely heavily on subjective **description**. Where is her focus on descriptive details most obvious? What is her purpose in describing particular individuals and objects as she does? How do these descriptive passages help support her essay's thesis?

Thematic Connections

- "Shall I compare thee to a summer's day?" (page 424)
- "The Ways We Lie" (page 463)

SHIRLEY JACKSON

The Lottery (Fiction)

Shirley Jackson (1916–1965) is best known for her subtly macabre stories of horror and suspense, most notably her best-selling novel *The Haunting of Hill House* (1959), which Stephen King has called "one of the greatest horror stories of all time." She also published wryly humorous reflections on her experiences as a wife and mother of four children. Many of her finest stories and novels were not anthologized until after her death.

Background on the initial reaction to "The Lottery" "The Lottery" first appeared in the *New Yorker* in 1948, three years after the end of World War II. Jackson was living somewhat uneasily in the New England college town of Bennington, Vermont, a village very similar to the setting of "The Lottery." She felt herself an outsider there, a sophisticated intellectual in an isolated, closely knit community that was suspicious of strangers. Here, Jackson (whose husband was Jewish) experienced frequent encounters with anti-Semitism. At the time, the full atrocity of Germany's wartime program to exterminate Jews, now called the Holocaust, had led many social critics to contemplate humanity's terrible capacity for evil. Most Americans, however, wished to put the horrors of the war behind them, and many readers reacted with outrage to Jackson's tale of an annual small-town ritual, calling it "nasty," "nauseating," and even "perverted." Others, however, immediately recognized its genius, its power, and its many layers of meaning. This classic tale is now one of the most widely anthologized of all twentieth-century short stories.

1 The morning of June 27th was clear and sunny, with the fresh warmth of a full-summer day; the flowers were blossoming profusely and the grass was richly green. The people of the village began to gather in the square, between the post office and the bank, around ten o'clock; in some towns there were so many people that the lottery took two days and had to be started on June 26th, but in this village, where there were only about three hundred people, the whole lottery took less than two hours, so it could begin at ten o'clock in the morning and still be through in time to allow the villagers to get home for noon dinner.

2 The children assembled first, of course. School was recently over for the summer, and the feeling of liberty sat uneasily on most of them; they tended to gather together quietly for a while before they broke into boisterous play, and their talk was still of the classroom and the teacher, of books and reprimands. Bobby Martin had already stuffed his pockets full of stones, and the other boys soon followed his example, selecting the smoothest and roundest stones; Bobby and Harry Jones and Dickie Delacroix—the villagers pronounced his name "Dellacroy"—eventually made a great pile of stones in one corner of the square and guarded it against the raids of the other boys. The girls stood aside, talking among themselves, looking over their shoulders at the boys, and the

very small children rolled in the dust or clung to the hands of their older brothers or sisters.

Soon the men began to gather, surveying their own children, speaking of   3
planting and rain, tractors and taxes. They stood together, away from the pile
of stones in the corner, and their jokes were quiet and they smiled rather than
laughed. The women, wearing faded house dresses and sweaters, came shortly
after their menfolk. They greeted one another and exchanged bits of gossip as
they went to join their husbands. Soon the women, standing by their husbands, began to call to their children, and the children came reluctantly, having to be called four or five times. Bobby Martin ducked under his mother's
grasping hand and ran, laughing, back to the pile of stones. His father spoke
up sharply, and Bobby came quickly and took his place between his father and
his oldest brother.

The lottery was conducted—as were the square dances, the teenage club,   4
the Halloween program—by Mr. Summers, who had time and energy to devote
to civic activities. He was a round-faced, jovial man and he ran the coal business, and people were sorry for him, because he had no children and his wife
was a scold. When he arrived in the square, carrying the black wooden box,
there was a murmur of conversation among the villagers, and he waved and
called "Little late today, folks." The postmaster, Mr. Graves, followed him, carrying a three-legged stool, and the stool was put in the center of the square and
Mr. Summers set the black box down on it. The villagers kept their distance,
leaving a space between themselves and the stool, and when Mr. Summers said,
"Some of you fellows want to give me a hand?" there was a hesitation before
two men, Mr. Martin and his oldest son, Baxter, came forward to hold the box
steady on the stool while Mr. Summers stirred up the papers inside it.

The original paraphernalia for the lottery had been lost long ago, and the   5
black box now resting on the stool had been put into use even before Old Man
Warner, the oldest man in town, was born. Mr. Summers spoke frequently to
the villagers about making a new box, but no one liked to upset even as much
tradition as was represented by the black box. There was a story that the present box had been made with some pieces of the box that had preceded it, the
one that had been constructed when the first people settled down to make a
village here. Every year, after the lottery, Mr. Summers began talking about a
new box, but every year the subject was allowed to fade off without anything's
being done. The black box grew shabbier each year; by now it was no longer
completely black but splintered badly along one side to show the original wood
color, and in some places faded and stained.

Mr. Martin and his oldest son, Baxter, held the black box securely on   6
the stool until Mr. Summers had stirred the papers thoroughly with his
hand. Because so much of the ritual had been forgotten or discarded, Mr.
Summers had been successful in having slips of paper substituted for the
chips of wood that had been used for generations. Chips of wood, Mr.
Summers had argued, had been all very well when the village was tiny, but
now that the population was more than three hundred and likely to keep
on growing, it was necessary to use something that would fit more easily
into the black box. The night before the lottery, Mr. Summers and

Mr. Graves made up the slips of paper and put them in the box, and it was then taken to the safe of Mr. Summers' coal company and locked up until Mr. Summers was ready to take it to the square the next morning. The rest of the year, the box was put away, sometimes one place, sometimes another; it had spent one year in Mr. Graves' barn and another year underfoot in the post office, and sometimes it was set on a shelf in the Martin grocery and left there.

There was a great deal of fussing to be done before Mr. Summers declared   7
the lottery open. There were the lists to make up — of heads of families, heads of households in each family, members of each household in each family. There was the proper swearing-in of Mr. Summers by the postmaster, as the official of the lottery; at one time, some people remembered, there had been a recital of some sort, performed by the official of the lottery, a perfunctory, tuneless chant that had been rattled off duly each year; some people believed that the official of the lottery used to stand just so when he said or sang it, others believed that he was supposed to walk among the people, but years and years ago this part of the ritual had been allowed to lapse. There had been, also, a ritual salute, which the official of the lottery had had to use in addressing each person who came up to draw from the box, but this also had changed with time, until now it was felt necessary only for the official to speak to each person approaching. Mr. Summers was very good at all this; in his clean white shirt and blue jeans, with one hand resting carelessly on the black box, he seemed very proper and important as he talked interminably to Mr. Graves and the Martins.

Just as Mr. Summers finally left off talking and turned to the assembled   8
villagers, Mrs. Hutchinson came hurriedly along the path to the square, her sweater thrown over her shoulders, and slid into place in the back of the crowd. "Clean forgot what day it was," she said to Mrs. Delacroix, who stood next to her, and they both laughed softly. "Thought my old man was out back stacking wood," Mrs. Hutchinson went on, "and then I looked out the window and the kids were gone, and then I remembered it was the twenty-seventh and came a-running." She dried her hands on her apron, and Mrs. Delacroix said, "You're in time, though. They're still talking away up there."

Mrs. Hutchinson craned her neck to see through the crowd and found her   9
husband and children standing near the front. She tapped Mrs. Delacroix on the arm as a farewell and began to make her way through the crowd. The people separated good-humoredly to let her through; two or three people said, in voices just loud enough to be heard across the crowd, "Here comes your Missus, Hutchinson," and "Bill, she made it after all." Mrs. Hutchinson reached her husband, and Mr. Summers, who had been waiting, said cheerfully, "Thought we were going to have to get on without you, Tessie." Mrs. Hutchinson said, grinning, "Wouldn't have me leave m'dishes in the sink, now, would you, Joe?" and soft laughter ran through the crowd as the people stirred back into position after Mrs. Hutchinson's arrival.

"Well, now," Mr. Summers said soberly, "guess we better get started, get   10
this over with, so's we can go back to work. Anybody ain't here?"

"Dunbar," several people said. "Dunbar, Dunbar."   11

Mr. Summers consulted his list. "Clyde Dunbar," he said. "That's right.   12
He's broke his leg, hasn't he? Who's drawing for him?"

"Me, I guess," a woman said, and Mr. Summers turned to look at her. "Wife   13
draws for her husband," Mr. Summers said. "Don't you have a grown boy to do
it for you, Janey?" Although Mr. Summers and everyone else in the village knew
the answer perfectly well, it was the business of the official of the lottery to ask
such questions formally. Mr. Summers waited with an expression of polite
interest while Mrs. Dunbar answered.

"Horace's not but sixteen yet," Mrs. Dunbar said regretfully. "Guess I gotta   14
fill in for the old man this year."

"Right," Mr. Summers said. He made a note on the list he was holding.   15
Then he asked, "Watson boy drawing this year?"

A tall boy in the crowd raised his hand. "Here," he said. "I'm drawing for   16
m'mother and me." He blinked his eyes nervously and ducked his head as several voices in the crowd said things like "Good fellow, Jack," and "Glad to see
your mother's got a man to do it."

"Well," Mr. Summers said, "guess that's everyone. Old Man Warner make it?"   17

"Here," a voice said, and Mr. Summers nodded.   18

A sudden hush fell on the crowd as Mr. Summers cleared his throat and   19
looked at the list. "All ready?" he called. "Now, I'll read the names — heads of
families first — and the men come up and take a paper out of the box. Keep the
paper folded in your hand without looking at it until everyone has had a turn.
Everything clear?"

The people had done it so many times that they only half listened to the direc-   20
tions; most of them were quiet, wetting their lips, not looking around. Then Mr.
Summers raised one hand high and said, "Adams." A man disengaged himself
from the crowd and came forward. "Hi, Steve," Mr. Summers said, and Mr. Adams
said, "Hi, Joe." They grinned at one another humorlessly and nervously. Then Mr.
Adams reached into the black box and took out a folded paper. He held it firmly
by one corner as he turned and went hastily back to his place in the crowd, where
he stood a little apart from his family, not looking down at his hand.

"Allen," Mr. Summers said. "Anderson. . . . Betham."   21

"Seems like there's no time at all between lotteries any more," Mrs. Delacroix   22
said to Mrs. Graves in the back row. "Seems like we got through the last one only
last week."

"Time sure goes fast," Mrs. Graves said.   23

"Clark. . . . Delacroix."   24

"There goes my old man," Mrs. Delacroix said. She held her breath while   25
her husband went forward.

"Dunbar," Mr. Summers said, and Mrs. Dunbar went steadily to the box   26
while one of the women said, "Go on, Janey," and another said, "There she
goes."

"We're next," Mrs. Graves said. She watched while Mr. Graves came around   27
from the side of the box, greeted Mr. Summers gravely, and selected a slip of paper
from the box. By now, all through the crowd there were men holding the small
folded papers in their large hands, turning them over and over nervously. Mrs.
Dunbar and her two sons stood together, Mrs. Dunbar holding the slip of paper.

"Harburt. . . . Hutchinson."   28

"Get up there, Bill," Mrs. Hutchinson said, and the people near her   29
laughed.

"Jones."   30

"They do say," Mr. Adams said to Old Man Warner, who stood next to him,   31
"that over in the north village they're talking of giving up the lottery."

Old Man Warner snorted. "Pack of crazy fools," he said. "Listening to the   32
young folks, nothing's good enough for *them*. Next thing you know, they'll be
wanting to go back to living in caves, nobody work any more, live *that* way for a
while. Used to be a saying about 'Lottery in June, corn be heavy soon.' First
thing you know, we'd all be eating stewed chickweed and acorns. There's *always*
been a lottery," he added petulantly. "Bad enough to see young Joe Summers
up there joking with everybody."

"Some places have already quit lotteries," Mrs. Adams said.   33

"Nothing but trouble in *that*," Old Man Warner said stoutly. "Pack of   34
young fools."

"Martin." And Bobby Martin watched his father go forward. "Overdyke. . . .   35
Percy."

"I wish they'd hurry," Mrs. Dunbar said to her older son. "I wish they'd   36
hurry."

"They're almost through," her son said.   37

"You get ready to run tell Dad," Mrs. Dunbar said.   38

Mr. Summers called his own name and then stepped forward precisely and   39
selected a slip from the box. Then he called, "Warner."

"Seventy-seventh year I been in the lottery," Old Man Warner said as he   40
went through the crowd. "Seventy-seventh time."

"Watson." The tall boy came awkwardly through the crowd. Someone said,   41
"Don't be nervous, Jack," and Mr. Summers said, "Take your time, son."

"Zanini."   42

After that, there was a long pause, a breathless pause, until Mr. Summers,   43
holding his slip of paper in the air, said, "All right fellows." For a minute, no
one moved, and then all the slips of paper were opened. Suddenly, all the
women began to speak at once, saying, "Who is it?," "Who's got it?," "Is it the
Dunbars?," "Is it the Watsons?" Then the voices began to say, "It's Hutchinson.
It's Bill," "Bill Hutchinson's got it."

"Go tell your father," Mrs. Dunbar said to her older son.   44

People began to look around to see the Hutchinsons. Bill Hutchinson was   45
standing quiet, staring down at the paper in his hand. Suddenly, Tessie
Hutchinson shouted to Mr. Summers, "You didn't give him time enough to
take any paper he wanted. I saw you. It
wasn't fair!"

"Be a good sport, Tessie," Mrs. Delacroix
called, and Mrs. Graves said, "All of us took
the same chance."

"Shut up, Tessie," Bill Hutchinson said.   47

"Well, everyone," Mr. Summers said,
"that was done pretty fast, and now we've
got to be hurrying a little more to get it

> "'Be a good sport,
> Tessie,' Mrs. Delacroix   46
> called, and Mrs. Graves
> said, 'All of us took the
> same chance.'"   48

done in time." He consulted his next list. "Bill," he said, "you draw for the Hutchinson family. You got any other households in the Hutchinsons?"

"There's Don and Eva," Mrs. Hutchinson yelled. "Make *them* take their chance!"   49

"Daughters draw with their husbands' families, Tessie," Mr. Summers said gently. "You know that as well as anyone else."   50

"It wasn't *fair*," Tessie said.   51

"I guess not, Joe," Bill Hutchinson said regretfully. "My daughter draws with her husband's family, that's only fair. And I've got no other family except the kids."   52

"Then, as far as drawing for families is concerned, it's you," Mr. Summers said in explanation, "and as far as drawing for households is concerned, that's you, too. Right?"   53

"Right," Bill Hutchinson said.   54

"How many kids, Bill?" Mr. Summers asked formally.   55

"Three," Bill Hutchinson said. "There's Bill, Jr., and Nancy, and little Dave. And Tessie and me."   56

"All right, then," Mr. Summers said. "Harry, you got their tickets back?"   57

Mr. Graves nodded and held up the slips of paper. "Put them in the box, then," Mr. Summers directed. "Take Bill's and put it in."   58

"I think we ought to start over," Mrs. Hutchinson said, as quietly as she could. "I tell you it wasn't *fair*. You didn't give him time enough to choose. *Every*body saw that."   59

Mr. Graves had selected the five slips and put them in the box, and he dropped all the papers but those onto the ground, where the breeze caught them and lifted them off.   60

"Listen, everybody," Mrs. Hutchinson was saying to the people around her.   61

"Ready, Bill?" Mr. Summers asked, and Bill Hutchinson, with one quick glance around at his wife and children, nodded.   62

"Remember," Mr. Summers said, "take the slips and keep them folded until each person has taken one. Harry, you help little Dave." Mr. Graves took the hand of the little boy, who came willingly with him up to the box. "Take a paper out of the box, Davy," Mr. Summers said. Davy put his hand into the box and laughed. "Take just *one* paper," Mr. Summers said. "Harry, you hold it for him." Mr. Graves took the child's hand and removed the folded paper from the tight fist and held it while little Dave stood next to him and looked up at him wonderingly.   63

"Nancy next," Mr. Summers said. Nancy was twelve, and her school friends breathed heavily as she went forward, switching her skirt, and took a slip daintily from the box. "Bill, Jr.," Mr. Summers said, and Billy, his face red and his feet over-large, nearly knocked the box over as he got a paper out. "Tessie," Mr. Summers said. She hesitated for a minute, looking around defiantly, and then set her lips and went up to the box. She snatched a paper out and held it behind her.   64

"Bill," Mr. Summers said, and Bill Hutchinson reached into the box and felt around, bringing his hand out at last with the slip of paper in it.   65

The crowd was quiet. A girl whispered, "I hope it's not Nancy," and the sound of the whisper reached the edges of the crowd.   66

"It's not the way it used to be," Old Man Warner said clearly. "People ain't   67
the way they used to be."

"All right," Mr. Summers said. "Open the papers. Harry, you open little   68
Dave's."

Mr. Graves opened the slip of paper and there was a general sigh through   69
the crowd as he held it up and everyone could see that it was blank. Nancy and
Bill, Jr., opened theirs at the same time, and both beamed and laughed, turning
around to the crowd and holding their slips of paper above their heads.

"Tessie," Mr. Summers said. There was a pause, and then Mr. Summers   70
looked at Bill Hutchinson, and Bill unfolded his paper and showed it. It was
blank.

"It's Tessie," Mr. Summers said, and his voice was hushed. "Show us her   71
paper, Bill."

Bill Hutchinson went over to his wife and forced the slip of paper out of   72
her hand. It had a black spot on it, the black spot Mr. Summers had made the
night before with the heavy pencil in the coal-company office. Bill Hutchinson
held it up, and there was a stir in the crowd.

"All right, folks," Mr. Summers said. "Let's finish quickly."   73

Although the villagers had forgotten the ritual and lost the original black   74
box, they still remembered to use stones. The pile of stones the boys had made
earlier was ready; there were stones on the ground with the blowing scraps of
paper that had come out of the box. Mrs. Delacroix selected a stone so large she
had to pick it up with both hands and turned to Mrs. Dunbar. "Come on," she
said. "Hurry up."

Mrs. Dunbar had small stones in both hands, and she said, gasping for   75
breath, "I can't run at all. You'll have to go ahead and I'll catch up with you."

The children had stones already, and someone gave little Davy Hutchinson   76
a few pebbles.

Tessie Hutchinson was in the center of a cleared space by now, and she   77
held her hands out desperately as the villagers moved in on her. "It isn't fair,"
she said. A stone hit her on the side of the head.

Old Man Warner was saying, "Come on, come on, everyone." Steve Adams   78
was in the front of the crowd of villagers, with Mrs. Graves beside him.

"It isn't fair, it isn't right," Mrs. Hutchinson screamed, and then they were   79
upon her.

· · ·

Reading Literature

1. List the stages in the process of the lottery. Then, identify passages that
   explain the reasoning behind each step. How logical are these explanations?
2. Why is it significant that the process has continued essentially unchanged
   for so many years? What does this fact suggest about the townspeople?
3. Do you see this story as an explanation of a brutal process carried out in one
   town, or do you see it as a universal statement about dangerous tendencies
   in modern society—or in human nature? Explain your reasoning.

Journal Entry

What do you think it would take to stop a process like this lottery? What would have to be done — and who would have to do it?

Thematic Connections

- "Thirty-Seven Who Saw Murder Didn't Call the Police" (page 127)
- "Shooting an Elephant" (page 132)

Writing Assignments for Process

1. Jessica Mitford describes the process of doing a job. Write an essay summarizing the steps you took in applying for, performing, or quitting a job.

2. Write a set of instructions explaining in objective terms how the lottery Shirley Jackson describes should be conducted. Imagine you are setting these steps down in writing for generations of your fellow townspeople to follow.

3. Write a process essay that describes a significant change you made in your personal, academic, or professional life. Include an explanation of your motivation for making the change.

4. List the steps in the process you follow when you study for an important exam. Then, interview two friends about how they study, and take notes about their usual routine. Finally, combine the most helpful strategies into a set of instructions aimed at students entering your school.

5. **Working with Sources.** Think of a series of steps in a bureaucratic process that you had to go through to accomplish something — getting a driver's license or becoming a U.S. citizen, for instance. Write an essay explaining that process, and include a thesis statement that evaluates the process's efficiency. Before you begin writing, consult a website that outlines the process, and refer to this explanation when necessary in your essay. Be sure to document any references to the site and to include a works-cited page. (See Chapter 18 for information on MLA documentation.)

6. Imagine you have encountered a visitor from another country (or another planet) who is not familiar with a social ritual you take for granted. Write a set of instructions outlining the steps involved in the ritual you are familiar with, such as choosing sides for a game or pledging a fraternity or sorority.

7. Write a process essay explaining how you went about putting together a collection, a scrapbook, a writing portfolio, a website, or an album of some kind. Be sure your essay makes clear why you collected or compiled your materials.

8. Explain how a certain ritual or ceremony is conducted in your religion. Make sure your explanation makes it possible for someone of another faith to understand the process, and include a thesis statement that explains why the ritual is important.

9. Think of a process you believe should be modified or discontinued. Formulate a thesis that presents your negative feelings, and then explain the process so that you make your objections clear to your readers.

10. Give readers instructions for the process of participating in a potentially dangerous but worthwhile physical activity such as skydiving, rock climbing, or white-water rafting. Be sure to include all necessary cautions.

Collaborative Activity for Process

Working with three other students, create an illustrated instructional pamphlet to help new students survive four of your school's first challenges, such as registering for classes, purchasing textbooks, eating in the cafeteria, or finding your way around campus. Before beginning, decide as a group which processes to write about, whether you want your pamphlet to be practical and serious or humorous and irreverent, and what kinds of illustrations it should include. Then, decide who will write about which process — each student should do one — and who will locate (or create) the illustrations. When all of you are ready, assemble your individual efforts into a single unified piece of writing.

Cause and Effect

What Is Cause and Effect?

Process explains *how* something happens; **cause and effect** analyzes *why* something happens. Cause-and-effect essays examine causes, describe effects, or do both. In the following paragraph, journalist Tom Wicker considers the effects of a technological advance on a village in India.

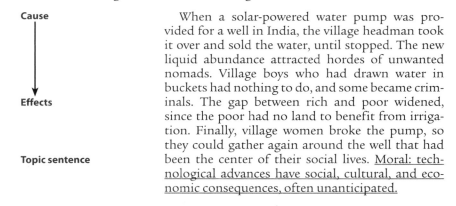

Cause

Effects

Topic sentence

When a solar-powered water pump was provided for a well in India, the village headman took it over and sold the water, until stopped. The new liquid abundance attracted hordes of unwanted nomads. Village boys who had drawn water in buckets had nothing to do, and some became criminals. The gap between rich and poor widened, since the poor had no land to benefit from irrigation. Finally, village women broke the pump, so they could gather again around the well that had been the center of their social lives. Moral: technological advances have social, cultural, and economic consequences, often unanticipated.

Cause and effect, like narration, links situations and events together in time, with causes preceding effects. But causality involves more than sequence: cause-and-effect analysis explains why something happened — or is happening — and predicts what probably will happen. Thus, an essay that examines causes and effects can focus on questions as varied as the following:

- What might be causing climate change, and what effects of climate change have been observed?
- What factors are responsible for the increase in gun violence?
- What changes might occur if the United States becomes a "majority minority" nation?
- What impact will the Black Lives Matter movement have on future local and national elections?
- How did the deregulation of the airline industry change air travel?

Sometimes many different causes can be responsible for one effect. For example, as the following diagram illustrates, many elements may contribute to an individual's decision to leave his or her country of origin and immigrate to the United States.

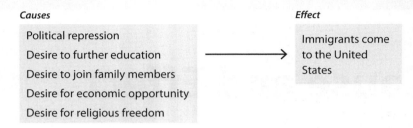

Similarly, a single cause can produce many different effects. Immigration, for instance, has had a variety of effects on the United States.

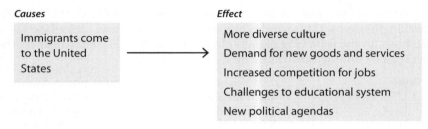

Using Cause and Effect

Causal relationships are rarely as neat as the preceding boxes suggest; in fact, such relationships are often subtle and complex. As you examine situations that seem suited to cause-and-effect analysis, you will discover that most complex situations involve numerous causes and many different effects.

Consider the following example.

The Case of the Car-Free Millennials

In recent years, all Americans—but particularly the generation known as millennials—have been driving less. Today, more than a fourth of people between age sixteen and thirty-four do not own cars. What has caused this decline in automobile ownership? One possible explanation is that it is expensive to buy and maintain a car, and as it has become harder for young people to find good jobs, many are unable to afford cars. For this reason, they may simply be delaying car purchases. Another possible explanation is that more young people are moving to big cities and close-in suburbs and therefore rely on public transportation, bicycles, and walking. Moreover, innovations such as car-sharing, bike-sharing, and ride-sharing programs and high-speed rail—as well as jobs that allow workers to telecommute—have made it possible for many to get along without owning a car. Even if they can afford cars, millennials might also not want to contribute to the negative impact that vehicles have on the environment. All in all, many young people seem to be managing without cars. What effects might this decline in automobile ownership have? Could it hurt the auto industry, thereby causing autoworkers to lose their jobs? Would it have a negative effect on other jobs, such as those in car dealerships or parts manufacturers? Could it encourage cities to fund more public transportation projects? Or, will the loss of revenue from gas taxes have the opposite effect, making cities and states unable to fund such projects? Finally, could this decline in car ownership (if it continues) contribute to saving the planet?

Cyclists ride with a street car in the Mid-Market neighborhood during Bike to Work Day in San Francisco, California, May 14, 2015.

Remember that when you write about situations such as the one described above you need to give a balanced analysis. In other words, you should try to consider all relevant causes and effects, not just the most obvious ones or the first ones you think of.

Understanding Main and Contributory Causes

Even when you have identified several causes of a particular effect, one is always more important than the others. Understanding the distinction between the **main** (most important) **cause** and the **contributory** (less important) **causes** is vital for planning a cause-and-effect essay because once you identify the main cause, you can emphasize it in your essay and downplay the other causes. How, then, can you tell which cause is most important? Sometimes the main cause is obvious, but often it is not, as the following example shows.

The Case of the Hartford Roof Collapse

During one winter a number of years ago, an unusually large amount of snow accumulated on the roof of the Civic Center in Hartford, Connecticut, and the roof fell in. Newspapers reported that the weight of the snow had caused the collapse, and they were partly right. Other buildings, however, had not been flattened by the snow, so the main cause seemed to lie elsewhere. Insurance investigators eventually determined that the roof design, not the weight of the snow (which was a contributory cause), was the main cause of the collapse.

These cause-and-effect relationships are shown in this diagram:

Main cause   *Contributory cause*

| Roof design | *Effect* | Weight of snow |

Roof collapse

Civic Center Roof Cleanup, Hartford, Connecticut, photographed by Richard Welling, 1978, color Polaroid instant print on paper, gift of the Richard Welling Family, copyright Debrah Welling and Lisa Welling Riss, courtesy of the Connecticut Historical Society, 2012.284.964.

Because the main cause is not always the most obvious one, you should consider the significance of each cause very carefully as you plan your essay—and you should continue to evaluate the importance of each cause as you write and revise.

Understanding Immediate and Remote Causes

Another important distinction is the difference between an immediate cause and a remote cause. An **immediate cause** closely precedes an effect and is therefore relatively easy to recognize. A **remote cause** is less obvious, perhaps because it occurred in the past or far away. Assuming that the most obvious cause is always the most important one can be dangerous as well as shortsighted.

Reconsidering the Hartford Roof Collapse

Most people agreed that the snow was the immediate cause of the roof collapse, but further study by insurance investigators suggested remote causes that were not as apparent. The design of the roof was the most important remote cause of the collapse, but other remote causes were also considered. Perhaps the materials used in the roof's construction were partly to blame. Maybe maintenance crews had not done their jobs properly or necessary repairs had not been made. If you were the insurance investigator analyzing the causes of this event, you would want to assess all possible contributing factors. If you did not consider the remote as well as the immediate causes, you would reach an oversimplified and perhaps incorrect conclusion.

This diagram summarizes the cause-and-effect relationships discussed above.

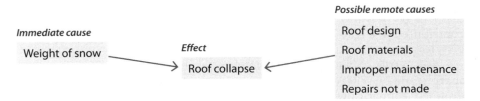

Remember that remote causes can be extremely important. In the Hartford roof collapse, as we have seen, a remote cause — the roof design — was actually the main cause of the accident.

Understanding Causal Chains

Sometimes an effect can also be a cause. This is true in a **causal chain**, where A causes B, B causes C, C causes D, and so on, as shown below.

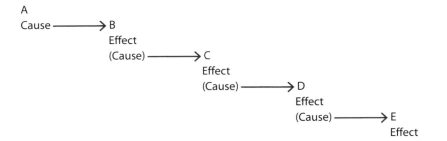

In causal chains, the result of one action is the cause of another. Leaving out any link in the chain, or failing to place any link in its proper order, destroys the logic and continuity of the chain.

An interesting example of a causal chain is the suggestion by a group of retired generals that global warming might be a threat to U.S. national security. According to these generals, global warming could cause worldwide climate changes, such as droughts, which in turn might lead to crop shortages, thereby creating a refugee crisis as people leave their homelands in search of food and clean water. The resulting refugee camps, the generals claim, could become a breeding ground for terrorists, and it is these terrorists who would threaten U.S. security.

Here is another example of a causal chain.

The Case of the Disappearing Bicycle

Today, the bicycle as a form of transportation for children is increasingly rare, with fewer than one percent of children now riding bicycles to school. In addition, fewer children ride bicycles for recreation today than in the past. Causes cited for this decline include the absence of sidewalks in many suburban communities, parents' rising fears about crime and traffic accidents, the rise in the number of students who schedule back-to-back after-school activities (perhaps due in part to the increased number of households with no stay-at-home parent), the popularity of social media and video games, and the increased reliance on after-school jobs by teenagers (who often need cars, not bikes, to get to work). The decreasing number of children who ride bikes has contributed to a corresponding steady decline, since the 1970s, in the sale of bicycles.

As a result of the decline in bicycle sales, bicycle thefts have decreased sharply, and bicycle deaths involving children younger than sixteen have also dropped dramatically (although this is due in part to the increased use of helmets). However, the number of American children who are obese has doubled since the mid-1980s, in part because children get less and less exercise. So, factors such as fewer sidewalks and more working teenagers may have led to a decline in bicycle sales, which in turn could have had a far-reaching impact on children's health.

If your analysis of a situation reveals a causal chain, this discovery can be useful as you plan your essay. The identification of a causal chain suggests an organizational pattern, and following the chain helps you to discuss items in their logical order. (Be careful, however, to keep your emphasis on the causal connections and not to lapse into narration.)

Avoiding *Post Hoc* Reasoning

When developing a cause-and-effect essay, you should not assume that just because event A *precedes* event B, event A has *caused* event B. This illogical assumption, called ***post hoc* reasoning**, equates a chronological sequence with causality. When you fall into this trap—assuming, for instance, that you failed an exam because a black cat crossed your path the day before—you are mistaking coincidence for causality.

Consider the two following examples of *post hoc* reasoning.

The Case of the Magical Maggots

Until the late nineteenth century, many scientists accepted the notion of spontaneous generation; that is, they believed living things could arise directly from nonliving matter. To support their beliefs, they pointed to specific situations. For instance, they observed that maggots, the larvae of the housefly, seemed to arise directly from the decaying flesh of dead animals.

These scientists were confusing sequence with causality, assuming that because the presence of decaying meat preceded the appearance of maggots, the two were connected in a causal relationship. In fact, because the dead animals were exposed to the air, flies were free to lay eggs in the animals' bodies, and these eggs hatched into maggots. Therefore, the living maggots were not a direct result of the presence of nonliving matter. Although these scientists were applying the best technology and scientific theory of their time, hindsight reveals that their conclusions were not valid.

The Case of the Female Centenarians

Several years ago, medical researchers published findings reporting that female centenarians—women who had reached the age of one hundred—were four times as likely to have given birth when they were past forty as were women in a control group who had died at the age of seventy-three. Researchers saw no causal connection between childbirth after forty and long life, suggesting only that the centenarians might have been predisposed to live longer because they had reached menopause later than the other women. Local television newscasts and tabloid newspapers, however, misinterpreted the study's implications, presenting the relationship between late childbearing and long life as a causal one. In a vivid example of *post hoc* reasoning, one promotional spot for a local television newscast proclaimed, "Having kids late in life can help you live longer."

In your writing, as well as in your observations, it is neither logical nor fair to assume that a causal relationship exists unless clear, strong evidence supports that connection. When you revise a cause-and-effect essay, make sure you have not confused words such as *because, therefore,* and *consequently* (words that indicate a causal relationship) with words such as *then, next, subsequently,* and *later* (words that indicate a chronological relationship). When you use a word like *because,* you are signaling to readers that you are telling *why* something happened; when you use a word like *then,* you are only indicating *when* it happened.

The ability to identify and analyze cause-and-effect relationships; to distinguish causes from effects and recognize causal chains; and to distinguish immediate from remote, main from contributory, and logical from illogical causes are all skills that will strengthen your writing.

Planning a Cause-and-Effect Essay

After you have sorted out the cause-and-effect relationships you will write about, you are ready to plan your essay. You have three basic options: to discuss causes, to discuss effects, or to discuss both causes and effects. Often, your assignment will suggest which of these options to use. Here are a few likely topics for cause-and-effect essays.

Focus on finding causes

{ Discuss the factors that contributed to the declining population of state mental hospitals in the 1960s. (social work)

Identify some possible causes of collective obsessional behavior. (psychology) }

Focus on describing or predicting effects

{ Evaluate the probable effects of moving elementary school children from a highly structured classroom to a relatively open classroom. (education)

Discuss the impact of World War I on two of Ernest Hemingway's characters. (literature) }

Focus on both causes and effects

{ The 1840s were volatile years in Europe. Choose one social, political, or economic event that occurred during those years; analyze its causes; and briefly note how the event influenced later developments in European history. (history) }

Developing a Thesis Statement

A cause-and-effect essay usually does more than just enumerate causes or effects; more often, it presents and supports a specific thesis. For example, an economics essay treating the major effects of the Vietnam War on the U.S. economy could be just a straightforward presentation of factual information — an attempt to inform readers of the war's economic impact. It is more likely, however, that the essay would not just enumerate the war's effects but also indicate their significance. In fact, cause-and-effect analysis often requires you to weigh various factors so that you can assess their relative significance.

When you draft your **thesis statement**, be sure it identifies the relationships among the specific causes or effects you will discuss. This thesis statement should ideally tell your readers three things: the issues you plan to consider; the position you will take; and whether your emphasis will be on causes, effects, or both. Your thesis statement may also indicate explicitly or implicitly the cause or effect you consider most important and the order in which you will present your points.

Arranging Causes and Effects

When deciding on the sequence in which you will present causes or effects, you have several options. One option is chronological order: you can present causes or effects in the order in which they occurred. Another option is to introduce the main cause first and then the contributory causes — or, you can do just the opposite. If you want to stress positive consequences, begin by briefly discussing the negative ones; if you plan to emphasize negative results, summarize the less important positive effects first. Still another possibility is to begin by dismissing any events that were not causes and then explain what the real causes were. (This method is especially effective if you think your readers are likely to jump to *post hoc* conclusions.) Finally, you can begin with the most obvious causes or effects and move on to more subtle (but perhaps more important) factors — and then to your analysis and conclusion.

Using Transitions

Cause-and-effect essays rely on clear transitions — *the first cause, the second cause; one result, another result* — to distinguish causes from effects and to help move readers from one cause or effect to the next. In essays that analyze complex causal relationships, transitions are even more important because they can help readers distinguish main from contributory causes (*the most important cause, another cause*) and immediate from remote causes (*the most obvious cause, a less apparent cause*). Transitions are also essential in a causal chain, where they can help readers sort out the sequence (*then, next*) as well as the causal relationships (*because, as a result, for this reason*). A more complete list of transitions appears on page 56.

Structuring a Cause-and-Effect Essay

Finding Causes

Suppose you are planning the social work essay mentioned earlier: "Discuss the factors that contributed to the declining population of state mental hospitals in the 1960s." Your assignment specifies an effect — the declining population of state mental hospitals — and asks you to discuss possible causes, which might include the following:

- An increasing acceptance of mental illness in our society
- Prohibitive costs of in-patient care
- Increasing numbers of mental health professionals, which made it possible to treat patients outside hospitals

Many health professionals, however, believe that the most important cause was the development and use of psychotropic drugs, such as chlorpromazine (Thorazine), which can alter behavior. To emphasize this cause in your essay, you could draft the following thesis statement.

Less important causes	Although society's increasing acceptance of mental illness, the high cost of in-patient care, and the rise in the number of mental health professionals were all
Effect	influential in reducing the population of state mental hospitals in the 1960s, the most important cause of this
Most important cause	decline was the development and use of psychotropic drugs.

This thesis statement fully prepares your readers for your essay. It identifies the points you will consider, and it reveals your position: your assessment of the relative significance of the causes you identify. It states the less important causes first and indicates their secondary importance with *although*. In the body of your essay, the less important causes would be discussed first so that the essay could gradually build up to the most convincing material. An informal outline for your essay might look like the one that follows.

SAMPLE OUTLINE: Finding Causes

INTRODUCTION

Thesis statement: Although society's increasing acceptance of mental illness, the high cost of in-patient care, and the rise in the number of mental health professionals were all influential in reducing the population of state mental hospitals in the 1960s, the most important cause of this decline was the development and use of psychotropic drugs.

FIRST CAUSE

Increasing acceptance of mental illness

SECOND CAUSE

High cost of in-patient care

THIRD CAUSE

Rise in the number of mental health professionals

FOURTH (AND MOST IMPORTANT) CAUSE

Development and use of psychotropic drugs

CONCLUSION

Restatement of thesis (in different words) or review of key points

Describing or Predicting Effects

Suppose you were planning an education essay on the topic mentioned earlier: "Evaluate the probable effects of moving elementary school children from a highly structured classroom to a relatively open classroom." The wording of this assignment tells you that you will focus on effects rather than on causes. After brainstorming to help you decide which specific points to discuss, you might draft this thesis statement.

Cause   Moving children from a highly structured classroom to a relatively open one is desirable because it is likely to encour-
Effects   age more independent play, more flexibility in forming friendship groups, and, ultimately, more creativity.

This thesis statement clearly tells readers the stand you will take and the main points you will consider in your essay. The thesis also clearly indicates that these points are *effects* of the open classroom. After introducing the cause, your essay would treat these three effects in the order in which they are presented in the thesis statement, building up to the most important effect. An informal outline of your essay might look like the one below.

SAMPLE OUTLINE: Describing or Predicting Effects

INTRODUCTION

Thesis statement: Moving children from a highly structured classroom to a relatively open one is desirable because it is likely to encourage more independent play, more flexibility in forming friendship groups, and, ultimately, more creativity.

FIRST EFFECT

More independent play

SECOND EFFECT

More flexibility in forming friendship groups

THIRD (AND MOST IMPORTANT) EFFECT

More creativity

CONCLUSION

Restatement of thesis (in different words) or review of key points

Revising a Cause-and-Effect Essay

When you revise a cause-and-effect essay, consider the items on Checklist: Revising on page 68. In addition, pay special attention to the items on the following checklist, which apply specifically to cause-and-effect essays.

> ✓ **REVISION CHECKLIST** **CAUSE AND EFFECT**
>
> ☐ Does your assignment call for a discussion of causes, effects, or both causes and effects?
> ☐ Does your essay have a clearly stated thesis that indicates whether you will focus on causes, effects, or both?
> ☐ Have you considered all possible causes and all possible effects?
> ☐ Have you distinguished between the main (most important) cause and the contributory (less important) causes?
> ☐ Have you distinguished between immediate and remote causes?
> ☐ Have you identified a causal chain in your reasoning?
> ☐ Have you avoided *post hoc* reasoning?
> ☐ Are the effects you're claiming supported by sources and proper documentation?
> ☐ Have you used transitional words and phrases to show how the causes and effects you discuss are related?

Editing a Cause-and-Effect Essay

When you edit your cause-and-effect essay, follow the guidelines on the editing checklists on pages 85, 88, and 92. In addition, focus on the grammar, mechanics, and punctuation issues that are particularly relevant to cause-and-effect essays. Two of these issues — avoiding faulty "the reason is because" constructions and using *affect* and *effect* correctly — are discussed here.

> 🔍 **GRAMMAR IN CONTEXT** **AVOIDING "THE REASON IS BECAUSE"; USING *AFFECT* AND *EFFECT* CORRECTLY**
>
> **Avoiding "the reason is because"** When you discuss causes and effects, you may find yourself using the phrase "the reason is." If you follow this phrase with *because* ("the reason is *because*"), you will create an error.
>
> The word *because* means "for the reason that." Therefore, it is redundant to say "the reason is because" (which literally means "the reason is for the reason that"). You can correct this error by substituting *that* for *because* ("the reason is *that*").
>
> **INCORRECT:** One reason for the famine in nineteenth-century Ireland was because the potato crop failed.
>
> **CORRECT:** One reason for the famine in nineteenth-century Ireland was that the potato crop failed.

Using Affect and Effect Correctly When you write a cause-and-effect essay, you will probably use the words *affect* and *effect* quite often. For this reason, it is important that you know the difference between *affect* and *effect*.

- *Affect*, usually a verb, means "to influence."

  Linda M. Hasselstrom believes that carrying a gun has <u>affected</u> her life in a positive way.

- *Effect*, usually a noun, means "a result."

- Linda M. Hasselstrom believes that carrying a gun has had a positive <u>effect</u> on her life.

NOTE: *Effect* can also be a verb meaning "to bring about" ("She worked hard to <u>effect</u> change in the community").

✔ **EDITING CHECKLIST** **CAUSE AND EFFECT**

- ☐ Have you used verb tenses correctly to distinguish among events that happened earlier, at the same time, and later?
- ☐ In a complex sentence that includes a dependent clause introduced by *because*, have you placed a comma after the dependent clause when it comes *before* the independent clause ("Because the party was so crowded, we left early")? Have you been careful *not* to use a comma when the dependent clause *follows* the independent clause ("We left early because the party was so crowded")?
- ☐ Have you used "the reason is that" (not "the reason is because")?
- ☐ Have you used *affect* and *effect* correctly?

A STUDENT WRITER: Cause and Effect

The following midterm exam, written for a history class, analyzes both the causes and the effects of the famine that occurred in Ireland during the 1840s. Notice how the writer, Evelyn Pellicane, concentrates on causes but also briefly discusses the effects of this tragedy, just as the exam question directs.

Question: The 1840s were volatile years in Europe. Choose one social, political, or economic event that occurred during those years, analyze its causes, and briefly note how the event influenced later developments in European history.

The Irish Famine, 1845–1849

Thesis statement   The Irish famine, which brought hardship and tragedy to   1
Ireland during the 1840s, was caused and prolonged by four basic
factors: the failure of the potato crop, the landlord-tenant system,
errors in government policy, and the long-standing prejudice of the
British toward Ireland.

First cause   The immediate cause of the famine was the failure of the   2
potato crop. In 1845, potato disease struck the crop, and potatoes
rotted in the ground. The 1846 crop also failed, and before long
people were eating weeds. The 1847 crop was healthy, but there were
not enough potatoes to go around, and in 1848 the blight struck
again, leading to more and more evictions of tenants by landlords.

Second cause   The tenants' position on the land had never been very secure.   3
Most had no leases and could be turned out by their landlords at any
time. If a tenant owed rent, he was evicted — or, worse, put in prison,
leaving his family to starve. The threat of prison caused many tenants
to leave their land; those who could leave Ireland did so, sometimes
with money provided by their landlords. Some landlords did try to
take care of their tenants, but most did not. Many were absentee
landlords who spent their rent money abroad.

Third cause   Government policy errors, although not an immediate cause of   4
the famine, played an important role in creating an unstable economy
and perpetuating starvation. In 1846, the government decided not to
continue selling corn, as it had during the first year of the famine,
claiming that low-cost purchases of corn by Ireland had paralyzed
British trade by interfering with free enterprise. Therefore, 1846 saw
a starving population, angry demonstrations, and panic; even those
with money were unable to buy food. Still, the government insisted
that if it sent food to Ireland, prices would rise in the rest of the
United Kingdom and that this would be unfair to hardworking English
and Scots. As a result, no food was sent. Throughout the years of the
famine, the British government aggravated an already grave situation:
they did nothing to improve agricultural operations, to help people
adjust to another crop, to distribute seeds, or to reform the landlord-
tenant system that made the tenants' position so insecure.

Fourth cause   At the root of this poor government policy was the long-   5
standing British prejudice against the Irish. Hostility between the

two countries went back some six hundred years, and the British were simply not about to inconvenience themselves to save the Irish. When the Irish so desperately needed grain to replace the damaged potatoes, it was clear that grain had to be imported from England. This meant, however, that the Corn Laws, which had been enacted to keep the price of British corn high by taxing imported grain, had to be repealed. The British were unwilling to repeal the Corn Laws. Even when they did supply cornmeal, they made no attempt to explain to the Irish how to cook this unfamiliar food. Moreover, the British government was determined to make Ireland pay for its own poor, so it forced the collection of taxes. Since many landlords could not collect the tax money, they were forced to evict their tenants. The British government's callous and indifferent treatment of the Irish has been called genocide.

Effects

As a result of this devastating famine, the population of   6
Ireland was reduced from about nine million to about six and one-half million. During the famine years, men roamed the streets looking for work, begging when they found none. Epidemics of "famine fever" and dysentery reduced the population drastically. The most important historical result of the famine, however, was the massive immigration to the United States, Canada, and Great Britain of poor, unskilled people who had to struggle to fit into a skilled economy and who brought with them a deep-seated hatred of the British. (This same hatred remained strong in Ireland itself — so strong that during World War II, Ireland, then independent, remained neutral rather than coming to England's aid.) Irish immigrants faced slums, fever epidemics, joblessness, and hostility — even anti-Catholic and anti-Irish riots — in Boston, New York, London, Glasgow, and Quebec. In Ireland itself, poverty and discontent continued, and by 1848 those emigrating from Ireland included a more highly skilled class of farmers, the ones Ireland needed to recover and to survive.

Conclusion (includes restatement of thesis)

The Irish famine, one of the great tragedies of the nineteenth   7
century, was a natural disaster compounded by the insensitivity of the British government and the archaic agricultural system of Ireland. Although the deaths that resulted depleted Ireland's resources even more, the men and women who immigrated to other countries permanently enriched those nations.

Points for Special Attention

Structure

This essay is relatively complex; if it were not so clearly organized, it might be difficult to follow. Because the essay was to focus primarily on causes, Evelyn first introduces the effect—the famine itself—and then considers its causes. After she examines each cause in turn, she moves on to the results of the famine, treating the most important result last. In this essay, then, the famine is first treated as an effect and later as a cause. In fact, the famine itself is the central link in a causal chain.

Evelyn devotes one paragraph to her introduction and one to each cause; she sums up the famine's results in a separate paragraph and devotes the final paragraph to her conclusion. (Depending on a particular essay's length and complexity, more—or less—than one paragraph may be devoted to each cause or effect.) An informal outline for her essay might look like this.

> The Irish Famine
> Introduction (including thesis statement)
> First cause: Failure of the potato crop
> Second cause: The landlord-tenant system
> Third cause: Errors in government policy
> Fourth cause: British prejudice
> Results of the famine
> Conclusion

Because Evelyn saw all the causes as important and interrelated, she decided not to present them in order of increasing importance. Instead, she begins with the immediate cause of the famine—the failure of the potato crop—and then digs more deeply until she arrives at the most remote cause, British prejudice.

Transitions

Because Evelyn considers a series of interrelated events as well as an intricate causal chain, the cause-and-effect relationships in this essay are both subtle and complex. Throughout the essay, many words suggest cause-and-effect connections: *brought, caused, leading to, therefore, as a result, so, since,* and the like. These words help readers to identify and understand the causal connections.

Answering an Exam Question

Before planning her answer, Evelyn read the exam question carefully. She saw that it asked for both causes and effects but that its wording directed her to spend more time on causes ("analyze") than on effects ("briefly note"), and this wording helped her to organize her discussion. In addition, she saw that she would need to indicate *explicitly* which were the causes ("government policy...played an important role") and which were the effects ("The most important historical result").

Evelyn's purpose was to convey factual information and thus to demonstrate her understanding of the course material. Rather than waste her limited time choosing a clever opening strategy or making elaborate attempts to engage her audience, she begins her essay with a direct statement of her thesis.

Working with Sources

Evelyn was obviously influenced by outside sources; the ideas in the essay are not completely her own. Because this was an exam, however, and because the instructor expected students to base their essays on class notes and assigned readings, Evelyn was not required to document her sources.

Focus on Revision

Because this essay was written for an exam, Evelyn had no time — and no need — to revise it further. If she had been preparing this assignment outside of class, however, she might have done more. For example, she could have added a more arresting opening, such as a brief eyewitness account of the famine's effects. Her conclusion — appropriately brief and straightforward for an exam answer — could also have been developed further, perhaps with the addition of information about the nation's eventual recovery. Finally, adding statistics, quotations by historians, or a brief summary of life in Ireland before the famine could have further enriched the essay.

PEER-EDITING WORKSHEET: CAUSE AND EFFECT

1. Paraphrase the essay's thesis. Is it explicitly stated? Should it be?

2. Does the essay focus on causes, effects, or both? Does the thesis statement clearly identify this focus? If not, how should the thesis statement be revised?

3. Does the writer consider *all* relevant causes or effects? Are any key causes or effects omitted? Are any irrelevant causes or effects included?

4. Make an informal outline of the essay. What determines the order of the causes or effects? Is this the most effective order? If not, what revisions do you suggest?

5. List the transitional words and phrases used to indicate causal connections. Are any additional transitions needed? If so, where?

6. Does the writer use *post hoc* reasoning? Point out any examples of illogical reasoning.

7. Are more examples or details needed to help readers understand causal connections? If so, where?

8. Do you find the writer's conclusions convincing? Why or why not?

9. Has the writer used any "the reason is because" constructions? If so, suggest revisions.

10. Are *affect* and *effect* used correctly? Point out any errors.

All the selections that follow focus on cause-and-effect relationships. Some readings focus on causes, others on effects. The first selection, a visual text, is followed by questions designed to illustrate how cause and effect can operate in visual form.

JEFFREY COOLIDGE

Rube Goldberg Machine (Photo)

Jeffrey Coolidge/Stone/Getty Images

. . .

Reading Images

1. This image shows a device inspired by Rube Goldberg, a cartoonist and inventor known for devising complex machines that carry out simple tasks in roundabout, overly complex ways. What task is depicted here? In what straightforward way could it be completed?
2. Study the image carefully. Does every event have a cause? Does every cause have a result? Does this diagram illustrate a causal chain? Why or why not?
3. What is the end result depicted here? Which event do you see as the main cause? Which events are remote causes?

Journal Entry

Write a paragraph summarizing the cause-and-effect relationships depicted in this image.

Thematic Connections

- "How to Make a Waste Pie Chart" (page 280)
- "Should Driverless Cars Kill Their Own Passengers to Save a Pedestrian?" (page 219)

RAY FISMAN AND MICHAEL LUCA

Did Free Pens Cause the Opioid Crisis?

Ray Fisman (b. 1970) is the Slater Family Professor in Behavioral Economics at Boston University. Before teaching at Boston University, he held positions at Columbia University, Harvard University, and the World Bank. He earned his B.A. from McGill University and his Ph.D. from Harvard University. His scholarly work has appeared in many academic journals, including the *Journal of Human Resources*; the *Journal of Law, Economics, and Organizations*; and the *Journal of Public Economics*. He has also coauthored several books, such as *The Inner Lives of Markets* (with Tim Sullivan; 2016) and *Corruption: What Everyone Needs to Know* (with Miriam A. Golden; 2017). Michael Luca is the Lee J. Styslinger III Associate Professor of Business Administration at Harvard University. His work has been published in academic journals such as *Management Science* and *Quantitative Marketing and Economics*. He received his B.A. from the University of Albany and his Ph.D. from Boston University. Along with Ray Fisman, he has published articles in various general-interest publications, including the *Wall Street Journal*, *Slate*, the *Harvard Business Review*, and *The Atlantic*.

Background on the Opioid Crisis Politicians, health experts, and the general public have all recognized the seriousness and scope of the opioid crisis. There are many ways to discuss and illustrate the problem, from painful personal stories to the position papers of policy experts. However, statistics from the Centers for Disease Control and Prevention (CDC) tell a story of their own. On average, roughly 130 people in the United States die of opioid overdoses every day. In 2017, more than 190 million opioid prescriptions were dispensed in the nation. According to the nonprofit United Hospital Fund, 2.2 million U.S. children have been directly affected by the opioid crisis — for example, when their parents were incarcerated or died of an overdose. Moreover, roughly 170,000 children either had abused opioids themselves or had accidentally taken them. People disagree over the causes and solutions for the crisis, but many blame doctors and profit-seeking pharmaceutical companies for the overprescription of powerful synthetic painkillers such as OxyContin. Indeed, the kind of pharmaceutical marketing discussed by Fisman and Luca is often viewed as a culprit in this context. To address the crisis, the CDC has released more stringent guidelines about prescribing opioids. In addition, law-enforcement agencies have worked to make their responses to the crisis more effective and humane. In the private sector, churches and other organizations have also tried to help address the issue in their communities and in the United States as a whole.

Early in *Dopesick*, a book examining how Purdue Pharma helped addict an 1 alarming number of Americans to opioids, Beth Macy writes about the army of drug reps who pushed the painkiller OxyContin. In its approach to sales, Macy shows, Purdue was scientific. Using information purchased from a data-mining firm, the company determined which physicians were prescribing the most of its competitors' painkillers, and dispatched sales reps to their practices. The more likely a doctor was to prescribe, the more often the reps darkened his door. The reps were highly motivated: Their bonuses were pegged to the milligrams of OxyContin a doctor prescribed.

The reps, traditionally known as "detail men" — though since the mid-   2
1990s, when OxyContin was introduced, the field has become more associated with young women — usually arrived bearing gifts. A rep might invite a doctor out to a fine restaurant, or on a junket in a desirable vacation destination. For doctors too busy for such gifts, work-arounds were devised. "Reps began coming by before holidays to drop off a turkey or beef tenderloin that a doctor could take home to the family — even a Christmas tree," Macy writes. To bend the ear of the most harried physicians, reps would invite them to meet at a nearby gas station, where they would buy the doctors a fill-up and pitch them on their wares as the fuel flowed into the tank.

In the years since OxyContin came to market, the industry has imple-   3
mented rules that forbid the most egregious forms of gift-giving. As early as 1991, the American Medical Association had issued recommendations: Ideally, gifts would benefit patients (free samples for those who otherwise couldn't afford them), but gifts to doctors were generally aboveboard as long as they were of "minimal value" — notepads and pens.

As the methods of Purdue's detailers make clear, the AMA's recommenda-   4
tions were honored in the breach through much of the '90s — and Purdue reps were hardly alone in using such methods to their advantage. In 2009, amid intensified government scrutiny of the industry, Big Pharma instituted a code that banned gifts large (tickets to sporting events or the theater) and small (coffee mugs).

Still, that code was itself full of loopholes. Pens were prohibited, but   5
meals — most often casual, in-office affairs — were still permissible. A 2017 article in the *Journal of the American Medical Association* found that in a single year (2015), nearly half the doctors in America received a payment from a drug rep. Close to 90 percent of those payments came in the form of free food and beverages.

You might reasonably ask whether a modest meal with a pharmaceutical sales rep matters all that much. You might also be surprised by what a small gift can buy. In recent years, social psychologists and marketers have demonstrated that the pull of reciprocity is exceedingly powerful in human beings, often acting on us in ways we may not consciously appreciate. Perhaps it's too much to suggest that free pens were responsible for   6
the opioid epidemic. But it's become more and more clear that a gift, even from a salesperson, can make the receiver feel obliged to give something in return.

> **"You might reasonably ask whether a modest meal with a pharmaceutical sales rep matters all that much."**

• • •

The potential conflicts of interest created by detailers' gifts have been rec-   7
ognized for as long as the money's been flowing. Doctors tend to prescribe

drugs from companies that give them gifts—but there could be harmless reasons for the pattern. Doctors who believe that Prozac is an effective drug might prescribe it a lot and also spend time with reps from Prozac's manufacturer, Eli Lilly, to learn about the latest research on how best to use it in treating patients.

Another 2017 study in *JAMA*, however, suggests that even small gifts can 8 cause doctors to change their script-writing behavior. It looked at what happened to the market share of brand-name drugs sold by reps at 19 academic medical centers from 2006 to 2012. Each institution in the study banned small gifts and regulated pharma reps' visits more strictly at some point during this time; the first enacted its prohibitions in October 2006, the last in May 2011. This staggered timeline allowed the researchers to examine how the rate of prescriptions for the repped drugs changed when the policies went into effect. They found that these drugs lost 1.67 percent in market share to cheap generics and drugs without a dedicated sales force. If that doesn't sound like a lot, think of it as a percentage of $60 billion, the 2010 sales revenue for the drugs covered by the study. It works out to a pretty handsome payback for some turkey sandwiches.

At a minimum, when doctors prescribe brand-name drugs rather than 9 generics, insurance companies' costs increase, as do your insurance premiums. Other recent research suggests more damaging consequences from gift-giving. One study found that placing limits on sales calls (including, in most cases, a ban on gifts) led to a decline in children being prescribed antidepressants and antipsychotics not approved by the FDA for pediatric use. (Such "off-label" prescribing is common, but the direct promotion of drugs for off-label uses is prohibited by federal law—there is insufficient evidence that these uses are effective.) Whether because they simply felt less beholden to salespeople, or perhaps because they were hearing fewer pitches for off-label uses, doctors prescribed these drugs to children less often when detailers' visits were restricted.

What about opioids? Well, there's this: A short paper published in *JAMA* 10 *Internal Medicine* in 2018 found that, while prescriptions have dropped across the country in response to their much-publicized abuse, among physicians who continued to receive gifts from opioid makers, prescriptions continued to see a modest rise.

•   •   •

The role of gifts in commerce dates back at least to ancient Rome. The 11 poet Catullus described the gifts Caesar deployed to cajole and manipulate others as "wicked generosity."

In recent decades, social psychologists have helped turn consumer-focused 12 gift-giving into a science. One of the godfathers of this field is Robert Cialdini. Early in his career, in the 1970s, he became intrigued by the various tactics that salespeople used to get consumers to buy stuff. He set out to explore whether these tricks actually worked. He went undercover, taking sales and marketing jobs at a used-car lot, a fund-raising organization, a telemarketing company. He cataloged the tactics he witnessed and began to test them at Arizona State University, where he was a faculty member.

This work culminated in 1984 with *Influence: The Psychology of Persuasion*, 13 which became a best seller and is still assigned and read in business schools today. The book lays out six principles that can make a pitch more persuasive. Among them is reciprocity, which Cialdini's book helped package as an explicit — and easy-to-implement — tactic for marketers.

More recent research has highlighted just how good an investment gifts can be — no matter what you're selling. In one experiment, the economist Armin Falk had a charity send about 10,000 letters to potential donors, asking them to give money. About a third of the would-be donors received only a letter. Another third received the letter accompanied by a postcard with a colorful drawing on it — a gift, the recipients were told, "from the children of Dhaka" that could be "kept or given to others." The final third received the letter and four postcards.

14

The postcards were not much of a gift — they cost pennies apiece. But they led to dramatically higher response rates. One postcard increased the response rate by 17 percent; four postcards raised the rate by 75 percent. According to Falk's back-of-the-envelope calculation, the four-postcard solicitation improved the profitability of the direct-mail campaign by about 55 percent relative to the no-postcard solicitation (after accounting for the cost of the postcards themselves).

15

Other fund-raising experiments leveraging reciprocity have seen similarly impressive results. In a study conducted by Michael Sanders of the Behavioural Insights Team — Britain's "Nudge Unit," dedicated to using behavioral insights to improve government policy — investment bankers were asked to donate a day's salary (roughly $750) to be split between two charities. Some were given a small packet of candy. The gift increased the likelihood of a full donation from 4.4 percent to roughly 11 percent — yielding a return on investment of more than 1,000 percent. (Like postcards, candy is cheap.) Clearly, even small gifts can have an outsize impact.

16

•   •   •

The prevalence and effectiveness of strategic gifts raise important questions for each of us as consumers, and for society at large: How can we protect ourselves from unwittingly falling prey to reciprocity? Should government regulators get more involved?

17

To some extent, regulators are already involved in reducing the use of gifts in the pharmaceutical industry. In 2003, the Department of Health and Human Services issued guidance about which industry marketing techniques violated federal anti-kickback laws. Recently, some states and even cities have imposed more stringent rules. Chicago, for example, has introduced a licensing system for pharmaceutical reps, aiming to mitigate "predatory marketing" of prescription drugs, with revenue from the licenses helping to fund opioid-addiction treatment.

18

While targeted regulation is a positive step, it's unlikely to solve the gift-giving problem entirely. It's hard to imagine legislation banning the World Wildlife Fund from sending you your annual batch of return-address labels, for instance.

19

So we must be on guard against salespeople — and our own instincts. Although some reciprocity can be explained by a natural desire to foster relationships with the people we interact with in our daily lives, studies have shown

20

that the impulse is more reflexive than pragmatic. Many people will recipro-
cate even in a onetime, completely anonymous transaction in which the gift
giver and the recipient never learn each other's identity.

The reciprocal pull may be impossible to overcome. But while the desire to   21
give back may be strong, it is also often short-lived. Research has shown that
the feeling can wear off quickly, which may explain why Purdue's sales reps
paid doctors so many visits.

• • •

Comprehension

1. According to Fishman and Luca, how did free pens "cause the opioid crisis"?
   Do the writers consider other causes? If so, where? If not, should they have
   done so?
2. What specific effects can the gifts the writers discuss have on doctors' behavior?
3. Do you see pharmaceutical sales representatives' gifts to doctors as an
   immediate or a remote cause of the problem the writers address? As a main
   or a contributory cause? Explain.
4. What negative results occur when doctors prescribe name-brand drugs
   instead of generics? What other negative consequences of gift giving do the
   writers identify?
5. Who (or what) do the writers blame for the situation they describe? What
   solutions do they suggest? Which do you think is most likely to solve the
   problem? Why?

Purpose and Audience

1. Why do Fishman and Luca open with two paragraphs about the book
   Dopesick? Is it an effective opening strategy? Why or why not? What other
   options did the writers have?
2. How do the writers expect you to react to the statement that the
   pharmaceutical representatives' bonuses "were pegged to the milligrams of
   OxyContin a doctor prescribed" (1)? How *did* you react?
3. Fisman and Luca provide expert opinion to support their points. Is it
   convincing? What other kinds of support could they have provided?
4. Are the writers mainly focused here on providing information, or do they
   have a persuasive purpose as well? Do they expect readers to take some kind
   of action? Explain.
5. In paragraph 11, the writers mention the long history of the "role of gifts in
   commerce." Why do they include this background information?
6. Does this essay present a fair, balanced view of the relationship between gift
   giving and opioid abuse? Why or why not?

Style and Structure

1. Does this essay focus primarily on causes or on effects? How can you tell?
2. Does this essay include a causal chain? If so, use arrows to diagram it (as
   shown on page 317).

3. Do you think Fishman and Luca commit the ***post hoc* fallacy**, or does the main causal connection they suggest seem logical? Explain.

4. **Vocabulary Project.** What do the writers mean by the phrase "the pull of reciprocity" (6)? In what sense is this phrase central to the point they are making?

5. Throughout this essay, the writers use terminology normally associated not with medicine but with sales and marketing — for example, "salespeople" (9) and "direct-mail campaign" (15). Identify a few other examples of such language, and explain why the writers use it. Is it an effective strategy?

Journal Entry

Should Fishman and Luca have discussed the *effects* of the opioid crisis in this essay — or at least explained the extent of the problem? Why or why not?

Writing Workshop

1. Suppose you have a new job as a sales rep for a pharmaceutical company. On your first day of work, your supervisor encourages you to offer gifts to the doctors you visit — meals, office supplies, and other items that are not specifically prohibited. What effect does this suggestion have on you? How is it likely to affect your behavior and your feelings about your job? Answer these questions in a cause-and-effect essay. (If you like, this essay can be written in the form of an email to your supervisor.)

2. **Working with Sources.** Do some research on the effects and extent of the opioid crisis. Then, write a cause-and-effect essay in which you explain how the spread of opioids has affected one U.S. community. Be sure to cite your sources and to include a works-cited page. (See Chapter 18 for information about MLA documentation.)

3. How do you think "Big Pharma" might justify the gift-giving practice described in this essay? Write a cause-and-effect essay citing the possible positive effects of this gift giving. If you like, you may write your essay in the form of a speech given by a pharmaceutical company executive at the company's annual sales meeting.

Combining the Patterns

Where in this essay could the writers add passages of **description**? *Should* they add such passages? What might they accomplish?

Thematic Connections

- "Job Application Letter" (page 209)
- "The Ways We Lie" (page 463)
- "Just Say No" (page 541)

MAGGIE KOERTH

Why Rational People Buy into Conspiracy Theories

Maggie Koerth (b. 1981) is a senior science writer at *FiveThirtyEight*, a statistics-focused website that analyzes polling, economics, and sports. Previously, she was a science writer and editor at *Boing Boing*, a blog that covers technology and culture, as well as a columnist for the *New York Times*. Her work has also appeared in *Discover*, *Popular Science*, and other publications. Koerth is also the author of *Before the Lights Go Out: Conquering the Energy Crisis Before It Conquers Us* (2012).

Background on famous conspiracy theories In her essay, Koerth refers to historian Richard Hofstadter's famous 1965 work, *The Paranoid Style in American Politics*. For Hofstadter, American politics — and implicitly, American life — was often marked by a sense of "heated exaggeration, suspiciousness, and conspiratorial fantasy." However, the belief in such fantasies knows no geographical or temporal boundaries. For example, anti-Semitic conspiracy theories stretch back to at least the Middle Ages and, later, were infamously promoted in *The Protocols of the Elders of Zion* (1903), a fraudulent text that claimed to reveal a scheme for Jewish world domination. Despite being a hoax, *The Protocols* appealed to prominent figures like Adolf Hitler and Henry Ford. As Hofstadter suggested, however, the United States has long been fertile ground for conspiracy theories, as in the case of nineteenth-century American fears of Catholics and Freemasons. In the twentieth century, many such theories flourished — often related to communism and the dangerous presence of internal enemies. For example, some Americans viewed the widespread fluoridation of the U.S. water supply in the 1950s and early 1960s as a subversive plot. Other conspiracies have focused on extraterrestrials and the government cover-up of alien activity, as in the case of Area 51, a military installation in Nevada that has long been a topic of conspiracy theorists. As Hofstadter noted, American politics (and political figures) has often attracted conspiratorial thinking. This is evident in such theories as the belief that President George W. Bush was actively complicit in the September 11, 2001, terrorist attacks; the claim that President Barack Obama is not a U.S. citizen; and the idea that a group of prominent politicians were involved in a human-trafficking ring operating in the basement of a pizza parlor in Washington, DC.

In the days following the bombings at the Boston Marathon, speculation online regarding the identity and motive of the unknown perpetrator or perpetrators was rampant. And once the Tsarnaev brothers were identified and the manhunt came to a close, the speculation didn't cease. It took a new form. A sampling: Maybe the brothers Tsarnaev were just patsies, fall guys set up to take the heat for a mysterious Saudi with high-level connections; or maybe they were innocent, but instead of the Saudis, the actual bomber had acted on behalf of a rogue branch of our own government; or what if the Tsarnaevs were behind the attacks, but were secretly working for a larger organization?

Crazy as these theories are, those propagating them are not — they're quite normal, in fact. But recent scientific research tells us this much: if you think one of the theories above is plausible, you probably feel the same way about the others, even though they contradict one another. And it's very likely that this isn't the only news story that makes you feel as if shadowy forces are behind major world events.   2

"The best predictor of belief in a conspiracy theory is belief in other conspiracy theories," says Viren Swami, a psychology professor who studies conspiracy belief at the University of Westminster in England. Psychologists say that's because a conspiracy theory isn't so much a response to a single event as it is an expression of an overarching worldview.   3

As Richard Hofstadter wrote in his seminal 1965 book, *The Paranoid Style in American Politics*, conspiracy theories, especially those involving meddlesome foreigners, are a favorite pastime in this nation. Americans have always had the sneaking suspicion that somebody was out to get us — be it Freemasons, Catholics, or communists. But in recent years, it seems as if every tragedy comes with a round of yarn-spinning, as the Web fills with stories about "false flag" attacks and "crisis actors" — not mere theorizing but arguments for the existence of a completely alternate version of reality.   4

Since Hofstadter's book was published, our access to information has vastly improved, which you would think would have helped minimize such wild speculation. But according to recent scientific research on the matter, it most likely only serves to make theories more convincing to the public. What's even more surprising is   5

> **"Conspiracy theories appear to be a way of reacting to uncertainty and powerlessness."**

that this sort of theorizing isn't limited to those on the margins. Perfectly sane minds possess an incredible capacity for developing narratives, and even some of the wildest conspiracy theories can be grounded in rational thinking, which makes them that much more pernicious. Consider this: 63 percent of registered American voters believe in at least one political conspiracy theory, according to a recent poll conducted by Fairleigh Dickinson University.

· · ·

While psychologists can't know exactly what goes on inside our heads, they have, through surveys and laboratory studies, come up with a set of traits that correlate well with conspiracy belief. In 2010, Swami and a co-author summarized this research in *The Psychologist*, a scientific journal. They found, perhaps surprisingly, that believers are more likely to be cynical about the world in general and politics in particular. Conspiracy theories also seem to be more compelling to those with low self-worth, especially with regard to their sense of agency in the world at large. Conspiracy theories appear to be a way of reacting to uncertainty and powerlessness.   6

Economic recessions, terrorist attacks, and natural disasters are massive, 7 looming threats, but we have little power over when they occur or how or what happens afterward. In these moments of powerlessness and uncertainty, a part of the brain called the amygdala kicks into action. Paul Whalen, a scientist at Dartmouth College who studies the amygdala, says it doesn't exactly do anything on its own. Instead, the amygdala jump-starts the rest of the brain into analytical overdrive — prompting repeated reassessments of information in an attempt to create a coherent and understandable narrative, to understand what just happened, what threats still exist, and what should be done now. This may be a useful way to understand how, writ large, the brain's capacity for generating new narratives after shocking events can contribute to so much paranoia in this country.

"If you know the truth and others don't, that's one way you can reassert 8 feelings of having agency," Swami says. It can be comforting to do your own research even if that research is flawed. It feels good to be the wise old goat in a flock of sheep.

Surprisingly, Swami's work has also turned up a correlation between conspiracy theorizing and strong support of democratic principles. But this isn't 9 quite so strange if you consider the context. Kathryn Olmsted, a historian at the University of California, Davis, says that conspiracy theories wouldn't exist in a world in which real conspiracies don't exist. And those conspiracies — Watergate or the Iran-Contra Affair — often involve manipulating and circumventing the democratic process. Even people who believe that the Sandy Hook shooting was actually a drama staged by actors couch their arguments in concern for the preservation of the Second Amendment.

• • •

Our access to high-quality information has not, unfortunately, ushered in 10 an age in which disagreements of this sort can easily be solved with a quick Google search. In fact, the Internet has made things worse. Confirmation bias — the tendency to pay more attention to evidence that supports what you already believe — is a well-documented and common human failing. People have been writing about it for centuries. In recent years, though, researchers have found that confirmation bias is not easy to overcome. You can't just drown it in facts.

In 2006, the political scientists Brendan Nyhan and Jason Reifler identi- 11 fied a phenomenon called the "backfire effect." They showed that efforts to debunk inaccurate political information can leave people more convinced that false information is true than they would have been otherwise. Nyhan isn't sure why this happens, but it appears to be more prevalent when the bad information helps bolster a favored worldview or ideology.

In that way, Swami says, the Internet and other media have helped perpet- 12 uate paranoia. Not only does more exposure to these alternative narratives help engender belief in conspiracies, he says, but the Internet's tendency toward tribalism helps reinforce misguided beliefs.

And that's a problem. Because while believing George W. Bush helped 13 plan the September 11 attacks might make you *feel* in control, it doesn't actually make you so. Earlier this year, Karen Douglas, a University of Kent psychologist, along with a student, published research in which they exposed people to conspiracy theories about climate change and the death of Princess Diana. Those who got information supporting the theories but not information debunking them were more likely to withdraw from participation in politics and were less likely to take action to reduce their carbon footprints.

Alex Jones, a syndicated radio host, can build fame as a conspiracy peddler;   14
politicians can hint at conspiracies for votes and leverage; but if conspiracy theories are a tool the average person uses to reclaim his sense of agency and access to democracy, it's an ineffective tool. It can even have dangerous health implications. For example, research has shown that African Americans who believe AIDS is a weapon loosed on them by the government (remembering the abuses of the Tuskegee experiment) are less likely to practice protected sex. And if you believe that governments or corporations are hiding evidence that vaccines harm children, you're less likely to have your children vaccinated. The result: pockets of measles and whooping-cough infections and a few deaths in places with low child-vaccination rates.

Psychologists aren't sure whether powerlessness causes conspiracy theo-   15
ries or vice versa. Either way, the current scientific thinking suggests these beliefs are nothing more than an extreme form of cynicism, a turning away from politics and traditional media — which only perpetuates the problem.

· · ·

Comprehension

1. What is a conspiracy theory? List some of the examples Koerth gives to illustrate this concept.
2. In paragraph 3, Koerth cites psychologists who say that "a conspiracy theory isn't so much a response to a single event as it is an expression of an overarching worldview." What do these psychologists mean?
3. What is "confirmation bias" (10)? What is the "backfire effect" (11)?
4. What traits "correlate well with conspiracy belief" (6)? How is belief in conspiracy theories related to "strong support of democratic principles" (9)?
5. How do the Internet and other media help "perpetuate paranoia" (12)?
6. According to Koerth, exactly why do "rational people buy into conspiracy theories"?
7. What effects of the belief in conspiracy theories does Koerth identify? Does she see these effects as generally positive or negative?

Purpose and Audience

1. This essay addresses a serious issue and relies for support on expert testimony, yet its style and tone are quite informal. What does this tell you about the writer's purpose and intended audience?
2. Koerth quotes psychology professor Viren Swami and political scientist Richard Hofstadter and also cites historians and scientists. How do the words of these experts support the point she is making?

3. Why do you think Koerth uses the phrase "rational people" (instead of just "people") in her title? How is her audience likely to respond to this phrase? How does she appeal to her audience in a similar way elsewhere in the essay—for example, with the statistic in paragraph 5?

4. Could any of the following sentences serve as the thesis of this essay?

   - "Crazy as these theories are, those propagating them are not—they're quite normal, in fact." (2)
   - " 'The best predictor of belief in a conspiracy theory is belief in other conspiracy theories.' " (3)
   - "Psychologists aren't sure whether powerlessness causes conspiracy theories or vice versa." (15)

   If not, can you suggest a more appropriate thesis statement for this essay?

Style and Structure

1. As the title suggests, this essay's primary focus is on the causes of conspiracy theories. Where does Koerth discuss the effects?

2. Could this essay be diagrammed as a causal chain? Try to create a diagram to illustrate such a chain.

3. **Vocabulary Project.** The word *paranoia* comes up several times in this essay—for example, in paragraph 7 and in paragraph 12. What is paranoia? Look up this word in a few different dictionaries—including a medical or psychological dictionary—and explain how it might be related to belief in conspiracy theories.

Journal Entry

Reread this essay's first paragraph. Do any of the rumors Koerth cites seem plausible to you? Why or why not?

Writing Workshop

1. Visit one of the many conspiracy theory sites on the web, and skim some of the theories described there. Identify one theory that you think makes sense. Then, write a cause-and-effect essay in which you explain what led you to accept this theory as true (or at least plausible).

2. **Working with Sources.** Conspiracy theories have been popular throughout history. Consult a few websites to get an overview of some popular conspiracy theories—for example, those surrounding the moon landing, 9/11, the assassination of JFK, or another historical event—and ask some of your friends which of these theories they find believable. Then, write an essay in which you try to account for what might have led to these theories and some possible effects of such beliefs. Be sure to provide parenthetical documentation for any references to Koerth's essay and to include a works-cited page. (See Chapter 18 for information on MLA documentation.)

Combining the Patterns

Koerth essay uses **exemplification** to illustrate the causes and effects of conspiracy theories. Does she include enough examples? Could she have included more, or better, examples?

Thematic Connections

- "The YouTube Effect" (page 20)
- "How to Spot Fake News" (page 289)
- "The Lottery" (page 303)
- "The Ways We Lie" (page 463)

ARTHUR W. LAMBERT

What Causes Cancer? It's Complicated

Arthur W. Lambert is a postdoctoral researcher at the Whitehead Institute, a nonprofit biomedical research institute affiliated with the Massachusetts Institute of Technology. He earned his undergraduate degree from the University of New Hampshire and his Ph.D. from the Boston University School of Medicine. His research focuses on the biology of cancer. He is the coauthor of several articles in journals such as *Molecular Cancer Research* and *Breast Cancer Research*.

Background on cancer research The history of cancer research stretches back to Hippocrates (460–370 B.C.E.), the ancient Greek physician known as the father of medicine. He believed that the body had four *humors* or bodily fluids: blood, phlegm, yellow bile, and black bile. Good health resulted from the balance between these substances, but excesses in black bile led to cancer. This theory of the humors — and this explanation of cancer's causes — persisted up through the eighteenth century. As medical scientists began to observe and apply the scientific method more judiciously, other explanations for the disease emerged, including infections, trauma, and chronic irritation. In 1882, William Halsted performed the first radical mastectomy to treat breast cancer. The twentieth century saw major progress in both understanding and treating the disease. For example, in 1955, researchers discovered that testosterone drives the growth of prostate cancer and that estrogen drives the growth of breast cancer. The first chemotherapy drug, 5-fluorouracil, was patented in 1956 and is still in use today. In the 1970s, researchers refined chemotherapy, which significantly improves the prognosis for adult lymphomas. They also developed a more sophisticated understanding of cancer's genetic factors. Today, although the disease remains the second leading cause of death in the United States, a cancer diagnosis is far from being an automatic death sentence. As our understanding deepens and treatments improve, that trend will likely continue — especially with recent developments in the field of big data oncology and the application of artificial intelligence.

A San Francisco jury decided last month that a plaintiff's case of non-Hodgkin lymphoma was caused by Bayer's Roundup weedkiller, which contains glyphosate, a probable carcinogen; last Wednesday the panel awarded him $80 million in damages. Less than a week before, a jury in Oakland, Calif., awarded $29 million to a woman who claimed her mesothelioma was caused by asbestos in Johnson & Johnson's talc powder. Last year in Missouri, Johnson & Johnson was ordered to pay $4.7 billion to 22 plaintiffs who believed the powder caused ovarian cancer. [1]

> "The truth is that we have no idea why some people develop cancer while others do not."

These decisions aren't the win for consumers that they might seem to be. Instead, they represent a search for a scapegoat that distorts the science of cancer as well as society's conception of the disease. [2]

I study the molecular mechanisms of cancer, and occasionally my job   3
comes up in casual conversation. More often than not, what follows is a question or comment along these lines: "Is it true that deodorant gives you cancer?"
"Eating organic can prevent cancer, right?" "My husband stopped eating sugar,
and I know it cured his cancer."

This line of thinking makes a certain sense, as many cancers are undoubtedly   4
linked to lifestyle choices and environmental exposure. Yet it is fundamentally
flawed because it overestimates the magnitude of these effects—assuming they
are real, which many probably aren't—and because it confuses measures of probability with direct causation.

Exposure to carcinogens influences the risk of developing cancer, which is   5
a function of many factors, including the dose and duration of the exposure.
Other factors, such as inherited genetic mutations, also create risk. To say
something is a carcinogen encompasses a wide spectrum of risk. A properly
conducted, well-controlled epidemiological study may reveal a statistically significant increase in risk related to a certain lifestyle choice or exposure, but it is
critical to consider the magnitude of the risk when applying this to any individual case of cancer.

Certain risk factors, like inheriting a mutant BRCA1 gene (which causes   6
breast and ovarian cancer), more or less ensure tumor development. Some, like
tobacco exposure, are clearly causal, even if most individuals exposed are
spared (80 percent to 90 percent of smokers do not develop cancer, but
lung-cancer rates are far higher than among nonsmokers). Yet many substances labeled "carcinogens" have relatively weak effects and must be judged
alongside the myriad other factors that increase or decrease cancer risk. With a
few exceptions, carcinogens work on the margins, acting as one of many factors tipping the scale toward cancer.

For glyphosate, the scientific evidence is decidedly mixed. A direct link to   7
cancer is still debatable, but even if one accepts the high end of the reported
risks the effects are, at best, modest. The upper estimate (relative risk of 1.3 to
1.4) is an order of magnitude lower than the risk associated with heavy smoking
(relative risk 15 to 30). To put it another way, the risk associated with
glyphosate falls somewhere between the small hazard that comes from eating a
considerable amount of bacon (for colorectal cancer) and consuming very hot
tea (for esophageal cancer).

Either directly or indirectly, many carcinogens lead to DNA damage, which is   8
the underlying cause of cancer. Assuming glyphosate could have inflicted some
genetic damage, it would still be difficult to say with any certainty that it actually
caused a cancer because an untold number of additional steps stand between an
exposure to carcinogenic agents and the diagnosed disease—a long and tortuous
road that stretches from the initially damaged cell to a resulting cancer.

Our bodies have many processes to repair cell damage or eliminate cells in   9
which repair has been unsuccessful. Even when damaged cells persist, they
have to circumvent additional biological barriers before a cell becomes
cancerous. The immune system is also adept at seeking out mutated cells and
eliminating them long before they develop into cancer. All this helps explain
why most cancers take decades to develop.

It isn't necessary to map every step of this journey to establish a connec-   10
tion between a carcinogenic exposure and cancer. But the smaller the risk associated with a carcinogen, the more important it is to account for the unknown.
Were additional carcinogens involved? How do lifestyle choices interact with
the initial exposures? What was the status of the immune system? Did other
pre-existing genetic differences play a role?

The truth is that we have no idea why some people develop cancer while   11
many others do not. Risk factors alter the odds but are hardly determinative.
For any individual case there is a sizable variable of uncertainty, representing
factors that are either poorly understood or truly random.

My principal concern isn't the liability of the companies involved. The most   12
important ramification of these lawsuits is their impact on the public psyche,
suggesting that there is a definitive explanation for every case of cancer.

Cancer is horrible, and the desire to find a clear and definable cause,   13
including factors that could have prevented it, is understandable. But these
cause-and-effect judicial decisions imply that it's possible to trace a straight
line from some specific event in the past leading straight to a cancer. That we
can break open a tumor, rewind it to the beginning, and see exactly when and
where things went wrong. In most cases this simply isn't possible.

And so we are left to deal with the uncomfortable reality that although we   14
have come far in our understanding of cancer, there is still so much that
remains a mystery.

·   ·   ·

Comprehension

1. In paragraph 2, Lambert calls the court decisions summarized in paragraph 1
   "a search for a scapegoat." What does he mean? Why does he characterize these
   decisions in this way?
2. What general causes of cancer does Lambert identify?
3. Why, according to Lambert, is identifying the causes of cancer "complicated"?
4. What does Lambert mean by "the magnitude of the risk" (5)? Why do we
   need to take this factor into account when considering the causes of cancer?
5. What is a carcinogen? In what sense do carcinogens "work on the margins" (6)?
6. Why, according to Lambert, do "most cancers take decades to develop" (9)?

Purpose and Audience

1. Why does Lambert present his professional credentials in paragraph 3? Is
   this information helpful? Is it necessary?
2. In one sentence, paraphrase this essay's thesis.
3. At several points in this essay, Lambert acknowledges the existence of a causal
   relationship between cancer and a particular substance or behavior. Give some
   examples. Do these admissions undercut his thesis? Why or why not?
4. In paragraph 12, Lambert notes that his "principal concern" about the
   lawsuits he observes "isn't the liability of the companies involved." What,
   then, *is* his main concern?

Style and Structure

1. In paragraph 8, Lambert uses the phrase "lead to" to denote a causal relationship; in paragraph 12, he uses "ramification" for the same purpose. What other words and phrase does he use to identify causality?
2. In what respects, if any, are the court decisions Lambert discusses in his introductory paragraphs based on **post hoc reasoning**?
3. **Vocabulary Project.** Lambert says, "Cancer is horrible" in paragraph 13. Is this an appropriate comment for a scientist to make in an essay aimed at an audience of nonscientists? Is it effective? What other words might Lambert have chosen to express this idea?
4. Throughout this essay, Lambert identifies various possible causes of cancer. Which of these possible causes do you see as the immediate cause, and which are remote causes? Which one do you think is the main cause, and which are contributory causes?
5. This essay focuses on causes. Does it also consider effects? If not, should it? Why or why not?

Journal Entry

What lifestyle changes have you made (or might you make in the future) to reduce our risk of developing cancer? Did reading this essay make you more or less likely to make such changes?

Writing Workshop

1. **Working with Sources.** Search for information about the 1964 Surgeon General's report on the relationship between cigarette smoking and cancer. How did people react to this report at the time? What new laws (and what changes in behavior) did this report eventually lead to? Write a cause-and-effect essay that examines some of the effects of the report in the years since it was released. Be sure to cite the sources you use and to include a works-cited page. (See Chapter 18 for information about MLA documentation.)
2. In the United States, many diseases have all but disappeared due to successful vaccination efforts, but in recent years, some parents and lawmakers have voiced their opposition to mandatory vaccination laws. What might be the results of such opposition? Write an essay that takes a dystopian view of the future as you trace the possible effects, both immediate and long term, of the suspension of mandatory vaccination requirements.

Combining the Patterns

Lambert is a scientist, but this essay is directed at the general public. Do you think he should have added sentences (or paragraphs) of **definition** anywhere in this essay? If so, where?

Thematic Connections

- "How to Tell a Mother Her Child Is Dead" (page 275)
- " 'Hope' is the thing with feathers" (page 514)

LINDA M. HASSELSTROM

A Peaceful Woman Explains Why She Carries a Gun

Linda M. Hasselstrom (b. 1943) grew up in rural South Dakota in a cattle ranching family. After receiving a master's degree in American literature from the University of Missouri, she returned to South Dakota to run her own ranch. A highly respected poet, essayist, and writing teacher, she often focuses on everyday life in the American West in her work. Her publications include the poetry collections *Caught by One Wing* (1984), *Roadkill* (1987), and *Dakota Bones* (1991); the essay collection *Land Circle* (1991); and several books about ranching, including *Between Grass and Sky: Where I Live and Work* (2002). Her most recent book is *Gathering from the Grassland* (2017), and she maintains the Windbreak House website, which offers writing retreats and advice.

Background on incidences of sexual assault Hasselstrom's gun ownership can certainly be considered in the context of the ongoing debate over how (and even whether) stricter gun safety measures should be enacted in the United States. In 2008, the Supreme Court overturned a thirty-two-year ban on handguns in Washington, DC, concluding that the ban violated individuals' right to keep and bear arms. In a ruling in 2010, it extended Second Amendment protection to every jurisdiction in the nation. Equally important, however, is that Hasselstrom's reason for carrying a gun is to protect herself from sexual assault. According to a National Crime Victimization survey, more than 300,000 people reported being sexually assaulted in the United States in 2018. It is estimated that only one in six instances of sexual assault is actually reported to the police, so the number of such attacks is, in reality, much higher. A 2009 study conducted by the National Shooting Sports Foundation found that gun purchases by women were increasing and that 80 percent of the female gun buyers who responded to the survey had purchased a gun for self-defense.

1   I am a peace-loving woman. But several events in the past ten years* have convinced me I'm safer when I carry a pistol. This was a personal decision, but because handgun possession is a controversial subject, perhaps my reasoning will interest others.

2   I live in western South Dakota on a ranch twenty-five miles from the nearest town: for several years I spent winters alone here. As a freelance writer, I travel alone a lot — more than 100,000 miles by car in the last four years. With women freer than ever before to travel alone, the odds of our encountering trouble seem to have risen. Distances are great, roads are deserted, and the terrain is often too exposed to offer hiding places.

---

* Eds. note — This essay was written in 2014.

A woman who travels alone is advised, usually by men, to protect herself by   3
avoiding bars and other "dangerous situations," by approaching her car like an
Indian scout, by locking doors and windows. But these precautions aren't
always enough. I spent years following them and still found myself in dangerous situations. I began to resent the idea that just because I am female, I have
to be extra careful.

A few years ago, with another woman, I camped for several weeks in the   4
West. We discussed self-defense, but neither of us had taken a course in it. She
was against firearms, and local police told us Mace was illegal. So we armed
ourselves with spray cans of deodorant tucked into our sleeping bags. We never
used our improvised Mace because we were lucky enough to camp beside people who came to our aid when men harassed us. But on one occasion we visited
a national park where our assigned space was less than fifteen feet from other
campers. When we returned from a walk, we found our closest neighbors were
two young men. As we gathered our cooking gear, they drank beer and loudly
discussed what they would do to us after dark. Nearby campers, even families,
ignored them: rangers strolled past, unconcerned. When we asked the rangers
point-blank if they would protect us, one of them patted my shoulder and said,
"Don't worry, girls. They're just kidding." At dusk we drove out of the park and
hid our camp in the woods a few miles away. The illegal spot was lovely, but our
enjoyment of that park was ruined. I returned from the trip determined to
reconsider the options available for protecting myself.

At that time, I lived alone on the ranch and taught night classes in town.   5
Along a city street I often traveled, a woman had a flat tire, called for help on
her CB radio, and got a rapist who left her beaten. She was afraid to call for
help again and stayed in her car until morning. For that reason, as well as
because CBs work best along line-of-sight, which wouldn't help much in the
rolling hills where I live, I ruled out a CB.

As I drove home one night, a car followed me. It passed me on a narrow   6
bridge while a passenger flashed a blinding spotlight in my face. I braked
sharply. The car stopped, angled across the bridge, and four men jumped out.
I realized the locked doors were useless if they broke the windows of my
pickup. I started forward, hoping to knock their car aside so I could pass. Just
then another car appeared, and the men hastily got back in their car. They
continued to follow me, passing and repassing. I dared not go home because
no one else was there. I passed no lighted houses. Finally they pulled over to
the roadside, and I decided to use their tactic: fear. Speeding, the pickup horn
blaring, I swerved as close to them as I dared as I roared past. It worked: they
turned off the highway. But I was frightened and angry. Even in my vehicle I
was too vulnerable.

Other incidents occurred over the years. One day I glanced out at a field   7
below my house and saw a man with a shotgun walking toward a pond full
of ducks. I drove down and explained that the land was posted. I politely
asked him to leave. He stared at me, and the muzzle of the shotgun began to
rise. In a moment of utter clarity I realized that I was alone on the ranch,
and that he could shoot me and simply drive away. The moment passed: the
man left.

One night, I returned home from teaching a class to find deep tire ruts in   8
the wet ground of my yard, garbage in the driveway, and a large gas tank empty.
A light shone in the house: I couldn't remember leaving it on. I was too embarrassed to drive to a neighboring ranch and wake someone up. An hour of cautious exploration convinced me the house was safe, but once inside, with the
doors locked, I was still afraid. I kept thinking of how vulnerable I felt, prowl-
ing around my own house in the dark.

My first positive step was to take a kung fu class, which teaches evasive or   9
protective action when someone enters your space without permission. I
learned to move confidently, scanning for possible attackers. I learned how to
assess danger and techniques for avoiding it without combat.

I also learned that one must practice several hours every day to be good at   10
kung fu. By that time I had married George: when I practiced with him, I
learned how *close* you must be to your attacker to use martial arts, and decided
a 120-pound woman dare not let a six-foot, 220-pound attacker get that close
unless she is very, very good at self-defense. I have since read articles by several
women who were extremely well trained in the martial arts, but were raped and
beaten anyway.

I thought back over the times in my life when I had been attacked or threat-   11
ened and tried to be realistic about my own behavior, searching for anything
that had allowed me to become a victim. Overall, I was convinced that I had
not been at fault. I don't believe myself to be either paranoid or a risk-taker, but
I wanted more protection.

With some reluctance I decided to try carrying a pistol. George had always   12
carried one, despite his size and his training in martial arts. I practiced shooting until I was sure I could hit an attacker who moved close enough to endanger me. Then I bought a license from the county sheriff, making it legal for me
to carry the gun concealed.

But I was not yet ready to defend myself. George taught me that the most   13
important preparation was mental: convincing myself I could actually *shoot a
person*. Few of us wish to hurt or kill another human being. But there is no
point in having a gun—in fact, gun possession might increase your
danger—unless you know you can use it. I got in the habit of rehearsing, as I
drove or walked, the precise conditions that would be required before I would
shoot someone.

People who have not grown up with the idea that they are capable of pro-   14
tecting themselves—in other words, most women—might have to work hard
to convince themselves of their ability, and of the necessity. Handgun ownership need not turn us into gunslingers, but it can be part of believing in, and
relying on, *ourselves* for protection.

To be useful, a pistol has to be available. In my car, it's within instant reach.   15
When I enter a deserted rest stop at night, it's in my purse, with my hand on
the grip. When I walk from a dark parking lot into a motel, it's in my hand,
under a coat. At home, it's on the headboard. In short, I take it with me almost
everywhere I go alone.

Just carrying a pistol is not protection; avoidance is still the best approach   16
to trouble. Subconsciously watching for signs of danger, I believe I've become

more alert. Handgun use, not unlike driving, becomes instinctive. Each time I've drawn my gun — I have never fired it at another human being — I've simply found it in my hand.

I was driving the half-mile to the highway mailbox one day when I saw a vehicle parked about midway down the road. Several men were standing in the ditch, relieving themselves. I have no objection to emergency urination, but I noticed they'd dumped several dozen beer cans in the road. Besides being ugly, cans can slash a cow's feet or stomach. 17

The men noticed me before they finished and made quite a performance out of zipping their trousers while walking toward me. All four of them gathered around my small foreign car, and one of them demanded what the hell I wanted. 18

"This is private land. I'd appreciate it if you'd pick up the beer cans." 19

"What beer cans?" said the belligerent one, putting both hands on the car door and leaning in my window. His face was inches from mine, and the beer fumes were strong. The others laughed. One tried the passenger door, locked; another put his foot on the hood and rocked the car. They circled, lightly thumping the roof, discussing my good fortune in meeting them and the benefits they were likely to bestow upon me. I felt very small and very trapped and they knew it. 20

"The ones you just threw out," I said politely. 21

"I don't see no beer cans. Why don't you get out here and show them to me, honey?" said the belligerent one, reaching for the handle inside my door. 22

"Right over there," I said, still being polite. " — there, and over there." I pointed with the pistol, which I'd slipped under my thigh. Within one minute the cans and the men were back in the car and headed down the road. 23

I believe this incident illustrates several important principles. The men were trespassing and knew it: their judgment may have been impaired by alcohol. Their response to the polite request of a woman alone was to use their size, numbers, and sex to inspire fear. The pistol was a response in the same language. Politeness didn't work: I couldn't match them in size or number. Out of the car, I'd have been more vulnerable. The pistol just changed the balance of power. It worked again recently when I was driving in a desolate part of Wyoming. A man played cat-and-mouse with me for thirty miles, ultimately trying to run me off the road. When his car passed mine with only two inches to spare, I showed him my pistol, and he disappeared. 24

When I got my pistol, I told my husband, revising the old Colt slogan, "God made men *and women,* but Sam Colt made them equal." Recently I have seen a gunmaker's ad with a similar sentiment. Perhaps this is an idea whose time has come, though the pacifist inside me will be saddened if the only way women can achieve equality is by carrying weapons. 25

> **"The pistol just changed the balance of power."**

We must treat a firearm's power with caution. "Power tends to corrupt, and absolute power corrupts absolutely," as a man (Lord Acton) once said. A 26 pistol is not the only way to avoid being raped or murdered in today's world, but, intelligently wielded, it can shift the balance of power and provide a measure of safety.

•   •   •

Comprehension

1. According to Hasselstrom, why does she carry a gun? In one sentence, summarize her rationale.
2. List the specific events that led Hasselstrom to her decision to carry a gun.
3. Other than carrying a gun, what means of protecting herself did Hasselstrom try? Why did she find these strategies unsatisfactory? Can you think of other strategies she could have adopted instead of carrying a gun?
4. Where in the essay does Hasselstrom express her reluctance to carry a gun?
5. In paragraph 13, Hasselstrom says that possessing a gun "might increase your danger — unless you know you can use it." Where else does she touch on the possible pitfalls of carrying a gun?
6. What does Hasselstrom mean when she says, "The pistol just changed the balance of power" (24)?

Purpose and Audience

1. How does paragraph 1 establish Hasselstrom's purpose for writing this essay? What other purpose might she have?
2. What purpose does paragraph 5 serve? Is it necessary?
3. Do you think this essay is aimed primarily at men or at women? Explain your conclusion.
4. Do you think Hasselstrom expects her readers to agree with her position? Where does she indicate that she expects them to challenge her? How does she address this challenge?

Style and Structure

1. This essay is written in the first person, and it relies heavily on personal experience. Do you see that as a strength or a weakness? Explain your position.
2. What is the main cause in this cause-and-effect essay — that is, what is the most important reason Hasselstrom gives for carrying a gun? Can you identify any contributory causes?
3. Could you argue that simply being a woman is justification enough for carrying a gun? Do you think this is Hasselstrom's position? Why or why not?
4. Think of Hasselstrom's essay as the first step in a possible causal chain. What situations might result from her decision to carry a gun?
5. In paragraph 25, Hasselstrom says that "the pacifist inside me will be saddened if the only way women can achieve equality is by carrying weapons." In her title and elsewhere in the essay, Hasselstrom characterizes herself as a "peaceful woman." Do you think she is successful in portraying herself as a peace-loving woman who only reluctantly carries a gun?

6. **Vocabulary Project.** Some of the words and phrases Hasselstrom uses in this essay suggest that she sees her pistol as an equalizer, something that helps to compensate for her vulnerability. Identify the words and phrases she uses to characterize her gun in this way.

Journal Entry

Do you agree that carrying a gun is Hasselstrom's only choice, or do you think she could take other steps to ensure her safety? Explain.

Writing Workshop

1. Hasselstrom lives in a rural area, and the scenarios she describes apply to rural life. Rewrite this essay as "A Peaceful Urban (or Suburban) Woman Explains Why She Carries a Gun."
2. **Working with Sources.** What reasons might a "peace-loving" *man* have for carrying a gun? Write a cause-and-effect essay outlining such a man's motives, using any of Hasselstrom's reasons that might apply to him as well. Be sure to include parenthetical documentation for any references to Hasselstrom's essay and to include a works-cited page. (See Chapter 18 for information on MLA documentation.)
3. Write a cause-and-effect essay presenting reasons to support a position that opposes Hasselstrom's: "A Peaceful Woman (or Man) Explains Why She (or He) Refuses to Carry a Gun."

Combining the Patterns

Several times in her essay, Hasselstrom uses **narration** to support her position. Identify these narrative passages. Are they absolutely essential to the essay? Could they be briefer? Could some be deleted? Explain.

Thematic Connections

- "Thirty-Seven Who Saw Murder Didn't Call the Police" (page 127)
- "Just Walk On By: A Black Man Ponders His Power to Alter Public Space" (page 231)
- Casebook: "How Can We Stem the Tide of Gun Violence?" (page 626)

KAREN MILLER PENSIERO

Photos That Change History

Karen Miller Pensiero (b. 1963) is the managing editor of the *Wall Street Journal*. She has held several different positions at that publication since 1985, including serving as money and markets editor of the *Wall Street Journal Europe*, director of corporate communications, and editor for newsroom standards. She is a graduate of the University of Missouri School of Journalism.

Background on the Syrian refugee crisis Although antigovernment protests in Syria began as a peaceful part of the 2011 Arab Spring, these uprisings against the regime of Bashar al-Assad ultimately degenerated into a complex and deadly civil war. Various factions, including the so-called Islamic State, the Free Syrian Army, government forces, and various other subfactions and ethnic groups, continue to battle throughout the country and in neighboring Iraq. As a result, close to half a million people have been killed, many of them civilians. According to the United Nations, more than 6.5 million Syrians are internally displaced. Many have fled to Lebanon, Jordan, and Turkey; many others have tried crossing the Mediterranean Sea to Greece, as in the case of Aylan Kurdi and his family. This crisis has led to social and political repercussions throughout Europe as well as in the United States, ranging from dilemmas about military intervention to ethical and practical questions about the obligation to accept refugees. For example, Germany's Chancellor Angela Merkel has expressed openness to accepting Syrian asylum seekers, while concerns about immigration, assimilation, and terrorism have led to contentious debates about the merits of such initiatives. Under the administration of President Donald Trump, the number of Syrian refugees accepted by the United States has dropped precipitously, from thousands annually to just dozens.

For years, the news media have published photos of Syrian refugees: 1
images of the dead, wounded, and displaced. But few of them seem to have made much of an impression — until last week,* when people around the world saw photos of a 3-year-old boy named Aylan Kurdi, whose lifeless body had washed up on a Turkish beach.

"Once in a while, an image breaks through the noisy, cluttered global 2
culture and hits people in the heart and not the head," says Douglas Brinkley, a professor of history at Rice University.

The boy had drowned, along with his brother and mother, while trying to 3
get from Turkey to the Greek island of Kos. The *Wall Street Journal* published an image of a Turkish officer carrying Aylan's dead body, with the boy's face not quite visible and the man looking away, as if not able to bring himself to look at the child. Other news organizations published an even more stark photo of the dead little boy, face down in the surf.

---

* Eds. note — This essay was written in 2015.

AP Photo/DHA/Nilufer Demir, File

A paramilitary police officer stands above the lifeless body of Aylan Kurdi, 3, who died after boats carrying desperate Syrian migrants to the Greek island of Kos capsized, near Bodrum, Turkey, Sept. 2.

Asked last week about this sudden shift in the migration debate, the docu-   4
mentary filmmaker and historian Ken Burns admitted that he once worried that the still image had been devalued, "that a picture was no longer worth a thousand words because there were so many of them." The photos of Aylan Kurdi are a reminder, he says, that "the power of the single image to convey complex information is still there. It has that power to shock and arrest us. To make us stop for just a second and interrupt the flow."

Though the issues have varied greatly over the decades, historians point to   5
other eras when photographs have resonated in the same transformative way, creating new social awareness and spurring changes in policy.

One iconic instance is "Migrant Mother," shot by Dorothea Lange in 1936   6
as part of her work for the federal government's Resettlement Administration. The picture of a woman and her children in a camp in the Central Valley of California vividly captured the plight of American migrants affected by the Great Depression, widespread drought, and the Dust Bowl.

"The photos were part of a government effort to shape and support" the   7
New Deal policies of President Franklin D. Roosevelt, says Joshua Brown, a professor of history at the Graduate Center of the City University of New York. "They were very carefully chosen for publication" to support those programs.

Library of Congress, Prints & Photographs Division, Reproduction number LC-DIG-fsa-8b29516 (digital file from original neg.)

"Migrant Mother": Florence Owens Thompson and her family during the Great Depression, photographed by Dorothea Lange in 1936, Nipomo, Calif. The photo was "part of a government effort to shape and support" the New Deal policies of President Franklin D. Roosevelt, says Prof. Brown.

Martha A. Sandweiss, a professor of history at Princeton University, recalls   8
a conversation she once had with Willard Van Dyke, a distinguished documentary filmmaker who, late in life, returned to his roots in photography. She asked him why, and he said, " 'Migrant Mother.' No film ever changed as many minds or touched as many people as that photograph did."

As World War II drew to a close, Dwight D. Eisenhower, then the command-   9
ing general of Allied forces in Western Europe, sent film crews to Nazi concentration camps. He believed, according to Prof. Brinkley, that "people will deny what's happening if you don't have photographic evidence of everything."

Before the release of the photos to the public, "people heard about the   10
tragedy of the Holocaust, and they heard statistics about it," Prof. Brinkley says, "but suddenly to see the degradation of human life to such a degree just sort of turned the whole world's head around. In many ways, it led to the creation of Israel."

Photography was also crucial in highlighting the injustice of Jim   11
Crow in the South and publicizing the efforts of the civil-rights movement.

AP Images

Gen. Dwight D. Eisenhower (center) views the dead in the courtyard of Ohrdruf, a sub-camp of the Buchenwald concentration camp, after its liberation by U.S. forces, Germany, April 12, 1945. When Eisenhower, then commanding general of Allied forces in Western Europe, learned of the concentration camps, he sent in film crews. "He made them take the Holocaust photos that shocked the world," says Douglas Brinkley, a professor of history at Rice University.

Prof. Brinkley sees similarities between those photos and last week's image of the dead Syrian boy.

"It all comes together with that photograph" of Aylan Kurdi, he says, "and that happens sometimes. It's still a rare moment, but it's something like the barking mad dogs of Bull Connor's Birmingham," referring to the white-supremacist public-safety commissioner who encouraged violence against peaceful protesters.   12

"The fire hoses had the same galvanizing effect," Prof. Brinkley says. "Once people saw those photos, they were repulsed by the Southern Jim Crow bigot system." Seeing such pictures "shifts people in the heart."   13

Prof. Brown says that the Student Nonviolent Coordinating Committee, a key group in the civil-rights movement, so valued the effect of photos that it had its own photographer. "There is no doubt," he says, "that the photographs of attacks on demonstrators played an important role in changing opinions."   14

Though many of history's most influential photos show the harsh reality of suffering or conflict, that's not the only way for images to make an impact. "Earthrise," the color photograph of our planet taken by astronaut Bill Anders on the *Apollo 8* mission in 1968, helped spark the global environmental movement, according to Prof. Brinkley.   15

AP Images/Bill Hudson

A 17-year-old civil-rights demonstrator is attacked by a police dog, May 3, 1963, Birmingham, Ala. President John F. Kennedy discussed this widely seen photo at a White House meeting the next afternoon. "Once people saw those photos," says Prof. Brinkley, "they were repulsed by the Southern Jim Crow bigot system."

16 Up to that point, "everybody thought going to the moon was about space exploration," he says. But many of the astronauts began speaking in terms of our "fragile planet." He believes that the image played a critical role in winning support for the creation of the Environmental Protection Agency in 1970.

17 As for last week's photos of Aylan Kurdi, why were they such an effective call to action? For Prof. Brown, the familiarity of the child, in his little Velcro-strap shoes and red shirt, is what made the photo resonate. "The child looks so much like children you know," he says. "That contrast with our former beliefs of refugees makes a big difference."

18 Mr. Burns describes such photographs as "symbols of a moment." They have "the power to transform the agonizingly slow conversation of politics and diplomacy to a kind of urgency that actually permits us as human beings to transcend the limitation" imposed by our own institutions.

19 Still photographs are "the DNA of our visual experience," says Mr. Burns. "We are brought together by them."

> "Still photographs are 'the DNA of our visual experience.'"

"Earthrise," taken by astronaut Bill Anders in 1968.

•   •   •

Comprehension

1. Why did the photo of Aylan Kurdi have such a great impact on people around the world, but other similar photos did not?
2. In paragraph 4, historian Ken Burns expresses concerns that still photos may have been "devalued." Do you think a photo can have as great an impact as a video? Do you think it can have a greater impact? Explain.
3. List the individual images Pensiero cites as having created "new social awareness" and led to "changes in policy" (5). Why did these particular images have such a great impact?
4. Why did General Dwight D. Eisenhower send film crews to Nazi concentration camps? How did these photos "change history"?
5. In paragraph 13, historian Douglas Brinkley says that when people saw photos of violence in Birmingham, Alabama, in 1963, "they were repulsed," and opinions of the "Southern Jim Crow bigot system" changed. Do you think Brinkley is exaggerating the impact of these photos? What other factors might have led to this change?
6. In paragraph 15, Pensiero shifts her discussion from one kind of photo to another. How does her emphasis change?

Purpose and Audience

1. What experts does Pensiero quote? What qualifies each of them as an "expert" on this subject?
2. Where does Pensiero discuss photos that had a *positive* impact? Why does she include this discussion? Do you think she should have spent more time on such photos? Why or why not?
3. What do you think Pensiero wants readers to take away from reading her essay? Do you think her primary purpose is to make a point about history or a point about photos?
4. In one sentence, summarize Pensiero's thesis.

Style and Structure

1. **Vocabulary Project.** What stronger words might be substituted for the word *change* in this essay's title? Given the possible alternatives, do you think *change* is the best choice? Explain.
2. Pensiero begins and ends her essay with a discussion of Aylan Kurdi. Why does she emphasize his story and not another?
3. Would this essay have had as great an impact if the photos it discusses were not included? Could detailed descriptions of the photos have had a similar impact?
4. Why does Pensiero focus on photos from various time periods? Would a group of contemporary photos work just as well? Why or why not?
5. Why does Pensiero place the photo *Earthrise* last?

Journal Entry

What one specific image might have the power to change Americans' views of immigration, animal testing, school shootings, capital punishment, or climate change? Why?

Writing Workshop

1. What photo published during your lifetime do you think has the power to "change history"? Why, and how? Write a cause-and-effect essay that begins with a description of the photo and provides its social and historical context. If possible, include the photo in your essay.
2. Write a cause-and-effect essay called "Videos That Change History." In your essay, explain the possible impact on history of two or three recent viral cell-phone videos. Do you expect the impact of these videos to last as long as some of the photos Pensiero discusses? Why or why not?
3. **Working with Sources.** Locate several iconic images, both positive and negative, of World War II, the Vietnam War, or the wars in Iraq or Afghanistan. Which images—the positive ones or the negative ones—do you think are likely to have the greatest impact on history? Why? Be sure to cite the source of the images you find and to include a works-cited list. (See Chapter 18 for information on MLA documentation.)

Combining the Patterns

Pensiero includes a good deal of **description** in this essay. Do you think she would have had to add more description if no pictures accompanied her essay? If so, where?

Thematic Connections

- "The YouTube Effect" (page 20)
- "Thirty-Seven Who Saw Murder Didn't Call the Police" (page 127)
- "How to Tell a Mother Her Child Is Dead" (page 275)
- "Emmett Till and Tamir Rice, Sons of the Great Migration" (page 414)
- "The Obligation to Endure" (page 554)
- "Letter from Birmingham Jail" (page 562)

MARTIN ESPADA

Why I Went to College (Poetry)

Martin Espada was born in 1957 in Brooklyn, New York. His father was a civil rights activist in the city's Puerto Rican community, and this informed Espada's political consciousness at an early age. Espada received his B.A. in history from the University of Wisconsin at Madison, and went on to earn a law degree from Northeastern University. He worked for years as tenant lawyer in Boston's Latinx community, and published his first book of poetry, *The Immigrant Iceboy's Bolero*, in 1982. His most recent poetry collections include *Vivas to Those Who Have Failed* (2016), *The Trouble Ball* (2011), and *The Republic of Poetry* (2006). He has also published several books of essays and worked on a number of books as an editor, including *What Saves Us: Poems of Empathy and Outrage in the Age of Trump* (2019). He received the 2018 Ruth Lilly Poetry Prize and currently teaches at the University of Massachusetts-Amherst.

Background on Latinx college attendance Hispanic and Latinx Americans make up the second-largest ethnic group in the United States, at approximately 17 percent of the national population. Rate of educational completion and college attendance has been a concern for this community, in large part because of economic disparity. Though high school dropout rates among this population have plummeted over the past few decades, economics still loom large: a 2014 poll showed that 66 percent of Hispanic/Latinx high school graduates who entered the workforce or the military directly cited a need to help support their family as a reason, compared with 39 percent of white graduates. This group's college enrollment has nonetheless gone up since the '90s, posting greater gains than other ethnic groups. Economic pressures can continue even for students who do enroll in higher education, with fewer Hispanic/Latinx students completing their degrees in four to six years, according to the U.S. Department of Education, and a smaller proportion of those students earning a bachelor's degree. Some schools with a growing Spanish-speaking population have added bilingual admissions counselors, produced Spanish-language recruitment materials, and tried to hire more diverse faculty to encourage student success and continue to close these gaps.

If you don't
My father said,
You better learn
To eat soup
Through a straw   5
'cause I'm gonna
break your jaw

• • •

Reading Literature

1. According to the speaker, why did he go to college? What other factors might have contributed to his decision?
2. What *effects* of this decision might the speaker's father be expecting to see?
3. What does this poem suggest about what kind of man the speaker's father is? About his attitude toward education? How does the speaker feel about him? How can you tell?

Journal Entry

Why did you decide to enroll in college? Consider both main and contributory causes.

Thematic Connections

- "How the Other Half Lives" (page 190)
- "What I Learned (and Didn't Learn) in College" (page 436)
- "The Dog Ate My Tablet, and Other Tales of Woe" (page 450)
- Debate: "Should Federal Student Loans Be Forgiven?" (page 576)

Writing Assignments for Cause and Effect

1. **Working with Sources.** Both "Thirty-Seven Who Saw Murder Didn't Call the Police" (page 127) and "On Dumpster Diving" (page 668) encourage readers, either directly or indirectly, to take action rather than remain uninvolved. Using information gleaned from these essays (or from others in the text) as support for your thesis, write an essay exploring the possible consequences of apathy, the possible causes of apathy, or both. Be sure to provide parenthetical documentation for any words or ideas that are not your own and to include a works-cited page. (See Chapter 18 for more information on MLA documentation.)

2. Identify a recent news article that you believe will have the power to "change history." In a cause-and-effect essay, explain why the news report you chose is so powerful.

3. What effects do student suicides have on college students, faculty, and administrators? Interview some people on your campus to see how they believe campus life would change (or has changed) in response to a student suicide.

4. How do you account for the popularity of one of the following: Twitter, Instagram, hip-hop, video games, home schooling, reality TV, fast food, vaping, flash mobs, or sensationalist tabloids such as the *Star*? Write an essay considering remote as well as immediate causes for the success of the phenomenon you choose.

5. Between 1946 and 1964, the U.S. birthrate increased considerably. Some of the effects attributed to this "baby boom" include the 1960s antiwar movement, an increase in the crime rate, and the development of the women's movement. Write an essay exploring some possible effects on the nation's economy and politics of this baby-boom generation as it ages. What trends would you expect to find now that the first baby boomers have passed age seventy?

6. Write an essay tracing a series of events in your life that constitutes a causal chain. Indicate clearly both the sequence of events and the causal connections among them, and be careful not to confuse coincidence with causality.

7. In recent years, almost half of American marriages ended in divorce. However, among married couples of generation X, born between 1965 and 1980, the divorce rate is considerably lower. To what do you attribute this decline in the divorce rate? Be as specific as possible, citing "case studies" of couples you are familiar with.

8. What do you see as the major cause of any one of these problems: binge drinking among college students, school shootings, childhood obesity, or academic cheating? Based on your identification of its cause, formulate some specific solutions for the problem you select.

9. Write an essay considering the likely effects of a severe, protracted shortage of one of the following commodities: clean water, rental housing,

cell phones, flu vaccine, or books. You may consider a community-, city-, or statewide shortage or a nation- or worldwide crisis.

10. Why do you think so many young adults do not vote? Explore the possible reasons for this situation, as well as its possible consequences (present and future).

Collaborative Activity for Cause and Effect

Working in groups of four, discuss your thoughts about the homeless population, and then list four effects the presence of homeless people is having on you, your community, and the nation. Assign each member of your group to write a paragraph explaining one of the effects the group identifies. Then, arrange the paragraphs in order of increasing importance, moving from the least to the most significant consequence. Finally, work together to turn your individual paragraphs into an essay: write an introduction, a conclusion, and transitions between paragraphs, and include a thesis statement in paragraph 1.

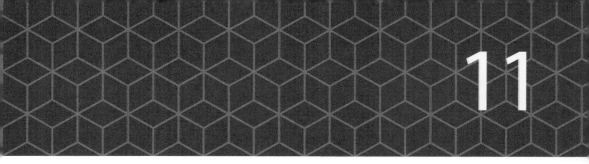

Comparison and Contrast

What Is Comparison and Contrast?

In the narrowest sense, *comparison* shows how two or more things are similar, and *contrast* shows how they are different. In most writing situations, however, the two related processes of **comparison and contrast** are used together. In the following paragraph from *Disturbing the Universe*, scientist Freeman Dyson compares and contrasts two different styles of human endeavor, which he calls "the gray and the green."

Topic sentence (outlines elements of comparison)

Point-by-point comparison

<u>In everything we undertake, either on earth or in the sky, we have a choice of two styles, which I call the gray and the green.</u> The distinction between the gray and green is not sharp. Only at the extremes of the spectrum can we say without qualification, this is green and that is gray. The difference between green and gray is better explained by examples than by definitions. Factories are gray, gardens are green. Physics is gray, biology is green. Plutonium is gray, horse manure is green. Bureaucracy is gray, pioneer communities are green. Self-reproducing machines are gray, trees and children are green. Human technology is gray, God's technology is green. Clones are gray, clades* are green. Army field manuals are gray, poems are green.

A special form of comparison, called **analogy**, explains an idea or thing by comparing it to a second, more familiar thing. In the following paragraph from *The Shopping Mall High School*, Arthur G. Powell, Eleanor Farrar, and David K. Cohen use analogy to shed light on the nature of contemporary American high schools.

---

* Eds. note — A group of organisms that evolved from a common ancestor.

Topic sentence (identifies elements of analogy)

If Americans want to understand their high schools at work, they should imagine them as shopping malls. Secondary education is another consumption experience in an abundant society. Shopping malls attract a broad range of customers with different tastes and purposes. Some shop at Target, others at Bloomingdale's. In high schools a broad range of students also shop. They too can select from an astonishing

Points of similarity

variety of products and services conveniently assembled in one place with ample parking. Furthermore, in malls and schools many different kinds of transactions are possible. Both institutions bring hopeful purveyors and potential purchasers together. The former hope to maximize sales but can take nothing for granted. Shoppers have a wide discretion not only about what to buy but also about whether to buy.

Using Comparison and Contrast

Throughout our lives, we are bombarded with information from newspapers, television, radio, the Internet, and personal experience: the police strike in Memphis; city workers walk out in Philadelphia; the Senate debates government spending; taxes are raised in New Jersey. Somehow we must make sense of the jumbled facts and figures that surround us. One way we have of understanding such information is to put it side by side with other information and then to compare and contrast. Do the police in Memphis have the same complaints as the city workers in Philadelphia? What are the differences between the two situations? Is the national debate on spending analogous to the New Jersey debate on taxes? How do they differ?

We apply comparison and contrast every day to matters that directly affect us. When we make personal decisions, we consider alternatives, asking ourselves whether one option seems better than another. Should I major in history or business? What job opportunities will each major offer me? Should I register to vote as a Democrat, a Republican, or an Independent? What are the positions of each political party on government spending, health care, and taxes? To answer questions like these, we use comparison and contrast.

Planning a Comparison-and-Contrast Essay

Because comparison and contrast is central to our understanding of the world, this way of thinking is often called for in essays and on essay exams.

Compare and contrast the attitudes toward science and technology expressed in Fritz Lang's *Metropolis* and George Lucas's *Star Wars*. (film)

What are the similarities and differences between mitosis and meiosis? (biology)

Discuss the advantages and disadvantages of establishing a partnership or setting up a corporation. (business law)

Discuss both the relative merits of charter schools and traditional public schools. (education)

Recognizing Comparison-and-Contrast Assignments

You are not likely to sit down and say to yourself, "I think I'll write a comparison-and-contrast essay today. Now what can I write about?" Instead, your assignment will suggest comparison and contrast, or you will decide comparison and contrast suits your purpose. In the preceding examples, for instance, the instructors phrased their questions to tell students how to treat the material. When you read these questions, certain keywords and phrases—*compare and contrast, similarities and differences, advantages and disadvantages, relative merits*—indicate that you should use a comparison-and-contrast pattern to organize your essay. Sometimes you may not even need a key phrase. Consider the question "Which of the two Adamses, John or Samuel, had the greater influence on the timing and course of the American Revolution?" Here the word *greater* is enough to suggest a contrast.

Even when your assignment is not worded to suggest comparison and contrast, your purpose may indicate this pattern of development. For instance, when you **evaluate**, you frequently use comparison and contrast. If, as a student in a management course, you are asked to evaluate two health-care systems, you can begin by researching the standards experts use in their evaluations. You can then compare each system's performance with those standards and contrast the systems with each other, concluding perhaps that both systems meet minimum standards but that one is more cost efficient than the other. Or if you are evaluating two energy drinks for a consumer newsletter, you can establish some criteria—ingredients, taste, health risks—and compare and contrast the drinks on each criterion. If each of the drinks is better in different categories, your readers will have to decide which qualities matter most to them.

Establishing a Basis for Comparison

Before you can compare and contrast two things, you must be sure a **basis for comparison** exists—that the two things have enough in common to justify the comparison. For example, although cats and dogs are very different, they share several significant elements: they are mammals, they make good pets, and they are intelligent. Without these shared elements, there would be no basis for comparison and nothing of importance to discuss.

A comparison should lead you beyond the obvious. For instance, at first the idea of a comparison-and-contrast essay based on an analogy between bees and people might seem absurd: after all, these two creatures differ in species, physical structure, and intelligence. In fact, their differences are so obvious that an essay based on them might seem pointless. After further analysis, however, you might decide that bees and people have quite a few things in common. Both are social animals that live in complex social structures, and both have tasks to perform and roles to fulfill in their respective societies. Therefore, you *could* write about them, but you would focus on the common elements that seem most similar — social structures and roles — rather than on dissimilar elements. If you tried to draw an analogy between bees and SUVs or humans and golf tees, however, you would run into trouble. Although some points of comparison could be found, they would be trivial. Why bother to point out that both bees and SUVs can travel great distances or that both people and tees are needed to play golf? Neither statement establishes a significant basis for comparison.

When two subjects are very similar, the differences may be worth writing about. On the other hand, when two subjects are not very much alike, you may find that the similarities are worth considering.

Selecting Points for Discussion

After you decide which subjects to compare and contrast, you need to select the points you want to discuss. You do this by determining your emphasis — on similarities, differences, or both — and the major focus of your essay. If your purpose in comparing two types of houseplants is to explain that one is easier to grow than the other, you would select points having to do with plant care, not those having to do with plant biology.

When you compare and contrast, make sure you treat the same (or at least similar) points for each subject you discuss. For instance, if you were going to compare and contrast two novels, you might consider the following points in both works.

NOVEL A	NOVEL B
Minor characters	Minor characters
Major characters	Major characters
Themes	Themes

Try to avoid the common error of discussing entirely different points for each subject. Such an approach obscures any basis for comparison that might exist. The two novels, for example, could not be meaningfully compared or contrasted if you discussed dissimilar points.

NOVEL A	NOVEL B
Minor characters	Author's life
Major characters	Plot
Themes	Symbolism

Developing a Thesis Statement

After selecting the points you want to discuss, you are ready to develop your thesis statement. This **thesis statement** should tell readers what to expect in your essay, identifying not only the subjects to be compared and contrasted but also the point you will make about them. Your thesis statement should also indicate whether you will concentrate on similarities, differences, or both. In addition, it may list the points of comparison and contrast in the order in which they will be discussed in the essay.

The structure of your thesis statement can indicate the emphasis of your essay. As the following sentences illustrate, a thesis statement can highlight the essay's central concern by presenting it in the independent, rather than the dependent, clause of the sentence. Notice that the structure of the first thesis statement emphasizes similarities, whereas the structure of the second highlights differences.

> Even though television and radio are distinctly different media, they use similar strategies to appeal to their audiences.

> Although Melville's *Moby-Dick* and London's *The Sea Wolf* are both about the sea, the minor characters, major characters, and themes of *Moby-Dick* establish its greater complexity.

Structuring a Comparison-and-Contrast Essay

Like every other type of essay in this book, a comparison-and-contrast essay has an **introduction**, several **body paragraphs**, and a **conclusion**. Within the body of your essay, you can use either of two basic comparison-and-contrast strategies — **subject by subject** or **point by point**.

As you might expect, each organizational strategy has advantages and disadvantages. In general, you should use subject-by-subject comparison when your purpose is to emphasize overall similarities or differences, and you should use point-by-point comparison when your purpose is to emphasize individual points of similarity or difference.

Using Subject-by-Subject Comparison

In a **subject-by-subject comparison**, you essentially write a separate section about each subject, and you discuss the same points for both subjects. Use your basis for comparison to guide your selection of points, and arrange these points in some logical order, usually in order of their increasing significance. The following informal outline illustrates a subject-by-subject comparison.

INTRODUCTION

Thesis statement: Even though television and radio are distinctly different media, they use similar strategies to appeal to their audiences.

SUBJECT 1: TELEVISION AUDIENCES

- Men
- Women
- Children

SUBJECT 2: RADIO AUDIENCES

- Men
- Women
- Children

CONCLUSION

Restatement of thesis (in different words) or review of key points

Subject-by-subject comparisons are most appropriate for short, uncomplicated essays. In longer essays, in which you might make many points about each subject, this organizational strategy demands too much of your readers, requiring them to keep track of all your points throughout your essay. In addition, because of the length of each section, your essay may seem like two completely separate essays. For longer or more complex essays, then, it is often best to use point-by-point comparison.

Using Point-by-Point Comparison

In a **point-by-point comparison**, you make a point about one subject and then follow it with a comparable point about the other. This alternating pattern continues throughout the body of your essay until all your points have been made. The following informal outline illustrates a point-by-point comparison.

INTRODUCTION

Thesis statement: Although Melville's *Moby-Dick* and London's *The Sea Wolf* are both about the sea, the minor characters, major characters, and themes of *Moby-Dick* establish its greater complexity.

MINOR CHARACTERS

First Subject: *The Sea Wolf*
Second Subject: *Moby-Dick*

MAJOR CHARACTERS

First Subject: *The Sea Wolf*
Second Subject: *Moby-Dick*

THEMES

First Subject: *The Sea Wolf*
Second Subject: *Moby-Dick*

CONCLUSION

Restatement of thesis (in different words) or review of key points

Point-by-point comparisons are useful for longer, more complicated essays in which you discuss many different points. (If you treat only one or two points of comparison, you should consider a subject-by-subject organization.) In a point-by-point essay, readers can follow comparisons or contrasts more easily and do not have to wait several paragraphs to find out, for example, the differences between minor characters in *Moby-Dick* and *The Sea Wolf* or to remember on page five what was said on page three. Nevertheless, it is easy to fall into a monotonous, back-and-forth movement between points when you write a point-by-point comparison. To avoid this problem, vary your sentence structure as you move from point to point—and be sure to use clear transitions.

Using Transitions

Transitions are especially important in comparison-and-contrast essays because readers need clear signals that identify individual similarities and differences. Without these cues, readers will have trouble following your discussion and may lose track of the significance of the points you are making. Some transitions indicating comparison and contrast are listed in the following box. (A more complete list of transitions appears on page 56.)

USEFUL TRANSITIONS FOR COMPARISON AND CONTRAST

COMPARISON

in comparison	like
in the same way	likewise
just as . . . so	similarly

CONTRAST

although	nevertheless
but	nonetheless
conversely	on the contrary
despite	on the one hand . . . on the other hand
even though	still
however	unlike
in contrast	whereas
instead	yet

Longer essays frequently include **transitional paragraphs** that connect one part of an essay to another. A transitional paragraph can be a single sentence that signals a shift in focus or a longer paragraph that provides a summary of what was said before. In either case, transitional paragraphs enable readers to pause and consider what has already been said before moving on to a new subject.

Revising a Comparison-and-Contrast Essay

When you revise your comparison-and-contrast essay, consider the items on Checklist: Revising on page 68. In addition, pay special attention to the items on the following checklist, which apply specifically to comparison-and-contrast essays.

 REVISION CHECKLIST **COMPARISON AND CONTRAST**

- ☐ Does your assignment call for comparison and contrast?
- ☐ What basis for comparison exists between the two subjects you are comparing?
- ☐ Does your essay have a clear thesis statement that identifies both the subjects you are comparing and the points you are making about them?
- ☐ Do you discuss the same or similar points for both subjects?
- ☐ If you have written a subject-by-subject comparison, have you included a transition paragraph that connects the two sections of the essay?
- ☐ If you have written a point-by-point comparison, have you included appropriate transitions and varied your sentence structure to indicate your shift from one point to another?
- ☐ Do you need to include a visual, or additional visuals?
- ☐ Do you need to add sources to support your thesis?
- ☐ Have you included transitional words and phrases that indicate whether you are discussing similarities or differences?

Editing a Comparison-and-Contrast Essay

When you edit your comparison-and-contrast essay, follow the guidelines on the editing checklists on pages 85, 88, and 92. In addition, focus on the grammar, mechanics, and punctuation issues that are particularly relevant to comparison-and-contrast essays. One of these issues — using parallel structure — is discussed on the next page.

GRAMMAR IN CONTEXT   USING PARALLELISM

Parallelism — the use of matching nouns, verbs, phrases, or clauses to express the same or similar ideas — is frequently used in comparison-and-contrast essays to emphasize the similarities or differences between one point or subject and another.

- Use parallel structure with paired items or with items in a series.

  "For women, as for girls, <u>intimacy is the fabric of relationships</u>, and <u>talk is the thread from which it is woven</u>" (Tannen 409).

  "Both were born on February 12, 1809 — <u>Darwin into a comfortable family in Shropshire, England</u>; <u>Lincoln into humble circumstances on the American frontier</u>" (Conn 420).

  According to Bruce Catton, Lee was <u>strong</u>, <u>aristocratic</u>, and <u>dedicated to the Confederacy</u>.

- Use parallel structure with paired items linked by correlative conjunctions (*not only/but also, both/and, neither/nor, either/or,* and so on).

  "In everything we undertake, **either** <u>on earth</u> **or** <u>in the sky</u>, we have a choice of two styles, which I call the gray and the green" (Dyson 367).

  According to Steven Conn, the Civil War changed the <u>social</u>, <u>political</u>, **and** <u>racial</u> landscape of the United States.

- Use parallel structure to emphasize the contrast between paired items linked by *as* or *than.*

  According to Deborah Tannen, conversation between men and women is **as** much <u>a problem for men</u> **as** <u>a problem for women</u>.

  As Deborah Tannen observes, most men are socialized <u>to communicate through actions</u> **rather than** <u>to communicate through conversation</u>.

EDITING CHECKLIST   COMPARISON AND CONTRAST

☐ Have you used parallel structure with parallel elements in a series?
☐ Have you used commas to separate three or more parallel elements in a series?
☐ Have you used parallel structure with paired items linked by correlative conjunctions?
☐ Have you used parallel structure with paired items linked by *as* or *than*?

A STUDENT WRITER: Subject-by-Subject Comparison

The following essay, by Mark Cotharn, is a subject-by-subject comparison. It was written for a composition class whose instructor asked students to write an essay comparing two educational experiences.

Brains versus Brawn

Introduction

When people think about discrimination, they usually associate it with race or gender. But discrimination can take other forms. For example, a person can gain an unfair advantage at a job interview by being attractive, by knowing someone who works at the company, or by being able to talk about something (like sports) that has nothing to do with the job. Certainly, the people who do not get the job would claim that they were discriminated against, and to some extent they would be right. As a high school athlete, I experienced both sides of discrimination. When I was a sophomore, I benefited from discrimination. When I was a junior, however, I was penalized by it, treated as if there were no place for me in a classroom. As a result, I learned that discrimination, whether it helps you or hurts you, is wrong.

Thesis statement (emphasizing differences)

First subject: Mark helped by discrimination

Status of football

At my high school, football was everything, and the entire town supported the local team. In the summer, merchants would run special football promotions. Adults would wear shirts with the team's logo, students would collect money to buy equipment, and everyone would go to the games and cheer the team on. Coming out of junior high school, I was considered an exceptional athlete who was eventually going to start as varsity quarterback. Because of my status, I was enthusiastically welcomed by the high school. Before I entered the school, the varsity coach visited my home, and the principal called my parents and told them how well I was going to do.

Treatment by teachers

I knew that high school would be different from junior high, but I wasn't prepared for the treatment I received from my teachers. Many of them talked to me as if I were their friend, not their student. My math teacher used to keep me after class just to talk football; he would give me a note so I could be late for my next class. My biology teacher told me I could skip the afternoon labs so that I would have some time for myself before practice. Several of my teachers told me that during football season, I didn't have to hand in homework because it might distract me during practice. My Spanish teacher even told me that if I didn't do well on a test, I could take it over after the season. Everything I did seemed to be perfect.

1

2

3

Mark's reaction to treatment

Despite this favorable treatment, I continued to study hard. 4
I knew that if I wanted to go to a good college, I would have to get good grades, and I resented the implication that the only way I could get good grades was by getting special treatment. I had always been a good student, and I had no intention of changing my study habits now that I was in high school. Each night after practice, I stayed up late outlining my notes and completing my class assignments. Any studying I couldn't do during the week, I would complete on the weekends. Of course my social life suffered, but I didn't care. I was proud that I never took advantage of the special treatment my teachers were offering me.

Transitional paragraph: signals shift from one subject to another

Then, one day, the unthinkable happened. The township redrew 5
the school-district lines, and I suddenly found myself assigned to a new high school — one that was academically more demanding than the one I attended and, worse, one that had a weak football team. When my parents appealed to the school board to let me stay at my current school, they were told that if the board made an exception for me, it would have to make exceptions for others, and that would lead to chaos. My principal and my coach also tried to get the board to change its decision, but they got the same response. So, in my junior year, at the height of my football career, I changed schools.

Second subject: Mark hurt by discrimination

Status of football

Unlike the people at my old school, no one at my new school 6
seemed to care much about high school football. Many of the students attended the games, but their primary focus was on getting into college. If they talked about football at all, they usually discussed the regional college teams. As a result, I didn't have the status I had when I attended my former school. When I met with the coach before school started, he told me the football team was weak. He also told me that his main goal was to make sure everyone on the team had a chance to play. So, even though I would start, I would have to share the quarterback position with two seniors. Later that day, I saw the principal, who told me that although sports were an important part of school, academic achievement was more important. He made it clear that I would play football only as long as my grades held up.

Treatment by teachers

Unlike the teachers at my old school, the teachers at my new 7
school did not give any special treatment to athletes. When I entered my new school, I was ready for the challenge. What I was not ready for was the hostility of most of my new teachers. From the first day, in just about every class, my teachers made it obvious that they had already made up their minds about what kind of student I was

Mark's reaction to treatment

going to be. Some teachers told me I shouldn't expect any special consideration just because I was the team's quarterback. One even said in front of the class that I would have to study as hard as the other students if I expected to pass. I was hurt and embarrassed by these comments. I didn't expect anyone to give me anything, and I was ready to get the grades I deserved. After all, I had gotten good grades up to this point, and I had no reason to think that the situation would change. Even so, my teachers' preconceived ideas upset me.

Just as I had in my old school, I studied hard, but I didn't know how to deal with the prejudice I faced. At first, it really bothered me and even affected my performance on the football field. However, after a while, I decided that the best way to show my teachers that I was not the stereotypical jock was to prove to them what kind of student I really was. In the long run, far from discouraging me, their treatment motivated me, and I decided to work as hard in the classroom as I did on the football field. By the end of high school, not only had the team won half of its games (a record season), but I had also proved to my teachers that I was a good student. (I still remember the surprised look on the face of my chemistry teacher when she handed my first exam back to me and told me that I had received the second-highest grade in the class.)

Conclusion

Before I graduated, I talked to the teachers about how they had treated me during my junior year. Some admitted they had been harder on me than on the rest of the students, but others denied they had ever discriminated against me. Eventually, I realized that some of them would never understand what they had done. Even so, my experience did have some positive effects. I learned that you should judge people on their merits, not by your own set of assumptions. In addition, I learned that although some people are talented intellectually, others have special skills that should also be valued. And, as I found out, discriminatory treatment, whether it helps you or hurts you, is no substitute for fairness.

Restatement of thesis

Points for Special Attention

Basis for Comparison

Mark knew he could easily compare his two experiences. Both involved high school, and both focused on the treatment he had received as an athlete. In one case, Mark was treated better than other students because he was the team's quarterback; in the other, he was stereotyped as a "dumb jock" because he was a football player. Mark also knew that his comparison would make an interesting (and perhaps unexpected) point — that discrimination is unfair even if it gives a person an advantage.

Selecting Points for Comparison

Mark wanted to make certain that he would discuss the same (or at least similar) points for the two experiences he was going to compare. As he planned his essay, he consulted his brainstorming notes and made the following informal outline.

EXPERIENCE 1 (gained an advantage)	EXPERIENCE 2 (was put at a disadvantage)
Status of football	Status of football
Treatment by teachers	Treatment by teachers
My reaction	My reaction

Structure

Mark's essay makes three points about each of the two experiences he compares. Because his purpose was to convey the differences between the two experiences, he decided to use a subject-by-subject strategy. In addition, Mark thought he could make his case more convincingly if he discussed the first experience fully before moving on to the next one, and he believed readers would have no trouble keeping his individual points in mind as they read. Of course, Mark could have decided to do a point-by-point comparison. He rejected this strategy, though, because he thought that shifting back and forth between subjects would distract readers from his main point.

Transitions

Without adequate transitions, a subject-by-subject comparison can read like two separate essays. Notice that in Mark's essay, paragraph 5 is a **transitional paragraph** that connects the two sections of the essay. In it, Mark sets up the comparison by telling how he suddenly found himself assigned to another high school.

In addition to connecting the sections of an essay, transitional words and phrases can identify individual similarities or differences. Notice, for example, how the transitional word *however* emphasizes the contrast between the following sentences from paragraph 1.

WITHOUT TRANSITION

When I was a sophomore, I benefited from discrimination. When I was a junior, I was penalized by it.

WITH TRANSITION

When I was a sophomore, I benefited from discrimination. When I was a junior, *however*, I was penalized by it.

Topic Sentences

Like transitional phrases, topic sentences can help guide readers through an essay. When reading a comparison-and-contrast essay, readers can easily forget the points being compared, especially if the essay is long. Direct, clearly stated topic sentences can act as guideposts, alerting readers to the comparisons and contrasts you are making. For example, Mark's straightforward topic sentence at the beginning of paragraph 5 dramatically signals the movement from one experience to the other ("Then, one day, the unthinkable happened"). In addition, as in any effective comparison-and-contrast essay, each point discussed in connection with one subject is also discussed in connection with the other. Mark's topic sentences reinforce this balance.

FIRST SUBJECT

At my high school, football was everything, and the entire town supported the local team.

SECOND SUBJECT

Unlike the people at my old school, no one at my new school seemed to care much about high school football.

Focus on Revision

In general, Mark's classmates thought he could have spent more time talking about what he did to counter the preconceptions about athletes that teachers in *both* his schools had.

One student in his peer-editing group pointed out that the teachers at both schools seemed to think athletes were weak students. The only difference was that the teachers at Mark's first school were willing to make allowances for athletes, while the teachers at his second school were not. The student thought that although Mark alluded to this fact, he should have made his point more explicitly.

Another classmate thought Mark should acknowledge that some student athletes *do* fit the teachers' stereotypes (although many do not). This information would reinforce his thesis and help him demonstrate how unfair his treatment was.

After rereading his essay, along with his classmates' comments, Mark decided to add information about how demanding football practice was. Without this information, readers would have a hard time understanding how difficult it was for him to keep up with his studies. He also decided to briefly acknowledge that although he did not fit the negative stereotype of student athletes, some other student athletes do. This fact, however, did not justify the treatment he received at the two high schools he attended. (A sample peer-editing worksheet for comparison and contrast appears on page 386.)

Working with Sources

One of Mark's classmates suggested that he add a quotation from Judith Ortiz Cofer's essay "The Myth of the Latin Woman: I Just Met a Girl Named Maria" (page 224) to his essay. The student pointed out that Cofer, like Mark, was a victim of discrimination on the basis of stereotyping. By referring to Cofer's essay, Mark could widen the scope of his remarks and show

how his experience was similar to that of someone who was stereotyped on the basis of ethnicity. Mark thought that was a good idea, and he decided to refer to Cofer's essay in the next draft of his essay. (Adding this reference would require him to include MLA parenthetical documentation and a works-cited page.)

A STUDENT WRITER: Point-by-Point Comparison

The following essay, by Maria Tecson, is a point-by-point comparison. It was written for a composition class whose instructor asked students to compare two websites about a health issue and to determine which is the more reliable information source.

A Comparison of Two Websites on Attention Deficit Disorder

Introduction

At first glance, the National Institute of Mental Health (NIMH) and ADD.com websites — two sites on Attention Deficit Disorder — look a lot alike. Both have attractive designs, headings, and links to other websites. Because anyone can publish on the Internet, however, websites cannot be judged just on how they look. Colorful graphics and an appealing layout can often hide shortcomings that make sites unsuitable research sources. As a comparison of the NIMH and ADD.com websites shows, the first

Thesis statement (emphasizing differences)

site is definitely a more reliable, useful source of information than the second.

First point: comparing home pages

The first difference between the two websites is the design of their home pages. The NIMH page looks clear and professional. For example, the logos, tabs, links, search boxes, and text columns

NIMH home page

are placed carefully on the page (see fig. 1). Words are spelled correctly; tabs help users to navigate; and content is arranged topically, with headings such as "Mental Health Information" and "Research." The page includes links to detailed reference lists and footnotes as well as to resources for further study. Finally, many of the pages associated with the NIMH site offer accessibility options, such as text in Spanish.

ADD home page

The ADD.com home page is more crowded than NIMH's ADHD/ ADD home page; although it has less text, it contains more design elements, including bright colors and a number of images (see fig. 2). The arrangement of these elements on the page, the focus of the information presented, and the lack of misspellings indicate that it has been carefully designed. This page is engaging and visually stimulating, and it contains headings and links to research studies. However, it is not always clear how the design elements and sidebars

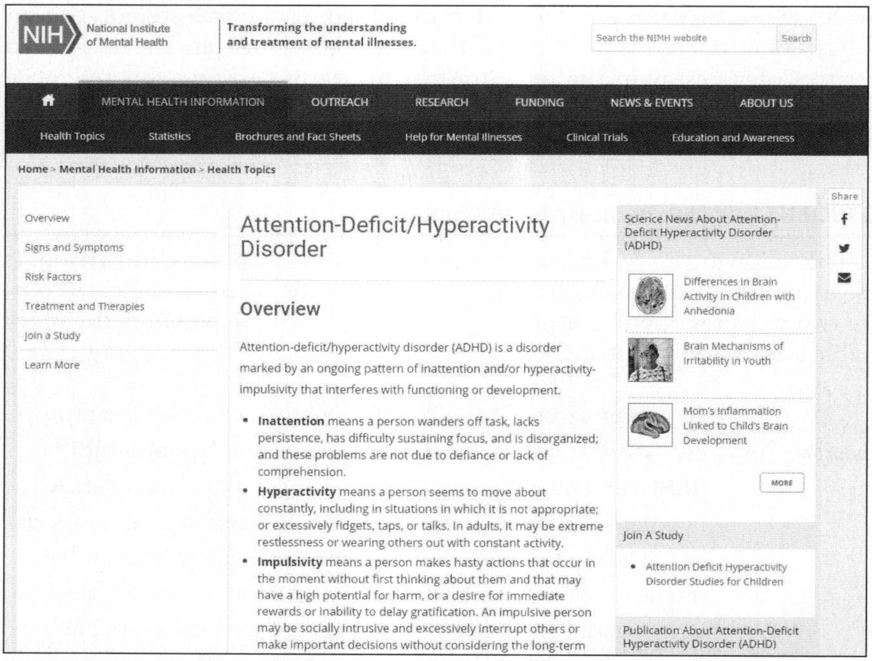

Fig. 1. Mental Health (NIMH) website from: National Institute of Mental Health. *Attention-Deficit/Hyperactivity Disorder, 2019,* nimh.nih.gov/health/topics/attention -deficit-hyperactivity-disorder-adhd/index.shtml.

are related to the information on the page. The home page also lacks any clear accessibility options, which limits the site's use by a wide audience.

Second point: comparing sponsors

NIMH site sponsor

Another difference between the two websites is their purposes. The URL for the NIMH website indicates that it is a *.gov* — a website created by a branch of the United States government. The logo at the top left of the home page identifies the National Institute of Mental Health (NIMH) as the sponsor of the site. The "About Us" tab on the upper right-hand side of the page links to a description of NIMH as well as to contact information for this organization. A notice at the bottom of the page informs visitors that NIMH is part of the National Institutes of Health, which is, in turn, a part of the U.S. Department of Health and Human Services. Furthermore, the "About Us" tab includes the NIMH Strategic Plan, which informs readers that NIMH is the "lead federal agency for research on mental and behavioral disorders." This

4

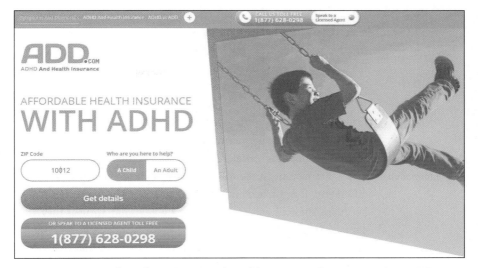

Fig. 2. ADD.com website from: "ADD and Health Insurance." *ADD.com*, 2019, ADD.com.

description clearly indicates that the site's purpose is to give the American public the latest information about ADHD. For this reason, the website lists treatments and therapies used to treat ADHD and objectively evaluates the various treatment options available to patients.

ADD site sponsor

The URL for ADD.com ends with *.com*, indicating that it is   5
a commercial site. The sponsor of this website is ADD.com. At the very bottom of the page, "Our Story" explains that the goal of ADD.com "is to help anyone with pre-existing medical conditions to get the help they want and need." A careful examination of the site, however, indicates that ADD.com's purpose is not just to deliver information about mental health and behavioral disorders. Although ADD.com treats some of the same topics as the NIMH site, its purpose is to sell insurance. This intention is made clear at the bottom the page with an appeal to parents of children suffering from ADHD: "Make sure an ADHD diagnosis doesn't ruin you financially and get covered."

Third point: how sites present information

A final difference between the two websites is how they   6
present the information. The ADHD information on the NIMH site is largely concentrated on a single page. The page is long, listing one topic after another. The links on the sidebar take readers down the

NIMH information   page to different sections, but the information is all included on the main page. Links on the right-hand side of the page take readers to other pages, both on the NIMH site and from outside sources, including other organizations working on ADHD, both governmental and academic. There are no ads of any kind on the NIMH website. Most of the sites linked to from the main page have an educational focus. In addition, the site clearly states that links to other sites "do not constitute an endorsement of their policies or products." In short, the NIMH site offers a straightforward presentation of material.

ADD information   Information on the ADD.com website, however, is presented   7
differently. It is arranged in short sections introduced by colorful headings. These illustrations break up the text, but at times they are distracting. In addition, text boxes, placed at various places on the page, ask readers to insert their zip codes so they can find "individual health insurance and family plans." Like the illustrations, these boxes are intrusive, interrupting the flow of the discussion and sometimes disrupting the clarity, focus, and usefulness of the ADD.com site. The boxes also make it clear that the purpose of the site is not just to inform readers about ADD but also to sell them health insurance.

Conclusion   A comparison of the NIMH website and ADD.com website   8
shows some clear differences between the two. The biggest difference is found in the reliability of information they present. The NIMH website makes it easy for users to understand where the information on the site comes from and why it is included. The ADD.com site, however, emphasizes its commercial associations, and this should cause readers to question the reliability of the information on the

Restatement   site. For this reason, the NIMH website is a much more useful source
of thesis   of information than the ADD.com website.

Points for Special Attention

Structure

Maria's purpose in writing this essay was to compare two websites that deal with Attention Deficit Hyperactivity Disorder and to determine which is the more useful, more reliable source of information. She structured her essay as a point-by-point comparison, carefully discussing the same point for each subject. With this method of organization, she can be sure her readers will understand the specific differences between the NIMH website and the ADD.com website. Had Maria used a subject-by-subject comparison, her readers would have had to keep turning back to compare the points she made about one website with those she made about the other.

Topic Sentences

Without clear topic sentences, Maria's readers would have had difficulty determining where each discussion of the NIMH website ended and each discussion about the ADD.com website began. Maria uses topic sentences to distinguish the two subjects of her comparison and to make the contrast between them clear.

Point 1

The NIMH page looks clear and professional.

The ADD.com home page is more crowded than NIMH's ADHD/ADD home page; although it has less text, it contains more design elements, including a number of images and sidebars.

Point 2

The URL for the NIMH website indicates that it is a *.gov* — a website created by a branch of the United States government.

The URL for ADD.com ends with *.com*, indicating that it is a commercial site.

Point 3

The ADHD information on the NIMH site is largely concentrated on a single page.

Information on the ADD.com website, however, is presented differently.

Transitions

In addition to clear and straightforward topic sentences, Maria included **transitional sentences** to help readers move through the essay. These sentences identify the three points of contrast in the essay, and by establishing a parallel structure, they form a pattern that reinforces the essay's thesis.

The first difference between the two websites is the design of their home pages.

Another difference between the two websites is their purposes.

A final difference between the two websites is how they present the information.

Working with Sources

Maria knew it would be easier for her to compare the NIMH and ADD.com websites if she included visuals in her essay. Because readers would be able to see the pages of the sites she was comparing, she would not have to include long passages of description. She could then concentrate on making specific points and not get sidetracked describing physical features. Her instructor pointed out that if she added these two visuals, she would have to include a label (*Fig. 1, Fig. 2,* and so on) along with a caption under each one. He also told her that if the caption included complete source information, there was no need to list the source on her works-cited page. (See Chapter 18 for a discussion of MLA documentation.)

Focus on Revision

Maria's classmates thought the greatest strength of her essay was its use of supporting examples, which made the contrast between the two websites clear, but they also thought that more detail would improve her essay. For example, in paragraph 6, Maria could include a list of the other kinds of sites linked to on the NIMH website. In paragraph 7, she could also list some of the specific information presented on the ADD.com website and explain why it might be problematic.

Maria thought these suggestions made sense. She also thought she could improve her conclusion: although it summed up the main points of her essay, it included little that would stay with readers after they finished. A sentence or two to caution readers about the need to carefully evaluate the information they find on websites would be a good addition.

PEER-EDITING WORKSHEET: COMPARISON AND CONTRAST

1. Does the essay have a clearly stated thesis? What is it?

2. What two things are being compared? What basis for comparison exists between the two?

3. Does the essay treat the same or similar points for each of its two subjects? List the points discussed.

   FIRST SUBJECT   **SECOND SUBJECT**
   a.   a.
   b.   b.
   c.   c.
   d.   d.

   Are these points discussed in the same order for both subjects? Are the points presented in parallel terms?

4. Does the essay use a point-by-point or subject-by-subject strategy? Is this strategy the best choice? Why?

5. Are transitional words and phrases used appropriately to identify points of comparison and contrast? List some of the transitions used.

6. Are additional transitions needed? If so, where?

7. Does the writer use parallelism to emphasize similarities or differences between one subject and another?

8. How could the introductory paragraph be improved?

9. How could the concluding paragraph be improved?

10. Does the writer use sources? Are they appropriate and helpful? Does the writer need to add additional sources?

11. Does the writer need to add a visual?

The selections that follow illustrate both subject-by-subject and point-by-point comparisons. The first selection, a pair of visual texts, is followed by questions designed to illustrate how comparison and contrast can operate in visual form.

AUGUSTE RODIN

The Kiss (Sculpture)

The Kiss, 1888–98 (marble)/Rodin, Auguste (1840–1917)/PHILIPPE GALARD/Musee Rodin, Paris, France/Bridgeman Images

ROBERT INDIANA

LOVE (Sculpture)

Amanda Hall/robertharding/Getty Images

. . .

Reading Images

1. What characteristics do the two sculptures pictured on the preceding pages share? Do they share enough characteristics to establish a basis for comparison? Explain.
2. Make a list of points you could discuss if you were comparing the two sculptures.
3. What general statement could you make about these two sculptures? Do the points you listed in response to question 2 provide enough support for this general statement?

Journal Entry

How does each sculpture convey the idea of love? Which one do you believe conveys this idea more effectively? Why?

Thematic Connections

- "The Storm" (page 194)
- "Sex, Lies, and Conversation" (page 408)
- "Shall I compare thee to a summer's day?" (page 424)

ROBERT WEISS

Closer Together or Further Apart: Digital Devices and the New Generation Gap

Robert Weiss is CEO of Seeking Integrity, an organization that works to promote healing from intimacy disorders. He earned his undergraduate degree at Emerson College and his master's degree in social work from the University of California, Los Angeles. He is a regular blogger for *Psychology Today* and the *Huffington Post*. His books include *Closer Together, Further Apart: The Effect of Technology and the Internet on Parenting, Work, and Relationships* (with Jennifer Schneider) (2014) and *Prodependence: Moving beyond Codependency* (2018).

Background on the generation gap The term *generation gap* is attributed to the anthropologist Margaret Mead, whose 1970 book *Culture and Commitment: A Study of the Generation Gap* looked at the tensions between generations as drivers of social change. Of course, people have been observing the relationships between the young and the old for thousands of years. The fourth-century Greek philosopher Aristotle wrote about this subject. Such social tensions have existed throughout the history of the United States. For example, older, more traditional Americans were shocked in the 1920s by "flappers": young women with short, "bobbed" haircuts, above-the-knee dresses, and rebellious, modern ideas about women, politics, and society. Mead's 1970 study emerged from the turmoil of the 1960s, a decade marked by cultural, social, and political upheaval driven by a younger generation of so-called baby boomers. Now, as the millennials and generation Zs mature into adulthood—and into the workforce and positions of social power—the baby boomers find themselves complaining about "kids today." For their part, tech-savvy millennials and others have responded to what they perceive as the condescending attitude of the older generation with the sarcastic, dismissive catchphrase: *"OK, boomer."*

Angry Birds: 1, Grandparents: 0

Last week Chuck and Janet Bloom gave their only daughter a night off by 1
taking their grandchildren out for dinner at a local pizza parlor. Both were looking forward to a playful evening with the kids. But as soon as they sat at the table, even before the menus appeared, they noted with dismay that their beloved grandkids were more engaged with and attentive to their holiday-acquired digital devices than to their loving, pizza-partying grandparents. Miriam, their sweet 14-year-old granddaughter, had her eyes intently focused on the contents of her iPad Facebook page. Briana, the 11-year-old, was posting her whereabouts on Twitter, Facebook, and Foursquare. And at the far end of the table, 7-year-old Sam's lips pursed in silent focus as he furiously engaged in a PlayStation cowboy shootout. Feeling frustrated, hurt, and angry—like

they might as well have dined alone — Chuck and Janet quietly launched into an oft-held discussion about how these devices are ruining not just their three grandkids, but young people in general.

At the very same moment and just one table over, half a dozen 20-something work friends were seated, also preparing to order pizza. And just one look over at that crowd affirmed Chuck and Janet's worries about a "lost generation." At that table, two of the diners amicably swapped office gossip, but the others were as engaged with their digital devices as the aforementioned grandkids. What the clucking Chuck and Janet failed to notice was that no one at this second table seemed even remotely concerned or bothered by the fact that technology held as much sway as actual people.

So, why were Chuck and Janet seething about the "digital snub" from their grandchildren, while everyone at the other table managed to enjoy themselves, completely unruffled by the ever-shifting sands of live conversation, texting, tweeting, and posting? In great part this difference stems from the fact that Chuck and Janet are digital immigrants, while their grandkids and the 20-somethings one table over are all digital natives — different generations divided by different definitions of personal respect, attentiveness, interpersonal communication, and what constitutes a meaningful relationship.

Digital Natives versus Digital Immigrants

Generally speaking, people born before 1980 are digital immigrants, and those born after are digital natives. This somewhat arbitrary dividing line attempts to separate those who grew up actively using the internet and those who did not. Another, and perhaps better, way of looking at things is to say that digital natives unquestioningly value and appreciate the role that digital technology plays in their lives, whereas digital immigrants hold mixed views on the subject. Not surprisingly, thanks to continual advances in digital technology (such as the introduction of internet-enabled smartphones a few years ago), the separation between digital natives and digital immigrants is widening almost by the day, resulting not so much in a generation gap as a generation chasm.

This new generation gap is evident in practically every facet of modern life. For instance, there are extreme differences in the ways digital natives and digital immigrants conduct business, gather news and information, and spend their paychecks. They also differ significantly in the ways they define personal privacy, experience entertainment, and socially engage (as evidenced in the pizza restaurant scenario above). Simply put, in a mere 25 years our basic forms of interpersonal communication and interaction have been drastically reformatted, and those who prefer the old ways of mostly face-to-face contact often feel left out and unappreciated.

> "Our basic forms of interpersonal communication and interaction have been drastically reformatted."

In some ways this new generation gap sounds a lot like every other generation gap in history. However, previous generation gaps have mostly centered on young people vocally, visually, and in-real-time challenging the beliefs and experiences of their elders. Today, the divide is more about the fact that young people neither see nor hear their elders because, from a communications standpoint, the two generations are not in the same room. For instance, in the pizza restaurant Chuck and Janet are "present" and interacting at the dinner table, while their grandkids are "present" and interacting in a completely different, entirely digital universe. In some ways, this means that Chuck and Janet are dinosaurs. Basically, because they're not texting, tweeting, or posting to social media, they're not effectively communicating with their grandkids. Thus it seems the 1960s mantra that Chuck and Janet used to utter, "Don't trust anyone over 30," has for their grandkids morphed into, "We don't care about anyone over 30 because we can't see or hear them."

Connection/Disconnection

Interestingly, many digital natives think that young people are isolated and disconnected—more interested in machines than people. In reality, nothing could be further from the truth. In fact, no generation in history has been more interconnected than Generations Y and Z. Statistics readily back this up. One study found that in 2009 more than half of American teens logged on to a social media site at least once per day, and nearly a quarter logged on 10 or more times per day. In the same year, a study by the Pew Internet and American Life Project found that more than three-quarters of U.S. teens owned a cellphone, with 88 percent texting regularly. Boys were sending and receiving 30 texts per day, with girls averaging 80. A more recent Pew study, this one conducted in 2012, finds these numbers are rising rapidly among every Gen Y and Z demographic. In fact, the first sentence of the 2012 study's overview reads: "Teens are fervent communicators." Indeed!

This same survey also reveals (to the chagrin of many digital immigrants) that texting is now the primary mode of communication between teens and their friends and family, far surpassing phone calls, emails, and face-to-face interactions. Depending on your age and point of view, of course, this may or may not be a bad thing.

Consider Brad, a tech-savvy digital immigrant who recently flew home from the West Coast to visit his family in Chicago. One evening at dinner there were three generations—his parents, him and his sister, and his sister's kids. During dinner the oldest child, 17, asked him via text: "Are you going to marry that girl you brought home last year?"

He texted back: "Yes, but no one else knows yet. Is that OK?"

In response, she typed: "I'm so excited. I know you don't want your mom and dad to know yet, but they are really hoping you will. They liked her. So just between us, can I be a bridesmaid?"

He texted: "I know my secret would be safe with you, and of course you will be a bridesmaid!"

For Brad, this poignant conversation with his niece was one of the more meaningful exchanges of his entire five-day visit. And it is possible that without the privacy shield provided by texting, his 17-year-old niece may not have had the courage to broach the subject, even if she'd been able to find a moment alone with him. For her, the digital buffer of texting made this sweet and intimate exchange possible. And the conversation was no less meaningful for either person just because it was conducted via text.

Talk versus Text: Does It Matter?

It is possible that human interactions are no less meaningful or productive   14
simply because they are digital rather than face-to-face. It is also possible the exact opposite is true. Frankly, it depends more on those doing the communicating than anything else. Most often, digital immigrants (Baby Boomer and Gen X types) tend to want/need/prefer in-person, live interactions, or at least telephone conversations where they can hear the other person's voice.

Digital natives, on the other hand, seem to feel that communication is   15
communication, no matter the venue. To them, it seems silly to wait until they run into someone when they can text that person right now and get an instant response. They ask: "Why would I be disconnected when I can post, tweet, and text to let my family and friends known what I'm doing and what I need, and they can do the same with me?" This, of course, is the crux of the current generation gap—shifting from a fully analog world to one that is increasingly digital.

In my recently released book *Closer Together, Further Apart*, my coauthor   16
Jennifer Schneider and I note that in today's world the best communicators are those who are willing and able to engage other people in whatever venue is most appropriate and useful at the time. They neither avoid nor insist on a particular mode of interaction. Instead, they work hard to make sure their message is fully understood by the intended audience no matter what. In other words, they embrace the idea that they need to live and communicate fluently in both the digital and analog worlds. As technology evolves, so do good communicators, and they do so without forgetting or discounting what has worked in the past, remaining constantly aware of the fact that some people may prefer the older methodology, while others prefer the new.

Unfortunately, as has always been the case when changes in technology   17
have swiftly and profoundly affected our day-to-day lives, many people, young and old alike, become entrenched in the belief that "the way we do it is the best way." The simple truth is that cultural/technological assimilation is rarely an easy task. Sometimes it can feel easier to judge and avoid, rather than to embrace and evolve. Thus we have the current communications-driven generation gap. That said, the effort of reaching out beyond our generational comfort zone is usually well worth the effort. Brad found that to be true with his niece, and Chuck and Janet might also find it to be the case if they were only willing to give it a shot.

∙   ∙   ∙

Comprehension

1. What is a "digital native"? How is a digital native different from a "digital immigrant"?
2. What is the "new generation gap"? Why, according to Weiss, is the new generation gap different from other generation gaps?

3. Do you agree with Weiss's assertion that "no generation in history has been more interconnected than Generations Y and Z" (7)? Why or why not?
4. According to Weiss, what are the qualities of "good communicators"? Do you agree?
5. What is the overall effect of digital devices on our communication? Does Weiss think that this effect has been positive or negative?

Purpose and Audience

1. Does Weiss expect his readers to be mostly digital natives, digital immigrants, or both? How do you know?
2. What attitudes does Weiss assume his readers have about his subject?
3. What is Weiss's purpose in writing his essay? Does he want to inform, enlighten, persuade, or accomplish something else?
4. Where does Weiss state his thesis? In one sentence, restate it in your own words.

Style and Structure

1. Throughout his essay, Weiss uses headings. How do these headings reinforce his comparison?
2. Is this essay structured as a subject-by-subject or a point-by-point comparison? Why do you think Weiss chose the strategy he did?
3. In paragraph 7, Weiss cites several studies. What point do these studies support? How effective is this support? Explain.
4. What idea does Weiss emphasize in his conclusion? Does his conclusion reinforce his thesis? Explain.
5. **Vocabulary Project**. In paragraph 4, Weiss says that the separation between digital natives and digital immigrants is not so much a generation gap as it is "a generation chasm." What are the **connotations** of "gap" and "chasm"? How do the different connotations help Weiss make his point?

Journal Entry

Is Weiss's assessment of the current digital environment accurate, or does he exaggerate the situation (or misrepresent its effects)?

Writing Workshop

1. Write an essay in which you compare how you communicate digitally with your friends with how you communicate face-to-face with them. What are the drawbacks and the advantages of each?
2. **Working with Sources.** Interview your parents about their attitudes toward digital communication. Are they digital immigrants (as Weiss suggests), or are they digital natives? Write an essay in which you compare their actual attitudes to the attitudes Weiss suggests they have. Include quotations from your interview as well as from Weiss's essay, and be sure to include parenthetical documentation and a works-cited page. (See Chapter 18 for information on MLA documentation.)

3. **Working with Sources.** Assume you are the CEO of a company that employs both baby boomers and generation Xers. Go online and research ways of helping workers communicate. Then, write an essay in which you compare the challenges you will face helping digital natives and digital immigrants with their day-to-day communication skills. Be sure to refer to Weiss in your essay and to include parenthetical documentation and a works-cited page. (See Chapter 18 for information on MLA documentation.)

Combining the Patterns

At two points in his essay, Weiss uses **narrative** anecdotes. What is the purpose of these anecdotes? How do they help Weiss make his point?

Thematic Connections

- "Call Me 'They'" (page 237)
- "Sex, Lies, and Conversation" (page 408)
- "Mother Tongue" (page 456)

AMY CHUA

Why Chinese Mothers Are Superior

Amy Chua was born in Champaign, Illinois, in 1962. She graduated from Harvard College and earned her J.D. at Harvard Law School, where she was executive editor of the *Harvard Law Review*. Chua is now the John M. Duff Professor of Law at Yale Law School, where she focuses on international law and business, ethnic conflict, and globalization and the law. Her books include *The Triple Package: How Three Unlikely Traits Explain the Rise and Fall of Cultural Groups in America* (with Jed Rubenfeld) (2014) and *Political Tribes: Group Instinct and the Fate of Nations* (2018). Chua is perhaps best known for her parenting memoir, *Battle Hymn of the Tiger Mother* (2011).

Background on parenting styles Chua writes disapprovingly about contemporary "Western" parents who, she claims, are "extremely anxious about their children's self-esteem." Such anxieties are relatively new, especially when one surveys the history of parenting — from the ancient Greeks, who commonly left unwanted children in the woods to die of exposure, to seventeenth-century American Puritans, who practiced a philosophy of visual "Better whipt than damned." French Enlightenment figure Jean-Jacques Rousseau (1712–1778) proposed a more sympathetic view of the child, writing that when "children's wills are not spoiled by our fault, children want nothing uselessly." In the nineteenth and early twentieth centuries, however, American parenting philosophies usually focused on discipline, emotional detachment, and the wisdom of experts. As Dr. Luther Emmett Holt wrote in *The Care and Feeding of Children* (1894), "Instinct and maternal love are too often assumed to be a sufficient guide for a mother." Pediatrician Benjamin Spock, who published his enormously influential *Baby and Child Care* in 1946, is often credited with — or blamed for — a social shift toward more permissive child-rearing, especially in the context of the baby-boom generation. Spock urged parents to trust their own judgment and to meet their children's needs rather than worrying about "spoiling" the child. In the decades that followed, this parenting approach accompanied an increasing emphasis on children's self-esteem, both at home and in school.

A lot of people wonder how Chinese parents raise such stereotypically successful kids. They wonder what these parents do to produce so many math whizzes and music prodigies, what it's like inside the family, and whether they could do it too. Well, I can tell them, because I've done it. Here are some things my daughters, Sophia and Louisa, were never allowed to do: 1

- attend a sleepover
- have a playdate
- be in a school play
- complain about not being in a school play
- watch TV or play computer games

- choose their own extracurricular activities
- get any grade less than an A
- not be the No. 1 student in every subject except gym and drama
- play any instrument other than the piano or violin
- not play the piano or violin.

I'm using the term "Chinese mother" loosely. I know some Korean, Indian, 2
Jamaican, Irish, and Ghanaian parents who qualify too. Conversely, I know
some mothers of Chinese heritage, almost always born in the West, who are
not Chinese mothers, by choice or otherwise. I'm also using the term "Western
parents" loosely. Western parents come in all varieties.

When it comes to parenting, the Chinese seem to produce children who 3
display academic excellence, musical mastery, and professional success — or so
the stereotype goes. *WSJ*'s* Christina Tsuei speaks to two moms raised by
Chinese immigrants who share what it was like growing up and how they hope
to raise their children.

All the same, even when Western parents think they're being strict, they 4
usually don't come close to being Chinese mothers. For example, my Western
friends who consider themselves strict make their children practice their
instruments 30 minutes every day. An hour at most. For a Chinese mother, the
first hour is the easy part. It's hours two and three that get tough.

Despite our squeamishness about cultural stereotypes, there are tons of 5
studies out there showing marked and quantifiable differences between
Chinese and Westerners when it comes to parenting. In one study of fifty
Western American mothers and forty-eight Chinese immigrant mothers,
almost 70 percent of the Western mothers said either that "stressing academic
success is not good for children" or that "parents need to foster the idea that
learning is fun." By contrast, roughly 0 percent of the Chinese mothers felt the
same way. Instead, the vast majority of the Chinese mothers said that they
believe their children can be "the best" students, that "academic achievement
reflects successful parenting," and that if children did not excel at school then
there was "a problem" and parents "were not doing their job." Other studies
indicate that compared to Western parents, Chinese parents spend approximately ten times as long every day drilling academic activities with their children. By contrast, Western kids are more likely to participate in sports teams.

What Chinese parents understand is that nothing is fun until you're good 6
at it. To get good at anything you have to work, and children on their own
never want to work, which is why it is crucial to override their preferences. This
often requires fortitude on the part of the parents because the child will resist;
things are always hardest at the beginning, which is where Western parents
tend to give up. But if done properly, the Chinese strategy produces a virtuous
circle. Tenacious practice, practice, practice is crucial for excellence; rote repetition is underrated in America. Once a child starts to excel at something —
whether it's math, piano, pitching, or ballet — he or she gets praise, admiration,

---

* Eds. note — *Wall Street Journal.*

and satisfaction. This builds confidence and makes the once not-fun activity fun. This in turn makes it easier for the parent to get the child to work even more.

Chinese parents can get away with things that Western parents can't. Once when I was young — maybe more than once — when I was extremely disrespectful to my mother, my father angrily called me "garbage" in our native Hokkien dialect. It worked really well. I felt terrible and deeply ashamed of what I had done. But it didn't damage my self-esteem or anything like that. I knew exactly how highly he thought of me. I didn't actually think I was worthless or feel like a piece of garbage. 7

> **"**What Chinese parents understand is that nothing is fun until you're good at it.**"**

As an adult, I once did the same thing to Sophia, calling her "garbage" in English when she acted extremely disrespectfully toward me. When I mentioned that I had done this at a dinner party, I was immediately ostracized. One guest named Marcy got so upset she broke down in tears and had to leave early. My friend Susan, the host, tried to rehabilitate me with the remaining guests. 8

The fact is that Chinese parents can do things that would seem unimaginable — even legally actionable — to Westerners. Chinese mothers can say to their daughters, "Hey fatty — lose some weight." By contrast, Western parents have to tiptoe around the issue, talking in terms of "health" and never ever mentioning the f-word, and their kids still end up in therapy for eating disorders and negative self-image. (I also once heard a Western father toast his adult daughter by calling her "beautiful and incredibly competent." She later told me that made her feel like garbage.) 9

Chinese parents can order their kids to get straight As. Western parents can only ask their kids to try their best. Chinese parents can say, "You're lazy. All your classmates are getting ahead of you." By contrast, Western parents have to struggle with their own conflicted feelings about achievement, and try to persuade themselves that they're not disappointed about how their kids turned out. 10

I've thought long and hard about how Chinese parents can get away with what they do. I think there are three big differences between the Chinese and Western parental mind-sets. 11

First, I've noticed that Western parents are extremely anxious about their children's self-esteem. They worry about how their children will feel if they fail at something, and they constantly try to reassure their children about how good they are notwithstanding a mediocre performance on a test or at a recital. In other words, Western parents are concerned about their children's psyches. Chinese parents aren't. They assume strength, not fragility, and as a result they behave very differently. 12

For example, if a child comes home with an A-minus on a test, a Western parent will most likely praise the child. The Chinese mother will gasp in horror and ask what went wrong. If the child comes home with a B on the test, some Western parents will still praise the child. Other Western parents will sit their 13 child down and express disapproval, but they will be careful not to make their child feel inadequate or insecure, and they will not call their child "stupid," "worthless," or "a disgrace." Privately, the Western parents may worry that their child does not test well or have aptitude in the subject or that there is something wrong with the curriculum and possibly the whole school. If the child's grades do not improve, they may eventually schedule a meeting with the school principal to challenge the way the subject is being taught or to call into question the teacher's credentials.

If a Chinese child gets a B—which would never happen—there would first be a screaming, hair-tearing explosion. The devastated Chinese mother would then get dozens, maybe hundreds of practice tests and work through them with her child for as long as it takes to get the grade up to an A.   14

Chinese parents demand perfect grades because they believe that their child can get them. If their child doesn't get them, the Chinese parent assumes it's because the child didn't work hard enough. That's why the solution to sub-standard performance is always to excoriate, punish, and shame the child. The Chinese parent believes that their child will be strong enough to take the shaming and to improve from it. (And when Chinese kids do excel, there is plenty of ego-inflating parental praise lavished in the privacy of the home.)   15

Second, Chinese parents believe that their kids owe them everything. The reason for this is a little unclear, but it's probably a combination of Confucian filial piety and the fact that the parents have sacrificed and done so much for their children. (And it's true that Chinese mothers get in the trenches, putting in long grueling hours personally tutoring, training, interrogating, and spying on their kids.) Anyway, the understanding is that Chinese children must spend their lives repaying their parents by obeying them and making them proud.   16

By contrast, I don't think most Westerners have the same view of children being permanently indebted to their parents. My husband, Jed, actually has the opposite view. "Children don't choose their parents," he once said to me. "They don't even choose to be born. It's parents who foist life on their kids, so it's the parents' responsibility to provide for them. Kids don't owe their parents anything. Their duty will be to their own kids." This strikes me as a terrible deal for the Western parent.   17

Third, Chinese parents believe that they know what is best for their children and therefore override all of their children's own desires and preferences. That's why Chinese daughters can't have boyfriends in high school and why Chinese kids can't go to sleepaway camp. It's also why no Chinese kid would ever dare say to their mother, "I got a part in the school play! I'm Villager Number Six. I'll have to stay after school for rehearsal every day from 3:00 to 7:00, and I'll also need a ride on weekends." God help any Chinese kid who tried that one.   18

Don't get me wrong: It's not that Chinese parents don't care about their children. Just the opposite. They would give up anything for their children. It's just an entirely different parenting model.   19

. . . Western parents worry a lot about their children's self-esteem. But as a parent, one of the worst things you can do for your child's self-esteem is to let them give up. On the flip side, there's nothing better for building confidence than learning you can do something you thought you couldn't.   20

There are all these new books out there portraying Asian mothers as   21
scheming, callous, overdriven people indifferent to their kids' true interests.
For their part, many Chinese secretly believe that they care more about their
children and are willing to sacrifice much more for them than Westerners, who
seem perfectly content to let their children turn out badly. I think it's a misunderstanding on both sides. All decent parents want to do what's best for their
children. The Chinese just have a totally different idea of how to do that.

Western parents try to respect their children's individuality, encouraging   22
them to pursue their true passions, supporting their choices, and providing
positive reinforcement and a nurturing environment. By contrast, the Chinese
believe that the best way to protect their children is by preparing them for the
future, letting them see what they're capable of, and arming them with skills,
work habits, and inner confidence that no one can ever take away.

• • •

Comprehension

1. What does Chua mean when she says, "What Chinese parents understand is
   that nothing is fun until you're good at it" (6)? Do you agree with her?
2. Does Chua's husband agree or disagree with her child-rearing methods?
   Why does he react the way he does?
3. According to Chua, why are Chinese parents able to do things that Western
   parents cannot?
4. How does Chua respond to the charge that Chinese parents don't care
   about their children?
5. According to Chua, how do Chinese child-rearing practices prepare children
   for life?

Purpose and Audience

1. What preconceptions about Chinese mothers does Chua think Westerners
   have? Do you think she is right?
2. Does Chua seem to expect her readers to be receptive, hostile, or neutral to
   her ideas? What evidence can you find to support your impression?
3. What is Chua's thesis? Where does she state it?
4. In an interview, Chua said that the editors of the *Wall Street Journal*, not she,
   chose the title of her essay. Why do you think the editors chose the title they
   did? What title do you think Chua would have chosen? What title would
   you give the essay?

Style and Structure

1. Why does Chua begin her essay with a list of things her two daughters were
   not allowed to do as they were growing up? How do you think she expects
   readers to react to this list? How do you react?
2. Is this essay a point-by-point comparison, a subject-by-subject comparison,
   or a combination of the two organizational strategies? Why does Chua
   arrange her comparison the way she does?

3. What evidence does Chua present to support her view that there are marked differences between the parenting styles of Chinese and Western parents?

4. Chua was born in the United States. Does this fact undercut her conclusions about the differences between Western and Chinese child-rearing? Explain.

5. What points does Chua emphasize in her conclusion? How else could she have ended her essay?

6. **Vocabulary Project.** In paragraph 2, Chua says she is using the terms "Chinese mother" and "Western parents" loosely. What does she mean? How does she define these two terms? How would you define them?

Journal Entry

Do you think Chua's essay perpetuates a cultural stereotype? Why or why not?

Writing Workshop

1. Write an essay in which you compare your upbringing to that of Chua's daughters. Were your parents "Western" or "Chinese" parents (or were they a combination of the two)? In your thesis, take a stand on the question of which kind of parent is "superior." Use examples from your childhood to support your thesis.

2. **Working with Sources.** Go online, find and read the poem "Suicide Note" by Janice Mirikitani. Then, write an essay in which you compare Chua's positive view of Asian child-rearing practices with the feelings expressed by the speaker in Mirikitani's poem. Be sure to include parenthetical documentation for any references to the two sources and a works-cited page. (See Chapter 18 for information on MLA documentation.)

3. When Chua's essay was published, it elicited thousands of responses, many of which were negative. For example, some readers thought her parenting methods were tantamount to child abuse, others admired Chua for her resolve and her emphasis on hard work, and still others said her methods reminded them of their own upbringings. Chua herself responded to readers' comments by saying her "tough love" approach was grounded in her desire to make sure her children were the best they could be. Write an email to Chua in which you respond to her essay. Be sure to address each of her major points and to compare your opinions to hers.

Combining the Patterns

Throughout her essay, Chua includes **exemplification** paragraphs. Identify two exemplification paragraphs, and explain how they help Chua make her point about the superiority of Chinese mothers.

Thematic Connections

- "How the Other Half Lives" (page 190)
- "Why I Went to College" (page 362)
- "Mother Tongue" (page 456)
- "Stop Calling It 'Vocational Training'" (page 502)

ELLEN LAIRD

I'm Your Teacher, Not Your Internet-Service Provider

Educator and essayist Ellen Laird believes that technology has forever changed both teaching and learning, as the following essay, originally published in the *Chronicle of Higher Education*, suggests. Laird is a professor of English at Hudson Valley Community College in New York.

Background on distance learning Correspondence schools began to appear in the United States in the late nineteenth century, facilitated to a large degree by an extensive and efficient national postal service. These schools allowed students to receive study materials by mail and to complete examinations and other written work that they then submitted, again by mail, to a central departmental office for grading by instructors. For the most part, correspondence schools tended to focus on technical curricula, although some programs were geared toward a more traditional liberal arts curriculum. By the 1930s, correspondence schools had entered a period of decline because of the rise of junior colleges that enabled students to have hands-on educational opportunities close to home. Then, beginning in the 1960s, the concept was revived through the broadcast of publicly funded televised courses, again with a mail-based system for transmitting written materials. Today, many universities have Internet-based distance-learning programs. They find that the Internet is a cost-effective, flexible, and efficient way to deliver courses to a large number of students, many of whom cannot commute to campus. Online education is not without problems, however. Some students complain that online classes do not provide the immediacy and intellectual stimulation of traditional classrooms. Moreover, students must be highly motivated and disciplined to complete online courses. Finally, discussion boards and email do not enable instructors to connect with students the way face-to-face settings do.

The honeymoon is over. My romance with distance teaching is losing its spark. Gone are the days when I looked forward to each new online encounter with students, when preparing and posting a basic assignment was a thrilling adventure, when my colleagues and friends were well-wishers, cautiously hopeful about my new entanglement. What remains is this instructor, alone, often in the dark of night, facing the reality of my online class and struggling to make it work.

After four years of Internet teaching, I must pause. When pressed to demonstrate that my online composition class is the equivalent of my classroom-based composition sections, I can do so professionally and persuasively. On the surface, course goals, objectives, standards, outlines, texts, Web materials, and so forth, are identical. But my fingers are crossed.

The two experiences are as different as a wedding reception and a rave. The nonlinear nature of online activity and the well-ingrained habits of Web use involve behavior vastly different from that which fosters success in the traditional college classroom. Last fall, my online students ranged from ages fifteen to fifty, from the home-schooled teen to the local union president. Yet all brought to class assumptions and habits that sometimes interfered with learning and often diminished the quality of the experience for all of us. As a seasoned online instructor, I knew what to expect and how to help students through the inevitable. But for the uninitiated, the reality of online teaching can be confounding and upsetting. It can make a talented teacher feel like an unmitigated failure. 3

If faculty members, whether well established or new, are to succeed in online teaching, they must be prepared for attitudes and behaviors that permeate Web use but undermine teaching and learning in the Web classroom. Potential online instructors are generally offered technical training in file organization, course-management software use, and the like. But they would be best served by an unfiltered look at what really happens when the student logs into class, however elegantly designed the course may be. A few declarative sentences drafted for my next online syllabus may suffice: 4

> "The honeymoon is over. My romance with distance teaching is losing its spark."

The syllabus is not a restaurant menu.

In sections offered in campus classrooms, my students regard the syllabus as a fixed set of requirements, not as a menu of choices. They accept the sequence and format in which course material is provided for them. They do not make selections among course requirements according to preference. 5

Online? Not so. Each semester, online students howl electronically about having to complete the same assignments in the same sequence required of my face-to-face students. Typical Internet users, these students are accustomed to choices online. They enjoy the nonlinear nature of Web surfing; they would be hard pressed to replicate the sequence of their activity without the down arrow beside the URL box on their browsers. 6

To their detriment, many of these students fail to consider that Web learning is different from Web use, particularly in a skills-based course like composition. They find it hard to accept, for example, that they must focus on writing a solid thesis before tackling a research paper. Most would prefer to surf from one module of material to the next and complete what appeals to them rather than what is required of them. 7

The difference between students' expectations and reality frustrates us all. In traditional classrooms, students do not pick up or download only the handouts that appeal to them; most do not try to begin the semester's final project without instruction in the material on which it is based. Yet, online students expect such options. 8

Even Cinderella had a deadline.

Students in my traditional classes certainly miss deadlines. But they gener-   9
ally regard deadlines as real, if not observable; they recognize an instructor's
right to set due dates; and they accept the consequences of missing them to be
those stated on the syllabus.

Not so with my online students. Neither fancy font nor flashing bullet can   10
stir the majority to submit work by the published deadline. Students seem to
extend the freedom to choose the time and place of their course work to every
aspect of the class. Few request extensions in the usual manner. Instead, they
announce them. One student, for example, emailed me days after a paper was
due, indicating that he had traveled to New York for a Yankees' game and
would submit the essay in a couple of weeks.

All course components do not function at the speed of the Internet.

As relaxed as my online students are about meeting deadlines, they begin   11
the course expecting instantaneous service. The speed of Internet transmission
seduces them into seeking and expecting speed as an element of the course.
Naturally, students' emphasis on rapidity works against them. The long, hard,
eventually satisfying work of thinking, doing research, reading, and writing
has no relationship to bandwidth, processor speed, or cable modems.

At the same time, it takes me a long time to respond thoughtfully to stu-   12
dents' work, particularly their writing. Each semester, online students require
help in understanding that waiting continues to be part of teaching and learning, that the instructor is not another version of an Internet-service provider,
to be judged satisfactory or not by processing speed and 24/7 availability.

There are no sick or personal days in cyberspace.

In my traditional classes, I refrain from informing students that I will be   13
out of town for a weekend, that I need a root canal, or that my water heater
failed before work. My face-to-face students can read my expression and bearing when they see me; thus, I can usually keep personal explanations to a professional minimum.

In my online class, however, students cannot see the bags under my eyes or   14
the look of exuberance on my face. They cannot hear the calm or the shake in
my voice. Thus, for the smooth functioning of the course, I willingly provide
details about where I am and what I am doing, so students can know what to
expect.

However, I am still troubled by the email message from an online student   15
that began, "I know you are at your father's funeral right now, but I just wondered if you got my paper." Surely, he hesitated before pushing "send," but his
need for reassurance prevailed. And so it goes, all semester long. There simply
isn't room in an online class for the messiness of ordinary life, the students' or
mine. Nor is there room for the extraordinary—the events of September 11, for
example. As long as the server functions, the course is always on, bearing down
hard on both students and instructor.

Still, students will register for online classes under circumstances that   16
would prohibit them from enrolling in a course on the campus. The welder
compelled to work mandatory overtime, the pregnant woman due before
midsemester, and the newly separated security guard whose wife will not surrender the laptop all arrive online with the hope and the illusion that, in cyber-
space, they can accomplish what is temporarily impossible for them on
campus.

I am not on your buddy list.

The egalitarian atmosphere of the Internet chat room transfers rapidly   17
and inappropriately to the online classroom. Faceless and ageless online, I am,
at first, addressed as a peer. If students knew that I dress like many of their
mothers, or that my hair will soon be more gray than brown, would their
exchanges with me be different? I reveal what I want them to know—the date
of my marathon, my now-deceased dog's consumption of a roll of aluminum
foil, my one gig as a cocktail-lounge pianist—but little of what one good look
at me, in my jumper and jewelry, would tell them.

They, on the other hand, hold back nothing. Confessional writing, always   18
a challenge in composition, can easily become the norm online. So can racist,
sexist, and otherwise offensive remarks—even admissions of crimes. The lack
of a face to match with a rhetorical voice provides the illusion of anonymity,
and thus the potential for a no-holds-barred quality to every discussion thread.
The usual restraint characterizing conversation among classroom acquaintances evaporates online within about two weeks. Private conversations fuse
with academic discussion before an instructor can log in.

Are there strategies to manage these and similar difficulties? Of course   19
there are. Thus, I continue with online teaching and welcome both its challenges and its rewards. But educators considering online teaching need to
know that instruction in person and online are day and night. They must brace
themselves for a marriage of opposites, and build large reserves of commitment, patience, and wherewithal if the relationship is to succeed.

· · ·

Comprehension

1. Why does Laird say that her "honeymoon" with online teaching is over (1)?
2. According to Laird, why are online teaching and classroom-based teaching
   different? How does she explain the differences?
3. What does Laird mean when she says that potential online instructors
   "would be best served by an unfiltered look at what really happens when the
   student logs into class" (4)?
4. In what way does classroom-based teaching limit students' choices? How is
   online teaching different?
5. In paragraph 11, Laird says, "The long, hard, eventually satisfying work of
   thinking, doing research, reading, and writing has no relationship to bandwidth, processor speed, or cable modems." What does she mean?

Purpose and Audience

1. What is the thesis of this essay?
2. To whom do you think Laird is addressing her essay? Instructors? Students? Both?
3. What do you think Laird is trying to accomplish in her essay? Is she successful?
4. Does Laird assume her readers are familiar with online teaching, or does she assume they are relatively unfamiliar with it? How can you tell?

Style and Structure

1. Is this essay a point-by-point or subject-by-subject comparison? Why do you think Laird chose this strategy?
2. Laird highlights a "few declarative sentences" (4) as boldfaced headings throughout her essay. What is the function of these headings?
3. Does Laird seem to favor one type of teaching over another? Is she optimistic or pessimistic about the future of online education? Explain.
4. Does Laird indicate how students feel about online teaching? Should she have spent more time exploring this issue?
5. In her conclusion, Laird asks, "Are there strategies to manage these and similar difficulties?" Her answer: "Of course there are" (19). Should she have listed some of these strategies in her conclusion? Why do you think she does not?
6. **Vocabulary Project.** In paragraph 3, Laird says, "The two experiences are as different as a wedding reception and a rave." What are the denotations and connotations of *wedding reception* and *rave*? What point is Laird trying to make with this comparison?

Journal Entry

Do you agree or disagree with Laird's assessment of distance learning and classroom-based learning? (If you have never taken an online course, discuss only her analysis of classroom-based learning.)

Writing Workshop

1. Write an essay in which you discuss whether you would like to take an online writing course. How do you think such a course would compare with a traditional classroom-based course? (If you are already taking such a course, compare it with a traditional writing course.)
2. **Working with Sources.** Write an email to Laird in which you explain that, like her, students also have difficulty adapting to online instruction. Address the specific difficulties students encounter in such courses, and compare these difficulties with those they experience when they take a classroom-based course. Include at least one quotation from Laird's essay, and be sure to include parenthetical documentation for the quotation and a works-cited page. (See Chapter 18 for information on MLA documentation.)

3. Read the following list of advantages of taking online courses:

   * A student who is ill will not miss classes.
   * Students who are employed and cannot come to campus can take courses.
   * Nontraditional students — people who are elderly or who have a disability, for example — can take courses.
   * Courses are taken at any time, day or night.
   * Guest speakers who cannot travel to campus can be integrated into the course.

   Then, make a list of disadvantages (for example, students never have face-to-face contact with an instructor). Finally, write an essay in which you discuss whether the advantages of online instruction outweigh the disadvantages.

Combining the Patterns

Laird begins her essay with two **narrative** paragraphs. What is the purpose of these paragraphs? What other strategy could Laird have used to introduce her essay?

Thematic Connections

* "What I Learned (and Didn't Learn) in College" (page 436)
* "The Dog Ate My Tablet, and Other Tales of Woe" (page 450)
* Debate: "Should Federal Student Loans Be Forgiven?" (page 576)

DEBORAH TANNEN

Sex, Lies, and Conversation

Deborah Tannen was born in Brooklyn, New York, in 1945 and is a professor of linguistics at Georgetown University. Tannen has written and edited several scholarly books on the problems of communicating across cultural, class, ethnic, and sexual divides. She has also presented her research to the general public in newspapers and magazines and in her best-selling books *That's Not What I Meant!: How Conversational Style Makes or Breaks Relationships* (1986), *You Just Don't Understand: Women and Men in Conversation* (1990), and *Talking from 9 to 5: Women and Men at Work* (1994), and *You Were Always Mom's Favorite: Sisters in Conversation throughout Their Lives* (2009). Her most recent book is *You're the Only One I Can Tell: Inside the Language of Women's Friendships* (2017).

Background on men's and women's communication styles Tannen wrote "Sex, Lies, and Conversation" because the chapter in *That's Not What I Meant!* on the difficulties men and women have communicating with one another got such a strong response. She realized the chapter might raise some controversy — that discussing their different communication styles might be used to malign men or to put women at a disadvantage — and indeed, some critics have seen her work as reinforcing stereotypes. Still, her work on the subject, along with that of other writers (most notably John Gray in his *Men Are from Mars, Women Are from Venus* series), has proved enormously popular. Much of the research about male and female differences in terms of brain function, relational styles and expectations, and evolutionary roles continues to stir debate.

I was addressing a small gathering in a suburban Virginia living room — a women's group that had invited men to join them. Throughout the evening, one man had been particularly talkative, frequently offering ideas and anecdotes, while his wife sat silently beside him on the couch. Toward the end of the evening, I commented that women frequently complain that their husbands don't talk to them. This man quickly concurred. He gestured toward his wife and said, "She's the talker in our family." The room burst into laughter; the man looked puzzled and hurt. "It's true," he explained. "When I come home from work I have nothing to say. If she didn't keep the conversation going, we'd spend the whole evening in silence." 1

This episode crystallizes the irony that although American men tend to talk more than women in public situations, they often talk less at home. And this pattern is wreaking havoc with marriage. 2

The pattern was observed by political scientist Andrew Hacker in the late '70s. Sociologist Catherine Kohler Riessman reports in her new book *Divorce Talk* that most of the women she interviewed — but only a few of the men — gave lack of communication as the reason for their divorces. Given the current divorce rate of nearly 50 percent, that amounts to millions of cases in the United States every year — a virtual epidemic of failed conversation. 3

In my own research, complaints from women about their husbands most   4
often focused not on tangible inequities such as having given up the chance for
a career to accompany a husband to his, or doing far more than their share of
daily life-support work like cleaning, cooking, social arrangements, and
errands. Instead, they focused on communication: "He doesn't listen to me,"
"He doesn't talk to me." I found, as Hacker observed years before, that most
wives want their husbands to be, first and foremost, conversational partners,
but few husbands share this expectation of their wives.

In short, the image that best represents the current crisis is the   5
stereotypical cartoon scene of a man sitting at the breakfast table with a
newspaper held up in front of his face, while a woman glares at the back of
it, wanting to talk.

Linguistic Battle of the Sexes

How can women and men have such different impressions of communi-   6
cation in marriage? Why the widespread imbalance in their interests and
expectations?

In the April issue of *American Psychologist*,   7
Stanford University's Eleanor Maccoby reports the results of her own and others'
research showing that children's development is most influenced by the social structure of peer interactions. Boys and girls tend
to play with children of their own gender,
and their sex-separate groups have different
organizational structures and interactive
norms.

> "How can women and men have such different impressions of communication in marriage? Why the widespread imbalance in their interests and expectations?"

I believe these systematic differences in   8
childhood socialization make talk between
women and men, like cross-cultural communication, heir to all the attraction
and pitfalls of that enticing but difficult enterprise. My research on men's and
women's conversations uncovered patterns similar to those described for children's groups.

For women, as for girls, intimacy is the fabric of relationships, and talk is   9
the thread from which it is woven. Little girls create and maintain friendships
by exchanging secrets; similarly, women regard conversation as the corner-
stone of friendship. So a woman expects her husband to be a new and improved
version of a best friend. What is important is not the individual subjects that
are discussed but the sense of closeness, of a life shared, that emerges when
people tell their thoughts, feelings, and impressions.

Bonds between boys can be as intense as girls', but they are based less on   10
talking, more on doing things together. Since they don't assume talk is the
cement that binds a relationship, men don't know what kind of talk women
want, and they don't miss it when it isn't there.

Boys' groups are larger, more inclusive, and more hierarchical, so boys   11
must struggle to avoid the subordinate position in the group. This may play a
role in women's complaints that men don't listen to them. Some men really

don't like to listen, because being the listener makes them feel one-down, like a child listening to adults or an employee to a boss.

But often when women tell men, "You aren't listening," and the men protest, "I am," the men are right. The impression of not listening results from misalignments in the mechanics of conversation. The misalignment begins as soon as a man and a woman take physical positions. This became clear when I studied videotapes made by psychologist Bruce Dorval of children and adults talking to their same-sex best friends. I found that at every age, the girls and women faced each other directly, their eyes anchored on each other's faces. At every age, the boys and men sat at angles to each other and looked elsewhere in the room, periodically glancing at each other. They were obviously attuned to each other, often mirroring each other's movements. But the tendency of men to face away can give women the impression they aren't listening even when they are. A young woman in college was frustrated: Whenever she told her boyfriend she wanted to talk to him, he would lie down on the floor, close his eyes, and put his arm over his face. This signaled to her, "He's taking a nap." But he insisted he was listening extra hard. Normally, he looks around the room, so he is easily distracted. Lying down and covering his eyes helped him concentrate on what she was saying.

Analogous to the physical alignment that women and men take in conversation is their topical alignment. The girls in my study tended to talk at length about one topic, but the boys tended to jump from topic to topic. The second-grade girls exchanged stories about people they knew. The second-grade boys teased, told jokes, noticed things in the room, and talked about finding games to play. The sixth-grade girls talked about problems with a mutual friend. The sixth-grade boys talked about fifty-five different topics, none of which extended over more than a few turns.

Listening to Body Language

Switching topics is another habit that gives women the impression men aren't listening, especially if they switch to a topic about themselves. But the evidence of the tenth-grade boys in my study indicates otherwise. The tenth-grade boys sprawled across their chairs with bodies parallel and eyes straight ahead, rarely looking at each other. They looked as if they were riding in a car, staring out the windshield. But they were talking about their feelings. One boy was upset because a girl had told him he had a drinking problem, and the other was feeling alienated from all his friends.

Now, when a girl told a friend about a problem, the friend responded by asking probing questions and expressing agreement and understanding. But the boys dismissed each other's problems. Todd assured Richard that his drinking was "no big problem" because "sometimes you're funny when you're off your butt." And when Todd said he felt left out, Richard responded, "Why should you? You know more people than me."

Women perceive such responses as belittling and unsupportive. But the boys seemed satisfied with them. Whereas women reassure each other by implying, "You shouldn't feel bad because I've had similar experiences," men do so by implying, "You shouldn't feel bad because your problems aren't so bad."

There are even simpler reasons for women's impression that men don't lis-   17
ten. Linguist Lynette Hirschman found that women make more listener-noise,
such as "mhm," "uhuh," and "yeah," to show "I'm with you." Men, she found,
more often give silent attention. Women who expect a stream of listener-noise
interpret silent attention as no attention at all.

Women's conversational habits are as frustrating to men as men's are to   18
women. Men who expect silent attention interpret a stream of listener-noise as
overreaction or impatience. Also, when women talk to each other in a close,
comfortable setting, they often overlap, finish each other's sentences, and
anticipate what the other is about to say. This practice, which I call "participa-
tory listenership," is often perceived by men as interruption, intrusion, and
lack of attention.

A parallel difference caused a man to complain about his wife, "She just   19
wants to talk about her own point of view. If I show her another view, she gets
mad at me." When most women talk to each other, they assume a conversa-
tionalist's job is to express agreement and support. But many men see their
conversational duty as pointing out the other side of an argument. This is
heard as disloyalty by women, and refusal to offer the requisite support. It is
not that women don't want to see other points of view, but that they prefer
them phrased as suggestions and inquiries rather than as direct challenges.

In his book *Fighting for Life*, Walter Ong points out that men use "agonis-   20
tic," or warlike, oppositional formats to do almost anything; thus discussion
becomes debate, and conversation a competitive sport. In contrast, women see
conversation as a ritual means of establishing rapport. If Jane tells a problem
and June says she has a similar one, they walk away feeling closer to each other.
But this attempt at establishing rapport can backfire when used with men.
Men take too literally women's ritual "troubles talk," just as women mistake
men's ritual challenges for real attack.

The Sounds of Silence

These differences begin to clarify why women and men have such different   21
expectations about communication in marriage. For women, talk creates intimacy. Marriage is an orgy of closeness: you can tell your feelings and thoughts,
and still be loved. Their greatest fear is being pushed away. But men live in a
hierarchical world, where talk maintains independence and status. They are on
guard to protect themselves from being put down and pushed around.

This explains the paradox of the talkative man who said of his silent wife,   22
"She's the talker." In the public setting of a guest lecture, he felt challenged to
show his intelligence and display his understanding of the lecture. But at
home, where he has nothing to prove and no one to defend against, he is free to
remain silent. For his wife, being home means she is free from the worry that
something she says might offend someone, or spark disagreement, or appear
to be showing off; at home she is free to talk.

The communication problems that endanger marriage can't be fixed by   23
mechanical engineering. They require a new conceptual framework about the
role of talk in human relationships. Many of the psychological explanations
that have become second nature may not be helpful, because they tend to

blame either women (for not being assertive enough) or men (for not being in touch with their feelings). A sociolinguistic approach by which male-female conversation is seen as cross-cultural communication allows us to understand the problem and forge solutions without blaming either party.

Once the problem is understood, improvement comes naturally, as it did   24
to the young woman and her boyfriend who seemed to go to sleep when she wanted to talk. Previously, she had accused him of not listening, and he had refused to change his behavior, since that would be admitting fault. But then she learned about and explained to him the differences in women's and men's habitual ways of aligning themselves in conversation. The next time she told him she wanted to talk, he began, as usual, by lying down and covering his eyes. When the familiar negative reaction bubbled up, she reassured herself that he really was listening. But then he sat up and looked at her. Thrilled, she asked why. He said, "You like me to look at you when we talk, so I'll try to do it." Once he saw their differences as cross-cultural rather than right and wrong, he independently altered his behavior.

Women who feel abandoned and deprived when their husbands won't lis-   25
ten to or report daily news may be happy to discover their husbands trying to adapt once they understand the place of small talk in women's relationships. But if their husbands don't adapt, the women may still be comforted that for men, this is not a failure of intimacy. Accepting the difference, the wives may look to their friends or family for that kind of talk. And husbands who can't provide it shouldn't feel their wives have made unreasonable demands. Some couples will still decide to divorce, but at least their decisions will be based on realistic expectations.

In these times of resurgent ethnic conflicts, the world desperately needs   26
cross-cultural understanding. Like charity, successful cross-cultural communication should begin at home.

· · ·

Comprehension

1. What pattern of communication does Tannen identify at the beginning of her essay?
2. According to Tannen, what do women complain about most in their marriages?
3. What gives women the impression that men do not listen?
4. What characteristics of women's speech do men find frustrating?
5. According to Tannen, what can men and women do to remedy the communication problems that exist in most marriages?

Purpose and Audience

1. What is Tannen's thesis?
2. What is Tannen's purpose in writing this essay? Do you think she wants to inform or to persuade? On what do you base your conclusion?
3. Is Tannen writing for an expert audience or for an audience of general readers? To men, women, or both? How can you tell?

Style and Structure

1. What does Tannen gain by stating her thesis in paragraph 2 of the essay? Would there be any advantage in postponing the thesis statement until the end? Explain.
2. Is this essay a subject-by-subject or a point-by-point comparison? What does Tannen gain by organizing her essay the way she does?
3. Throughout her essay, Tannen cites scholarly studies and quotes statistics. How effectively does this information support her points? Could she have made a strong case without this material? Why or why not?
4. Would you say Tannen's tone is hopeful, despairing, sarcastic, angry, or something else? Explain.
5. Tannen concludes her essay with a far-reaching statement. What do you think she hopes to accomplish with this conclusion? Is she successful? Explain your reasoning.
6. **Vocabulary Project.** Where does Tannen use professional **jargon** in this essay? Would the essay be more effective or less effective without these words? Explain.

Journal Entry

Based on your own observations of male-female communication, how accurate is Tannen's analysis? Can you relate an anecdote from your own life that illustrates (or contradicts) her thesis?

Writing Workshop

1. **Working with Sources.** In another essay, Tannen contrasts the communication patterns of male and female students in classroom settings. After observing students in a few of your own classes, write an essay of your own that draws a comparison between the communication patterns of your male and female classmates. Include quotations from both male and female students. Be sure to include parenthetical documentation for these quotations as well as for any references to Tannen's essay; also include a works-cited page. (See Chapter 18 for information on MLA documentation.)
2. Write an essay comparing the way male and female characters speak (or behave) in films or on television. Use examples to support your points.
3. Write an essay comparing the vocabulary used in two different sports. Does one sport use more violent language than the other? For example, baseball uses the terms *bunt* and *sacrifice*, and football uses the terms *blitz* and *bomb*. Use as many examples as you can to support your thesis.

Combining the Patterns

Tannen begins her essay with an anecdote. Why does she begin with this paragraph of **narration**? How does this story set the tone for the rest of the essay?

Thematic Connections

- "The Myth of the Latin Woman: I Just Met a Girl Named Maria" (page 224)
- "Mother Tongue" (page 456)
- "I Want a Wife" (page 494)

ISABEL WILKERSON

Emmett Till and Tamir Rice, Sons of the Great Migration

A native of Washington, DC, and a graduate of Howard University, Isabel Wilkerson (b. 1961) is a distinguished journalist and academic. She won a 1994 Pulitzer Prize for Feature Writing for her work as Chicago bureau chief of the *New York Times*. She is also the recipient of a George S. Polk Award and a Guggenheim Fellowship. Wilkerson has taught journalism at Emory University, Princeton University, Northwestern University, and Boston University. Her 2010 book, *The Warmth of Other Suns: The Epic Story of America's Great Migration*, focuses on two historical waves of African Americans who left the South for the Midwest and other regions of the country.

Background on Emmett Till In her essay, Wilkerson refers to the 1955 murder of Emmett Till as "a turning point in the civil rights movement." A Chicago native, the fourteen-year-old Till was visiting relatives in segregated Money, Mississippi, when he spoke to a white, married woman, Carolyn Bryant, in a grocery store. The specifics of the exchange are unclear: according to some accounts, Till touched her arm, propositioned her, or whistled at her. A few days later, Bryant's husband, Roy Bryant, and his half-brother J. W. Milam abducted Till. They beat him, shot him, and dumped his body in the Tallahatchie River, where it was discovered three days later. Tens of thousands of people attended Till's funeral, which startled and unified the Black community and drew sympathy from many whites across the country. Bryant and Milam were indicted for the murder, but were acquitted by an all-white Mississippi jury after only an hour of deliberation. Once acquitted — and immune from further prosecution — the two men admitted their guilt. Till's mother repeatedly tried to get prosecutors to reopen the case over the next several decades, but never succeeded. The brutal slaying of Emmett Till is still shocking, and it remains a foundational event of the early civil rights era.

In winter 1916, several hundred Black families from the Selma, Ala., Cotton Belt began quietly defecting from the Jim Crow South, with its night rides and hanging trees, some confiding to *The Chicago Defender* in February that the "treatment doesn't warrant staying." It was the start of the Great Migration, a leaderless revolution that would incite six million Black refugees over six decades to seek asylum within the borders of their own country.

"The horrors they were fleeing would follow them in freedom and into the current day."

1

They could not know what was in store for them or their descendants, nor   2
the hostilities they would face wherever they went. Consider the story of two
mothers whose lives bookend the migration and whose family lines would
meet similar, unimaginable fates. The horrors they were fleeing would follow
them in freedom and into the current day.

The first was Mamie Carthan Till, whose parents carried her from   3
Mississippi to Illinois early in the 1920s. In Chicago, she would marry and give
birth to a son, Emmett. In the summer of 1955, she would send him to visit
relatives back in Mississippi. Emmett had just turned 14, had been raised in
the new world and was unschooled in the "yes, sir, no, sir" ways of the Southern
caste system. That August, he was kidnapped, beaten, and shot to death, osten-
sibly for whistling at a white woman at a convenience store. His murder would
become a turning point in the civil rights movement.

Around that year, another woman, Millie Lee Wylie, left the bottomlands   4
of Sumter County, Ala., near where the migration had begun, and settled in
Cleveland. There, more than half a century later, just before Thanksgiving
2014, her 12-year-old great-grandson, bundled up in the cold, was playing with
a friend's pellet gun at a park outside a recreation center. His name was Tamir
Rice. A now familiar video shows a police officer shooting him seconds after
arrival, and an officer tackling his sister to the ground as she ran toward her
dying brother. Tamir's became one of the most recognizable names in a metro-
nome of unarmed Black people killed by the police in the last two years, further galvanizing the Black Lives Matter movement.

Tamir Rice would become to this young century what Emmett Till was to   5
the last. In pictures, the boys resemble each other, the same half-smiles on their
full moon faces, the most widely distributed photographs of them taken from
the same angle, in similar light, their clear eyes looking into the camera with
the same male-child assuredness of near adolescence. They are now tragic symbols of the search for Black freedom in this country.

It has been a century since the Great Migration that produced both boys   6
began. Our current era seems oddly aligned with that moment. The brutal
decades preceding the Great Migration — when a Black person was lynched on
average every four days — were given a name by the historian Rayford Logan.
He called them the Nadir. Today, in the era of the Charleston massacre, when,
according to one analysis of F.B.I. statistics, an African-American is killed by a
white police officer roughly every three and a half days, has the makings of a
second Nadir.

Or perhaps, in the words of Eric Foner, the leading scholar of Reconstruction,   7
a "second Redemption." That is what historians call the period of backlash
against the gains made by newly freedmen that led to Jim Crow.

Today, with Black advancement by an elite few extending as far as the   8
White House, we are seeing "a similar kind of retreat," Professor Foner said.
"The attack on voting rights, incarceration, obviously but even more intellectually and culturally, a sort of exhaustion with Black protest, an attitude of 'What
are these people really complaining about? Look at what we've done for you.'"

The country seems caught in a cycle. We leap forward only to slip back.   9
"We have not made anywhere near the progress we think we have," said Bryan

Stevenson of the Equal Justice Initiative in Alabama. "It's as if we're at half-time, and we started cheering as if we won the game."

What befell Emmett and Tamir reflects how racial interactions have   10
mutated over time, from the overt hatreds now shunned by most Americans to the unspoken, unconscious biases that are no less lethal and may be harder to fight. For all of its changes, the country remains in a similar place, a caste system based on what people look like.

The men and women of the Great Migration were asking questions that   11
remain unanswered today: What is to be the role of the people whom the country has marginalized by law and custom and with state-sanctioned violence for most of their time on this soil? How might these now 45 million people, still the most segregated of all groups in America, partake of the full fruits of citizenship? How can deeply embedded racial hierarchies be overcome?

Tamir Rice's great-grandmother, Millie Lee Wylie, was born into a family   12
of farm hands and sawmill workers. She married young and was left a widow when her husband died after a fall in a crooked river. With dreams of a new life, she packed up her belongings and left the tenant shacks of Alabama for the smokestacks of Cleveland, later sending for her three young sons. Like many of the women new to the north, she found work as a housekeeper and later as a hospital janitor. She would have two more children and marry a man named Robert Petty, who worked at the old Republic Steel plant and whose family had arrived years before from Mississippi by way of Kentucky.

They found themselves hemmed into the worn-out, predominantly Black   13
east side of Cleveland, with other refugees from the South. He worked the 7 A.M. to 3 P.M. shift; she worked from 3 P.M. to 11 P.M. He played the numbers and bet the horses at Thistledown to help make the rent on their apartment, in a dilapidated four-flat owned by an Eastern European woman who saw no need to keep it up.

They finally saved up for a two-story house with aluminum siding in the sub-   14
urbs. The white neighbors began moving out shortly thereafter, a common response to Black efforts to move up in most every receiving station in the North.

Millie—now Mrs. Petty—went about re-creating the things she missed from   15
the "old country." She planted collard greens and watermelons and raised chickens in the backyard. She cooked neck bone and made hogshead cheese, singing hymns—"I'm coming up on the rough side of the mountain"—as she worked. Sundays, she ushered at a storefront Baptist church in her belted navy dress with white gloves and collar, perfumed with her one indulgence, Chanel No. 5.

After lives of work and want, both she and her husband died in their 50s,   16
she of cancer and he of a heart attack after losing a lung from asbestos exposure at the plant. Their early deaths left the family ungrounded, without the close networks that had sustained their Southern ancestors. The daughter, Darlette Pinkston, suffered for it. Her marriage did not last, and she began living with a man who beat and threatened her until, fearing for her life, she killed him. Her daughter, Samaria, was 12 when she testified at the trial to the abuse she had witnessed and then lost her mother to prison for 15 years.

Samaria moved between foster homes and then to the streets. She dropped   17
out of school in ninth grade, worked odd jobs, cleaning and doing clerical work, and had four children, the youngest of whom was Tamir.

She got tutors for her children, managed to get the oldest through high   18
school and the others on track to finish. Tamir had swimming and soccer lessons and "Iron Man" DVDs. He had suffered such separation anxiety that she
had to send him to nursery school with a picture of herself so he would know
he would see her again.

On the afternoon of Nov. 22, 2014, a Saturday, she let Tamir and his sister   19
Tajai go to the recreation center by the park across the street before dinner. She
was starting the lasagna when there was a knock at the door. Two children told
her that Tamir had been shot. She didn't believe them. "No, not my kids," she
told them. "My kids are in the park." A neighbor boy had let Tamir play with
his pellet gun without her knowing it. "I hadn't seen the gun before," she told
me. "They knew better than to let me see it."

When she arrived, the officers would not let her near her son to comfort   20
him as he lay bleeding on the ground, she said. They told her they would put
her in the squad car if she didn't stay back.

As in the majority of the twenty-first century cases of police shootings in   21
the North, no one was prosecuted in the death of Tamir Rice. Late last
December, a grand jury declined to indict the officer who killed him. Decades
ago, in the Jim Crow South, Emmett Till's killers were acquitted by an all-white
jury, but at least they had gone to trial.

I asked Michael Petty, Tamir's great-uncle and a retired chaplain's assis-   22
tant in the Navy, how Millie, his mother, would have borne what happened
to the great-grandson she never lived to see, in the place she traveled so far
to reach. It would have crushed her, Mr. Petty said. "My mother would have
carried that hurt," he said, "and felt the pain of the generations."

· · ·

Comprehension

1. What is the "Great Migration"? Why did it occur?
2. In paragraph 1, Wilkerson mentions "night rides and hanging trees." Why
   do you think she doesn't explain these references? Should she have?
3. How were Mamie Carthan Till and Millie Lee Wylie alike? How were they
   different?
4. Wilkerson says, "Tamir Rice would become to this young century what
   Emmett Till was to the last" (5). What point is she making?
5. What does Wilkerson mean when she says that today "has the makings of a
   second Nadir" (6)? Why does she believe this?
6. How does Eric Foner define the "second Redemption" (7)? How, according
   to Wilkerson, is the United States "caught in a cycle" (9)?

Purpose and Audience

1. Is Wilkerson writing primarily for a white audience, an African American
   audience, or both? How do you know?
2. Do you think Wilkerson expects her readers to be receptive or hostile to her
   ideas? How can you tell?

3. Where does Wilkerson state her thesis? In your own words, summarize this thesis.
4. What do you think Wilkerson hoped to accomplish with her essay? Is her purpose to persuade? To inform? To enlighten? Or did she have some other motive? Explain.

Style and Structure

1. Wilkerson's introduction consists of two paragraphs. What does each of these paragraphs accomplish?
2. In comparing her two subjects, Wilkerson relies mainly on a point-by-point structure. What are the advantages and disadvantages of this organization?
3. Underline the transitional words and phrases that indicate the contrast between Wilkerson's two subjects in this essay. Should she have used more transitions, or does she have enough?
4. In paragraphs 19 and 20, Wilkerson tells how Tamir Rice's mother found out her son had been shot by police, but Wilkerson gives no details about the incident itself or its aftermath. Should she have? Why do you think she does not supply this information? (Before answering this question, do some research to find out more about Tamir Rice's killing.)
5. What points does Wilkerson emphasize in her conclusion? Is it an effective concluding strategy? Would another strategy have been better? Explain.
6. **Vocabulary Project.** In paragraph 10, Wilkerson says the United States remains "a caste system based on what people look like." What is a caste system? Do you think Wilkerson's use of this term is accurate?

Journal Entry

Wilkerson's essay discusses the families of both Emmett Till and Tamir Rice. What does each boy's upbringing tell you about his family?

Writing Workshop

1. Write an essay in which you compare Emmett Till's upbringing with Tamir Rice's.
2. **Working with Sources.** Wilkerson says that six million African Americans who took part in the Great Migration "could not know what was in store for them or their descendants" (2). Interview one of your grandparents (or an older relative) and find out what this person once envisioned for future generations of his or her family. Did they accurately predict what lay ahead? Then, write an essay in which you compare your relative's expectations with what actually happened. Be sure to document your interview and to include a works-cited page. (See Chapter 18 for information on MLA documentation.)
3. **Working with Sources.** Go to YouTube and listen to "The Death of Emmett Till" by Bob Dylan. Then, read the lyrics online. Write an essay in which you compare Wilkerson's treatment of Emmett Till to Dylan's. What does each hope to accomplish by telling Till's story? Do they each have the same purpose?

Are they successful? Be sure to document all references to Wilkerson's essay and to include a works-cited page. (See Chapter 18 for information on MLA documentation.)

Combining the Patterns

Much of this essay consists of **narrative** paragraphs. How do these narratives help Wilkerson develop her thesis?

Thematic Connections

- "Just Walk On By: A Black Man Ponders His Power to Alter Public Space" (page 231)
- "How to Tell a Mother Her Child Is Dead" (page 275)
- The Declaration of Independence (page 548)
- "Letter from Birmingham Jail" (page 562)

STEVEN CONN

The Twin Revolutions of Lincoln and Darwin

Steven Conn is the W. E. Smith Professor of History at Miami University in Oxford, Ohio. Conn received his undergraduate degree from Yale University and his Ph.D. from the University of Pennsylvania. He has written and edited several books, including *History's Shadow: Native Americans and Historical Consciousness in the Nineteenth Century* (2004), *Do Museums Still Need Objects?* (2010), and *Americans Against the City: Anti-Urbanism in the Twentieth Century* (2014). Conn is a frequent contributor to the *Huffington Post* and the *Chronicle of Higher Education*.

Background on the world in 1809 Abraham Lincoln and Charles Darwin were both born in 1809. But other major figures were also born that year, among them the British poet Alfred Tennyson, the future prime minister of the United Kingdom William Gladstone, and the German composer Felix Mendelssohn. In 1809, the Napoleonic Wars raged in Europe, while the Treaty of the Dardanelles ended the war between the Ottoman Empire and the United Kingdom. In the sciences, the French naturalist Jean-Baptiste Lamarck published *Philosophie Zoologique*, which outlined an early theory of evolution. Throughout the world, life expectancy was less than forty years. In the United States, American inventor and designer Robert Fulton patented his steamboat, which revolutionized domestic travel and commercial transportation. In March 1809, James Madison was sworn in as the fourth U.S. president, but as tensions over commerce and western expansion heightened, the country was on course for another war with Britain in 1812.

1 Abraham Lincoln, the Great Emancipator, has been much on our minds recently. Today, exactly 200 years after Lincoln's birth, Barack Obama's presidency is one fulfillment of the work Lincoln started.

2 Lincoln shares his birthday with Charles Darwin, the other Great Emancipator of the nineteenth century. In different ways, each liberated us from tradition.

3 Charles Darwin and Abraham Lincoln were exact contemporaries. Both were born on February 12, 1809 — Darwin into a comfortable family in Shropshire, England; Lincoln into humble circumstances on the American frontier.

4 They also came to international attention at virtually the same moment. Darwin published his epochal book, *On the Origin of Species*, in 1859. The following year, Lincoln became the sixteenth president of the United States. Also in 1860, Harvard botanist Asa Gray wrote the first review of Darwin's book to appear in this country.

5 Lincoln and Darwin initiated twin revolutions. One brought the Civil War and the emancipation of roughly four million slaves; the other, a new

explanation of the natural world. Lincoln's war transformed the social, political, and racial landscape in ways that continue to play out. Darwin transformed our understanding of biology, paving the way for countless advances in science, especially medicine.

> "Lincoln and Darwin initiated twin revolutions."

With his powerful scientific explanation of the origins of species, Darwin dispensed with the pseudoscientific assertions of African American inferiority. In this way, Darwin provided the scientific legitimacy for Lincoln's political and moral actions.   6

The two revolutions shared a commitment to one proposition: that all human beings are fundamentally equal. In this sense, both Lincoln and Darwin deserve credit for emancipating us from the political and intellectual rationales for slavery.   7

For Lincoln, this was a political principle and a moral imperative. He was deeply ambivalent about the institution of slavery. As the war began, he believed that saving the Union, not abolishing slavery, was the cause worth fighting for. But as the war ground gruesomely on, he began to see that ending slavery was the only way to save the Union without making a mockery of the nation's founding ideals.   8

This is what Lincoln meant when he promised, in the 1863 Gettysburg Address, that the war would bring "a new birth of freedom." He was even more emphatic about it in his second inaugural address, in 1865. Slavery could not be permitted to exist in a nation founded on the belief that we are all created equal.   9

Darwin, for his part, was a deeply committed abolitionist from a family of deeply committed abolitionists. Exposed to slavery during his travels in South America, Darwin wrote, "It makes one's blood boil." He called abolishing slavery his "sacred cause." In some of his first notes about evolution, he railed against the idea that slaves were somehow less than human.   10

For Darwin, our shared humanity was a simple biological fact. Whatever variations exist among the human species—what we call *races*—are simply the natural variations that occur within all species. Like it or not, in a Darwinian world we are all members of one human family. This truth lay at the center of Darwin's science and his abolitionism.   11

That understanding of human equality—arrived at from different directions and for different reasons—helps explain the opposition to the revolutions unleashed by Lincoln and Darwin. It's also why many Americans—virtually alone in the developed world—continue to deny Darwinian science.   12

Many white Southerners never accepted Lincoln's basic proposition about the political equality of Black Americans. In the years after the Civil War and Reconstruction, they set up the brutal structures and rituals of segregation. All of the elaborate laws, customs and violence of the segregated South served to deny the basic truth that all Americans are created equal. Most Northerners, meanwhile, didn't care much about the "Southern problem."   13

No wonder, then, that many Americans simply rejected Darwin's insights   14
out of hand. Slavery and segregation rested on the assumption that Black
Americans were not fully human. Darwinian science put the lie to all that.

Lincoln insisted on equality as a political fact. Darwin demonstrated it as a   15
biological fact. In their shared commitment to human equality, each in his
own realm, these two Great Emancipators helped us break free from the shackles of the past.

· · ·

Comprehension

1. Why, according to Conn, should Lincoln have been "much on our minds"
   with the election of Barack Obama as president (1)?
2. What does Conn mean when he says, "Darwin provided the scientific legitimacy for Lincoln's political and moral values" (6)?
3. How did Lincoln's attitude toward slavery change as the Civil War pro-
   gressed? Was Lincoln's opinion of slavery different from Darwin's? If so,
   how?
4. In what sense did both Lincoln and Darwin initiate "twin revolutions"?
5. Why, according to Conn, do many Americans "continue to deny Darwinian
   science" (12). Do you find his explanation credible?

Purpose and Audience

1. Restate this essay's thesis in your own words.
2. What prompted Conn to write his essay? What did he hope to accomplish?
3. Does Conn expect his readers to be familiar with the accomplishments of
   both Lincoln and Darwin? How do you know?

Style and Structure

1. Does Conn use subject-by-subject or point-by-point comparison? Why do
   you think he chose the strategy he did?
2. Conn states his thesis in paragraph 5. Why does he wait so long to state it?
3. Identify several instances of parallelism in this essay, and explain what ideas
   this strategy emphasizes in each instance.
4. What support does Conn provide for his points? Should he have provided
   more support? Does the fact that Conn is a professor of history eliminate
   the need for certain kinds of support? Explain.
5. What point does Conn make in his conclusion? Does his conclusion
   reinforce his thesis? Explain.
6. **Vocabulary Project.** Look up synonyms for the following words. Then,
   determine if each synonym would be as effective as the word used.
   emancipator (1)
   epochal (4)
   pseudoscientific (6)
   imperative (8)
   shackles (15)

Journal Entry

Do you accept Darwinian science as fact? If so, why? If not, why not?

Writing Workshop

1. Write an essay in which you compare two people you know well—two teachers, your parents, two relatives, two friends, or two fictional characters. Be sure to include a thesis statement.
2. Compare the music you listened to when you were much younger to the music you listen to now. What do these two types of music reveal about you and about how you have changed? In what sense does this change constitute a "revolution"?
3. **Working with Sources.** Using language and syntax appropriate for middle-school students, revise this essay for that audience, making the same points that Conn does about Lincoln and Darwin. Be sure to include documentation for any references to Conn's essay as well as a works-cited page. (See Chapter 18 for information on MLA Documentation.)

Combining the Patterns

Throughout his essay, Conn uses **exemplification** to structure paragraphs. Identify several paragraphs that use examples to support their topic sentences, and bracket the examples. How do these examples reinforce the point Conn is making?

Thematic Connections

- "Soweto" (page 175)
- "Emmett Till and Tamir Rice, Sons of the Great Migration" (page 414)
- "The Untouchable" (page 487)
- The Declaration of Independence (page 548)
- "Letter from Birmingham Jail" (page 562)

WILLIAM SHAKESPEARE

Shall I compare thee to a summer's day? (Poetry)

Generally considered the greatest writer in the English language, William Shakespeare (1564–1616) was a poet, playwright, actor, and theatrical businessman. Born and raised in Stratford-on-Avon, he wrote his plays between 1588 and 1613. His surviving works include roughly 38 plays and 154 sonnets, as well as two narrative poems, "Venus and Adonis" and "The Rape of Lucrece." Other texts exist as well, but their authorship remains uncertain. His comedies, tragedies, histories, and romances, from *A Midsummer Night's Dream* and *Hamlet* to *Henry the V* and *The Tempest*, are performed today more than any other playwright's work.

Background on the sonnet In "Scorn Not the Sonnet," the English poet William Wordsworth (1770–1850) writes that "with this key / Shakespeare unlocked his heart." By the time Shakespeare wrote his sonnets in the 1590s, the sonnet form was already centuries old. The sonnet — from *sonneto*, Italian for "little song" — originated in Italy in the thirteenth century; it was refined and innovated by writers like Dante (1265–1321) and Petrarch (1304–1374). The sonnet arrived in England in the 1500s when English writers such as Sir Thomas Wyatt (1503–1542) and Henry Howard, the Earl of Surrey (c. 1516–1547), began retooling it for the English language. Later in the century, it became a common form for poets, such as Sir Philip Sidney, Edmund Spenser, and William Shakespeare.

Consisting of three four-line stanzas followed by a rhymed couplet, Shakespeare's sonnets are timeless meditations on beauty, love, time, and death. They are thought to have been written in 1590 and were formally published in 1609. The real-life historical characters of the sonnets remain mysterious. The first 126 are addressed to a "fair youth" or young man, whom the poet urges to marry and have children; the final 28, which are more overtly erotic, are thought to be directed at a woman, often referred to as the "dark lady." The sonnets have been translated into almost every written language and even now continue to fascinate and inspire contemporary readers and writers. As Virginia Woolf suggests in her novel *To the Lighthouse*, they are "beautiful and reasonable, clear and complete, the essence sucked out of life and rounded here."

Shall I compare thee to a summer's day?
Thou art more lovely and more temperate:
Rough winds do shake the darling buds of May,*
And summer's lease hath all too short a date;
Sometime too hot the eye of heaven shines,   5
And often is his gold complexion dimmed;
And every fair from fair sometimes declines,
By chance or nature's changing course untrimmed;**
But thy eternal summer shall not fade,
Nor lose possession of that fair thou ow'st;***   10
Nor shall death brag thou wand'rest in his shade,
When in eternal lines† to time thou grow'st:
    So long as men can breathe, or eyes can see,
    So long lives this, and this gives life to thee.

• • •

Reading Literature

1. What two subjects is Shakespeare comparing? How do you know when the speaker shifts from one subject to the other?
2. Is this poem a subject-by-subject or point-by-point comparison? Why do you think Shakespeare chose this organization?
3. What comment do you think the poem is making about a summer's day? About youth? About death? About poetry?

Journal Entry

Many people see this poem as celebrating love, but others see it differently. What do you think this poem is really about?

Thematic Connections

- "My Mother Never Worked" (page 122)
- "The Myth of the Latin Woman: I Just Met a Girl Named Maria" (page 224)
- "Flick Chicks" (page 444)

---

* Eds. note — At the time Shakespeare wrote, May was considered a summer month.
** Eds. note — Without decoration.
*** Eds. note — Own or ownest.
† Eds. note — Lines of poetry, lines of descent.

Writing Assignments for Comparison and Contrast

1. Find a description of the same news event in two different magazines or newspapers. Write a comparison-and-contrast essay discussing the similarities and differences between the two stories.

2. **Working with Sources.** In your local public library, locate two children's books on the same subject — one written in the 1950s and one written within the past ten years. Write an essay discussing which elements are the same and which are different. Include a thesis statement about the significance of the differences between the two books. Be sure to document all material you take from the two books and create a works-cited page. (See Chapter 18 for information on MLA documentation.)

3. Write an essay about a relative or friend you have known since you were a child. Consider how your opinion of this person is different now from what it was then.

4. Write an essay comparing and contrasting the expectations that college instructors and high school teachers have for their students. Cite your own experiences as examples.

5. Since you started college, how have you changed? Write a comparison-and-contrast essay that answers this question.

6. Taking careful notes, watch a local television news program and then a national news broadcast. Write an essay comparing the two programs, paying particular attention to the news content and to the journalists' broadcasting styles.

7. Write an essay comparing your own early memories of school with those of a parent or an older relative.

8. How are the attitudes toward education different among students who work to finance their own education and students who do not? Your thesis statement should indicate what differences exist and why.

9. Compare and contrast the college experiences of commuters and students who live in dorms on campus. Interview people in your classes to use as examples.

10. Write an essay comparing any two groups that have divergent values — vegetarians and meat eaters or smokers and nonsmokers, for example.

11. How is being a participant — playing a sport or acting in a play, for instance — different from being a spectator? Write a comparison-and-contrast essay in which you answer this question.

Collaborative Activity for Comparison and Contrast

Form groups of four students each. Assume your college has hired these groups as consultants to suggest solutions for several problems students have been complaining about. Select the four areas — food, campus safety, parking, and class scheduling, for example — you think need improvement. Then, as a group, write a short report to your college describing the present conditions in these areas, and compare them to the improvements you envision. (Be sure to organize your report as a comparison-and-contrast essay.) Finally, have one person from each group read the group's report to the class. Decide as a class which group has the best suggestion.

12

Classification and Division

What Is Classification and Division?

Division is the process of breaking a whole into parts; **classification** is the process of sorting individual items into categories. In the following paragraph from "Pregnant with Possibility," Gregory J. E. Rawlins divides Americans into categories based on their access to computer technology.

Topic sentence identifies categories

<u>Today's computer technology is rapidly turning us into three completely new races: the superpoor, the rich, and the superrich.</u> The superpoor are perhaps eight thousand in every ten thousand of us. The rich — me and you — make up most of the remaining two thousand, while the superrich are perhaps the last two of every ten thousand. Roughly speaking, the decisions of two superrich people control what almost two thousand of us do, and our decisions, in turn, control what the remaining eight thousand do. These groups are really like races since the group you're born into often determines which group your children will be born into.

Through **classification and division**, we can make sense of seemingly random ideas by putting scattered bits of information into useful, coherent order. By breaking a large group into smaller categories and assigning individual items to larger categories, we can identify relationships between a whole and its parts and relationships among the parts themselves.

In countless practical situations, classification and division bring order to chaos. For example, your music can be *divided* into distinct genres: hip-hop, pop, rock, country, reggae, and so on. Similarly, phone numbers listed in your cell phone's address book can be *classified* according to four clearly defined categories: home, work, mobile, and other. Thus, order can be brought to your music and your phone numbers—just as it is brought to newspapers, department stores, supermarkets, biological hierarchies, and libraries—when a whole is divided into categories or sections and individual items are assigned to one or another of these subgroups.

Understanding Classification

Even though the interrelated processes of classification and division invariably occur together, they are two separate operations. When you **classify**, you begin with individual items and sort them into categories. Because a given item invariably has several different attributes, it can be classified in various ways. For example, the most obvious way to classify the students who attend your school might be according to their year. However, you could also classify students according to their major, grade-point average, or any number of other principles. The **principle of classification** that you choose—the quality your items have in common—depends on how you wish to approach the members of this large and diverse group.

Understanding Division

Division is the opposite of classification. When you **divide**, you start with a whole (an entire class) and break it into its individual parts. For example, you might start with the large general class *television shows* and divide it into categories: *sitcoms, action/adventure, reality shows*, and so forth. You could then divide each of these categories even further. *Action/adventure programs*, for example, might include *Westerns, crime dramas, spy dramas*, and so on—and each of these categories could be further divided as well. Eventually, you would need to identify a particular principle of classification to help you assign specific programs to one category or another—that is, to classify them.

Using Classification and Division

Whenever you write an essay, you use classification and division to bring order to the invention stage of the writing process. For example, when you brainstorm, as Chapter 2 explains, you begin with your topic and list all the ideas you can think of. Next, you *divide* your topic into logical categories and *classify* the items in your brainstorming notes into one category or another, perhaps narrowing, expanding, or eliminating some categories—or some ideas—as you go along. This sorting and grouping enables you to condense and shape your material until it eventually suggests a thesis and the main points your essay will develop.

More specifically, certain topics and questions, because of the way they are worded, immediately suggest a classification-and-division pattern. Suppose, for example, you are asked, "What kinds of policies can government implement to reduce the threat posed by climate change?" Here the word *kinds* suggests classification and division. Other words — such as *types*, *varieties*, *aspects*, and *categories* — can also indicate that this pattern of development is called for.

Planning a Classification-and-Division Essay

Once you decide to use a classification-and-division pattern, you need to identify a **principle of classification**. Every group of people, things, or ideas can be categorized in many different ways. For example, when deciding which textbooks to purchase first, you could classify books according to their *usefulness*, considering whether they are required, recommended, or optional. You could also classify books according to their *relevance* to your coursework, considering which books will be used in courses in your major, which will be used in other required courses, and which will be used in electives. Of course, if you have limited funds, you might want to classify books according to their *cost*, buying the less expensive ones first. In each case, your purpose would determine how you classify the items.

Selecting and Arranging Categories

After you define your principle of classification and apply it to your topic, you should decide on your categories by dividing a whole class into parts and grouping a number of different items together within each part. Next, you should decide how you will treat the categories in your essay. Just as a comparison-and-contrast essay makes comparable points about its subjects, so your classification-and-division essay should treat all categories similarly. When you discuss comparable points for each category, your readers are able to understand your distinctions among categories as well as your definition of each category.

Finally, you should arrange your categories in some logical order so that readers can see how the categories are related and what their relative importance is. Whatever order you choose, it should be consistent with your purpose and with your essay's thesis.

Developing a Thesis Statement

Like other kinds of essays, a classification-and-division essay should have a thesis. Your **thesis statement** should identify your subject and perhaps introduce the categories you will discuss; it may also suggest the relationships of your categories to one another and to the subject as a whole. In addition, your thesis statement should tell your readers why your classification is significant, and it might also establish the relative value of your categories. For example, if you were writing an essay about investment strategies, a thesis statement that simply listed different kinds of investments would be pointless. Instead, your thesis statement might note their relative strengths and weaknesses and perhaps make recommendations based on this assessment. Similarly, a research essay about a writer's major works would accomplish little if it merely categorized his or her writings. Instead, your thesis statement should communicate your evaluation of these different kinds of works, perhaps demonstrating that some deserve higher public regard than others.

✓ **CHECKLIST**   **ESTABLISHING CATEGORIES**

☐ **All the categories should derive from the same principle.** If you decide to divide *television shows* into *sitcoms, reality shows*, and the like, it is not logical to include *children's programs* because this category results from one principle (target audience), whereas the others result from another principle (genre). Similarly, if you were classifying undergraduates at your school according to their year, you would not include the category *students receiving financial aid*.

☐ **All the categories should be at the same level.** In the series *sitcoms, action/ adventure*, and *Westerns*, the last item, *Westerns*, does not belong because it is at a lower level — that is, it is a subcategory of *action/adventure*. Likewise, *sophomores* (a subcategory of *undergraduates*) does not belong in the series *undergraduates, graduate students*, and *continuing education students*.

☐ **You should treat all categories that are significant and relevant to your discussion.** Include enough categories to make your point, with no important omissions and no overlapping categories. In a review of a network's fall television lineup, the series *sitcoms, reality shows, crime shows*, and *detective shows* is incomplete because it omits important categories such as *news programs, game shows*, and *documentaries*; moreover, *detective shows* may overlap with *crime shows*. In the same way, the series *freshmen, sophomores, juniors*, and *transfers* is illogical: the important group *seniors* has been omitted, and *transfers* may include *freshmen, sophomores*, and *juniors*.

Using Transitions

When you write a classification-and-division essay, you use transitional words and phrases both to introduce your categories (the *first* category, *one* category, and so on) and to move readers from one category to the next (*the second* category, *another* category, and so on). In addition, transitional words and expressions can show readers the relationships among categories — for example, whether one category is more important than another (*a more important* category, the *most important* category, and so on). A more complete list of transitions appears on page 56.

Structuring a Classification-and-Division Essay

Once you have drafted your essay's thesis statement and established your categories, you should plan your classification-and-division essay around the same three major sections that other kinds of essays have: *introduction, body*, and *conclusion*. Your **introduction** should orient your readers by identifying your topic, the principle for classifying your material, and the individual categories you plan to discuss; your thesis is also usually stated in the introduction. In the **body paragraphs**, you should discuss your categories one by one, in the same order in which you mentioned them in your introduction. Finally, your **conclusion** should restate your thesis in different words, summing up the points you have made and perhaps considering their implications.

Suppose you are preparing a research essay on Mark Twain's nonfiction works for an American literature course. You have read selections from *Roughing It, Life on the Mississippi*, and *The Innocents Abroad*. Besides these travel narratives, you have read parts of Twain's autobiography and some of his correspondence and essays. When you realize that the works you have studied can easily be classified as four different types of Twain's nonfiction — travel narratives, essays, letters, and autobiography — you decide to use classification and division to structure your essay. So, you first divide the large class *Twain's nonfiction prose* into major categories: his travel narratives, essays, autobiography, and letters. Then, you classify the individual works, assigning each work to one of these categories, which you will discuss one at a time. Your purpose is to persuade readers to reconsider the reputations of some of these works, and you word your thesis statement accordingly. You might then prepare a formal outline like the one that follows.

SAMPLE OUTLINE: Classification and Division

INTRODUCTION

Thesis statement: Most readers know Mark Twain as a novelist, but his nonfiction works — his travel narratives, essays, letters, and especially his autobiography — deserve more attention.

FIRST CATEGORY: TRAVEL NARRATIVES

- *Roughing It*
- *The Innocents Abroad*
- *Life on the Mississippi*

SECOND CATEGORY: ESSAYS

- "Fenimore Cooper's Literary Offenses"
- "How to Tell a Story"
- "The Awful German Language"

THIRD CATEGORY: LETTERS

- To W. D. Howells
- To his family

FOURTH CATEGORY: AUTOBIOGRAPHY

CONCLUSION

Restatement of thesis (in different words) or review of key points

Because this will be a long essay, each of the outline's divisions will have several subdivisions, and each subdivision might require several paragraphs.

This outline illustrates the characteristics of an effective classification-and-division essay. First, Twain's nonfiction works are classified according to a single principle of classification — literary genre. (Depending on your purpose, another principle — such as theme or subject matter — could work just as well.) The outline also reveals that the essay's four categories are on the same level (each is a different literary genre) and that all relevant categories are included. Had you left out *essays*, for example, you would have been unable to classify several significant works of nonfiction.

This outline also arranges the four categories so that they will support your thesis most effectively. Because you believe Twain's travel narratives are somewhat overrated, you plan to discuss them early in your essay. Similarly, because you think the autobiography would make your best case for the merit of the nonfiction works as a whole, you decide it should be placed last. (Of course, you could arrange your categories in several other orders, such as from shorter to longer works or from least to most popular, depending on the thesis your essay will support.)

Finally, this outline reminds you to treat all categories comparably in your essay. Your case would be weakened if, for example, you did not consider style in your discussion of Twain's letters while discussing style for every other category. This omission might lead your readers to suspect that you had not done enough research on the letters — or that the style of Twain's letters did not measure up to the style of his other works.

Revising a Classification-and-Division Essay

When you revise a classification-and-division essay, consider the items on Checklist: Revising on page 68. In addition, pay special attention to the items on the following checklist, which apply specifically to revising classification-and-division essays.

✓ **REVISION CHECKLIST**   **CLASSIFICATION AND DIVISION**

☐ Does your assignment call for classification and division?
☐ Have you identified a **principle of classification** for your material?
☐ Have you identified the categories you plan to discuss and decided how you will treat them?
☐ Have you arranged your categories in a logical order?
☐ Have you treated all categories similarly?
☐ Does your essay have a clearly stated thesis that identifies the subject of your classification (perhaps listing the categories you will discuss) and indicates why it is important?
☐ Have you used transitional words and phrases to show the relationships among categories?
☐ Do you need to add references to one or more sources?
☐ Do you need to add a visual?

Editing a Classification-and-Division Essay

When you edit your classification-and-division essay, you should follow the guidelines on the editing checklists on pages 85, 88, and 92. In addition, you should focus on the grammar, mechanics, and punctuation issues that are particularly relevant to classification-and-division essays. One of these issues — using a colon to introduce your categories — is discussed below.

🔍 **GRAMMAR IN CONTEXT**   **USING A COLON TO INTRODUCE YOUR CATEGORIES**

When you state the thesis of a classification-and-division essay, you often give readers an overview by listing the categories you will discuss. You introduce this list of categories with a **colon**, a punctuation mark whose purpose is to direct readers to look ahead for a series, list, clarification, or explanation.

When you use a colon to introduce your categories, the colon must be preceded by a complete sentence.

CORRECT: Carolyn Foster Segal's essay identifies kinds of student excuses with five headings: The Family, The Best Friend, The Evils of Dorm Life, The Evils of Technology, and The Totally Bizarre.

INCORRECT: The headings that Carolyn Foster Segal uses to identify kinds of student excuses are: The Family, The Best Friend, The Evils of Dorm Life, The Evils of Technology, and The Totally Bizarre.

In any list or series of three or more categories, the categories should be separated by commas, with a comma preceding the *and* that separates the last two items. This last comma prevents confusion by ensuring that readers will be able to see at a glance exactly how many categories you are discussing.

CORRECT: The Family, The Best Friend, The Evils of Dorm Life, The Evils of Technology, and The Totally Bizarre (five categories)

INCORRECT: The Family, The Best Friend, The Evils of Dorm Life, The Evils of Technology and The Totally Bizarre (without the final comma, it might appear you are only discussing four categories)

NOTE: Items on a list or in a series are always expressed in **parallel** terms. See the Grammar in Context box on page 375.

✓ **EDITING CHECKLIST** **CLASSIFICATION AND DIVISION**

☐ Do you introduce your list of categories with a colon preceded by a complete sentence?
☐ Are the items on your list of categories separated by commas?
☐ Do you include a comma before the *and* that connects the last two items on your list?
☐ Do you express the items on your list in parallel terms?

A STUDENT WRITER: Classification and Division

The following classification-and-division essay was written by Josie Martinez for an education course. Her assignment was to look back at her own education and to consider what she had learned so far, referring in her essay to Leon Wieseltier's "Perhaps Culture Is Now the Counterculture," a college commencement address reprinted in the *New Republic*. Josie's essay divides a whole — her college classes — into four categories.

What I Learned (and Didn't Learn) in College

Introduction   In "Perhaps Culture Is Now the Counterculture," Leon Wieseltier   1
defends the study of the humanities, opening his remarks by asking,
"Has there ever been a moment in American life when the humanities
were cherished less, and . . . needed more?" (Wieseltier) He goes
on to stress the importance of balancing science and technology
courses (which are increasingly popular with today's students) with
humanities courses. Even though not every class will be rewarding

or even enjoyable, taking a variety of courses in different disciplines will expose students to a wide range of subjects and also teach them about themselves.

Categories listed and explained

Despite the variety of experiences that different students have with different courses, most college classes can be classified into one of four categories: ideal classes, worthless classes, disappointing classes, and unexpectedly valuable classes. First are courses that students love — ideal learning environments in which they enjoy both the subject matter and the professor-student interaction. Far from these ideal courses are those that students find completely worthless in terms of subject matter, atmosphere, and teaching style. Somewhere between these two extremes are two kinds of courses that can be classified into another pair of opposites: courses that students expect to enjoy and to learn much from but are disappointing and courses that students are initially not interested in but that exceed

Thesis statement

their expectations. Understanding these four categories can help students accept the fact that one disappointing class is not a disaster and can encourage them to try classes in different disciplines as well as those with different instructors and formats.

2

First category: ideal class

One of the best courses I have taken so far as a college student was my Shakespeare class. The professor who taught it had a great sense of humor and was liberal in terms of what she allowed in her classroom — for example, excerpts from controversial film adaptations and virtually any discussion, relevant or irrelevant. The students in the class — English majors and non-English majors, those who were interested in the plays as theater and those who preferred to study them as literature — shared an enthusiasm for Shakespeare, and they were eager to engage in lively discussions. This class gave us a thorough knowledge of Shakespeare's plays (tragedies, histories, comedies) as well as an understanding of his life. We also developed our analytical skills through our discussions of the plays and films as well as through special projects — for example, a character profile presentation and an abstract art presentation relating a work of art to one of the plays. This class was an ideal learning environment not only because of the wealth of material we were exposed to but also because of the respect with which our professor treated us: we were her colleagues, and she was as willing to learn from us as we were to learn from her.

3

Second category: worthless class

In contrast to this ideal class, one of the most worthless courses I have taken in college was Movement Education. As an education major, I expected to like this class, and several other

4

students who had taken it told me it was both easy and enjoyable. The class consisted of playing children's games and learning what made certain activities appropriate and inappropriate for children of various ages. The only requirement for this class was that we had to write note cards explaining how to play each game so that we could use them for reference in our future teaching experiences. Unfortunately, I never really enjoyed the games we played, and I have long since discarded my note cards and forgotten how to play the games — or even what they were.

Third category: disappointing class

Although I looked forward to taking Introduction to Astronomy, I was very disappointed in this class. I had hoped to satisfy my curiosity about the universe outside our solar system, but the instructor devoted most of the semester to a detailed study of the Earth and the other bodies in our own solar system. In addition, a large part of our work included charting orbits and processing distance equations — work that I found both difficult and boring. Furthermore, we spent hardly any class time learning how to use a telescope and how to locate objects in the sky. In short, I gained little information from the class, learning only how to solve equations I would never confront again and how to chart orbits that had already been charted.

5

Fourth category: unexpectedly valuable class

In direct contrast to my astronomy class, a religion class called Paul and the Early Church was much more rewarding than I had anticipated. Having attended Catholic school for thirteen years, I assumed this course would offer little that was new to me. However, because the class took a historical approach to studying Paul's biblical texts, I found that I learned more about Christianity than I had in all my previous religion classes. We learned about the historical validity of Paul and other texts in the Bible and how they were derived from various sources and passed orally through several generations before being written down and translated into different languages. We approached the texts from a linguistic perspective, exploring the significance of certain words and learning how various meanings can be derived from different translations of the same passage. This class was unlike any of my other religion classes in that it encouraged me to study the texts objectively, leaving me with a new and valuable understanding of material I had been exposed to for most of my life.

6

Conclusion

Although each student's learning experience in college will be different — because every student has a different learning style, is

7

Summary of four categories   interested in different subjects, and takes courses at different schools taught by different professors — all college students' experiences are similar in one respect. All students will encounter the same kinds

Thesis statement   of courses: those that are ideal, those that are worthless, those that they learn little from despite their interest in the subject, and those that they learn from and become engaged in despite their low

Restatement of thesis   expectations. Understanding that these categories exist is important because it gives students the freedom and courage to try new things, as college students did years ago. After all, even if one course is a disappointment, another may be more interesting — or even exciting. For this reason, college students should not be discouraged by a course they do not like; the best classes are almost certainly still in their future.

Works-cited list (begins new page)

Work Cited

Wieseltier, Leon. "Perhaps Culture Is Now the Counterculture: A Defense of the Humanities." *New Republic.* 28 May 2013. newrepublic .com/article/113299/leon-wieseltier-commencement-speech -brandeis-university-2013

Points for Special Attention

Working with Sources

Josie's teacher asked students to cite Leon Wieseltier's "Perhaps Culture Is Now the Counterculture," which they had just discussed, somewhere in their essays. Josie knew that the passage she chose to quote or paraphrase would have to be directly relevant to her own essay's subject, so she knew it would have to focus on academic (rather than economic or social) issues. When she read Wieseltier's opening comments on the need for exposure to a wide variety of subjects, she knew she had found something that could give her essay a more global, less personal focus. For this reason, she decided to refer to Wieseltier in her essay's first paragraph. (Note that she includes parenthetical documentation and a work-cited page.)

Thesis and Support

Josie's purpose in writing this essay was to communicate to her professor and the other students in her education class what she had learned from the classes she had taken so far in college, and both the thesis she states in paragraph 2 and the restatement of this thesis in her conclusion make this point clear: what she has learned is to take a wide variety of courses. Knowing that few, if any, students in her class would have taken any of the courses she took, Josie realized she had to provide a lot of detail to show what these classes taught her.

Organization

As she reviewed the various courses she had taken and assessed their strengths and weaknesses, Josie saw a classification scheme emerging. As soon as she noticed it, she organized her material into four categories. Rather than discuss the four kinds of classes from best to worst or from worst to best, Josie decided to present them as two opposing pairs: ideal class and worthless class, and surprisingly disappointing class and unexpectedly worthwhile class. In paragraph 2, Josie lists the four categories she plans to discuss in her essay and gives readers an overview of these categories to help prepare them for her thesis.

Transitions between Categories

Josie uses clear topic sentences to move readers from one category to the next and to indicate the relationship of each category to another.

> One of the best courses I have taken so far as a college student was my Shakespeare class. (3)

> In contrast to this ideal class, one of the most worthless courses I have taken in college was Movement Education. (4)

> Although I looked forward to taking Introduction to Astronomy, I was very disappointed in this class. (5)

> In direct contrast to my astronomy class, a religion class called Paul and the Early Church was much more rewarding than I had anticipated. (6)

These four sentences distinguish the four categories from one another and also help to communicate Josie's direction and emphasis.

Focus on Revision

An earlier draft of Josie's essay, which she discussed with her instructor in a conference, did not include very specific topic sentences. Instead, the sentences were vague and unfocused:

> One class I took in college was a Shakespeare course.

> Another class I took was Movement Education.

> I looked forward to taking Introduction to Astronomy.

> My experience with a religion class was very different.

Although her essay's second paragraph listed the categories and explained how they differed, Josie's instructor advised her to revise her topic sentences so that it would be clear which category she was discussing in each body paragraph. Josie took his advice and revised these topic sentences. After reading her next draft, she felt confident that her categories—listed in paragraph 2 and repeated in her topic sentences and in her conclusion—were clear and distinct.

Even after making these revisions, however, Josie felt her essay needed some additional fine-tuning. For example, in her final draft, she planned to add some material to paragraphs 4 and 5. At first, because she had dismissed Movement Education as completely worthless and Introduction to Astronomy as disappointing, Josie felt she did not have to say much about them. When she reread her essay, however, she realized she needed to explain the shortcomings of the two classes more fully so that her readers would understand why these classes had little value for her.

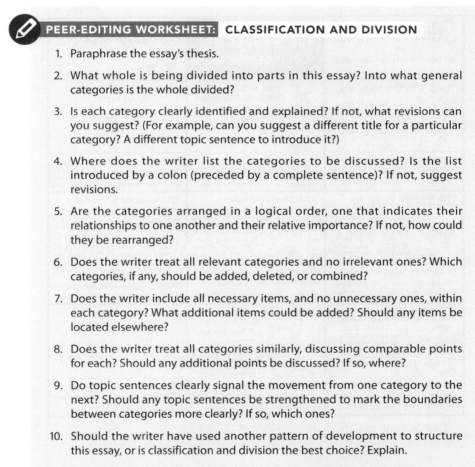

PEER-EDITING WORKSHEET: **CLASSIFICATION AND DIVISION**

1. Paraphrase the essay's thesis.

2. What whole is being divided into parts in this essay? Into what general categories is the whole divided?

3. Is each category clearly identified and explained? If not, what revisions can you suggest? (For example, can you suggest a different title for a particular category? A different topic sentence to introduce it?)

4. Where does the writer list the categories to be discussed? Is the list introduced by a colon (preceded by a complete sentence)? If not, suggest revisions.

5. Are the categories arranged in a logical order, one that indicates their relationships to one another and their relative importance? If not, how could they be rearranged?

6. Does the writer treat all relevant categories and no irrelevant ones? Which categories, if any, should be added, deleted, or combined?

7. Does the writer include all necessary items, and no unnecessary ones, within each category? What additional items could be added? Should any items be located elsewhere?

8. Does the writer treat all categories similarly, discussing comparable points for each? Should any additional points be discussed? If so, where?

9. Do topic sentences clearly signal the movement from one category to the next? Should any topic sentences be strengthened to mark the boundaries between categories more clearly? If so, which ones?

10. Should the writer have used another pattern of development to structure this essay, or is classification and division the best choice? Explain.

11. Should the writer have added one or more sources — or a visual?

Each of the following selections is developed by means of classification and division. In some cases, the pattern is used to explain ideas; in others, it is used to persuade the reader. The first selection, a visual text, is followed by questions designed to illustrate how classification and division can operate in visual form.

MATT GROENING

The 9 Types of College Teachers (Cartoon)

• • • •

Reading Images

1. In this image, Matt Groening identifies nine types of college teachers. What principles of classification does the image use to determine these categories? Do any of these categories overlap, or are they all distinct?
2. Are there types of teachers you believe are missing from Groening's system of classification? What does the visual gain or lose by focusing primarily on negative caricatures?
3. How do the illustrations add to (or take away from) the categories represented here? What does the drawing style say about the overall point of view of this classification?

Journal Entry

Identify a few categories of *good* college teachers, and write a few sentences explaining each category.

Thematic Connections

- "I'm Your Teacher, Not Your Internet-Service Provider" (page 402)
- "The Dog Ate My Tablet, and Other Tales of Woe" (page 450)

MINDY KALING

Flick Chicks: A Guide to Women in the Movies

Comedian, actor, writer, and producer Mindy Kaling was born in 1979 in Cambridge, Massachusetts. Her parents, immigrants from India, moved to the United States the year she was born. Kaling graduated from Dartmouth College, where she worked on the college's humor magazine and participated in improvisational comedy. As a sophomore, she interned for NBC's *Late Night With Conan O'Brien*. After graduation, she moved to Brooklyn, New York, where she worked behind the scenes on television shows while also working on her writing and stand-up comedy. Her major break came in 2005 when she joined the cast of the NBC sitcom *The Office*, where she eventually became a writer, director, and executive producer. From 2012 to 2017, she created and starred in her own show, *The Mindy Project*. Kaling has also written several books, including *Is Everyone Hanging Out without Me? (and Other Concerns)* (2011) and *Why Not Me?* (2015).

Background on women in television As was the case in the Hollywood film industry, women have long been underrepresented in television's directorial, production, and writing positions. Still, there were some early pioneers. For example, in 1948, Lucille Ball and Desi Arnez created Desilu Productions and produced *I Love Lucy*, which was the first television show that included a woman, Madelyn Pugh, among its head writers. In the 1960s, Ball took sole ownership of the Desilu studio as it produced successful programs like *Mission: Impossible* and *Star Trek*. Later in her career, movie star Ida Lupino moved behind the television camera to direct a variety of shows in the 1960s and 1970s, such as *The Twilight Zone*, *Bewitched*, and *The Fugitive*. In the 1970s and 1980s, female directors and producers became more common — and more respected. For example, Joan Darling, who directed episodes of *M*A*S*H*, *Taxi*, and *Magnum, P.I.*, became the first woman to win an Emmy award for directing in 1976 for her work on the *Mary Tyler Moore Show*. This behind-the-scenes segment of the television industry still remains overwhelmingly male. In recent years, however, several women have risen to prominence as writers, directors, and producers including Tina Fey, Lena Dunham, Amy Poehler, and Mindy Kaling.

A few years ago, I sat down for a meeting with some executives at a movie studio that I will call Thinkscope Visioncloud. Thinkscope Visioncloud had put out several of my favorite movies, and they wanted to see if I had any feature ideas. I was very excited. I have a great job writing for *The Office*, but, really, all television writers do is dream of one day writing movies. I'll put it this way: At the Oscars the most famous person in the room is, like, Angelina Jolie. At the Emmys the huge exciting celebrity is Bethenny Frankel. You get what I mean. It's snobby and grossly aspirational, but it's true.

The junior executives' office at Thinkscope Visioncloud was nicer than any room within a fifty-mile radius of the *Office* studio. After I finished pitching one of my ideas for a low-budget romantic comedy, I was met with silence. One of the execs sheepishly looked at the other execs. He finally said, "Yeah, but we're really trying to focus on movies about board games. People really seem to respond to those."

For the rest of the meeting, we talked about whether there was any poten-   3
tial in a movie called *Yahtzee!* I made some polite suggestions and left.

I am always surprised at what movie   4
studios think people will want to see. I'm even more surprised at how often they are correct. Based on what I've learned from my time in Hollywood, the following titles are my best guess as to what may soon be coming to a theater near you:

> "I am always surprised at what movie studios think people will want to see."

Bananagrams 3D

Apples to Apples 4D (The audience is pummelled with apples at the end of the movie.)

Crest Whitestrips

Sharks vs. Volcanoes

King Tut vs. King Kong

Streptococcus vs. Candidiasis (Strep Throat vs. Yeast Infection)

The Do-Over

The Switcheroo

Street Smart

Street Stupid ("Street Smart" sequel)

Fat Astronaut

The Untitled Liam Neeson Vendetta Project

Human Quilt (horror movie)

The Cute Bear from Those Toilet-Paper Ads Movie

Those movies all sound great to me, and, incidentally, I am prepared to   5
write any of them, if there is interest. But what I'd really like to write is a romantic comedy. This is my favorite kind of movie. I feel almost embarrassed revealing this, because the genre has been so degraded in the past twenty years that saying you like romantic comedies is essentially an admission of mild stupidity. But that has not stopped me from enjoying them.

I like watching people fall in love onscreen so much that I can suspend   6
my disbelief in the contrived situations that occur only in the heightened world of romantic comedies. I have come to enjoy the moment when the male lead, say, slips and falls right on top of the expensive wedding cake. I actually feel robbed when the female lead's dress doesn't get torn open at a baseball game while the JumboTron camera is on her. I regard romantic comedies as a subgenre of sci-fi, in which the world operates according to different rules than my regular human world. For me, there is no difference between Ripley from *Alien* and any Katherine Heigl character. They are equally implausible. They're all participating in a similar level of fakey razzle-dazzle, and I enjoy every second of it.

It makes sense, then, that in the romantic-comedy world there are many 7
specimens of women who — like Vulcans or Mothra — do not exist in real life.
Here are some examples:

The Klutz

When a beautiful actress is cast in a movie, executives rack their brains to 8
find some kind of flaw in the character she plays that will still allow her to be
palatable. She can't be overweight or not perfect-looking, because who would
pay to see that? A female who is not one hundred per cent perfect-looking in
every way? You might as well film a dead squid decaying on a beach somewhere
for two hours.

So they make her a Klutz. 9

The hundred-percent-perfect-looking female is perfect in every way except 10
that she constantly bonks her head on things. She trips and falls and spills
soup on her affable date (Josh Lucas. Is that his name? I know it's two first
names. Josh George? Brad Mike? Fred Tom? Yes, it's Fred Tom). The Klutz
clangs into stop signs while riding her bike and knocks over giant displays of
fine china in department stores. Despite being five feet nine and weighing a
hundred and ten pounds, she is basically like a drunk buffalo who has never
been a part of human society. But Fred Tom loves her anyway.

The Ethereal Weirdo

The smart and funny writer Nathan Rabin coined the term Manic Pixie 11
Dream Girl to describe this archetype after seeing Kirsten Dunst in the movie
"Elizabethtown." This girl can't be pinned down and may or may not show up
when you make concrete plans with her. She wears gauzy blouses and braids.
She likes to dance in the rain and she weeps uncontrollably if she sees a sign for
a missing dog or cat. She might spin a globe, place her finger on a random
spot, and decide to move there. The Ethereal Weirdo appears a lot in movies,
but nowhere else. If she were from real life, people would think she was a homeless woman and would cross the street to avoid her. But she is essential to the
male fantasy that even if a guy is boring he deserves a woman who will find him
fascinating and perk up his dreary life by forcing him to go skinny-dipping in a
stranger's pool.

The Woman Who Is Obsessed with Her Career and Is No Fun at All

I regularly work sixteen hours a day. Yet, like most people I know who are 12
similarly busy, I'm a pleasant, pretty normal person. But that's not how working women are depicted in movies. I'm not always barking orders into my
hands-free phone device and yelling, "I have no time for this!" Often, a script
calls for this uptight career woman to "relearn" how to seduce a man, and she
has to do all sorts of crazy degrading crap, like eat a hot dog in a sexy way or
something. And since when does holding a job necessitate that a woman pull
her hair back in a severe, tight bun? Do screenwriters think that loose hair
makes it hard to concentrate?

The Forty-Two-Year-Old Mother of the Thirty-Year-Old Male Lead

If you think about the backstory of a typical mother character in a   13
romantic comedy, you realize this: when "Mom" was an adolescent, the very
week she started to menstruate she was impregnated with a baby who would
grow up to be the movie's likable brown-haired leading man. I am fascinated
by Mom's sordid early life. I would rather see this movie than the one I bought
a ticket for.

I am so brainwashed by the young-mom phenomenon that when I saw the   14
poster for *The Proposal* I wondered for a second if the proposal in the movie was
Ryan Reynolds' suggesting that he send his mother, Sandra Bullock, to an
old-age home.

The Sassy Best Friend

You know that really hilarious and horny best friend who is always asking   15
about your relationship and has nothing really going on in her own life? She
always wants to meet you in coffee shops or wants to go to Bloomingdale's to
sample perfumes? She runs a chic dildo store in the West Village? Nope? O.K.,
that's this person.

The Skinny Woman Who Is Beautiful and Toned but Also Gluttonous and Disgusting

Again, I am more than willing to suspend my disbelief for good set decora-   16
tion alone. One pristine kitchen from a Nancy Meyers movie like *It's Complicated*
compensates for five scenes of Diane Keaton being caught half naked in a topi-
ary. But I can't suspend disbelief enough, for instance, if the gorgeous and
skinny heroine is also a ravenous pig when it comes to food. And everyone in
the movie — her parents, her friends, her boss — are all complicit in this huge
lie. They constantly tell her to stop eating. And this actress, this poor skinny
actress who obviously lost weight to play the likable lead character, has to say
things like "Shut up, you guys! I love cheesecake! If I want to eat an entire
cheesecake, I will!" If you look closely, you can see this woman's ribs through
the dress she's wearing — that's how skinny she is, this cheesecake-loving cow.

The Woman Who Works in an Art Gallery

How many freakin' art galleries are out there? Are people buying visual art   17
on a daily basis? This posh/smart/classy profession is a favorite in movies. It's in
the same realm as kindergarten teacher or children's-book illustrator in terms
of accessibility: guys don't really get it, but it is likable and nonthreatening.

Art Gallery Woman: "Dust off the Warhol. You know, that Campbell's   18
Soup one in the crazy color! We have an important buyer coming into town,
and this is a really big deal for my career. I have no time for this!"

The Gallery Worker character is the rare female movie archetype that has a   19
male counterpart. Whenever you meet a handsome, charming, successful man
in a romantic comedy, the heroine's friend always says the same thing: "He's
really successful. He's" — *say it with me* — "an architect!"

There are, like, nine people in the entire world who are architects, and one   20
of them is my dad. None of them look like Patrick Dempsey.

· · ·

Comprehension

1. This essay classifies "flick chicks." What exactly is a "flick chick"?
2. In paragraph 4, Kaling says, "I am always surprised at what movie studios think people would like to see." How does this statement prepare readers for the categories she names?
3. Why does Kaling like romantic comedies? What does she mean when she says that she sees them as "a subgenre of sci-fi" (6)? Is that a serious observation? Explain.
4. Can you think of any additional categories that Kaling doesn't discuss?

Purpose and Audience

1. Does Kaling simply want to provide an overview of the state of women in movies, or does she want to change her audience's mind or convince readers to take some kind of action? Explain.
2. What does Kaling expect to accomplish in paragraph 4 by presenting a list of movie titles? How do you react to this list?
3. What point does Kaling make about the difference between "flick chicks" and women in real life?
4. In one sentence, state this essay's thesis. Does the essay include an explicit thesis statement? If so, where? If not, does it need one?

Style and Structure

1. Do you think the term *flick chicks* has a positive, a negative, or a neutral connotation? Explain.
2. Kaling introduces her classification in paragraph 7 with "Here are some examples." What purpose do the paragraphs that precede the actual classification serve?
3. Does Kaling cover too many (or too few) categories? Do any of her categories overlap? Explain.
4. **Vocabulary Project.** One of Kaling's categories is "The Klutz." What is a klutz? What is the origin of this word? Based on information provided in paragraph 10, write a one-sentence formal definition of the word *klutz*.
5. This essay is written in the first person and is generally quite informal. Does this informality strengthen or undercut Kaling's point?
6. Does Kaling treat each category in the same way, devoting the same amount of attention to each? If not, why not?
7. Does Kaling introduce her categories in any particular order? What, if anything, determines how she arranges them?

Journal Entry

"Flick chicks" is a play on the expression "chick flicks." Do you see either (or both) of these terms as sexist? Why or why not?

Writing Workshop

1. **Working with Sources.** Research the top American films of one decade, or one year, of the twentieth century. Choose one film to watch, and then write a classification essay in which you consider the kinds of stereotypes (of gender, race, ethnicity, sexual orientation, and so on) portrayed in this film. Be sure to acknowledge the sources you use (the film itself as well as critical commentary) and to include a works-cited page. (See Chapter 18 for information on MLA documentation.)

2. Write a classification essay that explores the different categories of *men* depicted in contemporary films or television shows. Give each category a distinctive name, and use several examples to illustrate each category.

3. This essay was written in 2011. Write an update, creating four or five new categories and discussing several examples of how women are portrayed in twenty-first-century films.

Combining the Patterns

Where in this essay does Kaling use **exemplification**? Where does she use **description**? What other patterns of development can you identify in this essay?

Thematic Connections

- "The Myth of the Latin Woman: I Just Met a Girl Named Maria" (page 224)
- "'Girl'" (page 251)
- "The Rule" (page 492)
- "I Want a Wife" (page 494)

CAROLYN FOSTER SEGAL

The Dog Ate My Tablet, and Other Tales of Woe

Carolyn Foster Segal (b. 1950) is a professor emeritus of English at Cedar Crest College and currently teaches at Muhlenberg College in Allentown, Pennsylvania. Segal has published poetry, fiction, and essays in a number of publications, including *Inside Higher Ed*, *Salon*, the *Huffington Post*, and the *Chronicle of Higher Education*, where the following essay originally appeared. She sums up her ideas about writing as follows: "Writing — and it does not matter if it is writing about a feature of the landscape, an aspect of human nature, or a work of literature — begins with observation. The other parts are curiosity, imagination, and patience." She has received hundreds of responses from other instructors corroborating the experiences she describes here.

Background on academic integrity and honor codes Although making up an excuse for being unprepared for class may seem like a minor infraction, it may still be considered a breach of academic integrity. At many colleges, honor codes define academic integrity and set penalties for those who violate its rules. The concept of college honor codes in the United States goes back to one developed by students at the University of Virginia in 1840, but reports of widespread cheating on college campuses in the early 1990s brought renewed interest in such codes. (Surveys show that more than three-quarters of college students have cheated at least once during their schooling, and an even greater number see cheating as the norm among successful students.) According to one 2017 survey, for example, more than 80 percent of college students acknowledged cheating in some form. Significant percentages of students admitted to purchasing research papers online, using smartphones to cheat in class, and paying services to take their online classes for them. Administrators and professors have worked to stem such practices with online tools such as Turnitin.com, a widely used plagiarism detection system, but colleges have also strived to cultivate a culture of academic honesty. For example, the International Center for Academic Integrity (established in 1992) helps colleges and universities find ways to promote "honesty, trust, fairness, respect, and responsibility" among students and faculty members. Its original twenty-five-member group has grown to include more than two hundred institutions, and many other colleges have adopted its goals as well. The main focus of most honor codes is on discouraging plagiarism — copying the work of others and presenting the work of others as one's own — and various forms of cheating on tests. The International Center for Academic Integrity sees promoting individual honesty as the fundamental issue underlying all of these concerns.

Taped to the door of my office is a cartoon that features a cat explaining to 1
his feline teacher, "The dog ate my homework." It is intended as a gently humorous reminder to my students that I will not accept excuses for late work, and it,

like the lengthy warning on my syllabus, has had absolutely no effect. With a show of energy and creativity that would be admirable if applied to the (missing) assignments in question, my students persist, week after week, semester after semester, year after year, in offering excuses about why their work is not ready. Those reasons fall into several broad categories: the family, the best friend, the evils of dorm life, the evils of technology, and the totally bizarre.

The Family

The death of the grandfather/grandmother is, of course, the grandmother of all excuses. What heartless teacher would dare to question a student's grief or veracity? What heartless student would lie, wishing death on a revered family member, just to avoid a deadline? Creative students may win extra extensions (and days off) with a little careful planning and fuller plot development, as in the sequence of "My grandfather/grandmother is sick"; "Now my grandfather/grandmother is in the hospital"; and finally, "We could all see it coming—my grandfather/grandmother is dead."

> "Those reasons fall into several broad categories: the family, the best friend, the evils of dorm life, the evils of technology, and the totally bizarre."

2

Another favorite excuse is "the family emergency," which (always) goes like this: "There was an emergency at home, and I had to help my family." It's a lovely sentiment, one that conjures up images of Louisa May Alcott's* little women rushing off with baskets of food and copies of *Pilgrim's Progress,*** but I do not understand why anyone would turn to my most irresponsible students in times of trouble.

3

The Best Friend

This heartwarming concern for others extends beyond the family to friends, as in, "My best friend was up all night and I had to (a) stay up with her in the dorm, (b) drive her to the hospital, or (c) drive to her college because (1) her boyfriend broke up with her, (2) she was throwing up blood [no one catches a cold anymore; everyone throws up blood], or (3) her grandfather/grandmother died."

4

At one private university where I worked as an adjunct, I heard an interesting spin that incorporated the motifs of both best friend and dead relative: "My best friend's mother killed herself." One has to admire the cleverness here: A mysterious woman in the prime of her life has allegedly committed suicide, and no professor can prove otherwise! And I admit I was moved, until finally I had to point out to my students that it was amazing how the simple act of my assigning a topic for a paper seemed to drive large numbers of otherwise happy

5

---

* Eds. note—Nineteenth-century sentimental novelist, author of *Little Women*.
** Eds. note—Eighteenth-century allegory by John Bunyan describing a Christian's journey from the City of Destruction to the Celestial City.

and healthy middle-aged women to their deaths. I was careful to make that point during an off week, during which no deaths were reported.

The Evils of Dorm Life

These stories are usually fairly predictable; almost always feature the evil 6
roommate or hallmate, with my student in the role of the innocent victim; and
can be summed up as follows: My roommate, who is a horrible person, likes to
party, and I, who am a good person, cannot concentrate on my work when he
or she is partying. Variations include stories about the two people next door
who were running around and crying loudly last night because (a) one of them
had boyfriend/girlfriend problems; (b) one of them was throwing up blood; or
(c) someone, somewhere, died. A friend of mine in graduate school had a
student who claimed that his roommate attacked him with a hammer. That, in
fact, was a true story; it came out in court when the bad roommate was tried
for killing his grandfather.

The Evils of Technology

The computer age has revolutionized the student story, inspiring almost 7
as many new excuses as it has Internet businesses. Here are just a few electronically enhanced explanations:

- The computer wouldn't let me save my work.
- The printer wouldn't print.
- The printer wouldn't print this file.
- The printer wouldn't give me time to proofread.
- The printer made a black line run through all my words, and I know you
  can't read this, but do you still want it, or wait, here, take my tablet. File
  name? I don't know what you mean.
- I swear I attached it.
- It's my roommate's computer, and she usually helps me, but she had to
  go to the hospital because she was throwing up blood.
- I did write to the listserv, but all my messages came back to me.
- I just found out that all my other listserv messages came up under a
  diferent name. I just want you to know that its really me who wrote all
  those messages, you can tel which ones our mine because I didnt use the
  spelcheck! But it was yours truely :) Anyway, just in case you missed those
  messages or dont belief its my writting. I'll repeat what I sad: I thought
  the last movie we watched in clas was borring.

The Totally Bizarre

I call the first story "The Pennsylvania Chain Saw Episode." A commuter 8
student called to explain why she had missed my morning class. She had gotten up early so that she would be wide awake for class. Having a bit of extra
time, she walked outside to see her neighbor, who was cutting some wood. She
called out to him, and he waved back to her with the saw. Wouldn't you know
it, the safety catch wasn't on or was broken, and the blade flew right out of the

saw and across his lawn and over her fence and across her yard and severed a tendon in her right hand. So she was calling me from the hospital, where she was waiting for surgery. Luckily, she reassured me, she had remembered to bring her paper and a stamped envelope (in a plastic bag, to avoid bloodstains) along with her in the ambulance, and a nurse was mailing everything to me even as we spoke.

That wasn't her first absence. In fact, this student had missed most of the   9
class meetings, and I had already recommended that she withdraw from the course. Now I suggested again that it might be best if she dropped the class. I didn't harp on the absences (what if even some of this story were true?). I did mention that she would need time to recuperate and that making up so much missed work might be difficult. "Oh, no," she said, "I can't drop this course. I had been planning to go on to medical school and become a surgeon, but since I won't be able to operate because of my accident, I'll have to major in English, and this course is more important than ever to me." She did come to the next class, wearing—as evidence of her recent trauma—a bedraggled Ace bandage on her left hand.

You may be thinking that nothing could top that excuse, but in fact I have   10
one more story, provided by the same student, who sent me a letter to explain why her final assignment would be late. While recuperating from her surgery, she had begun corresponding on the Internet with a man who lived in Germany. After a one-week, whirlwind Web romance, they had agreed to meet in Rome, to rendezvous (her phrase) at the papal Easter Mass. Regrettably, the time of her flight made it impossible for her to attend class, but she trusted that I—just this once—would accept late work if the pope wrote a note.

. . .

Comprehension

1. What exactly is Segal classifying in this essay?
2. In paragraph 3, Segal says, "I do not understand why anyone would turn to my most irresponsible students in times of trouble." Do you see this comment as fair? Is she making fun of her students?
3. Which of the excuses Segal discusses do you see as valid? Which do you see as just excuses? Why?
4. Do you see Segal as rigid and unsympathetic, or do you think her frustration is justified? Do you think her students are irresponsible procrastinators or simply overworked?
5. What lessons do you think Segal would like her students to learn from her? Would reading this essay teach them what she wants them to learn?

Purpose and Audience

1. This essay was originally published in the *Chronicle of Higher Education*, a periodical for college teachers and administrators. How do you think these readers responded to the essay? Why? How do you respond?

2. Do you think Segal's purpose here is to entertain, to let off steam, to warn, to criticize, to change students' habits — or something else? Explain.

3. In paragraph 7, Segal lists some specific excuses in the "evils of technology" category, paraphrasing students' remarks and even imitating their grammar and style. Why does she do this? Considering her likely audience, is this an effective strategy?

Style and Structure

1. In paragraph 1, Segal lists the five categories she plans to discuss. Is this list necessary? Why or why not?

2. Are Segal's categories mutually exclusive, or do they overlap? Could she combine any categories? Can you think of any categories she does not include?

3. What determines the order in which Segal introduces her categories? Is this order logical, or should she present her categories in a different order?

4. Does Segal discuss comparable points for each category? What points, if any, need to be added?

5. Segal frequently uses **sarcasm** in this essay. Give some examples. Given her intended audience, do you think this tone is appropriate? How do you react to her sarcasm?

6. **Vocabulary Project.** Every profession has its own unique **jargon**. What words and expressions in this essay characterize the writer as a college professor?

7. Throughout her essay, Segal returns again and again to two excuses: "my grandfather/grandmother died" and "throwing up blood." Locate different versions of these excuses in the essay. Why do you think she singles out these two excuses?

8. Although Segal deals with a serious academic problem, she includes many expressions — such as "Wouldn't you know it" (8) — that give her essay an informal tone. Identify some other examples. What is your reaction to the essay's casual, offhand tone?

9. Review the category Segal calls "The Evils of Technology." Can you add to (and update) her list? Can you create subcategories?

Journal Entry

Do you think this essay is funny? Explain your reaction.

Writing Workshop

1. **Working with Sources.** Write an email to Segal explaining why your English paper will be late, presenting several different kinds of original excuses for your paper's lateness. Before you present your own superior excuses, be sure to acknowledge the inadequacies of the excuses Segal lists, quoting a few and including parenthetical documentation and a works-cited page. (See Chapter 18 for information about MLA documentation.)

2. Write an essay identifying four or five categories of legitimate excuses for handing in work late. If you like, you can use narrative examples from your own life as a student to explain each category.
3. Using a humorous (or even sarcastic) tone, write an essay identifying several different categories of teachers in terms of their shortcomings — for instance, teachers who do not cover the assigned work or teachers who do not grade papers in a timely fashion. Be sure to give specific examples of teachers in each category.

Combining the Patterns

In paragraphs 8 through 10, Segal uses **narration** to tell two stories. What do these stories add to her essay? Do you think she should have added more stories like these to her essay? If so, where?

Thematic Connections

* "Cutting and Pasting: A Senior Thesis by (Insert Name)" (page 17)
* "The Price of Silence" (page 78)
* "I'm Your Teacher, Not Your Internet-Service Provider" (page 402)
* "The Ways We Lie" (page 463)

AMY TAN

Mother Tongue

Amy Tan was born in 1952 in Oakland, California, the daughter of recent Chinese immigrants. When she began to write fiction, she started to explore the contradictions she faced as a Chinese American who was also the daughter of immigrant parents. In 1989, she published *The Joy Luck Club*, a best-selling novel about four immigrant Chinese women and their American-born daughters. Her most recent books are the novels *Saving Fish from Drowning* (2005), *Rules for Virgins* (2011), *The Valley of Amazement* (2013), and *The Memory of Desire* (2017). Her memoir, *Where the Past Begins: A Writer's Memoir*, was published in 2017. In the following 1990 essay, Tan considers her mother's heavily Chinese-influenced English, as well as the different "Englishes" she herself uses, especially in communicating with her mother. She then discusses the potential limitations of growing up with immigrant parents who do not speak fluent English.

Background on Asian Americans and standardized tests The children of Asian immigrants tend to be highly assimilated and are often outstanding students, in part because their parents expect them to work hard and do well. Most who were born in the United States speak and read English fluently, yet on standardized tests, they have generally scored higher in math than in English. For example, the average SAT scores nationally in 2018 were 531 in math and 536 in evidence-based reading and writing. Asian-American students had average scores of 635 in math and 588 in evidence-based reading and writing. (The verbal scores represent an improvement over earlier years, in which Asian-American students generally scored lower than average in the verbal sections of the SAT.) In some cases, as Tan suggests, the perception that Asian-American students have greater skill in math than in reading and writing, based on average standardized test scores, may lead teachers to discourage these students from pursuing degrees in fields outside of math and science.

1   I am not a scholar of English or literature. I cannot give you much more than personal opinions on the English language and its variations in this country or others.

2   I am a writer. And by that definition, I am someone who has always loved language. I am fascinated by language in daily life. I spend a great deal of my time thinking about the power of language — the way it can evoke an emotion, a visual image, a complex idea, or a simple truth. Language is the tool of my trade. And I use them all — all the Englishes I grew up with.

3   Recently, I was made keenly aware of the different Englishes I do use. I was giving a talk to a large group of people, the same talk I had already given to half a dozen other groups. The nature of the talk was about my writing, my life, and my book, *The Joy Luck Club*. The talk was going along well enough, until I remembered one major difference that made the whole talk sound wrong. My

mother was in the room. And it was perhaps the first time she had heard me give a lengthy speech, using the kind of English I have never used with her. I was saying things like, "The intersection of memory upon imagination" and "There is an aspect of my fiction that relates to thus-and-thus"—a speech filled with carefully wrought grammatical phrases, burdened, it suddenly seemed to me, with nominalized forms, past perfect tenses, conditional phrases, all the forms of standard English that I had learned in school and through books, the forms of English I did not use at home with my mother.

Just last week, I was walking down the street with my mother, and I again found myself conscious of the English I was using, and the English I do use with her. We were talking about the price of new and used furniture and I heard myself saying this: "Not waste money that way." My husband was with us as well, and he didn't notice any switch in my English. And then I realized why. It's because over the twenty years we've been together I've often used that same kind of English with him, and sometimes he even uses it with me. It has become our language of intimacy, a different sort of English that relates to family talk, the language I grew up with.   4

So you'll have some idea of what this family talk I heard sounds like, I'll quote what my mother said during a recent conversation which I videotaped and then transcribed. During this conversation my mother was talking about a political gangster in Shanghai who had the same last name as her family's, Du, and how the gangster in his early years wanted to be adopted by her family, which was rich by comparison. Later, the gangster became more powerful, far richer than my mother's family, and one day showed up at my mother's wedding to pay his respects. Here's what she said in part: 5

"Du Yusong having business like fruit stand. Like off the street kind. He is Du like Du Zong—but not Tsung-ming Island people. The local people call putong, the river east side, he belong to that side local people. The man want to ask Du Zong father take him in like become own family. Du Zong father wasn't looking down on him, but didn't take seriously, until that man big like become a mafia. Now important person very hard to inviting him. Chinese way, come only to show respect, don't stay for dinner. Respect for making big celebration, he shows up. Mean gives lots of respect. Chinese custom. Chinese social life that way. If too important won't have to stay too long. He come to my wedding. I didn't see. I heard it. I gone to boy's side, they have YMCA dinner. Chinese age I was nineteen."   6

You should know that my mother's expressive command of English belies how much she actually understands. She reads the *Forbes* report, listens to *Wall Street Week*, converses daily with her stockbroker, reads all of Shirley MacLaine's books with ease—all kinds of things I can't begin to understand. Yet some of my friends tell me they understand 50 percent of what my mother says. Some say they understand 80 to 90 percent. Some say they understand none of it, as if she were speaking pure Chinese. But to me, my mother's English is perfectly clear, perfectly natural. It's my mother's tongue. Her language, as I hear it, is vivid, direct, full of observation and imagery. This was the language that helped shape the way I saw things, expressed things, made sense of the world.   7

Lately, I've been giving more thought to the kind of English my mother   8
speaks. Like others, I have described it to people as "broken" or "fractured"
English. But I wince when I say that. It has always bothered me that I can think
of no way to describe it other than "broken," as if it were damaged and needed
to be fixed, as if it lacked a certain wholeness and soundness. I've heard other
terms used, "limited English," for example. But they seem just as bad, as if
everything is limited, including people's perceptions of the limited English
speaker.

I know this for a fact, because when I was growing up, my mother's "lim-   9
ited" English limited *my* perception of her. I was ashamed of her English. I
believed that her English reflected the quality of what she had to say. That is,
because she expressed them imperfectly her thoughts were imperfect. And I
had plenty of empirical evidence to support me: the fact that people in department stores, at banks, and at restaurants did not take her seriously, did not
give her good service, pretended not to understand her, or even acted as if they
did not hear her.

My mother has long realized the limitations of her English as well. When I   10
was fifteen, she used to have me call people on the phone to pretend I was she.
In this guise, I was forced to ask for information or even complain and yell at
people who had been rude to her. One time it was a call to her stockbroker in
New York. She had cashed out her small portfolio and it just so happened we
were going to go to New York the next week, our very first trip outside
California. I had to get on the phone and say in an adolescent voice that was
not very convincing, "This is Mrs. Tan."

And my mother was standing in the back whispering loudly, "Why he   11
don't send me check, already two weeks late. So mad he lie to me, losing me
money."

And then I said in perfect English, "Yes, I'm getting rather concerned. You   12
had agreed to send the check two weeks ago, but it hasn't arrived."

Then she began to talk more loudly. "What he want, I come to New York   13
tell him front of his boss, you cheating me?" And I was trying to calm her down,
make her be quiet, while telling the stockbroker, "I can't tolerate any more
excuses. If I don't receive the check immediately I am going to have to speak to
your manager when I'm in New York next week." And sure enough, the following week there we were in front of this astonished stockbroker, and I was sitting there red-faced and quiet, and my mother, the real Mrs. Tan, was shouting
at his boss in her impeccable broken English.

We used a similar routine just five days ago, for a situation that was far less   14
humorous. My mother had gone to the hospital for an appointment, to find
out about a benign brain tumor a CAT scan had revealed a month ago. She
said she had spoken very good English, her best English, no mistakes. Still, she
said, the hospital did not apologize when they said they had lost the CAT scan
and she had come for nothing. She said they did not seem to have any sympathy
when she told them she was anxious to know the exact diagnosis, since her
husband and son had both died of brain tumors. She said they would not give
her any more information until the next time and she would have to make
another appointment for that. So she said she would not leave until the doctor

called her daughter. She wouldn't budge. And when the doctor finally called her daughter, me, who spoke in perfect English—lo and behold—we had assurances the CAT scan would be found, promises that a conference call on Monday would be held, and apologies for any suffering my mother had gone through for a most regrettable mistake.

I think my mother's English almost had an effect on limiting my possibilities in life as well. Sociologists and linguists probably will tell you that a person's developing language skills are more influenced by peers. But I do think that the language spoken in the family, especially in immigrant families which are more insular, plays a large role in shaping the language of the child. And I believe that it affected my results on achievement tests, IQ tests, and the SAT. While my English skills were never judged as poor, compared to math, English could not be considered my strong suit. In grade school I did moderately well, getting perhaps B's, sometimes B-pluses, in English and scoring perhaps in the sixtieth or seventieth percentile on achievement tests. But those scores were not good enough to override the opinion that my true abilities lay in math and science, because in those areas I achieved A's and scored in the ninetieth percentile or higher.

This was understandable. Math is precise; there is only one correct answer. Whereas, for me at least, the answers on English tests were always a judgment call, a matter of opinion and personal experience. Those tests were constructed around items like fill-in-the-blank sentence completion, such as "Even though Tom was _____, Mary thought he was _____." And the correct answer always seemed to be the most bland combinations of thoughts, for example, "Even though Tom was shy, Mary thought he was charming," with the grammatical structure "even though" limiting the correct answer to some sort of semantic opposites, so you wouldn't get answers like, "Even though Tom was foolish, Mary thought he was ridiculous." Well, according to my mother, there were very few limitations as to what Tom could have been and what Mary might have thought of him. So I never did well on tests like that.

The same was true with word analogies, pairs of words in which you were supposed to find some sort of logical, semantic relationship—for example, "*Sunset* is to *nightfall* as _____ is to _____." And here you would be presented with a list of four possible pairs, one of which showed the same kind of relationship: *red* is to *stoplight*, *bus* is to *arrival*, *chills* is to *fever*, *yawn* is to *boring*. Well, I could never think that way. I knew what the tests were asking, but I could not block out of my mind the images already created by the first pair, "*sunset* is to *nightfall*"—and I would see a burst of colors against a darkening sky, the moon rising, the lowering of a curtain of stars. And all the other pairs of words—red, bus, stoplight, boring—just threw up a mass of confusing images, making it impossible for me to sort out something as logical as saying: "A sunset precedes nightfall" is the same as "a chill precedes a fever." The only way I would have gotten that answer right would have been to imagine an associative situation, for example, my being disobedient and staying out past sunset, catching a chill at night, which turns into feverish pneumonia as punishment, which indeed did happen to me.

15

16

17

I have been thinking about all this lately, about my mother's English, about achievement tests. Because lately I've been asked, as a writer, why there are not more Asian Americans represented in American literature. Why are there few Asian Americans enrolled in creative writing programs? Why do so many Chinese students go into engineering? Well, these are broad sociological questions I can't begin to answer. But I have noticed in surveys—in fact, just last week—that Asian students, as a whole, always do significantly better on math achievement tests than in English. And this makes me think that there are other Asian-American students whose English spoken in the home might also be described as "broken" or "limited." And perhaps they also have teachers who are steering them away from writing and into math and science, which is what happened to me.

> "Why are there few Asian Americans enrolled in creative writing programs? Why do so many Chinese students go into engineering?"

18

Fortunately, I happen to be rebellious in nature and enjoy the challenge of disproving assumptions made about me. I became an English major my first year in college, after being enrolled as pre-med. I started writing nonfiction as a freelancer the week after I was told by my former boss that writing was my worst skill and I should hone my talents toward account management.

19

But it wasn't until 1985 that I finally began to write fiction. And at first I wrote using what I thought to be wittily crafted sentences, sentences that would finally prove I had mastery over the English language. Here's an example from the first draft of a story that later made its way into *The Joy Luck Club*, but without this line: "That was my mental quandary in its nascent state." A terrible line, which I can barely pronounce.

20

Fortunately, for reasons I won't get into today, I later decided I should envision a reader for the stories I would write. And the reader I decided upon was my mother because these were stories about mothers. So with this reader in mind—and in fact she did read my early drafts—I began to write stories using all the Englishes I grew up with: the English I spoke to my mother, which for lack of a better term might be described as "simple"; the English she used with me, which for lack of a better term might be described as "broken"; my translation of her Chinese, which could certainly be described as "watered down"; and what I imagined to be her translation of her Chinese if she could speak in perfect English, her internal language, and for that I sought to preserve the essence, but neither an English nor a Chinese structure. I wanted to capture what language ability tests can never reveal: her intent, her passion, her imagery, the rhythms of her speech, and the nature of her thoughts.

21

Apart from what any critic had to say about my writing, I knew I had succeeded where it counted when my mother finished reading my book and gave me her verdict: "So easy to read."

22

· · ·

Comprehension

1. What is Tan classifying in this essay? What individual categories does she identify?
2. Where does Tan identify the different categories she discusses in "Mother Tongue"? Should she have identified these categories earlier? Explain your reasoning.
3. Does Tan illustrate each category she identifies? Does she treat all categories equally? If she does not, do you see this as a problem? Explain.
4. In what specific situations does Tan say her mother's "limited English" was a handicap? In what other situations might Mrs. Tan face difficulties?
5. What effects has her mother's limited English had on Tan's life?
6. How does Tan account for the difficulty she had in answering questions on achievement tests, particularly word analogies? Do you think her problems in this area can be explained by the level of her family's language skills, or might other factors also be to blame? Explain.
7. In paragraph 18, Tan considers the possible reasons for the relatively few Asian Americans in the fields of language and literature. What explanations does she offer? What other explanations can you think of?

Purpose and Audience

1. Why do you suppose Tan begins her essay by explaining her qualifications? Why, for example, does she tell her readers she is "not a scholar of English or literature" (1) but rather a writer who is "fascinated by language in daily life" (2)?
2. Do you think Tan expects most of her readers to be Asian American? To be familiar with Asian-American languages and culture? How can you tell?
3. Is Tan's primary focus in this essay on language or on her mother? Explain your conclusion.

Style and Structure

1. This essay's style is relatively informal. For example, Tan uses *I* to refer to herself and addresses her readers as *you*. Identify other features that characterize her style as informal. Do you think a more formal style would strengthen her credibility? Explain your reasoning.
2. In paragraph 6, Tan quotes a passage of her mother's speech. What purpose does Tan say she wants this quotation to serve? What impression does it give of her mother? Do you think this effect is what Tan intended? Explain.
3. In paragraph 8, Tan discusses the different words and phrases that might be used to describe her mother's spoken English. Which of these terms seems most accurate? Do you agree with Tan that these words are unsatisfactory? What other term for her mother's English would be both neutral and accurate?
4. In paragraphs 10 through 13, Tan juxtaposes her mother's English with her own. What point do these quoted passages make?

5. **Vocabulary Project.** Consider the expression *Mother Tongue* in Tan's title. What does this expression usually mean? What does it seem to mean here?

6. In paragraph 20, Tan quotes a "terrible line" from an early draft of part of her novel *The Joy Luck Club*. Why do you suppose she quotes this line? How is its style different from the writing style she uses in "Mother Tongue"?

Journal Entry

In paragraph 9, Tan says that when she was growing up she was sometimes ashamed of her mother because of her limited English proficiency. Have you ever felt ashamed of a parent (or a friend) because of his or her inability to "fit in" in some way? How do you feel now about your earlier reaction?

Writing Workshop

1. What different "Englishes" (or other languages) do you use in your day-to-day life as a student, employee, friend, and family member? Write a classification-and-division essay identifying, describing, and illustrating each kind of language and explaining the purpose it serves.

2. **Working with Sources.** What kinds of problems does a person whose English is as limited as Mrs. Tan's face in the age of social media and instant communication? Write a classification-and-division essay that identifies and explains the kinds of problems you might encounter today if the level of your spoken English were comparable to Mrs. Tan's. Try to update some of the specific situations Tan describes, quoting Tan where necessary, and be sure to document any borrowed words or ideas and to include a works-cited page. (See Chapter 18 for information on MLA documentation.)

3. Tan's essay focuses on spoken language, but people also use different kinds of *written* language in different situations. Write a classification-and-division essay that identifies and analyzes three different kinds of written English that you might use: one appropriate for your parents, one for a teacher or employer, and one for a friend. Illustrate each kind of language with a few sentences directed at each audience about your plans for your future. In your thesis statement, explain why all three kinds of language are necessary.

Combining the Patterns

Tan develops her essay with a series of anecdotes about her mother and about herself. How does this use of **narration** strengthen her essay? Could she have made her point about the use of different "Englishes" without these anecdotes? What other strategy could she have used?

Thematic Connections

- "Why Chinese Mothers Are Superior" (page 396)
- "The Park" (page 663)

STEPHANIE ERICSSON

The Ways We Lie

Stephanie Ericsson (b. 1953) grew up in San Francisco and began writing as a teenager. She has been a screenwriter and an advertising copywriter and has published several books based on her own life. *Shame Faced: The Road to Recovery* and *Women of AA: Recovering Together* (both 1985) focus on her experiences with addiction; *Companion through the Darkness: Inner Dialogues on Grief* (1993) deals with the sudden death of her first husband; and *Companion into the Dawn: Inner Dialogues on Loving* (1994) is a collection of essays.

Background on lies in politics and business The following piece originally appeared in the *Utne Reader* as the cover article of the January 1993 issue, which was devoted to the theme of lies and lying. The subject had particular relevance after a year when the honesty of Bill Clinton — the newly elected U.S. president — had been questioned. (It also followed the furor surrounding the confirmation hearings of U.S. Supreme Court nominee Clarence Thomas, who denied allegations by attorney Anita Hill of workplace sexual harassment; here the question was who was telling the truth and who was not.) Six years later, Clinton was accused of perjury and faced a Senate impeachment trial. In subsequent years, lying was featured prominently in the news as executives at a number of major corporations were charged with falsifying records at the expense of employees and shareholders, and George W. Bush's administration was accused of lying about the presence of weapons of mass destruction in Iraq to justify going to war. More recently, President Donald Trump and his administration have been regularly charged with lying about everything from inauguration-crowd sizes to the withholding of funds to Ukraine — the latter led to Trump's impeachment. Kellyanne Conway, counselor to the president, even unintentionally coined a new phrase for lies in 2017: "alternative facts."

The bank called today and I told them my deposit was in the mail, even 1 though I hadn't written a check yet. It'd been a rough day. The baby I'm pregnant with decided to do aerobics on my lungs for two hours, our three-year-old daughter painted the living-room couch with lipstick, the IRS put me on hold for an hour, and I was late to a business meeting because I was tired.

I told my client the traffic had been bad. When my partner came home, his 2 haggard face told me his day hadn't gone any better than mine, so when he asked, "How was your day?" I said, "Oh, fine," knowing that one more straw might break his back. A friend called and wanted to take me to lunch. I said I was busy. Four lies in the course of a day, none of which I felt the least bit guilty about.

We lie. We all do. We exaggerate, we minimize, we avoid confrontation, we   3
spare people's feelings, we conveniently forget, we keep secrets, we justify lying
to the big-guy institutions. Like most people, I indulge in small falsehoods and
still think of myself as an honest person. Sure I lie, but it doesn't hurt anything.
Or does it?

I once tried going a whole week without
telling a lie, and it was paralyzing. I discov-   4
ered that telling the truth all the time is nearly
impossible. It means living with some serious
consequences: The bank charges me $60 in
overdraft fees, my partner keels over when I
tell him about my travails, my client fires me
for telling her I didn't feel like being on time,

> **"I once tried going a whole week without telling a lie, and it was paralyzing."**

and my friend takes it personally when I say I'm not hungry. There must be some
merit to lying.

But if I justify lying, what makes me any different from slick politicians or   5
the corporate robbers who raided the S&L industry? Saying it's okay to lie one
way and not another is hedging. I cannot seem to escape the voice deep inside
me that tells me: When someone lies, someone loses.

What far-reaching consequences will I, or others, pay as a result of my lie?   6
Will someone's trust be destroyed? Will someone else pay *my* penance because I
ducked out? We must consider the *meaning of our actions*. Deception, lies, capital
crimes, and misdemeanors all carry meanings. *Webster's* definition of *lie* is
specific:

1. a false statement or action especially made with the intent to deceive;
2. anything that gives or is meant to give a false impression.

A definition like this implies that there are many, many ways to tell a lie.   7
Here are just a few.

The White Lie

A man who won't lie to a woman has very little consideration for her feelings.

— BERGEN EVANS

The white lie assumes that the truth will cause more damage than a sim-   8
ple, harmless untruth. Telling a friend he looks great when he looks like hell
can be based on a decision that the friend needs a compliment more than a
frank opinion. But, in effect, it is the liar deciding what is best for the lied to.
Ultimately, it is a vote of no confidence. It is an act of subtle arrogance for
anyone to decide what is best for someone else.

Yet not all circumstances are quite so cut-and-dried. Take, for instance, the   9
sergeant in Vietnam who knew one of his men was killed in action but listed
him as missing so that the man's family would receive indefinite compensation instead of the lump-sum pittance the military gives widows and children.
His intent was honorable. Yet for twenty years this family kept their hopes
alive, unable to move on to a new life.

Facades

Et tu, Brute?

— CAESAR*

We all put up facades to one degree or another. When I put on a suit to go   10
to see a client, I feel as though I am putting on another face, obeying the expectation that serious businesspeople wear suits rather than sweatpants. But I'm a
writer. Normally, I get up, get the kid off to school, and sit at my computer in
my pajamas until four in the afternoon. When I answer the phone, the caller
thinks I'm wearing a suit (though the UPS man knows better).

But facades can be destructive because they are used to seduce others into   11
an illusion. For instance, I recently realized that a former friend was a liar. He
presented himself with all the right looks and the right words and offered lots
of new consciousness theories, fabulous books to read, and fascinating
insights. Then I did some business with him, and the time came for him to pay
me. He turned out to be all talk and no walk. I heard a plethora of reasonable
excuses, including in-depth descriptions of the big break around the corner. In
six months of work, I saw less than a hundred bucks. When I confronted him,
he raised both eyebrows and tried to convince me that I'd heard him wrong,
that he'd made no commitment to me. A simple investigation into his past
revealed a crowded graveyard of disenchanted former friends.

Ignoring the Plain Facts

Well, you must understand that Father Porter is only human. . . .

— A MASSACHUSETTS PRIEST

In the '60s, the Catholic Church in Massachusetts began hearing com-   12
plaints that Father James Porter was sexually molesting children. Rather than
relieving him of his duties, the ecclesiastical authorities simply moved him
from one parish to another between 1960 and 1967, actually providing him
with a fresh supply of unsuspecting families and innocent children to abuse.
After treatment in 1967 for pedophilia, he went back to work, this time in
Minnesota. The new diocese was aware of Father Porter's obsession with children, but they needed priests and recklessly believed treatment had cured him.
More children were abused until he was relieved of his duties a year later. By his
own admission, Porter may have abused as many as a hundred children.

Ignoring the facts may not in and of itself be a form of lying, but consider   13
the context of this situation. If a lie is *a false action done with the intent to deceive*,
then the Catholic Church's conscious covering for Porter created irreparable
consequences. The church became a co-perpetrator with Porter.

---

* Eds. note — "And you, Brutus?" (Latin). In Shakespeare's play *Julius Caesar*, Caesar asks
this question when he sees Brutus, whom he has believed to be his friend, among the
conspirators who are stabbing him.

Deflecting

> When you have no basis for an argument, abuse the plaintiff.
>
> — CICERO

I've discovered that I can keep anyone from seeing the true me by being selectively blatant. I set a precedent of being up-front about intimate issues, but I never bring up the things I truly want to hide; I just let people assume I'm revealing everything. It's an effective way of hiding. 14

Any good liar knows that the way to perpetuate an untruth is to deflect attention from it. When Clarence Thomas exploded with accusations that the Senate hearings were a "high-tech lynching," he simply switched the focus from a highly charged subject to a radioactive subject. Rather than defending himself, he took the offensive and accused the country of racism. It was a brilliant maneuver. Racism is now politically incorrect in official circles — unlike sexual harassment, which still rewards those who can get away with it. 15

Some of the most skillful deflectors are passive-aggressive people who, when accused of inappropriate behavior, refuse to respond to the accusations. This you-don't-exist stance infuriates the accuser, who, understandably, screams something obscene out of frustration. The trap is sprung and the act of deflection successful, because now the passive-aggressive person can indignantly say, "Who can talk to someone as unreasonable as you?" The real issue is forgotten and the sins of the original victim become the focus. Feeling guilty of name-calling, the victim is fully tamed and crawls into a hole, ashamed. I have watched this fighting technique work thousands of times in disputes between men and women, and what I've learned is that the real culprit is not necessarily the one who swears the loudest. 16

Omission

> The cruelest lies are often told in silence.
>
> — R. L. STEVENSON

Omission involves telling most of the truth minus one or two key facts whose absence changes the story completely. You break a pair of glasses that are guaranteed under normal use and get a new pair, without mentioning that the first pair broke during a rowdy game of basketball. Who hasn't tried something like that? But what about omission of information that could make a difference in how a person lives his or her life? 17

For instance, one day I found out that rabbinical legends tell of another woman in the Garden of Eden before Eve. I was stunned. The omission of the Sumerian goddess Lilith from Genesis — as well as her demonization by ancient misogynists as an embodiment of female evil — felt like spiritual robbery. I felt like I'd just found out my mother was really my stepmother. To take seriously the tradition that Adam was created out of the same mud as his equal counterpart, Lilith, redefines all of Judeo-Christian history. 18

Some renegade Catholic feminists introduced me to a view of Lilith that   19
had been suppressed during the many centuries when this strong goddess was
seen only as a spirit of evil. Lilith was a proud goddess who defied Adam's need
to control her, attempted negotiations, and when this failed, said adios and left
the Garden of Eden.

This omission of Lilith from the Bible was a patriarchal strategy to keep   20
women weak. Omitting the strong-woman archetype of Lilith from Western
religions and starting the story with Eve the Rib has helped keep Christian and
Jewish women believing they were the lesser sex for thousands of years.

Stereotypes and Clichés

> Where opinion does not exist, the status quo becomes stereotyped and all origi-
> nality is discouraged.
>
> — BERTRAND RUSSELL

Stereotype and cliché serve a purpose as a form of shorthand. Our need for   21
vast amounts of information in nanoseconds has made the stereotype vital to
modern communication. Unfortunately, it often shuts down original thinking, giving those hungry for the truth a candy bar of misinformation instead of
a balanced meal. The stereotype explains a situation with just enough truth to
seem unquestionable.

All the "isms" — racism, sexism, ageism, et al. — are founded on and fueled   22
by the stereotype and the cliché, which are lies of exaggeration, omission, and
ignorance. They are always dangerous. They take a single tree and make it a
landscape. They destroy curiosity. They close minds and separate people. The
single mother on welfare is assumed to be cheating. Any Black male could tell
you how much of his identity is obliterated daily by stereotypes. Fat people,
ugly people, beautiful people, old people, large-breasted women, short men,
the mentally ill, and the homeless all could tell you how much more they are
like us than we want to think. I once admitted to a group of people that I had a
mouth like a truck driver. Much to my surprise, a man stood up and said, "I'm
a truck driver, and I never cuss." Needless to say, I was humbled.

Groupthink

> Who is more foolish, the child afraid of the dark, or the man afraid of the light?
>
> — MAURICE FREEHILL

Irving Janis, in *Victims of GroupThink*, defines this sort of lie as a psychological   23
phenomenon within decision-making groups in which loyalty to the group has
become more important than any other value, with the result that dissent and
the appraisal of alternatives are suppressed. If you've ever worked on a committee or in a corporation, you've encountered groupthink. It requires a combination of other forms of lying — ignoring facts, selective memory, omission, and
denial, to name a few.

The textbook example of groupthink came on December 7, 1941. From as   24
early as the fall of 1941, the warnings came in, one after another, that Japan
was preparing for a massive military operation. The Navy command in Hawaii
assumed Pearl Harbor was invulnerable — the Japanese weren't stupid enough
to attack the United States' most important base. On the other hand, racist
stereotypes said the Japanese weren't smart enough to invent a torpedo effective in less than 60 feet of water (the fleet was docked in 30 feet); after all, U.S.
technology hadn't been able to do it.

On Friday, December 5, normal weekend leave was granted to all the com-   25
manders at Pearl Harbor, even though the Japanese consulate in Hawaii was
busy burning papers. Within the tight, good-ole-boy cohesiveness of the U.S.
command in Hawaii, the myth of invulnerability stayed well entrenched. No
one in the group considered the alternatives. The rest is history.

Out-and-Out Lies

The only form of lying that is beyond reproach is lying for its own sake.

— OSCAR WILDE

Of all the ways to lie, I like this one the best, probably because I get tired of   26
trying to figure out the real meanings behind things. At least I can trust the
bald-faced lie. I once asked my five-year-old nephew, "Who broke the fence?"
(I had seen him do it.) He answered, "The murderers." Who could argue?

At least when this sort of lie is told it can be easily confronted. As the per-   27
son who is lied to, I know where I stand. The bald-faced lie doesn't toy with my
perceptions — it argues with them. It doesn't try to refashion reality, it tries to
refute it. *Read my lips.* . . . No sleight of hand. No guessing. If this were the only
form of lying, there would be no such thing as floating anxiety or the adult-
children of alcoholics movement.

Dismissal

Pay no attention to that man behind the curtain! I am the Great Oz!

— THE WIZARD OF OZ

Dismissal is perhaps the slipperiest of all lies. Dismissing feelings, percep-   28
tions, or even the raw facts of a situation ranks as a kind of lie that can do as
much damage to a person as any other kind of lie.

The roots of many mental disorders can be traced back to the dismissal   29
of reality. Imagine that a person is told from the time she is a tot that her
perceptions are inaccurate. *"Mommy, I'm scared."* "No, you're not, darling."
"I don't like that man next door, he makes me feel icky." "Johnny, that's a terrible
thing to say, of course you like him. You go over there right now and be nice
to him."

I've often mused over the idea that madness is actually a sane reaction to   30
an insane world. Psychologist R. D. Laing supports this hypothesis in *Sanity,
Madness & the Family*, an account of his investigations into families of
schizophrenics. The common thread that ran through all of the families he
studied was a deliberate, staunch dismissal of the patient's perceptions from a
very early age. Each of the patients started out with an accurate grasp of reality,
which, through meticulous and methodical dismissal, was demolished until
the only reality the patient could trust was catatonia.

Dismissal runs the gamut. Mild dismissal can be quite handy for forgiving   31
the foibles of others in our day-to-day lives. Toddlers who have just learned to
manipulate their parents' attention sometimes are dismissed out of necessity.
Absolute attention from the parents would require so much energy that no
one would get to eat dinner. But we must be careful and attentive about how
far we take our "necessary" dismissals. Dismissal is a dangerous tool, because
it's nothing less than a lie.

Delusion

> We lie loudest when we lie to ourselves.
>
> — ERIC HOFFER

I could write the book on this one. Delusion, a cousin of dismissal, is the   32
tendency to see excuses as facts. It's a powerful lying tool because it filters out
information that contradicts what we want to believe. Alcoholics who believe
that the problems in their lives are legitimate reasons for drinking rather than
results of the drinking offer the classic example of deluded thinking. Delusion
uses the mind's ability to see things in myriad ways to support what it wants to
be the truth.

But delusion is also a survival mechanism we all use. If we were to fully con-   33
template the consequences of our stockpiles of nuclear weapons or global warming, we could hardly function on a day-to-day level. We don't want to incorporate
that much reality into our lives because to do so would be paralyzing.

Delusion acts as an adhesive to keep the status quo intact. It shamelessly   34
employs dismissal, omission, and amnesia, among other sorts of lies. Its most
cunning defense is that it cannot see itself.

> The liar's punishment . . . is that he cannot believe anyone else.
>
> — GEORGE BERNARD SHAW

These are only a few of the ways we lie. Or are lied to. As I said earlier, it's   35
not easy to entirely eliminate lies from our lives. No matter how pious we may
try to be, we will still embellish, hedge, and omit to lubricate the daily machinery
of living. But there is a world of difference between telling functional lies and
living a lie. Martin Buber* once said, "The lie is the spirit committing treason

---

* Eds. note — Austrian-born Judaic philosopher (1878–1965).

against itself." Our acceptance of lies becomes a cultural cancer that eventually shrouds and reorders reality until moral garbage becomes as invisible to us as water is to a fish.

How much do we tolerate before we become sick and tired of being sick and   36
tired? When will we stand up and declare our *right* to trust? When do we stop accepting that the real truth is in the fine print? Whose lips do we read this year when we vote for president? When will we stop being so reticent about making judgments? When do we stop turning over our personal power and responsibility to liars?

Maybe if I don't tell the bank the check's in the mail I'll be less tolerant of   37
the lies told me every day. A country song I once heard said it all for me: "You've got to stand for something or you'll fall for anything."

·   ·   ·

Comprehension

1. List and briefly define each of the ten kinds of lies Ericsson identifies.
2. Why, in Ericsson's view, is each kind of lie necessary?
3. According to Ericsson, what is the danger of each kind of lie?
4. Why does Ericsson like "out-and-out lies" (26–27) best?
5. Why is "dismissal" the "slipperiest of all lies" (28)?

Purpose and Audience

1. Is Ericsson's thesis simply that "there are many, many ways to tell a lie" (7)? Or, is she defending — or attacking — the practice of lying? Try to state her thesis in a single sentence.
2. Do you think Ericsson's choice of examples reveals a political bias? If so, do you think she expects her intended audience to share her political views? Explain your conclusion.

Style and Structure

1. Despite the seriousness of her subject matter, Ericsson's essay is informal; her opening paragraphs are especially personal and breezy. Why do you think she chose to use this kind of style, particularly in her introductory paragraphs? Do you think her decision makes sense?
2. Ericsson introduces each category of lie with a quotation. What function do these quotations serve? Do you think her essay would be less (or more) effective without them? Why or why not?
3. In addition to a heading and a quotation, what other elements does Ericsson include in her treatment of each kind of lie? Are all the discussions parallel — that is, does her discussion of each category include the same elements? If not, do you think this lack of balance is a problem? Explain.
4. What, if anything, determines the order in which Ericsson arranges her categories in this essay? Do you think any category should be relocated? If so, why — and where should it be placed?

5. Throughout her essay, Ericsson uses **rhetorical questions**. Why do you suppose she uses this stylistic device?

6. **Vocabulary Project.** Ericsson uses many **colloquialisms** in this essay, such as "I could write the book on this one" (32). Identify as many of these informal expressions as you can. Why do you think she uses colloquialisms instead of more formal expressions? Do they have a positive or negative effect on your reaction to her ideas? Explain.

7. Ericsson occasionally cites the views of experts. Why does she include these references? If she wanted to cite additional experts, what professional backgrounds or fields of study do you think they should represent? Why?

8. In paragraph 29, Ericsson says, "Imagine that a person is told from the time she is a tot. . . ." Does she use *she* in similar contexts elsewhere in the essay? Do you find the feminine form of the personal pronoun appropriate or distracting? What other options does Ericsson have? Explain.

9. Paragraphs 35 through 37 constitute Ericsson's conclusion. How does this conclusion parallel the essay's introduction in terms of style, structure, and content?

Journal Entry

In paragraph 3, Ericsson says, "We lie. We all do." Later in the paragraph, she comments, "Sure I lie, but it doesn't hurt anything. Or does it?" Answer her question.

Writing Workshop

1. **Working with Sources.** Choose three or four of Ericsson's categories, and write a classification-and-division essay called "The Ways I Lie." Base your essay on personal experience, and include an explicit thesis statement that either defends your own lies or is sharply critical of their use. Be sure to document Ericsson's essay when you cite her categories and to include a works-cited page. (See Chapter 18 for information on MLA documentation.)

2. In paragraph 22, Ericsson condemns stereotypes. Write a classification-and-division essay with the following thesis statement: "Stereotypes are usually inaccurate, often negative, and always dangerous." In your essay, consider the kinds of stereotypes applied to one of the following groups: people who are disabled, overweight, or elderly; urban teenagers; politicians; stay-at-home mothers (or fathers); or immigrants.

3. Using the thesis provided in question 2, write a classification-and-division essay that considers the stereotypes applied to three or four of the following occupations: police officers, librarians, used-car dealers, flight attendants, lawyers, construction workers, rock musicians, accountants, and telemarketers.

Combining the Patterns

A dictionary **definition** is a familiar — even tired — strategy for an essay's introduction. Do you think Ericsson should delete the definition in paragraph 6 for this reason, or do you believe it is necessary? Explain.

Thematic Connections

- "'What's in a Name?'" (page 2)
- "The Money" (page 113)
- "The Hidden Life of Garbage" (page 185)
- "How to Spot Fake News" (page 289)
- "Did Free Pens Cause the Opioid Crisis?" (page 332)

AMY LOWELL

Patterns (Poetry)

The poet Amy Lowell (1874–1925) was born and raised in Brookline, Massachusetts. The Lowells were prominent "Boston Brahmins": wealthy, accomplished, upper-class families who traced their lineage back to the early years of colonial settlement. Encouraged as a child to write, Lowell studied literature in her family's seven-thousand-book home library and published a book (cowritten with her sister and mother) by the time she was thirteen. As she once supposedly said, "God made me a business woman, and I made myself a poet." Her career as a serious writer truly began after she met the modernist poet and critic Ezra Pound in 1912. At the time, Pound was a proponent of "Imagism," a style of poetry that stressed clarity, simplicity, and precision by focusing on concrete images instead of description and abstraction. Lowell became an enthusiastic practitioner of this aesthetic as well as a celebrity lecturer on poetry, both in the United States and abroad. Lowell's collections include *A Dome of Many-Coloured Glass* (1912), *Sword Blades and Poppy Seed* (1914), *Tendencies in Modern American Poetry* (1917), and *What's O'Clock* (1925).

Background on the Battle of Ypres In the preface to her book *Women and Ghosts* (1916), Lowell wrote, "No one writing today can fail to be affected by the great war raging in Europe at this time. We are too near it to do more than touch upon it. But, obliquely, it is suggested in many of these poems . . ." That is certainly the case with "Patterns." Although the poem never specifies a particular war, it does provide a clue: "For the man who should loose me is dead, / Fighting with the Duke in Flanders." These lines allude to the battle of the Yser (a river running from Belgium to the North Sea), a 1914 clash that took place in the region of Belgium known as Flanders, a major theater of World War I's Western Front. The Germany army, led by Albrecht, Duke of Württemberg, fought with Belgian forces at the Yser Canal as part of a wider attempt to invade Belgium. The battle, known as the first battle of Ypres, lasted from October 19 to November 22. The Germans were ultimately repelled by Allied forces, but only at great cost to both sides. The Belgian, French, and British suffered well over 100,000 casualties and deaths, as did the German forces. The second battle of Ypres, in which the Germans suffered a more decisive defeat, occurred the next year. As Lowell suggests, the war had a great influence on poets, novelists, and other writers, both during and in the years after the war. Lieutenant Colonel John McCrae's 1915 "In Flanders Fields," perhaps the most famous poem inspired by World War I, offers a response to "Patterns." Informed by McCrae's own experience on the Western Front, the poem's speaker says: "We are the Dead. Short days ago / We lived, felt dawn, saw sunset glow, / Loved and were loved, and now we lie / In Flanders fields."

I walk down the garden paths,
And all the daffodils
Are blowing, and the bright blue squills.
I walk down the patterned garden paths
In my stiff, brocaded gown.   5
With my powdered hair and jewelled fan,
I too am a rare
Pattern. As I wander down
The garden paths.

My dress is richly figured,   10
And the train
Makes a pink and silver stain
On the gravel, and the thrift
Of the borders.
Just a plate of current fashion,   15
Tripping by in high-heeled, ribboned shoes.
Not a softness anywhere about me,
Only whale-bone and brocade.
And I sink on a seat in the shade
Of a lime tree. For my passion   20
Wars against the stiff brocade.
The daffodils and squills
Flutter in the breeze
As they please.
And I weep;   25
For the lime tree is in blossom
And one small flower has dropped upon my bosom.

And the splashing of waterdrops
In the marble fountain
Comes down the garden paths.   30
The dripping never stops.
Underneath my stiffened gown
Is the softness of a woman bathing in a marble basin,
A basin in the midst of hedges grown
So thick, she cannot see her lover hiding,   35
But she guesses he is near,
And the sliding of the water
Seems the stroking of a dear
Hand upon her.
What is Summer in a fine brocaded gown!   40
I should like to see it lying in a heap upon the ground.
All the pink and silver crumpled up on the ground.
I would be the pink and silver as I ran along the paths,

And he would stumble after,
Bewildered by my laughter.   45
I should see the sun flashing from his sword-hilt and the buckles on his shoes.
I would choose
To lead him in a maze along the patterned paths,
A bright and laughing maze for my heavy-booted lover,
Till he caught me in the shade,   50
And the buttons of his waistcoat bruised my body as he clasped me,
Aching, melting, unafraid.
With the shadows of the leaves and the sundrops,
And the plopping of the waterdrops,
All about us in the open afternoon —   55
I am very like to swoon
With the weight of this brocade,
For the sun sifts through the shade.

Underneath the fallen blossom
In my bosom,   60
Is a letter I have hid.
It was brought to me this morning by a rider from the Duke.
"Madam, we regret to inform you that Lord Hartwell
Died in action Thursday sen'night."
As I read it in the white, morning sunlight,   65
The letters squirmed like snakes.
"Any answer, Madam," said my footman.
"No," I told him.
"See that the messenger takes some refreshment.
No, no answer."   70
And I walked into the garden,
Up and down the patterned paths,
In my stiff, correct brocade.
The blue and yellow flowers stood up proudly in the sun,
Each one.   75
I stood upright too,
Held rigid to the pattern
By the stiffness of my gown.
Up and down I walked,
Up and down.   80

In a month he would have been my husband.
In a month, here, underneath this lime,
We would have broke the pattern;
He for me, and I for him,
He as Colonel, I as Lady,   85
On this shady seat.
He had a whim

That sunlight carried blessing.
And I answered, "It shall be as you have said."
Now he is dead.   90

In Summer and in Winter I shall walk
Up and down
The patterned garden paths
In my stiff, brocaded gown.
The squills and daffodils   95
Will give place to pillared roses, and to asters, and to snow.
I shall go
Up and down,
In my gown.
Gorgeously arrayed,   100
Boned and stayed.
And the softness of my body will be guarded from embrace
By each button, hook, and lace.
For the man who should loose me is dead,
Fighting with the Duke in Flanders,   105
In a pattern called a war.
Christ! What are patterns for?

·   ·   ·

Reading Literature

1. This poem's speaker has lost her fiancé in World War I. Do the patterns she identifies help her cope, or do they make her situation worse? Explain.
2. In what sense is the speaker herself "a rare / pattern" (lines 7–8)? In what sense is war a pattern?
3. Answer the questions the speaker asks in the poem's last line.

Journal Entry

What kinds of patterns (for example, patterns of dress or behavior) can you identify in your own life? Which of these have you chosen, and which have been chosen for you?

Thematic Connections

- "My Mother Never Worked" (page 122)
- "Call Me 'They'" (page 237)
- "'Girl'" (page 251)
- "The Lottery" (page 303)

Writing Assignments for Classification and Division

1. Choose a film you have seen recently, and list all the elements you consider significant: plot, direction, acting, special effects, and so on. Then, further subdivide each category (for instance, listing each of the major special effects). Using this list as an outline, write a review of the film.

2. Write an essay classifying the teachers or bosses you have had into several distinct categories, and form a judgment about the relative effectiveness of the individuals in each group. Give each category a name, and be sure your essay has a thesis statement.

3. What fashion styles do you observe on your college campus? Establish four or five distinct categories, and write an essay classifying students on the basis of how they dress. Give each group of students a descriptive title.

4. **Working with Sources.** Look through this book's thematic table of contents (page xxxiii), and choose three essays on the same general subject. Then, write a classification-and-division essay discussing the different ways writers can explore the same theme. Be sure your topic sentences clearly define your three categories, and be sure to include parenthetical documentation for all references to the essays you choose and a works-cited page. (See Chapter 18 for information on MLA documentation.)

5. Many consider violence in sports to be a serious problem. Write an essay expressing your views on this problem. Using a classification-and-division structure, categorize information according to sources of violence (such as the players, the nature of the game, and the fans).

6. **Working with Sources.** Review "Patterns," and find two or three other poems about the negative effects of war. Then, write a classification-and-division essay in which you discuss your reactions to these poems and your view of what they say about war. Taken together, what common sentiments do the three communicate? Be sure to document all references to the poems and to include a works-cited list. (See Chapter 18 for information on MLA documentation.)

7. Write a lighthearted classification-and-division essay discussing kinds of snack foods, cartoons, pets, status symbols, shoppers, vacations, weight-loss diets, hairstyles, or drivers.

8. Write a classification-and-division essay assessing the relative merits of several different politicians, websites, blogs, or academic majors.

9. What kinds of survival skills does a student need to get through college successfully? Write a classification-and-division essay identifying and discussing several kinds of skills and indicating why each category is important. If you like, you may write your essay in the form of an orientation guide for beginning college students.

10. Divide your social media friends into categories according to some logical principle. Then, write a classification-and-division essay that includes a thesis statement indicating how different the various groups are.

Collaborative Activity for Classification and Division

Working in a group of four students, devise a classification system encompassing all the different kinds of popular music the members of your group favor. You may begin with general categories, such as country, rock, rap, or metal, but you should also include more specific categories, such as honky tonk, punk rock, Motown, and death metal, in your classification system. After you decide on categories and subcategories that represent the tastes of all group members, fill in examples for each category. Then, devise several different options for arranging your categories into an essay.

Definition

What Is Definition?

A **definition** tells what a term means and how it differs from other terms in its class. In the following paragraph from "Altruistic Behavior," anthropologist Desmond Morris defines *altruism*, the key term of his essay.

Topic sentence	Altruism is the performance of an unselfish act. As a pattern of behavior, this act must have two properties: it must benefit someone else, and it must do so to the disadvantage of the benefactor. It is not merely a matter of being helpful; it is helpfulness at a cost to yourself.
Extended definition defines term by *enumeration* **and** *negation*	

Most people think of definition in terms of dictionaries, which give brief, succinct explanations — called **formal definitions** — of what words mean, but a definition can also explain what something, or even someone, *is* — that is, its essential nature. Sometimes a definition requires a paragraph, an essay, or even a whole book. These longer, more complex definitions are called **extended definitions**.

Understanding Formal Definitions

Many definitions have a standard three-part structure. First, they present the *term* to be defined, then the general *class* it is a part of, and finally the *qualities that differentiate it* from the other terms in the same class.

TERM	CLASS	DIFFERENTIATION
behaviorism	a theory	that regards the objective facts of a subject's actions as the only valid basis for psychological study
cell	a unit of protoplasm	with a nucleus, cytoplasm, and an enclosing membrane

naturalism	a literary movement	whose original adherents believed writers should treat life with scientific objectivity
mitosis	a process	of nuclear division of cells, consisting of prophase, metaphase, anaphase, and telophase
authority	a power	to command and require obedience

Remember to provide a true definition (like those illustrated above), not just a descriptive statement such as "Happiness is a four-day weekend." Also keep in mind that repetition is not definition, so don't include the term you are defining in your definition. (For instance, the statement "Abstract art is a school of artists whose works are abstract" clarifies nothing for your readers.) Finally, define as precisely as possible. Name the class of the term you are defining — "mitosis is *a process* of cell division" — and define this class as narrowly and as accurately as you can, clearly differentiating your term from other members of its class. Careful attention to the language and structure of your formal definition will help readers understand your meaning.

Understanding Extended Definitions

Many extended-definition essays include short formal definitions like those found in dictionaries. In such an essay, a brief formal definition can introduce readers to the extended definition, or it can help to support the essay's thesis. However, providing a formal definition of each term you use is seldom necessary or desirable. Readers will either already know what a word means or be able to look it up. Still, it is often helpful to provide a brief definition of any term that is key to your readers' understanding of your essay, especially if a key term has more than one meaning, if you are using it in an unusual way, or if you are fairly certain that the term will be unfamiliar to your readers.

An extended definition does not follow a set **pattern of development**. Instead, it uses whatever strategies best suit the writer's purpose, the term being defined, and the writing situation. In fact, any one (or more than one) of the essay patterns illustrated in this book can be used to structure a definition essay.

Using Definition

Many situations call for extended definitions. On an exam, for example, you might be asked to define *behaviorism*, tell what a *cell* is, explain the meaning of the literary term *naturalism*, include a comprehensive definition of *mitosis* in your answer, or define *authority*. Such exam questions cannot always be answered in a sentence or two. In fact, the definitions they call for often require a full paragraph or even several paragraphs.

Extended definitions are useful in many academic assignments besides exams. For example, definitions can explain abstractions such as *freedom*, controversial terms such as *right to life*, or **slang** terms (informal expressions whose meanings may vary from locale to locale or change as time passes).

Planning a Definition Essay

Developing a Thesis Statement

The thesis of a definition essay should do more than simply identify the term to be defined and more than just define it. The thesis statement needs to make clear to readers the larger purpose for which you are defining the term. For example, assume you set out to write an extended definition of *behaviorism*. If your goal is to show its usefulness for treating patients with certain psychological disorders, a statement like "This essay will define behaviorism" will not be very helpful. Even a formal definition — "Behaviorism is a theory that regards the objective facts of a subject's actions as the only valid basis for psychological study" — is not enough. Your thesis statement needs to suggest the *value* of this kind of therapy, not just tell what it is — for example, "Contrary to some critics' objections, behaviorism is a valid approach for treating a wide variety of psychological dysfunctions."

Deciding on a Pattern of Development

You can organize a definition essay according to one or more of the patterns of development described in this book. As you plan your essay and jot down your ideas about the term or subject you will define, you will see which pattern or patterns are most useful. For example, each of the formal definitions illustrated on pages 479–80 could be expanded with a different pattern of development:

• **Exemplification**   To explain *behaviorism*, you could give **examples**. Carefully chosen cases could show exactly how behaviorism works and how this theory of psychology applies to different situations. Often, examples are the clearest way to explain something. For instance, defining dreams as "the symbolic representation of mental states" might convey little to readers who do not know much about psychology, but a few examples would help you make your meaning clear. Many students have dreams about taking exams — perhaps dreaming that they are late for the test, that they remember nothing about the course, or that they are writing their answers in disappearing ink. You might explain the nature of dreams by interpreting these particular dreams, which may reflect anxiety about a course or about school in general.

• **Description**   You can explain the nature of something by **describing** it. For example, the concept of a *cell* is difficult to grasp from just a formal definition, but your readers would understand the concept more clearly if you were to describe what a cell looks like, possibly providing a diagram. Concentrating on the cell membrane, cytoplasm, and nucleus, you could detail each structure's appearance and function. These descriptions would enable readers to visualize the whole cell and understand its workings. Of course, description involves more than the visual: a definition of a tsunami might describe the sounds and the appearance of this enormous ocean wave, and a definition of Parkinson's disease might include a description of its symptoms.

• **Comparison and contrast**   An extended definition of *naturalism* could use a **comparison-and-contrast** structure. Naturalism is one of several major movements in American literature, so its literary aims could be contrasted with those of other literary movements, such as romanticism or realism. Or, you might compare and contrast the plots and characters of several naturalistic works with those of romantic or realistic works. Anytime you need to define something unfamiliar, you can use an **analogy** to compare it to something that is likely to be familiar to your readers. For example, your readers may never have heard of the Chinese dish sweet-and-sour cabbage, but you can help them imagine it by saying that its texture is similar to that of coleslaw. You can also define a thing by contrasting it with something unlike it, especially if the two have some qualities in common. For instance, one way to explain the British sport of rugby might be to contrast it with American football, which is not as violent.

• **Process**   Because mitosis is a process, an extended definition of *mitosis* can be organized as an explanation of a **process**. By tracing the process from stage to stage, you would clearly define this type of cell division for your readers. Process is also a suitable pattern for defining objects in terms of what they do. For example, because a computer carries out various processes, an extended definition of a computer would probably include a process explanation.

• **Classification and division**   You could define *authority* by using **classification and division**. Basing your extended definition on the model developed by the German sociologist Max Weber, you could divide the class *authority* into the subclasses *traditional authority*, *charismatic authority*, and *legal-bureaucratic authority*. By explaining each type of authority, you could clarify this very broad term for your readers. In both extended and formal definitions, classification and division can be very useful. By identifying the class something belongs to, you are explaining what kind of thing it is. For instance, *monetarism* is an economic theory, *The Adventures of Huckleberry Finn* is a novel, and *emphysema* is a disease. Likewise, by dividing a class into subclasses, you are defining something more specifically. Emphysema, for instance, is a disease of the lungs and can therefore be classified with tuberculosis but not with appendicitis.

Structuring a Definition Essay

Like other essays, a definition essay should have an introduction, a body, and a conclusion. Although a formal definition strives for objectivity, an extended definition usually does not. Instead, it is likely to define a term in a way that reflects your attitude toward the subject or your reason for defining it. For example, your extended-definition essay about literary naturalism might argue that the significance of this movement's major works has been underestimated by literary scholars, or your definition of *authority* might criticize its abuses. In such cases, the **thesis statement** provides a focus for your definition essay, showing readers your approach to the definition.

The **introduction** identifies the term to be defined, perhaps presents a brief formal definition, and goes on to state the essay's thesis. The body of the essay expands the definition, using any one (or several) of the patterns of development explained and illustrated in this text.

In addition to using various patterns of development, you can expand the **body** of your definition by using any of the following strategies:

- You can define a term by using **synonyms** (words with similar meanings).
- You can define a term by using **negation** (telling what it is *not*).
- You can define a term by using **enumeration** (listing its characteristics).
- You can define a term by discussing its **origin and development** (the word's derivation, original meaning, and usages).

NOTE: If you are describing something that is unfamiliar to your readers, you can also include a **visual** — a drawing, painting, diagram, or photograph — to help them understand your definition.

Your essay's **conclusion** reminds readers why you have chosen to define the term, perhaps restating your thesis in different words.

Suppose your assignment is to write a short essay for your introductory psychology course. You decide to examine *behaviorism*. Of course, you can define the word in one or two sentences. To explain the *concept* of behaviorism and its status in the field of psychology, however, you must go beyond the dictionary.

Now, you have to decide what kinds of explanations are most suitable for your topic and for your intended audience. If you are trying to define *behaviorism* for readers who know very little about psychology, you might use analogies that relate behaviorism to your readers' experiences, such as how they were raised or how they train their pets. You might also use examples, but the examples would relate not to psychological experiments or clinical treatment but to experiences in everyday life. If, however, you are directing your essay to your psychology instructor, who obviously already knows what behaviorism is, your purpose is to show that you know, too. One way to do this is to compare behaviorism with other psychological theories, another way is to give examples of how behaviorism works in practice, and another way is to briefly summarize the background and history of the theory. (In a long essay, you might use all these strategies.)

After considering your essay's scope and audience, you might decide that because behaviorism has been somewhat controversial, your best strategy is to supplement a formal definition with examples showing how behaviorist assumptions and methods are applied in specific situations. These examples, drawn from your class notes and textbook, would support your thesis that behaviorism is a valid approach for treating certain psychological dysfunctions. Together, your examples would define *behaviorism* as it is understood today.

An informal outline for your essay might look like the following.

SAMPLE OUTLINE: Definition

INTRODUCTION

Thesis statement: Contrary to its critics' objections, behaviorism is a valid approach for treating a wide variety of psychological dysfunctions.

BACKGROUND

Definition of behaviorism, including its origins and evolution

FIRST EXAMPLE

Use of behaviorism to help psychotic patients function in an institutional setting

SECOND EXAMPLE

Use of behaviorism to treat neurotic behavior, such as chronic anxiety, a phobia, or a pattern of destructive acts

THIRD EXAMPLE

Use of behaviorism to treat normal but antisocial or undesirable behavior, such as heavy smoking or overeating

CONCLUSION

Restatement of thesis (in different words) or review of key points

Notice how the three examples in this essay define behaviorism with the kind of complexity, detail, and breadth that a formal definition could not duplicate. This definition is more like a textbook explanation — and, in fact, textbook explanations are often written as extended definitions.

Revising a Definition Essay

When you revise a definition essay, consider the items on Checklist: Revising on page 68. In addition, pay special attention to the items on the following checklist, which apply specifically to revising definition essays.

✔ **REVISION CHECKLIST** **DEFINITION**

- ☐ Does your assignment call for definition?
- ☐ Does your essay include a clearly worded thesis statement — one that identifies the term you will be defining and tells readers why you are defining it?
- ☐ Have you included a formal definition of your subject? Have you defined other key terms that may not be familiar to your readers?
- ☐ Have you used appropriate patterns of development to expand your definition?
- ☐ Do you need to use other strategies — such as synonyms, negation, or enumeration — to expand your definition?
- ☐ Do you need to discuss the origin and development of the term you are defining?
- ☐ Do you need to include a visual?
- ☐ Do you need to include sources?

Editing a Definition Essay

When you edit your definition essay, follow the guidelines on the editing checklists on pages 85, 88, and 92. In addition, focus on the grammar, mechanics, and punctuation issues that are particularly relevant to definition essays. One of these issues — avoiding the phrases *is when* and *is where* in formal definitions — is discussed below.

 GRAMMAR IN CONTEXT **AVOIDING *IS WHEN* AND *IS WHERE***

Many extended definitions include a one-sentence formal definition. As you have learned, such definitions must include the term you are defining, the class to which the term belongs, and the characteristics that distinguish the term from other terms in the same class.

Sometimes, however, when you are defining a term or concept, you may find yourself departing from this structure and using the phrase *is when* or *is where*. If so, your definition is not complete because it omits the term's class. (In fact, the use of *is when* or *is where* indicates that you are actually presenting an example of the term and not a definition.)

You can avoid this error by making certain that the form of the verb *be* in your definition is always followed by a noun.

INCORRECT: As described by Ajoy Mahtab in his essay "The Untouchable," *prejudice* is when someone forms an irrational bias or negative opinion of a person or group.

CORRECT: As described by Ajoy Mahtab in his essay "The Untouchable," *prejudice* is an irrational bias or negative opinion of a person or group.

INCORRECT: As Richard A. Posner defines it, *plagiarism* is where someone copies from a work without acknowledging the source.

CORRECT: As Richard A. Posner defines it, plagiarism is "unacknowledged copying" from a source.

✓ **EDITING CHECKLIST** **DEFINITION**

☐ Have you avoided using *is when* and *is where* in your formal definitions?
☐ Have you used the present tense for your formal definition — even if you have used the past tense elsewhere in your essay?
☐ In your formal definition, have you italicized the term you are defining?
☐ If you included a visual, is it appropriate and helpful?
☐ If you used sources, have you documented them?

A STUDENT WRITER: Definition

The following student essay, written by Ajoy Mahtab for a composition course, defines the untouchables, members of a caste that is shunned in India. In his essay, Ajoy, who grew up in Calcutta (now Kolkata), presents a thesis that is sharply critical of the practice of ostracizing untouchables. Note that he includes a photograph to help readers understand the unfamiliar term he is defining.

The Untouchable

Introduction:
background

A word that is extremely common in India yet uncommon to   1
the point of incomprehension in the West is the word *untouchable*.
It is a word that has had very sinister connotations throughout
India's history. A rigorously worked-out caste system has traditionally
existed in Indian society. At the top of the social ladder sat the
Brahmins, the clan of the priesthood. These people had renounced
the material world for a spiritual one. Below them came the
Kshatriyas, or the warrior caste. This caste included the kings and all
their nobles, along with their armies. Third on the social ladder were
the Vaishyas, who were the merchants of the land. Trade was their
only form of livelihood. Last came the Shudras — the menials. Shudras
were employed by the prosperous as sweepers and laborers. Originally
a person's caste was determined only by his profession. This meant
that if the son of a merchant joined the army, he automatically
converted from a Vaishya to a Kshatriya. However, the system soon
became hereditary and rigid. Whatever one's occupation, one's caste
was determined from birth according to the caste of one's father.

Outside of this structure were a group of people, human beings   2
treated worse than dogs and shunned far more than lepers, people
who were not considered even human, people who defiled with their
very touch. These were the Achhoots: the untouchables, one of whom

Formal definition

Historical
background

is shown in fig. 1. The word *untouchable* is commonly defined as
"that which cannot or should not be touched." In India, however,
it was taken to a far greater extreme. The untouchables of a village
lived in a separate community downwind of the borders of the village.
They had a separate water supply, for they would make the village
water impure if they were to drink from it. When they walked, they
were made to bang two sticks together continuously so that passersby
could hear them coming and thus avoid an untouchable's shadow.
Tied to their waists, trailing behind them, was a broom that would
clean the ground they had walked on. The penalty for not following
these or any other rules was death for the untouchable and, in many
instances, for the entire untouchable community.

Present situation

One of the pioneers of the fight against untouchability was   3
Mahatma Gandhi. Thanks to his efforts and those of many others,
untouchability no longer presents anything like the horrific picture
described above. In India today, in fact, recognition of untouchability is
punishable by law. Theoretically, there is no such thing as untouchability
anymore. But old traditions linger on, and a deep-rooted fear passed

Sean Sprague/The Image Works

Fig. 1. Sean Sprague. *Untouchable Woman Sweeping in Front of Her House in a Village in Tamil Nadu, India.* 2003. The Image Works, theimageworks.com/fotoweb/grid.fwx? SF_FIELD1=untouchable+woman+sweeping&SF_FIELD1_MATCHTYPE=all#Preview1.

down from generation to generation does not disappear overnight. Even today, for example, caste is an important factor in most marriages. Most Indian surnames reveal a person's caste immediately, so it is a difficult thing to hide. The shunning of the untouchable is more prevalent in South India, where people are much more devout, than in the North. Some people would rather starve than share food and water with an untouchable. This concept is very difficult to accept in the West, but it is true all the same.

Example

I remember an incident from my childhood. I could not have   4
been more than eight or nine at the time. I was on a holiday staying at my family's house on the river Ganges. A festival was going on, and, as is customary, we were giving the servants small presents. I was handing them out when an old woman, bent with age, slowly

hobbled into the room. She stood in the far corner of the room all alone, and no one so much as looked at her. When the entire line ended, she stepped hesitantly forward and stood in front of me, looking down at the ground. She then held a cloth stretched out in front of her. I was a little confused about how I was supposed to hand her her present since both her hands were holding the cloth. Then, with the help of prompting from someone behind me, I learned that I was supposed to drop the gift into the cloth without touching the cloth itself. It was only later that I found out that she was an untouchable. This was the first time I had actually come face to face with such prejudice, and it felt like a slap in the face. That incident was burned into my memory, and I do not think I will ever forget it.

Conclusion begins   The word *untouchable* is not often used in the West, and when   5 it is, it is generally used as a complimentary term. For example, an avid fan might say of an athlete, "He was absolutely untouchable. Nobody could even begin to compare with him." It seems rather ironic that a word could be so favorable in one culture and so negative in another. Why does a word that gives happiness in one part of the world cause pain in another? Why does the same word have different meanings to different people around the globe? Why do certain words cause rifts and others forge bonds? I do not think anyone can tell me the answers to these questions.

Conclusion continues   No actual parallel can be found today that compares to the   6 horrors of untouchability. For an untouchable, life itself was a

Thesis statement   crime. The day was spent just trying to stay alive. From the misery of the untouchables, the world should learn a lesson: isolating and punishing any group of people is dehumanizing and immoral.

Points for Special Attention

Thesis Statement

Ajoy Mahtab's assignment was to write an extended definition of a term he assumed would be unfamiliar to his audience. Because he had definite ideas about the unjust treatment of the untouchables, Ajoy wanted his essay to have a strong thesis that communicated his disapproval. Still, because he knew his American classmates would need a good deal of background information before they would understand the context for such a thesis, he decided not to present it in his introduction. Instead, he decided to lead up to his thesis gradually and state it at the end of his essay. When other students in the class reviewed his draft, this subtlety was one of the points they reacted to most favorably.

Structure

Ajoy's introduction establishes the direction of his essay by introducing the word he will define; he then places this word in context by explaining India's rigid caste system. In paragraph 2, he gives the formal definition of the word *untouchable* and goes on to sketch the term's historical background. Paragraph 3 explains the status of the untouchables in present-day India, and paragraph 4 gives a vivid example of Ajoy's first encounter with an untouchable. As he begins his conclusion in paragraph 5, Ajoy brings his readers back to the word his essay defines. Here he uses two strategies to add interest: he contrasts a contemporary American usage of *untouchable* with its pejorative meaning in India, and he asks a series of **rhetorical questions** (questions asked for effect and not meant to be answered). In paragraph 6, Ajoy presents a summary of his position to lead into his thesis statement.

Patterns of Development

This essay uses a number of strategies commonly incorporated into extended definitions: it includes a formal definition, explains the term's origin, and explores some of the term's connotations. The essay also uses several familiar patterns of development. For instance, paragraph 1 uses classification and division to explain India's caste system; paragraphs 2 and 3 use brief examples to illustrate the plight of the untouchable; and paragraph 4 presents a narrative. Each of these patterns enriches the definition.

Working with Sources

Ajoy includes a visual — a photograph of an untouchable — to supplement his passages of description and to help his readers understand this very unfamiliar concept. He places the photograph early in his essay, where it will be most helpful, and he refers to it in paragraph 2 with the phrase "one of whom is shown in fig. 1." In addition, he includes a caption below the photo with full source information.

Focus on Revision

Because the term Ajoy defined was so unfamiliar to his classmates, many of the peer-editing worksheets students filled in asked for more information. One suggestion in particular — that he draw an analogy between the unfamiliar term *untouchable* and a concept more familiar to American students — appealed to Ajoy as he planned his revision. Another student suggested that Ajoy could compare untouchables to other groups who have been shunned, such as people with AIDS. Although Ajoy states in his conclusion that no parallel exists, an attempt to find common ground between untouchables and other groups could make his essay more meaningful to his readers and bring home to them a distinctly unfamiliar idea.

PEER-EDITING WORKSHEET: DEFINITION

1. What term is the writer defining? Does the essay include a formal definition? If so, where? If no formal definition is included, should one be added?

2. For what purpose is the writer defining the term? Does the essay include a thesis statement that makes this purpose clear? If not, suggest revisions.

3. What patterns does the writer use to develop the definition? What other patterns could be used? Would a visual be helpful?

4. Does the writer use analogies to develop the definition? If so, where? Do you find these analogies helpful? What additional analogies might help readers understand the term more fully?

5. Does the essay define the term in language and content appropriate for its audience? Does the definition help readers understand the meaning of the term?

6. Does the writer use synonyms to develop the definition? If so, where? If not, where could synonyms be used to help communicate the term's meaning?

7. Does the writer use negation to develop the definition? If so, where? If not, could the writer strengthen the definition by explaining what the term is not?

8. Does the writer use enumeration to develop the definition? If so, where? If not, where in the essay might the writer list the term's special characteristics?

9. Does the writer explain the term's origin and development? If so, where? If not, do you believe this information should be added?

10. If the writer includes sources, are they helpful and appropriate? Are they documented fully and correctly?

11. If the writer includes a visual, does it help to define the essay's subject?

The selections that follow use exemplification, description, narration, and other methods of developing extended definitions. The first selection, a visual text, is followed by questions designed to illustrate how definition can operate in visual form.

The Rule (Comic Strip)

FIG. 13.2

Reading Images

1. This classic 1985 comic strip introduces three criteria for evaluating movies from a feminist perspective. What term does the comic strip define? Write a one-sentence definition of that term.
2. A 2017 article in the *National Review* refers to the Bechdel rule as "a meaningless way to measure whether movies pass the feminist litmus test." (For example, the rule doesn't assess a film's worth or take into account whether the film actually focuses on a woman.) How do you react to that characterization? Why?
3. Could Bechdel's criteria be applied to romance novels? To science fiction? To video games? To TV sitcoms? Why or why not?

Journal Entry

Apply the Bechdel rule to a movie that you know well. Does the film meet Bechdel's three criteria? Does your understanding of the rule change your assessment of the film? Does it help you to evaluate the film fairly and accurately? Explain.

Thematic Connections

- from *Persepolis II* (page 111)
- "Sex, Lies, and Conversation" (page 408)
- "Flick Chicks" (page 444)

JUDY BRADY

I Want a Wife

Judy Brady (1937–2017) published articles on many social issues. Diagnosed with breast cancer in 1980, she became active in the politics of cancer and edited *Women and Cancer* (1990) and *One in Three: Women with Cancer Confront an Epidemic* (1991). She also helped found the Toxic Links Coalition, an organization devoted to lobbying for cancer and environmental issues.

Background on the status of women Brady had been active in the women's movement since 1969, and "I Want a Wife" first appeared in the premiere issue of the feminist *Ms.* magazine in 1972. That year represented perhaps the height of the feminist movement in the United States. The National Organization for Women, established in 1966, had hundreds of chapters around the country. The Equal Rights Amendment, barring discrimination against women, passed in Congress (although by its 1982 deadline it was ratified by only thirty-five of the necessary thirty-eight states), and Congress also passed Title IX of the Education Amendments of 1972, which required equal opportunity (in sports as well as academics) for all students in any school that receives federal funding. At that time, women accounted for just under 40 percent of the labor force (up from 23 percent in 1950); this number has grown to almost 50 percent today, in part because of the severe recession that started in 2008, which has caused more job losses for men than for women. Of mothers with children under age eighteen, fewer than 40 percent were employed in 1970; today, around 70 percent work, and around half work full-time. As for stay-at-home fathers, their numbers have increased from virtually zero to more than two million.

1 I belong to that classification of people known as wives. I am A Wife. And, not altogether incidentally, I am a mother.

2 Not too long ago a male friend of mine appeared on the scene fresh from a recent divorce. He had one child, who is, of course, with his ex-wife. He is looking for another wife. As I thought about him while I was ironing one evening, it suddenly occurred to me that I, too, would like to have a wife. Why do I want a wife?

3 I would like to go back to school so that I can become economically independent, support myself, and, if need be, support those dependent upon me. I want a wife who will work and send me to school. And while I am going to school I want a wife to take care of my children. I want a wife to keep track of the children's doctor and dentist appointments. And to keep track of mine, too. I want a wife to make sure my children eat properly and are kept clean. I want a wife who will wash the children's clothes and keep them mended. I want a wife who is a good nurturant attendant to my children, who arranges for their schooling, makes sure that they have an adequate social life with their peers, takes them to the park, the zoo, etc. I want a wife who takes care of the

children when they are sick, a wife who arranges to be around when the children need special care, because, of course, I cannot miss classes at school. My wife must arrange to lose time at work and not lose the job. It may mean a small cut in my wife's income from time to time, but I guess I can tolerate that. Needless to say, my wife will arrange and pay for the care of the children while my wife is working.

I want a wife who will take care of *my* physical needs. I want a wife who will 4 keep my house clean. A wife who will pick up after my children, a wife who will pick up after me. I want a wife who will keep my clothes clean, ironed, mended, replaced when need be, and who will see to it that my personal things are kept in their proper place so that I can find what I need the minute I need it. I want a wife who cooks the meals, a wife who is a *good* cook. I want a wife who will plan the menus, do the necessary grocery shopping, prepare the meals, serve them pleasantly, and then do the cleaning up while I do my studying. I want a wife who will care for me when I am sick and sympathize with my pain and loss of time from school. I want a wife to go along when our family takes a vacation so that someone can continue to care for me and my children when I need a rest and change of scene.

I want a wife who will not bother me with rambling complaints about a 5 wife's duties. But I want a wife who will listen to me when I feel the need to explain a rather difficult point I have come across in my course of studies. And I want a wife who will type my papers for me when I have written them.

I want a wife who will take care of the details of my social life. When my 6 wife and I are invited out by my friends, I want a wife who will take care of the babysitting arrangements. When I meet people at school that I like and want to entertain, I want a wife who will have the house clean, will prepare a special meal, serve it to me and my friends, and not interrupt when I talk about things that interest me and my friends. I want a wife who will have arranged that the children are fed and ready for bed before my guests arrive so that the children do not bother us. I want a wife who takes care of the needs of my guests so that they feel comfortable, who makes sure that they have an ashtray, that they are passed the hors d'oeuvres, that they are offered a second helping of the food, that their wine glasses are replenished when necessary, that their coffee is served to them as they like it. And I want a wife who knows that sometimes I need a night out by myself.

I want a wife who is sensitive to my sexual needs, a wife who makes love 7 passionately and eagerly when I feel like it, a wife who makes sure that I am satisfied. And, of course, I want a wife who will not demand sexual attention when I am not in the mood for it. I want a wife who assumes the complete responsibility for birth control, because I do not want more children. I want a wife who will remain sex-

> **"My God, who wouldn't want a wife?"**

ually faithful to me so that I do not have to clutter up my intellectual life with jealousies. And I want a wife who understands that *my* sexual needs may entail more than strict adherence to monogamy. I must, after all, be able to relate to people as fully as possible.

If, by chance, I find another person more suitable as a wife than the wife I   8
already have, I want the liberty to replace my present wife with another one.
Naturally, I will expect a fresh new life; my wife will take the children and be
solely responsible for them so that I am left free.

When I am through with school and have a job, I want my wife to quit   9
working and remain at home so that my wife can more fully and completely
take care of a wife's duties.

My God, who *wouldn't* want a wife?   10

· · ·

Comprehension

1. In one sentence, define what Brady means by *wife*. Does this ideal wife
   actually exist? Explain.
2. List some of the specific duties of the wife Brady describes. Into what five
   general categories does Brady arrange these duties?
3. What complaints does Brady apparently have about the life she actually
   leads? To what does she seem to attribute her problems?
4. Under what circumstances does Brady say she would consider leaving her
   wife? What would happen to the children if she left?

Purpose and Audience

1. This essay was first published in *Ms.* magazine. In what sense is it appropriate for the audience of this feminist publication? Where might it appear if it
   were written today?
2. Does this essay have an explicitly stated thesis? If so, where is it? If the thesis
   is implied, paraphrase it.
3. Do you think Brady *really* wants the kind of wife she describes? Explain your
   response.

Style and Structure

1. Throughout the essay, Brady repeats the words "I want a wife." What is the
   effect of this repetition?
2. The first and last paragraphs of this essay are quite brief. Are these paragraphs effective, or should one or both be developed further?
3. In enumerating a wife's duties, Brady frequently uses the verb *arrange*. What
   other verbs does she use repeatedly? How do these verbs help her make her
   point?
4. Brady never uses the personal pronouns *he* or *she* to refer to the wife she
   defines. Why not?

5. **Vocabulary Project.** Going beyond the dictionary definitions, decide what Brady means to suggest by each of the following words. Is she using any of these terms sarcastically?

proper (4)	necessary (6)	suitable (8)
pleasantly (4)	demand (7)	free (8)
bother (6)	clutter up (7)	

Journal Entry

How accurate is Brady's 1972 characterization of a wife today? Which of the characteristics she describes have remained the same? Which have changed? Why?

Writing Workshop

1. Write an essay defining your ideal boss, parent, teacher, or pet.
2. Write an essay titled "I Want a Husband." Taking an **ironic** stance, use society's notions of the ideal husband to help you shape your definition.
3. **Working with Sources.** Find information online about the 1972 premiere issue of *Ms.* magazine. What articles and features appeared there? How did contemporary critics react to the magazine's content and philosophy at the time? Referring to the information you find, write an essay in which you define *Ms.* as a feminist magazine. Be sure to provide a clear definition of *feminist magazine* early in your essay. Be sure to cite your sources and to include a works-cited page. (See Chapter 18 for information on MLA documentation.)

Combining the Patterns

Like most definition essays, "I Want a Wife" uses several patterns of development. Which ones does it use? Which of these do you consider most important for supporting Brady's thesis? Why?

Thematic Connections
- "My Mother Never Worked" (page 122)
- "Sex, Lies, and Conversation" (page 408)
- "Flick Chicks" (page 444)

JOSÉ ANTONIO BURCIAGA

Tortillas

José Antonio Burciaga (1940–1996) was the founder of *Diseños Literarios*, a publishing company in California, as well as one of the founders of the comedy troupe Culture Clash. He contributed fiction, poetry, and articles to many anthologies, as well as to journals and newspapers. He also published several books of poems, drawings, and essays, including the poetry collection *Undocumented Love* (1992) and the essay collection *Drink Cultura* (1993). "Tortillas," originally titled "I Remember Masa," was first published in *Weedee Peepo* (1988), a collection of essays in Spanish and English. A posthumous edition of Burciaga's work, *The Last Supper of Chicano Heroes: The Selected Works of José Antonio Burciaga*, appeared in 2008.

Background on tortillas Tortillas have been a staple of Mexican cooking for thousands of years. These thin, round griddle cakes made of cornmeal (*masa*) are often eaten with every meal, and the art of making them is still passed from generation to generation (although they now are widely available commercially as well). The earliest Mexican immigrants introduced them to the United States, and today, tortillas, along with many other popular items of Mexican cuisine, are part of the country's culinary landscape (as are a wide variety of other "ethnic" foods, such as pizza, egg rolls, bagels, sushi, and gyros). Still, tortillas have special meaning for Mexican Americans, and in this essay Burciaga discusses the role of the tortilla within his family's culture.

My earliest memory of *tortillas* is my *Mamá* telling me not to play with them. I had bitten eyeholes in one and was wearing it as a mask at the dinner table. 1

As a child, I also used *tortillas* as hand warmers on cold days, and my family claims that I owe my career as an artist to my early experiments with *tortillas*. According to them, my clowning around helped me develop a strong artistic foundation. I'm not so sure, though. Sometimes I wore a *tortilla* on my head, like a *yarmulke*, and yet I never had any great urge to convert from Catholicism to Judaism. But who knows? They may be right. 2

For Mexicans over the centuries, the *tortilla* has served as the spoon and the fork, the plate and the napkin. *Tortillas* originated before the Mayan civilizations, perhaps predating Europe's wheat bread. According to Mayan mythology, the great god Quetzalcoatl, realizing that the red ants knew the secret of using maize as food, transformed himself into a black ant, infiltrated the colony of red ants, and absconded with a grain of corn. (Is it any wonder that to this day, black ants and red ants do not get along?) Quetzalcoatl then put maize on the lips of the first man and woman, Oxomoco and Cipactonal, so that they would become strong. Maize festivals are still celebrated by many Indian cultures of the Americas. 3

When I was growing up in El Paso, *tortillas* were part of my daily life. I used   4
to visit a *tortilla* factory in an ancient adobe building near the open *mercado* in
Ciudad Juárez. As I approached, I could hear the rhythmic slapping of the *masa*
as the skilled vendors outside the factory formed it into balls and patted them
into perfectly round corn cakes between the palms of their hands. The wonderful aroma and the speed with which the women counted so many dozens of *tortillas* out of warm wicker baskets still linger in my mind. Watching them at work
convinced me that the most handsome and *deliciosas tortillas* are handmade.
Although machines are faster, they can never adequately replace generation-
to-generation experience. There's no place in the factory assembly line for the
tender slaps that give each *tortilla* character. The best thing that can be said
about mass-producing *tortillas* is that it makes it possible for many people to
enjoy them.

In the *mercado* where my mother shop-   5
ped, we frequently bought *taquitos de nopalitos*,
small tacos filled with diced cactus, onions,
tomatoes, and *jalapeños*. Our friend Don
Toribio showed us how to make delicious,
crunchy *taquitos* with dried, salted pumpkin
seeds. When you had no money for the filling, a poor man's *taco* could be made by placing a warm *tortilla* on the left palm, applying
a sprinkle of salt, then rolling the *tortilla* up

> "For Mexicans over the centuries, the tortilla has served as the spoon and the fork, the plate and the napkin."

quickly with the fingertips of the right hand. My own kids put peanut butter
and jelly on *tortillas*, which I think is truly bicultural. And speaking of fast foods
for kids, nothing beats a *quesadilla*, a *tortilla* grilled-cheese sandwich.

Depending on what you intend to use them for, *tortillas* may be made in   6
various ways. Even a run-of-the-mill *tortilla* is more than a flat corn cake. A
skillfully cooked homemade *tortilla* has a bottom and a top; the top skin forms
a pocket in which you put the filling that folds your *tortilla* into a taco. Paper-
thin *tortillas* are used specifically for *flautas*, a type of taco that is filled, rolled,
and then fried until crisp. The name *flauta* means *flute*, which probably refers to
the Mayan bamboo flute; however, the only sound that comes from an edible
flauta is a delicious crunch that is music to the palate. In México *flautas* are
sometimes made as long as two feet and then cut into manageable segments.
The opposite of *flautas* is *gorditas*, meaning *little fat ones*. These are very thick
small *tortillas*.

The versatility of *tortillas* and corn does not end here. Besides being tasty   7
and nourishing, they have spiritual and artistic qualities as well. The
Tarahumara Indians of Chihuahua, for example, concocted a corn-based beer
called *tesgüino*, which their descendants still make today. And everyone has
read about the woman in New Mexico who was cooking her husband a *tortilla*
one morning when the image of Jesus Christ miraculously appeared on it.
Before they knew what was happening, the man's breakfast had become a local
shrine.

Then there is *tortilla* art. Various Chicano artists throughout the Southwest   8
have, when short of materials or just in a whimsical mood, used a dry *tortilla* as

a small, round canvas. And a few years back, at the height of the Chicano movement, a priest in Arizona got into trouble with the Church after he was discovered celebrating mass using a *tortilla* as the host. All of which only goes to show
that while the *tortilla* may be a lowly corn cake, when the necessity arises, it can
reach unexpected distinction.

· · ·

Comprehension

1. What exactly is a tortilla?
2. List the functions — both practical and whimsical — that tortillas serve.
3. In paragraph 7, Burciaga cites the "spiritual and artistic qualities" of
   tortillas. Do you think he is being serious? Explain your reasoning.

Purpose and Audience

1. Burciaga states his thesis explicitly in his essay's final sentence. Paraphrase
   this thesis. Why do you think he does not state it sooner? Do you think it
   was the right decision? Why or why not?
2. Do you think Burciaga expects most of his readers to be of Hispanic
   descent? To be familiar with tortillas? How can you tell?
3. Why do you think Burciaga uses humor in this essay? Is it consistent with
   his essay's purpose? Could the humor have a negative effect on his audience? Explain.
4. Why are tortillas so important to Burciaga? Is it just their versatility he
   admires, or do they represent something more to him?

Style and Structure

1. Where does Burciaga provide a formal definition of *tortilla*? Why does he
   locate this formal definition where he does?
2. Burciaga uses many Spanish words, but he defines only some of them — for
   example, *taquitos de nopalitos* and *quesadilla* in paragraph 5 and *flautas* and
   gorditas in paragraph 6. Why do you think he defines some Spanish terms
   but not others? Should he have defined them all?
3. Does Burciaga use synonyms or negation to define *tortilla*? Does he discuss
   the word's origin and development? If so, where? If not, do you think any of
   these strategies would improve his essay? Explain.
4. **Vocabulary Project.** Look up each of the following words in a Spanish-
   English dictionary, and try to supply its English equivalent.

   mercado (4)   deliciosas (4)

   masa (4)   jalapeños (5)

Journal Entry

Explore some additional uses — practical or frivolous — for tortillas that Burciaga does not discuss.

Writing Workshop

1. **Working with Sources.** Find information about a food that is important to your family, ethnic group, or circle of friends, and write an essay that defines that food. Begin with your own "earliest memory" of the food, and then provide background information on the food's origin and history. As you develop your definition, use several patterns of development, as Burciaga does. Assume your audience is not familiar with the food you define. Your thesis should indicate why the food is so important to you. Be sure to document references to Burciaga's essay and to include a works-cited page. (See Chapter 18 for information on MLA documentation.)

2. Relying primarily on description and exemplification, define a food that you assume is familiar to all your readers. Do not name the food until your essay's last sentence.

3. Write an essay defining a food — but include a thesis statement that paints a very favorable portrait of a much-maligned food (for example, Spam or scrapple) or a very negative picture of a popular food (for example, chocolate or ice cream).

Combining the Patterns

Burciaga uses several patterns of development in his extended definition. Where, for example, does he use **description**, **narration**, **process**, and **exemplification**? Does he use any other patterns?

Thematic Connections

- "The Secret Lion" (page 140)
- "Goodbye to My Twinkie Days" (page 171)
- "The Park" (page 663)

VIRGINIA FOXX

Stop Calling It "Vocational Training"

Virginia Foxx, a Republican U.S. representative from North Carolina, was born in 1943 in the Bronx, New York, but grew up in rural North Carolina. The first person in her family to attend college, she earned her undergraduate and graduate degrees at the University of North Carolina at Chapel Hill. Before entering politics, Foxx ran a nursery and landscaping business with her husband, taught at Appalachian State University, and served as president of Maryland Community College. Foxx then spent ten years in the North Carolina State Senate, where she sponsored many bills, opposed tax increases, and initiated legislation to make government more efficient. Currently, she is the Republican leader of the House Education and Labor Committee. From 2013 to 2016, she served as secretary of the House Republican Conference. A staunch conservative, she has won the U.S. Chamber of Commerce's Spirit of Enterprise Award and the Family Research Council's True Blue Award.

Background on vocational training The term *vocational training* usually refers to postsecondary education focused on acquiring skills and knowledge for a specific job (such as x-ray technician) or a particular trade (such as welding). Institutions that provide this training are called vocational schools, technical schools, or vocational colleges. Their degree and licensing programs generally range from about eight months to two years. The history of this formal vocational training stretches back to the "schools of industry" in eighteenth-century Germany and England. In these institutions, students — most of them poor — did industrial-wage work along with their coursework, allowing them to pay their tuition. Women in these schools learned trades like sewing and knitting, and men learned to become furniture makers or woodworkers. In the United States, after the Civil War, the trade-school movement (backed in large part by philanthropists and union leaders) emerged as a response to the need for workers in a rapidly expanding industrial economy. Trade schools were also seen as a way to assimilate new immigrants to the United States — as well as a vehicle for teaching values such as the Protestant work ethic, temperance, and productivity. Over the last couple of decades, Americans have witnessed a revival of interest in trade schools, especially in the wake of the 2008 financial crisis, ever-rising tuition costs for four-year degrees, and concerns about student-loan debt. In fact, enrollment in vocational training programs has doubled since the late 1990s, and more than sixteen million students now attend these postsecondary institutions, where the training costs much less than a traditional bachelor's degree and takes much less time. Moreover, many jobs now require specialized training that traditional college programs cannot provide, particularly in fields such as infrastructure, technology, and transportation.

I know how it feels to be the only woman in a room of powerful men. I also know how it feels to be tuned out because of how I look or where I'm from. For these reasons I'm sympathetic to those who are passionate about changing culture for the better by promoting "inclusive" language. But the focus on inclusivity hasn't extended to the way we talk about education.

> "Whether an individual acquires a skill credential, a bachelor's degree, a postgraduate degree, or anything in between, it's all education."

Education has always been the key to opportunity in America, rightly called "the great equalizer." But the sociologist Herbert Spencer once noted "how often misused words generate misleading thoughts." By placing descriptors like "vocational" and "technical" in front of the word "education," we generate misleading thoughts about the types of people who enroll in such programs.

Those who earn what people usually call vocational and technical degrees have long been viewed as inferior to those who graduate with a series of letters after their names. If you went to school to learn a trade, you must be lesser, because someone long ago decided that college should be called "higher" education. Considering the state of colleges and universities today, the word "higher" may be the most misleading of them all.

The way we speak about education is inherently classist. When a student of lesser means attends a traditional four-year school, we say she "overcame her circumstances." When a student from a wealthy background chooses a trade school we say he didn't "live up to expectations." We are all but telling people that the trade jobs this country needs are dirty, and that skills-based education is for people without means or, much worse, without potential. We have perpetuated the idea that baccalaureate degrees and desk jobs are for middle-class and affluent people; community college and technical pursuits are for the poor.

I ended up with a series of abbreviations after my name because I wanted to teach. One of the few lessons that stuck with me from all the courses I took on the way to earning my Ed.D. came during a classroom discussion that sparked my passion for changing the way we talk about education. I'll never forget how the professor responded to a student who used the word "training." Training, the professor admonished, was for animals. Humans receive an education.

We can't keep speaking of people as if they are animals. Whether an individual acquires a skill credential, a bachelor's degree, a postgraduate degree, or anything in between, it's all education. We need to think about the words we use and why we use them if we are to break the stigma around all forms of education. If we don't, we will never overcome the abiding sense of inequality and unfairness that so many Americans feel.

Individual potential transcends all demographics. It's time that we speak honestly about the educational paths we set for Americans — and the paths they should be commended for choosing for themselves.

. . .

Comprehension

1. Why does Foxx see "'inclusive' language" (1) as limited?
2. Why does Foxx quote Herbert Spencer in paragraph 2?
3. In paragraph 3, Foxx criticizes the term *"higher" education*. On what basis does she do so?
4. Why, according to Foxx, are our discussions of education "inherently classist" (4)? Do you agree with her? Why or why not?
5. Do you think Fox's real subject here is education, language, or class conflict? Explain your conclusion.
6. In paragraph 7, Foxx says, "Individual potential transcends all demographics." What does she mean? Is she correct, or is she being unrealistic?

Purpose and Audience

1. Virginia Foxx is a Republican member of Congress who has a B.A. from the University of North Carolina as well as a master's degree in sociology and a Ph.D. in education. Where in the essay does she allude to her academic degrees? Why does she do so?
2. Why do you suppose Foxx opens with references to her own experiences? Is it an effective opening strategy? Why or why not?
3. What does Foxx hope to accomplish in this essay? For example, do you think she wants to change readers' minds? Inspire them to take action? Modify their goals? What makes you think so?
4. In paragraph 6, Foxx says, "Whether an individual acquires a skill credential, a bachelor's degree, a postgraduate degree, or anything in between, it's all education." What does she mean? Is that her essay's thesis?

Style and Structure

1. **Vocabulary Project.** What connotations do you associate with the word *training*? Do you think the professor that Foxx refers to in paragraph 5 was right to discourage the use of this word? Why or why not?
2. Where in her definition does Foxx use **negation**? Where does she use comparison? What other strategies does she use to develop her definition?
3. Would you characterize the overall tone of this essay as optimistic or pessimistic? Explain.
4. In one sentence, define *education* as Foxx would define it. Then, write your own definition of *education*. How are these two definitions alike? How are they different?

Journal Entry

Do you see vocational and technical programs as education? Or do you see these alternatives to college as training rather than education?

Writing Workshop

1. Write your own extended definition of *education*, using exemplification and narration to trace your own experiences with education, both inside and outside the classroom.

2. Write a proposal for an innovative new elementary, middle, or high school. In your proposal, define the kind of education you plan to offer students, and give examples of the kinds of opportunities your brand of education will provide.

3. **Working with Sources.** Research the history of vocational education in the United States (or in another country). Then, write an essay that defines *vocational education* by tracing its origin and development. Be sure to document all references to sources and to include a works-cited page. (See Chapter 18 for information on MLA documentation.

Combining the Patterns

How could this brief definition essay be expanded with **narration**? With **exemplification**?

Thematic Connections

- "Why I Went to College" (page 362)
- "What I Learned (and Didn't Learn) in College" (page 436)
- "The Dog Ate My Tablet, and Other Tales of Woe" (page 450)
- Debate: "Should Federal Student Loans Be Forgiven?" (page 576)

TONI MORRISON

Goodness: Altruism and the Literary Imagination

A Nobel laureate in literature and a towering figure in contemporary American fiction, Toni Morrison (1931–2019) was born and raised in Lorain, Ohio. She earned her B.A. at Howard University and her M.A. from Cornell University. After teaching English at Texas Southern University and Howard University, she began a decades-long career as an editor at Random House publishing, where she became the first Black editor in the fiction department. At Random House, Morrison championed many African American writers, including Toni Cade Bambara, Angela Davis, and Gayl Jones. She published her own first novel, *The Bluest Eye*, in 1970. Over the next several years, the acclaimed novels *Sula* (1973), *Song of Solomon* (1977), and *Tar Baby* (1981) followed. Morrison reached the height of her acclaim and popularity with the *Beloved* trilogy: *Beloved* (1987), *Jazz* (1992), and *Paradise* (1997). These novels wove together intense love stories with wider social, political, and cultural themes of African American history. From 1989 to 2006, she also taught creative writing courses at Princeton University. In addition to her 1993 Nobel Prize in Literature, she won countless other awards, including the Pulitzer Prize for Fiction, the American Book Award, and the Library of Congress Creative Achievement Award for Fiction. Awarding her a 2012 Presidential Medal of Freedom, President Barack Obama said, "Toni Morrison's prose brings us that kind of moral and emotional intensity that few writers ever attempt."

Background on poetic justice As Morrison writes in paragraph 11 of the following essay, "In nineteenth-century novels, regardless of what acts of wickedness or cruel indifference controlled the plot, the ending was almost always the triumph of goodness." The term for this distribution of rewards to the good and punishments for the bad is *poetic justice*. Fables, fairy tales, and parables often make the device obvious, as these forms explicitly teach moral lessons. For example, in *Cinderella*, Cinderella's evil stepmother and abusive sisters must watch at the end of the story as Cinderella becomes the queen. Poetic justice operates in modern films, too, as when the wrongly accused and imprisoned protagonist of *The Shawshank Redemption* escapes after twenty years in prison and lives happily ever after while a corrupt prison official is punished. But another powerful tradition exists in our storytelling, whether in print, in film, or on television: the lure of the morally ambiguous protagonist, or antihero. Television, in particular, has featured many such characters and stories that toy with our sense of poetic justice, including *The Sopranos*, *The Wire*, *Mad Men*, and *The Walking Dead*. Although some may insist that this moral framework is false or naive, others argue that it remains a central value and purpose in literature. As the literary critic and scholar Jonathan Gottschall writes, stories working on the principle of poetic justice "make us believe in a lie: that the world is more just than it actually is. But believing that lie has important effects for society — and it may even help explain why humans tell stories in the first place."

On an October morning in 2006, a young man backed his truck into the driveway of a one-room schoolhouse. He walked into the school and after ordering the boy students, the teacher, and a few other adults to leave, he lined up 10 girls, ages 9 to 13, and shot them. The mindless horror of that attack drew intense and sustained press as well as, later on, books and film. Although there had been two other, school shootings only a few days earlier, what made this massacre especially notable was the fact that its landscape was an Amish community—notoriously peaceful and therefore the most unlikely venue for such violence.

> "Goodness sits in the audience and watches, assuming it even has a ticket to the show."

1

Before the narrative tracking the slaughter had been exhausted in the press, another rail surfaced, one that was regarded as bizarre and somehow as shocking as the killings. The Amish community forgave the killer, refused to seek justice, demand vengeance, or even to judge him. They visited and comforted the killer's widow and children (who were not Amish), just as they embraced the relatives of the slain. There appeared a number of explanations for their behavior—their historical aversion to killing anyone at all for any reason and their separatist convictions. More to the point, the Amish community had nothing or very little to say to outside inquiry except that it was God's place to judge, not theirs. And, as one cautioned, "Do not think evil of this man." They held no press conferences and submitted to no television interviews. They quietly buried the dead, attended the killer's funeral, then tore down the old schoolhouse and built a new one.

2

Their silence following the slaughter, along with their deep concern for the killer's family, seemed to me at the time characteristic of genuine "goodness." And I became fascinated with the term and its definition.

3

Thinkers, of whom none was as uninformed as I was, have long analyzed what constitutes goodness, what good is good, and what its origins are or may be. The myriad theories I read overwhelmed me, and to reduce my confusion I thought I should just research the term "altruism." I quickly found myself on a frustrating journey into a plethora of definitions and counterdefinitions. I began by thinking of altruism as a more or less faithful rendition of its Latin root: alter/other; selfless compassion for the "other." That route was not merely narrow; it led to a swamp of interpretations, contrary analyses, and doubt. A few of these arguments posited wildly different explanations: (1) Altruism is not an instinctive act of selflessness, but a taught and learned one. (2) Altruism might actually be narcissism, ego enhancement, even a mental disorder made manifest in a desperate desire to think well of oneself to erase or diminish self-loathing. (3) Some of the most thought-provoking theories came from scholarship investigating the DNA, if you will, seeking evidence of an embedded gene automatically firing to enable the sacrifice of oneself for the benefit of others; a kind of brother or sister to Darwin's "survival of the fittest." Examples of confirmation or contradiction of the Darwinian theory came primarily from the animal and insect kingdoms: squirrels deliberately attracting

4

predators to themselves to warn the other squirrels; birds as well and especially ants, bees, bats all in service to the colony, the collective, the swarm. Such behavior is very common among humans. But the question being put seemed to be whether such sacrifice for kin and/or community is innate, built, as it were, into our genes just as individual conquest of others is held to be a natural, instinctive drive that serves evolution. Is there a "good" gene along with a "selfish" gene? The further question for me was the competition between the gene and the mind.

I confess I was unable and ill equipped to understand much of the scholarship on altruism, but I did learn something about its weight, its urgency, and its relevance and irrelevance in contemporary thought.   5

Keeping those Amish in mind, I wondered why the narrative of that event, in the press and visual media, quickly ignored the killer and the slaughtered children and began to focus almost exclusively on the shock of forgiveness. As I noted earlier, mass shootings at schools were perhaps too ordinary; there had been two such shootings elsewhere during that same time, but the Amish community's unwillingness to clamor for justice/vengeance/retribution, or even to judge the killer was the compelling story. The shock was that the parents of the dead children took pains to comfort the killer's widow, her family, and her children, to raise funds for them, not themselves. Of the victimized community's response to that almost classic example of evil, in addition to their refusal to fix blame, the most extraordinary element was their silence. It was that silence (that refusal to be lionized, televised) that caused me to think differently about goodness.   6

Of course thinking about goodness implies, indeed requires, a view of its opposite.   7

I have never been interested in or impressed by evil itself, but I have been confounded by how attractive it is to others. I am stunned by the attention given to its every whisper and shout. Which is not to deny its existence and ravage, nor to suggest evil does not demand confrontation, but simply to wonder why it is so worshiped, especially in literature. Is it its theatricality, its costume, its blood spray, the emotional satisfaction that comes with its investigation more than with its collapse? (The ultimate detective story, the paradigm murder mystery.) Perhaps it is how it dances, the music it inspires, its clothing, its nakedness, its sexual disguise, its passionate howl, and its danger. The formula in which evil reigns is bad versus good, but the deck is stacked because goodness in contemporary literature seems to be equated with weakness, as pitiful (a girl running frightened and helpless through the woods while the pursuing villain gets more of our attention than her savior).   8

Evil has a blockbuster audience; Goodness lurks backstage. Evil has vivid speech; Goodness bites its tongue. It is Billy Budd, who can only stutter. It is Coetzee's Michael K, with a harelip that so limits his speech that communication with him is virtually impossible. It is Melville's Bartleby, confining language to repetition. It is Faulkner's Benjy, an idiot.   9

Rather than rummage through the exquisite and persuasive language of religions—all of which implore believers to rank goodness as the highest and holiest of human achievement, and many of which identify their saints and   10 icons of worship as examples of pure altruism — I decided to focus on the role goodness plays in literature using my own line of work — fiction — as a test.

In nineteenth-century novels, regardless of what acts of wickedness or   11
cruel indifference controlled the plot, the ending was almost always the triumph of goodness. Dickens, Hardy, and Austen all left their readers with a sense of the restoration of order and the triumph of virtue, even Dostoyevsky. Note that Svidrigailov in *Crime and Punishment*, exhausted by his own evil and the language that supports it, becomes so bored by his terminal acts of charity, he commits suicide. He cannot live without the language of evil, nor within the silence of good deeds. There are famous exceptions to what could be called a nineteenth-century formula invested in identifying clearly who or what is good. Obviously *Don Quixote* and *Candide* both mock the search for pure goodness. Other exceptions to that formula remain puzzles in literary criticism: Melville's *Billy Budd* and *Moby-Dick*, both of which support multiple interpretations regarding the rank, the power, the meaning that goodness is given in these texts. The consequence of Billy Budd's innocence is execution. Is Ishmael good? Is Ahab a template for goodness, fighting evil to the death? Or is he a wounded, vengeful force outfoxed by indifferent nature, which is neither good nor bad? Innocence represented by Pip we know is soon abandoned, swallowed by the sea without a murmur. Generally, however, in nineteenth-century literature, whatever the forces of malice the protagonist is faced with, redemption and the triumph of virtue was his or her reward.

Twentieth-century novelists were unimpressed. The movement away   12
from happy endings or the enshrining of good over evil was rapid and stark after World War I. *That* catastrophe was too wide, too deep to ignore or to distort with a simplistic gesture of goodness. Many early modern novelists, especially Americans, concentrated on the irredeemable consequences of war — the harm it did to its warriors, to society, to human sensibility. In those texts, acts of sheer goodness, if not outright comical, are treated with irony at best or ladled with suspicion and fruitlessness at worst. One thinks of Faulkner's *A Fable* and the mixed reviews it received, most of which were disdainful of the deliberate armistice between soldiers in trench warfare against each other driven by a Christ-like character. The term "hero" seems to be limited these days to the sacrificing dead: first responders running into fiery buildings, mates throwing themselves on grenades to save the lives of others, rescuing the drowning, the wounded. Faulkner's character would never be seen or praised as a hero.

Evil grabs the intellectual platform and its energy; it demands careful   13
examinations of its consequences, its techniques, its motives, its successes however short-lived or temporary. Grief, melancholy, missed chances for personal happiness often seem to be contemporary literature's concept of evil. It hogs the stage. Goodness sits in the audience and watches, assuming it even has a ticket to the show. A most compelling example of this obsession with evil is Umberto Eco's *The Prague Cemetery*. Brilliant as it is, never have I read a more deeply disturbing fascination with the nature of evil; disturbing precisely because it is treated as a thrilling intelligence scornful of the monotony and stupidity of good intentions.

Contemporary literature is not interested in goodness on a large or even   14
limited scale. When it appears, it is with a note of apology in its hand and has
trouble speaking its name. For every *To Kill a Mockingbird*, there is a Flannery
O'Connor's *Wise Blood* or "A Good Man Is Hard to Find," striking goodness
down with a well-honed literary ax. Many of the late twentieth-, early twenty-
first-century heavyweights—Philip Roth, Norman Mailer, Saul Bellow, and
so on—are masters at exposing the frailty, the pointlessness, the comedy of
goodness.

I thought it would be interesting and possibly informative to examine my   15
thesis on the life and death of goodness in literature using my own work. I
wanted to measure and clarify my understanding by employing the definitions
of altruism that I gleaned from my tentative research. To this end, I selected
three:

1. Goodness taught and learned (a habit of helping strangers and/or
   taking risks for them).
2. Goodness as a form of narcissism, ego enhancement or even a mental
   disorder.
3. Goodness as instinct, as a result of genetics (protecting one's kin or
   one's group).

An example of the first: A learned habit of goodness can be found in   16
A Mercy. There a priest, at some danger to himself, teaches female slaves to read
and write. Lest this be understood as simple kindness, here is a sample of punishments levied on white people who risked promoting literacy among Black
people: "Any white person assembling with slaves or free Negroes for purpose
of instructing them to read or write, or associating with them in any unlawful
assembly, shall be confined in jail not exceeding six months and fined not
exceeding $100.00." That text appeared in Virginia's criminal law as late
as 1848.

Examples of the third: Instinctive kin protection is the most common rep-   17
resentative of goodness—and I acknowledge several areas of failure to articulate them. From the deliberate sticking of one's leg under a train for insurance
money to raise their family in *Sula*, to setting a son on fire to spare him and
others the sight of his self-destruction. Note this is the same mother who
throws herself out of a window to save a daughter from fire. These acts are far
too theatrical and are accompanied by no compelling language. On the other
hand, there is the giving away of one's child to a stranger in order to save her
from certain molestation in *A Mercy*. The motive that impels Florens's mother,
a *minha mae*, seems to me quite close to altruism, and most importantly is given
language which I hoped would be a profound, a literal definition of freedom:
"To be given dominion over another is a hard thing; to wrest dominion over
another is a wrong thing; to give dominion of yourself to another is an evil
thing."

Another example of the third: Unquestioning compassion in support of not   18
just kin but of members of the group in general. In *Home*, for example, women
provide unsolicited but necessary nursing care to a member of the collective
who has spent a lifetime despising them; their "reason" being responsibility to

God: "They did not want to meet their Maker and have nothing to say when He asked, 'What have you done?'" A further instance of innate group compassion is the healing of Cee, physically as well as mentally. It was important to me to give that compassion voice: "Look to yourself," Miss Ethel tells her. "You free. Nothing and nobody is obliged to save you but you . . . You young and a woman and there is serious limitation in both but you a person, too . . . Somewhere inside you is that free person . . . Locate her and let her do some good in the world."

An example of the second: Goodness as a form of narcissism, perhaps   19 mental disorder, occurs in the very first novel I wrote. Determined to erase his self-loathing, Soaphead Church, a character in *The Bluest Eye*, chooses to "give," or pretend to give, blue eyes to a little girl in psychotic need of them. In his letter to God, he imagines himself doing the good God refuses. Misunderstood as it is, it has language.

Over time, these last 40 years, I have become more and more invested in   20 making sure acts of goodness (however casual or deliberate or misapplied or, like the Amish community, blessed) produce language. But even when not articulated, like the teaching priest in *A Mercy*, such acts must have a strong impact on the novel's structure and on its meaning. Expressions of goodness are never trivial or incidental in my writing. In fact, I want them to have life-changing properties and to illuminate decisively the moral questions embedded in the narrative. It was important to me that none of these expressions be handled as comedy or irony. And they are seldom mute.

Allowing goodness its own speech does not annihilate evil, but it does   21 allow me to signify my own understanding of goodness: the acquisition of self-knowledge. A satisfactory or good ending for me is when the protagonist learns something vital and morally insightful that she or he did not know at the beginning.

Claudia's words, at the end of *The Bluest Eye*: "I even think now that the   22 land of the entire country was hostile to marigolds that year. This soil is bad for certain kinds of flowers. Certain seeds it will not nurture, certain fruit it will not bear, and when the land kills of its own volition, we acquiesce and say the victim had no right to live. We are wrong of course but it doesn't matter. It's too late. At least on the edge of my town, among the garbage and sunflowers of my town, it's much, much, much too late."

Such insight has nothing to do with winning, and everything to do with   23 the acquisition of knowledge. Knowledge on display in the language of moral clarity — of goodness.

· · ·

Comprehension

1. How does Morrison explain her fascination with goodness — "with the term and its definition" (3)?
2. What is *altruism*? How is it related to goodness?
3. How would Morrison define *evil*? Why does she discuss evil in an essay on goodness?

4. According to Morrison, "Evil has a blockbuster audience; Goodness lurks backstage" (9). Later, she says that evil "hogs the stage. Goodness sits in the audience and wonders" (13). With statements like these, Morrison questions why evil gets so much attention, in literature as well as in life. What does she conclude?
5. How do nineteenth-century novels differ from twentieth-century novels in their view of goodness? How does Morrison account for this difference?
6. In paragraph 20, Morrison expresses her growing interest in "making sure acts of goodness . . . produce language." What does she mean?

Purpose and Audience

1. Morrison begins her comments with a three-paragraph narrative. Why? What does this passage accomplish? How else might she have opened her essay?
2. This essay was originally presented as a 2012 lecture at Harvard Divinity School. How might Morrison's expectations about this audience have influenced her remarks? What changes might she have needed to make to accommodate an audience of college professors? Of college students?
3. Beginning in paragraph 11, Morrison focuses on goodness in literature. Do you see this material as intrusive, or do you think it is clearly related to the real-life examples she cites in paragraphs 1 through 3?
4. Starting in paragraph 15, Morrison applies her "thesis on the life and death of goodness in literature" to her own work. Do you think that is a good strategy? Why or why not?
5. In one sentence, write a thesis statement for this essay.

Style and Structure

1. Make an outline of this essay, including its thesis and key supporting points. Use the outline on page 484 as a model.
2. Where does Morrison use narration? Where does she use exemplification? Classification?
3. Where does Morrison explore a term's origin? Where does she define by negation?
4. **Vocabulary Project.** Write your own one-sentence formal definitions of *goodness*, *altruism*, and *evil*, following the models on pages 479–80.

Journal Entry

Which has had the greater impact on your life, goodness or evil? Why?

Writing Workshop

1. **Working with Sources.** Research the Amish people in an attempt to learn about their history and their beliefs. Then, write a definition essay that defines *goodness* from their point of view. Be sure to cite the sources you use

and to include a works-cited page. (See Chapter 18 for information on MLA documentation.)

2. Write a definition essay that defines *evil* by focusing on a fictional character. Use narration, description, and exemplification to create a portrait of an individual who is the very definition of evil.

3. Write a definition essay that defines *goodness* by focusing on someone you know or have read about. As in question 2 above, use narration, description, and exemplification to shape your essay.

Combining the Patterns

This definition essay uses a variety of different patterns of development, including narration, exemplification, and classification. How (and where) might Morrison have used **description** or **process** to further develop her essay?

Thematic Connections

- "Shooting an Elephant" (page 132)
- "The Lottery" (page 303)
- "Emmett Till and Tamir Rice, Sons of the Great Migration" (page 414)
- "Letter from Birmingham Jail" (page 562)
- Casebook: "How Can We Stem the Tide of Gun Violence?" (page 626)

EMILY DICKINSON

"Hope" is the thing with feathers (Poetry)

Emily Dickinson (1830–1886) is one of the most distinctive voices in all American poetry. Dickinson was born in Amherst, Massachusetts, to a well-known and public-spirited family (her father served in Congress as a representative from Massachusetts). Although she was well-read and well-educated for a woman of her time, she spent much of her life as a recluse in Amherst, reading, corresponding, spending time with her family, and writing nearly eighteen hundred poems. She was not recognized for her writing in her lifetime: nearly all Dickinson's poems were discovered — and published — after her death. Along with the unmistakable style of her work, its timeless themes — nature, love, personal identity, mortality — continue to startle and fascinate readers.

Background on the idea of hope Many of our earliest myths and stories explore the idea of hope. In Greek mythology, for example, Pandora opens a forbidden box (or jar), releasing evils into the world; after the lid is closed, only hope is left behind. Among early philosophers, Greek and Roman stoics believed hope was dangerous and misleading. In the Christian tradition, hope is one of the three theological virtues (faith, hope, and charity), bound up with the certainty of salvation: "By whom also we have access by faith into this grace wherein we stand, and rejoice in hope of the glory of God" Romans 5:2. Buddhists believe hope must be liberated from personal desires and discontent with the present, even if it aims toward enlightenment in the next earthly life. Of course, hope is also significant outside religious traditions. Marxist thinkers, for example, have placed hope in the utopian transformation of society. A perennial theme of self-help and motivational experts, hope — as a function of cognition and culture — has also become a focus of study for neurologists, anthropologists, and psychologists. In an influential essay, the psychologist Richard Lazarus wrote, "To hope is to believe that something positive, which does not presently apply to one's life, could still materialize, and so we yearn for it."

"Hope" is the thing with feathers —
That perches in the soul —
And sings the tune without the words —
And never stops — at all —

And sweetest — in the Gale — is heard —   5
And sore must be the storm —
That could abash the little Bird
That kept so many warm —

I've heard it in the chillest land —
And on the strangest Sea —   10
Yet — never — in Extremity,
It asked a crumb — of me.

•   •   •

Reading Literature

1. This poem defines *hope* by drawing an **analogy** between hope and a bird. What does the poem suggest these two things have in common?
2. How does hope "perch" in the soul? What other words could you substitute for "perches" (line 2)?
3. What kind of "tune" (3) does hope sing? What kind of "Gale" (5) and "storm" (6) might threaten hope?

Journal Entry

Write a one-paragraph definition of *hope*. Develop your paragraph with examples and analogies.

Thematic Connections

- "My Field of Dreams" (page 106)
- "My Mother Never Worked" (page 122)
- "How to Tell a Mother Her Child Is Dead" (page 275)
- The Declaration of Independence (page 548)

Writing Assignments for Definition

1. Choose a document or ritual that is a significant part of your religious or cultural heritage. Define it, using any pattern or combination of patterns you choose, but be sure to include a formal definition somewhere in your essay. Assume your readers are not familiar with the term you are defining.

2. Define an abstract term — for example, *stubbornness, security, courage,* or *fear* — by making it concrete. You can develop your definition with a series of brief examples or with an extended narrative that illustrates the characteristic you are defining.

3. The readings in this chapter define (among other things) a food and a family role. Write an essay using examples and description to define one of these topics, such as ramen noodles (food) or a stepmother (family role).

4. **Working with Sources.** Visit webmd.com (for adult health issues) or kidshealth.org (for children's health issues) to learn about one of these medical conditions: angina, migraine, Down syndrome, attention deficit disorder, schizophrenia, autism, or Alzheimer's disease. Then, write an extended definition essay explaining the condition to an audience of high school students. Be sure to include parenthetical documentation for references to your source and a works-cited page. (See Chapter 18 for information on MLA documentation.)

5. Use a series of examples to support a thesis in an essay that defines *racism, sexism, ageism, homophobia,* or another type of bigotry.

6. Choose a term that is central to one of your courses — for instance, *naturalism, behaviorism,* or *authority* — and write an essay defining the term. Assume your audience is made up of students who have not yet taken the course. You may begin with an overview of the term's origin if you believe this information is appropriate. Then, develop your essay with examples and analogies that will facilitate your audience's understanding of the term. Your purpose is to convince readers that understanding the term you are defining is important.

7. Assume your audience is from a culture unfamiliar with present-day American children's pastimes. Write a definition essay for this audience describing the form and function of a Frisbee, a Barbie doll, an action figure, a skateboard, or a video game.

8. Review any one of the following narrative essays in Chapter 6, and use it to help you develop an extended definition of one of the following terms.

   - "The Money" — revenge
   - "My First Police Stop" — stereotyping
   - "My Mother Never Worked" — work
   - "Thirty-Seven Who Saw Murder Didn't Call the Police" — apathy
   - "Shooting an Elephant" — power

   Be sure to document any words or ideas you borrow from a source and to include a works-cited page. (See Chapter 18 for information on MLA documentation.)

9. What constitutes an education? Define the term *education* by identifying several different sources of knowledge, formal or informal, and explaining what each contributes. To get ideas for your essay, look at the excerpt from *Persepolis II* (page 111) or "Just Walk On By: A Black Man Ponders His Power to Alter Public Space" (page 231).

10. What qualifies someone as a hero? Developing your essay with a series of examples, define the word *hero*. Include a formal definition, and try to incorporate at least one paragraph defining the term by explaining and illustrating what a hero is *not*.

Collaborative Activity for Definition

Working as a group, choose one of the following words to define: *pride*, *hope*, *sacrifice*, or *justice*. Then, define the term with a series of extended examples drawn from films your group members have seen, with each of you developing an illustrative paragraph based on a different film. (Before beginning, your group may decide to focus on one particular genre of film.) When everyone in the group has read each paragraph, work together to formulate a thesis that asserts the vital importance of the quality your examples have defined. Finally, write suitable opening and closing paragraphs for the essay, and arrange the body paragraphs in a logical order, adding transitions where necessary.

Argumentation

What Is Argumentation?

Argumentation is a logical way of asserting the soundness of a debatable position, belief, or conclusion. Argumentation takes a stand — supported by evidence — and urges people to share the writer's perspective and insights. In the following paragraph from *To Sell Is Human: The Surprising Truth about Moving Others*, Daniel Pink argues that the impact of the smartphone has been much greater than most people realize.

<table>
<tr>
<td valign="top">

Topic sentence (takes a stand)

Background presents both sides of issue

Evidence (examples)

</td>
<td>

<u>While the Web has enabled more microentrepreneurs to flourish, its overall impact might seem quaint compared with the smartphone.</u> As Marc Andreessen, the venture capitalist who in the early 1990s created the first Web browser, has said, "The smartphone revolution is *under*hyped." These hand-held mini-computers certainly can destroy certain aspects of sales. Consumers can use them to conduct research, comparison-shop, and bypass salespeople altogether. But once again, the net effect is more creative than destructive. The same technology that renders certain types of salespeople obsolete has turned even more people into potential sellers. For instance, the existence of smartphones has birthed an entire app economy that didn't exist before 2007, when Apple shipped its first iPhone. Now the production of apps itself is responsible for nearly half a million jobs in the United States alone, most of them created by bantamweight entrepreneurs. Likewise, an array of new technologies, such as Square from one of the founders of Twitter, PayHere from eBay, and GoPayment from Intuit, make it easier for individuals to accept credit card payments directly on their mobile devices — allowing anyone with a phone to become a shopkeeper.

</td>
</tr>
</table>

Argumentation can be used to convince other people to accept (or at least acknowledge the validity of) your position; to defend your position, even if you cannot convince others to agree; or to question or refute a position you believe to be misguided, untrue, dangerous, or evil (without necessarily offering an alternative).

Understanding Argumentation and Persuasion

Although the terms *persuasion* and *argumentation* are frequently used interchangeably, they do not mean the same thing. **Persuasion** is a general term that refers to how a writer influences an audience to adopt a belief or follow a course of action. To persuade an audience, a writer relies on various kinds of appeals — appeals based on emotion (***pathos***), on logic (***logos***), and on the character reputation of the writer (***ethos***).

- ***Logos*** — the appeal to logic — focuses on the logical structure of the argument. It relies on evidence and formal reasoning to reach a logical conclusion.
- ***Pathos*** — the appeal to emotion — focuses on the emotional dimension of an issue. It relies on a person's ability to move an audience by eliciting an emotional response, such as fear, anger, sadness, or empathy.
- ***Ethos*** — the appeal to authority — focuses on the character of the speaker. It relies on a person's trustworthiness, expertise, and credibility to influence an audience.

Argumentation is the appeal to reason (*logos*). In an argument, a writer connects a series of statements so that they lead logically to a conclusion. Argumentation is different from persuasion in that it does not try to move an audience to action; its primary purpose is to demonstrate that certain ideas are valid and others are not. Moreover, unlike persuasion, argumentation has a formal structure: an argument makes points, supplies evidence, establishes a logical chain of reasoning, refutes opposing arguments, and accommodates the audience's views.

As the selections in this chapter demonstrate, however, most effective arguments combine two or more appeals: even though their primary appeal is to reason, they may also appeal to emotions. For example, you could use a combination of logical and emotional appeals to argue against lowering the drinking age in your state from twenty-one to eighteen. You could appeal to *reason* by constructing an argument leading to the conclusion that the state should not condone policies that have a high probability of injuring or killing citizens.

You could support your conclusion by presenting statistics showing that alcohol-related traffic accidents kill more teenagers than disease does. You could also cite a study showing that when the drinking age was raised from eighteen to twenty-one, fatal accidents declined. In addition, you could include an appeal to the *emotions* by telling a particularly poignant story about an eighteen-year-old alcoholic or by pointing out how an increased number of accidents involving drunk drivers would cost some innocent people their lives. Keep in mind, however, that although appeals to your audience's emotions may reinforce the central point of your argument, they do not take the place of sound logic and compelling evidence. The appeals you choose and how you balance them depend on your purpose and your sense of your audience.

As you consider what strategies to use, remember that some extremely effective appeals are unfair. Although most people would agree that lies, threats, misleading statements, and appeals to greed and prejudice are unacceptable ways of reaching an audience, such appeals are used in daily conversation, in political campaigns, and even in international diplomacy. Nevertheless, in your college writing you should use only those appeals that most people would consider fair. To do otherwise will undercut your audience's belief in your trustworthiness and weaken your argument.

Planning an Argumentative Essay

Choosing a Topic

In an argumentative essay, as in all writing, choosing the right topic is important. Ideally, you should have an intellectual or emotional stake in your topic. Still, you should be open-minded and willing to consider all sides of a question. In other words, you should be able, from the outset, to consider your topic from other people's viewpoints; doing so will help you determine what their beliefs are and how they are likely to react to your argument. You can then use this knowledge to build your case and to address opposing viewpoints. If you cannot be open-minded, you should choose another topic you can deal with more objectively.

Other factors should also influence your selection of a topic. First, you should be well informed about your topic. In addition, you should choose an issue narrow enough to be treated in the space available to you or be willing to confine your discussion to one aspect of a broad issue. It is also important to consider what you expect your argument to achieve. If your topic is so far-reaching that you cannot identify what point you want to make, or if your position is overly idealistic or unreasonable, your essay will suffer.

Developing a Thesis

After you have chosen your topic, you are ready to state the position you will argue in the form of a **thesis**. Keep in mind that in an argumentative essay, your thesis must take a stand — in other words, it must be **debatable**. A good argumentative thesis states a proposition that at least some people will object to. Arguing a statement of fact or an idea that most people accept as self-evident is pointless. Consider the following thesis statement:

Education is the best way to address the problem of increased drug use among teenagers.

This thesis statement presents ideas that some people might take issue with: it says that increased drug use is a problem among teenagers, that more than one possible solution to this problem exists, and that education is a better solution than any other. Your argumentative essay should go on to support each of these three points logically and persuasively.

A good way to test the suitability of your thesis for an argumentative essay is to formulate an **antithesis**, a statement that asserts the opposite position. If you think some people would support the antithesis, you can be certain your thesis is indeed debatable.

> Thesis: Education is the best way to address the problem of increased drug use among teenagers.
>
> Antithesis: Education is not the best way to address the problem of increased drug use among teenagers.

Analyzing Your Audience

Before writing any essay, you should analyze the characteristics, values, and interests of your audience. In argumentation, it is especially important to consider what beliefs or opinions your readers are likely to have and whether your audience is likely to be *friendly*, *neutral*, or *hostile* to your thesis.

- A **friendly audience** is sympathetic to your argument. This audience might already agree with you or have an emotional or intellectual attachment to you or to your position.
- A **neutral audience** has few or no preconceived opinions about the issue you are going to discuss. This audience is undecided and will consider your position, given the chance.
- A **hostile audience** disagrees with your position and does not accept the underlying assumptions of your argument. This audience is unlikely to change its mind no matter how much evidence you provide.

In an argumentative essay, you face a dual challenge. You must appeal to readers who are neutral or even hostile to your position, and you must influence those readers so that they are more receptive to your viewpoint. For example, it would be relatively easy to convince college students that tuition should be lowered or to convince instructors that faculty salaries should be raised. You could be reasonably sure, in advance, that each group would agree with your position. But argument requires more than just telling people what they already believe. It would be much harder to convince college students that tuition should be raised to pay for an increase in instructors' salaries or to persuade instructors to forgo raises so that tuition can remain the same. Remember that your audience will not just take your word for the claims you make. You must provide evidence that will support your thesis and establish a line of reasoning that will lead logically to your conclusion.

It is probably best to assume that some, if not most, of your readers are **skeptical** — that they are open to your ideas but need to be convinced. This assumption will keep you from making claims you cannot support. If your position is controversial, you should assume an informed (and possibly determined) opposition is looking for holes in your argument.

Gathering and Documenting Evidence

All the points you make in your essay must be supported. If they are not, your audience will dismiss them as unfounded, irrelevant, or unclear. Sometimes you can support a statement with appeals to emotion, but most of the time you support your argument's points by appealing to reason — by providing **evidence**: facts and opinions in support of your position.

As you gather evidence and assess its effectiveness, keep in mind that evidence in an argumentative essay never proves anything conclusively. If it did, there would be no debate — and hence no point in arguing. The best that evidence can do is convince your audience that an assertion is reasonable and worth considering.

Kinds of Evidence

Evidence can be *fact* or *opinion*. **Facts** are statements that people generally agree are true and that can be verified independently. In other words, they can be measured, observed, and supported by evidence or statistics. For example, it is a fact that fewer people were killed in U.S. automobile accidents in 2018 than in 1975. It is also a fact that this decrease came about, in part, because of better-engineered cars.

Facts are often accompanied by **opinions** — subjective statements or assumptions about something or someone. Opinions express how a person feels and are influenced by beliefs and values — and sometimes by preconceived ideas or attitudes. Keep in mind that there is a difference between an unsupported statement of opinion and an opinion supported by factual evidence. Unsupported opinions do not carry much weight, but supported opinions can be very persuasive — particularly when they are the opinions of experts in a relevant field. For example, you could offer the opinion that automobile deaths could be reduced if all vehicles were equipped with crash-avoidance systems. You could then make this statement more persuasive by supporting it with **expert opinion** — for example, by saying that David Zuby, the chief researcher at the Insurance Institute for Highway Safety, believes crash-avoidance systems should be standard equipment for all automobiles.

Keep in mind that not all opinions are equally convincing. The opinions of experts are more convincing than are those of individuals who have limited knowledge of an issue. Your personal opinions can be evidence (provided you are knowledgeable about your subject), but they are usually less convincing to your audience than an expert's opinion. In the final analysis, what is important is not just the quality of the evidence but also the **credibility** (or believability) of the person offering it.

What kind of evidence might change readers' minds? That depends on the readers, the issue, and the facts at hand. Put yourself in the place of your readers, and ask what would make them receptive to your thesis. Why, for example, should a student agree to pay higher tuition? You might concede that tuition is high but point out that it has not been raised for three years while the college's costs have kept going up. Your research shows that cost of heating and maintaining the buildings has increased, and professors' salaries have not, with the result that several excellent instructors have recently left the college for higher-paying jobs. Furthermore, cuts in federal and state funding have already caused a reduction in the number of courses offered. Similarly, how could you convince a professor to agree to accept no raise at all, especially because faculty salaries have not kept up with inflation? You could say that because cuts in government funding have already reduced course offerings and because the government has also reduced funds for student loans, any further increase in tuition to pay faculty salaries would cause some students to drop out, which in turn would eventually cost some instructors their jobs. As you can see, the evidence you use in an argument depends to a great extent on whom you want to convince and what you know about them.

Criteria for Evidence

As you select and review material, choose your evidence with the following three criteria in mind.

1. Your evidence should be **relevant**. It should support your thesis and be pertinent to your argument. As you present evidence, be careful not to concentrate so much on a single example that you lose sight of the broader position you are supporting. Such digressions may confuse your readers. For example, in arguing for more medical aid to Central and South America, one student made the point that the Zika virus epidemic is spreading to many countries in this region. To support his point, he discussed the recent spread of dengue fever. Although interesting, this example is not relevant. To show its relevance, the student would have to link his discussion to his assertions about the Zika epidemic, possibly by pointing out that both diseases are tropical, transmitted by mosquitoes, and relatively recent in origin.

2. Your evidence should be **representative**. It should represent the full range of opinions about your subject, not just one side. For example, in an essay arguing against the use of animals in medical experimentation, you would not just use information provided by animal rights activists. You would also use information supplied by medical researchers, pharmaceutical companies, and medical ethicists.

The examples and expert opinions you include should also be **typical**, not aberrant. Suppose you are writing an essay in support of creating bike lanes on your city's streets. To support your thesis, you present the example of Philadelphia, which has a successful bike-lane program. As you consider your evidence, ask yourself if Philadelphia's experience with bike lanes is typical. Did other cities have less success? Take a close look at the opinions that disagree with the position you plan to take. If you understand your opposition, you can refute it effectively when you write your paper.

3. Your evidence should be **sufficient**. It should include enough facts, opinions, and examples to support your claims. The amount of evidence you need depends on the length of your essay, your audience, and your thesis. It stands to reason that you would use fewer examples in a two-page essay than

in a ten-page essay. Similarly, an audience that is favorably disposed to your thesis might need only one or two examples to be convinced, whereas a skeptical or hostile audience would need many more. As you develop your thesis, think about the amount of support you will need to write your essay. You may decide that a narrower, more limited thesis will be easier to support than a more inclusive one.

Documentation of Evidence

After you decide on a topic, you should begin to gather evidence. Sometimes you can use your own ideas and observations to support your claims. Most of the time, however, you will have to use the print and electronic resources of the library or search the Internet to locate the information you need.

Whenever you use such evidence in your essay, you have to **document** it by providing the source of the information. (When documenting sources, follow the MLA documentation format explained in Chapter 18 of this book.) If you don't document your sources, your readers are likely to question or dismiss your evidence, thinking that it may be inaccurate, unreliable, or simply false. **Documentation** gives readers the ability to evaluate the sources you cite and to consult them if they wish. When you document sources, you establish credibility by showing readers that you are honest and have nothing to hide.

Documentation also helps you avoid **plagiarism** — presenting the ideas or words of others as if they were your own. Certainly you don't have to document every idea you use in your paper. For example, **common knowledge** — information you could easily find in several reference sources — can be presented without documentation, and so can your own ideas. You must, however, document any use of a direct quotation and any ideas, statistics, charts, diagrams, or pictures that you obtain from your source. (See Chapter 17 for information on plagiarism.)

Dealing with the Opposition

When gathering evidence, you should always try to identify the most obvious — and even the not-so-obvious — objections to your position. By directly addressing these objections in your essay, you will help convince readers that your own position is valid. This part of an argument, called **refutation**, is essential to making the strongest case possible.

Refutation enables you to anticipate doubts and to address objections that skeptical readers may have. It strengthens your case by presenting you as a person who understands both sides of an argument and who weighs alternatives before arguing for one or the other. Notice, in the following passage from the classic essay "Politics and the English Language," how George Orwell refutes an opponent's argument.

> I said earlier that the decadence of our language is probably curable. Those who deny this would argue, if they produced an argument at all, that language merely reflects existing social conditions, and that we cannot influence its development by any direct tinkering with words and constructions. So far as the general tone or spirit of a language goes, this may be true, but it is not true in detail. Silly words and expressions have often disappeared, though not through any evolutionary process but owing to the conscious actions of a minority.

In the excerpt above, Orwell begins by stating the point he wants to make, goes on to define the argument against his position, and then identifies the weakness of this opposing argument. Later in the essay, Orwell strengthens his argument by presenting examples that support his point.

When an opponent's argument is so compelling that it cannot be easily dismissed, you should **concede** its strength (admit that it is valid). By acknowledging that a point is well taken, you reinforce the impression that you are a fair-minded person. After conceding the strength of the opposing argument, try to identify its limitations and then move your argument to more solid ground. (Often an opponent's strong point addresses only *one* facet of a multifaceted problem.) Notice in the example above that Orwell concedes an opposing argument when he says, "So far as the general tone or spirit of a language goes, this may be true." Later in his discussion, he refutes this argument by pointing out its shortcomings.

Strategies for Refuting Opposing Arguments

You can refute opposing arguments by showing that they are unsound, unfair, or inaccurate. Begin by listing all the arguments against your position that you can think of. Then, as you gather your evidence, decide which of these points you will refute, keeping in mind that careful readers will expect you to address the most compelling arguments against your position. Be sure not to distort an opposing argument by making it seem weaker than it actually is. This technique, called **creating a straw man**, can backfire and turn fair-minded readers against you.

WEAKNESS IN OPPOSING ARGUMENT	REFUTATION STRATEGY
Factual errors	Identify and correct factual errors, perhaps explaining how they call the writer's credibility into question.
Insufficient support	Point out that more evidence is needed; note the kind of support (for example, statistics) that is missing.
Illogical reasoning	Identify the fallacies in the writer's argument, and explain why the logic is flawed. For example, is the writer setting up a straw man or committing the *ad hominem* fallacy? (See pages 532–35 for more on logical fallacies.)
Exaggerated claims	Identify exaggerated statements, and explain why they overstate the case.
Biased statements	Identify biased statements, and show how they undermine the writer's credibility. (See pages 712–13 for a discussion of bias in research sources.)
Irrelevant arguments	Identify irrelevant points, and make clear why they are not related to the writer's central argument.

Understanding Rogerian Argument

Not all arguments are (or should be) confrontational. Psychologist Carl Rogers has written about how to argue without assuming an adversarial relationship. According to Rogers, traditional strategies of argument rely on confrontation — trying to prove that an opponent's position is wrong. With this method of arguing, one person is "wrong" and one is "right." By attacking an opponent and repeatedly hammering home the message that his or her arguments are incorrect or misguided, a writer forces the opponent into a defensive position. The result is conflict, disagreement, and frequently ill will and hostility.

Rogers recommends that you think of those who disagree with you as colleagues, not adversaries. With this approach, now known as **Rogerian argument**, you enter into a cooperative relationship with opponents. Instead of aggressively refuting opposing arguments, you emphasize points of agreement and try to find common ground. Thus, you collaborate to find mutually satisfying solutions. By adopting a conciliatory attitude, you demonstrate your respect for opposing viewpoints and your willingness to compromise and work toward a position that both you and those who disagree with you will find acceptable. To use a Rogerian strategy in your writing, follow the guidelines below.

✓ **CHECKLIST**   **GUIDELINES FOR USING ROGERIAN ARGUMENT**

☐ Begin by summarizing opposing viewpoints.
☐ Carefully consider the position of those who disagree with you. What are their legitimate concerns? If you were in their place, how would you react?
☐ Present opposing viewpoints accurately and fairly. Demonstrate your respect for the ideas of those who disagree with you.
☐ Concede the strength of a compelling opposing argument.
☐ Acknowledge the concerns you and your opposition share.
☐ Point out to readers how they will benefit from the position you are defining.
☐ Present the evidence that supports your viewpoint.

Using Deductive and Inductive Arguments

In an argument, you move from evidence to a conclusion in two ways. One method, called **deductive reasoning**, proceeds from a general premise or assumption to a specific conclusion. Deduction is what most people mean when they speak of logic. Using strict logical form, deduction holds that if all the statements in the argument are true, the conclusion must also be true.

The other method of moving from evidence to conclusion is called **inductive reasoning**. Induction proceeds from individual observations to a more general conclusion and uses no strict form. It requires only that all the relevant evidence be stated and that the conclusion fit the evidence better than any other conclusion would.

Most written arguments use a combination of deductive and inductive reasoning, but it is simpler to discuss and illustrate them separately.

Using Deductive Arguments

The basic form of a deductive argument is a **syllogism**. A syllogism consists of a **major premise**, which is a general statement; a **minor premise**, which is a related but more specific statement; and a **conclusion**, which is drawn from those premises. Consider the following example.

Major premise:	All Olympic runners are fast.
Minor premise:	Jesse Owens was an Olympic runner.
Conclusion:	Therefore, Jesse Owens was fast.

As you can see, if you grant both the major and minor premises, you must also grant the conclusion. In fact, it is the only conclusion you can properly draw. You cannot reasonably conclude that Jesse Owens was slow because that conclusion contradicts the premises. Nor can you conclude (even if it is true) that Jesse Owens was tall because that conclusion includes information that is not in the premises.

Of course, this argument seems obvious, and it is much simpler than an argumentative essay would be. In fact, a deductive argument's premises can be fairly elaborate. The Declaration of Independence, which appears later in this chapter, has at its core a deductive argument that could be summarized in this way:

Major premise:	Tyrannical rulers deserve no loyalty.
Minor premise:	King George III is a tyrannical ruler.
Conclusion:	Therefore, King George III deserves no loyalty.

The major premise is a statement that the Declaration claims is **self-evident**—so obvious it needs no proof. Much of the Declaration consists of evidence to support the minor premise that King George is a tyrannical ruler. The conclusion, because it is drawn from those premises, has the force of irrefutable logic: the king deserves no loyalty from his American subjects, who are therefore entitled to revolt against him.

When a conclusion follows logically from the major and minor premises, the argument is said to be **valid**. But if the syllogism is not logical, the argument is not valid, and the conclusion is not sound. For example, the following syllogism is not logical:

Major premise:	All dogs are animals.
Minor premise:	All cats are animals.
Conclusion:	Therefore, all dogs are cats.

Of course, the conclusion is absurd. But how did we wind up with such a ridiculous conclusion when both premises are obviously true? The answer is that the syllogism actually contains two major premises. (Both the major and minor premises begin with *all.*) Therefore, the syllogism is defective, and the argument is invalid. Consider the following example of an invalid argument:

Major premise:	All dogs are animals.
Minor premise:	Ralph is an animal.
Conclusion:	Therefore, Ralph is a dog.

Here, an error in logic occurs because the minor premise refers to a term in the major premise that is **undistributed** — that is, it covers only some of the items in the class it denotes. (To be valid, the minor premise must refer to the term in the major premise that is **distributed** — that is, it covers *all* the items in the class it denotes.) In the major premise, *dogs* is the distributed term; it designates *all dogs*. The minor premise, however, refers to *animals*, which is undistributed because it refers only to animals that are dogs. As the minor premise establishes, Ralph is an animal, but it does not logically follow that he is a dog. He could be a cat, a horse, or even a human being.

Even if a syllogism is valid — that is, correct in its form — its conclusion will not necessarily be **true**. The following syllogism draws a false conclusion:

Major premise:	All dogs are brown.
Minor premise:	My poodle Toby is a dog.
Conclusion:	Therefore, Toby is brown.

As it happens, Toby is black. The conclusion is false because the major premise is false: many dogs are *not* brown. If Toby were actually brown, the conclusion would be correct, but only by chance, not by logic. To be **sound**, a syllogism must be both logical and true.

The strength of a deductive argument is that if readers accept your major and minor premises, they must grant your conclusion. Therefore, you should try to select premises that you know your readers will accept or that are self-evident — that is, premises most people believe to be true. Do not assume, however, that "most people" refers only to your friends and acquaintances. Consider those who may hold different views. If you think your premises are too controversial or difficult to establish firmly, you should use inductive reasoning.

Using Inductive Arguments

Unlike deduction, induction has no distinctive form, and its conclusions are less definitive than those of syllogisms. Still, much inductive thinking (and writing based on that thinking) tends to follow a particular process.

- First, you decide on a question to be answered or, especially in the sciences, a tentative answer to such a question, called a **hypothesis**.
- Then, you gather the evidence that is relevant to the question and that may be important to finding the answer.
- Finally, you move from your evidence to your conclusion by making an **inference** — a statement about the unknown based on the known — that answers the question and takes the evidence into account.

Here is a very simple example of the inductive process:

Question:	How did that living-room window get broken?
Evidence:	There is a baseball on the living-room floor.
	The baseball was not there this morning.
	Some children were playing baseball this afternoon.
	They were playing in the vacant lot across from the window.
	They stopped playing a little while ago.
	They aren't in the vacant lot now.
Conclusion:	One of the children hit or threw the ball through the window; then, they all ran away.

The conclusion, because it takes all the evidence into account, seems obvious, but if it turned out that the children had been playing volleyball, not baseball, this additional piece of evidence would undercut the conclusion. Even if the conclusion is believable, you cannot necessarily assume it is true: after all, the window could have been broken in some other way. For example, perhaps a bird flew against it, and perhaps the baseball in the living room had gone unnoticed for days, making the second piece of "evidence" on the list not true.

Because inductive arguments tend to be more complicated than the example above, it is not always easy to move from the evidence you have collected to a sound conclusion. The more pertinent information you gather, the smaller the gap between your evidence and your conclusion; the less pertinent evidence you have, the larger the gap and the weaker your conclusion. To bridge this gap, you have to make what is called an **inductive leap**—a stretch of the imagination that enables you to draw a sound conclusion. Remember, however, that inductive conclusions are only probable, never certain. The more evidence you provide, the stronger your conclusion. When the gap between your evidence and your conclusion is too great, you reach a weak conclusion that is not supported by the facts. This well-named error is called **jumping to a conclusion** because it amounts to a premature inductive leap. You can avoid reaching an unjustified or false conclusion by making sure you have collected enough evidence to justify your conclusion.

Using Toulmin Logic

Another approach for structuring arguments has been advanced by philosopher Stephen Toulmin. According to Toulmin, arguments are more complex than formal logic suggests. In order to more thoroughly analyze and develop arguments, he created a method of inquiry known as **Toulmin logic**. This method looks at the elements of an argument as well as the underlying assumptions that cause readers to respond the way they do. In its simplest terms, Toulmin's model divides arguments into three parts: the *claim*, the *grounds*, and the *warrant*.

- The **claim** is the main point of the essay. Usually the claim is stated directly as the thesis, but in some arguments it may be implied.
- The **grounds** — the material a writer uses to support the claim — can be evidence (facts or expert opinion) or appeals to the emotions or values of the audience.
- The **warrant** is the inference that connects the claim to the grounds. (According to Toulmin, the warrant is the glue that holds the argument together.) The warrant can be a belief that is taken for granted or an assumption that underlies the argument.

In its most basic form, an argument following Toulmin logic would look like this example.

Claim:	Carol should be elected class president.
Grounds:	Carol is an honor student.
Warrant:	A person who is an honor student would make a good class president.

When you formulate an argument using Toulmin logic, you can still use inductive and deductive reasoning. You derive your claim inductively from facts and examples, and you connect the grounds and warrant to your claim deductively. For example, the deductive argument in the Declaration of Independence that was summarized on page 528 can be represented as shown here.

Claim:	King George III deserves no loyalty.
Grounds:	King George III is a tyrannical ruler.
Warrant:	Tyrannical rulers deserve no loyalty.

As Toulmin points out, the clearer your warrant, the more likely readers will be to agree with it. Notice that in the two preceding examples, the warrants are very explicit.

Real arguments — the ones you encounter in print or online — are not as simple as the three-part model above suggests. To account for the complexity of these arguments, Toulmin expanded his model to include the following three elements: *the backing, qualifiers,* and *rebuttals*.

- The **backing** consists of additional statements that support the warrant.
- The **qualifiers** are statements that limit the claim. By using words such as *most, some, sometimes, often,* and *usually,* they acknowledge that a claim might not be true in all circumstances.
- The **rebuttals** are statements that address (and refute) arguments against the claim.

Using this expanded Toulmin model, you could construct the following argument in favor of paid parental leave.

Claim:	Companies should institute paid parental leave for all families.
Grounds:	Studies have shown that companies that have instituted paid parental leave for parents have experienced increased productivity.
Warrant:	Paid parental leave benefits both companies and their employees.
Backing:	Only 5 percent of low-wage earners get paid parental leave. One study showed that in countries that have paid parental leave, mothers were more likely to work full time, work longer hours, and earn more money than mothers in countries that did not have paid leave.
Qualifiers:	In some situations, however, paid parental leave can have drawbacks. Sometimes an employee's earnings can suffer. Also, employees who take parental leave can be passed over for raises or promotions.
Rebuttals:	As time goes on, however, these problems tend to dissipate. Studies show that the more employees take paid parental leave, the more accepted it becomes.

Recognizing Fallacies

Fallacies are flaws in reasoning that undermine your argument's logic. They may sound reasonable or true but are actually deceptive and dishonest. When readers detect them, such statements can turn even a sympathetic audience against your position by causing them to question your fairness and your judgment. Here are some of the more common fallacies that you should avoid.

Begging the Question

This fallacy assumes that a statement is true when it actually requires proof. It requires readers to agree that certain points are self-evident when in fact they are not.

Unfair and shortsighted policies that limit free trade are a threat to the U.S. economy.

Restrictions against free trade may or may not be unfair and shortsighted, but emotionally loaded language does not constitute proof. The statement begs the question because it assumes what it should be proving — that policies that limit free trade are unfair and shortsighted.

Argument from Analogy

An **analogy** explains something unfamiliar by comparing it to something familiar. Although analogies can help explain abstract or unclear ideas, they do not constitute proof. An argument based on an analogy frequently ignores important dissimilarities between the two things being compared. When this occurs, the argument is fallacious.

> Overcrowded conditions in some parts of our city have forced people together like rats in a cage. Like rats, they will eventually turn on one another, fighting and killing until a balance is restored. It is therefore necessary that we vote to appropriate funds to build low-cost housing.

No evidence is offered to establish that people behave like rats under these or any other conditions. Just because two things have some characteristics in common, you should not assume they are alike in other respects.

Personal Attack (Argument *Ad Hominem*)

This fallacy tries to divert attention from the facts of an argument by attacking the motives or character of the person making the argument.

> The public should not take seriously Dr. Mason's plan for improving county health services. He is overweight and a smoker.

This attack on Dr. Mason's character says nothing about the quality of his plan. Sometimes a connection exists between a person's private and public lives — for example, in a case of conflict of interest. However, no evidence of such a connection is presented here.

Jumping to a Conclusion

Sometimes called a *hasty* or *sweeping generalization*, this fallacy occurs when a conclusion is reached on the basis of too little evidence.

> Because our son benefited from home schooling, every child should be educated in this way.

Perhaps other children would benefit from home schooling, and perhaps not, but no conclusion about children in general can be reached on the basis of just one child's experience.

False Dilemma (Either/Or Fallacy)

This fallacy occurs when a writer suggests that only two alternatives exist even though there may be others.

> We must choose between life and death, between intervention and genocide. No one can be neutral on this issue.

An argument like this oversimplifies an issue and forces people to choose between extremes instead of exploring more moderate positions.

Equivocation

This fallacy occurs when the meaning of a key term changes at some point in an argument. Equivocation makes it seem as if a conclusion follows from premises when it actually does not.

> As a human endeavor, computers are a praiseworthy and even remarkable accomplishment. But how human can we hope to be if we rely on computers to make our decisions?

The use of *human* in the first sentence refers to the entire human race. In the second sentence, *human* means "merciful" or "civilized." By subtly shifting this term to refer to qualities characteristic of people as opposed to machines, the writer makes the argument seem more sound than it is.

Red Herring

This fallacy occurs when the focus of an argument is shifted to divert the audience from the actual issue.

> The mayor has proposed building a new sports stadium. How can he consider allocating millions of dollars to this scheme when so many professional athletes are being paid such high salaries?

The focus of this argument should be the merits of the sports stadium. Instead, the writer shifts to the irrelevant issue of athletes' high salaries.

You Also (*Tu Quoque*)

This fallacy asserts that an opponent's argument has no value because the opponent does not follow his or her own advice.

> How can that judge favor stronger penalties for convicted drug dealers? During his confirmation hearings, he admitted to smoking marijuana when he was in college.

Appeal to Doubtful Authority

Often people will attempt to strengthen an argument with references to experts or famous people. These appeals have merit when the person referred to is an expert in the area being discussed. They do not have merit, however, when the individuals cited have no expertise on the issue.

> According to Jenny McCarthy, childhood vaccines cause autism in children.

Although Jenny McCarthy is a model, actress, and radio host, she is not a physician or a research scientist. Therefore, her pronouncements about vaccines are no more than personal opinions or, at best, educated guesses.

Misleading Statistics

Although statistics are a powerful form of factual evidence, they can be misrepresented or distorted in an attempt to influence an audience.

> Women will never be competent firefighters; after all, 50 percent of the women in the city's training program failed the exam.

Here, the writer has neglected to mention that there were only two women in the program. Because this statistic is not based on a large enough sample, it cannot be used as evidence to support the argument.

Post Hoc, Ergo Propter Hoc (After This, Therefore Because of This)

This fallacy, known as *post hoc* **reasoning**, assumes that because two events occur close together in time, the first must be the cause of the second.

> Every time a Republican is elected president, a recession follows. If we want to avoid another recession, we should elect a Democrat.

Even if it were true that recessions always occur during the tenure of Republican presidents, no causal connection has been established. (See pages 318–19.)

Non Sequitur (It Does Not Follow)

This fallacy occurs when a statement does not logically follow from a previous statement.

> Disarmament weakened the United States after World War I. Disarmament also weakened the United States after the Vietnam War. For this reason, the city's efforts to limit gun sales will weaken the United States.

The historical effects of disarmament have nothing to do with current efforts to control the sale of guns. Therefore, the conclusion is a *non sequitur*.

Bandwagon (Argument *Ad Populum*)

The **bandwagon fallacy** asserts that something is true because many people believe it is true. The underlying assumption is that if a belief is widely held, then it must be so. Without supporting evidence, however, this kind of argument cannot be valid.

> The federal government should forgive all student loans. Everyone agrees that this would help the economy.

Clearly, not everyone believes that forgiving all student loans would help the economy. In any case, the writer would need to supply statistical evidence to validate the position that loan forgiveness would actually help the economy.

Stacking the Deck (Cherry Picking)

Stacking the deck occurs when an argument includes only evidence that supports its thesis and ignores evidence that does not. This technique is frequently employed by those who oppose early childhood vaccinations. For example, they often cite individual cases of young children being diagnosed with autism after receiving vaccines but neglect to establish a causal link. In addition, they ignore the fact that millions of children who are vaccinated each year experience no ill effects.

Using Transitions

Transitional words and **phrases** are extremely important in argumentative essays. Without these words and phrases, readers could easily lose track of your argument.

Argumentative essays use transitions to signal a shift in focus. For example, paragraphs that present the specific points in support of your argument can signal this purpose with transitions such as *first, second, third, in addition,* and *finally*. In the same way, paragraphs that refute opposing arguments can signal this purpose with transitions such as *still, nevertheless, however,* and *yet*. Transitional words and phrases — such as *therefore* and *for these reasons* — can indicate that you are presenting your argument's conclusions.

USEFUL TRANSITIONS FOR ARGUMENTATION

all in all	in conclusion
as a result	in other words
finally	in short
first, second, third	in summary
for example	nevertheless
for instance	on the one hand . . . on the other hand
for these reasons	still
however	therefore
in addition	thus
in brief	yet

A more complete list of transitions appears on page 56.

Structuring an Argumentative Essay

An argumentative essay, like other kinds of essays, has an **introduction**, a **body**, and a **conclusion**. However, an argumentative essay has its own special structure, one that ensures that ideas are presented logically and convincingly. The Declaration of Independence follows the typical structure of many classic arguments.

SAMPLE OUTLINE: Argumentation

INTRODUCTION

Introduces the issue

States the thesis

BODY

Induction — offers evidence to support the thesis

Deduction — uses syllogisms to support the thesis

States the arguments against the thesis and refutes them

CONCLUSION

Restates the thesis (in different words); reviews key points; ends with a forceful closing statement

Jefferson begins the Declaration by presenting the issue that the document addresses: the obligation of the people of the American colonies to tell the world why they must separate from Great Britain. Next, Jefferson states his thesis that because of the tyranny of the British king, the colonies must replace his rule with another form of government. In the body of the Declaration, he offers as evidence twenty-eight examples of injustice endured by the colonies. Following the evidence, Jefferson refutes counterarguments by explaining how again and again the colonists have appealed to the British for redress, but without result. In his concluding paragraph, he restates the thesis and reinforces it one final time. He ends with a flourish: speaking for the representatives of the United States, he explicitly dissolves all political connections between England and America.

Not all arguments, however, follow this pattern. Your material, your thesis, your purpose, your audience, the type of argument you are writing, and the limitations of your assignment all help you determine the strategies you use. If your thesis is especially novel or controversial, for example, the refutation of opposing arguments may come first. In this instance, opposing positions might even be mentioned in the introduction — provided they are discussed more fully later in the argument.

Suppose your journalism instructor gives you the following assignment:

> Select a controversial topic that interests you, and write a brief editorial about it. Direct your editorial to readers who do not share your views, and try to convince them that your position is reasonable. Be sure to acknowledge the view your audience holds and to refute possible criticisms of your argument.

You are well informed about one local issue because you have just read a series of articles on it. A citizens' group is lobbying for a local ordinance that would authorize government funding for religious schools. Because you have also recently studied the doctrine of separation of church and state in your American government class, you know you could argue fairly and strongly against the position taken by this group.

An informal outline of your essay might look like the following:

SAMPLE OUTLINE: Argumentation

INTRODUCTION

Introduce the issue: Should public tax revenues be spent on aid to religious schools?

State the thesis: Despite the pleas of citizen groups like Religious School Parents United, using tax dollars to support church-affiliated schools violates the U.S. Constitution.

POINT 1

Evidence (deduction): Explain the general principle of separation of church and state.

POINT 2

Evidence (induction): Present recent examples of court cases interpreting and applying this principle.

POINT 3

Evidence (deduction): Explain how the court cases apply to your community's situation.

OPPOSING ARGUMENTS REFUTED

Identify and refute arguments used by Religious School Parents United. Concede the point that religious schools educate many children who would otherwise have to be educated in public schools at taxpayers' expense. Then, explain the limitations of this argument.

CONCLUSION

Restate the thesis (in different words); review key points; end with a strong closing statement.

Revising an Argumentative Essay

When you revise an argumentative essay, consider the items on Checklist: Revising on page 68. In addition, pay special attention to the items on the following checklist, which apply specifically to argumentative essays.

> ✔ **REVISION CHECKLIST**   **ARGUMENTATION**
>
> ☐ Does your assignment call for argumentation?
> ☐ Have you chosen a topic you can argue about effectively?
> ☐ Do you have a debatable thesis?
> ☐ Have you considered the beliefs and opinions of your audience?
> ☐ Is your evidence relevant, representative, and sufficient?
> ☐ Have you documented evidence you have gathered from sources? Have you included a works-cited page?
> ☐ Have you made an effort to address your audience's possible objections to your position?
> ☐ Have you refuted opposing arguments?
> ☐ Have you used inductive or deductive reasoning (or a combination of the two) to move from your evidence to your conclusion?
> ☐ Do you need to add sources to support your thesis?
> ☐ Do you need to include a visual, or additional visuals?
> ☐ Have you checked for logical fallacies?
> ☐ Have you used appropriate transitional words and phrases?

Editing an Argumentative Essay

When you edit your argumentative essay, follow the guidelines on the editing checklists on pages 85, 88, and 92. In addition, focus on the grammar, mechanics, and punctuation issues that are particularly relevant to argumentative essays. One of these issues — using coordinating and subordinating conjunctions to link ideas — is discussed in the pages that follow.

GRAMMAR IN CONTEXT USING COORDINATING AND SUBORDINATING CONJUNCTIONS

When you write an argumentative essay, you often have to use **conjunctions** — words that join other words or groups of words — to express the logical and sequential relationships between ideas in your sentences. Conjunctions are especially important because they help readers follow the logic of your argument. For this reason, you should be certain the conjunctions you select clearly and accurately communicate the connections between the ideas you are discussing.

Using Coordinating Conjunctions A **compound sentence** is made up of two or more independent clauses (simple sentences) connected by a coordinating conjunction. **Coordinating conjunctions** join two independent clauses that express ideas of equal importance, and they also indicate how those ideas are related.

independent clause   *independent clause*
[People can disobey unjust laws], <u>or</u> [they can be oppressed by them].

COORDINATING CONJUNCTIONS

and (*indicates addition*)
but, yet (*indicate contrast or contradiction*)
or (*indicates alternatives*)
nor (*indicates an elimination of alternatives*)
so, for (*indicate a cause-and-effect connection*)

According to Thomas Jefferson, the king has refused to let governors pass important laws, <u>and</u> he has imposed taxes without the consent of the people.

Rachel Carson says human beings use pesticides to control insects, <u>but</u> these chemicals can damage the environment.

Martin Luther King Jr. does not believe that all laws are just, <u>nor</u> does he believe that it is wrong to protest unjust laws.

When you use a coordinating conjunction to join together two independent clauses, you should always place a comma before the coordinating conjunction.

Using Subordinating Conjunctions A **complex sentence** is made up of one independent clause (simple sentence) and one or more dependent clauses. (A dependent clause cannot stand alone as a sentence.) Subordinating conjunctions link dependent and independent clauses that express ideas of unequal importance, and they also indicate how those ideas are related.

independent clause
[According to Martin Luther King Jr., he led protests]

dependent clause
[<u>so that</u> he could fight racial injustice].

SUBORDINATING CONJUNCTIONS

SUBORDINATING CONJUNCTION	RELATIONSHIP BETWEEN CLAUSES
after, before, since, until, when, whenever, while	Time
as, because, since, so that	Cause or effect
even if, if, unless	Condition
although, even though, though	Contrast

"All segregation statutes are unjust <u>because</u> segregation distorts the soul and damages the personality" (King 566).

"<u>If</u> this philosophy had not emerged, by now many streets of the South would, I am convinced, be flowing with blood" (King 569).

"<u>Before</u> the pen of Jefferson etched the majestic words of the Declaration of Independence across the pages of history, we were here" (King 572).

When you use a subordinating conjunction to join two clauses, place a comma after the dependent clause when it comes *before* the independent clause. Do not use a comma when the dependent clause comes *after* the independent clause.

<u>When</u> they signed the Declaration of Independence, Thomas Jefferson and the others knew they were committing treason. (*comma*)

Thomas Jefferson and the others knew they were committing treason <u>when</u> they signed the Declaration of Independence. (*no comma*)

✓ **EDITING CHECKLIST** **ARGUMENTATION**

☐ Have you used coordinating conjunctions correctly to connect two or more independent clauses?

☐ Do the coordinating conjunctions accurately express the relationship between the ideas in the independent clauses?

☐ Have you placed a comma before the coordinating conjunction?

☐ Have you used subordinating conjunctions correctly to connect an independent clause and one or more dependent clauses?

☐ Do the subordinating conjunctions accurately express the relationship between the ideas in the dependent and independent clauses?

☐ Have you placed a comma after the dependent clause when it comes before the independent clause?

☐ Have you remembered not to use a comma when the dependent clause comes after the independent clause?

A STUDENT WRITER: Argumentation

The following essay, written by Marta Ramos for her composition course, illustrates the techniques discussed earlier in this chapter.

Just Say No

Introduction

Recently, use of so-called "study drugs" has become a hotly debated subject. Many students now routinely take prescription medications such as Ritalin or Adderall to improve their academic *Summary of* performance (Brennan). On the one hand, students who take these *controversy* medications say that they help them concentrate and improve their ability to study and to get high grades (Sison). On the other hand, medical professionals warn that the effects of prolonged exposure to these drugs can be harmful and in some cases even fatal. Unfortunately, these warnings have not stopped an ever-increasing number of students — both in high school and in college — from taking such drugs. They argue that parental pressure and the need *Thesis statement* to succeed have forced them to take extreme measures. In the final analysis, however, the risks of these drugs far outweigh their supposed advantages.

1

Argument (inductive)

Despite the claims of users, there is little empirical evidence to show that study drugs actually improve attention or enhance memory. A recent article in the *Daily Beast* examined a range of research on the effectiveness of Ritalin and Adderall. It concluded, "In study after study examining the effect of the drugs on so-called *Evidence* healthy subjects, the findings have been underwhelming. At best, the drugs show a small effect; more often, researchers come up with negative findings. . . ." Moreover, researchers have concluded that Adderall, in particular, "makes you think you're doing better than you actually are" (Schwartz). This probably accounts for the anecdotal evidence of the drug's effectiveness. In short, even though students who take study drugs think they work, there is little hard evidence to suggest they actually do.

2

Argument (inductive)

Adding to the problem, study drugs are often obtained illegally or under false pretenses. Students either buy them from friends or fake conditions such as Attention Deficit Disorder (ADD) to get doctors to prescribe them. Because Adderall is an amphetamine, its side effects are unpredictable — especially when it is abused or mixed with alcohol. For this reason, taking drugs like Adderall *Evidence* without proper medical supervision can — and often does — have severe physical and mental consequences (Sison). For example, Steven Roderick, a student, began taking Adderall during his first

3

year in college. In the beginning, a small amount of the drug seemed to improve his academic performance, but as time went on, he needed to increase the dosage to experience the same effect. By his senior year, Roderick was taking large amounts of Adderall in the morning before classes and taking other drugs at night to get to sleep. Eventually, the Adderall stopped working, and because he could not concentrate without it, he was forced to drop out of school (Cohen).

Argument (deductive)

Even though the physical effects of study drugs are obvious, other negative effects can be subtle and quite insidious. Current research suggests that study drugs can "alter personality and constrain the very self that should be supported to live authentically" (Graf et al. 1257). In other words, study drugs provide a false sense of self to students at a time when they should be testing their abilities and pursuing authenticity. It goes without saying that college is a time of self-discovery and that any substance that interferes with this process is, therefore, harmful and should be avoided. Unfortunately, the temptation to take study drugs is encouraged by a society that values superficiality over depth, instant gratification over determination, and winning at all costs over fairness and personal development.   4

Refutation of opposing argument

Of course, not everyone agrees with this assessment of study drugs. Some argue that concerns about these medications are overblown and that they are more like caffeinated drinks than steroids or amphetamines. In an article on Slate.com, Will Oremus asks, "What if Adderall turns out to be the new coffee — a ubiquitous, mostly harmless little helper that enables us to spend more time poring over spreadsheets and less time daydreaming or lolling about in bed?" The answer to this question is simple. Unlike drinking coffee, the abuse of illicitly obtained prescription drugs is not "mostly harmless." On the contrary, it can undermine the academic mission of colleges; it can damage the physical and mental well-being of students; and it can hurt society as a whole by compromising its core values.   5

Conclusion

Because of the dangers of study drugs, educators, medical professionals, and parents should inform students of the risks and discourage their use. Medical professionals should be on the lookout for students who are trying to fool them into prescribing Adderall. Parents should be educated to recognize the behavior associated with the excessive use of study drugs. Finally, colleges should make it clear to students that the use of study drugs is unacceptable and will not be tolerated. Only by adopting these measures can the use of study drugs be curtailed — and, eventually, eliminated.   6

Works Cited

Works-cited list (begins new page)

Brennan, Collin. "Popping Pills: Examining the Use of 'Study Drugs' during Finals." *USA Today College*, 16 Dec. 2015, college. www.usatoday.com/2015/12/16/popping-pills-examining-the -use-of-study-drugs-during-fnals/.

Cohen, Roger. "The Competition Drug." *The New York Times*, 4 Mar. 2013, www.nytimes.com/2013/03/05/opinion/global/roger -cohen-adderall-the-academic-competition-drug.html?_r=0.

Graf, William D., et al. "Pediatric Neuroenhancement: Ethical, Legal, Social, and Neurodevelopmental Implications." *Neurology*, vol. 80, no. 13, 26 Mar. 2013, pp. 1251–60.

Oremus, Will. "The New Stimulus Package." *Slate*, 27 Mar. 2013, www .slate.com/articles/technology/superman/2013/03/adderall _ritalin_vyvanse_do_smart_pills_work_if_you_don_t _have_adhd.html.

Schwartz, Casey. "Busting the Adderall Myth." *The Daily Beast*, 20 Dec. 2010, www.thedailybeast.com/articles/2010/12/21 /adderall-concentration-benefits-in-doubt-new-study.html.

Sison, Geraldo. "Adderall Abuse among College Students." *American Addiction Centers*, 3 Sept. 2019, www.americanaddictioncenters .org/adderall/adderall-abuse-among-college-students.

Points for Special Attention

Choosing a Topic

For her composition course, Marta Ramos was asked to write an argumentative essay on a topic of her choice. Because her college newspaper had recently run an editorial on the use of study drugs, she decided to explore this topic. Although Marta had no direct experience with study drugs, such as Adderall and Ritalin, she knew people who used them. Given the timeliness and seriousness of the issue, Marta thought it would be a good topic for her to write about. Because she had read the article in her school newspaper, as well as the many responses (both pro and con) that it elicited, she thought she understood both sides of the controversy. She knew she was against the use of study drugs, but even so, she believed she could approach the topic with an open mind and would be able to reconsider her opinion if the evidence led her in a different direction.

Gathering Evidence

Marta realized she could not rely on personal experience to support her position. For this reason, she used information from several outside sources to develop her argument. For example, she found an article in the academic journal *Neurology* that increased her understanding of her subject. She also found a newspaper article about a student whose story illustrated the practical dangers of study drugs. In addition, she decided to address Will Oremus's 2013 defense of study drugs, which she found both interesting and troubling. She took notes on her sources and recorded their bibliographic information for her works-cited page.

Organization

Marta begins her essay by providing the context for her argument and then stating her thesis:

> In the final analysis, however, the risks of these drugs far outweigh their supposed advantages.

In her first body paragraph, Marta addresses the misconception that study drugs are effective. She includes material from an article by Casey Schwartz that summarizes several studies on the use of Ritalin and Adderall by college students, and she combines this information with her own ideas to make the point that study drugs give users a false sense of confidence.

Marta goes on to discuss the harmful physical and psychological effects of study drugs. She begins by saying that because study drugs are often obtained illegally or under false pretenses, their use is extremely risky. She illustrates this point with an anecdote about a student who began taking Adderall to improve his academic performance but eventually had to drop out of college because he could no longer concentrate.

Finally, Marta explains how study drugs have insidious effects on users. In this paragraph, she presents a deductive argument:

Major premise:	Students should discover their authentic selves in college.
Minor premise:	Any substance that interferes with this discovery process is harmful to students.
Conclusion:	Therefore, study drugs are harmful and should be avoided.

Refuting Opposing Arguments

Marta spends one paragraph addressing Will Oremus's point that taking study drugs may be no more harmful than drinking coffee. She refutes this claim by pointing out that unlike coffee, study drugs can do real harm to students as well as to colleges and to society. Here, as in the rest of her essay, Marta is careful to appear both reasonable and respectful. She makes her points clearly and concisely, taking care to avoid name-calling, personal attacks, and jumping to conclusions.

Focus on Revision

When Marta's instructor returned her essay along with his comments, he told her that she had made a very strong argument but that the argument would have been even stronger had she refuted more than one opposing argument. For example, she could have addressed the argument that taking study drugs is not unethical because these medications only help you if you have studied in the first place. Marta could also have considered other issues related to this controversy. For instance, is it unfair for some students to use study drugs while others do not? Does the increasing use of study drugs indicate a problem with the educational system? Does pressure to excel put students under too much pressure? Should colleges be doing more to limit the number of courses that students can carry? Would more student aid enable students to concentrate more on studying and less on earning money to pay tuition?

✎ PEER-EDITING WORKSHEET   ARGUMENTATION

1. Does the essay take a stand on an issue? What is it? At what point does the writer state his or her thesis? Is the thesis debatable?

2. What evidence does the writer include to support his or her position? What additional evidence could the writer supply?

3. Has the writer used information from outside sources? If so, is documentation included? Identify any information the writer should have documented but did not.

4. Does the essay summarize and refute the opposing arguments? List these arguments.

5. How effective are the writer's refutations? Should the writer address any other arguments?

6. Does the essay use inductive reasoning? Deductive reasoning? Both? Provide an example of each type of reasoning used in the essay.

7. Does the writer use sources? Do they reinforce the writer's argument? Does the writer need to add additional sources?

8. Does the writer need to add a visual?

9. Does the essay include any logical fallacies? If so, how would you correct these fallacies?

10. Do coordinating and subordinating conjunctions convey the logical and sequential connections between ideas?

11. How could the introduction be improved?

12. How could the conclusion be improved?

The essays that follow represent a wide variety of topics, and the purpose of each essay is to support a debatable thesis. In addition to three classic arguments, this chapter also includes two debates and two casebooks that focus on current issues. Each of the debates pairs two essays that take opposing stands on the same issue. In the casebooks, four essays as well as a visual text on a single topic offer a greater variety of viewpoints. The first selection, a visual text, is followed by questions designed to illustrate how argumentation can operate in visual form.

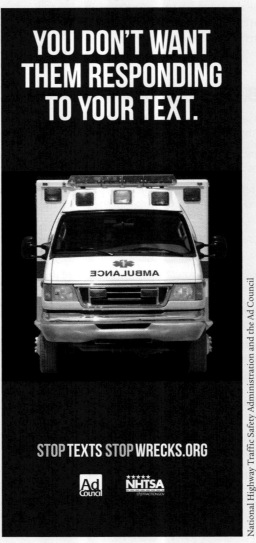

National Highway Traffic Safety Administration and the Ad Council

Reading Images

1. At whom is this ad directed?
2. What point does the headline make? How does the image support this point?
3. Does this ad appeal primarily to logic, to emotion, or to both? Explain.
4. Visit the website StopTextsStopWrecks.org. What additional information does the site include that supports the message of the advertisement?

Journal Entry

Do you have additional suggestions about how to address the problem of texting while driving? Post your comments in the "Talk to Us" box on StopTextsStop-Wrecks.org.

Thematic Connections

- "The YouTube Effect" (page 20)
- "Ten Ways We Get the Odds Wrong" (page 242)
- "The Embalming of Mr. Jones" (page 296)

THOMAS JEFFERSON

The Declaration of Independence

Thomas Jefferson was born in 1743 in what is now Albemarle County, Virginia. A lawyer, he was elected to Virginia's colonial legislature in 1768 and began a distinguished political career that strongly influenced the early development of the United States. In addition to his participation in the Second Continental Congress of 1775–1776, which ratified the Declaration of Independence, he served as governor of Virginia; as minister to France; as secretary of state under President George Washington; as vice president under John Adams; and, finally, as president from 1801 to 1809. After his retirement, he founded the University of Virginia. He died on July 4, 1826.

Background on the struggle for American independence By the early 1770s, many residents of the original thirteen American colonies were convinced that King George III and his ministers wielded too much power over the colonists. In particular, they objected to a series of taxes imposed by the British Parliament to offset the cost of protecting the colonies during the French and Indian War. Being without representation in Parliament, the colonists asserted that "taxation without representation" amounted to tyranny. In response to a series of laws Parliament passed in 1774 to limit the political and geographic freedom of the colonists, representatives of each colony met at the Continental Congress of 1774 to draft a plan of reconciliation, but it was rejected.

As cries for independence increased, British soldiers and state militias began to engage in armed conflict, which by 1776 had become a full-fledged war. On June 11, 1776, the Second Continental Congress chose Jefferson, Benjamin Franklin, and several other delegates to draft a declaration of independence. The draft was written by Jefferson, with suggestions and revisions contributed by other commission members. Jefferson's Declaration of Independence challenges a basic assumption of its time — that the royal monarch ruled by divine right — and, in so doing, it became one of the most important political documents in world history.

As you read, keep in mind that to the British, the Declaration of Independence was a call for open rebellion. For this reason, the Declaration's final sentence, in which the signatories pledge their lives, fortunes, and honor, is no mere rhetorical flourish. Had England defeated the colonists, everyone who signed the Declaration of Independence would have been arrested, charged with treason or sedition, stripped of his property, and probably hanged.

When in the course of human events, it becomes necessary for one people   1
to dissolve the political bonds which have connected them with another, and to assume among the powers of the earth, the separate and equal station to which the Laws of Nature and of Nature's God entitle them, a decent respect to the opinions of mankind requires that they should declare the causes which impel them to the separation.

We hold these truths to be self-evident, that all men are created equal, that they are endowed by their Creator with certain unalienable rights, that among these are life, liberty, and the pursuit of happiness. That to secure these rights, governments are instituted among men, deriving their just powers from the consent of the governed. That whenever any form of government becomes destructive to these ends, it is the right of the people to alter or to abolish it, and to institute new government, laying its foundation on such principles and organizing its powers in such form, as to them shall seem most likely to effect their safety and happiness. Prudence, indeed, will dictate that governments long established should not be changed for light and transient causes; and accordingly all experience hath shown, that mankind are more disposed to suffer, while evils are sufferable, than to right themselves by abolishing the forms to which they are accustomed. But when a long train of abuses and usurpations, pursuing invariably the same object, evinces a design to reduce them under absolute despotism, it is their right, it is their duty, to throw off such government, and to provide new guards for their future security. Such has been the patient sufferance of these Colonies; and such is now the necessity which constrains them to alter their former systems of government. The history of the present king of Great Britain is a history of repeated injuries and usurpations, all having in direct object the establishment of an absolute tyranny over these States. To prove this, let facts be submitted to a candid world.

> "We hold these truths to be self-evident, that all men are created equal. . . ."

2

He has refused his assent to laws, the most wholesome and necessary for the public good.

3

He has forbidden his Governors to pass laws of immediate and pressing importance, unless suspended in their operation till his assent should be obtained; and when so suspended, he has utterly neglected to attend to them.

4

He has refused to pass other laws for the accommodation of large districts of people, unless those people would relinquish the right of representation in the legislature, a right inestimable to them and formidable to tyrants only.

5

He has called together legislative bodies at places unusual, uncomfortable, and distant from the depository of their public records, for the sole purpose of fatiguing them into compliance with his measure.

6

He has dissolved representative houses repeatedly, for opposing with manly firmness his invasions on the rights of people.

7

He has refused for a long time, after such dissolutions, to cause others to be elected; whereby the legislative powers, incapable of annihilation, have returned to the people at large for their exercise; the State remaining in the meantime exposed to all the dangers of invasion from without, and convulsions within.

8

He has endeavoured to prevent the population of these states; for that purpose obstructing the laws for naturalization of foreigners; refusing to pass others to encourage their migration hither, and raising the conditions of new appropriations of lands.

9

He has obstructed the administration of justice, by refusing his assent to   10
laws for establishing judiciary powers.

He has made judges dependent on his will alone, for the tenure of their   11
offices, and the amount and payment of their salaries.

He has erected a multitude of new offices, and sent hither swarms of offi-   12
cers to harass our people, and eat out their substance.

He has kept among us, in times of peace, standing armies without the con-   13
sent of our legislatures.

He has affected to render the military independent of and superior to the   14
civil power.

He has combined with others to subject us to a jurisdiction foreign to our   15
constitution, and unacknowledged by our laws; giving his assent to their acts
of pretended legislation:

For quartering large bodies of troops among us: 16

For protecting them, by a mock trial, from punishment for any murders   17
which they should commit on the inhabitants of these States:

For cutting off our trade with all parts of the world: 18

For imposing taxes on us without our consent: 19

For depriving us in many cases, of the benefits of trial by jury: 20

For transporting us beyond seas to be tried for pretended offences: 21

For abolishing the free system of English laws in a neighbouring Province,   22
establishing therein an arbitrary government, and enlarging its boundaries so
as to render it at once an example and fit instrument for introducing the same
absolute rule into these Colonies:

For taking away our Charters, abolishing our most valuable laws, and   23
altering fundamentally the forms of our governments:

For suspending our own legislatures, and declaring themselves invested   24
with power to legislate for us in all cases whatsoever.

He has abdicated government here, by declaring us out of his protection   25
and waging war against us.

He has plundered our seas, ravaged our coasts, burnt our towns, and   26
destroyed the lives of our people.

He is at this time transporting large armies of foreign mercenaries to com-   27
plete the works of death, desolation and tyranny, already begun with circumstances of cruelty and perfidy scarcely paralleled in the most barbarous ages,
and totally unworthy the head of a civilized nation.

He has constrained our fellow citizens taken captive on the high seas to   28
bear arms against their country, to become the executioners of their friends
and brethren, or to fall themselves by their hands.

He has excited domestic insurrections amongst us, and has endeavoured   29
to bring on the inhabitants of our frontiers, the merciless Indian savages,
whose known rule of warfare, is an undistinguished destruction of all ages,
sexes, and conditions.

In every stage of these oppressions we have petitioned for redress in the   30
most humble terms: our repeated petitions have been answered only by
repeated injury. A prince whose character is thus marked by every act which
may define a tyrant, is unfit to be the ruler of a free people.

Nor have we been wanting in attentions to our British brethren. We have   31
warned them from time to time of attempts by their legislature to extend an
unwarrantable jurisdiction over us. We have reminded them of the circumstances of our emigration and settlement here. We have appealed to their
native justice and magnanimity, and we have conjured them by the ties of our
common kindred to disavow these usurpations, which would inevitably interrupt our connections and correspondence. They too have been deaf to the
voice of justice and of consanguinity. We must, therefore, acquiesce in the
necessity, which denounces our separation, and hold them, as we hold the rest
of mankind, enemies in war, in peace friends.

We, therefore, the Representatives of the United States of America, in   32
General Congress, assembled, appealing to the Supreme Judge of the world for
the rectitude of our intentions, do, in the name, and by authority of the good
people of these Colonies, solemnly publish and declare, That these United
Colonies are, and of right ought to be Free and Independent States; that they
are absolved from all allegiance to the British Crown, and that all political connection between them and the state of Great Britain, is and ought to be totally
dissolved; and that as Free and Independent States, they have full power to levy
war, conclude peace, contract alliances, establish commerce, and to do all other
acts and things which Independent States may of right do. And for the support
of this declaration, with a firm reliance on the protection of divine Providence,
we mutually pledge to each other our lives, our fortunes, and our sacred honor.

•   •   •

Comprehension

1. What "truths" does Jefferson say are "self-evident" (2)?
2. What does Jefferson say is the source from which governments derive their
   powers?
3. What reasons does Jefferson give to support his premise that the United
   States should break away from Great Britain?
4. What conclusions about British rule does Jefferson draw from the evidence
   he presents?

Purpose and Audience

1. What is the major premise of Jefferson's argument? Should Jefferson have
   done more to establish the truth of this premise?
2. The Declaration of Independence was written during a period now referred
   to as the Age of Reason. In what ways has Jefferson tried to make his document appear reasonable?
3. For what audience (or audiences) was the document intended? Which
   groups of readers would have been most likely to accept it? Explain.
4. How effectively does Jefferson anticipate and refute the opposition?
5. In paragraph 31, following the list of grievances, why does Jefferson address
   his "British brethren"?
6. At what point does Jefferson state his thesis? Why does he state it where he
   does?

Style and Structure

1. Does the Declaration of Independence rely primarily on inductive reasoning or deductive reasoning? Identify examples of each.
2. What techniques does Jefferson use to create smooth and logical transitions from one paragraph to another?
3. Why does Jefferson list his twenty-eight grievances? Why doesn't he just summarize them or mention a few representative grievances?
4. Jefferson begins the last paragraph of the Declaration of Independence with "We, therefore." How effective is this conclusion? Explain.
5. **Vocabulary Project.** Underline ten words that have negative connotations. How does Jefferson use these words to help him make his point? Do you think words with more neutral connotations would strengthen or weaken his case? Why?
6. **Vocabulary Project.** What words does Jefferson use that are rarely used today? Would the Declaration of Independence be more meaningful to today's readers if it were updated, with more familiar words substituted? To help you formulate your response, try rewriting a paragraph or two, and assess your updated version. Look up any unfamiliar words in an online dictionary such as dictionary.com.

Journal Entry

Do you think Jefferson is being fair to the king? Do you think he should have been?

Writing Workshop

1. Following Jefferson's example, write a declaration of independence from your school, job, family, or any other institution with which you are associated.
2. **Working with Sources.** Go to the website ushistory.org/declaration, and look at the revisions Congress made to Jefferson's original draft of the Declaration of Independence. Decide which version you think is better. Then, write an essay in which you present your case. Be sure to document references to both versions of the Declaration and to include a works-cited page. (See Chapter 18 for information on MLA documentation.)
3. **Working with Sources.** In an argumentative essay written from the viewpoint of King George III, answer Jefferson. Try to convince the colonists that they should not break away from Great Britain. If you can, refute some of the points Jefferson makes. Be sure to include parenthetical documentation for all references to the Declaration and a works-cited page. (See Chapter 18 for information on MLA documentation.)

Combining the Patterns

The middle section of the Declaration of Independence is developed by means of **exemplification**: it presents a series of examples to support Jefferson's assertion that the colonists have experienced "repeated injuries and usurpations" (2). Are these examples relevant? Representative? Sufficient? What other pattern of development could Jefferson have used to support his assertion?

Thematic Connections
- from *Persepolis II* (page 111)
- "Photos That Change History" (page 354)
- "The Twin Revolutions of Lincoln and Darwin" (page 420)
- "Letter from Birmingham Jail" (page 562)

RACHEL CARSON

The Obligation to Endure

A marine biologist, conservationist, and author, Rachel Carson (1907–1964) was a foundational figure in the modern environmental movement. While working for the U.S. Bureau of Fisheries in the 1930s, she began writing for general-interest publications and newspapers like the *Baltimore Sun*, *The Atlantic*, and *Collier's*. Her first book, an accessible but scientifically accurate work about fish and seabirds, was published in 1941. After World War II, she became more focused on nature conservation and the widespread use of synthetic and chemical pesticides like DDT (dichlorodiphenyltrichloroethane). Those preoccupations led to Carson's most famous work, *Silent Spring*, which was serialized in the *New Yorker* magazine and then published as a book in 1962. *Silent Spring* not only raised awareness of environmental issues but also influenced national policy. Her other works include *The Edge of the Sea* (1955) and *Lost Woods: The Discovered Writing of Rachel Carson* (1998).

Background on the environmental movement in the United States The history of environmental awareness in the United States stretches back to the nation's founding. For example, Thomas Jefferson was a naturalist, botanist, and farmer who envisioned the United States as an agrarian republic. Industrialization and urbanization in the nineteenth century, however, spurred both skepticism about progress and a more urgent sense that nature needed protection. Henry David Thoreau published *Walden*, a philosophical manifesto about living close to nature, in 1854; President Ulysses S. Grant established Yellowstone National Park as protected wilderness in 1872. Author and activist John Muir, the most important American conservationist of the late nineteenth and early twentieth centuries, founded the Sierra Club — the largest environmental organization in the United States — in 1892. During his term as president, Theodore Roosevelt created the United States Forest Service and established several national parks, forests, and reserves. Wisconsin Senator Gaylord Nelson founded Earth Day in 1970, the beginning of a decade that witnessed the creation of the Environmental Protection Agency, Clean Air Act, and other initiatives. But writers, in particular, have played a significant role in conservation and environmentalism. For example, ecologist Aldo Leopold's *Sand County Almanac* (1949) and activist and writer Edward Abbey's *Desert Solitaire* (1968) shaped public attitudes about nature and influenced government policies toward the environment. Perhaps no single book was as influential as Carson's *Silent Spring*, however, from which the following selection is excerpted.

The history of life on earth has been a history of interaction between living   1
things and their surroundings. To a large extent, the physical form and the habits of the earth's vegetation and its animal life have been molded by the environment. Considering the whole span of earthly time, the opposite effect, in which life actually modifies its surroundings, has been relatively slight. Only

within the moment of time represented by the present century has one species — man — acquired significant power to alter the nature of his world.

During the past quarter century this power has not only increased to one of disturbing magnitude but it has changed in character. The most alarming of all man's assaults upon the environment is the contamination of air, earth, rivers, and sea with dangerous and even lethal materials. This pollution is for the most part irrecoverable; the chain of evil it initiates not only in the world that must support life but in living tissues is for the most part irreversible. In this now universal contamination of the environment, chemicals are the sinister and little-recognized partners of radiation in changing the very nature of the world — the very nature of its life. Strontium 90, released through nuclear explosions into the air, comes to earth in rain or drifts down as fallout, lodges in soil, enters into the grass or corn or wheat grown there, and in time takes up its abode in the bones of a human being, there to remain until his death. Similarly, chemicals sprayed on croplands or forests or gardens lie long in soil, entering into living organisms, passing from one to another in a chain of poisoning and death. Or they pass mysteriously by underground streams until they emerge and, through the alchemy of air and sunlight, combine into new forms that kill vegetation, sicken cattle, and work unknown harm on those who drink from once pure wells. As Albert Schweitzer has said, "Man can hardly even recognize the devils of his own creation."

It took hundreds of millions of years to produce the life that now inhabits the earth — eons of time in which that developing and evolving and diversifying life reached a state of adjustment and balance with its surroundings. The environment, rigorously shaping and directing the life it supported, contained elements that were hostile as well as supporting. Certain rocks gave out dangerous radiation; even within the light of the sun, from which all life draws its energy, there were short-wave radiations with power to injure. Given time — time not in years but in millennia — life adjusts, and a balance has been reached. For time is the essential ingredient; but in the modern world there is no time.

The rapidity of change and the speed with which new situations are created follow the impetuous and heedless pace of man rather than the deliberate pace of nature. Radiation is no longer merely the background radiation of rocks, the bombardment of cosmic rays, the ultraviolet of the sun that have existed before there was any life on earth; radiation is now the unnatural creation of man's tampering with the atom. The chemicals to which life is asked to make its adjustment are no longer merely the calcium and silica and copper and all the rest of the minerals washed out of the rocks and carried in rivers to the sea; they are the synthetic creations of man's inventive mind, brewed in his laboratories, and having no counterparts in nature.

> **"The rapidity of change and the speed with which new situations are created follow the impetuous and heedless pace of man rather than the deliberate pace of nature."**

To adjust to these chemicals would require time on the scale that is 5 nature's; it would require not merely the years of a man's life but the life of generations. And even this, were it by some miracle possible, would be futile, for the new chemicals come from our laboratories in an endless stream; almost five hundred annually find their way into actual use in the United States alone. The figure is staggering and its implications are not easily grasped — 500 new chemicals to which the bodies of men and animals are required somehow to adapt each year, chemicals totally outside the limits of biologic experience.

Among them are many that are used in man's war against nature. Since the 6 mid-1940s over 200 basic chemicals have been created for use in killing insects, weeds, rodents, and other organisms described in the modern vernacular as "pests"; and they are sold under several thousand different brand names.

These sprays, dusts, and aerosols are now applied almost universally to 7 farms, gardens, forests, and homes — nonselective chemicals that have the power to kill every insect, the "good" and the "bad," to still the song of birds and the leaping of fish in the streams, to coat the leaves with a deadly film, and to linger on in soil — all this though the intended target may be only a few weeds or insects. Can anyone believe it is possible to lay down such a barrage of poisons on the surface of the earth without making it unfit for all life? They should not be called "insecticides," but "biocides."

The whole process of spraying seems caught up in an endless spiral. Since 8 DDT was released for civilian use, a process of escalation has been going on in which ever more toxic materials must be found. This has happened because insects, in a triumphant vindication of Darwin's principle of the survival of the fittest, have evolved super races immune to the particular insecticide used, hence a deadlier one has always to be developed — and then a deadlier one than that. It has happened also because, for reasons to be described later, destructive insects often undergo a "flareback," or resurgence, after spraying, in numbers greater than before. Thus the chemical war is never won, and all life is caught in its violent crossfire.

Along with the possibility of the extinction of mankind by nuclear war, the 9 central problem of our age has therefore become the contamination of man's total environment with such substances of incredible potential for harm — substances that accumulate in the tissues of plants and animals and even penetrate the germ cells to shatter or alter the very material of heredity upon which the shape of the future depends.

Some would-be architects of our future look toward a time when it will be 10 possible to alter the human germ plasm by design. But we may easily be doing so now by inadvertence, for many chemicals, like radiation, bring about gene mutations. It is ironic to think that man might determine his own future by something so seemingly trivial as the choice of an insect spray.

All this has been risked — for what? Future historians may well be amazed 11 by our distorted sense of proportion. How could intelligent beings seek to control a few unwanted species by a method that contaminated the entire environment and brought the threat of disease and death even to their own kind? Yet this is precisely what we have done. We have done it, moreover, for reasons that collapse the moment we examine them. We are told that the enormous and expanding use of pesticides is necessary to maintain farm production. Yet is our real problem not one of *overproduction*? Our farms, despite measures to remove acreages from production and to pay farmers *not* to produce, have yielded such a staggering excess of crops that the American taxpayer in 1962 is paying out more than one billion dollars a year as the total carrying cost of the surplus-food storage program. And is the situation helped when one branch of the Agriculture Department tries to reduce production while another states, as it did in 1958, "It is believed generally that reduction of crop acreages under provisions of the Soil Bank will stimulate interest in use of chemicals to obtain maximum production on the land retained in crops."

All this is not to say there is no insect problem and no need of control. I am   12
saying, rather, that control must be geared to realities, not to mythical situations, and that the methods employed must be such that they do not destroy us along with the insects.

The problem whose attempted solution has brought such a train of disas-   13
ter in its wake is an accompaniment of our modern way of life. Long before the age of man, insects inhabited the earth — a group of extraordinarily varied and adaptable beings. Over the course of time since man's advent, a small percentage of the more than half a million species of insects have come into conflict with human welfare in two principal ways: as competitors for the food supply and as carriers of human disease.

Disease-carrying insects become important where human beings are   14
crowded together, especially under conditions where sanitation is poor, as in time of natural disaster or war or in situations of extreme poverty and deprivation. Then control of some sort becomes necessary. It is a sobering fact, however, as we shall presently see, that the method of massive chemical control has had only limited success, and also threatens to worsen the very conditions it is intended to curb.

Under primitive agricultural conditions the farmer had few insect prob-   15
lems. These arose with the intensification of agriculture — the devotion of immense acreages to a single crop. Such a system set the stage for explosive increases in specific insect populations. Single-crop farming does not take advantage of the principles by which nature works; it is agriculture as an engineer might conceive it to be. Nature has introduced great variety into the landscape, but man has displayed a passion for simplifying it. Thus he undoes the built-in checks and balances by which nature holds the species within bounds. One important natural check is a limit on the amount of suitable habitat for each species. Obviously then, an insect that lives on wheat can build up its population to much higher levels on a farm devoted to wheat than on one in which wheat is intermingled with other crops to which the insect is not adapted.

The same thing happens in other situations. A generation or more ago, the   16
towns of large areas of the United States lined their streets with the noble elm tree. Now the beauty they hopefully created is threatened with complete destruction as disease sweeps through the elms, carried by a beetle that would have only limited chance to build up large populations and to spread from tree to tree if the elms were only occasional trees in a richly diversified planting.

Another factor in the modern insect problem is one that must be viewed   17
against a background of geologic and human history: the spreading of thousands of different kinds of organisms from their native homes to invade new
territories. This worldwide migration has been studied and graphically
described by the British ecologist Charles Elton in his recent book *The Ecology
of Invasions*. During the Cretaceous Period, some hundred million years ago,
flooding seas cut many land bridges between continents and living things
found themselves confined in what Elton calls "colossal separate nature
reserves." There, isolated from others of their kind, they developed many new
species. When some of the land masses were joined again, about 15 million
years ago, these species began to move out into new territories—a movement
that is not only still in progress but is now receiving considerable assistance
from man.

The importation of plants is the primary agent in the modern spread of   18
species, for animals have almost invariably gone along with the plants, quarantine being a comparatively recent and not completely effective innovation. The
United States Office of Plant Introduction alone has introduced almost
200,000 species and varieties of plants from all over the world. Nearly half of
the 180 or so major insect enemies of plants in the United States are accidental
imports from abroad, and most of them have come as hitchhikers on plants.

In new territory, out of reach of the restraining hand of the natural ene-   19
mies that kept down its numbers in its native land, an invading plant or animal
is able to become enormously abundant. Thus it is no accident that our most
troublesome insects are introduced species.

These invasions, both the naturally occurring and those dependent on   20
human assistance, are likely to continue indefinitely. Quarantine and massive
chemical campaigns are only extremely expensive ways of buying time. We are
faced, according to Dr. Elton, "with a life-and-death need not just to find new
technological means of suppressing this plant or that animal"; instead we need
the basic knowledge of animal populations and their relations to their surroundings that will "promote an even balance and damp down the explosive
power of outbreaks and new invasions."

Much of the necessary knowledge is now available but we do not use it. We   21
train ecologists in our universities and even employ them in our governmental
agencies but we seldom take their advice. We allow the chemical death rain to
fall as though there were no alternative, whereas in fact there are many, and our
ingenuity could soon discover many more if given opportunity.

Have we fallen into a mesmerized state that makes us accept as inevitable   22
that which is inferior or detrimental, as though having lost the will or the
vision to demand that which is good? Such thinking, in the words of the ecologist Paul Shepard, "idealizes life with only its head out of water, inches above
the limits of toleration of the corruption of its own environment. . . . Why
should we tolerate a diet of weak poisons, a home in insipid surroundings, a
circle of acquaintances who are not quite our enemies, the noise of motors
with just enough relief to prevent insanity? Who would want to live in a world
which is just not quite fatal?"

Yet such a world is pressed upon us. The crusade to create a chemically   23
sterile, insect-free world seems to have engendered a fanatic zeal on the part of
many specialists and most of the so-called control agencies. On every hand
there is evidence that those engaged in spraying operations exercise a ruthless
power. "The regulatory entomologists . . . function as prosecutor, judge and
jury, tax assessor and collector and sheriff to enforce their own orders," said
Connecticut entomologist Neely Turner. The most flagrant abuses go
unchecked in both state and federal agencies.

It is not my contention that chemical insecticides must never be used. I do   24
contend that we have put poisonous and biologically potent chemicals indis-
criminately into the hands of persons largely or wholly ignorant of their poten-
tials for harm. We have subjected enormous numbers of people to contact with
these poisons, without their consent and often without their knowledge. If the
Bill of Rights contains no guarantee that a citizen shall be secure against lethal
poisons distributed either by private individuals or by public officials, it is
surely only because our forefathers, despite their considerable wisdom and
foresight, could conceive of no such problem.

I contend, furthermore, that we have allowed these chemicals to be used   25
with little or no advance investigation of their effect on soil, water, wildlife, and
man himself. Future generations are unlikely to condone our lack of prudent
concern for the integrity of the natural world that supports all life.

There is still very limited awareness of the nature of the threat. This is an   26
era of specialists, each of whom sees his own problem and is unaware of or
intolerant of the larger frame into which it fits. It is also an era dominated by
industry, in which the right to make a dollar at whatever cost is seldom challenged. When the public protests, confronted with some obvious evidence of
damaging results of pesticide applications, it is fed little tranquilizing pills of
half truth. We urgently need an end to these false assurances, to the sugar coating of unpalatable facts. It is the public that is being asked to assume the risks
that the insect controllers calculate. The public must decide whether it wishes
to continue on the present road, and it can do so only when in full possession
of the facts. In the words of Jean Rostand, "The obligation to endure gives us
the right to know."

• • •

Comprehension

1. How, according to Carson, have people "acquired significant power to alter
   the nature of [the] world" (1)?
2. What does Carson mean when she says that "in the modern world there is
   no time" (3)?
3. Why does Carson think "insecticides" should be called "biocides" (7)? What
   new problems do pesticides create?
4. What does Carson see as "the central problem of our age" (9)?
5. How do increased human populations create the conditions for increased
   insect populations? Why, according to Carson, is this situation a problem?

6. Why is single-crop farming dangerous? What effect does it have on the environment? On insect populations?
7. What are the "false assurances" (26) to which Carson refers in her conclusion? What does she say we should do to end them?

Purpose and Audience

1. What is Carson's thesis? At what point does she state it? Why does she state it where she does?
2. What is Carson's purpose? Do you think she expects to change people's ideas or behavior, or does she have some other idea in mind?
3. Does Carson see her audience as receptive, hostile, or neutral? How can you tell?

Style and Structure

1. What is the significance of the essay's title?
2. Why does Carson begin her essay by discussing the history of life on earth? How does this introduction set up the discussion to follow?
3. Throughout her essay, Carson cites statistics and includes the opinions of experts. How effective is this support?
4. Where in her essay does Carson appeal to logic? To emotions? To ethics? What does each of these appeals accomplish?
5. In paragraph 12, Carson concedes the point that insects can cause problems. Does she adequately refute this point? Explain your answer.
6. What points does Carson emphasize in her conclusion? Why?
7. **Vocabulary Project.** In paragraph 13, Carson uses the metaphor "train of disaster" to describe the impact of using pesticides to destroy insects. What does she mean? How effective is this use of **figurative language**?

Journal Entry

What environmental issue today is as serious as the one Carson discusses in her essay?

Writing Workshop

1. In paragraph 6, Carson says that she thinks man "is in a war against nature." Write an argumentative essay in which you take a stand for and against her position.
2. Do you think this essay is as relevant today as it was when it appeared in 1962? Write an argumentative essay in which you answer this question.
3. **Working with Sources.** *Silent Spring*, the book from which this essay is excerpted, is credited with launching the modern environmental movement. This book is not without its critics, however. Some, such as the entomologist J. Gordon Edwards, have asserted that it is full of omissions, faulty logic, and fabrications. Go online and read Edwards's 1992 essay, "The Lies of Rachel Carson." Then, do further research on the accuracy of Carson's claims.

Finally, write an essay in which you argue whether Carson's legacy has been positive or negative. Be sure to document all your sources and to include a works-cited page. (See Chapter 18 for information on MLA documentation.)

Combining the Patterns

Carson uses **cause and effect** extensively in this essay, especially when she discusses the detrimental effects of using "nonselective chemicals" (7). Find two examples of her use of cause and effect, and consider what each cause-and-effect discussion adds to her essay.

Thematic Connections

- "The Hidden Life of Garbage" (page 185)
- "Ten Ways We Get the Odds Wrong" (page 242)
- "On Dumpster Diving" (page 668)
- "Long Live the Albatross" (page 683)

MARTIN LUTHER KING JR.

Letter from Birmingham Jail

Martin Luther King Jr. was born in Atlanta, Georgia, in 1929. After receiving his doctorate in theology from Boston University in 1955, he became pastor of the Dexter Avenue Baptist Church in Montgomery, Alabama. There, he organized a 382-day bus boycott that led to the 1956 Supreme Court decision outlawing segregation on Alabama's buses. As leader of the Southern Christian Leadership Conference, he was instrumental in securing the civil rights of Black Americans, using methods based on a philosophy of nonviolent protest. His books include *Stride toward Freedom* (1958) and *Why We Can't Wait* (1964). In 1964, King was awarded the Nobel Peace Prize. He was assassinated in 1968 in Memphis, Tennessee.

Background on racial segregation In 1896, the Supreme Court ruled in *Plessy v. Ferguson* that "separate but equal" accommodations on railroad cars gave African Americans the equal protection guaranteed by the Fourteenth Amendment of the United States Constitution. This decision was used to justify separate public facilities — including schools — for Blacks and whites well into the twentieth century.

In the mid-1950s, state support for segregation and discrimination against Blacks had begun to be challenged. Supreme Court decisions in 1954 and 1955 declared segregation in public schools and other publicly financed venues unconstitutional, while Blacks and whites alike were calling for an end to discrimination. Their actions took the form of marches, boycotts, and sit-ins (organized protests whose participants refuse to move from a public area). Many whites, however, particularly in the South, vehemently resisted any change in race relations.

By 1963, when King organized a campaign against segregation in Birmingham, Alabama, tensions ran deep. He and his followers met fierce opposition from the police, as well as from white moderates, who considered him an "outside agitator." During the demonstrations, King was arrested and jailed for eight days. While imprisoned, he wrote his "Letter from Birmingham Jail" to white clergymen to explain his actions and to answer those who urged him to call off the demonstrations.

April 16, 1963

My Dear Fellow Clergymen:

While confined here in the Birmingham city jail, I came across your recent   1
statement calling my present activities "unwise and untimely." Seldom do I pause to answer criticism of my work and ideas. If I sought to answer all the criticisms that cross my desk, my secretaries would have little time for anything other than such correspondence in the course of the day, and I would have no time for constructive work. But since I feel that you are men of genuine good will and that your criticisms are sincerely set forth, I want to try to answer your statement in what I hope will be patient and reasonable terms.

I think I should indicate why I am here in Birmingham, since you have been influenced by the view which argues against "outsiders coming in." I have the honor of serving as president of the Southern Christian Leadership Conference, an organization operating in every southern state, with headquarters in Atlanta, Georgia. We have some eighty-five affiliated organizations across the South, and one of them is the Alabama Christian Movement for Human Rights. Frequently we share staff, educational, and financial resources with our affiliates. Several months ago the affiliate here in Birmingham asked us to be on call to engage in a nonviolent direct-action program if such were deemed necessary. We readily consented, and when the hour came we lived up to our promise. So I, along with several members of my staff, am here because I was invited here. I am here because I have organizational ties here.

But more basically, I am in Birmingham because injustice is here. Just as the prophets of the eighth century B.C. left their villages and carried their "thus saith the Lord" far beyond the boundaries of their home towns, and just as the Apostle Paul left his village of Tarsus and carried the gospel of Jesus Christ to the far corners of the Greco-Roman world, so am I compelled to carry the gospel of freedom beyond my own home town. Like Paul, I must constantly respond to the Macedonian call for aid.

Moreover, I am cognizant of the interrelatedness of all communities and states. I cannot sit idly by in Atlanta and not be concerned about what happens in Birmingham. Injustice anywhere is a threat to justice everywhere. We are caught in an inescapable network of mutuality, tied in a single garment of destiny. Whatever affects one directly, affects all indirectly. Never again can we afford to live with the narrow, provincial, "outside agitator" idea. Anyone who lives inside the United States can never be considered an outsider anywhere within its bounds.

You deplore the demonstrations taking place in Birmingham. But your statement, I am sorry to say, fails to express a similar concern for the conditions that brought about the demonstrations. I am sure that none of you would want to rest content with the superficial kind of social analysis that deals merely with effects and does not grapple with underlying causes. It is unfortunate that demonstrations are taking place in Birmingham, but it is even more unfortunate that the city's white power structure left the Negro community with no alternative.

In any nonviolent campaign there are four basic steps: collection of the facts to determine whether injustices exist; negotiation; self-purification; and direct action. We have gone through all these steps in Birmingham. There can be no gainsaying the fact that racial injustice engulfs this community. Birmingham is probably the most thoroughly segregated city in the United States. Its ugly record of brutality is widely known. Negroes have experienced grossly unjust treatment in courts. There have been more unsolved bombings of Negro homes and churches in Birmingham than in any other city in the nation. These are the hard, brutal facts of the case. On the basis of these conditions, Negro leaders sought to negotiate with the city fathers. But the latter consistently refused to engage in good-faith negotiation.

Then, last September, came the opportunity to talk with leaders of   7
Birmingham's economic community. In the course of the negotiations, certain
promises were made by the merchants—for example, to remove the stores'
humiliating racial signs. On the basis of these promises, the Reverend Fred
Shuttlesworth and the leaders of the Alabama Christian Movement for Human
Rights agreed to a moratorium on all demonstrations. As the weeks and
months went by, we realized that we were the victims of a broken promise. A
few signs, briefly removed, returned; the others remained.

As in so many past experiences, our hopes had been blasted, and the   8
shadow of deep disappointment settled upon us. We had no alternative except
to prepare for direct action, whereby we would present our very bodies as
means of laying our case before the conscience of the local and the national
community. Mindful of the difficulties involved, we decided to undertake a
process of self-purification. We began a series of workshops on nonviolence,
and we repeatedly asked ourselves: "Are you able to accept blows without retal-
iating?" "Are you able to endure the ordeal of jail?" We decided to schedule our
direct-action program for the Easter season, realizing that except for
Christmas, this is the main shopping period of the year. Knowing that a strong
economic-withdrawal program would be the by-product of direct action, we
felt that this would be the best time to bring pressure to bear on the merchants
for the needed change.

Then it occurred to us that Birmingham's mayoral election was coming up   9
in March, and we speedily decided to postpone action until after election day.
When we discovered that the Commissioner of Public Safety, Eugene "Bull"
Connor, had piled up enough votes to be in the run-off, we decided again to
postpone action until the day after the run-off so that the demonstrations
could not be used to cloud the issues. Like many others, we waited to see Mr.
Connor defeated, and to this end we endured postponement after postponement. Having aided in this community need, we felt that our direct-action program could be delayed no longer.

You may well ask, "Why direct action? Why sit-ins, marches, and so forth?   10
Isn't negotiation a better path?" You are quite right in calling for negotiation.
Indeed, this is the very purpose of direct action. Nonviolent direct action seeks
to create such a crisis and foster such a tension that a community which has
constantly refused to negotiate is forced to confront the issue. It seeks so to
dramatize the issue that it can no longer be ignored. My citing the creation of
tension as part of the work of the nonviolent-resister may sound rather shocking. But I must confess that I am not afraid of the word "tension." I have earnestly opposed violent tension, but there is a type of constructive, nonviolent
tension which is necessary for growth. Just as Socrates felt that it was necessary to create a tension in the mind so that individuals could rise from the
bondage of myths and half-truths to the unfettered realm of creative analysis
and objective appraisal, so must we see the need for nonviolent gadflies to
create the kind of tension in society that will help men rise from the dark
depths of prejudice and racism to the majestic heights of understanding and
brotherhood.

The purpose of our direct-action program is to create a situation so 11
crisis-packed that it will inevitably open the door to negotiation. I therefore con-
cur with you in your call for negotiation. Too long has our beloved Southland
been bogged down in a tragic effort to live in monologue rather than dialogue.

One of the basic points in your statement is that the action that I and my 12
associates have taken in Birmingham is untimely. Some have asked: "Why
didn't you give the new city administration time to act?" The only answer that
I can give to this query is that the new Birmingham administration must be
prodded about as much as the outgoing one, before it will act. We are sadly
mistaken if we feel that the election of Albert Boutwell as mayor will bring the
millennium to Birmingham. While Mr. Boutwell is a much more gentle person
than Mr. Connor, they are both segregationists, dedicated to maintenance of
the status quo. I have hoped that Mr. Boutwell will be reasonable enough to see
the futility of massive resistance to desegregation. But he will not see this without pressure from devotees of civil rights. My friends, I must say to you that we
have not made a single gain in civil rights without determined legal and nonviolent pressure. Lamentably, it is an historical fact that privileged groups seldom give up their privileges voluntarily. Individuals may see the moral light
and voluntarily give up their unjust posture; but, as Reinhold Niebuhr* has
reminded us, groups tend to be more immoral than individuals.

We know through painful experience that freedom is never voluntarily 13
given by the oppressor; it must be demanded by the oppressed. Frankly, I have
yet to engage in a direct-action campaign that was "well timed" in the view of
those who have not suffered unduly from the disease of segregation. For years
now I have heard the word "Wait!" It rings in the ear of every Negro with piercing familiarity. This "Wait" has almost always meant "Never." We must come
to see, with one of our distinguished jurists, that "justice too long delayed is
justice denied."

We have waited for more than 340 years for our constitutional and God- 14
given rights. The nations of Asia and Africa are moving with jetlike speed
toward gaining political independence, but
we still creep at horse-and-buggy pace
toward gaining a cup of coffee at a lunch
counter. Perhaps it is easy for those who
have never felt the stinging darts of segregation to say, "Wait." But when you have seen
vicious mobs lynch your mothers and
fathers at will and drown your sisters and
brothers at whim; when you have seen hate-
filled policemen curse, kick, and even kill
your Black brothers and sisters; when you

> **"**We must come to
> see, with one of our
> distinguished jurists,
> that 'justice too long
> delayed is justice
> denied.'**"**

see the vast majority of your twenty million Negro brothers smothering in an
airtight cage of poverty in the midst of an affluent society; when you suddenly
find your tongue twisted and your speech stammering as you seek to explain

---

* Eds. note — American religious and social thinker (1892–1971).

to your six-year-old daughter why she can't go to the public amusement park that has just been advertised on television, and see tears welling up in her eyes when she is told that Funtown is closed to colored children, and see ominous clouds of inferiority beginning to form in her little mental sky, and see her beginning to distort her personality by developing an unconscious bitterness toward white people; when you have to concoct an answer for a five-year-old son who is asking, "Daddy, why do white people treat colored people so mean?"; when you take a cross-country drive and find it necessary to sleep night after night in the uncomfortable corners of your automobile because no motel will accept you; when you are humiliated day in and day out by nagging signs reading "white" and "colored"; when your first name becomes "nigger," your middle name becomes "boy" (however old you are), and your last name becomes "John," and your wife and mother are never given the respected title "Mrs."; when you are harried by day and haunted at night by the fact that you are a Negro, living constantly at tiptoe stance, never quite knowing what to expect next, and are plagued with inner fears and outer resentments; when you are forever fighting a degenerating sense of "nobodiness"—then you will understand why we find it difficult to wait. There comes a time when the cup of endurance runs over, and men are no longer willing to be plunged into the abyss of despair. I hope, sirs, you can understand our legitimate and unavoidable impatience.

You express a great deal of anxiety over our willingness to break laws. This   15 is certainly a legitimate concern. Since we so diligently urge people to obey the Supreme Court's decision of 1954 outlawing segregation in the public schools, at first glance it may seem rather paradoxical for us consciously to break laws. One may well ask: "How can you advocate breaking some laws and obeying others?" The answer lies in the fact that there are two types of laws: just and unjust. I would be the first to advocate obeying just laws. One has not only a legal but a moral responsibility to obey just laws. Conversely, one has a moral responsibility to disobey unjust laws. I would agree with St. Augustine* that "an unjust law is no law at all."

Now, what is the difference between the two? How does one determine   16 whether a law is just or unjust? A just law is a man-made code that squares with the moral law or the law of God. An unjust law is a code that is out of harmony with the moral law. To put it in the terms of St. Thomas Aquinas:** An unjust law is a human law that is not rooted in eternal law and natural law. Any law that uplifts human personality is just. Any law that degrades human personality is unjust. All segregation statutes are unjust because segregation distorts the soul and damages the personality. It gives the segregator a false sense of superiority and the segregated a false sense of inferiority. Segregation, to use the terminology of the Jewish philosopher Martin Buber, substitutes an "I-it" relationship for an "I-thou" relationship and ends up relegating persons to the status of things. Hence segregation is not only politically, economically, and

---

* Eds. note—Early church father and philosopher (354–430).
** Eds. note—Italian philosopher and theologian (1225–1274).

sociologically unsound, it is morally wrong and sinful. Paul Tillich* has said that sin is separation. Is not segregation an existential expression of man's tragic separation, his awful estrangement, his terrible sinfulness? Thus it is that I can urge men to obey the 1954 decision of the Supreme Court, for it is morally right; and I can urge them to disobey segregation ordinances, for they are morally wrong.

Let us consider a more concrete example of just and unjust laws. An unjust law is a code that a numerical or power majority group compels a minority group to obey but does not make binding on itself. This is *difference* made legal. By the same token, a just law is a code that a majority compels a minority to follow and that it is willing to follow itself. This is *sameness* made legal. 17

Let me give another explanation. A law is unjust if it is inflicted on a minority that, as a result of being denied the right to vote, had no part in enacting or devising the law. Who can say that the legislature of Alabama which set up that state's segregation laws was democratically elected? Throughout Alabama all sorts of devious methods are used to prevent Negroes from becoming registered voters, and there are some counties in which, even though Negroes constitute a majority of the population, not a single Negro is registered. Can any law enacted under such circumstances be considered democratically structured? 18

Sometimes a law is just on its face and unjust in its application. For instance, I have been arrested on a charge of parading without a permit. Now, there is nothing wrong in having an ordinance which requires a permit for a parade. But such an ordinance becomes unjust when it is used to maintain segregation and to deny citizens the First-Amendment privilege of peaceful assembly and protest. 19

I hope you are able to see the distinction I am trying to point out. In no sense do I advocate evading or defying the law, as would the rabid segregationist. That would lead to anarchy. One who breaks an unjust law must do so openly, lovingly, and with a willingness to accept the penalty. I submit that an individual who breaks a law that conscience tells him is unjust, and who willingly accepts the penalty of imprisonment in order to arouse the conscience of the community over its injustice, is in reality expressing the highest respect for law. 20

Of course, there is nothing new about this kind of civil disobedience. It was evidenced sublimely in the refusal of Shadrach, Meshach, and Abednego** to obey the laws of Nebuchadnezzar, on the ground that a higher moral law was at stake. It was practiced superbly by the early Christians, who were willing to face hungry lions and the excruciating pain of chopping blocks rather than submit to certain unjust laws of the Roman Empire. To a degree, academic freedom is a reality today because Socrates practiced civil disobedience. In our own nation, the Boston Tea Party represented a massive act of civil disobedience. 21

---

* Eds. note — American philosopher and theologian (1886–1965).
** Eds. note — In the Book of Daniel, three men who were thrown into a blazing fire for refusing to worship a golden statue.

We should never forget that everything Adolph Hitler did in Germany was   22
"legal" and everything the Hungarian freedom fighters did in Hungary was
"illegal." It was "illegal" to aid and comfort a Jew in Hitler's Germany. Even so,
I am sure that, had I lived in Germany at the time, I would have aided and comforted my Jewish brothers. If today I lived in a Communist country where certain principles dear to the Christian faith are suppressed, I would openly
advocate disobeying that country's antireligious laws.

I must make two honest confessions to you, my Christian and Jewish   23
brothers. First, I must confess that over the past few years I have been gravely
disappointed with the white moderate. I have almost reached the regrettable
conclusion that the Negro's great stumbling block in his stride toward freedom is not the White Citizens Counciler or the Ku Klux Klanner, but the white
moderate, who is more devoted to "order" than to justice; who prefers a negative peace which is the absence of tension to a positive peace which is the presence of justice; who constantly says, "I agree with you in the goal you seek, but
I cannot agree with your methods of direct action"; who paternalistically
believes he can set the timetable for another man's freedom; who lives by a
mythical concept of time and who constantly advises the Negro to wait for a
"more convenient season." Shallow understanding from people of good will is
more frustrating than absolute misunderstanding from people of ill will.
Lukewarm acceptance is much more bewildering than outright rejection.

I had hoped that the white moderate would understand that law and order   24
exist for the purpose of establishing justice and that when they fail in this purpose they become the dangerously structured dams that block the flow of social
progress. I had hoped that the white moderate would understand that the present tension in the South is a necessary phase of the transition from an obnox-
ious negative peace, in which the Negro passively accepted his unjust plight, to a
substantive and positive peace, in which all men will respect the dignity and
worth of human personality. Actually, we who engage in nonviolent direct
action are not the creators of tension. We merely bring to the surface the hidden
tension that is already alive. We bring it out in the open, where it can be seen and
dealt with. Like a boil that can never be cured so long as it is covered up but
must be opened with all its ugliness to the natural medicines of air and light,
injustice must be exposed, with all the tension its exposure creates, to the light
of human conscience and the air of national opinion, before it can be cured.

In your statement you assert that our actions, even though peaceful, must   25
be condemned because they precipitate violence. But is this a logical assertion?
Isn't this like condemning a robbed man because his possession of money precipitated the evil act of robbery? Isn't this like condemning Socrates because
his unswerving commitment to truth and his philosophical inquiries precipitated the act by the misguided populace in which they made him drink hem-
lock? Isn't this like condemning Jesus because his unique God-consciousness
and never-ceasing devotion to God's will precipitated the evil act of crucifix-
ion? We must come to see that, as the federal courts have consistently affirmed,
it is wrong to urge an individual to cease his efforts to gain his basic constitutional rights because the quest may precipitate violence. Society must protect
the robbed and punish the robber.

I had also hoped that the white moderate would reject the myth concern-   26
ing time in relation to the struggle for freedom. I have just received a letter
from a white brother in Texas. He writes: "All Christians know that the colored
people will receive equal rights eventually, but it is possible that you are in too
great a religious hurry. It has taken Christianity almost two thousand years to
accomplish what it has. The teachings of Christ take time to come to earth."
Such an attitude stems from a tragic misconception of time, from the strangely
irrational notion that there is something in the very flow of time that will inevitably cure all ills. Actually, time itself is neutral; it can be used either destruc-
tively or constructively. More and more I feel that the people of ill will have
used time much more effectively than have the people of good will. We will
have to repent in this generation not merely for the hateful words and actions
of the bad people, but for the appalling silence of the good people. Human
progress never rolls in on wheels of inevitability; it comes through the tireless
efforts of men willing to be coworkers with God, and without this hard work,
time itself becomes an ally of the forces of social stagnation. We must use time
creatively, in the knowledge that the time is always ripe to do right. Now is the
time to make real the promise of democracy and transform our pending
national elegy into a creative psalm of brotherhood. Now is the time to lift our
national policy from the quicksand of racial injustice to the solid rock of
human dignity.

You speak of our activity in Birmingham as extreme. At first I was rather   27
disappointed that fellow clergymen would see my nonviolent efforts as those of
an extremist. I began thinking about the fact that I stand in the middle of two
opposing forces in the Negro community. One is a force of complacency, made
up in part of Negroes who, as a result of long years of oppression, are so drained
of self-respect and a sense of "somebodiness" that they have adjusted to segregation; and in part of a few middle-class Negroes who, because of a degree of
academic and economic security and because in some ways they profit by segregation, have become insensitive to the problems of the masses. The other force
is one of bitterness and hatred, and it comes perilously close to advocating violence. It is expressed in the various Black nationalist groups that are springing
up across the nation, the largest and best-known being Elijah Muhammad's
Muslim movement. Nourished by the Negro's frustration over the continued
existence of racial discrimination, this movement is made up of people who
have lost faith in America, who have absolutely repudiated Christianity, and
who have concluded that the white man is an incorrigible "devil."

I have tried to stand between these two forces, saying that we need emulate   28
neither the "do-nothingism" of the complacent nor the hatred and despair of
the Black nationalist. For there is the more excellent way of love and nonviolent protest. I am grateful to God that, through the influence of the Negro
church, the way of nonviolence became an integral part of our struggle.

If this philosophy had not emerged, by now many streets of the South   29
would, I am convinced, be flowing with blood. And I am further convinced
that if our white brothers dismiss as "rabble-rousers" and "outside agitators"
those of us who employ nonviolent direct action, and if they refuse to support
our nonviolent efforts, millions of Negroes will, out of frustration and despair,

seek solace and security in Black-nationalist ideologies—a development that would inevitably lead to a frightening racial nightmare.

Oppressed people cannot remain oppressed forever. The yearning for freedom   30
eventually manifests itself, and that is what has happened to the American Negro. Something within has reminded him of his birthright of freedom, and something without has reminded him that it can be gained. Consciously or unconsciously, he has been caught up by the *Zeitgeist*, and with his Black brothers of Africa and his brown and yellow brothers of Asia, South America, and the Caribbean, the United States Negro is moving with a sense of great urgency toward the promised land of racial justice. If one recognizes this vital urge that has engulfed the Negro community, one should readily understand why public demonstrations are taking place. The Negro has many pent-up resentments and latent frustrations, and he must release them. So let him march; let him make prayer pilgrimages to the city hall; let him go on freedom rides—and try to understand why he must do so. If his repressed emotions are not released in nonviolent ways, they will seek expression through violence; this is not a threat but a fact of history. So I have not said to my people, "Get rid of your discontent." Rather, I have tried to say that this normal and healthy discontent can be channeled into the creative outlet of nonviolent direct action. And now this approach is being termed extremist.

But though I was initially disappointed at being categorized as an extrem-   31
ist, as I continued to think about the matter I gradually gained a measure of satisfaction from the label. Was not Jesus an extremist for love: "Love your enemies, bless them that curse you, do good to them that hate you, and pray for them which despitefully use you, and persecute you." Was not Amos an extremist for justice: "Let justice roll down like waters and righteousness like an ever-flowing stream." Was not Paul an extremist for the Christian gospel: "I bear in my body the marks of the Lord Jesus." Was not Martin Luther an extremist: "Here I stand; I cannot do otherwise, so help me God." And John Bunyan: "I will stay in jail to the end of my days before I make a butchery of my conscience." And Abraham Lincoln: "This nation cannot survive half slave and half free." And Thomas Jefferson: "We hold these truths to be self-evident, that all men are created equal. . . ." So the question is not whether we will be extremists, but what kind of extremists we will be. Will we be extremists for hate or for love? Will we be extremists for the preservation of injustice or for the extension of justice? In that dramatic scene of Calvary's hill three men were crucified. We must never forget that all three were crucified for the same crime—the crime of extremism. Two were extremists for immorality, and thus fell below their environment. The other, Jesus Christ, was an extremist for love, truth, and goodness, and thereby rose above his environment. Perhaps the South, the nation, and the world are in dire need of creative extremists.

I hoped that the white moderate would see this need. Perhaps I was too   32
optimistic; perhaps I expected too much. I suppose I should have realized that few members of the oppressor race can understand the deep groans and passionate yearnings of the oppressed race, and still fewer have the vision to see that injustice must be rooted out by strong, persistent, and determined action. I am thankful, however, that some of our white brothers in the South have grasped the meaning of this social revolution and committed themselves to it.

They are still all too few in quantity, but they are big in quality. Some — such as Ralph McGill, Lillian Smith, Harry Golden, James McBride Dabbs, Ann Braden, and Sarah Patton Boyle — have written about our struggle in eloquent and prophetic terms. Others have marched with us down nameless streets of the South. They have languished in filthy, roach-infested jails, suffering the abuse and brutality of policemen who view them as "dirty nigger-lovers." Unlike so many of their moderate brothers and sisters, they have recognized the urgency of the movement and sensed the need for powerful "action" antidotes to combat the disease of segregation.

33   Let me take note of my other major disappointment. I have been so greatly disappointed with the white church and its leadership. Of course, there are some notable exceptions. I am not unmindful of the fact that each of you has taken some significant stands on this issue. I commend you, Reverend Stallings, for your Christian stand on this past Sunday, in welcoming Negroes to your worship service on a nonsegregated basis. I commend the Catholic leaders of this state for integrating Spring Hill College several years ago.

34   But despite these notable exceptions, I must honestly reiterate that I have been disappointed with the church. I do not say this as one of those negative critics who can always find something wrong with the church. I say this as a minister of the gospel, who loves the church; who was nurtured in its bosom; who has been sustained by its spiritual blessings and who will remain true to it as long as the cord of life shall lengthen.

35   When I was suddenly catapulted into the leadership of the bus protest in Montgomery, Alabama, a few years ago, I felt we would be supported by the white church. I felt that the white ministers, priests, and rabbis of the South would be among our strongest allies. Instead, some have been outright opponents, refusing to understand the freedom movement and misrepresenting its leaders; all too many others have been more cautious than courageous and have remained silent behind the anesthetizing security of stained-glass windows.

36   In spite of my shattered dreams, I came to Birmingham with the hope that the white religious leadership of this community would see the justice of our cause and, with deep moral concern, would serve as the channel through which our just grievances could reach the power structure. I had hoped that each of you would understand. But again I have been disappointed.

37   There was a time when the church was very powerful — in the time when the early Christians rejoiced at being deemed worthy to suffer for what they believed. In those days the church was not merely a thermometer that recorded the ideas and principles of popular opinion; it was a thermostat that transformed the mores of society. Whenever the early Christians entered a town, the people in power became disturbed and immediately sought to convict the Christians for being "disturbers of the peace" and "outside agitators." But the Christians pressed on, in the conviction that they were "a colony of heaven," called to obey God rather than man. Small in number, they were big in commitment. They were too God-intoxicated to be "astronomically intimidated." By their effort and example they brought an end to such ancient evils as infanticide and gladiatorial contests.

Things are different now. So often the contemporary church is a weak, ineffectual voice with an uncertain sound. So often it is an archdefender of the status quo. Far from being disturbed by the presence of the church, the power structure of the average community is consoled by the church's silent—and often even vocal—sanction of things as they are.

But the judgment of God is upon the church as never before. If today's church does not recapture the sacrificial spirit of the early church, it will lose its authenticity, forfeit the loyalty of millions, and be dismissed as an irrelevant social club with no meaning for the twentieth century. Every day I meet young people whose disappointment with the church has turned into outright disgust.

Perhaps I have once again been too optimistic. Is organized religion too inextricably bound to the status quo to save our nation and the world? Perhaps I must turn my faith to the inner spiritual church, the church within the church, as the true *ekklesia** and the hope of the world. But again I am thankful to God that some noble souls from the ranks of organized religion have broken loose from the paralyzing chains of conformity and joined us as active partners in the struggle for freedom. They have left their secure congregations and walked the streets of Albany, Georgia, with us. They have gone down the highways of the South on tortuous rides for freedom. Yes, they have gone to jail with us. Some have been dismissed from their churches, have lost the support of their bishops and fellow ministers. But they have acted in the faith that right defeated is stronger than evil triumphant. Their witness has been the spiritual salt that has preserved the true meaning of the gospel in these troubled times. They have carved a tunnel of hope through the dark mountain of disappointment.

I hope the church as a whole will meet the challenge of this decisive hour. But even if the church does not come to the aid of justice, I have no despair about the future. I have no fear about the outcome of our struggle in Birmingham, even if our motives are at present misunderstood. We will reach the goal of freedom in Birmingham and all over the nation, because the goal of America is freedom. Abused and scorned though we may be, our destiny is tied up with America's destiny. Before the pilgrims landed at Plymouth, we were here. Before the pen of Jefferson etched the majestic words of the Declaration of Independence across the pages of history, we were here. For more than two centuries our forebears labored in this country without wages; they made cotton king; they built the homes of their masters while suffering gross injustice and shameful humiliation—and yet out of a bottomless vitality they continued to thrive and develop. If the inexpressible cruelties of slavery could not stop us, the opposition we now face will surely fail. We will win our freedom because the sacred heritage of our nation and the eternal will of God are embodied in our echoing demands.

Before closing I feel impelled to mention one other point in your statement that has troubled me profoundly. You warmly commended the Birmingham police for keeping "order" and "preventing violence." I doubt that you would

38

39

40

41

42

---

* Eds. note—Greek word for the early Christian church.

have so warmly commended the police force if you had seen its dogs sinking their teeth into unarmed, nonviolent Negroes. I doubt that you would so quickly commend the policemen if you were to observe their ugly and inhumane treatment of Negroes here in the city jail; if you were to watch them push and curse old Negro women and young Negro girls; if you were to see them slap and kick old Negro men and young boys; if you were to observe them, as they did on two occasions, refuse to give us food because we wanted to sing our grace together. I cannot join you in your praise of the Birmingham police department.

It is true that the police have exercised a degree of discipline in handling   43
the demonstrators. In this sense they have conducted themselves rather "nonviolently" in public. But for what purpose? To preserve the vile system of segregation. Over the past few years I have consistently preached that nonviolence demands that the means we use must be as pure as the ends we seek. I have tried to make clear that it is wrong to use immoral means to attain moral ends. But now I must affirm that it is just as wrong, or perhaps even more so, to use moral means to preserve immoral ends. Perhaps Mr. Connor and his policemen have been rather nonviolent in public, as was Chief Pritchett in Albany, Georgia, but they have used the moral means of nonviolence to maintain the immoral end of racial injustice. As T. S. Eliot has said, "The last temptation is the greatest treason: To do the right deed for the wrong reason."

I wish you had commended the Negro sit-inners and demonstrators of   44
Birmingham for their sublime courage, their willingness to suffer, and their amazing discipline in the midst of great provocation. One day the South will recognize its real heroes. They will be the James Merediths,* with the noble sense of purpose that enables them to face jeering and hostile mobs, and with the agonizing loneliness that characterizes the life of the pioneer. They will be old, oppressed, battered Negro women, symbolized in a seventy-two-year-old woman in Montgomery, Alabama, who rose up with a sense of dignity and with her people decided not to ride segregated buses, and who responded with ungrammatical profundity to one who inquired about her weariness: "My feets is tired, but my soul is at rest." They will be the young high school and college students, the young ministers of the gospel and a host of their elders, courageously and nonviolently sitting in at lunch counters and willingly going to jail for conscience's sake. One day the South will know that when these disinherited children of God sat down at lunch counters, they were in reality standing up for what is best in the American dream and for the most sacred values in our Judaeo-Christian heritage, thereby bringing our nation back to those great wells of democracy which were dug deeply by the founding fathers in their formulation of the Constitution and the Declaration of Independence.

Never before have I written so long a letter. I'm afraid it is much too long to   45
take your precious time. I can assure you that it would have been much shorter if I had been writing from a comfortable desk, but what else can one do when he is alone in a narrow jail cell, other than write long letters, think long thoughts, and pray long prayers?

---

* Eds. note — James Meredith was the first African American to enroll at the University of Mississippi.

If I have said anything in this letter that overstates the truth and indicates   46
an unreasonable impatience, I beg you to forgive me. If I have said anything
that understates the truth and indicates my having a patience that allows me
to settle for anything less than brotherhood, I beg God to forgive me.

I hope this letter finds you strong in the faith. I also hope that circum-   47
stances will soon make it possible for me to meet each of you, not as an integra-
tionist or a civil-rights leader but as a fellow clergyman and a Christian brother.
Let us all hope that the dark clouds of racial prejudice will soon pass away and
the deep fog of misunderstanding will be lifted from our fear-drenched communities, and in some not too distant tomorrow the radiant stars of love and
brotherhood will shine over our great nation with all their scintillating beauty.

Yours for the cause of Peace and Brotherhood,
Martin Luther King Jr.

· · ·

Comprehension

1. King says he seldom answers criticism. Why not? Why does he decide to do
   so in this instance?
2. Why do the other clergymen consider King's activities to be "'unwise and
   untimely'" (1)?
3. What reasons does King give for the demonstrations? Why does he think it
   is too late for negotiations?
4. What does King say *wait* means to Black people?
5. What are the two types of laws King defines? What is the difference between
   the two?
6. What does King find illogical about the claim that the actions of his followers precipitate violence?
7. Why is King disappointed in the white church?

Purpose and Audience

1. Why, in the first paragraph, does King establish his setting (the Birmingham city jail) and define his intended audience?
2. Why does King begin his letter with a reference to his audience as "men of
   genuine good will" (1)? Is this phrase **ironic** in light of his later criticism of
   them? Explain.
3. What indicates that King is writing his letter to an audience other than his
   fellow clergymen?
4. What is the thesis of this letter? Is it stated or implied?

Style and Structure

1. Where does King seek to establish that he is a reasonable person?
2. Where does King address the objections of his audience?
3. As in the Declaration of Independence, transitions are important in King's
   letter. Identify the transitional words and phrases that connect the different
   parts of his argument.

4. Why does King cite Jewish, Catholic, and Protestant philosophers to support his position?
5. Throughout his letter, King cites theologians and philosophers (Augustine, Aquinas, Buber, Tillich, and others). Why do you think he does that?
6. King uses both induction and deduction in his letter. Find an example of each, and explain how they function in his argument.
7. Throughout the body of his letter, King criticizes his audience of white moderates. In his conclusion, however, he seeks to reestablish a harmonious relationship with them. How does he do that? Is he successful?
8. **Vocabulary Project.** Locate five **allusions** to the Bible in this essay. (For example, in paragraph 14, King refers to his "cup of endurance.") Look up these allusions. Then, determine how they help King express his ideas.

Journal Entry

Do you believe King's remarks go too far? Do you believe they do not go far enough? Explain.

Writing Workshop

1. Write an argumentative essay supporting a deeply held belief of your own. Assume your audience, like King's, is not openly hostile to your position.
2. **Working with Sources.** Assume you are a militant political leader responding to Martin Luther King Jr. Argue that King's methods do not go far enough. Be sure to address potential objections to your position. You might want to consult a website such as kinginstitute.stanford.edu or read some newspapers and magazines from the 1960s to help you prepare your argument. Be sure to document all references to your sources and to include a works-cited page. (See Chapter 18 for information on MLA documentation.)
3. **Working with Sources.** Read your local newspaper for several days, collecting articles about a controversial subject that interests you. Using information from the articles, take a position on the issue, and write an essay supporting it. Be sure to document all references to your sources and to include a works-cited page. (See Chapter 18 for information on MLA documentation.)

Combining the Patterns

In "Letter from Birmingham Jail," King includes several passages of **narration**. Find two of these passages, and discuss what use King makes of narration. Why do you think narration plays such an important part in King's argument?

Thematic Connections

- "Just Walk On By: A Black Man Ponders His Power to Alter Public Space" (page 231)
- "Photos That Change History" (page 354)
- "Emmett Till and Tamir Rice, Sons of the Great Migration" (page 414)
- The Declaration of Independence (page 548)

Should Federal Student Loans Be Forgiven?

Education should not be a debt sentence.

Alex Arnold/Alamy

Student loans were once framed as a solution to higher education affordability issues. After years of escalating tuition costs and accompanying debt, some students have become more vocal in their demands for alternate solutions.

• • •

Student-loan debt has become a major problem in the United States. Tales of overburdened, loan-saddled students and graduates seem to be common — and statistics bear them out. Overall, student debt in the United States now tops $1.4 billion, with more than 44 million individuals currently owing on their loans. The typical college senior graduates with almost $30,000 in student debt, while 14 percent of parents take out an average of

$35,000 in federal Parent PLUS loans. The sad fact is that many students seeking higher education face a choice between being unable to afford tuition or submitting to what some have called a "debt-for-diploma system."

Many factors have contributed to this situation. College tuition rates have almost quadruped over the last ten years, and as a result, financial assistance has become a necessity for those seeking degrees. At the same time, states have cut higher education funding, which has made even public institutions difficult to afford. Indeed, according to the Center on Budget Priorities, state funding for two- and four-year colleges is almost $9 billion below 2008 levels. Critics argue that personal responsibility (or lack thereof) is a large part of the problem. They say that too many high school graduates are taking out loans to get impractical degrees that will make them unable to pay back their debts. In many cases, students — and their cosigning parents — do not fully understand the implications of taking on large student debt.

Politicians, reformers, and others have proposed a number of solutions to this problem. Some argue that the government should forgive all student-loan debt and absorb the cost of public higher education, whereas others suggest that repayment should be tied to the financial condition of borrowers. Supporters of these suggestions say that colleges and universities create economic opportunity, not only for graduates, but also for society as a whole. Opponents, however, are quick to point out that these proposals do nothing more than transfer the financial burden of higher education from students and their parents to taxpayers.

The two selections in this debate take opposing points of view on this issue. In "No, Your Student Loans Should Not Be Forgiven," Mary Clare Amselem argues that although debt forgiveness may seem attractive, it will cause more problems than it solves. According to Amselem, loan forgiveness will "cost more than projected and more students will enroll in college who may have otherwise been gainfully employed in the workforce." In "Let's Cancel Everyone's Student Debt, for the Economy's Sake," Eric Levitz says that the government should forgive all student loan debt and make public universities free. According to Levitz, the high cost of college "has depressed the purchasing power of a broad, and growing, part of the labor force," and this situation will negatively affect the nation's overall economy.

MARY CLARE AMSELEM

No, Your Student Loans Should Not Be Forgiven

Mary Clare Amselem is a policy analyst in the Center for Education Policy at the Heritage Foundation, a conservative research and policy advocacy organization. A native of Potomac, Maryland, Amselem graduated from the College of the Holy Cross and earned a master's degree from George Washington University's Trachtenberg School of Public Policy and Administration. Her work focuses on ways in which free market principles can inform higher education policy, especially the cost of college. She has written for the *Boston Herald*, the *Washington Times*, and the Heritage Foundation's *Daily Signal*. She has also appeared on C-Span and Fox News.

Background on the Public Service Loan Forgiveness Program Started in 2007, the Public Service Loan Forgiveness (PSLF) program was created as part of the College Cost Reduction and Access Act of 2007. It enables graduates to lessen their federal student loan debt by working full time in public service. If participants spend ten years teaching, nursing, or working in a government agency or nonprofit and make 120 payments on their student loans, the federal government will forgive their remaining student debt. The program's critics argue that taxpayers' dollars should not promote public service jobs and that the program is too expensive, citing Congressional Budget Office estimates that it will cost $23 billion over the first eight years. Others claim that because it helps just college graduates, it is unfair to lower-income families. Despite these objections, supporters of PSLF see it as a work in progress that can help students deal with the rising costs of higher education.

1   Senators Bernie Sanders of Vermont and Elizabeth Warren of Massachusetts are making headlines with their plans to forgive student loan debt and make public colleges tuition-free.

2   While many agree removing financial responsibility on the part of the student is bad policy, the 45 million Americans holding student loans undoubtedly see debt forgiveness as attractive.

3   Burdensome student loan debt is indeed problematic. Studies show it has discouraged desirable economic activity such as starting a business or buying a home. But loan forgiveness will cause more problems than it solves.

> "Burdensome loan debt is indeed problematic."

4   Both Warren and Sanders propose to pay for their plans by raising taxes. Why should American taxpayers have to pay off loans that students took on voluntarily?

5   Two-thirds of Americans do not hold bachelor's degrees. Their choice not to go to college, whatever the reason may be, in

many cases may have involved a desire to avoid the high cost of higher education.

These Americans are statistically less likely to earn as much as Americans   6
who *do* hold bachelor's degrees. It is regressive, or taking a larger percentage from low-income earners, to ask Americans who purposely avoided the high cost of college to pay for students who chose to take on mountains of debt.

Loan forgiveness rewards fiscal irresponsibility.   7

Senator Sanders proposes eliminating all $1.6 trillion in student loan   8
debt, regardless of student need.

Many students decided to take a frugal path through higher education,   9
which should be encouraged. Perhaps they decided to go to a less expensive school and took on a part time job. If loan forgiveness becomes universal, students who made those smart financial decisions, ensuring they make their loan payments on time, will be given the same benefit as students who went to the most expensive university and have defaulted on their loan payments every month. Why would any student going forward decide to go the responsible route? And why work, knowing taxpayers will pick up the tab?

Not to mention the millions of members of our military who receive   10
tuition-free college as a benefit earned for serving our country. This benefit would be rendered useless if it is granted to everyone.

Loan forgiveness programs already exist, and even these limited programs   11
are extremely problematic.

For example, there's the Public Service Loan Forgiveness (PSLF) program,   12
which discharges the loans of public sector employees after just 10 years of government employment. The Congressional Budget Office projects this program alone will cost $24 billion over the next 10 years.

The generous terms of PSLF yielded many unintended consequences — one   13
of them being many more students enrolled in the program than originally anticipated and took on far more debt.

As AEI's Jason Delisle has written: "60,000 new borrowers enroll in PSLF   14
every quarter. Other Department statistics show that most participants borrowed well in excess of $50,000 in federal loans and one-third borrowed more than $100,000. Such high debt levels indicate that the program is mostly benefiting borrowers with graduate degrees."

Importantly, borrowers with graduate degrees earn more on average than   15
those with fewer years of education. It seems troublesome that those best equipped to pay off their loans will benefit the most from a student loan bailout.

PSLF should serve as a cautionary tale.   16

Loan forgiveness will undoubtedly cost more than projected and more   17
students will enroll in college who may have otherwise been gainfully employed in the workforce.

To pay for this the Sanders's plan calls for a tax on Wall Street trading.   18

Heritage's Adam Michel argues that, historically, such taxes increase mar-   19
ket volatility and do not generate nearly as much revenue as expected. Inevitably, the middle class ends up stuck with the tab, either through tax increases or damage to the economy.

While loan forgiveness sounds attractive, we should focus instead on how   20
we got here.

Federal student loans offer colleges and universities excessive funds that   21
enable them to raise their tuition without fear of losing customers. Instead,
Americans should be holding colleges and universities accountable by tighten-
ing the purse strings coming from Washington.

Eliminating federal student loans will encourage colleges to step up their   22
game, lower their prices, and maybe even begin teaching marketable skills.
Loan forgiveness doubles down on the failed federal policies that led to the
$1.6 trillion student loan crisis.

•   •   •

Comprehension

1. How many Americans currently have student loans? How do they view
   proposals by Senators Bernie Sanders and Elizabeth Warren to forgive
   student-loan debt?
2. Why, according to Amselem, is burdensome student-loan debt "problematic" (3)?
3. How will forgiving student debt affect students? How will it affect the
   military and military veterans?
4. What solutions does Amselem favor to address the problem of student
   debt?

Purpose and Audience

1. This essay originally appeared in *Human Events*, an online publication
   devoted to conservative news and analysis. In what sense, if any, does this
   article convey a conservative point of view?
2. Does Amselem assume her readers are hostile, indifferent, or sympathetic to
   her ideas? How can you tell?
3. What is Amselem's purpose? Does she want to convey information?
   Persuade? Move people to action? Something else? Explain.

Style and Structure

1. Why does Amselem mention Senators Elizabeth Warren and Bernie Sanders
   in her introduction? How does this introduction prepare readers for the rest
   of the essay? Would another strategy have been more effective? Why or why
   not?
2. Where is Amselem's thesis statement? Why does she place it where she does?
   Restate her thesis in your own words.
3. How does Amselem use **rhetorical questions** to advance her argument?
   Identify a specific example. Is this strategy effective? Explain.
4. **Vocabulary Project.** In paragraph 6, Amselem describes proposals to
   forgive student debt as "regressive." What does this term mean? Does
   Amselem's use of this term make sense in the context of her argument?
   Explain.

5. What evidence does Amselem use to support her points? Does she present enough evidence? Explain.
6. In paragraph 16, Amselem says, "PSLF should serve as a cautionary tale." What does she mean?

Journal Entry

Amselem suggests that student loan forgiveness rewards irresponsible people and places an unfair burden on taxpayers — most of whom do not have college degrees. Do you agree? For example, if you chose a frugal path through college and repaid your loans, would you resent loan forgiveness?

Writing Workshop

1. According to Amselem, the two-thirds of Americans who do not hold bachelor's degrees should not be forced to subsidize students who choose to take on mountains of debt. Write an essay on which you agree or disagree with her contention. Use your own experiences to support your thesis.
2. **Working with Sources.** Go online and look at the proposals to forgive student debt from Elizabeth Warren and Bernie Sanders. Next, write a one-paragraph summary of each. Then, write an essay in which you agree or disagree with one of these proposals. (You can also use information from the two essays in this debate to support your points.) Be sure to document all ideas that you borrow from your sources and to include a works-cited page. (See Chapter 18 for information on MLA documentation.)
3. In addition to forgiving student debt, both Warren and Sanders want to make public colleges tuition free. Do you think public colleges should be free? Write an argumentative essay that presents your position. Be sure to address and refute the strongest arguments against your thesis.

Combining the Patterns

Where in the essay does Amselem use **cause and effect**? Why is this pattern of development so important to her argument?

Thematic Connections
- "The Money" (page 113)
- "Should Driverless Cars Kill Their Own Passengers to Save a Pedestrian?" (page 219)
- "What Causes Cancer? It's Complicated" (page 344)
- "Why Chinese Mothers Are Superior" (page 396)

ERIC LEVITZ

We Must Cancel Everyone's Student Debt, for the Economy's Sake

Eric Levitz is a senior writer and associate editor of the Intelligencer at *New York Magazine*. Previously, he held positions at MSNBC, the Salon Media Group, and Heavy.com. He earned both his undergraduate degree and his master's at Johns Hopkins University, where he has also taught as a visiting lecturer.

Background on the skills gap In his essay, Levitz refers to the so-called skills gap, which became a catchphrase in the wake of the 2008 financial crash and subsequent Great Recession. Proponents of this idea argue that workers simply need to gain the skills for which great market demand exists, and they will find jobs. From another perspective, it implies that companies and businesses are struggling to find skilled, qualified people to fill existing jobs. President Barack Obama lamented this problem in 2015 as he proposed $100 million for workforce technical training. Although a skills gap may be the cause of some unemployment, economic research over the past several years suggests a more complex picture of the labor market. For example, other barriers to stable employment exist, including the proliferation of low-wage positions, the slumping of regional economies, and the lack of access to childcare. According to studies of those who were laid off during or after the financial crash of 2008, many companies showed little or no interest in retraining former workers for future employment. Moreover, if there were a skills gap, the wages of those with marketable skills would have risen as companies competed for a small pool of talent, but labor department statistics show that this did not happen.

In 2017, congressional Republicans passed a $1.5 trillion tax cut, which delivered the lion's share of its benefits to the wealthy and corporations. The GOP did not justify this policy on the grounds that all corporate shareholders and trust-fund hipsters *deserved* to have their wealth increased. Rather, the party argued that, however one felt about making the rich richer, the tax cuts would ultimately benefit *all* Americans by increasing economic growth and lowering unemployment.

But what if we could have achieved those objectives, at roughly the same price, by forgoing tax cuts—and wiping out every penny of student debt in the United States, instead?

A new research paper from the Levy Economics Institute of Bard College suggests this was, in fact, an option.

In America today, 44 million people collectively carry $1.4 trillion in student debt. That giant pile of financial obligations isn't just a burden on individual borrowers, but on the nation's entire economy. The astronomical rise in the cost of college tuition—combined with the stagnation of entry-level wages for college graduates—has depressed the purchasing power of a broad, and growing, part of the labor force. Many of these workers are struggling to keep their heads above water; 11 percent of aggregate student loan debt is now more than 90 days past due, or delinquent. Others are unable to invest in a home, vehicle, or start a family (and engage in all the myriad acts of consumption that go with that).

> "In America today, 44 million people collectively carry $1.4 trillion in student debt."

Thus, if the government were to forgive all the student debt it owns (which makes up more than 90 percent of all outstanding student debt), and bought out all private holders of such debt, a surge in consumer demand—and thus, employment and economic growth—would ensue.   5

According to the Levy Institute paper, authored by economists Scott Fullwiler, Stephanie Kelton, Catherine Ruetschlin, and Marshall Steinbaum, canceling all student debt would increase GDP by between $86 billion and $108 billion per year, over the next decade. This would add between 1.2 and 1.5 million jobs to the economy, and reduce the unemployment rate by between 0.22 and 0.36 percent.   6

So, the macroeconomic upside of canceling all student debt would be substantial. The primary (supposed) downsides of such a policy would be a higher deficit, the potentially regressive distributional consequences of debt forgiveness, and (relatedly) the unfairness of rewarding certain well-off borrowers who don't "deserve" it. Of course, all of these critiques would apply more powerfully to the recently passed tax cut bill. Few people would argue that increasing Harvey Weinstein's after-tax income was a laudable public policy goal. But no one thinks that we should judge the merits of a tax cut on the basis of whether it rewards *any* unsavory individuals.   7

And in the case of student debt forgiveness, concerns about unfairness are largely informed by status quo bias. It's true that increasing the net worth of some upper-middle-class Harvard graduates by $200,000—while giving nothing to working-class City College graduates who already paid off their student loans—is not, in and of itself, a progressive proposition. But viewed in its totality, the post-debt cancellation world is considerably more egalitarian than the one we live in now.   8

While the top 20 percent of earners do have the largest absolute student-debt loads, low-income minority borrowers have the highest delinquency rates. This disparity is rooted in structural, race-based disadvantages, including, according to Marshall Steinbaum's research, "segregation within higher education, which relegates minority students to the worst-performing institutions, discrimination in both credit and labor markets, and the underlying racial wealth gap that means Black and Hispanic students have a much smaller cushion of family wealth to fall back on, both to finance higher education in the first place and also should any difficulty with debt repayment arise."   9

One implication of this, as the policy analyst Matt Bruenig has demonstrated, is that student debt is significantly increasing the racial wealth gap among younger Americans.   10

More broadly, the explosion of student debt in America was orchestrated   11
by deliberate government policies, which were justified on premises that have
proven to be false. Specifically, the government encouraged young Americans
to view even high student-debt loads as a safe investment in their own futures,
on the grounds that the economy was suffering from a "skills gap"—there was
an abundance of high wage, white-collar jobs to be created or filled, if only the
supply of highly educated workers would rise to meet demand. This turned
out to be a fiction—one that victimized a generation of working-class college
students. As Steinbaum writes:

> The reason for [the] vast enlargement of the population of [student loan]
> borrowers is the worsening labor market. Scarce jobs are allocated to the
> most credentialed applicants, which triggers a rat race of credentialization,
> and that rat race is worst for minorities. That young cohorts are better edu-
> cated than their predecessors *should* result in higher lifetime earnings, if the
> "skills gap" mythology that motivated the expansion of the federal student
> loan programs were true. Instead, more and more expensive credentials result
> in jobs that pay the same or worse, leading to the escalation of debt loads.

Student debtors were, in many, many cases, persuaded to make poor finan-   12
cial decisions by their own government—which, as the owner of their debts,
now stands to profit from those mistakes. By wiping the slate clean, Uncle Sam
wouldn't just improve the macroeconomy, but also increase its fairness, and
reduce racial inequality.

And once that's done, the government can turn its attention toward ensur-   13
ing that no future college students are burdened by such massive debt loads
ever again. To make public education work as a vehicle for socioeconomic
mobility—in a world of ever-rising tuition rates and stagnant wages for college
graduates—we're going to need a new model for financing higher education.
A simple and remarkably affordable option would be to make public
universities free.

Doing all this would probably require a few significant tax increases.   14
Fortunately, there are now a great many pass-through business owners and
corporate shareholders who could sorely use one of those.

· · ·

Comprehension

1. What two factors have "depressed the purchasing power of a broad, and
   growing, part of the labor force" (4)?
2. What is "status quo bias"(8)? Why is this term significant in the debate
   about student loan forgiveness?
3. Which group of student-loan borrowers has the highest delinquency rate?
   How does Levitz explain this phenomenon?
4. What role have government policies played in perpetuating the idea of a
   skills gap?
5. According to Levitz, what is the simplest and most affordable way to finance
   higher education?

Purpose and Audience

1. Where does Levitz state his thesis? Why does he place it where he does?
2. Does Levitz appeal mainly to logic, to the emotions, or to character and authority? Explain.
3. What is Levitz's purpose in writing his essay? Is he simply seeking to inform his audience about different ways that student debt is distributed, or does he have some other purpose in mind? Explain.

Style and Structure

1. In his introduction, Levitz discusses a Republican tax cut passed during the first year of the Trump administration. Why does Levitz begin this way? What preconceptions does he think his readers have? What preconceptions does he have?
2. Where does Levitz use inductive reasoning? Where does he use deductive reasoning? Point to a specific example of each, and explain why he uses each strategy.
3. Levitz uses former film producer Harvey Weinstein as an example in this essay. Why do you think he focuses on this individual? (If you are not familiar with Weinstein, research him online.) What point is Levitz trying to make?
4. How does Levitz address arguments against his position? Does he present them fairly and refute them persuasively? What other arguments could Levitz have addressed? Should he have included them?
5. **Vocabulary Project.** In paragraph 7, Levitz refers to the "macroeconomic upside of canceling all student debt." What does the term *macroeconomic* mean in the context of this essay? What point is Levitz making by using this term?
6. Throughout his essay, Levitz uses statistics to support his points. How persuasive is this evidence? What are the strengths and weaknesses of this type of evidence?.

Journal Entry

In paragraph 13, Levitz writes, "And once [students and graduates are freed from debt], the government can turn its attention toward ensuring that no future college students are burdened by such massive debt loads ever again." How do you respond to this idea? Do you believe that it is the government's role to make sure college students stay out of debt?

Writing Workshop

1. **Writing with Sources.** Both Amselem and Levitz discuss the idea of "fairness." What are their respective notions of fairness? How do their ideas about the student debt crisis follow from their conceptions of fairness? Which version of "fairness" do you find more convincing? Write an essay that answers these questions. Be sure to document all ideas that you borrow

from your sources and to include a works-cited page. (See Chapter 18 for information on MLA documentation.)

2. **Writing with Sources.** Levitz suggests that public education should "work as a vehicle for socioeconomic mobility" (13). Do you think the primary purpose of public schools and universities is to allow graduates to rise socially and economically? Should public education have other functions as well? Write an essay in which you argue for or against Levitz's position. Be sure to document all ideas that you borrow from your sources and to include a works-cited page. (See Chapter 18 for information on MLA documentation.)

3. In paragraph 12, Levitz asserts that in many cases, student debtors were "persuaded to make poor financial decisions by their own government." Do you find this claim credible? Is Levitz making a valid point, or is he simply enabling borrowers to avoid taking responsibility for their financial choices?

Combining the Patterns

Where in the essay does Levitz use **comparison and contrast**? Point to a specific example. Why is this pattern, in particular, important to his argument?

Thematic Connections
- "Ten Ways We Get the Odds Wrong" (page 242)
- "Steps to the Dream" (page 264)
- "Why Rational People Buy into Conspiracy Theories" (page 338)
- "Stop Calling It 'Vocational Training'" (page 502)

Can Individuals Do Anything to Resolve the Climate Crisis?

Paul Souders/Corbis Documentary/Getty Images

According to recent analysis, polar ice caps are melting at a higher rate than they were throughout the 1990s. This could eventually lead to a catastrophic rise in sea levels.

●　　●　　●

As Americans have become more environmentally conscious, caring for the environment has often been framed in terms of individual responsibility. For example, in the 1970s and 1980s, public service announcements featured Woodsy Owl imploring Americans, "Give a hoot—don't pollute." As climate change has emerged as an urgent problem, people have taken a similar approach by recycling, eating less meat, using LED lightbulbs, buying hybrid and electric cars, installing solar panels on their homes, and making countless other choices to reduce their carbon footprints and live more sustainable lives. There's no doubt that such efforts have many real benefits. For example, recycling reduces litter, creates jobs, and saves much of the energy that would be needed to produce glass, steel, and plastic from raw materials. Now, however, responsibility is rightfully shifting away from individuals and toward the one hundred companies that have been responsible for the vast majority of global carbon emissions over the last three decades. Moreover, the kind of action necessary to address a global threat is now seen as collective and international rather than individual. "Only you can prevent forest fires," claimed Smokey Bear—but only the massive effort of international governments can fully address the effects of climate change.

The two essays in this debate consider the challenges to the individual posed by climate change. In "Reducing Your Carbon Footprint Still Matters," Leor Hackel and Gregg Sparkman assert that individual choices and actions do matter, particularly because they effect changes in norms that can lead to wide-scale changes in behavior. Natasha Geiling ("The Only Individual Action That Matters Is Voting for People Who Care about Climate Change") takes a different perspective, arguing that well-meaning individual actions are all but irrelevant at a time when collective national effort is so necessary.

LEOR HACKEL AND GREGG SPARKMAN

Reducing Your Carbon Footprint Still Matters

Leor Hackel is an assistant professor of psychology at the University of Southern California. His research focuses on decision making, cooperation, and learning in the context of social settings, behavioral experiments, and neuroimaging. He earned his B.S. from Columbia University and his Ph.D. from New York University. He has published in a variety of academic journals, including the *Journal of Experimental Social Psychology*, *Current Opinion in Psychology*, and *Psychological Science*. Gregg Sparkman is a Ph.D. candidate in the psychology department at Stanford University. He received his undergraduate degree from the University of California, Berkeley. Before pursuing his doctorate, Sparkman worked as a research associate and volunteered for Berkeley's Greater Good Science Center.

Background on changing norms around smoking Hackel and Sparkman refer to previous "cultural shifts" in norms around behaviors such as smoking. Indeed, the decline of tobacco use provides a remarkable example of such a shift. In 1954, adult smoking peaked at 45 percent in the United States and remained at around 40 percent into the 1970s. Over the next six decades, however, the habit declined steadily. According to the U.S. Centers for Disease Control and Prevention, the rate is now 13.7 percent. Many different factors contributed to this decrease in smoking, including strong warning labels on cigarette packages, high taxes on cigarettes, antismoking campaigns that focused on young people, and laws that banned smoking from public spaces. Over time, the scientific evidence prevailed over pseudoscience and misleading propaganda promulgated by the tobacco industry. Just as important, however, is that norms and customs also changed. Today, as the scope of smoking bans has increased, smoking has become far less socially acceptable.

Two weeks ago, the Intergovernmental Panel on Climate Change released a dire report that made crystal clear that we have about a decade to stop catastrophic levels of climate change. The report caught fire for another extremely near deadline: It suggests that if we *don't* manage to dramatically shift carbon emissions, we'll start feeling the brunt of the effects as soon as 2040. These dates have prompted a more urgent asking of the oft-discussed question: How do we start this herculean task? 1

Recent articles in *Vox*, the *Guardian*, and the *Outline* have warned that individuals "going green" in daily life won't make enough of a difference to be worth the effort. In fact, they argue, such efforts could actually make matters worse, as focusing on individual actions might distract people from pressuring corporations and government officials to lower greenhouse gas emissions and enact the broader policy change we need to meet our climate goals. These 2 articles and others like them (including in *Slate*) tend to conclude that the only truly meaningful action people can take to influence our climate future is to vote.

Voting is crucial, but this perspective misses a large point of individual   3
actions. We don't recommend taking personal actions like limiting plane rides, eating less meat, or investing in solar energy because all of these small tweaks will build up to enough carbon savings (though it could help). We do so because people taking action in their personal lives is actually one of the best ways to get to a society that implements the policy-level change that is truly needed. Research on social behavior suggests lifestyle change can build momentum for systemic change. Humans are social animals, and we use social cues to recognize emergencies. People don't spring into action just because they see smoke; they spring into action because they see others rushing in with water. The same principle applies to personal actions on climate change.

Psychologists Bibb Latane and John Darley tested this exact scenario in a   4
now-classic study. Participants filled out a survey in a quiet room, which suddenly began to fill with smoke (from a vent set up by the experimenters). When alone, participants left the room and reported the apparent fire. But in the presence of others who ignored the smoke, participants carried on as though nothing were wrong.

The IPCC has sent up a flare on climate change, but this warning is not   5
enough. Many people will need to see others making real changes instead of carrying on with business as usual. Ask yourself: Do you believe politicians and businesses will act as urgently as they need to if we keep living our lives as though climate change were not happening? Individual acts of conservation — alongside intense political engagement — are what signal an emergency to those around us, which will set larger changes in motion.

It's true that fossil fuel companies bear the lion's share of responsibility for   6
this crisis, and that consumers buying efficient light bulbs will not set things right; we need government action to shift our energy sources from coal and gas to sunlight and wind. It's also true that shortsighted campaigns for lifestyle change can backfire. When campaigns focus only on easy consumer tweaks and say nothing about policy, they imply climate change requires little real effort and that consumers can fix this crisis alone.

But when individuals supplement policy efforts with substantial, sus-   7
tained, and wide-ranging action, they inspire new social norms. These norms can then aggregate to large-scale impacts. For instance, mass lifestyle change — flying and driving less, eating less meat, heating and cooling homes less, reducing food waste — helps cover gaps where policy change would fall short of our climate goals. More importantly, social norms can spark collective action and move the needle on policy.

As in previous cultural shifts — like those around smoking or drunk   8
driving — more people will need to see fossil fuels as an extreme danger to human health and safety. A powerful way to spread this attitude is to act like it in our own lives, minimizing the fossil fuels we burn. Climate scientist Peter Kalmus — who has not flown since 2012 — summarizes this attitude: "I try to avoid burning fossil fuels, because it's clear that doing so causes real harm . . . . I don't like harming others, so I don't fly." One person skipping a flight will

not solve global warming alone, but when one person withdraws from a system that causes harm, they make that harm palpable to others.

How can we get large numbers of people to make such changes? Psychologists find that conservation behavior spreads across people. It's not enough to tell people they *should* conserve; people have to see what others *do*. For instance, the odds of someone buying solar panels for their roof go up for each home in the neighborhood that already has them. In fact, homes with solar panels more visible from the street have an even larger impact on neighbors. This is because people's actions reveal what they value. When people see their neighbors conserve energy, they infer that their community values environmental action.

Advocates similarly gain credibility by walking the walk. In a study released this week, community organizers who owned solar panels themselves recruited 63 percent more homeowners to install solar panels than community organizers who did not. Again, people inferred that advocates with solar panels believed more in the importance of the issue.

What can you do when current norms promote unsustainable behaviors like frequent flying or eating large amounts of meat? Change the norms. And people will likely rapidly adapt. In one recent study, café patrons learned that 30 percent of Americans had recently changed their behavior by eating less meat. These patrons were twice as likely to order a meatless lunch compared with a control group (1 in 3 people versus 1 in 6). Why? Changing a habit takes effort; when people do it, they signal the importance of change. Change also signals that more people will curb their meat eating in the future, and people conform to this anticipated norm as if it were a current reality. Finally, change signals that anyone can take climate action, and eating less meat is not just for vegetarians.

As a rule of thumb, the more substantial the change you make, the more you signal the need for change. Recycling matters, but it is common and easy. When you order the veggie burger even though you're a meat lover, take a bus instead of an Uber, or skip a professional conference that requires air travel, you deliver a message that fossil fuels are dangerous and that climate change requires an urgent response.

How many people does it take to start change? Just one. This insight comes from research on "social dilemmas," or situations in which people can contribute towards communal well-being—as in reducing emissions and calling representatives—or can ride along for free while others do the work. Psychologists study these situations using tasks that pit individual gains against collective good. In one task, anonymous players can contribute money to a collective fund, which gets doubled and redistributed, or they can keep their money and benefit from the contributions of their fellows. Share more and the group benefits; keep more and you benefit. In general, people contribute more when they see others do it too—even if only one other person starts the trend at first. Climate change scholar Steve Westlake found this exact pattern in a recent survey: Among respondents who knew one person who gave up flying for the environment, half flew less themselves.

> **"How many people does it take to start change? Just one."**

9

10

11

12

13

Flying less does reduce emissions. Crucially, though, social norms provide a   14
backdrop for policy change. When people forge an initial commitment to a cause,
like buying less meat, they often proceed to political commitments, like contact-
ing a senator. People don't like to be hypocrites; they like harmony between their
lifestyles and their politics. Rather than undermining political action, sustainable living prompts sustainable voting. A caveat: These benefits emerge when
conservation requires some sacrifice. Easy, single-shot actions (like buying
efficient lightbulbs) make us feel like we have done our part and can disengage.
More challenging, ongoing actions (like changing our diets) propel us forward
into action. Just as sacrifice convinces others that climate action is important, it
convinces us of our own commitment; we start to see ourselves as climate advocates. Eating less meat creates a gateway to workplace advocacy — like encouraging digital meetings or lobbying for solar panels — which opens a door to signing
petitions or protesting.

If people act on climate change in their daily lives, they will expect industry   15
to do its part. People value reciprocity: We punish free riders who don't do
their part and reward those who chip in — and businesses know it. They also
pay attention to trends. For example, after roughly a decade of decline in per
capita meat consumption, the CEO of Tyson Foods — the world's second-
largest producer of chicken, beef, and pork — announced that the company
would shift to more plant-based alternatives. Lyft recently announced it would
offset carbon emissions from its rides. Google, Apple, Sony, T-Mobile, and others have committed to buying renewable energy. Did these companies make
changes solely out of the goodness of their hearts? Of course not. Every company follows incentives — to manage public relations, meet consumer demand,
and stand out from competitors. Where consumers go, industry incentives
follow.

Politicians run a similar calculus to decide if environmental policies will   16
get them re-elected. When we enact personal change out of climate concern, we
show that there is real support for laws aimed at enacting societal change.
Personal conservation might not achieve our climate goals, but it can convince
politicians to pass laws that will.

For instance, California just passed a law known as SB 100: By 2045,   17
the fifth-largest economy in the world will be powered by 100 percent
renewable electricity. The bill was sponsored by state Sen. Kevin De León,
who has challenged Dianne Feinstein for her Senate seat — a tough race in
which any challenger needs good PR. If Californians had no reputation for
energy conservation and environmental concern, would De León have
taken a political risk anyway and prioritized passing SB 100? Perhaps not.
In anonymous interviews, politicians who personally care about climate
change have expressed hesitation to sponsor laws when they perceive
insufficient constituent concern. Each individual's choices, especially
when amplified through social influence, help create a social environment
ripe for political change.

There are plenty of things to do about climate change beyond voting. Take   18
a train or bus instead of a plane, even if inconvenient — in fact, especially when
inconvenient. Take a digital meeting instead of an in-person one, even if you

give up expensed travel. Go to a protest, invest in noncarbon energy, buy solar panels, eat at meatless restaurants, canvass for climate-conscious candidates. Do whichever of these you can, as conspicuously as you can. With each step, you communicate an emergency that needs all hands on deck. Individual action — across supermarkets, skies, roads, homes, workplaces, and ballot boxes — sounds an alarm that might just wake us from our collective slumber and build a foundation for the necessary political change.

. . .

Comprehension

1. Two deadlines are mentioned in Hackel and Sparkman's introduction. Why are they important?
2. What misunderstanding or misguided belief do the writers hope to correct?
3. Why do Hackel and Sparkman think it is important for individuals to take "personal actions like limiting plane rides, eating less meat, or investing in solar energy" (3)?
4. According to Hackel and Sparkman, who bears "the lion's share of responsibility for [the climate] crisis" (6)? Does this acknowledgment undercut the writers' argument? Why or why not?
5. Hackel and Sparkman ask, "How many people does it take to start change" (13)? What is their answer?

Purpose and Audience

1. What is the essay's thesis? How would you restate it in your own words?
2. Given the premises of the first paragraph, what do the authors seem to assume about their readers?
3. What purpose does paragraph 2 serve?
4. Hackel and Sparkman not only want to change readers' view of individual action but also encourage them to take specific action. Will this essay influence the way you think about climate change? Might it influence your actions? If so, how?

Style and Structure

1. **Vocabulary Project.** In this essay, Hackel and Sparkman focus on the relationship between changing norms and changes in behavior. What does the word *norm* mean?
2. How do the writers use **rhetorical questions** to organize their argument? Point to a specific example.
3. How do the writers use **analogy** in paragraph 3? On what do they base this analogy? Do you find it persuasive? Why or why not?
4. In what respects is this essay an **inductive argument**? Where do the writers use induction?
5. Hackel and Sparkman claim, "In general, people contribute more when they see others do it too" (13). Do you think they provide enough evidence to support this generalization? Explain.

6. The writers frequently move from general claims to specific evidence. What transitional words and phrases do they use to make this shift?

7. How would you describe the tone of this essay? Is this tone appropriate for the writers' purpose? Explain.

Journal Entry

Hackel and Sparkman write, "Humans are social animals, and we use social cues to recognize emergencies" (3). Write about a time (not necessarily an "emergency") when the words or actions of another person (or group) led you to think or act in a certain way.

Writing Workshop

1. **Working with Sources.** In paragraph 11, Hackel and Sparkman write, "What can you do when current norms promote unsustainable behaviors like frequent flying or eating large amounts of meat? Change the norms. And people will likely rapidly adapt." Here, the writers discuss shifts in our norms that promote unsustainable behavior, such as smoking and drunk driving. Identify another social or cultural behavior that you think needs to be changed, and consider the norms that support that behavior. Then, write an essay in which you propose two or three ways to change those norms to help change people's unsustainable behaviors. Be sure to document the sources you use and to include a works-cited page. (See Chapter 18 for information on MLA documentation.)

2. According to the writers, politicians use information on people's attitudes and behaviors about climate change "to decide if environmental policies will get them re-elected" (16). Although there is an international scientific consensus on climate change among experts in the field, that body of research and its attendant warnings have failed to motivate large-scale action on the part of the U.S. government. How do you explain that disconnect? What, if anything, do you think could eliminate it? Write an essay that addresses these questions.

3. Over the years, have you observed a shift in the norms that influence the beliefs and actions related to climate change held by people you know? Write an essay in which you trace support for climate change initiatives among your friends and family members, discussing changes in their behavior as well as in their beliefs.

Combining the Patterns

The writers rely extensively on **exemplification** to make their argument. How effective are their examples? Which examples seem the strongest? Why?

Thematic Connections

- "Thirty-Seven Who Saw Murder Didn't Call the Police" (page 127)
- "Shooting an Elephant" (page 132)
- "Ten Ways We Get the Odds Wrong" (page 242)
- "The Lottery" (page 303)

NATASHA GEILING

The Only Individual Action That Matters Is Voting for People Who Care about Climate Change

Oregon native Natasha Geiling is an environmental journalist as well as a J.D. candidate at the University of California, Berkeley, School of Law. Previously, she was a climate reporter for ThinkProgress and an online reporter for *Smithsonian* magazine. Her work has also appeared in *Slate*, *Modern Farmer*, *Atlas Obscura*, and *Bustle*. She earned her undergraduate degree at Wellesley College.

Background on the Intergovernmental Panel on Climate Change and International Action According to its website, the Intergovernmental Panel on Climate Change (IPCC) is a body of the United Nations designed to "provide policymakers with regular scientific assessments on climate change, its implications and potential future risks, as well as to put forward adaptation and mitigation options." In 2018, the IPCC released a special report on the effects of a 1.5 degree Celsius and 2 degree Celsius increase in global temperature above preindustrial levels. As Geiling notes, the outlook is dire, particularly with regard to human health, the sustainability of the oceans, and the perilous position of low-lying areas prone to flooding. Such temperature changes will create food insecurity and massive population displacement, among other problems. Avoiding or even limiting these consequences will require massive international effort on the part of countries throughout the world. So far, however, responses have been sluggish. The United States has been especially intractable on this issue — for example, withdrawing from the 2015 Paris Agreement, which aimed to keep the increase in global average temperature to below 2° Celsius above preindustrial levels. In 2019, however, Senator Edward Markey and Representative Alexandria Ocasio-Cortez released a fourteen-page resolution for a "Green New Deal," one of whose goals was to shift the United States to 100 percent renewable, zero-emission energy sources.

On October 7, 2018, the United Nations' Intergovernmental Panel on Climate Change released a massive report that, through careful consideration of more than 6,000 scientific studies, contained a bleak message for anyone who lives on planet Earth. The IPCC, a notoriously staid scientific body, wrote that we have put off acting on climate change for long enough that it's almost certain that the planet will face catastrophic consequences like global food shortages, mass migration, and destruction of ecosystems in a just few decades.

While the report cautions that it's not too late to stop the very worst consequences of climate change from coming to fruition, the solution that it gives, from a practical standpoint, isn't very encouraging. Basically, we have a

> " Stop voting for politicians who don't treat climate change like the immediate, existential threat that it is. "

decade to get our act together before the planet warms to a temperature that will drown entire islands; a decade to beat back climate change denial enough to switch completely from fossil fuels to clean energy, and completely remake almost every sector of human life.

Grasping for a silver lining in the darkness, some outlets responded to the IPCC report's depressing news with tips about steps that individuals can take to slow climate change. CNN, for instance, published a list with suggestions for personal action like consuming fewer meat products, switching from flying to driving, and replacing old, inefficient technology with newer, more energy efficient pieces. Those are all good ideas, but they're also almost certainly useless at this point. Individual action on climate change is literally an outmoded '80s idea from a previous IPCC report when things were not so dire. Switching to a plant-based diet saves 0.7 metric tons of carbon dioxide each year—about the same as burning 90 gallons of gas. Giving up a car entirely saves the average person about 2.1 metric tons of carbon dioxide—the same as burning 270 gallons of gas. The United States as a whole, emitted 6.87 billion metric tons of carbon dioxide equivalent in 2014. Only 100 corporations worldwide are responsible for a whopping 71 percent of global emissions. Laying the responsibility of climate change at the feet of individual people by telling them to tinker around the margins of their own actions is like telling someone to stop a reckless driver by turning down the radio or turning up the air conditioning.

There is really only one thing that individuals can do to prevent the worst of climate change from becoming a reality—and really, it's the only way out of this mess: stop voting for politicians who don't treat climate change like the immediate, existential threat that it is.

This should, in theory, be easy. There are hundreds of politicians up for re-election who have shown that they don't believe in climate change despite overwhelming evidence to the contrary. In the House of Representatives, 232 elected officials, or a little more than half, are climate deniers. In the Senate, 53 are. These are people who, unlike the average individual, actually have the power to create the kinds of policy changes needed to avert the worst of climate change. They could pass a tax on carbon, or pass a bill investing in green infrastructure—policies that, unlike switching your thermostat to a smart thermostat, would have an actionable impact on the amount of carbon dioxide our country spews into the atmosphere each year.

The current Congress—for a number of reasons, from sheer cravenness to fossil fuel money in politics to the fact that most representatives are so old that they won't feel the consequences of climate change anyway—isn't going to do that. A nationwide price on carbon, one of the IPCC's primary policy suggestions for getting a handle on rampant climate change, is a political anathema. This summer, 229 representatives voted for a resolution that condemned a carbon tax as "not in the best interest of the United States." And following the release of the IPCC report, Sen. Roger Wicker (R-MS) told the *Huffington Post* that the report "might as well be calling on me to sprout wings and fly to Canada for the summer."

Replacing these people with politicians who actually care about the future   7 of our planet is not as easy as it sounds. Historically, voters — even liberal Democrats, the demographic most likely to care about environmental issues at the polls — have prioritized things like the economy, or national security, over issues like climate change. Candidates don't help the problem, because they rarely, if ever, talk about it — even when it seems ridiculous not to, like one Democrat running for the House in the North Carolina district that received 30 inches of rain during Hurricane Florence only weeks ago who doesn't even list climate change as an issue on his campaign website. If there's any personal action we aren't taking that we should be, it's demanding that candidates take an aggressive, uncompromising stance on climate change immediately, and showing up to vote for them when they do.

We have 12 years to act before climate change becomes catastrophic.   8 That's six midterm elections. Three presidential elections. A handful of chances to elect people who care more about the planet than corporations or political donations. We can start in a month. Or we can keep electing people who ignore reality for their own comfort. Either way, we can't say we weren't warned.

· · ·

Comprehension

1. According the report of the Intergovernmental Panel on Climate Change (IPCC), what "catastrophic consequences" will the planet face in the coming decades?
2. Why is individual action on climate change now an "outmoded . . . idea" (3)?
3. In paragraph 3, Geiling writes that CNN "published a list with suggestions for personal action like consuming fewer meat products, switching from flying to driving, and replacing old, inefficient technology with newer, more energy efficient pieces." What does she think of these recommendations? Why?
4. What practical political solutions does Geiling propose? Do you see her suggestions as feasible? Why or why not?

Purpose and Audience

1. What is Geiling's thesis? Where does she place her thesis statement? Why do you think she chose to locate it at this point in her essay?
2. What is the purpose of paragraph 3? What role does it play in Geiling's argument?

3. Do you think this essay is likely to persuade those who are skeptical about climate change? Why or why not? Is Geiling writing for that group of readers? How can you tell?

Style and Structure

1. **Vocabulary Project.** Geiling describes the IPCC as "notoriously staid" (1). What does the word *staid* mean? What point is Geiling trying to make by labeling the IPCC in this way?
2. Geiling writes, "Laying the responsibility of climate change at the feet of individual people by telling them to tinker around the margins of their own actions is like telling someone to stop a reckless driver by turning down the radio or turning up the air conditioning" (3). Do you find this **analogy** persuasive? Explain.
3. Does Geiling commit an **either-or** fallacy in this essay? Explain.
4. Geiling refers to politicians who ignore climate change as people who "ignore reality for their own comfort" (8). Does that seem like a fair characterization? Why or why not?

Journal Entry

According to Geiling, "Historically, voters . . . have prioritized things like the economy, or national security, over issues like climate change" (7). Where do you prioritize climate change?

Writing Workshop

1. **Working with Sources.** Hackel and Sparkman (page 589) view individual choice and behavior as a key element in addressing climate change. In contrast, Geiling argues that practices like reducing meat consumption are "good ideas, but they're also almost certainly useless" (3). Which essay do you find more persuasive? Write an essay that evaluates the two positions on this issue. Be sure to document all words and ideas that you borrow from the essays, and include a works-cited page. (See Chapter 18 for information on MLA documentation.)
2. Geiling writes that it "should, in theory, be easy" (5) to vote in "candidates [who] take an aggressive, uncompromising stance on climate change immediately" (7). In your view, why is it so difficult to get politicians to take such a stance?
3. **Working with Sources.** Write a letter to your congressional representative in which you support or challenge his or her general position and specific statements on climate change. Begin by looking at the legislator's website and reading news articles that discuss his or her views on this issue. Be sure to document references to those sources and to include a works-cited page. (See Chapter 18 for information on MLA documentation.)

Combining the Patterns

Where does Geiling use **cause and effect** in this essay? Do you find her causal relationships and connections logical?

Thematic Connections

- "How to Spot Fake News" (page 289)
- "Why Rational People Buy into Conspiracy Theories" (page 338)
- "The Ways We Lie" (page 463)
- "The Obligation to Endure" (page 554)

Is Free Speech on Campus in Peril?

zimmytws/Shutterstock

Citizens' legal and social expectations regarding free speech do not always match up.

• • •

Before the fall 2016 semester began at the University of Chicago, dean of students, John Ellison, sent all incoming students a letter that affirmed the school's dedication to open discussion and rigorous intellectual debate. Ellis wrote, "Our commitment to academic freedom means that we do not support so-called 'trigger warnings,' we do not cancel invited speakers because their topics might prove controversial, and we do not condone the creation of intellectual 'safe spaces' where individuals can retreat from ideas and perspectives at odds with their own." Ellison's letter was part of an ongoing national debate about speech on college campuses that still engages educators, opinion columnists, politicians, legal experts, and students.

Ellison expresses the views of many who see the current academic climate as overprotective. These critics view trigger warnings (that is, the identification of course content that might offend or otherwise upset students), the creation of "safe spaces," the policing of "microaggressions," and charges of "hate speech" as synonymous with censorship. They argue that these measures go beyond the realm of courtesy and instead encourage people to be oversensitive to perceived offenses, particularly in the context of race, ethnicity, gender, and sexual orientation. In short, these measures cut against the grain of America's tradition of free speech, which seems especially important in an academic context: students and scholars should have a space to discuss a wide range of ideas, even unsavory and unpopular ideas.

Others disagree, contending that critics of trigger warnings and other related practices ignore the pedagogical usefulness of these tools. They point out that creating a safe space for discussion does not necessarily mean shielding students from unpleasant or upsetting topics. On the contrary, students can't learn if they feel threatened or vulnerable. In this sense, hateful and harmful speech can shut down discussion and undercut the educational mission of a university. If students are going to learn, they have to be able to express themselves in classrooms that encourage free and open expression as well as civil disagreement.

The selections in this casebook examine the topic of free speech on campus from a number of different perspectives. Geoffrey R. Stone's "Free Expression in Peril" charts the history of free speech on college campuses in the United States and expresses his concern that this hard-fought right might be slipping away. In "The Case for Restricting Hate Speech," Laura Beth Nielsen argues that the American legal tradition of protecting speech rights protects the power and privilege of the "haves" at the expense of the "have-nots." In "Trigger Warnings, Safe Spaces, and Free Speech, Too," University of Chicago senior Sophie Downes defines important terms in the debate over trigger warnings and questions the motivations behind the Ellison letter. In "The Latest Study on Trigger Warnings Finally Convinced Me They're Not Worth It," Shannon Palus looks at recent research about the efficacy — and unintended side effects — of trigger warnings.

GEOFFREY R. STONE

Free Expression in Peril

Geoffrey R. Stone is an author and educator. After graduating from the University of Chicago Law School, he served as a law clerk for the U.S. Court of Appeals for the D.C. Circuit and to Supreme Court Justice William J. Brennan Jr. He returned to teaching at the University of Chicago, where he is currently the Edward H. Levi Distinguished Service Professor. He is the editor of the *Supreme Court Review* and has authored a number of books, including *Top Secret: When Our Government Keeps Us in the Dark* (2007) and *Speaking Out: Reflections of Law, Liberty, and Justice* (2010).

Background on the Report of the Committee on Freedom of Expression In 2014, Robert Zimmer, the president of the University of Chicago, appointed a Committee on Freedom of Expression at his school. This committee was asked to create a statement "articulating the University's overarching commitment to free, robust, and uninhibited debate and deliberation among all members of the University's community." Geoffrey R. Stone was the chair of this committee, which included six other University of Chicago professors. The three-page report was lauded by some in the press, in part because it was published only a day before the 2015 attacks on the offices of French satirical magazine *Charlie Hebdo*, which were viewed by many as a direct assault on freedom of speech. The editorial board at the University of Chicago student newspaper, however, criticized the report for failing to differentiate "between acceptable and unacceptable speech."

1 Until recently, and for roughly half a century, American universities enjoyed an era of relatively robust academic freedom. In the past few years, though, that has changed. Ironically, the threat to academic freedom in the United States today comes not from government and not from the institutions themselves but from a new generation of students who do not understand the nature, the fragility, and the importance of this principle.

2 Universities must educate our students to understand that academic freedom is not a law of nature. It is not something to be taken for granted. It is, rather, a hard-won acquisition in a lengthy struggle for academic integrity.

3 Students today seem not to understand that, until well into the nineteenth century, real freedom of thought was neither practiced nor professed in American universities. Before then, any freedom of inquiry or expression in American colleges was smothered by the prevailing theory of "doctrinal moralism," which assumed that the worth of an idea must be judged by what the institution's leaders considered its moral value. Through the first half of the nineteenth century, American higher education squelched any notion of free discussion or intellectual curiosity. Indeed, as the nation moved toward the Civil War, any professor or student in the North who defended slavery, or any professor or student in the South who challenged slavery, could readily be dismissed, disciplined, or expelled.

Between 1870 and 1900, however, there was a genuine revolution in   4
American higher education. With the battle over Darwinism, new academic
goals came to be embraced. For the first time, to criticize as well as to preserve
traditional moral values and understandings became an accepted function of
higher education.

In 1892, William Rainey Harper, the first president of the University of   5
Chicago, could boldly assert: "When for any reason the administration of a
university attempts to dislodge a professor or punish a student because of his
political or religious sentiments, at that moment the institution has ceased to
be a university." But, despite such sentiments, the battle for academic freedom
has been a contentious and a continuing one.

For example, in the closing years of the nineteenth century, businessmen   6
who had accumulated vast industrial wealth began to support universities on
an unprecedented scale. But that support was not without strings, and professors who offended wealthy trustees by criticizing the ethics of their business
practices were dismissed from such leading universities as Cornell and Stanford.

Then, during World War I, when patriotic zealots persecuted and even   7
prosecuted those who questioned the wisdom or the morality of the war, universities collapsed almost completely in their defense of academic freedom.
Students and professors were systematically expelled or fired at even such distinguished institutions as Columbia University and the University of Virginia
merely for "encouraging a spirit of indifference toward the war."

Similar issues arose again, with a vengeance, during the post–World War II   8
Red Scare. In the late 1940s and the 1950s, most universities excluded from
academic life those even suspected of entertaining Communist sympathies.
Yale's president, Charles Seymour, went so far as to boast that "there will be no
witch hunts at Yale, because there will be no witches. We will neither admit nor
hire anyone with Communist sympathies."

We now face a similar set of challenges. We live today in an era of political   9
correctness in which students themselves demand censorship, and colleges,
afraid to offend those students, too often surrender academic freedom.

In recent years, student pressure thwarted speakers' scheduled appear-   10
ances at Brown University, Johns Hopkins, Williams, and elsewhere. Colorado
College suspended a student for making a joke considered antifeminist and
racist. William & Mary, De Paul University, and the University of Colorado all
disciplined students for criticizing affirmative action, and the University of
Kansas disciplined a professor for condemning the National Rifle Association.

At Wesleyan University, after the school newspaper published a student   11
op-ed criticizing the Black Lives Matter movement, students demanded that
administrators defund the paper. At Amherst College, students demanded
that the administration remove posters stating that "All Lives Matter." At
Emory University, students demanded that the university punish whoever had
chalked "Trump 2016" on campus sidewalks because, in the words of one, "I'm
supposed to feel comfortable and safe. . . . I don't deserve to feel afraid at my
school." And at Harvard, African-American students demanded that a professor be taken to the woodshed for saying in class that he would be "lynched" if
he gave a closed-book examination.

The latter is an example of a so-called "microaggression" — words or   12
phrases that may make students feel uncomfortable or "unsafe." Such microaggressions, whether uttered by students or faculty members, have been
deemed punishable by colleges and universities across the nation. A recent survey revealed that 72 percent of current college students support disciplinary
action against any student or faculty member who expresses views that they
deem "racist, sexist, homophobic, or otherwise offensive."

Another recent innovation is the much-discussed "trigger warning." A   13
trigger warning is a requirement that before professors assign readings or hold
classes that might make some students feel uncomfortable, they must warn
students that the readings or the class will deal with sensitive topics like rape,
affirmative action, abortion, murder, slavery, the Holocaust, religion, homosexuality, or immigration.

And then there's disruption: If students who disagree with a speaker's   14
views can't get a speech canceled, they disrupt the event to silence that speaker.
Too often, college administrators, fearful of seeming unsympathetic to the
protesters, terminate the events because of the disruptions and then fail to discipline the disrupters for their behavior.

How did we get here? It was not long ago when college students were   15
demanding the right to free speech. Now they demand the right to be free from
speech that they find offensive or upsetting.

One often-expressed theory is that students of this generation, unlike   16
their predecessors, are weak, fragile, and emotionally unstable. They've been
raised, the argument goes, by parents who have protected, rewarded, and celebrated them in every way from the time they were infants. Therefore they've
never learned to deal with challenge, defeat, uncertainty, anxiety, stress, insult,
or fear. They are emotionally incapable of dealing with challenge.

But if that is so, then the proper role of a university is not to protect and   17
pamper them but to prepare them for the difficulties of the real world. The
goal should not be to shield them from discomfort, insult, and insecurity, but
to enable them to be effective citizens. If their parents have, indeed, failed
them, then their colleges and universities should save them from themselves.

There is, however, another possibility. It is that students, or at least some   18
students, have always felt this way, but until now they were too intimidated,
too shy, too deferential to speak up. If so, this generation of college students
deserves credit, because instead of remaining silent and oppressed, they have
the courage to demand respect, equality, and safety.

I think there is an element of truth in both of these perspectives, but I am   19
inclined to think that the former explains more than the latter.

Faced with the continuing challenges to academic freedom at American   20
universities, the University of Chicago's president, Robert J. Zimmer, charged a
faculty committee last year with the task of drafting a formal statement on
freedom of expression. The goal of that committee, which I chaired, was to
stake out Chicago's position on these issues. That statement has since become
a model for a number of other universities. Here are some examples of its
central principles.

- "It is not the proper role of the University to attempt to shield individuals from ideas and opinions they find unwelcome, disagreeable, or even deeply offensive."
- "Concerns about civility and mutual respect can never be used as a justification for closing off discussion of ideas, however offensive or disagreeable those ideas may be to some members of our community."
- "The University may restrict expression that violates the law, that falsely defames a specific individual, that constitutes a genuine threat or harassment, that unjustifiably invades substantial privacy or confidentiality interests, or that is otherwise directly incompatible with the core functioning of the university. But these are narrow exceptions to the general principle of freedom of expression."
- "The university's fundamental commitment is to the principle that robust debate and deliberation may not be suppressed because the ideas put forth are thought by some or even by most members of the University community to be offensive, unwise, immoral, or wrong-headed. It is for the individual members of the community, not for the university as an institution, to make those judgments for themselves, and to act on those judgments not by seeking to suppress speech, but by openly and vigorously contesting the ideas that they oppose."
- "Although members of the university are free to criticize and contest the views expressed on campus, and to criticize and contest speakers who are invited to express their views on campus, they may not obstruct or otherwise interfere with the freedom of others to express views they reject or even loathe."

Why should a university embrace these principles? 21

First, bitter experience has taught that even the ideas we hold to be most 22 certain often turn out to be wrong. As confident as we might be in our own wisdom, certainty is different from truth. The core obligation of a university is to invite challenge to the accepted wisdom.

Second, history shows that suppression of speech breeds suppression of 23 speech. If today I am permitted to silence those whose views I find distasteful, I have then opened the door to allow others down the road to silence me. The neutral principle, no suppression of ideas, protects us all.

Third, a central precept of free expression is the possibility of a chilling effect. That problem is especially acute today because of social media. Students and faculty members used to be willing to take controversial positions because the risks were relatively modest. After all, one could say something provocative, and the statement soon disappeared from view. But now, every comment you make can be circulated to the world and called up

> **"**Should students be allowed to express whatever views they want, however offensive? Yes. Absolutely.**"** 24

with a click by prospective employers or graduate schools or neighbors. The potential costs of speaking courageously, of taking controversial positions, of taking risks, is greater than ever. Indeed, according to a recent survey, about half of American college students now say that it is unsafe for them to express unpopular views. Many faculty members clearly share that sentiment. In this climate, it is especially important for universities to stand up for free expression.

How should this work in practice? Should students and faculty be allowed   25
to express whatever views they want, however offensive they might be to others?

Yes. Absolutely.   26

Should those who disagree and who are offended be allowed to condemn   27
that speech and those speakers in the most vehement terms? Yes. Absolutely.

Should those who are offended and who disagree be allowed to demand   28
that the university punish those who have offended them? Yes. Absolutely.

Should the university punish those whose speech annoys, offends, and   29
insults others? Absolutely not.

That is the core meaning of academic freedom.   30

Does that mean the university's hands are tied? No.   31

A university should educate its students about the importance of civility   32
and mutual respect. These values should be reinforced by education and exam-ple, not by censorship.

A university should encourage disagreement, argument, and debate. It   33
should instill in its students and faculty members the importance of winning the day by facts, by ideas, and by persuasion, rather than by force, obstruction, or censorship. For a university to fulfill its most fundamental mission, it must be a safe space for even the most loathsome, odious, offensive, disloyal argu-ments. Students should be encouraged to be tough, fearless, rigorous, and effective advocates and critics.

At the same time, a university has to recognize that in our society, flawed   34
as it is, the costs of free speech will fall most heavily on those who feel the most marginalized and unwelcome. All of us feel that way sometimes, but the indi-viduals who bear the brunt of free speech — at least of certain types of free speech — often include racial minorities; religious minorities; women; gay men, lesbians, and transsexuals; and immigrants. Universities must be sensitive to that reality.

Although they should not attempt to "solve" this problem by censorship,   35
universities should support students who feel vulnerable, marginalized, silenced, and demeaned. They should help them learn how to speak up, how to respond effectively, how to challenge those whose attitudes, whose words, and whose beliefs offend and appall them. The world is not a safe space, and we must enable our graduates to win the battles they'll have to fight in years to come.

But hard cases remain. As simple as it may be to state a principle, it is   36
always much more difficult to apply it to concrete situations. So let me leave you with a few cases to ponder.

A sociology professor gives a talk on campus condemning homosexuality   37
as immoral and calling on "normal" students to steer clear of "fags, perverts,
and sexual degenerates." What, if anything, should the chair of the sociology
department do? In my judgment, this is a classic case of academic freedom.
The professor is well within his rights to offer such opinions, however offensive others might find them.

A student hangs a Confederate flag, a swastika, an image of an aborted   38
fetus, or a "Vote for Trump" sign on the door of his dorm room. What, if anything, should administrators do? The university should not pick and choose
which messages to permit and which to ban. That is classic censorship. But in
the context of a residence hall, where students are a bit of a captive audience,
the university can have a content-neutral rule that bans all signs on dorm-
room doors.

The dean of a university's law school goes on Fox News and says "Abortion   39
is murder. We should fire any female faculty member and expel any female student who has had an abortion." The university president is then inundated
with complaints from alumni saying, in effect, "I'll never give another nickel to
your damn school as long as she remains dean." What should the president
do? A dean or other administrator at a university has distinctive responsibilities. If she engages in behavior, including expression, that renders her effectively incapable of fulfilling her administrative responsibilities, then she can be
removed from her position. This is necessary to the core functioning of the
institution. At the same time, though, if the dean is also a faculty member, she
cannot be disciplined as a faculty member for the exercise of academic freedom.

We needn't rely solely on hypotheticals. There was the situation at DePaul   40
University in which a student group invited a highly controversial speaker who
maintains, among other things, that there is no wage gap for women, that as a
gay man he can attest that one's sexual orientation is purely a matter of choice,
and that white men have fewer advantages than women and African-
Americans. A group of student protesters disrupted the event by shouting,
ultimately causing the talk to be canceled. They maintained that their shouting was merely the exercise of free speech.

What should the university do in such circumstances? Should it permit   41
the protest? Arrest the protesters on the spot? Allow them to protest and then
punish them after the fact?

Such a disruption is not in any way an exercise of free expression. Although   42
students can protest the event in other ways, they cannot prevent either speakers
or listeners from engaging in a dialogue they wish to engage in without obstruction. In such circumstances, the protesters should be removed and disciplined
for their behavior. (DePaul's president, the Rev. Dennis H. Holtschneider, apolo-
gized to the speaker but also criticized "speakers of his ilk" for being "more
entertainers and self-serving provocateurs than the public intellectuals they
purport to be.")

Or consider the incident last year at the University of Oklahoma when a   43
group of fraternity brothers, in a private setting, chanted a racist song.
Someone who was present at the time filmed the event and circulated it online.

Was the university's president, David Boren, right to expel the students? In my judgment, no.

As these examples attest, there are, in fact, marginal cases. But we should not let them obscure the clarity of our commitment to academic freedom. That commitment is now seriously and dangerously under attack. It will be interesting to see whether our universities today have the courage, the integrity, and the fortitude — sometimes lacking in the past — to live up to the highest ideals of a "true" university.

44

• • •

Comprehension

1. According to Stone, what kind of intellectual climate do colleges create by sanctioning "safe space[s]" and "trigger warnings"?
2. What theories does Stone propose to explain why students are demanding safe spaces and trigger warnings?
3. In paragraph 23, Stone says that "suppression of speech breeds suppression of speech." What does he mean?
4. Stone implies that the debates about free speech in higher education have implications for all Americans. What are these implications?
5. What does Stone mean when he says that "the costs of free speech will fall most heavily on those who feel the most marginalized and unwelcome" (34)? Do you agree?

Purpose and Audience

1. Does Stone expect his audience to be in favor of free speech? Does he expect them to be sympathetic to the rest of his argument, or more neutral? How can you tell?
2. Where does Stone state his thesis? Why do you think he places it where he does?
3. Does Stone appeal mainly to logic, to emotions, or to character and authority? Explain.
4. Stone concedes in paragraph 36 that "hard cases remain" and presents several examples of controversy over free speech. How might this information undermine his case? How might it support his case?

Style and Structure

1. Why does Stone quote some central principles from the University of Chicago's statement on freedom of expression?
2. Stone presents a brief history of free speech on college campuses, including the rise of Darwinism and the Red Scare. How do these historical examples support his overall point? What other examples might he have chosen?
3. In paragraphs 15 through 18, Stone presents two possible causes for recent student movements in favor of safe spaces and trigger warnings.

In paragraph 19, he acknowledges that he finds truth in both options, but feels that the first one is a stronger explanation. Why do you think he presented both of these causes?

4. **Vocabulary Project.** In his closing paragraph, Stone calls on schools "to live up to the highest ideals of a 'true' university." Write a paragraph-length definition of a *true university* according to Stone's view.

Journal Entry

Do you think students in your class are able to "express whatever views they want" (paragraph 25)? Or do you think your school is one of those that "too often surrender academic freedom" (9)?

Writing Workshop

1. According to Stone, colleges are "fearful of seeming unsympathetic" (14) and so they inhibit free speech. Do you think students should be allowed to say anything they want to in class, or do you think faculty and administrators should place limits on speech? Write an argumentative essay that presents your position. Be sure to include specific examples to support your thesis.

2. **Working with Sources.** Stone refers to the University of Chicago's 2015 Report of the Committee on Freedom of Expression as a model for administrators and faculty. Find this document online and read it, paying close attention to the restrictions on expression that it allows. If your university has such a statement, read it. If not, find two similar documents from other schools. Then, using these statements as source material, write your own statement on principles of free expression. Be sure to document all references to your sources and to include a works-cited page. (See Chapter 18 for information on MLA documentation.)

3. In paragraph 25, Stone argues that "students and faculty be allowed to express whatever views they want, however offensive they might be to others." Do you think faculty members should be allowed to say anything they want in class? Or, do you think there should be limits? Write an argumentative essay that presents your opinion. Be sure to include specific examples to support your thesis.

Combining the Patterns

Where in this essay does Stone use **exemplification**? Does he provide enough examples to support his claims? Explain your answer.

Thematic Connections

- "Call Me 'They'" (page 237)
- "How to Spot Fake News" (page 289)
- "Sex, Lies, and Conversation" (page 408)

LAURA BETH NIELSEN

The Case for Restricting Hate Speech

Laura Beth Nielsen is a professor and director of legal studies in the sociology department of Northwestern University. Nielsen is also a lawyer and a research professor at the American Bar Foundation. She earned her undergraduate, J.D., and Ph.D. degrees from the University of California, Berkeley. Nielsen's research focuses on the law's capacity for social change, including issues of sexual harassment in the workplace and employment civil rights. Her books include *Handbook of Employment Discrimination Research: Rights and Realities* (with Robert L. Nelson, 2005) and *Theoretical and Empirical Studies of Rights* (2007). Her work has appeared in academic journals such as the *Law and Society Review*, the *Journal of Empirical Legal Studies*, and *Law and Social Inquiry*.

Background on the Supreme Court's history of decisions addressing hate speech Even though the First Amendment allows for restrictions on certain types of speech, such as libel and obscenity, "hate speech"— public utterances that express hate or encourage violence toward a person or group — is protected by the Constitution. The U.S. Supreme Court has addressed this issue on several occasions. For example, in 1964, an Ohio Ku Klux Klan leader spoke at a rally and was later charged with breaking a state law advocating violence. He was convicted, fined, and sentenced to prison. But a 1969 Supreme Court ruling reversed this decision, saying that a state cannot forbid speech unless it is "directed to inciting or producing imminent lawlessness." Even so, many states have tried to enact hate-speech laws, but they rested on shaky legal ground. In 1992, the Court struck down a St. Paul, Minnesota, ordinance that banned cross burning and other expressions of racial supremacy after a cross was burned on a Black family's lawn. Speaking for the majority, Justice Antonin Scalia said, "The First Amendment does not permit St. Paul to impose special prohibitions on those speakers who express views on disfavored subjects." At the root of this legal tradition is the simple adage, "Sticks and stones may break my bones, but words will never hurt me." Later Supreme Court rulings, such as *Virginia v. Black* (2003) and *Snyder v. Phelps* (2011), have upheld this principle. More recently, however, some legal scholars — including Nielsen — have questioned this distinction between words and actions and have argued in favor of banning certain types of hate speech.

As a sociologist and legal scholar, I struggle to explain the boundaries of free speech to undergraduates. Despite the 1st Amendment — I tell my students — local, state, and federal laws limit all kinds of speech. We regulate advertising, obscenity, slander, libel, and inciting lawless action to name just a few. My students nod along until we get to racist and sexist speech. Some can't grasp why, if we restrict so many forms of speech, we don't also restrict hate speech. Why, for example, did the Supreme Court on Monday rule that the trademark office cannot reject "disparaging" applications — like a request from an Oregon band to trademark "the Slants" as in Asian "slant eyes."

The typical answer is that judges must balance benefits and harms. If judges are asked to compare the harm of restricting speech — a cherished core constitutional value — to the harm of hurt feelings, judges will rightly choose to protect free expression. But perhaps it's nonsense to characterize the nature of the harm as nothing more than an emotional scratch; that's a reflection of the deep inequalities in our society, and one that demonstrates a profound misunderstanding of how hate speech affects its targets.

Legally, we tell members of traditionally disadvantaged groups that they must live with hate speech except under very limited circumstances. The KKK can parade down Main Street. People can't falsely yell fire in a theater but can yell the N-word at a person of color. College women are told that a crowd of frat boys chanting "no means yes and yes means anal" is something they must tolerate in the name of (someone else's) freedom.

At the same time, our regime of free speech protects the powerful and popular. Many city governments, for instance, have banned panhandling at the behest of their business communities. The legal justification is that the targets of begging (commuters, tourists, and consumers) have important and legitimate purposes for being in public: to get to work or to go shopping. The law therefore protects them from aggressive requests for money.

Consider also the protections afforded to soldiers' families in the case of Westboro Baptist anti-gay demonstrations. When the Supreme Court in 2011 upheld that church's right to stage offensive protests at veterans' funerals, Congress passed the Honoring America's Veterans' Act, which prohibits any protests 300 to 500 feet around such funerals. (The statute made no mention of protecting LGBTQ funeral attendees from hate speech, just soldiers' families.)

So soldiers' families, shoppers, and workers are protected from troubling speech. People of color, women walking down public streets or just living in their dorm on a college campus are not. The only way to justify this disparity is to argue that commuters asked for money on the way to work experience a tangible harm, while women catcalled and worse on the way to work do not — as if being the target of a request for change is worse than being racially disparaged by a stranger.

In fact, empirical data suggest that frequent verbal harassment can lead to various negative consequences. Racist hate speech has been linked to cigarette smoking, high blood pressure, anxiety, depression, and post-traumatic stress disorder, and requires complex coping strategies. Exposure to racial slurs also diminishes academic performance. Women subjected to sexualized speech may develop a phenomenon of "self-objectification," which is associated with eating disorders.

These negative physical and mental health outcomes — which embody the historical roots of race and gender oppression — mean that hate speech is not "just speech." Hate speech is doing something. It results in tangible harms that are serious in and of themselves and that collectively amount to the harm of subordination. The harm of perpetuating discrimination. The harm of creating inequality.

Instead of characterizing racist and sexist hate speech as "just speech," courts and legislatures need to account for this research and, perhaps, allow the restriction of hate speech as do all of the other economically advanced democracies in the world. 9

> **"Many readers will find this line of reasoning repellent."**

Many readers will find this line of thinking repellent. They will insist that protecting hate speech is consistent with and even central to our founding principles. They will argue that regulating hate speech would amount to a serious break from our tradition. They will trivialize the harms that social science research undeniably associates with being the target of hate speech, and call people seeking recognition of these affronts "snowflakes." 10

But these free-speech absolutists must at least acknowledge two facts. First, the right to speak already is far from absolute. Second, they are asking disadvantaged members of our society to shoulder a heavy burden with serious consequences. Because we are "free" to be hateful, members of traditionally marginalized groups suffer. 11

· · ·

Comprehension

1. What "struggle" does Nielsen describe in the first paragraph of her essay? Why does she begin her essay by talking about her students?
2. Although the First Amendment broadly protects freedom of expression, what kinds of speech can be regulated by state, local, and federal laws?
3. According to Nielsen, what things must judges balance when considering speech restrictions?
4. What legal status does the "harm of hurt feelings" have in the context of speech restrictions?
5. In paragraph 7, Nielsen cites empirical data. What data does she cite? What point does she make with this evidence?
6. According to Nielsen, what "two facts" must "free-speech absolutists" acknowledge (11)?

Purpose and Audience

1. What is Nielsen's purpose in writing this essay? For example, is she writing to inform, persuade, or compel readers to action?
2. Where does Nielsen state her thesis? Why does she state it where she does?
3. In paragraph 10, Nielsen says, "Many readers will find this line of thinking repellent." Who are the readers she is referring to, and what will they find repellent? Why do you think she makes this statement?

Style and Structure

1. Does Nielsen begin this essay with an appeal to *logos, ethos,* or *pathos*? Do you find this strategy effective? Explain.
2. Where in this essay does Nielsen use inductive reasoning? Where does she use deductive reasoning?
3. What is the relationship between paragraphs 3 and 4? What difference do they highlight? Why is this distinction important to Nielsen's argument?
4. Where does Nielsen address opposing viewpoints? How effectively does she refute these counterarguments?
5. **Vocabulary Project.** In paragraph 10, Nielsen says, "[Many readers] will trivialize the harms that social science research undeniably associates with being the target of hate speech, and call people seeking recognition of these affronts 'snowflakes.'" What does the term *snowflake* mean to you? In a paragraph, write a brief definition of *snowflake*, and explain its connotation in the essay.
6. What point (or points) does Nielsen emphasize in her conclusion? Should she have emphasized something else? Why or why not?

Journal Entry

In her introduction Nielsen says, "We regulate advertising, obscenity, slander, libel, and inciting lawless action to name just a few. My students nod along until we get to racist and sexist speech. Some can't grasp why, if we restrict so many forms of speech, we don't also restrict hate speech" (1). Do you agree or disagree with her statement?

Writing Workshop

1. According to the Nielsen, our current legal conception of free speech "protects the powerful and popular" (4) while "we tell members of traditionally disadvantaged groups that they must live with hate speech except under very limited circumstances" (3). She cites examples to support her view. Do you agree? Write an essay that supports or refutes Nielsen's argument. Make sure to include examples from your own experience to support your thesis.
2. **Working with Sources.** Go online and read about the following four landmark U. S. Supreme Court hate speech cases:

    - *Brandenburg v. Ohio* (1969)
    - *Nationalist Socialist Party v. Skokie* (1977)
    - *Virginia v. Black* (2003)
    - *Snyder v. Phelps* (2011)

    After reading about these cases, write an argumentative essay in which you respond to Nielson's contention that hate speech should be regulated. Be sure to document all references to your sources and to include a works-cited page. (See Chapter 18 for information on MLA documentation.)
3. **Working with Sources.** Survey some students, instructors, and administrators at your school. What range of opinion do you find regarding free

speech on campus? Then, using your research, write an essay in which you argue for or against limiting certain kinds of speech at your school. Be sure to document all references to your sources and to include a works-cited page. (See Chapter 18 for information on MLA documentation.)

Combining the Patterns

Where does Nielsen use **compare and contrast** in her essay? What conclusion does she want her readers to draw from the contrasts?

Thematic Connections

- "Thirty-Seven Who Saw Murder Didn't Call the Police" (page 127)
- "Call Me 'They'" (page 237)
- "Emmett Till and Tamir Rice, Sons of the Great Migration" (page 414)

SOPHIE DOWNES

Trigger Warnings, Safe Spaces, and Free Speech, Too

Sophie Downes is a recent graduate from the University of Chicago, where she was a senior English major at the time she wrote this article. While there, she was a head editor and contributor for the *Chicago Maroon*, a student newspaper.

Background on the 2016 welcome letter from the University of Chicago In August 2016, John "Jay" Ellison, dean of students at the University of Chicago, sent a letter to the incoming class of 2020. In part, this letter contained a message of welcome and congratulated students on their acceptance to the school. The communication then outlined the university's "commitment to freedom of inquiry and expression," inviting members of the campus community "to speak, write, listen, challenge, and learn, without fear of censorship." This message touched off a flurry of responses, as supporters held up the letter as a robust defense of free speech. Critique of the letter focused around its controversial second paragraph, which stated, "Our commitment to academic freedom means that we do not support so-called 'trigger warnings,' we do not cancel invited speakers because their topics might prove controversial, and we do not condone the creation of intellectual 'safe spaces' where individuals can retreat from ideas and perspectives at odds with their own." The letter was not officially published by the University of Chicago, but the *Chicago Maroon*, the university's independent student newspaper, shared a photo of it on its Twitter feed.

1   I didn't get the University of Chicago welcome letter that made the rounds on the internet earlier this summer. I'm a senior this year, and the message from Jay Ellison, the dean of undergraduate students, was for the incoming class: Don't expect trigger warnings or safe spaces here. The university, he said, was committed to free expression and would not shield students from ideas they disagreed with or found offensive.

2   The implication was that students who support trigger warnings and safe spaces are narrow-minded, oversensitive, and opposed to dialogue. The letter betrayed a fundamental misunderstanding of what the terms "trigger warnings" and "safe spaces" mean, and came across as an embarrassing attempt to deflect attention from serious issues on campus.

3   A trigger warning is pretty simple: It consists of a professor's saying in class, "The reading for this week includes a graphic description of sexual assault," or a note on a syllabus that reads, "This course deals with sensitive material that may be difficult for some students."

A safe space is an area on campus where students—especially but not limited to those who have endured trauma or feel marginalized—can feel comfortable talking about their experiences. This might be the Office of Multicultural Student Affairs or it could be Hillel House, but in essence, it's a place for support and community.

This spring, I was in a seminar that dealt with gender, sexuality, and disability. Some of the course reading touched on disturbing subjects, including sexual violence and child abuse. The instructor told us that we could reach out to her if we had difficulty with the class materials, and that she'd do everything she could to make it easier for us to participate. She included a statement to this effect on the syllabus and repeated it briefly at the beginning of each class. Nobody sought to "retreat from ideas and perspectives at odds with their own," as Dean Ellison put it in the letter, nor did these measures hinder discussion or disagreement, both of which were abundant.

> "[S]upport systems can be a lifeline in the tumultuous environment of college."

Of course, not every class calls out for trigger warnings—I've never heard of them for an economics course. Likewise, plenty of students will never need to visit a safe space. But for those who do, support systems can be a lifeline in the tumultuous environment of college, and are important precisely because they encourage a free exchange of ideas.

A little heads-up can help students engage with uncomfortable and complex topics, and a little sensitivity to others, at the most basic level, isn't coddling. Civic discourse in this country has become pretty ugly, so maybe it's not surprising that students are trying to create ways to have compassionate, civil dialogue.

The really strange thing about the Ellison letter, though, is that it positioned itself in opposition to resources the University of Chicago has already built: Instructors already choose whether to use trigger warnings in their classes, and there are many safe spaces on campus. Dean Ellison is even listed as a "safe space ally" on the website of one program run by the Office of L.G.B.T.Q. Student Life.

If, as a university spokesman says, no program or policy is set to change, why release this condemnation at all?

The administration wants to appear as an intellectual force beating back destabilizing waves of political correctness that have rocked college campuses. But the focus of student protests hasn't been the lack of trigger warnings and safe spaces. Instead, many protesters want the university to evaluate how it invests its money, improve access for students with mental illnesses and disabilities, support low-income and first-generation students, and pay its employees fair wages. They have been pushing for more transparency in the school's private police force, which has resisted making most of its policies public in the face of complaints. The university is also under federal investigation over its handling of sexual assault cases.

Yet, the administration has refused to meet with student groups who have asked to discuss these issues, and it has threatened to discipline students who staged a sit-in protest. The university even hired a provost who specializes in corporate crisis management and dealing with "activist pressure." While the university accuses students of silencing opposing voices, it continues to insulate itself against difficult questions.

In this context, it's hard to see the dean's letter as anything other than a public relations maneuver. While students are being depicted as coddled and fragile, the administration is stacking bricks in its institutional wall to avoid engaging with their real concerns.   12

It's too bad, because there are certainly legitimate debates to be had over speech in academic settings. The Ellison letter, for example, included a denunciation of attempts by students to disrupt university-sponsored events featuring controversial speakers. But that has little to do with trigger warnings and safe spaces.   13

Regardless of the posturing of academic administrations, in trigger warnings and safe spaces, students have carved out ways to help, accommodate, and listen to those around them. Campus advocacy groups will not be deterred by a letter, as their goals have nothing to do with censorship and everything to do with holding universities accountable to the communities they are supposed to foster.   14

• • •

Comprehension

1. Downes argues that the Ellison letter "came across as an embarrassing attempt to deflect attention from serious issues on campus" (2). What does she mean? How does this claim set up her main argument?
2. Why does Downes mention that Dean Ellison is listed as a "safe space ally" (8) on a school website?
3. In what sense could the Ellison letter be seen as "a public relations maneuver" (12)? Why does Downes consider this a bad thing?
4. Why does Downes argue that denouncing "attempts by students to disrupt university-sponsored events . . . has little to do with trigger warnings and safe spaces" (13)? Do you agree?
5. How does Downes think students on campus will respond to the Ellison letter?

Purpose and Audience

1. Why does Downes mention that she did not receive Jay Ellison's welcome letter? How does her status as a senior at the University of Chicago strengthen or weaken her *ethos*?
2. What is Downes's purpose in writing this article? What does she want to accomplish?
3. Does Downes consider her audience friendly, hostile, or neutral? How can you tell?

Style and Structure

1. Where does Downes present her thesis? Why do you think she chose to place it there?
2. Downes offers a personal anecdote from her seminar on gender, sexuality, and disability. How does this example support her argument? What other information from the seminar could she have included?
3. In paragraph 12, Downes says the administration at the University of Chicago "is stacking bricks in its institutional wall to avoid engaging with their real concerns." To what logical fallacy is she referring? Why does Downes imply that the university might actually prefer to take on the wrong issues?
4. How would Downes's essay be different if she structured it as a Rogerian argument? What changes would she have to make? Do you think this strategy would be more or less effective than the one she uses?
5. How does Downes use transitions to move readers through her essay? Where might additional transitions have helped you follow her argument more easily?

Journal Entry

How do you define "free speech"? Does this term have a different meaning on college campuses than it does in the "real world"?

Writing Workshop

1. According to Downes, "support systems can be a lifeline in the tumultuous environment of college, and are important precisely because they encourage a free exchange of ideas" (6). She also says, "Civic discourse in this country has become pretty ugly, so maybe it's not surprising that students are trying to create ways to have compassionate, civil dialogue" (7). How do you respond to these statements? Do you think civic discourse has become "ugly"? Do you think the support systems Downes outlines are the solution? Write an essay in which you agree or disagree with Downes's point.
2. **Working with Sources.** According to Downes, the University of Chicago "hired a provost who specializes in corporate crisis management and dealing with 'activist pressure.'" Do some research on the field of corporate crisis management. Then, write an essay explaining why a provost with this focus would or would not be a benefit for the school. Be sure to document all references to your sources and to include a works-cited page. (See Chapter 18 for information on MLA documentation.)
3. **Working with Sources.** Downes agrees that "there are certainly legitimate debates to be had over speech in academic settings" (13). Do some research on one of these other "legitimate debates," and write an argument for why this issue would have been a stronger focus for administrators at the University of Chicago. Include quotations from your research to support your argument and document them in a works-cited page. (See Chapter 18 for information on MLA documentation.)

Combining the Patterns

Where does Downes use **definition** in this essay? How do these definitions support her main argument?

Thematic Connections

SHANNON PALUS

The Latest Study on Trigger Warnings Finally Convinced Me They're Not Worth It

Shannon Palus is a staff writer at *Slate* who often covers science. Previously, she was a writer for *Wirecutter*, a product-review website owned by the *New York Times*. Palus's work has also appeared in *Scientific American, Discover, The Atlantic*, and other magazines. She earned her undergraduate degree from McGill University.

Background on parental advisories and the movie ratings system In some ways, trigger warnings resemble the ratings systems that are used for movies and television shows. For movies, the current rating system — which ranges from G (for general audiences) to R (for viewers seventeen or older) — was established in 1968 by the Motion Picture Association of America. These ratings replaced the complex and fussy moral judgments of the Hays Code, a set of guidelines that operated from 1934 to 1968, with a rating system that allows audiences — especially parents — to decide for themselves what is appropriate and what is not. Similarly, the TV Parental Guidelines, a television rating system, provides guidance on sexual content, violence, and profanity in television programs. This rating system, proposed by the U.S. Congress in 1996 and adopted by networks in 1997, is used by most broadcast and cable networks. It requires icons indicating content to appear at the beginning of all rated programs. According to the TV Parental Guidelines website, 77 percent of parents use the ratings system to inform their viewing choices.

1   "Trigger warnings just don't help," Payton Jones, a clinical psychology doctoral student at Harvard, tweeted alongside a preprint of his new paper. He further explained that the paper actually suggests that trigger warnings might even be *harmful*.

2   When I saw the tweet, my gut reaction was that Jones was wrong. I have been for trigger warnings even before the Year of the Trigger Warning, which according to *Slate* was 2013. Opponents of trigger warnings tend to argue that they are an unnecessary concession that only serves to further coddle already sheltered college students. I figure they might be a good way to help people with mental injuries such as post-traumatic stress disorder stay safer as they move around the world, the same way that a person with a broken leg uses crutches. But after considering Jones' paper, and chatting with him, I've been convinced that we'd do better to save the minimal effort it takes to affix trigger warnings to college reading assignments or put up signs outside of theater productions and apply it to more effective efforts to care for one another.

Research that trigger warnings might not be all that helpful has been mounting over a few studies, including the one that Jones and his colleagues published last year titled "Trigger Warning: Empirical Evidence Ahead." Yes, that title is trollish, but here is what they did: They had a few hundred participants read several passages, some of which were potentially disturbing. Half

> "Research that trigger warnings might not be all that helpful has been mounting."

3

received no heads up before the passages, and half got a label ahead of the iffy ones that read: "TRIGGER WARNING: The passage you are about to read contains disturbing content and may trigger an anxiety response, especially in those who have a history of trauma." The results suggested that trigger warnings could actually help *generate* anxiety, thus making them counterproductive. But there was a major limitation in that study: It didn't focus on people who had experienced trauma. Two studies written up in the *New York Times* in March had similar limitations (those both concluded that trigger warnings didn't do anything, good or bad).

So what about people who actually might be, you know, triggered by the   4
material? Jones' latest paper addresses just that question. The methods are the same as the 2018 paper, but with a pool of 451 participants who had experienced trauma. (A consent form required for ethical purposes did require that participants acknowledge that they would be reading emotional material, Jones told me, which is sort of a trigger warning all on its own but a required step of the process.) In this population, trigger warnings still failed to lessen the emotional distress from reading a passage. The authors also found evidence, they wrote, that trigger warnings "countertherapeutically reinforce survivors' view of their trauma as central to their identity." Though more evidence is needed to say for sure, their research suggests that trigger warnings could be actively harmful to the very people for whom they are meant.

I then wondered if trigger warnings might help folks simply avoid the trig-   5
gering material, a sort of opt-out system for people who aren't up for dealing with it. But the evidence on whether people actually avoid material based on trigger warnings is mixed, Jones outlines in the paper. It could be that most people who have been through trauma see trigger warnings and plow ahead regardless. If they do end up avoiding the material and the associated adverse reaction, that's not a good thing, either. "Cognitive avoidance is really counterproductive," psychologist Darby Saxbe told Katy Waldman for a 2016 *Slate* story on the then-current science of trigger warnings, a point Jones also made to me. I know this extremely well from my days avoiding public speaking: Having an anxious reaction, and living to tell the tale, is actually an important part of learning to live with one's brain.

That's not to say that people who have experienced trauma should be left   6
on their own to have that panicked response and just get over it. "Rather than issuing trigger warnings, universities can best serve students by facilitating access to effective and proven treatments for P.T.S.D. and other mental health problems," Richard McNally, a Harvard psychologist and co-author on the

paper with Jones, wrote in the *New York Times* in 2016. He argued that emotional reactions to assigned readings were "a signal that students need to prioritize their mental health and obtain evidence-based, cognitive-behavioral therapies that will help them overcome P.T.S.D." In other words, if you feel you need a trigger warning, maybe what you really need is better medical care.

My last justification: Could trigger warnings simply be important because 7
they signal that you are in a space where your feelings and mental health needs are going to be respected and taken seriously? "I don't think trigger warnings are the best way to do that," Jones told me. "Making a statement to that effect sends the same signal." It could also help build more broadly inclusive spaces. Teachers and professors could make a general announcement about the atmosphere they are hoping to cultivate at the beginning of a class. Colleges could take requests for trigger warnings as a sign that they need to bolster access to mental health professionals. Theaters could find a way to offer people the explicit option to gracefully step out and reenter, no questions asked, for any kind of medical need.

There are other problems with trigger warnings. Even if they did work, 8
how would we go about issuing them for all possible triggers? Different people have different triggers, which are based on personal experiences and may or may not be connected to what the average person considers disturbing or explicit. "My experience is that the audience can do a better job than I can at figuring out what kind of content will upset them by reading the headline than I ever could randomly guessing what blog posts count as triggering," Amanda Marcotte wrote in *Slate* in 2013. If you're still wondering if a polite heads up might be in order — one that doesn't invoke the language about anxiety that the explicit warning in Jones' study does — then consider that we do live in a world with headlines, and book jackets, and movie previews, and graphic content advisories. The world naturally comprises signals about what we are about to experience.

Trigger warnings may have been developed under incredibly well-meaning 9
pretenses, but they have now failed to prove useful in study after study. Like many a random supplement, trigger warnings are probably useless for most people and potentially, though not definitively, a little harmful to some. So, with no clear upside, why risk it? Perhaps because it is certainly easy to issue one and feel like you're doing something helpful. Just remember that this might come at the expense of doing something that would actually help.

· · ·

Comprehension

1. Palus describes the title of a research study as "trollish" (3). What does she mean?
2. What did the researchers who published "Trigger Warning: Empirical Evidence Ahead" discover during their study? What effects did trigger warnings have on subjects?

3. What is "cognitive avoidance" (5), and what are its effects? How is it related to trigger warnings?
4. What does Palus think should take the place of trigger warnings? Does her proposal seem realistic? Why or why not?
5. In her last paragraph, Palus compares trigger warnings to "a random [nutritional] supplement." Does this comparison make sense? What other comparison could she have made?

Purpose and Audience

1. Where does Palus state her thesis? Why do you think she states it where she does?
2. Does Palus expect her audience to be in favor of trigger warnings? How do you know?
3. What is Palus's purpose in writing this essay? What does she want to accomplish?

Style and Structure

1. Palus begins her essay with a quotation from a doctoral student at Harvard. Why does she use this strategy for her introduction? What other strategy could she have used?
2. What rhetorical appeal does Palus make in paragraph 2: *logos*, *ethos*, or *pathos*? Explain.
3. In paragraph 2, Palus compares trigger warnings to crutches. Does this comparison make sense? What does she want to accomplish with this comparison?
4. Where does Palus address opposing arguments? How effectively does she refute them?
5. Does Palus make concessions to those with opposing points of view? If so, how do these concessions affect your view of her argument?
6. **Vocabulary Project.** Throughout her essay, Palus uses informal language — for example, "gut reaction" (2), "I figure" (2), and "folks" (5). What does she hope to accomplish with this strategy?

Journal Entry

In paragraph 6, Palus says, "In other words, if you feel you need a trigger warning, maybe what really need is better medical care." Do you agree or disagree with her statement? Do you think she is being too glib? Explain.

Writing Workshop

1. **Working with Sources.** What is your own position on trigger warnings? Are they a reasonable response to provocative texts and images, or do they stifle free speech and "coddle" students? To support your points, use your own experiences as well as material from the essays in this casebook. (You may also want to speak to instructors who use trigger warnings.) Be sure to

document all references to your sources and to include a works-cited page. (See Chapter 18 for information on MLA documentation.)

2. In this essay, Palus describes the way new information caused her to change her mind about trigger warnings. Have you ever had this experience? Write an argumentative essay organized in a similar way: state your thesis, and then trace the process of changing your mind. Keep in mind that you will be trying to change the reader's mind about the subject as well.

3. **Working with Sources.** How do you respond to those who view contemporary college students as coddled and sheltered? Do you think this characterization is fair? Write an argument that takes a position on this stereotype. Use material from the other essays in this casebook to support your points. Be sure to document all references to your sources and to include a works-cited page. (See Chapter 18 for information on MLA documentation.)

Combining the Patterns

How does Palus use **classification and division** to structure this essay? Is this pattern an effective way of organizing her argument?

Thematic Connections

- "Should Driverless Cars Kill Their Own Passengers to Save a Pedestrian?" (page 219)
- "Call Me 'They'" (page 237)
- "Ten Ways We Get the Odds Wrong" (page 242)
- "The Only Individual Action That Matters Is Voting for People Who Care about Climate Change" (page 595)

BEN HEINE

Censorship (Illustration)

©Ben Heine

Reading Images

1. What point is this visual making about free speech? Who is its intended audience?
2. How do the words and images work together to communicate the central message about free speech?
3. Does the visual appeal mainly to logic or to emotion?
4. What words could you substitute for the ones in the visual? Would your words be more or less effective? Explain.

Journal Entry

Do you think the visual is effective? Is it likely to have the intended effect on its intended audience?

Thematic Connections

- "Call Me 'They'" (page 237)
- "How to Spot Fake News" (page 289)
- "Sex, Lies, and Conversation" (page 408)
- "Patterns" (page 473)

How Can We Stem the Tide of Gun Violence?

Vesnaandjic/iStock/Getty Images

Despite concerns about gun violence, unrelated crises can still lead Americans to arm themselves. At the onset of the recent COVID-19 pandemic, U.S. background checks spiked, indicating a surge in gun sales.

·   ·   ·

Mass shootings in the United States have occurred for centuries. More recently, however, they seem to have become a permanent fixture of our lives—a situation amplified by social media as well as by traditional news outlets. Seven of the ten worst mass shootings in American history have occurred in the last 15 years, and just mentioning the place names brings to mind the horrific events now associated with them: Columbine. Virginia Tech. Fort Hood. Aurora. Sandy Hook. Orlando. Las Vegas. Parkland. El Paso. Dayton. School shootings have had an especially strong impact—and provoked very strong responses. Now, even kindergartners regularly practice lockdown- and shelter-in-place drills, while schools consider design features to make them safer in active-shooter situations, and businesses promote bullet-proof backpacks.

Two things are worth keeping in mind. First, violent crime has been declining over the last three decades. Second, the majority of gun-related deaths occur not in mass shootings but in suicides (23,854 per year) or individual incidents involving handguns (10,982). Still, the rate of gun deaths in the United States remains far higher than that of other developed countries, such as Australia, France, Canada, and Germany. Some observers have identified a range of factors that might be contributing to the high levels of gun violence, from violent films and video games to mental illness. Others, however, point out that countries with lower levels of gun violence have access to much of the same violent media and that the prevalence of mental illnesses is not determined by national boundaries. Many people believe that America's relationship with guns and gun culture is unique in that gun ownership is seen by many as a fundamental right established in the Second Amendment of the Constitution. Indeed, much of the political debate stems from differing interpretations of that Amendment, which says: "A well-regulated Militia, being necessary to the security of a free State, the right of the people to keep and bear Arms, shall not be infringed." Legal scholars, politicians, gun-rights supporters, and gun-regulation activists all struggle with the meaning of this text, even as the U.S. Supreme Court has taken a broader view of the Amendment and struck down state and local laws that restrict guns. One thing is certain: hundreds of millions of guns are now in circulation in the United States, and no legislation or other solution is likely to make guns—or gun violence—disappear in the near future.

The four essays in this casebook explore this issue from a variety of viewpoints. In "Guns Are the Problem," German Lopez sees no mystery in why there is so much gun violence in the United States: "What is unique about the U.S. is that it makes it so easy for people with any motive or problem to obtain a gun." In "6 Real Ways We Can Reduce Gun Violence in America," Sean Gregory and Chris Wilson argue for a shift in thinking about gun violence that would make addressing the problem a public health issue rather than a contentious political issue. William V. Glastris Jr. ("A Real Long-Term Solution to Gun Violence") proposes a more radical solution: nationalizing the firearms industry. As he writes, "The scope of our imagination ought to match the scope of the epidemic." Finally, journalist Clifton Leaf examines how Australia's gun policies have differed from the U.S., and have been met with great success.

GERMAN LOPEZ

Guns Are the Problem

A senior correspondent at the news and opinion website *Vox*, German Lopez's writing focuses on criminal justice, guns, and drugs. Prior to working at *Vox*, he covered local, city, and state politics at the *CityBeat Cincinnati*. Lopez received his undergraduate degree from the University of Cincinnati.

Background on gun laws in other countries As Lopez points out, the United States is unique in its approach to regulating firearms, in part because of the legal tradition originating in the Second Amendment of the U.S. Constitution. A survey of other countries shows a variety of regulatory regimes. In Canada, which has relatively high gun ownership per capita (although nowhere near the U.S. rate), federal laws require all gun owners to be at least eighteen years old, to obtain a license (which includes a background check), and to take a public safety course. Japan has some of the strictest firearms regulations in the world, which may help explain its low rate of gun-related homicides. That country's laws ban all guns except shotguns, air guns, and firearms related to other, specific purposes. Essentially, only the military and the police have access to legal handguns and rifles in Japan. The civilians who do own guns are subject to instruction, registration, and inspections. In the United Kingdom, which also has a relatively low rate of gun-related deaths, most guns are prohibited, and those who do own firearms go through a rigorous process to obtain a license. Moreover, anyone who had been convicted of a crime cannot handle a gun for five years thereafter. It is worth noting that the United Kingdom, Norway, and Australia all instituted stricter regulations after terrible mass shootings. For example, the 1996 Port Arthur massacre, in which a mentally ill man killed thirty-five people and injured twenty-three others, led Australia to radically reshape its gun laws. Not only did new legislation prohibit automatic and semiautomatic rifles (along with increased restrictions on handguns), but the government also sponsored a gun buyback program that took a significant percentage of assault weapons out of circulation.

1 Mass shootings in America seem like a never-ending nightmare.

2 On Saturday, a shooting in El, Paso, Texas, killed 20 people and injured 26 more. On Sunday, a shooting in Dayton, Ohio, killed at least 10 and injured 26 more. The weekend before, a shooting in Gilroy, California, killed four and wounded 13 others, while yet another shooting in Chippewa Falls, Wisconsin, killed six and injured two.

3 That doesn't even account for the average 100-plus gun deaths that aren't part of mass shootings but happen every day in the U.S.

> "Why does this keep happening?"

4 Why does this keep happening? In the aftermath of a shooting, many Americans focus on the shooter's motive. That leads to some legitimate questions, like whether the gunman in El Paso was motivated by white

supremacy and racism that President Donald Trump has enabled, or what role, if any, mental illness played. It's also led to some less valid contributions, such as House Minority Leader Kevin McCarthy and Texas Lt. Gov. Dan Patrick's bizarre comments suggesting violent video games are to blame.

But the reason for the ceaseless death toll is simpler: It ultimately comes down to America's lax access to a large supply of guns.   5

Many factors can of course play a role in any individual shooting. But when you want to explain why America sees so many of these mass shootings in general — more than 250 so far in 2019, by one estimate — and why America suffers more gun violence than other developed nations, none of these factors gives a satisfying answer. Only guns are the common variable.   6

To put it another way: America doesn't have a monopoly on racism, sexism, other kinds of bigotry, mental illness, or violent video games. All of those things exist in countries across the world, many with much less gun violence. What is unique about the U.S. is that it makes it so easy for people with any motive or problem to obtain a gun.   7

America's Gun Problem, Briefly Explained

It comes down to two basic problems.   8

First, America has uniquely weak gun laws. Other developed nations at the very least require one or more background checks and almost always something more rigorous beyond that to get a gun, from specific training courses to rules for locking up firearms to more arduous licensing requirements to specific justifications, besides self-defense, for owning a gun.   9

In the U.S., even a background check isn't an absolute requirement; the current federal law is riddled with loopholes and hampered by poor enforcement, so there are many ways around even a basic background check. And if a state enacts stricter measures than federal laws, someone can simply cross state lines to buy guns in a jurisdiction with looser rules. There are simply very few barriers, if any, to getting a gun in the U.S.   10

Second, the U.S. has a ton of guns. It has far more than not just other developed nations but any other country, period. In 2017, the estimated number of civilian-owned firearms in the U.S. was 120.5 guns per 100 residents, meaning there were more firearms than people. The world's second-ranked country was Yemen, a quasi-failed state torn by civil war, where there were 52.8 guns per 100 residents, according to an analysis from the Small Arms Survey.   11

Both of these factors come together to make it uniquely easy for someone with violent intent to find a firearm, allowing them to carry out a horrific shooting.   12

This is borne out in the statistics, which show America has far more gun violence than other developed nations. The U.S. has nearly six times the gun homicide rate of Canada, more than seven times that of Sweden, and nearly 16 times that of Germany, according to United Nations data for 2012 compiled by the Guardian. (These gun deaths are one reason America has a much higher overall homicide rate, which includes non-gun deaths, than the rest of the developed world.)   13

Homicides by firearm per 1 million people
In advanced countries according to the Human Development Index.
Numbers are for 2012.

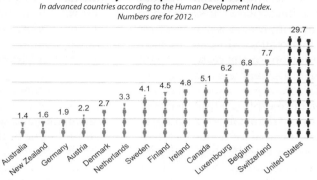

SOURCE: UNODC, Small Arms Survey, via The Guardian.

If having so many guns around actually made the U.S. safer, as the National   14
Rifle Association and pro-gun politicians claim, America would have one of
the lowest rates of gun violence in the world. But the statistics suggest that, in
fact, the opposite is true.

The research, compiled by the Harvard School of Public Health's Injury   15
Control Research Center, is also pretty clear: After controlling for variables
such as socioeconomic factors and other crime, places with more guns
have more gun deaths. Researchers have found this to be true not just with
homicides but also with suicides (which in recent years were around
60 percent of U.S. gun deaths), domestic violence, violence against police,
and mass shootings.

As a breakthrough analysis by UC Berkeley's Franklin Zimring and   16
Gordon Hawkins in the 1990s found, it's not even that the U.S. has more crime
than other developed countries. This chart, based on data from Jeffrey
Swanson at Duke University, shows that the U.S. is not an outlier when it
comes to overall crime:

CRIME in 15 industrialized countries
12-month prevalence rates for 11 index-crimes (year 2000)

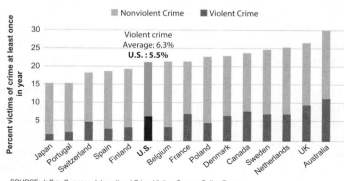

SOURCE: Jeffrey Swanson. International Crime Victims Survey. Gallup Europe.

Instead, the U.S. appears to have more lethal violence—and that's driven   17
in large part by the prevalence of guns.

"A series of specific comparisons of the death rates from property crime   18
and assault in New York City and London show how enormous differences in
death risk can be explained even while general patterns are similar," Zimring
and Hawkins wrote. "A preference for crimes of personal force and the willingness and ability to use guns in robbery make similar levels of property crime 54
times as deadly in New York City as in London."

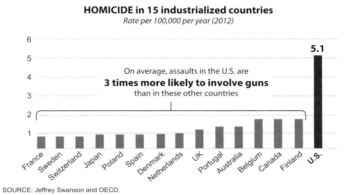

HOMICIDE in 15 industrialized countries
Rate per 100,000 per year (2012)

On average, assaults in the U.S. are
3 times more likely to involve guns
than in these other countries

SOURCE: Jeffrey Swanson and OECD.

This is in many ways intuitive: People of every country get into argu-   19
ments and fights with friends, family, and peers. Every country has extremists and other hateful individuals. But in the U.S. it's much more likely that
someone who's angry or hateful will be able to pull out a gun and kill someone, because there are so many guns around and few barriers to getting the
weapons.

Researchers have found that stricter gun laws could help. A 2016 review of   20
130 studies in 10 countries, published in *Epidemiologic Reviews,* found that new
legal restrictions on owning and purchasing guns tended to be followed by a
drop in gun violence—a strong indicator that restricting access to guns can
save lives. A review of the U.S. evidence by RAND also linked some gun control
measures, including background checks, to reduced injuries and deaths. A
growing body of evidence, from Johns Hopkins researchers, also supports laws
that require a license to buy and own guns.

That doesn't mean that bigots and extremists will never be able to carry   21
out a shooting in places with stricter gun laws. Even the strictest gun laws can't
prevent every shooting.

Guns are also not the only contributor to violence. Other factors include,   22
for example, poverty, urbanization, alcohol consumption, and the strength of
criminal justice systems.

But when researchers control for other confounding variables, they have   23
found time and again that America's loose access to guns is a major reason the
U.S. is so much worse in terms of gun violence than its developed peers.

So America, with its lax laws and abundance of firearms, makes it uniquely   24
easy for people to commit horrific gun violence. Until the U.S. confronts that
issue, it will continue to see mass shooting after mass shooting.

•   •   •

Comprehension

1. What important distinction between the United States and other countries
   does Lopez make in paragraph 6?
2. What "two basic problems" (8) account for the frequency of gun violence in
   the United States compared with other countries?
3. According to Lopez in paragraph 14, the National Rifle Association claims
   that guns make the country safer. How does he dispute that argument?
4. In paragraph 14, Lopez cites research indicating that "the U.S. is not an outlier when it comes to overall crime." Why is this information important to
   Lopez's argument about guns and gun violence?

Purpose and Audience

1. How do the first three paragraphs establish the premises of Lopez's
   argument?
2. What is the purpose of paragraph 3 in this essay? Why does Lopez include
   it? How is it related to the essay's overall purpose?
3. What is the thesis of this essay? Is it stated explicitly, or is it implied?
4. This essay was published in *Vox,* an online publication that (in its own
   words) seeks to "explain the news." Does this essay achieve that goal?
   If so, how?

Style and Structure

1. Where in the essay does Lopez qualify his argument? Do you find these
   qualifications necessary and adequate? Why or why not?
2. How would describe the writer's tone and style, given the argument and subject matter of the essay? Is Lopez objective, biased, angry, or ironic? Point to
   a specific example that illustrates your description.
3. **Vocabulary Project.** In paragraph 19, the writer describes the results of a
   gun violence study as "intuitive." What does this word mean? What are the
   benefits and drawbacks of data and arguments that are intuitive?
4. What strategy does the writer use in the conclusion of the essay? Is it
   effective? Explain.

Journal Entry

Discussions of gun violence often center on the tension between concerns about
preventing violence and concerns about maintaining individual rights. Which of
these two issues concerns you more? Why?

Writing Workshop

1. **Working with Sources.** In paragraph 14, Lopez refers to the National Rifle Association and "pro-gun politicians," both of whom generally argue for liberalizing gun laws. What is your position on this issue? Do you think guns should be subjected to stricter regulation or less regulation? After consulting other essays in this casebook for background information and additional perspectives, write an argumentative essay expressing your own view on the question of liberalizing gun laws. Be sure to provide parenthetical references to source material and to include a works-cited page. (See Chapter 18 for information on MLA documentation.)

2. **Working with Sources.** Lopez establishes that the problem of gun violence in the United States is a unique phenomenon. How would you propose to solve this problem? Write an argumentative essay that makes three specific proposals for addressing gun violence. Refer to essays in this casebook as well as to other sources, and be sure to include parenthetical references for all source material as well as a works-cited page. (See Chapter 18 for information on MLA documentation.)

3. Today's millennials, generally described as those born between 1981 and 1996, grew up at a time of horrifying and sensational mass shootings, beginning with Columbine High School in 1999. Today's college students have grown up against a backdrop of the more recent shootings cited by Lopez. How do you think these shootings have shaped your own political views, perspectives, and attitudes, as well as those of others your age? Write an argumentative essay that explores this question.

Combining the Patterns

In what sense is this a **cause-and-effect** essay? Why is that pattern of development important to Lopez's argument and purpose?

Thematic Connections

- "My First Police Stop" (page 117)
- "How to Tell a Mother Her Child Is Dead" (page 275)
- "Did Free Pens Cause the Opioid Crisis?" (page 332)
- "A Peaceful Woman Explains Why She Carries a Gun" (page 348)

From the pages of

SEAN GREGORY AND CHRIS WILSON

6 Real Ways We Can Reduce Gun Violence in America

Sean Gregory is a senior writer at *TIME* magazine and an adjunct professor at Columbia University's School of Journalism. Before working for *TIME,* Gregory wrote for the Associated Press and for *Sports Illustrated* magazine. He also worked in finance. He earned his undergraduate degree from Princeton University and his master's from Columbia University's Graduate School of Journalism. Chris Wilson is an interactive graphics editor and a director of data journalism at TIME.com. Previously, he was a columnist for Yahoo! News and a senior editor at *Slate.* Wilson received his undergraduate degree from the University of Virginia.

Background on mass shootings in the twentieth century Although Americans might be inclined to see mass shootings (defined as shootings in which four or more people are killed) as a contemporary phenomenon, such incidents are not unique to our time. In the twentieth century, the first mass shooting occurred in 1903, when troubled Spanish-American war veteran Gilbert Twigg killed nine people, including himself, with a 12-gauge shotgun at a Winfield, Kansas, concert. Similar events occurred in every subsequent decade, including the Kelayres massacre of 1934, in which a Democratic political parade was attacked, and Howard Unruh's 1949 "Walk of Death" in Camden, New Jersey: Unruh, enraged by disputes with his neighbors and suffering from psychological problems, killed thirteen people, including a two-year-old boy. Unruh is notable for fitting the archetype that is familiar to us today: the frustrated, aggrieved, and isolated lone wolf who attacks a neighborhood, a workplace, or a school. Indeed, several twentieth-century shootings occurred on school and college campuses. One of the best-known took place at the University of Texas in 1966, when Charles Whitman used multiple firearms to kill fourteen people on campus, many of them shot from the observation deck of the school's Main Building tower. Shootings took place at a somewhat greater frequency in the 1970s, 1980s, and 1990s. The most shocking, perhaps, was the 1999 Columbine High School massacre, in which two students, Eric Harris and Dylan Kiebold, shot and killed twelve students and one teacher — and injured many others — before killing themselves.

Columbine. Sandy Hook. Virginia Tech. Las Vegas. The names of America's mass shootings have become as hauntingly familiar as the responses to them—a now predictable cycle of thoughts and prayers, calls for new gun laws, debate over their need and then, usually, little else. Until the next one.

> "No other developed country has such a high rate of gun violence."

1

No other developed country has such a high rate of gun violence. A March 2016 study in the American Journal of Medicine found that Americans are 25 times more likely to die from gun homicide than people in other wealthy countries. There are commonsense steps we can take to reduce that toll, but they require acknowledging certain truths. The right to bear arms is enshrined in the Constitution, and there are approximately 265 million privately owned guns in the U.S., according to researchers from Northeastern and Harvard universities. Any sensible discussion about America's gun-violence problem must acknowledge that guns aren't going away. "We have to admit to ourselves that in a country with so many guns, progress is going to be measured incrementally," says Jeff Swanson, a professor of psychiatry and behavioral sciences at Duke University School of Medicine.

2

What does that mean in practice? It requires a shift in our collective perspective. While legislators in statehouses and Washington can pass laws that may—or may not—help, the most effective way to tackle our national problem is to stop thinking of gun control as a political battle and instead see gun violence as a public-health issue. "The public-health model says you intervene in as many places as possible," says Dr. Liza Gold, a clinical professor of psychiatry at Georgetown University School of Medicine. "There are no magic solutions. There are a lot of solutions."

3

Here are six steps that we can take to reduce America's shameful gun-violence problem.

4

1. Buying a gun should be like buying a car

The reduction in U.S. motor-vehicle deaths over the past 50 years is one of the great triumphs of public-health intervention. Safer cars, stronger seat-belt laws, and fewer teenage drivers have helped reduce car fatalities, which dropped from 33.5 deaths per billion miles traveled in 1975 to 11.8 in 2016. Gun deaths have increased steadily since 2009 and are now nearly as lethal as traffic accidents, according to the Centers for Disease Control and Prevention (CDC).

5

Lawmakers can learn lessons from auto safety. To start, they can put in effect more rigorous requirements for owning firearms. "For the most part, it is much easier to be a legal gun owner in America than it is to be a legal driver," says David Hemenway, director of the Injury Control Research Center at the Harvard T.H. Chan School of Public Health.

6

Some measures, like Walmart's lifting its minimum age for purchasing a gun from 18 to 21, may sound good but likely won't do much to combat gun

7

violence. According to FBI reports, handguns were responsible for 90 percent of homicides in 2016. Walmart sells handguns only in Alaska.

A more effective policy would require every buyer, of any age, to obtain a license that includes a registration of all purchases and at least a modest training program. According to the State Firearms Law project, just seven states require a permit to possess a gun of any kind. A 2014 study in the Journal of Urban Health found that Missouri's 2007 repeal of its permit-to-purchase handgun law was associated with a 25 percent increase in firearms homicide rates. 8

2. Pass gun laws that actually reduce gun violence

Not all gun laws are created equal. The military-grade rifles used in many mass shootings may dominate the political debate, but they account for less than 5 percent of homicides. Meanwhile, research published in *JAMA Internal Medicine* in early March found that strong firearms laws in a state, such as background checks for all private sales and restrictions on multiple purchases, were associated with lower rates of gun homicides. 9

Researchers are also finding links between right-to-carry laws—which require governments to issue concealed-carry permits to citizens who meet certain requirements—and spikes in firearms crime. A 2017 National Bureau of Economic Research working paper estimates that 10 years after the adoption of right-to-carry laws, violent crime is 13 percent to 15 percent higher than it would have been without those policies. 10

Another measure that has attracted lawmakers' attention is extreme-risk protection orders, also known as gun-violence restraining orders. These allow family members or law enforcement to petition a court to temporarily bar an at-risk person from buying firearms. Police may also be permitted to confiscate their guns. Before the shooting in Parkland, Fla., California, Oregon, Washington, Indiana, and Connecticut all had some version on the books. Florida adopted one on March 9. 11

Evidence suggests that these orders save lives. A 2017 study in *Law and Contemporary Problems* estimated that in Connecticut, every 10 to 20 gun seizures averted a suicide. In California, the San Diego city attorney's office has issued 20 gun-violence restraining orders since mid-December. In one instance, an employee of a car dealership had praised the Las Vegas gunman and said that if he were fired, he'd return to the dealership with a gun. After the city obtained a gun-violence restraining order, the man surrendered a semiautomatic rifle. 12

3. Doctors can help reduce gun violence. Let them

Doctors can play a key role in educating families about gun safety, particularly when it comes to keeping guns out of the hands of young children. Studies show that some 3-year-olds are strong enough to shoot a gun. By the time they reach school age, about 75 percent can fire a weapon. As a result, the American Academy of Pediatrics (AAP) recommends that pediatricians start asking about firearms in the home when children are 3 years old and curious about the world—and objects—around them. 13

But some states have sought to prevent doctors from talking about guns   14
with patients, even though they present a health risk. A 2011 Florida law
threatened physicians with suspending their medical license and fines if they
inquired about and discussed a family's firearms. Doctors sued, claiming that
the statute violated their First Amendment rights. A federal appeals court settled the "Docs v. Glocks" case in February, siding with the physicians and
overturning the law. Minnesota, Missouri, and Montana also limit doctors'
ability to address guns with patients in different ways.

Doctors say such gag laws and restrictions hamper their ability to discuss   15
issues that can affect patient safety; after all, they talk about the dangers of smoking or of not wearing a seat belt in a car. "My role is not to be judgmental," says
Dr. Joseph Wright, chair of the committee on emergency medicine for the AAP.
"We are asking about and providing information about what science has demonstrated as the most effective ways to keep children safe in homes with guns."

4. Invest in smart gun technology

"If we can set it up so you can't unlock your phone unless you've got the   16
right fingerprint," President Barack Obama asked in January 2013, "why can't
we do the same thing for our guns?" More than five years and too many tragedies later, guns aren't much smarter now than they were at the time of the Sandy
Hook school massacre. In fact, no truly smart guns are on the market in the U.S.

All the pieces appear to be in place. The safety technology is available.   17
Entrepreneurs have introduced products that use biometrics to identify a
weapon's rightful owner while locking it for everyone else. Such smart guns
may not prevent mass shootings with firearms purchased legally. But they can
prevent crimes or suicides with weapons owned by somebody else. They can
also cut down on accidental shootings. According to the CDC, an average of
500 people are shot to death unintentionally every year.

If the benefits seems obvious, why aren't smart guns available? Some gun   18
owners worry that the technology will fail when they need it most, like during a
home invasion. Others fear government overreach. New Jersey passed a law in
2002 requiring that the state's retailers sell only personalized, or smart, guns
within three years of their being available for sale elsewhere in the U.S. The
mandate backfired, mobilizing opposition to smart guns from the firearms
lobby and stunting investment in the technology. Similarly, when Smith &
Wesson, one of the largest handgun manufacturers in the U.S., agreed to
develop smart-gun technology in the wake of the Columbine school shooting
in 2000, the National Rifle Association condemned the company. Gun owners
boycotted, and sales plummeted. No major gun manufacturers have invested
in the technology since.

In early March, Smith & Wesson's parent company, American Outdoor   19
Brands Corp., reaffirmed its stance. "We are a manufacturing company, not a
technology company," it wrote in a response to the investment-management
firm BlackRock, which had inquired about the gunmaker's plans to address
safety concerns.

Support for smart guns, however, could be building. A 2016 study from   20
Johns Hopkins University found that almost 60 percent of Americans

considering purchasing a new handgun would be willing to make it a smart gun. "The time for smart guns," says Stephen Teret, founding director of the school's Center for Gun Policy and Research, "is now." Such numbers mean that smart guns could be a prime market opportunity. "This isn't just a great gun-safety mission," says Gareth Glaser, CEO of LodeStar Firearms, which is developing a smart gun. "It could be a hell of a business."

5. Eliminate funding restrictions on gun violence research

According to a 2017 study published in the *Journal of the American Medical Association*, gun violence should have received $1.4 billion in federal research money from 2004 to 2015, on the basis of mortality rates and funding levels for other leading causes of death. Instead, such projects received $22 million — just 1.6 percent of the projected amount. Gun violence received 5.3 percent of the federal research funds allocated for motor-vehicle accidents, even though they kill similar numbers of Americans per year.

"We know far less about gun violence as a cause of injury and death than we do about almost every medical problem," says Dr. Elinore Kaufman, chief resident in surgery at NewYork-Presbyterian/Weill Cornell Medical Center.

There is a reason for this lack of knowledge. In 1996, Congress, with a push from the NRA, passed the Dickey Amendment — named after its author, former Republican Representative Jay Dickey from Arkansas — which mandated that no CDC funds could be spent on research that "may be used to advocate or promote gun control." Congress also cut $2.6 million from the CDC budget, which was equal to the federal agency's expenditure on firearm-injury research the prior year. The message to researchers was clear: study the gun problem at your own risk. "The effect of the Dickey Amendment was beyond chilling," says Dr. Eric Fleegler, a pediatric emergency physician and health services researcher at Boston Children's Hospital.

The restrictions on research funding have had devastating consequences on what we know — and what we don't. In early March, the Rand Corp., a non-partisan think tank, released a sweeping two-year examination of U.S. gun laws. The main takeaway: there's a dearth of evidence on their impact. Few studies, for example, test the argument that gun restrictions thwart people's ability to defend themselves. "There are thousands of studies waiting to be performed," says Fleegler. "But you can't do them because of the money." Toward the end of his life, even Dickey, who died in April 2017, said he regretted the amendment that bears his name.

Some states are trying to pick up the slack. California recently opened the nation's first state-funded firearms-violence research center, on the Sacramento campus of the University of California, Davis. Such investments are urgent as the failure to find answers carries a steep cost. "People are dead today," says Dr. Garen Wintemute, director of the new center, "as a result."

6. End legal immunity for gun manufacturers

Federal law offers the gun industry extraordinary protections. In 2005, Congress passed the Protection of Lawful Commerce in Arms Act, which shields gun manufacturers and sellers from civil claims brought by victims of gun violence. NRA CEO Wayne LaPierre hailed the law as the most significant piece of pro-gun legislation in 20 years.

No one benefits from frivolous lawsuits. But holding manufacturers liable   27
for the misuse of their products, experts say, would incentivize them to make firearms safer. "If pillows caused fatalities at that level, those companies would be bankrupt," says Fleegler of Boston Children's Hospital. "If there were 500 deaths a year associated with any consumer product, it would be banned, regulated, fixed. But here, nothing."

•   •   •

Comprehension

1. According to Gregory and Wilson, what fact must "any sensible" discussion (2) of gun laws and gun violence take into account?
2. In the writers' view, what is the most effective way to address the problem of gun violence? What shift in thinking does this strategy require?
3. What kinds of firearms tend to dominate the political debate? Why, according to the writers, is this focus a problem?
4. What role can doctors play in addressing gun violence?
5. The technology to create "smart guns," which only work for their owners and lock out other users, already exists. Why, then, do "smart guns" remain unavailable?
6. What is the "Dickey amendment," and what consequences has it had?

Purpose and Audience

1. How would you characterize the audience Gregory and Wilson are trying to reach? For example, are strong gun-rights advocates or Second Amendment absolutists likely to be swayed by their argument? Why or why not?
2. What is the essay's thesis? Where do the writers locate it? Why do they place it there?
3. How would you classify Gregory and Wilson's argument as inductive, deductive, or a combination of the two strategies? Explain.
4. Where do the writers use *logos*? *Pathos*? *Ethos*? What is the primary rhetorical appeal used in this essay?
5. Would you describe this essay as a **Rogerian argument**? Why or why not?

Style and Structure

1. Why do you think Gregory and Wilson structured their argument as a numbered list? What are the advantages and disadvantages of this organizing principle? Do the headings help the writers make their case, or are they unnecessary — or even distracting?
2. Do Gregory and Wilson address any counterarguments? If so, are their refutations convincing? Explain.

3. Gregory and Wilson propose an analogy between obtaining a car and obtaining a gun. How effective is this analogy? What are its limitations? How might a gun rights advocate respond to it?

4. **Vocabulary Project.** In paragraph 4, introducing their recommendations, Gregory and Wilson characterize our nation's gun-violence problem as "shameful." Is the word *shameful* appropriate here? Is it perhaps too strong? Not strong enough? Suggest some alternatives, and consider how they might change the point the writers are making here.

Journal Entry

In their introduction, Gregory and Wilson imply that we have become desensitized to mass shootings and gun violence. Do you agree?

Writing Workshop

1. **Working with Sources.** Gregory and Wilson propose six possible solutions they believe will help reduce gun violence. Choose one of these proposals to research further, considering how effective it would be, how feasible it would be to implement, and what obstacles it would have to overcome. Be sure to consider and refute opposing arguments and to include parenthetical references to source material and a works-cited page. (See Chapter 18 for information on MLA documentation.)

2. Gregory and Wilson claim that Americans must "stop thinking of gun control as a political battle and instead see gun violence as a public health issue" (3). Is this a realistic goal? Do you think the issues of gun rights, gun violence, and gun regulations can be removed from political battles? Write an essay that responds to the writers' recommendation — either agreeing with it or challenging it.

3. **Working with Sources.** Read all the selections in the casebook, and come up with your own three-point plan for reducing gun violence, supporting your claims with evidence and examples. Include parenthetical references to source material and a works-cited page. (See Chapter 18 for information on MLA documentation.)

Combining the Patterns

How do Gregory and Wilson use **exemplification** to support their argument? Do their examples support their main claims and generalizations? Would additional examples be helpful? If so, where?

Thematic Connections

- "Ten Ways We Get the Odds Wrong" (page 242)
- "What Causes Cancer? It's Complicated" (page 344)
- "Emmett Till and Tamir Rice, Sons of the Great Migration" (page 414)

WILLIAM V. GLASTRIS JR.

A Real Long-Term Solution to Gun Violence

William V. Glastris Jr. is a managing member at Evanston Partners, LLC, a private equity investment firm. A founding principal of Prospect Partners, LLC, he has spent nearly four decades as a private equity investor. Glastris is also a chairman of the board of the Fabretto Children's Foundation, a nonprofit organization that serves children in Nicaragua. He received his undergraduate degree from Northwestern University and his M.B.A. from Northwestern's Kellogg Graduate School of Management.

Background on gun deaths in the United States Although mass shootings understandably attract intense media attention, most gun deaths in the United States are not the result of such high-profile incidents. According to the Federal Bureau of Investigation and the Centers for Disease Control and Prevention, 39,773 people died from gun-related injuries in 2017 (the most recent year for which comprehensive data are available). Notably, however, suicides accounted for about 60 percent of all gun deaths (28,854), as has long been the case, and murders accounted for about 37 percent (14,542) of these deaths. (The rest involved law enforcement, were unintentional, or had unknown causes.) Total gun deaths in 2017 were the highest since 1968, but that is primarily because of a high number of suicides. In fact, gun murders have remained well below their 1993 peak of 18,253. This trend is consistent with an overall decline in violent crime over the last three decades. Still, the U.S. gun death rate remains higher than that of most other nations, particularly developed countries such as Canada, France, and Germany.

The debate about gun violence in America has fallen into a depressingly 1 familiar routine. After every horrendous mass shooting, like the recent one at the Tree of Life synagogue in Pittsburgh, or weekend spree of violence in Chicago, the media commences a few days of wall-to-wall coverage. Large numbers of Americans demand changes in gun laws. Experts debate various reforms on TV. When no changes are forthcoming, attention lags until the next mass shooting. Rinse and repeat.

There are two principal reasons why we are stuck in this painful rut. The 2 first is that the National Rifle Association, via its influence primarily within the Republican Party, has effective veto power over any gun legislation at the national level and in many states. The second is that the solutions that are typically discussed fail to match the scale of the problem. Banning military-style semiautomatic weapons, regulating magazine clips, closing the gun show loophole, and preventing people with domestic violence restraining orders from acquiring weapons might well reduce levels of gun violence — to some extent. But it is hard to argue that these reforms, even if they all went into effect, would do much more than put a modest dent in the problem, and for a simple reason: there are just too many guns floating around.

In total, Americans possess as many as 393 million guns—almost half of   3 all civilian-owned guns around the world—despite making up only 4.4 percent of the world's population. In such an environment, it's simply too easy for someone determined to do harm to get a gun. States with more guns experience more gun-related deaths, including homicides. According to the *American Journal of Public Health*, a 1 percent increase in a state's gun ownership rate equates to a roughly 1 percent increase in firearm homicides. States with the most guns also report the most completed suicides, which account for the majority of gun-related deaths. This is partly because guns make it much easier for people to kill themselves. Over 85 percent of suicides attempted with a firearm prove fatal. By contrast, the fatality rate of poison-related suicide attempts is 7.4 percent. For cutting, it's 5.1 percent. Gun violence did drop substantially in the 1990s before stabilizing—at a rate vastly higher than in any other developed country—during the first decade and a half of this century. But since 2014, gun violence rates have again spiked.

> **"The stalemate on gun legislation will not last forever."**

The stalemate on gun legislation will   4 not last forever. A point will come, as it has several times in America's past, when Washington will be politically ready to act— most likely the next time Democrats control both the White House and Congress. When that moment arrives, wouldn't it be better if, instead of debating marginal fixes, there were new ideas on the table to actually address the root of the problem by substantially reducing the number of guns in circulation?

In that spirit, I would like to float such an idea. It is not one that comes   5 from deep expertise in gun policy, which I cannot claim. Rather, it emerges from my experience in the private equity business.

After our small company buyout firm purchased an importer of night vision   6 monoculars, a product popular with hunters, we began to get approached by business brokers about small arms manufacturers that were for sale. One such company—which we later visited—was a well-run, highly profitable, and rather intimidating manufacturer of sniper rifles. At first the notion of competing in a market as large as the firearms industry didn't seem to make sense. We soon learned, however, that the U.S. firearm manufacturing industry is relatively small. The market capitalizations of the two largest U.S. firearm manufacturers— Sturm, Ruger & Co. and Smith & Wesson, public companies that together produce approximately 50 percent of all handguns manufactured in the United States—total less than $3 billion. To put that in perspective, the market cap of General Motors is roughly $50 billion. In fact, the vast majority of U.S.-made handguns are produced by fewer than fifty, mostly small, private companies.

In the end, we chose not to invest in the firearms industry. But the exercise   7 drove a thought. To shift the supply and demand dynamics of firearms in America, and thereby reduce gun violence, what if somebody acquired every handgun manufacturer in America? And what if that somebody were the federal government?

Sniper rifles are fearsome weapons, made specifically to kill unsuspecting   8
humans. But they are not seriously contributing to the gun violence problem
in the U.S. Nor are hunting rifles, shotguns, or truly automatic weapons (the
latter are heavily regulated and seldom in civilian hands). Rather, most gun
violence is perpetrated with handguns. In the ten states with the most gun
homicides, handguns are responsible for roughly 80 percent.

Semiautomatic assault rifles, like the AR-15 and its competitors, are at the   9
center of the gun debate, primarily because of their role in recent mass shootings. But mass shootings make up a small fraction of gun injuries and deaths
in America. Moreover, according to a 2013 government report, a handgun was
involved in roughly two-thirds of mass shootings in the U.S. since the 1999
Columbine High School massacre.

The number of handguns in circulation is astonishing. According to the   10
Bureau of Alcohol, Tobacco, Firearms and Explosives (ATF), since 1986 over
100 million handguns have been manufactured and imported into the
U.S. — approximately one for every household in America during that period.

To bring down the level of gun violence, we need to have fewer handguns   11
in circulation. To that end, I propose that Congress pass legislation directing
the federal government to take three major steps: purchase the entire domestic
handgun manufacturing industry; ban the import of all handguns; and offer
cash buybacks for all handguns in circulation. Over time, this would allow the
government to significantly lower the supply — and thereby raise the price — of
handguns, all without infringing on Americans' right to bear arms.

Let's take these steps in turn, beginning with the first: empowering the fed-   12
eral government to buy out the domestic handgun industry. Constitutionally,
there's no reason why this could not happen. Washington nationalized the
railroads temporarily during World War I, bailed Chrysler out of bankruptcy in
the late 1970s, and bought out the insurance company AIG in 2008 before selling its shares in 2012.

Under law, the government would have to offer "just compensation" to   13
shareholders of the handgun businesses, but the cost would be quite modest.
In many instances, it would not even be necessary to purchase the entire
companies — only the handgun assets. These manufacturers could continue to
make and sell hunting rifles, shotguns, ammunition, and accessories. Indeed,
even at a price of two to three times current market valuation (which may be
necessary because prices will certainly rise in anticipation of the sale), the
entirety of U.S. handgun manufacturing capacity — literally every producer,
large and small — could be acquired for around $5 billion. That's big money,
for sure, but within the context of the federal government it's not so much.

Then bring in a smart, highly experienced team of managers from the   14
industry to pull the new federal handgun manufacturing holding company
together. Maintain brands and models, run some of the divisions independently, but create efficiencies at the same time — just as is done in private
industry. Build a board of directors with relevant experience. Continue to
manufacture and sell handguns under existing laws to all of the usual customers, including national retail chains, independent gun stores and dealers, individuals who pass background checks, and federal, state, and local government

agencies. Reaffirm every American's Second Amendment rights to own a gun (or as many guns as you want) along with the enforcement of existing laws.

The second step in this long-term solution to gun violence is to ban the importation of handguns, which accounts for a growing proportion of the American market. Of the more than nine million handguns introduced to the U.S. market in 2016, about 40 percent were imported, predominantly from allies like Austria, Germany, Italy, Croatia, and Brazil.   15

Again, there is no constitutional reason why this could not happen. In 1989, George H. W. Bush declared a permanent ban on almost all foreign-made semiautomatic weapons. In 1998, Bill Clinton affirmed Bush's ban, adjusting it to include weapons that could be easily converted to and from military-grade capacity. Banning handgun importation would require considerable political capital, possibly including new legislation and changes to existing trade agreements. But the fact remains that these countries and, in most cases, these foreign private companies, are supplying the United States with roughly four out of ten handguns being sold in our country every year and are a major contributor to the gun violence epidemic we are seeking to solve.   16

At this point, we would control our own destiny with regard to the supply of handguns in the country. With the elimination of imported handguns, the federally owned factories would experience significantly higher demand and the ability to raise prices. And when the price of something goes up, the public buys less of it.   17

Higher prices for handguns would dramatically increase the profitability of the new federal handgun manufacturing holding company. And who would be the owners of these American factories? That's right—you and I. The increased profitability of the U.S. handgun industry would inure directly to the benefit of the American taxpayer and likely lead to a boost in jobs in the domestic handgun manufacturing industry. Significantly, existing gun owners would also benefit from this shift in supply and demand, since the value of all existing handguns, both foreign made and domestic, would rise.   18

Of course, if new domestic companies were allowed to jump back into the handgun manufacturing business, they would flood the market, undercutting the government's prices and spoiling the entire effort. So the legislation would also have to grant the government a monopoly on the manufacturing of handguns. Constitutionally, this would be controversial. Liberal jurists would point out that Congress has this power under the interstate commerce clause and argue that the Second Amendment protects the right to keep and bear arms—not to manufacture and sell them. Conservative judges might argue the opposite: that restricting supply more than what "the market" dictates unduly impinges on the right to obtain a gun. With conservatives dominating the Supreme Court, the legislation would face rough sledding. But that would be true of almost any ambitious progressive policy one can think of. Eventually, the more conservative reading of the Second Amendment will have to be overcome.   19

The third step is legislation that authorizes a long-term, nationwide federal buyback of handguns. Gun buybacks are nothing new; local governments have been running them for years, offering citizens cash for any guns they bring to the police department, no questions asked. There is scant evidence that local   20 buybacks achieve their stated aim of reducing the number of guns on the streets, however, for the simple reason that the gun industry just fills the void by selling fresh weapons. But with the overall supply now restricted by the import ban and federal ownership of the domestic handgun business, every gun purchased through the federal buyback could mean one fewer in circulation.

This program would only be effective if the prices paid — with no questions 21 asked, no IDs required, and for cash — were attractive. And they would be, thanks to steps one and two. With the supply of new guns restricted, the buyback program would pay the now much higher market price for pre-owned handguns. A run-of-the-mill used handgun that was purchased legally for around $200 might fetch a buyback price of around $500. More expensive handguns could bring $1,000 or more.

According to a 2015 analysis by the *Washington Post*, the average gun- 22 owning American household owns about eight guns. Most gun owners bought all their guns lawfully and are highly responsible. If you are one of the millions of people who own a number of guns, the opportunity to sell down your collection at a significant profit and still remain well armed could be very attractive. On the other end of the spectrum, the communities where violence involving illegal guns is most severe are disproportionately poor and heavily African American and Hispanic. Changing the market dynamics to get handguns off the street and out of households — and dramatically raising the cost of obtaining one — would benefit these communities most of all.

Weapons purchased by the government would be imaged, their serial 23 numbers entered into a centralized system, and in most cases transferred to secure regional processing centers, like existing armories. Usable pre-owned weapons would be re-marketed to federal agencies, the military, state and local police departments, and private security agencies. Others might be sold to foreign governments at export market prices, never to be imported back to the U.S. Those that had been stolen would be held at the local buyback location — in most cases a police station — and returned to their rightful owners. Excess or unusable inventory would be systematically destroyed.

Once in place, the system would necessarily be managed, through trial and 24 error, with an eye toward its market effects. The aim would be to slowly, over many years, diminish the number of handguns in circulation, but not so much that rising prices caused a spike in gun theft or made a black market in smuggled or illegally fabricated weapons highly lucrative. (It almost goes without saying that manufacturing 3-D printable handguns, which the courts have already begun to crack down on, should remain illegal.)

The total long-term cost of this solution is difficult to measure with much 25 intellectual honesty, but some aspects can be estimated. The federal purchase of the handgun manufacturers, as we've seen, would cost from about $5 billion to perhaps as much as $8 billion. But the ban on imports would effectively reduce that cost by increasing the value and profitability of the new taxpayer-owned federal handgun holding company. In other words, the federal government would overpay for the private manufacturing assets and then improve the profitability of those assets by limiting foreign supply. American taxpayers would subsequently own a very valuable and profitable business.

The cost of the third part of the legislation, the nationwide handgun buy-   26
back, is the most difficult to estimate. Setting up and staffing 500 to 1,000
buyback locations around the country—even if they are in existing police
departments or similar protected buildings—would be expensive. So would
establishing regional secure processing locations. Purchasing pre-owned handguns at now higher market prices would be the most costly, especially since we
can expect that many individuals would stock up on handguns in anticipation
of the legislation going into effect.

But, again, keep in mind that all these costs would be offset in three funda-   27
mental ways. First, a government-controlled monopoly handgun industry would
be highly profitable, providing substantial recurring revenue. Second, most of the
bought-back handguns would be resold at market prices, including as exports.

Third, and most importantly, there would be enormous savings gained by   28
a reduction in gun violence. The Giffords Law Center estimates that such violence costs the American economy at least $229 billion every year. This figure
takes into account many factors, including the costs of taxpayer-paid emergency and other medical care, lost productivity, and courts and incarceration.
It does not attempt to measure the pain of a life-altering injury, or the horror
of losing a loved one to murder, accident, or suicide. The benefits of reducing
gun violence are greater than what can be put in absolute dollar terms. What's
clear is that in the end, the long-term value to the American people of slowly
but surely reducing the number of handguns in circulation and the resulting
reduction in gun violence would be a tremendous bargain.

The politics of a federal purchase of all handgun manufacturers, an import   29
ban, and a federal buyback will obviously play badly with the gun rights movement and its standard-bearing organization, the NRA—which would face losing
a major source of funding and thus a loss of political power. These politics could
well stop the idea in its tracks. At the same time, this approach has something
going for it that no other gun violence solution can claim: it provides direct,
immediate, and substantial economic benefits to the owners of handgun manufacturers and every American handgun owner. The more handguns you own, the
more money you stand to make. It would be instructive to observe how Second
Amendment–focused gun enthusiasts weigh their ideological principles against
the prospect of having existing gun collections rise substantially in value. We may
never know until we put forth the proposal. It may be that American voters will
recoil at the idea. But what about younger voters, who polls show are less skeptical
about government and more sympathetic to gun violence legislation? And what
happens when, a couple decades from now, these voters make up the majority?

Gun violence has woven its way into the fabric of American culture. It's not   30
simply a familiar breed of tragedy; it's one we've come to expect. The possibilities
I've described are not modest, but neither are the ramifications of gun violence.
In the face of such thoroughly normalized violence, Americans deserve broad,
sweeping reforms. As a country, we've experienced far too many years of pains-
taking incrementalism, of NRA stalemates masquerading as compromises.
The scope of our imagination ought to match the scope of the epidemic. That
way, when the moment for change comes—likely, when Democrats once again
control Washington—we all can say we left no stone unturned.

· · ·

Comprehension

1. Glastris opens his essay by describing a "depressingly familiar routine." Why, according to him, are we stuck in this "painful rut" (2)?
2. For Glastris, what is the problem with most of the solutions to gun violence that are typically proposed?
3. What type of firearm is responsible for most homicides in the ten states with the highest murder rate? Given this fact, why are assault rifles "at the center of the gun debate" (9)?
4. What three specific steps does Glastris propose the federal government take to reduce gun violence?
5. How would the costs of the writer's ambitious proposal be offset?
6. In his concluding paragraph, Glastris writes, "The scope of our imagination ought to match the scope of the epidemic." What does he mean by this statement?

Purpose and Audience

1. Does Glastris seem to have a political bias on the topic of gun control, or does he seem politically neutral? Explain.
2. What purpose do paragraphs 8 and 9 serve? What point is Glastris trying to make?
3. What is the thesis of this essay? Why do you think Glastris chose to place it where he does? Was that a good decision?
4. How does Glastris address possible objections to granting the government a "monopoly on the manufacturing of handguns" (19)? Do you find his refutation persuasive? Why or why not?

Style and Structure

1. How does Glastris appeal to *ethos* in paragraph 5? Do you find the appeal persuasive? Why or why not?
2. Where does Glastris use **exemplification**? Are his examples effective? Why or why not?
3. Where does Glastris use **cause-and-effect**? Does he use the pattern effectively? Why or why not?
4. **Vocabulary Project.** Glastris ends paragraph 1 with the sentence, "Rinse and repeat." What does he mean? What is the origin of this expression? Given its usual connotation, is its use in the context of this serious essay appropriate? Explain.

Journal Entry

Glastris points out that "Americans possess as many as 393 million guns—almost half of all civilian-owned guns around the world—despite making up only 4.4 percent of the world's population" (3). Did you grow up around people who owned firearms? What is your general attitude toward guns and gun ownership?

Writing Workshop

1. **Working with Sources.** In paragraph 12, Glastris provides some background for his proposal:

   > Let's take these steps in turn, beginning with the first: empowering the federal government to buy out the domestic handgun industry. Constitutionally, there's no reason why this could not happen. Washington nationalized the railroads temporarily during World War I, bailed Chrysler out of bankruptcy in the late 1970s, and bought out the insurance company AIG in 2008 before selling its shares in 2012.

   Do you think it is acceptable and appropriate for the government to "buy out" particular companies and even (as in this case) entire industries? Write an essay that addresses this question in the context of Glastris's examples in paragraph 12. How is his proposal similar to and different from the examples he mentions? What are the relative risks and rewards of nationalizing industries in this way? Be sure to include parenthetical references to source material and to include a works-cited page. (See Chapter 18 for information on MLA documentation.)

2. **Working with Sources.** Glastris begins with the premise that the United States is in a repetitive cycle — particularly in the context of our politics and political institutions, which are failing to address the problem of gun violence. However, he also writes, "The stalemate on gun legislation will not last forever" (4). Do you agree? What do you think could end this stalemate? Write an essay that examines the political impasse on gun legislation and proposes at least one idea for overcoming it. Be sure to use parenthetical references to document your sources, and include a works-cited page. (See Chapter 18 for information on MLA documentation.)

3. As Glastris notes, Americans own an enormous number of firearms — many more, per person, than residents of any other country. What do you think accounts for this situation? Why are guns so prevalent in the United States? Write an argumentative essay that answers the question, Why are guns so important in American culture?

Combining the Patterns

Where does Glastris use **process** to develop his essay? How does process help him to make his case?

Thematic Connections

- "Did Free Pens Cause the Opioid Crisis?" (page 332)
- "A Peaceful Woman Explains Why She Carries a Gun" (page 348)
- "Photos That Change History" (page 354)
- "Patterns" (page 473)

CLIFTON LEAF

How Australia All but Ended Gun Violence

Clifton Leaf is an American journalist and author. After graduating from Williams College, he worked as a journalist and editor specializing in business at *The New York Times* op-ed page and *Sunday Review*; *The Wall Street Journal*'s *SmartMoney* magazine; and *Fortune* magazine. His experience beating cancer eventually inspired his book *The Truth in Small Doses: Why We're Losing the War on Cancer — and How to Win It*, which was published in 2013. In 2017, he was named editor-in-chief of *Fortune*.

Background on the of the Second Amendment debate Gun laws in Australia tightened throughout the 1980s and 1990s in response to multiple instances of mass killings. Several Australian states enacted gun registration and limited the availability of semi-automatic weapons—measures that have often been suggested for the United States. The Second Amendment of the U.S. Constitution is often cited as the reasoning behind the lack of more stringent gun regulation. Its language is relatively straightforward: "A well-regulated Militia, being necessary to the security of a free State, the right of the people to keep and bear Arms, shall not be infringed." This basic principle has its roots in English common law, which recognizes the rights of self-defense, resistance to oppression, and the collective obligation to defend one's state or country, but the correct interpretation of the amendment's wording has long been hotly debated. Some argue that the phrase "well-regulated militia" limits weapons to organized military units, such as the National Guard. Others see it as guaranteeing an individual right to bear arms that "shall not be infringed." Over the last two hundred years, American jurisprudence has wrestled with the tension between these two positions. For example, in the 1876 case *United States v. Cruikshank,* the Supreme Court ruled that the Amendment only applied to the federal government; in other words, individual states and private entities were free to regulate guns as they saw fit. Throughout the twentieth century, legislation and judicial rulings generally allowed for laws such as the 1934 National Firearms Act, which placed rigorous restrictions on fully automatic "machine guns." But in recent years, gun control legislation has been limited, and the Court has taken a more expansive view of the Second Amendment. In the landmark 2008 case *District of Columbia v. Heller,* for example, the Court held that the Second Amendment guaranteed an individual right to bear arms. Canada, meanwhile, responded to a 2020 mass shooting quickly and decisively by banning assault weapons outright.

On April 28, 1996, a 28-year-old man named Martin Bryant drove his yellow Volvo to a popular tourist spot in Port Arthur, Australia, a former penal colony on the island state of Tasmania, and opened fire with a semi-automatic weapon. 1

Before the day was through, he had shot dead 35 people and wounded 18 others. Twelve of those deaths came at the Broad Arrow Café, where Bryant first ate lunch and then sprayed bullets with his Colt AR-15 SP1, which he had stowed in a tennis bag. At the gift shop next door, he murdered eight more people. Later, he shot a young mother running away with her two children—all three at close range.

He was a loner, with a clean-shaven face and wavy blond hair. His IQ was said to be 66. By all accounts, he was a terrible shot. But with the weapons he carried—the AR-15 and a second, self-loading military-style rifle—aim was almost immaterial. The SP1 could fire several rounds per second with little recoil. Pointing the gun at a crowd of tourists, it was hard not to hit somebody. 2

If all this sounds too horrifically familiar—an estranged loner, an AR-15, dozens dead in a matter of minutes—there is a remarkable twist to the story. In the wake of the Port Arthur massacre, Australian lawmakers did something about it. 3

Within just weeks of that tragedy, elected officials in each of Australia's six states and two mainland territories—pressed forward by police chiefs across the continent and by the then-newly elected prime minister—banned semi-automatic and other military-style weapons across the country. The federal government of Australia prohibited their import, and lawmakers introduced a generous nationwide gun buyback program, funded with a Medicare tax, to encourage Australians to freely give up their assault-style weapons. Amazingly, many of them did. 4

> **"In the wake of the Port Arthur massacre, Australian lawmakers did something about it."**

A land of roughneck pioneers and outback settlers, Australia had never embraced much government regulation and certainly not about their guns. This was a land of almost cartoonish toughness and self-reliance, home of Crocodile Dundee and Australian rules football. Here even the kangaroos box. But Port Arthur had followed too many prior deadly shooting sprees and Australians were clearly sick to death of them. 5

So what happened after the assault-weapon ban? Well therein lies the other half of the story twist noted above: *Nothing.* 6

Nothing, that is, in a good way. 7

Australian independence didn't end. Tyranny didn't come. Australians still hunted and explored and big-wave surfed to their hearts' content. Their economy didn't crash; Invaders never arrived. Violence, in many forms, went down across the country, not up. Somehow, lawmakers on either side of the gun debate managed to get along and legislate. 8

As for mass killings, there were no more. Not one in the past 22 years. 9

In 2002, a mentally impaired student at Monash University in Melbourne shot two people dead and injured five others. He came to his rampage with six handguns, not an assault rifle. Had he been carrying an AR-15, the toll would have been far worse. But even so, Australian lawmakers added a new National Handgun Agreement, a separate buyback act, and a reformulated gun trafficking policy to their legislative arsenal. 10

There has been no similar shooting spree since.   11

But it wasn't just the murderous rampages that faded away. Gun violence   12
in general declined over the following two decades to a nearly unimaginable
degree. In 2014, the latest year for which final statistics are available, Australia's
murder rate fell to less than 1 killing per 100,000 people—a murder rate one-
fifth the size of America's.

Just 32 of those homicides—in a nation of 24 million people—were com-   13
mitted with guns. By comparison, more than 500 people were shot dead last
year in the city of Chicago alone. (Chicago has about 2.7 million residents.)

Perhaps most remarkable is what happened with gun suicides in Australia   14
in the wake of the post–Port Arthur firearm legislation. They dropped by some
80 percent, according to one analysis.

What stopped many of those would-be suicides—quite straightforwardly,   15
it seems—was the lack of access to a gun, a generally immediate and effective
method of killing. (Nine out of 10 suicide attempts with a firearm result in
death, a far higher share than attempts by other methods.) Public health
experts call such an effect "means restriction." Some Australians found other
ways to take their own lives—but for many, that acute moment of sadness and
resolve passed in the absence of a gun.

Suicide "is commonly an impulsive act by a vulnerable individual," explain   16
E. Michael Lewiecki and Sara A. Miller in the *American Journal of Public Health*.
"The impulsivity of suicide provides opportunities to reduce the risk of suicide
by restricting access to lethal means."

Which brings us back to the here and now. In 2015, an unthinkable 22,103   17
Americans shot themselves to death with a gun—accounting for just over half
of the suicides in the country that year.

It isn't hard to imagine what would happen without all those guns at the   18
ready. In a world of raging hypotheticals, we actually have some good, hard
answers for this. All we have to do is look down under. There are millions of
American families begging us to do it.

·   ·   ·

Comprehension

1. In paragraph 2, following a paragraph that describes the Port Arthur massacre, Leaf points out the gunman's weaknesses. What are these weaknesses?
   Why does Leaf provide this information?
2. What actions did lawmakers take after the attack? What were the results of
   their actions?
3. What does Leaf mean in paragraph 8 when he says that nothing happened
   as a result of the assault-weapon ban?
4. How is the 2002 shooting described in paragraph 10 different from the Port
   Arthur shooting? How does this example help Leaf make his point?
5. How are the attitudes toward gun legislation different in Australia and the
   United States? How do you account for this difference?

Purpose and Audience

1. This essay—published in 2018 in *Fortune*, an American magazine that focuses on business—describes events that occurred in Australia in 1996. Why do you think *Fortune* decided to publish this essay at this time?
2. Do you think Leaf expects his readers to be familiar with the events he describes? How can you tell?
3. At times, Leaf cites the opinions of experts. Why does he do this? Do you think he needs to refer to additional experts?
4. How might Leaf expect his American readers to react to paragraphs 8 and 9? To the essay as a whole? Explain.
5. This essay takes a clear stand on the issue of gun violence. What is Leaf's position—and why does he use the situation in Australia to make his point? Was this a good decision?

Style and Structure

1. Why does Leaf open his essay with a graphic description of the Port Arthur massacre? Do you see this as an effective opening strategy, or do you think readers may react negatively?
2. Paragraph 6 is only two sentences long, and other paragraphs consist of just a single sentence. Why does Leaf keep these paragraphs so short? Should they be combined with adjacent paragraphs, or are they effective as is? Explain.
3. **Vocabulary Project.** Consider Leaf's use of the term "shooting spree" in paragraph 11. What exactly is a "shooting spree"? What connotations does this expression have? Do you think this term accurately characterizes the Port Arthur massacre? Why or why not?
4. In his conclusion, Leaf refers to "a world of raging hypotheticals" (18). Explain what he means, giving an example of a "raging hypothetical."

Journal Entry

Do you think the United States could enact legislation similar to that enacted in Australia? Do you think it should?

Writing Workshop

1. **Working with Sources.** In paragraph 5, Leaf provides some very general information about Australian culture and spirit, suggesting parallels with the United States in terms of the two nations' common "toughness and self-reliance." Do some research about the early days of each country's history to learn how these shared values developed. Then, write an essay in which you take a stand for or against these values, tying them (as Leaf does) to the attitudes toward gun violence in the two countries. Include in-text citations for your sources, and include a works-cited page as well. (See Chapter 18 for information on MLA documentation.)

2. Whenever the topic of gun control is brought up, people seem to split into two camps; one supporting legislation that will limit the number of guns in society, and the other upholding the second-amendment right to "bear arms." Write an essay in which you present your views on the issue of gun control. Do you think it is a necessary step to control gun violence, or do you think it infringes on your constitutional rights? Be specific, and include examples from your own experience (and from the news) to support your points.

3. **Working with Sources.** Having read the essays in this casebook and considered the problem from different perspectives, write an argumentative essay that answers the question, "How Can We Stem the Tide of Gun Violence?" Your essay should include at least two or three specific recommendations on how to solve the problems you identify. You may cite outside sources as well as the essays in this casebook, but be sure to include parenthetical citations for all your sources and to include a works-cited page. (See Chapter 18 for information on MLA documentation.)

Combining the Patterns

Where does Leaf use **cause and effect?** Where does he use **comparison and contrast?** How does he use each of these patterns to support his thesis?

Thematic Connections

- "How to Tell a Mother Her Child Is Dead" (page 275)
- "A Peaceful Woman Explains Why She Carries a Gun" (page 348)
- "Photos That Change History" (page 354)
- ·"Patterns" (page 473)

From "The Ghastlygun Tinies" (Illustrated Poem)

O is for OWEN learning about states

P is for PAULA protecting classmates

Q is for QUINN whose life had just begun

R is for REID, valued less than a gun

S is for STEPHEN who's planning for prom

T is for TINA who's texting her mom

• • •

Reading Images

1. This visual text is an excerpt from a 26-panel parody of an illustrated alphabet book in rhyming couplets. The original picture book, *The Gashlycrumb Tinies*, by Edward Gorey, enumerates a variety of terrible fates that could befall children. Find the original illustrated poem online. Do you think the subject of *MAD*'s version is appropriate for a reworking of the original? Why or why not?
2. What argument does this visual text make? How does it support that argument?
3. How are the images in the panels for the letters O, Q, and S different from those in the panels for P, R, and T? How do the differences between them create **irony**?

Journal Entry

Focusing on one panel of the excerpt, describe the effect it has on you, and explain how the panel's images help to convey that effect.

Thematic Connections

- "How to Tell a Mother Her Child Is Dead" (page 275)
- "A Peaceful Woman Explains Why She Carries a Gun" (page 348)
- "Patterns" (page 473)
- "Guns Are the Problem" (page 628)

Writing Assignments for Argumentation

1. Write an argumentative essay discussing whether parents have a right to spank their children. If your position is that they do, under what circumstances? What limitations should exist? If your position is that they do not, how should parents discipline children? How should they deal with inappropriate behavior?

2. Visit the American Library Association's website at ala.org, and read the list of banned and challenged books of the twenty-first century. Choose a book from the list that you have read. Assume a library in your town has decided that the book you have chosen is objectionable and has removed it from the shelves. Write an email to your local newspaper arguing for or against the library's actions. Make a list of the major arguments that might be advanced against your position, and try to refute some of them in your email.

3. In Great Britain, cities began installing video surveillance systems in public areas in the 1970s. Police departments claim these cameras help them do their jobs more efficiently. For example, such cameras enabled police to identify and capture the two terrorists who bombed the Boston Marathon in 2013. Opponents of the cameras say the police are creating a society that severely compromises the right of personal privacy. How do you feel about this issue? Assume the police department in your city is proposing to install cameras in the downtown and other pedestrian areas. Write an editorial for your local paper presenting your views on the topic.

4. Write an essay discussing under what circumstances, if any, animals should be used for scientific experimentation.

5. **Working with Sources.** Each year, a growing number of high school graduates are choosing to take a year off before going to college. The idea of this kind of "gap year" has been the source of some debate. Proponents say a gap year gives students time to mature, time to decide what they want to get out of their education. It also gives them the opportunity to travel or to save some money for college. Detractors of a gap year point out that some students have trouble getting back into the academic routine when the year is over. In addition, students who take a year off are a year behind their classmates when they return. Research the pros and cons of the gap year. Then, write an essay in which you argue for or against taking a year off before college. Be sure to document your sources and to include a works-cited page. (See Chapter 18 for information on MLA documentation.)

6. **Working with Sources.** Visit the website deathpenalty.org, and research some criminal cases that resulted in the death penalty. Write an essay using these accounts to support your arguments either for or against the death penalty. Be sure to document your sources and to include a works-cited page. (See Chapter 18 for information about MLA documentation.)

7. Write an argumentative essay discussing under what circumstances a nation has an obligation to go (or not to go) to war.

8. **Working with Sources.** Gasoline-powered cars account for more than half the oil consumed in the United States and almost 25 percent of the greenhouse gases. As a result, carmakers, such as Tesla, BMW, and General Motors, have spent considerable time and money trying to develop practical and efficient electric vehicles. Supporters say these electric-driven vehicles could reduce pollution significantly over the next ten years. Detractors say electric cars come with a cost, one that cancels out any possible benefits they may have. Research the pros and cons of electric vehicles. Then, write an essay in which you argue for or against the move toward electric cars. Be sure to document your sources and to include a works-cited page. (See Chapter 18 for information on MLA documentation.)

9. In the Declaration of Independence, Jefferson says all individuals are entitled to "life, liberty, and the pursuit of happiness." Write an essay arguing that these rights are not absolute.

10. Write an argumentative essay on one of these topics:

- Should high school students be required to recite the Pledge of Allegiance at the start of each school day?
- Should college students be required to do community service?
- Should public school teachers be required to pass periodic competency tests?
- Should the legal drinking age be raised (or lowered)?
- Should the children of undocumented immigrants qualify for in-state tuition rates at public colleges?
- Should sugary drinks be banned in all public schools and government workplaces?
- Do Facebook and other social networking sites do more harm than good?

Collaborative Activity for Argumentation

Working with three other students, select a controversial topic — one not covered in any of the debates in this chapter — that interests all of you. (You can review the Writing Assignments for Argumentation to get ideas.) State your topic the way a topic is stated in a formal debate:

Resolved: The federal government should censor Internet content.

Then, divide into two-member teams, and decide which team will take the pro position and which will take the con. Each team should list the arguments on its side of the issue and then write two or three paragraphs summarizing its position. Finally, the teams should stage a ten-minute debate — five minutes for each side — in front of the class. (The pro side presents its argument first.) At the end of each debate, the class should decide which team has presented the stronger arguments.

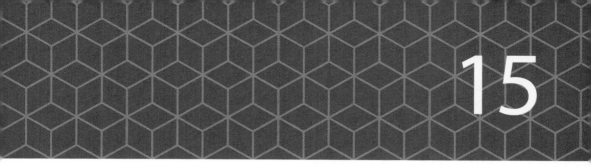

Combining the Patterns

Many paragraphs combine several patterns of development. In the following paragraph, for example, Paul Hoffman uses narration, exemplification, and cause and effect to explain why we tend to see numbers as more than "instruments of enumeration."

Topic sentence	<u>The idea that numbers are not mere instruments of enumeration but are sacred, perfect,</u>
Narration	<u>friendly, lucky, or evil goes back to antiquity</u>. In the sixth century B.C. Pythagoras, whom schoolchildren associate with the famous theorem that in a right triangle the square of the hypotenuse always equals the sum of the squares of its sides, not only performed brilliant mathematics but
Exemplification	made a religion out of numbers. In numerology, the number 12 has always represented completeness, as in the 12 months of the year, the 12 signs of the zodiac, the 12 hours of the day, the 12 gods of Olympus, the 12 labors of Hercules, the 12 tribes of Israel, the 12 apostles of Jesus, the 12 days of Christmas, and, more recently perhaps, the 12 eggs in an egg carton. Since 13 exceeds 12
Cause and effect	by only one, the number lies just beyond completeness and, hence, is restless to the point of being evil.

Like paragraphs, essays do not usually follow a single pattern of development; in fact, nearly every essay, including the ones in this text, combines a variety of patterns. Even though an essay may be structured according to one dominant pattern, it is still likely to include paragraphs, and even groups of paragraphs, shaped by other patterns of development. For example, a process essay can use **cause and effect** to show the results of the process, and a cause-and-effect essay can use **exemplification** to illustrate possible causes or effects. In many cases, a dominant pattern is supported by other patterns; in fact, combining various patterns in a single essay gives writers the flexibility to express their ideas most effectively. For this reason, each essay in Chapters 6 through 14 of this text is followed by a Combining the Patterns question that focuses on how the essay uses (or might use) other patterns of development along with its dominant pattern.

Structuring an Essay by Combining the Patterns

Essays that combine various patterns of development, like essays structured primarily by a single pattern, include an **introduction**, several **body paragraphs**, and a **conclusion**. The introduction typically ends with the thesis statement that gives the essay its focus, and the conclusion often reviews that thesis in different words or reviews the essay's key points. Each body paragraph (or group of paragraphs) is structured according to the pattern of development that best suits the material it develops.

Suppose you are planning your answer to the following question on a take-home essay exam for a sociology of religion course.

> For what reasons are people attracted to cults? Why do they join? Support your answer with specific examples that illustrate how cults recruit and retain members.

The wording of this exam question ("for what reasons") suggests that the essay's dominant pattern of development will be **cause and effect**; the wording also suggests that this cause-and-effect structure will include **exemplification** ("specific examples"). In addition, you may decide to develop your essay with **definition** and **process**.

An informal outline for your essay might look like this one:

SAMPLE OUTLINE: Combining the Patterns

INTRODUCTION

Definition of *cult* (defined by negation — telling what it is *not* — and by comparison and contrast with *religion*)

Thesis statement (suggests cause and effect): Using aggressive recruitment tactics and isolating potential members from their families and past lives, cults appeal to new recruits by offering them a highly structured environment.

CAUSE AND EFFECT

Why people join cults

> **PROCESS**
>
> How cults recruit new members

> **EXEMPLIFICATION**
>
> Tactics various cults use to retain members (series of brief examples)

> **CONCLUSION**
>
> **Restatement of thesis** or review of key points

Combining the Patterns: Revising and Editing

When you revise an essay that combines several patterns of development, consider the items on Checklist: Revising on page 68, as well as any of the more specific revision checklists in Chapters 6 through 14 that apply to the patterns in your essay. As you edit your essay, refer to the editing checklists on pages 85, 88, and 92 and to the individual editing checklists in Chapters 6 through 14. You may also wish to consult the Grammar in Context sections that appear throughout the book, as well as the one that follows.

GRAMMAR IN CONTEXT **AGREEMENT WITH INDEFINITE PRONOUNS**

A **pronoun** is a word that takes the place of a noun or another pronoun in a sentence. Unlike most pronouns, an **indefinite pronoun** (*anyone, either, each,* and so on) does not refer to a specific person or thing.

Subject-Verb Agreement Pronoun subjects must agree in number with their verbs: singular pronouns (*I, he, she, it,* and so on) take singular verbs, and plural pronouns (*we, they,* and so on) take plural verbs.

"I have learned much as a scavenger" (Eighner 669).

We were super ninjas one day and millionaires the next; we became the heroes we idolized and lived the lives we dreamed about (Truong 664).

Indefinite pronoun subjects must also agree in number with their verbs: singular indefinite pronouns take singular verbs, and plural indefinite pronouns take plural verbs. Most indefinite pronouns are singular, but some are plural.

SINGULAR INDEFINITE PRONOUNS

Another	anyone	everyone	one	each
either	neither	anything	everything	

"Everyone was darker or lighter than we were" (Truong 665).

"Everything seems to stink" (Eighner 674).

PLURAL INDEFINITE PRONOUNS

Both	many	few	several	others

"Many are discarded for minor imperfections that can be pared away" (Eighner 671).

NOTE: A few indefinite pronouns — *some, all, any, more, most,* and *none* — may be either singular or plural, depending on their meaning in the sentence.

> **SINGULAR:**   According to David Kirby, some of the history of tattoos is surprising. (*Some* refers to *history,* so the verb is singular.)

> **PLURAL:**   Some of the tattoos David Kirby discusses serve as a kind of "record book," while others create a "canvas" (690). (*Some* refers to *tattoos,* so the verb is plural.)

Pronoun-Antecedent Agreement An **antecedent** is the noun or pronoun that a pronoun refers to in a sentence. Pronouns must agree in number with their antecedents.

Use a singular pronoun to refer to a singular indefinite pronoun antecedent.

Each day has its surprises for Lars Eighner and his dog, Lizbeth.

Use a plural pronoun to refer to a plural indefinite pronoun antecedent.

Many of the people who pass Eighner and Lizbeth avert their eyes.

NOTE: Although the indefinite pronoun *everyone* is singular, it is often used with a plural pronoun in everyday speech and informal writing; increasingly, this usage is seen in more formal contexts as well. Similarly, the plural pronoun "they" is often now used as a gender-neutral singular term.

Everyone turns their heads when Eighner and Lizbeth walk by.

However, college writing still generally calls for the use of standard pronoun-antecedent agreement.

People turn their heads when Eighner and Lizbeth walk by.

The essays in this chapter illustrate how different patterns of development work together in a single piece of writing. The first two essays—"The Park" by Michael Huu Truong, a student, and "On Dumpster Diving" by Lars Eighner—include marginal annotations that identify the various patterns these writers use. Truong's essay relies primarily on narration, but he also uses description and exemplification to convey his memories of childhood. Eighner's essay combines sections of definition, exemplification, classification and division, cause and effect, comparison and contrast, and process; at the same time, he tells a story (narration) and provides vivid details (description) of his life as a homeless person.

Following these annotated essays are three additional selections that combine patterns: Olivia Judson's "Long Live the Albatross," David Kirby's "Inked Well," and Jonathan Swift's classic satire "A Modest Proposal." Each of the essays in this chapter is followed by the same types of questions that accompany the reading selections that appear elsewhere in the text.

A STUDENT WRITER: Combining the Patterns

This essay was written by Michael Huu Truong for a first-year composition course in response to the assignment "Write an essay about the person and/or place that defined your childhood."

The Park

Background

My childhood did not really begin until I came to this country   1
from the jungle of Vietnam. I can't really remember much from this
period, and the things I do remember are vague images that I have no
desire or intention to discuss. However, my childhood in the States

Thesis statement

was a lot different, especially after I met my friend James. While it
lasted, it was paradise.

Narrative begins

It was a cold wintry day in February after a big snowstorm — the   2
first I'd ever seen. My lips were chapped, my hands were frozen stiff,

*Description:
effects of cold*

and my cheeks were burning from the biting wind, and yet I loved
it. I especially loved the snow. I had come from a country where the

*Comparison and
contrast: U.S. vs.
Vietnam*

closest things to snow were white paint and cotton balls. But now I
was in America. On that frosty afternoon, I was determined to build a
snowman. I had seen them in books, and I had heard they could talk.
I knew they could come alive, and I couldn't wait.

"Eyryui roeow ierog," said a voice that came out of nowhere. I   3
turned around, and right in my face was a short, red-faced (probably

*Description:
James*

from the cold wind) Korean kid with a dirty, runny nose. I responded,
"Wtefkjkr ruyjft gsdfr" in my own tongue. We understood each other

*Narration: the
first day*

perfectly, and we expressed our understanding with a smile. Together,
we built our first snowman. We were disappointed that evening when

the snowman just stood there; however, I was happy because I had made my first friend.

Analogies

Ever since then we've been a team like Abbott and Costello (or, when my cousin joined us, the Three Stooges). The two of us were inseparable. We could've made the greatest Krazy Glue commercial ever.   4

Narration: what they did that summer

The summer that followed the big snowstorm, from what I can recall, was awesome. We were free like comets in the heavens, and we did whatever our hearts wanted. For the most part, our desires were fulfilled in a little park across the street. This park was ours; it was like our own planet guarded by our own robot army (disguised as trees). Together we fought against the bigger people who always tried to invade and take over our world. The enemy could never conquer our fortress because they would have to destroy our robots, penetrate our force field, and then defeat us; this last feat would be impossible.   5

Narrative continues

Examples: what they banished

This park was our fantasy land where everything we wished for came true and everything we hated was banished forever. We banished vegetables, cheese, bigger people, and — of course — girls. The land was enchanted, and we could be whatever we felt like. We were super ninjas one day and millionaires the next; we became the heroes we idolized and lived the lives we dreamed about. I had the strength of Bruce Lee and Superman; James possessed the power of Clint Eastwood and the Bionic Man. My weapons were the skills of Bruce and a cape. James, however, needed a real weapon for Clint, and the weapon he made was awesome. The Death Ray could destroy a building with one blast, and it even had a shield so that James was always protected. Even with all his mighty weapons and gadgets, though, he was still no match for Superman and Bruce Lee. Every day, we fought until death (or until our parents called us for dinner).   6

Examples: superhero fantasies

Narrative continues

Examples: new worlds and planets

When we became bored with our super powers, the park became a giant spaceship. We traveled all over the Universe, conquering and exploring strange new worlds and mysterious planets. Our ship was a top-secret indestructible space warship called the X–007. We went to Mars, Venus, Pluto, and other alien planets, destroying all the monsters we could find. When necessary, our spacecraft was transformed into a submarine for deep-sea adventures. We found lost cities, unearthed treasures, and saved Earth by destroying all the sea monsters that were plotting against us. We became heroes — just like Superman, Bruce Lee, the Bionic Man, and Clint Eastwood.   7

Cause and effect: prospect of school leads to problems

James and I had the time of our lives in the park that summer. It was great — until we heard about the horror of starting school. Shocked and terrified, we ran to our fortress to escape. For some   8 reason, though, our magic kingdom had lost its powers. We fought hard that evening, trying to keep the bigger people out of our planet, but the battle was soon lost. Bruce Lee, Superman, the Bionic Man, and Clint Eastwood had all lost their special powers.

Narrative continues

School wasn't as bad as we'd thought it would be. The first day, James and I sat there with our hands folded. We didn't talk or move, and we didn't dare look at each other (we would've cracked up because we always made these goofy faces). Even though we had pens that could be transformed into weapons, we were still scared.   9

Description: school

Everyone was darker or lighter than we were, and the teacher was speaking a strange language (English). James and I giggled as she talked. We giggled softly when everyone else talked, and they laughed out loud when it was our turn to speak.   10

Narrative continues

The day dragged on, and all we wanted to do was go home and rebuild our fortress. Finally, after an eternity, it was almost three o'clock. James and I sat at the edge of our seats as we counted under our breath: "10, 9, 8, 7, 6, 5, 4, 3, 2, 1." At last, the bell sounded. We dashed for the door and raced home and across the street—and then we stopped. We stood still in the middle of the street with our hearts pounding like the beats of a drum. The cool September wind began to pick up, and   11

Description: the fence

everything became silent. We stood there and watched the metal of the fence reflect the beautiful colors of the sun. It was beautiful, and yet we hated everything about it. The new metal fence separated us from our fortress, our planet, our spaceship, our submarine—and, most important of all, from our heroes and our dreams.

We stood there for a long time. As the sun slowly turned red and sank beneath the ground, so did our dreams, heroes, and hearts. Darkness soon devoured the park, and after a while we walked home with only the memories of the summer that came after the big snowstorm.   12

Points for Special Attention

Writing a Personal Experience Essay

Michael's instructor specified that he was to write an essay about a person or place in order to help his readers—other students—understand what his childhood was like. Because the assignment called for a personal experience essay, Michael was free to use the first-person pronouns *I* and *we*, as well as contractions, although neither would be acceptable in a more formal essay.

Thesis Statement

Because Michael's primary purpose in this essay was to communicate personal feelings and impressions, an argumentative thesis statement (such as

"If every cell phone and video game in the United States disappeared, more people would have childhoods like mine") would have been inappropriate. Still, Michael states his thesis explicitly in order to unify his essay around the dominant impression he wants to convey: "While it lasted, it was paradise."

Combining the Patterns

Michael also had more specific purposes, and they determined the patterns that shape his essay. His essay's dominant pattern is *narration,* but to help students visualize the person (James) and the place (the park) he discusses, he includes sections that *describe* and give concrete, specific *examples* as well as summarize his daily routine. These patterns work together to create an essay that conveys a clear sense of his childhood to readers.

Transitions

The transitional words and phrases that connect the individual sentences and paragraphs of Michael's essay—"But now," "Ever since," "The summer that followed the big snowstorm"—serve primarily to move readers through time. Such transitions are appropriate because narration is the dominant pattern of this essay.

Detail

"The Park" is full of specific detail—for example, the quoted bits of dialogue and the names of Michael's heroes and of particular games (and related equipment and weapons). The descriptive details that re-create the physical scenes—in particular, the snow, cold, frost, and wind of winter and the sun reflected on the fence—are vivid enough to help readers visualize the places Michael writes about.

Figures of Speech

Michael's essay describes a time when his imagination wandered without the restraints of adulthood. Appropriately, he uses **simile**, **metaphor**, and **personification**—"We were free like comets in the heavens"; "the park became a giant spaceship"; "We found lost cities, unearthed treasures, and saved Earth"; "Darkness soon devoured the park"—to evoke the time and place he describes.

Working with Sources

Michael's assignment did not require him to consult any outside sources. If it had, he could have included background information about immigration from Vietnam to the United States—particularly data about when Vietnamese people first came to the United States, where immigrants settled, how children adjusted to school and learned English, and how quickly they assimilated. Such information could have provided some context for his childhood memories.

Focus on Revision

Michael's assignment asked him to write about his childhood, and he chose to focus on his early years in the United States. When his peer-editing group discussed his essay, however, a number of students were curious about his life in Vietnam. Some of them thought he should add a paragraph summarizing the "vague images" he remembered of his earlier childhood, perhaps contrasting these images with details about his life in the United States, as he does in passing in paragraph 2. When Michael discussed this idea with his instructor, she suggested instead that he consider deleting the sentence in paragraph 1 that states he has "no desire or intention to discuss" this part of his life because it raises issues his essay does not address. After thinking about these suggestions, Michael decided to delete this sentence in his next draft but also to add a brief paragraph about his life in Vietnam, contrasting the park and his friendship with James with some of his earlier, less idyllic memories.

PEER-EDITING WORKSHEET | **COMBINING THE PATTERNS**

1. Using the annotations for "The Park" (page 663) or "On Dumpster Diving" (page 668) as a guide, annotate the essay to identify the patterns of development it uses.

2. What is the essay's thesis? Is it explicitly stated? If not, state it in your own words. What pattern or patterns of development are suggested by the wording of the thesis statement?

3. What dominant pattern of development determines the essay's overall structure?

4. What patterns does the writer use to develop the body paragraphs of the essay? Why is each pattern used in a particular paragraph or group of paragraphs?

5. What patterns are *not* used? Where, if anywhere, might using one of these patterns serve the writer's purpose?

6. Review the essay's topic sentences. Is the wording of each topic sentence consistent with the particular pattern that structures the paragraph? If not, suggest possible ways some of the topic sentences might be reworded.

7. Should the writer consider adding one or more visuals?

8. If the writer uses sources, are they well chosen and helpful? Are they documented fully and appropriately? Does the essay need additional sources?

Each of the following essays combines several patterns, blending strategies to achieve the writer's purpose.

LARS EIGHNER

On Dumpster Diving

Lars Eighner (b. 1948) dropped out of the University of Texas at Austin after his third year and took a job at a state mental hospital. After leaving his job over a policy dispute in 1988 and falling behind in his rent payments, Eighner became homeless. For three years, he traveled between Austin and Los Angeles with his dog, Lizbeth, earning what money he could from writing stories for magazines. Eighner's *Travels with Lizbeth* (1993), memories of his experiences living on the street, was written on a computer he found in a Dumpster. The following chapter from that book details the practical dangers as well as the many possibilities he discovered in his "Dumpster diving." Eighner now lives in Austin and works as a freelance writer and writing coach.

Background on the homeless Although the number of homeless people in the United States is difficult to measure accurately, homelessness has become a highly visible issue. It is estimated, for example, that as many as ten million people experienced homelessness in the United States in the late 1980s, when Eighner himself was homeless. This surge in homelessness had a number of causes. Perhaps most important was a booming real estate market that led to a significant drop in affordable housing in many areas of the country. In several cities, single-room-occupancy hotels, which had long provided cheap lodging, were demolished or converted into luxury apartments. At the same time, new technologies left many unskilled workers jobless. Government policies against detaining the nondangerous mentally ill against their will also played a significant role. (About a fourth of all homeless people are thought to be mentally ill.) A real estate bubble and the subsequent foreclosure crisis then forced hundreds of thousands out of their houses, leading many cities to report increased demand for emergency shelter. Currently, the U.S. Department of Health and Human Services estimates that homelessness affects around 500,000 people on any given night. Approximately 40 percent of the homeless population are children.

This chapter was composed while the author was homeless. The present tense has been preserved.

Definition: Dumpster

Long before I began Dumpster diving I was impressed 1 with Dumpsters, enough so that I wrote the Merriam-Webster research service to discover what I could about the word *Dumpster*. I learned from them that it is a proprietary word belonging to the Dempsey Dumpster company. Since then I have dutifully capitalized the word, although it was lowercased in almost all the citations Merriam-Webster photocopied for me. Dempsey's word is too apt. I have never heard these things called anything but

Dumpsters. I do not know anyone who knows the generic name for these objects. From time to time I have heard a wino or hobo give some corrupted credit to the original and call them Dipsy Dumpsters.

Narration: *Eighner's story begins*

I began Dumpster diving about a year before I became homeless.   2

Definition: Dumpster diving

I prefer the word *scavenging* and use the word *scrounging*   3
when I mean to be obscure. I have heard people, evidently meaning to be polite, use the word *foraging*, but I prefer to reserve that word for gathering nuts and berries and such, which I do also according to the season and the opportunity. *Dumpster diving* seems to me to be a little too cute and, in my case, inaccurate because I lack the athletic ability to lower myself into the Dumpsters as the true divers do, much to their increased profit.

I like the frankness of the word *scavenging,* which I can   4
hardly think of without picturing a big black snail on an aquarium wall. I live from the refuse of others. I am a scavenger. I think it a sound and honorable niche, although if I could I would naturally prefer to live the comfortable consumer life, perhaps — and only perhaps — as a slightly less wasteful consumer, owing to what I have learned as a scavenger.

Narration: *story continues*

While Lizbeth and I were still living in the shack on   5
Avenue B as my savings ran out, I put almost all my sporadic income into rent. The necessities of daily life I began to extract from Dumpsters. Yes, we ate from them. Except for jeans, all my clothes came from Dumpsters. Boom boxes, candles, bedding, toilet paper, a virgin male love doll, medicine, books, a typewriter, dishes, furnishings, and change, sometimes amounting to many dollars — I acquired many things from Dumpsters.

Exemplification: *things found in Dumpsters*

Thesis statement

I have learned much as a scavenger. I mean to put   6
some of what I have learned down here, beginning with the practical art of Dumpster diving and proceeding to the abstract.

What is safe to eat?   7

After all, the finding of objects is becoming something of an urban art. Even respectable employed people   8
will sometimes find something tempting sticking out of a Dumpster or standing beside one. Quite a number of people, not all of them of the bohemian type, are willing to brag that they found this or that piece of trash. But eating from Dumpsters is what separates the dilettanti from the professionals. Eating safely from the Dumpsters involves three principles: using the senses and common sense to

evaluate the condition of the found materials, knowing the Dumpsters of a given area and checking them regularly, and seeking always to answer the question "Why was this discarded?"

Comparison and contrast: Dumpster divers vs. others

Perhaps everyone who has a kitchen and a regular supply   9
of groceries has, at one time or another, made a sandwich and eaten half of it before discovering mold on the bread or got a mouthful of milk before realizing the milk had turned. Nothing of the sort is likely to happen to a Dumpster diver because he is constantly reminded that most food is discarded for a reason. Yet a lot of perfectly good food can be found in Dumpsters.

Classification and division: different kinds of food found in Dumpsters and their relative safety

Canned goods, for example, turn up fairly often in the   10
Dumpsters I frequent. All except the most phobic people will be willing to eat from a can, even if it came from a Dumpster. Canned goods are among the safest foods to be found in Dumpsters but are not utterly foolproof.

Although very rare with modern canning methods,   11
botulism is a possibility. Most other forms of food poisoning seldom do lasting harm to a healthy person, but botulism is almost certainly fatal and often the first symptom is death. Except for carbonated beverages, all canned goods should contain a slight vacuum and suck air when first punctured. Bulging, rusty, and dented cans and cans that spew when punctured should be avoided, especially when the contents are not very acidic or syrupy.

Heat can break down the botulin, but this requires   12
much more cooking than most people do to canned goods. To the extent that botulism occurs at all, of course, it can occur in cans on pantry shelves as well as in cans from Dumpsters. Need I say that home-canned goods are simply too risky to be recommended.

From time to time one of my companions, aware of   13
the source of my provisions, will ask, "Do you think these crackers are really safe to eat?" For some reason it is most often the crackers they ask about.

This question has always made me angry. Of course   14
I would not offer my companion anything I had doubts about. But more than that, I wonder why he cannot evaluate the condition of the crackers for himself. I have no special knowledge and I have been wrong before. Since he knows where the food comes from, it seems to me he ought to assume some of the responsibility for deciding what he will put in his mouth. For myself I have few qualms about dry foods such as crackers, cookies, cereal, chips, and pasta if they are free of visible contaminates and still dry and crisp. Most often such things are found

in the original packaging, which is not so much a positive sign as it is the absence of a negative one.

Raw fruits and vegetables with intact skins seem per- 15
fectly safe to me, excluding of course the obviously rotten. Many are discarded for minor imperfections that can be pared away. Leafy vegetables, grapes, cauliflower, broccoli, and similar things may be contaminated by liquids and may be impractical to wash.

Candy, especially hard candy, is usually safe if it 16
has not drawn ants. Chocolate is often discarded only because it has become discolored as the cocoa butter de-emulsified. Candying, after all, is one method of food preservation because pathogens do not like very sugary substances.

All of these foods might be found in any Dumpster 17
and can be evaluated with some confidence largely on the basis of appearance. Beyond these are foods that cannot be correctly evaluated without additional information.

I began scavenging by pulling pizzas out of the Dump- 18
ster behind a pizza delivery shop. In general, prepared food requires caution, but in this case I knew when the shop closed and went to the Dumpster as soon as the last of the help left.

Such shops often get prank orders; both the orders 19
and the products made to fill them are called *bogus*. Because help seldom stays long at these places, pizzas are often made with the wrong topping, refused on delivery for being cold, or baked incorrectly. The products to be discarded are boxed up because inventory is kept by count-ing boxes: A boxed pizza can be written off; an unboxed pizza does not exist.

I never placed a bogus order to increase the supply 20
of pizzas and I believe no one else was scavenging in this Dumpster. But the people in the shop became suspicious and began to retain their garbage in the shop overnight. While it lasted I had a steady supply of fresh, sometimes warm pizza. Because I knew the Dumpster I knew the source of the pizza, and because I visited the Dumpster regularly I knew what was fresh and what was yesterday's.

Cause and effect: why Eighner visits certain Dumpsters; why students throw out food

The area I frequent is inhabited by many affluent col- 21
lege students. I am not here by chance; the Dumpsters in this area are very rich. Students throw out many good things, including food. In particular they tend to throw everything out when they move at the end of a semester, before and after breaks, and around midterm, when many of them despair of college. So I find it advantageous to keep an eye on the academic calendar.

Students throw food away around breaks because they 22
do not know whether it has spoiled or will spoil before
they return. A typical discard is a half jar of peanut butter.
In fact, nonorganic peanut butter does not require refrig-
eration and is unlikely to spoil in any reasonable time.
The student does not know that, and since it is Daddy's
money, the student decides not to take a chance. Opened
containers require caution and some attention to the
question "Why was this discarded?" But in the case of discards from student apartments, the answer may be that
the item was thrown out through carelessness, ignorance,
or wastefulness. This can sometimes be deduced when the
item is found with many others, including some that are
obviously perfectly good.

Some students, and others, approach defrosting a 23
freezer by chucking out the whole lot. Not only do the circumstances of such a find tell the story, but also the mass
of frozen goods stays cold for a long time and items may
be found still frozen or freshly thawed.

Yogurt, cheese, and sour cream are items that are 24
often thrown out while they are still good. Occasionally
I find cheese with a spot of mold, which of course I just
pare off, and because it is obvious why such a cheese was
discarded, I treat it with less suspicion than an apparently
perfect cheese found in similar circumstances. Yogurt is
often discarded, still sealed, only because the expiration
date on the carton had passed. This is one of my favorite finds because yogurt will keep for several days, even in
warm weather.

Students throw out canned goods and staples at the 25
end of semesters and when they give up college at midterm. Drugs, pornography, spirits, and the like are often
discarded when parents are expected — Dad's Day, for
example. And spirits also turn up after big party weekends,
presumably discarded by the newly reformed. Wine and
spirits, of course, keep perfectly well even once opened, but
the same cannot be said of beer.

My test for carbonated soft drinks is whether they 26
still fizz vigorously. Many juices or other beverages are
too acidic or too syrupy to cause much concern, provided

Examples: liquids
that require care

they are not visibly contaminated. I have discovered nasty
molds in the vegetable juices, even when the product was
found under its original seal; I recommend that such
products be decanted slowly into a clear glass. Liquids
always require some care. One hot day I found a large jug
of Pat O'Brien's Hurricane mix. The jug had been opened
but was still ice cold. I drank three large glasses before it

became apparent to me that someone had added rum to the mix, and not a little rum. I never tasted the rum, and by the time I began to feel the effects I had already ingested a very large quantity of the beverage. Some divers would have considered this a boon, but being suddenly intoxicated in a public place in the early afternoon is not my idea of a good time.

I have heard of people maliciously contaminating discarded food and even handouts, but mostly I have heard of this from people with vivid imaginations who have had no experience with Dumpsters themselves. Just before the pizza shop stopped discarding its garbage at night, jalapeños began showing up on most of the thrown-out pizzas. If indeed this was meant to discourage me, it was a wasted effort because I am a native Texan.   27

For myself, I avoid game, poultry, pork, and egg-based foods, whether I find them raw or cooked. I seldom have the means to cook what I find, but when I do I avail myself of plentiful supplies of beef, which is often in very good condition. I suppose fish becomes disagreeable before it becomes dangerous. Lizbeth is happy to have any such thing that is past its prime and, in fact, does not recognize fish as food until it is quite strong.   28

Home leftovers, as opposed to surpluses from restaurants, are very often bad. Evidently, especially among students, there is a common type of personality that carefully wraps up even the smallest leftover and shoves it into the back of the refrigerator for six months or so before discarding it. Characteristic of this type are the reused jars and margarine tubs to which the remains are committed. I avoid ethnic foods I am unfamiliar with. If I do not know what it is supposed to look like when it is good, I cannot be certain I will be able to tell if it is bad.   29

No matter how careful I am I still get dysentery at least once a month, oftener in warmer weather. I do not want to paint too romantic a picture. Dumpster diving has serious drawbacks as a way of life.   30

Process: how to scavenge

I learned to scavenge gradually, on my own. Since then I have initiated several companions into the trade. I have learned that there is a predictable series of stages a person goes through in learning to scavenge.   31

At first the new scavenger is filled with disgust and self-loathing. He is ashamed of being seen and may lurk around, trying to duck behind things, or he may try to dive at night. (In fact, most people instinctively look away from a scavenger. By skulking around, the novice calls attention   32 to himself and arouses suspicion. Diving at night is ineffective and needlessly messy.)

Every grain of rice seems to be a maggot. Everything 33
seems to stink. He can wipe the egg yolk off the found can,
but he cannot erase from his mind the stigma of eating
garbage.

That stage passes with experience. The scavenger finds 34
a pair of running shoes that fit and look and smell brand-
new. He finds a pocket calculator in perfect working order.
He finds pristine ice cream, still frozen, more than he can
eat or keep. He begins to understand: People throw away
perfectly good stuff, a lot of perfectly good stuff.

At this stage, Dumpster shyness begins to dissipate. 35
The diver, after all, has the last laugh. He is finding all
manner of good things that are his for the taking. Those
who disparage his profession are the fools, not he.

He may begin to hang on to some perfectly good 36
things for which he has neither a use nor a market. Then
he begins to take note of the things that are not perfectly
good but are nearly so. He mates a Walkman with broken earphones and one that is missing a battery cover. He
picks up things that he can repair.

At this stage he may become lost and never recover. 37
Dumpsters are full of things of some potential value to
someone and also of things that never have much intrin-
sic value but are interesting. All the Dumpster divers I have
known come to the point of trying to acquire everything
they touch. Why not take it, they reason, since it is all free?
This is, of course, hopeless. Most divers come to realize that
they must restrict themselves to items of relatively immediate utility. But in some cases the diver simply cannot control himself. I have met several of these pack-rat types. Their
ideas of the values of various pieces of junk verge on the
psychotic. Every bit of glass may be a diamond, they think,
and all that glisters,* gold.

Cause and effect: why Eighner gains weight when he scavenges

I tend to gain weight when I am scavenging. Partly 38
this is because I always find far more pizza and dough-
nuts than water-packed tuna, nonfat yogurt, and fresh
vegetables. Also I have not developed much faith in the
reliability of Dumpsters as a food source, although it has
been proven to me many times. I tend to eat as if I have no
idea where my next meal is coming from. But mostly I just
hate to see food go to waste and so I eat much more than I
should. Something like this drives the obsession to collect
junk.

---

* Eds. note — Glitters.

As for collecting objects, I usually restrict myself to collecting one kind of small object at a time, such as pocket calculators, sunglasses, or campaign buttons. To live on the street I must anticipate my needs to a certain extent: I must pick up and save warm bedding I find in August because it will not be found in Dumpsters in November. As I have no access to health care, I often hoard essential drugs, such as antibiotics and antihistamines. (This course can be recommended only to those with some grounding in pharmacology. Antibiotics, for example, even when indicated are worse than useless if taken in insufficient amounts.) But even if I had a home with extensive storage space, I could not save everything that might be valuable in some contingency.

Cause and effect: why Eighner saves items

I have proprietary feelings about my Dumpsters. As I have mentioned, it is no accident that I scavenge from ones where good finds are common. But my limited experience with Dumpsters in other areas suggests to me that even in poorer areas, Dumpsters, if attended with sufficient diligence, can be made to yield a livelihood. The rich students discard perfectly good kiwi fruit; poorer people discard perfectly good apples. Slacks and Polo shirts are found in one place; jeans and T-shirts in the other. The population of competitors rather than the affluence of the dumpers most affects the feasibility of survival by scavenging. The large number of competitors is what puts me off the idea of trying to scavenge in places like Los Angeles.

Comparison and contrast: Dumpsters in rich and poorer areas

Curiously, I do not mind my direct competition, other scavengers, so much as I hate the can scroungers.

People scrounge cans because they have to have a little cash. I have tried scrounging cans with an able-bodied companion. Afoot a can scrounger simply cannot make more than a few dollars in a day. One can extract the necessities of life from the Dumpsters directly with far less effort than would be required to accumulate the equivalent value in cans. (These observations may not hold in places with container redemption laws.)

Cause and effect: why people scrounge cans

Can scroungers, then, are people who must have small amounts of cash. These are drug addicts and winos, mostly the latter because the amounts of cash are so small. Spirits and drugs do, like all other commodities, turn up in Dumpsters and the scavenger will from time to time have a half bottle of a rather good wine with his dinner. But the wino cannot survive on these occasional finds; he must have his daily dose to stave off the DTs. All the cans he can carry will buy about three bottles of Wild Irish Rose.

Comparison and contrast: can scroungers vs. true scavengers

I do not begrudge them the cans, but can scroungers 44 tend to tear up the Dumpsters, mixing the contents and littering the area. They become so specialized that they can see only cans. They earn my contempt by passing up change, canned goods, and readily hockable items.

There are precious few courtesies among scavengers. 45 But it is common practice to set aside surplus items: pairs of shoes, clothing, canned goods, and such. A true scavenger hates to see good stuff go to waste, and what he cannot use he leaves in good condition in plain sight.

Can scroungers lay waste to everything in their path 46 and will stir one of a pair of good shoes to the bottom of a Dumpster, to be lost or ruined in the muck. Can scroungers will even go through individual garbage cans, something I have never seen a scavenger do.

Cause and effect: why scavengers do not go through individual garbage cans

Individual garbage cans are set out on the public 47 easement only on garbage days. On the other days going through them requires trespassing close to a dwelling. Going through individual garbage cans without scattering litter is almost impossible. Litter is likely to reduce the public's tolerance of scavenging. Individual cans are simply not as productive as Dumpsters; people in houses and duplexes do not move so often and for some reason do not tend to discard as much useful material. Moreover, the time required to go through one garbage can that serves one household is not much less than the time required to go through a Dumpster that contains the refuse of twenty apartments.

But my strongest reservation about going through 48 individual garbage cans is that this seems to me a very personal kind of invasion to which I would object if I were a householder. Although many things in Dumpsters are obviously meant never to come to light, a Dumpster is somehow less personal.

I avoid trying to draw conclusions about the people 49 who dump in the Dumpsters I frequent. I think it would be unethical to do so, although I know many people will find the idea of scavenger ethics too funny for words.

Examples: things found in Dumpsters

Dumpsters contain bank statements, correspon- 50 dence, and other documents, just as anyone might expect. But there are also less obvious sources of information. Pill bottles, for example. The labels bear the name of the patient, the name of the doctor, and the name of the drug. AIDS drugs and antipsychotic medicines, to name but two groups, are specific and are seldom prescribed for any other disorders. The plastic compacts for birth-control pills usually have complete label information.

Despite all of this sensitive information, I have had   51
only one apartment resident object to my going through
the Dumpster. In that case it turned out the resident was a
university athlete who was taking bets and who was afraid
I would turn up his wager slips.

Occasionally a find tells a story. I once found a small   52
paper bag containing some unused condoms, several partial tubes of flavored sexual lubricants, a partially used
compact of birth-control pills, and the torn pieces of a picture of a young man. Clearly she was through with him
and planning to give up sex altogether.

Dumpster things are often sad — abandoned teddy   53
bears, shredded wedding books, despaired-of sales kits.
I find many pets lying in state in Dumpsters. Although I
hope to get off the streets so that Lizbeth can have a long
and comfortable old age, I know this hope is not very realistic. So I suppose when her time comes she too will go
into a Dumpster. I will have no better place for her. And
after all, it is fitting, since for most of her life her livelihood
has come from the Dumpster. When she finds something
I think is safe that has been spilled from a Dumpster, I let
her have it. She already knows the route around the best
ones. I like to think that if she survives me she will have a
chance of evading the dog catcher and of finding her sustenance on the route.

Silly vanities also come to rest in the Dumpsters. I am   54
a rather accomplished needleworker. I get a lot of material
from the Dumpsters. Evidently sorority girls, hoping to
impress someone, perhaps themselves, with their mastery
of a womanly art, buy a lot of embroider-by-number kits,
work a few stitches horribly, and eventually discard the
whole mess. I pull out their stitches, turn the canvas over,
and work an original design. Do not think I refrain from
chuckling as I make gifts from these kits.

I find diaries and journals. I have often thought of   55
compiling a book of literary found objects. And perhaps
I will one day. But what I find is hopelessly commonplace
and bad without being, even unconsciously, camp. College
students also discard their papers. I am horrified to discover the kind of paper that now merits an A in an undergraduate course. I am grateful, however, for the number
of good books and magazines the students throw out.

In the area I know best I have never discovered vermin   56
in the Dumpster, but there are two kinds of kitty surprise.
One is alley cats whom I meet as they leap, claws first, out
of Dumpsters. This is especially thrilling when I have Lizbeth in tow. The other kind of kitty surprise is a plastic

garbage bag filled with some ponderous, amorphous mass. This always proves to be used cat litter.

City bees harvest doughnut glaze and this makes   57
the Dumpster at the doughnut shop more interesting. My faith in the instinctive wisdom of animals is always shaken whenever I see Lizbeth attempt to catch a bee in her mouth, which she does whenever bees are present. Evidently some birds find Dumpsters profitable, for birdie surprise is almost as common as kitty surprise of the first kind. In hunting season all kinds of small game turn up in Dumpsters, some of it, sadly, not entirely dead. Curiously, summer and winter, maggots are uncommon.

The worst of the living and near-living hazards of the   58
Dumpsters are the fire ants. The food they claim is not much of a loss, but they are vicious and aggressive. It is very easy to brush against some surface of the Dumpster and pick up half a dozen or more fire ants, usually in some sensitive area such as the underarm. One advantage of bringing Lizbeth along as I make Dumpster rounds is that, for obvious reasons, she is very alert to ground-based fire ants. When Lizbeth recognizes a fire-ant infestation around our feet, she does the Dance of the Zillion Fire Ants. I have learned not to ignore this warning from Lizbeth, whether I perceive the tiny ants or not, but to remove ourselves at Lizbeth's first *pas de bourée.** All the more so because the ants are the worst in the summer months when I wear flip-flops if I have them. (Perhaps someone will misunderstand this. Lizbeth does the Dance of the Zillion Fire Ants when she recognizes more fire ants than she cares to eat, not when she is being bitten. Since I have learned to react promptly, she does not get bitten at all. It is the isolated patrol of fire ants that falls in Lizbeth's range that deserves pity. She finds them quite tasty.)

Process: how to go through a Dumpster

By far the best way to go through a Dumpster is to   59
lower yourself into it. Most of the good stuff tends to settle at the bottom because it is usually weightier than the rubbish. My more athletic companions have often demonstrated to me that they can extract much good material from a Dumpster I have already been over.

To those psychologically or physically unprepared to   60
enter a Dumpster, I recommend a stout stick, preferably with some barb or hook at one end. The hook can be used to grab plastic garbage bags. When I find canned goods or other objects loose at the bottom of a Dumpster, I lower

---

* Eds. note — A ballet step.

a bag into it, roll the desired object into the bag, and then hoist the bag out — a procedure more easily described than executed. Much Dumpster diving is a matter of experience for which nothing will do except practice.

Dumpster diving is outdoor work, often surprisingly 61 pleasant. It is not entirely predictable; things of interest turn up every day and some days there are finds of great value. I am always very pleased when I can turn up exactly the thing I most wanted to find. Yet in spite of the element of chance, scavenging more than most other pursuits tends to yield returns in some proportion to the effort and intelligence brought to bear. It is very sweet to turn up a few dollars in change from a Dumpster that has just been gone over by a wino.

The land is now covered with cities. The cities are full 62 of Dumpsters. If a member of the canine race is ever able to know what it is doing, then Lizbeth knows that when we go around to the Dumpsters, we are hunting. I think of scavenging as a modern form of self-reliance. In any event, after having survived nearly ten years of government service, where everything is geared to the lowest common denominator, I find it refreshing to have work that rewards initiative and effort. Certainly I would be happy to have a sinecure again, but I am no longer heartbroken that I left one.

Cause and effect: results of Eighner's experiences as a scavenger

I find from the experience of scavenging two rather 63 deep lessons. The first is to take what you can use and let the rest go by. I have come to think that there is no value in the abstract. A thing I cannot use or make useful, perhaps by trading, has no value however rare or fine it may be. I mean useful in some broad sense — some art I would find useful and some otherwise.

I was shocked to realize that some things are not 64 worth acquiring, but now I think it is so. Some material things are white elephants that eat up the possessor's substance. The second lesson is the transience of material being. This has not quite converted me to a dualist,* but it has made some headway in that direction. I do not suppose that ideas are immortal, but certainly mental things are longer lived than other material things.

Once I was the sort of person who invests objects with 65 sentimental value. Now I no longer have those objects, but I have the sentiments yet.

---

* Eds. note — Someone who believes that the world consists of two opposing forces, such as mind and matter.

Many times in our travels I have lost everything but   66
the clothes I was wearing and Lizbeth. The things I find
in Dumpsters, the love letters and rag dolls of so many
lives, remind me of this lesson. Now I hardly pick up a
thing without envisioning the time I will cast it aside. This
I think is a healthy state of mind. Almost everything I have
now has already been cast out at least once, proving that
what I own is valueless to someone.

Anyway, I find my desire to grab for the gaudy bauble   67
has been largely sated. I think this is an attitude I share
with the very wealthy — we both know there is plenty more
where what we have came from. Between us are the rat-race
millions who nightly scavenge the cable channels looking
for they know not what.

I am sorry for them.   68

•   •   •

Comprehension

1. Using your own words, write a one-sentence definition of *Dumpster diving*.
2. List some of Eighner's answers to the question "Why was this discarded?"
   (8). What additional reasons can you think of?
3. What foods does Eighner take particular care to avoid? Why?
4. In paragraph 30, Eighner comments, "Dumpster diving has serious drawbacks as a way of life." What drawbacks does he cite in his essay? What additional drawbacks are implied? Can you think of others?
5. Summarize the stages in the process of learning to scavenge.
6. In addition to food, what else does Eighner scavenge for? Into what general
   categories do these items fall?
7. Why does Eighner hate "can scroungers" (44)?
8. What lessons has Eighner learned as a Dumpster diver?

Purpose and Audience

1. In paragraph 6, Eighner states his purpose: to record what he has learned as
   a Dumpster diver. What additional purposes do you think he had in setting
   his ideas down on paper?
2. Do you think most readers are likely to respond to Eighner's essay with
   sympathy? Pity? Impatience? Contempt? Disgust? How do you react? Why?
3. Why do you think Eighner chose not to provide much background about
   his life — his upbringing, education, or work history — before he became
   homeless? Do you think this decision was a wise one? How might such
   information (for example, any of the details provided in the headnote that
   precedes the essay) have changed readers' reactions to his discussion?
4. In paragraph 8, Eighner presents three principles one must follow to eat
   safely from a Dumpster; in paragraphs 59 and 60, he explains how to
   go through a Dumpster; and throughout the essay, he includes many

cautions and warnings. Clearly, he does not expect his audience to take up Dumpster diving. Why, then, does he include this kind of detailed information?
5. When Eighner begins paragraph 9 with "Perhaps everyone who has a kitchen," he encourages readers to identify with him. Where else does he make efforts to help readers imagine themselves in his place? Are these efforts successful? Explain your response.
6. What effect do you think the essay's last sentence is calculated to have on readers? What effect does it have on you?

Style and Structure

1. Eighner opens his essay with a fairly conventional strategy: extended definitions of *Dumpster* and *Dumpster diving*. What techniques does he use in paragraphs 1 through 3 to develop these definitions? Is beginning with definitions the best strategy for this essay? Explain your answer.
2. **Vocabulary Project.** In paragraph 3, Eighner suggests several alternative words for *diving* as he uses it in his essay. Consult an unabridged dictionary to determine the connotations of each of his alternatives. What are the pros and cons of substituting one of these words for *diving* in Eighner's title and throughout the essay?
3. This long essay contains three one-sentence paragraphs. Why do you think Eighner isolates these three sentences? Do you think any of them should be combined with an adjacent paragraph? Explain your reasoning.
4. As the introductory note explains, Eighner chose to retain the present tense even though he was no longer homeless when the essay was published. Why do you think he decided to preserve the present tense?
5. Eighner's essay includes a number of lists that catalog items he came across (for example, in paragraphs 5 and 50). Identify as many of these lists as you can. Why do you think Eighner includes such extensive lists?

Journal Entry

In paragraphs 21 through 25, Eighner discusses the discarding of food by college students. Do your own experiences support his observations? Do you think he is being too hard on students, or does his characterization seem accurate?

Writing Workshop

1. Write an essay about a homeless person you have seen in your community. Use any patterns you like to structure your paper. When you have finished, annotate your essay to identify the patterns you have used.
2. Write an email to your school's dean of students recommending steps that can be taken on your campus to redirect discarded (but edible) food to the homeless. Use process and exemplification to structure your message, and use information from Eighner's essay to support your points. (Be sure to acknowledge your source.)

3. **Working with Sources.** Taking Eighner's point of view and using information from his essay, as well as information (for example, statistics) you find online, write an argumentative essay with a thesis statement that takes a strong stand for ending homelessness and recommends government or private measures that should be taken to accomplish this goal. If you like, you may write your essay in the form of a statement by Eighner to a congressional committee. Be sure to document any words or ideas you borrow from Eighner or from other sources and to include a works-cited page. (See Chapter 18 for information on MLA documentation.)

Combining the Patterns

Review the annotations that identify each pattern of development used in this essay. Which patterns seem to be most effective in helping you understand and empathize with the life of a homeless person? Why?

Thematic Connections
- "Stability in Motion" (page 179)
- "The Hidden Life of Garbage" (page 185)
- "Food Insecurity on Campus" (page 211)
- "Photos That Change History" (page 354)
- "The Untouchable" (page 487)
- The Declaration of Independence (page 548)

OLIVIA JUDSON

Long Live the Albatross

Olivia Judson (b. 1970) is an evolutionary biologist and writer. A graduate of Stanford University, Judson went on to receive her doctorate from Oxford University. Her scientific writing has appeared in *Nature*, *Science*, *National Geographic*, and *The Economist*, where she worked as a science writer from 1995 to 1997. She has also worked as an online columnist for the *New York Times*. Judson's books include *Dr. Tatiana's Sex Advice to All Creation* (2002) and *Dinosaur Eggs for Breakfast* (2009); she has also appeared on television in an adaptation of her *Dr. Tatiana* book, as well as on the PBS series *Nova*. She is currently a research fellow at Imperial College in London.

Background on animal species in danger of extinction The term *endangered species* is familiar to many people, but the origins of its official designation may not be. Species are categorized as "endangered" by the International Union for the Conservation of Nature (IUCN), which was founded in 1948. The IUCN's headquarters are in Switzerland, but it employs about a thousand full-time staff members around the globe and claims more than fourteen hundred organizations (some governmental, some not) as members. "Endangered" is IUCN's best-known classification, but the organization designates species on a schema that also includes "least concern" (no immediate threat), "near-threatened" (may become threatened in the near future), "vulnerable" (a high risk of becoming endangered), "critically endangered" (facing a high risk of extinction), "extinct in the wild" (existing in captivity but not in a free-living population), and "extinct" (no remaining individuals). More than 50 percent of the world's species are considered to be at some risk of extinction, caused by industrialization, overhunting, and invasive species, among other factors.

I remember the first albatross I ever saw. I was on a small boat a few miles off the coast of New Zealand. As the bird sailed past, gliding on the wind, it skimmed low over the waves, the tip of one wing so close to the water that I thought it must touch. But it never did.

> "I remember the first albatross I ever saw."

1

I no longer know which species it was — there are 20 or so, and the encounter was years ago — but I remember my excitement at seeing a bird at once majestic and mythic. Carl Linnaeus, the Swede who, in the eighteenth century, invented the system of Latin names by which different species are known, called the group *Diomedea*, a reference to the Greek legend in which the companions of the warrior Diomedes are transformed into birds. Perhaps he was inspired by stories then reaching Europe, which told how the huge birds — the largest can have a wingspan of nearly 12 feet — would sometimes fly alongside ships struggling through the tempests of the southern seas.

2

One of these accounts certainly inspired the Romantic poet Samuel Taylor 3
Coleridge. In *The Rime of the Ancient Mariner*, published in 1798, Coleridge
describes an albatross following a ship in a storm. On impulse, one of the sailors
shoots the bird. This turns out to be a crime against nature, and is met with
divine retribution. As the first installment of his penance, the sailor explains,
"Instead of the cross, the Albatross / About my neck was hung." Henceforth, the
name of this magnificent creature would be synonymous with "terrible burden."

"I remember the first albatross I ever saw," says the narrator of Herman 4
Melville's *Moby-Dick*. "It was during a prolonged gale, in waters hard upon the
Antarctic Seas." He goes on to relate that the bird was captured "with a treach-
erous hook and line." Happily, it was soon released, albeit — in a sly inversion of
Coleridge — bearing a leather strap around its neck listing the ship's time and
place.

These days, certainly, albatrosses are burdened by humans more often 5
than the other way around. In 1989, six members of the species *Diomedea exu-
lans*, also known as the wandering albatross, became the first birds ever successfully fitted with satellite trackers. The devices showed that the birds ranged
farther, and traveled faster, than anyone had thought: In one 33-day trip, an
individual covered more than 9,000 miles, reaching speeds of 50 miles an hour.
Subsequent research has shown that over the course of their long lives — the
birds can live for more than 50 years — wandering albatrosses may travel more
than 5.2 million miles, which is about 11 round trips to the moon. They cover
almost all this distance by soaring effortlessly upon the wind.

Wandering albatrosses are slow to reach maturity, and breed slowly once 6
they do. In a given breeding attempt, the female lays a single egg, which the
parents take turns incubating until, more than two and a half months later, it
hatches. If all goes well, the chick will fledge about nine months after that. The
effort to raise a chick is so long and strenuous that, after doing so, both parents
take a sabbatical year, which they spend entirely at sea.

Like so many other life-forms now, almost half of all albatross species are 7
endangered, some critically. With his "treacherous hook and line," Melville was
prescient: For wandering albatrosses, as well as several related species, longline
fisheries are one of the main causes of death. The birds take the bait, get caught
on the hooks, and drown. Moreover, because they live so long and prey on fish
and squid, albatrosses are among the birds most contaminated with mercury.
In many ways, they are mirrors of the ways that humans treat the sea.

While I don't believe in divine punishment, I do read *The Rime* as a warning 8
against ecological destruction. If, through our actions, the albatross were to
pass entirely into legend, we would have diminished the richness not only of
nature but of ourselves. These birds have an important cultural dimension;
if they vanish, a tangible part of human culture vanishes too. More generally, if
we lose these marvelous and beautiful organisms, which have evolved over
such a long period and which have never existed anywhere else in our cosmos
and never will, we erode our capacity for wonder, knowledge, and inspiration,
and diminish the planet for those who come after us.

But it is not too late; the albatross is not gone yet. Efforts to protect the   9
birds are under way, and an international treaty (the Agreement on the
Conservation of Albatrosses and Petrels) is in force. As a result, a number of
fisheries have started setting bait at night, using weighted hooks, and flying
streamers that scare the birds away. All of these measures reduce the number of
birds caught, and suggest a way to create more general mechanisms of plane-
tary care. We still have time to stop the ransacking of nature and ensure that,
for generations to come, people will be able to exclaim with delight and awe, "I
remember the first albatross I ever saw!"

• • •

Comprehension

1. Why was Judson's first sight of an albatross so memorable?
2. In what sense is the albatross "at once majestic and mythic" (2)?
3. How did the word *albatross* come to mean a "terrible burden" (3)?
4. Judson sees Coleridge's poem as "a warning against ecological destruction"
   (8). Why?
5. How has the albatross been used to advance scientific research?
6. What efforts are being made to protect the albatross from extinction? What
   is Judson's opinion of these efforts?

Purpose and Audience

1. Why does Judson focus on the albatross? What does she expect readers to
   take away from her essay?
2. Why does Judson provide a summary of Coleridge's poem in paragraphs
   3 and 4? Is this summary necessary, or do you think she could reasonably
   expect her readers to be familiar with this poem?
3. Judson opens paragraph 5 by saying that today, "albatrosses are burdened
   by humans more than the other way around." How does she support this
   statement? In what sense is the statement **ironic**?
4. Is this essay's central focus on the albatross's value as an enduring literary
   symbol or on its status as an endangered species? Explain.

Style and Structure

1. **Vocabulary Project.** What does the word *endangered* mean to you? In what
   contexts is it most often used? What words (in addition to *species*) does it
   generally modify?
2. What does the scientific information about the albatross's biological development in paragraph 6 contribute to the essay? Is it necessary? Why or why not?
3. Judson covers a variety of topics related to the albatross, focusing on everything from her personal experience to etymology to scientific research. If
   you were to divide the essay into sections, where would you place headings,
   and how would you word them?

4. Judson uses several different patterns to develop her essay. Which do you see as the essay's *primary* pattern of development? Why?

5. Judson introduces her essay with the sentence, "I remember the first albatross I ever saw." Where else does this sentence appear? What does this repetition accomplish?

Journal Entry

Do you see this essay as primarily optimistic or pessimistic? Why?

Writing Workshop

1. **Working with Sources.** Read Samuel Taylor Coleridge's "The Rime of the Ancient Mariner," the narrative poem discussed in paragraphs 3 and 4. Then, write an essay in which you discuss the effect the albatross had on the sailors in the poem and how it changed them. Be sure to document all references to the poem and to include a works-cited page. (See Chapter 18 for information on MLA documentation.)

2. In her conclusion, Judson states, "We still have time to stop the ransacking of nature." Do you agree? Write an essay in which you argue that in fact it is too late to stop this "ransacking of nature" — or that, although time is running out, the process can still be slowed down.

3. Choose an animal you know a lot about, and write a similar tribute (serious or humorous) to that animal. Call your essay "Long Live the _____." If possible, consider some of the same topics Judson examines in her discussion of the albatross.

Combining the Patterns

What patterns of development does Judson use in her essay? Annotate the essay to identify each pattern. Use the annotations accompanying "On Dumpster Diving" (page 668) as a guide.

Thematic Connections

- "The Twin Revolutions of Lincoln and Darwin" (page 420)
- "The Obligation to Endure" (page 554)
- Debate: "Can Individuals Do Anything to Resolve the Climate Crisis?" (page 587)

DAVID KIRBY

Inked Well

Poet David Kirby is a longtime professor of English at Florida State University, where he teaches nineteenth-century American literature and creative writing. He has authored or coauthored twenty-nine books, including the poetry collections *The Ha-Ha* (2003), *The House on Boulevard Street* (2007), and *Talking about Movies with Jesus*; literary studies such as *Mark Strand and the Poet's Place in Contemporary Culture* (1990) and *Herman Melville* (1993); the essay collection *Ultra-Talk: Johnny Cash, the Mafia, Shakespeare, Drum Music, St. Teresa of Avila, and 17 Other Colossal Topics of Conversation* (2007); and the biography *Little Richard: The Birth of Rock 'n' Roll* (2009).

Background on tattoos People have sported tattoos for more than five thousand years. In some cultures, tattoos have marked a rite of passage into adulthood. They have also symbolized spiritual protection, status within a clan, fertility, and social ostracism, among other things. (Interestingly, the teachings of both Judaism and Islam specifically prohibit tattooing.) In modern Western culture, tattoos primarily serve as body adornment, although there are some exceptions — for example, the Nazis forcibly tattooed identifying numbers on many Jews, and members of some street gangs wear tattoos that signify membership. In the United States today, the most popular tattoos include skulls, hearts, eagles, and crosses as well as abstract tribal designs based on motifs that originated among Polynesian Islanders (historically, some of the most heavily tattooed people in the world). Celtic designs, flowers and butterflies, angels, stars, dragons, Chinese characters, and swallows are also popular, and anchors, once staples among sailors, are now making a comeback. Increasingly, tattoo artists are being taken seriously, and an original design may be worth thousands of dollars, or even more. Today, conventions of tattoo enthusiasts, such as the traveling Bodyart Expo, draw millions of participants each year. The cost of getting a tattoo can be as much as two hundred dollars an hour. (Getting rid of a tattoo can cost considerably more.)

1   Some tattooed people are easier to read than others.

2   When Richard Costello tried to sell stolen motorcycle parts on eBay earlier this year, he put the items on the floor and photographed them, though the photos also included his bare feet, with the word *White* tattooed on one and *Trash* on the other. The bike's lawful owner did a Web search, found what appeared to be the stolen parts, and notified the Clearwater, Florida, police department. Since jail records typically include identifying marks, it didn't take long for local detectives to identify Mr. Costello and set up a sting. He was arrested after showing up with a van full of stolen parts and is now facing trial. According to Sgt. Greg Stewart, Mr. Costello "just tiptoed his way back to jail."

3   L'Affaire White Trash confirmed just about everything that I thought about tattoos until recently; namely, that in addition to being nasty and

unsanitary, tattoos only grace the skins of either bottom feeders or those who want to pretend they are. Richard Costello's phenomenal act of self-betrayal wouldn't have been a surprise at all to modernist architect Adolph Loos, whose influential 1908 essay "Ornament and Crime" is still cited today as a potent argument against frills and fancy stuff. Mr. Loos wrote in effect a manifesto opposing decoration, which he saw as a mark of primitive cultures, and in favor of simplicity, which is a sign of, well, modernism. Thus, Mr. Loos reasoned, it's OK for a Pacific Islander to cover himself and all his possessions with ink and carvings, whereas "a modern person [i.e., a European] who tattoos himself is either a criminal or a degenerate. . . . People with tattoos not in prison are either latent criminals or degenerate aristocrats."

So, presuming the kid with a Tweety Bird tattoo on his forearm who delivered your pizza last night isn't a down-on-his-luck baronet who's trying to earn enough money to return to his ancestral estate in Northumberland and claim his seat on the Queen's Privy Council, does the fact that he's slinging pies mean that he simply hasn't lived long enough to commit his first murder? Not necessarily: tattoos have a richer social history than one might think.   4

Tattoos were brought to Europe from Polynesia by eighteenth-century British explorers, as Margo DeMello writes in *Bodies of Inscription: A Cultural History of the Modern Tattoo Community* (2000). Europeans who had tattoos in those days were not social bottom dwellers. And as Charles C. Mann points out in *1491* (2005), Americans first saw tattoos in the New World on their conflicted Indian hosts as early as 1580. To Protestants of ascetic temperaments, these exotic displays were of a piece with the colonists' propensity to see Indians as primeval savages.   5

Perhaps predictably, however, tattoos came ultimately to signify patriotism rather than exoticism in the United States. The first known professional tattoo artist in the United States was one Martin Hildebrandt, who set up shop in New York City in 1846. Mr. Hildebrandt became instrumental in establishing the tradition of the tattooed serviceman by practicing his craft on soldiers and sailors on both sides in the Civil War as he migrated from one camp to another.   6

And then occurred one of those curious little shifts that make history so delicious. Tattoos became fashionable among members of the European aristocracy, who encountered the practice during nineteenth-century trips to the Far East.   7

By the beginning of World War I, though, the lords and ladies had all but abandoned bodily decoration. Why? Because by then, anybody could get a tattoo. The laborious process involving hand-tapping ink into the skin with a single needle was made obsolete with the invention of the electric tattoo machine in 1891. Tattooing suddenly became easier, less painful, and, mainly, cheaper. This led to the speedy spread of the practice throughout the working class and its abandonment by the rich.   8

By the middle of the twentieth century, tattooing seemed largely the province of bikers, convicts, and other groups on the margins of society, much as Mr. Loos had predicted. Except for all those patriotic servicemen, a century ago tattoos were the tribal marks that you paid somebody to cut into your skin so   9 that everyone would know you belonged to a world populated by crooks and creeps, along with a few bored aristocrats who would probably have been attracted to living a life of crime had their trust funds not rendered it redundant. And if things had stayed that way, I wouldn't be writing this essay: tattoos would be simply one more way of differentiating "Them" from "Us."

But "We" are the ones who are tattooed now: in the late twentieth century, the middle class began showing up in droves at tattoo parlors. A study in the June 2006 issue of the *Journal of the American Academy of Dermatology* reveals that as many as 24 percent of men and women between the ages of eighteen and fifty have one or more tattoos—up from just 15 to 16 percent in 2003. Men and women are equally likely to be tattooed, though the women surveyed are more likely to have body piercings, as well.

How did this change come to pass? Those of us who are certain we'll never get a tattoo will always shudder with joy when we read about knuckleheads like Richard Costello. But more and more people who wouldn't have dreamed of being tattooed a few years back are paying good money to have sketches of boom boxes, court jesters, and spider webs incised into their hides. Why, and what does it say about the world we live in?

To answer these questions, I walked the streets of Tallahassee, Florida, accosting total and sometimes menacing-looking strangers with the intent of asking them questions about the most intimate parts of their bodies. Any stereotypes of tattooed "victims" I had fell by the wayside rather quickly.

One of my first lessons was that people can get the biggest, most colorful tattoos either for exceedingly complex reasons or none at all. Jen (I'll use first names only), a pretty, slender brunette in her late twenties, said getting a tattoo was simply on a list of things she wanted to do. Melissa, a grad student in modern languages whom I spied in a bookstore wearing a pair of low-slung jeans, got a black and blue love knot high on one hip because she and her friend wanted identical tattoos, "even though she's not my friend anymore." Becky wanted a tattoo that would be a means of "making a promise to myself that I would become the person I wanted to be, that I would improve my life through hard work."

Of the dozen or so subjects I interviewed, Jodie was the sweetest, the most articulate, and the most heavily inked—her arms were fully sleeved in tattoos, and she was making plans to get started on her hands and neck. Jodie explained that she had been a "cutter" who "was having a lot of trouble with hurting myself physically for various reasons, so I began to get tattooed. It didn't take me long to realize that getting tattooed was quite comparable to cutting myself; it was a way for me to 'bleed out' the emotional pains which I was unable to deal with otherwise."

Jodie is smart as well as troubled. She knew she was hurting herself and would continue to do so, so she sublimated her self-destruction and made art of it, as surely as, say, poet Sylvia Plath* did—temporarily, anyway.

---

* Eds. note—American confessional poet who committed suicide in 1963 at the age of thirty.

It seems that more and more people from every walk of life in these United   16
States are getting tattooed. These pioneers are "deterritorializing" tattoos, in
Ms. DeMello's words, liberating them from patriotic sailors and dim-bulb
motorcycle thieves and making them available to soccer moms and dads.

Tattoos have always been a means of identifying oneself, notes Ms. DeMello,   17
and are always meant to be read—even a tattoo that's hidden becomes a secret
book of sorts. When you get a tattoo, you write yourself, in a manner of speaking, and make it possible for others to read you, which means that every tattoo
has a story.

There are primarily two types of tattoo narratives, the Record Book and   18
the Canvas. Melissa, the young woman who got her tattoo to signify bonding
with a friend, was capturing a relationship as one might with a photograph. In
the pop music world, rap artists and other musicians sometimes get tattoos of
friends or relatives who have died violently or merely passed away. The Dixie
Chicks agreed to get a little chick footprint on the insteps of their feet for every
No. 1 album they had.

If your body is a Record Book, then you and everyone who sees you is look-   19
ing back at the events depicted there. But if you see your body as a Canvas, then
the story you tell is, at least in its conception and execution, as inner-driven as
any by Faulkner or Hemingway. Jodie, for example, is going over every inch of
her body, using it as a way to tell herself a story she's beginning to understand
only gradually. The more she understands, the more she "revises," just as any
other artist might: her first tattoo was "a horrible butterfly thing," she told me,
"which has since been covered up with a lovely raven."

Every person with a tattoo is a link in a chain of body modification that   20
goes back to the dawn of human history. Researchers have found sharpened
pieces of manganese dioxide—black crayons,
really—that Neanderthals may have used to
color animal skins as well as their own. The
ancient Egyptians practiced simple tattooing. Today, radically different cultures share
an obsession with body remodeling that
goes far beyond mere tattooing. African
tribes pierce and scar the body routinely;
weightlifters pump their pecs until they bulge like grapefruit; women pay for
cosmetic breast enlargement or reduction. And if that's not enough evidence
that body modification is endemic, I have one word for you: *Botox.*

> "In a word, tattoos
> are now officially OK
> by me."

The point of all this is self-expression—and we seem to be living in a time   21
where that's what nearly everybody (word carefully chosen) wants to do, in
one way or another. As with all lifestyle changes, the tricky part is knowing
when to stop.

As I said, I used to think tattoos were for either lowlifes or those who   22
wanted to pretend they were, but my mind now stands changed by the thoughtful, articulate people I talked to and the spectacular designs that had been
inked into their bodies. In a word, tattoos are now officially OK by me.

Does that mean I'd get one? Not on your life.   23

· · ·

Comprehension

1. Explain the possible meanings of "Inked Well," the essay's title.
2. Kirby opens his essay with a narrative that recounts "L'Affaire White Trash" (3). Why does he begin with this narrative? What does it illustrate about tattoos?
3. Where does Kirby present information on the history of tattoos? Why does he include this background? Is it necessary? Why does he return to this historical background in paragraph 20?
4. According to Kirby, how has the tattooed population changed over the years? What factors explain these changes?
5. What does Kirby mean when he says, " 'We' are the ones who are tattooed now" (10)?
6. What two kinds of "tattoo narratives" does Kirby identify? How are they different?
7. According to Kirby, for what reasons do people get tattoos? Can you think of additional reasons?
8. How have Kirby's ideas about tattoos changed over the years? *Why* have they changed?

Purpose and Audience

1. Is Kirby's primary purpose to provide information about tattoos, to entertain readers, to explore his own feelings about tattoos, or to persuade readers to consider getting (or not getting) tattoos? Explain.
2. In paragraph 4, Kirby says that "tattoos have a richer social history than one might think." Is this his essay's thesis? If not, what is the thesis of "Inked Well"?
3. Why do you think Kirby mentions the universal "obsession with body remodeling" in paragraph 20? How do you think he expects this reference to affect his audience's reactions to his thesis? How do you react?

Style and Structure

1. **Vocabulary Project.** What is the origin of the word *tattoo*? Check a dictionary to find out. Then, visit a tattoo website such as tattoos.com, and list some words and phrases that are part of the vocabulary of the tattoo industry. Define several of these words and expressions in layperson's terms.
2. What do you see as this essay's dominant pattern of development? Why?
3. Kirby's first and last paragraphs are each just one sentence long. Are his short introduction and conclusion effective? If you were to expand them, what would you add? Why?
4. Where does Kirby cite experts? Where does he include statistics? What do these kinds of information add to his essay?

Journal Entry

Do you see tattoos as art or as a kind of defacement or self-mutilation? Explain your feelings.

Writing Workshop

1. **Working with Sources.** Find some pictures of tattoos online. Then, write a classification-and-division essay that discusses the kinds of tattoos you discover. Be sure your essay has a thesis statement that makes a point about tattoos, and use exemplification, description, and comparison and contrast to support your thesis. If you like, you may illustrate your essay with photos or drawings. If you use visuals you find online or in print, be sure to document your sources and to include a works-cited page. (See Chapter 18 for information on MLA documentation.)

2. In paragraph 11, Kirby asks what the prevalence of tattoos says about the world we live in. Using cause and effect as your dominant pattern of development, write an essay that tries to explain what accounts for this phenomenon. Use description and exemplification to support your points.

3. In paragraph 17, Kirby says, "When you get a tattoo, you write yourself, in a manner of speaking, and make it possible for others to read you, which means that every tattoo has a story." What story would you like your own tattoo (or tattoos) to tell? Write an essay that answers this question, using description, exemplification, and cause and effect as well as narration.

Combining the Patterns

What patterns of development does Kirby use in his essay? Annotate the essay to identify each pattern. Use the annotations accompanying "On Dumpster Diving" (page 668) as a guide.

Thematic Connections

* "Medium Ash Brown" (page 269)
* "Patterns" (page 473)

JONATHAN SWIFT

A Modest Proposal

Jonathan Swift (1667–1745) was born in Dublin, Ireland, and spent much of his life journeying between his homeland, where he had a modest income as an Anglican priest, and England, where he wished to be part of the literary establishment. The author of many satires and political pamphlets, he is best known today for *Gulliver's Travels* (1726), a sharp satire that, except among academics, is now read primarily as a fantasy for children.

Background on the English-Irish conflict At the time Swift wrote "A Modest Proposal," Ireland had been essentially under British rule since 1171, with the British often brutally suppressing rebellions by the Irish people. When Henry VIII of England declared a Protestant Church of Ireland, many of the Irish remained fiercely Roman Catholic, which led to even greater contention. By the early 1700s, the English-controlled Irish Parliament had passed laws that severely limited the rights of Irish Catholics, and British trade policies had begun to seriously depress the Irish economy. A fierce advocate for the Irish people in their struggle under British rule, Swift published several works supporting the Irish cause. The following sharply ironic essay was written during the height of a terrible famine in Ireland, when the British were proposing a devastating tax on the impoverished Irish citizenry. Note that Swift does not write in his own voice here but adopts the persona of one who does not recognize the barbarity of his "solution."

1   It is a melancholy object to those who walk through this great town* or travel in the country, when they see the streets, the roads, and cabin doors, crowded with beggars of the female sex, followed by three, four, or six children, all in rags and importuning every passenger for an alms. These mothers, instead of being able to work for their honest livelihood, are forced to employ all their time in strolling to beg sustenance for their helpless infants, who, as they grow up, either turn thieves for want of work, or leave their dear native country to fight for the Pretender in Spain, or sell themselves to the Barbadoes.**

2   I think it is agreed by all parties that this prodigious number of children in the arms, or on the backs, or at the heels of their mothers, and frequently of their fathers, is in the present deplorable state of the kingdom a very great additional grievance; and therefore whoever could find out a fair, cheap, and easy method of making these children sound, useful members of the commonwealth would deserve so well of the public as to have his statue set up for a preserver of the nation.

---

* Eds. note — Dublin.
** Eds. note — Many young Irishmen left their country to fight as mercenaries in Spain's civil war or to work as indentured servants in the West Indies.

But my intention is very far from being confined to provide only for the children of professed beggars; it is of a much greater extent, and shall take in the whole number of infants at a certain age who are born of parents in effect as little able to support them as those who demand our charity in the streets. 3

As to my own part, having turned my thoughts for many years upon this important subject, and maturely weighed the several schemes of the other projectors, I have always found them grossly mistaken in their computation. It is true, a child just dropped from its dam may be supported by her milk for a solar year, with little other nourishment; at most not above the value of two shillings, which the mother may certainly get, or the value in scraps, by her lawful occupation of begging; and it is exactly at one year old that I propose to provide for them in such a manner as instead of being a charge upon their parents or the parish, or wanting food and raiment for the rest of their lives, they shall on the contrary contribute to the feeding, and partly to the clothing, of many thousands. 4

There is likewise another great advantage in my scheme, that it will prevent those involuntary abortions, and that horrid practice of women murdering their bastard children, alas, too frequent among us, sacrificing the poor innocent babies, I doubt, more to avoid the expense than the shame, which would move tears and pity in the most savage and inhuman breast. 5

The number of souls in this kingdom being usually reckoned one million and a half, of these I calculate there may be about two hundred thousand couples whose wives are breeders, from which number I subtract thirty thousand couples who are able to maintain their own children, although I apprehend there cannot be so many under the present distress of the kingdom; but this being granted, there will remain an hundred and seventy thousand breeders. I again subtract fifty thousand for those women who miscarry, or whose children die by accident or disease within the year. There only remain an hundred and twenty thousand children of poor parents annually born. The question therefore is, how this number shall be reared and provided for, which, as I have already said, under the present situation of affairs, is utterly impossible by all the methods hitherto proposed. For we can neither employ them in handicraft nor agriculture; we neither build houses (I mean in the country) nor cultivate land. They can very seldom pick up livelihood by stealing till they arrive at six years old, except where they are of towardly parts,* although I confess they learn the rudiments much earlier, during which time they can however be looked upon only as probationers, as I have been informed by a principal gentleman in the country of Cavan, who protested to me that he never knew above one or two instances under the age of six, even in a part of the kingdom so renowned for the quickest proficiency in that art. 6

I am assured by our merchants that a boy or a girl before twelve years old is no salable commodity; and even when they come to this age, they will not yield above three pounds, or three pounds and half a crown at most on the Exchange; which cannot turn to account either to the parents or the kingdom, the charge of nutriment and rags having been at least four times that value. 7

---

* Eds. note—Precocious.

I shall now therefore humbly propose my own thoughts, which I hope will   8
not be liable to the least objection.

I have been assured by a very knowing American of my acquaintance in   9
London, that a young healthy child well nursed is at a year old a most delicious, nourishing, and wholesome food, whether stewed, roasted, baked, or
boiled; and I make no doubt that it will equally serve in fricassee or a ragout.

I do therefore humbly offer it to public consideration that of the hundred   10
and twenty thousand children, already computed, twenty thousand may be
reserved for breed, whereof only one fourth part to be males, which is more
than we allow to sheep, black cattle, or swine; and my reason is that these children are seldom the fruits of marriage, a circumstance not much regarded by
our savages, therefore one male will be sufficient to serve four females. That
the remaining hundred thousand may at a year old be offered in sale to the
persons of quality and fortune through the
kingdom, always advising the mother to let
them suck plentifully in the last month, so
as to render them plump and fat for a good
table. A child will make two dishes at an
entertainment for friends; and when the
family dines alone, the fore or hind quarter
will make a reasonable dish, and seasoned
with a little pepper or salt, will be very good
boiled on the fourth day, especially in
winter.

> "I grant this food will be somewhat dear, and therefore very proper for landlords, who, as they have already devoured most of the parents, seem to have the best title to the children."   11

I have reckoned upon a medium that a
child just born will weigh twelve pounds,
and in a solar year if tolerably nursed
increaseth to twenty-eight pounds.

"I grant this food will be somewhat   12
dear, and therefore very proper for landlords, who, as they have already
devoured most of the parents, seem to have the best title to the children."

Infant's flesh will be in season throughout the year, but more plentiful in   13
March, and a little before and after. For we are told by a grave author, an eminent French physician,* that fish being a prolific diet, there are more children
born in Roman Catholic countries about nine months after Lent, than at any
other season; therefore, reckoning a year after Lent, the markets will be more
glutted than usual, because the number of popish infants is at least three to
one in this kingdom; and therefore it will have one other collateral advantage,
by lessening the number of Papists** among us.

I have already computed the charge of nursing a beggar's child (in which   14
list I reckon all cottagers, laborers, and four fifths of the farmers) to be about
two shillings per annum, rags included; and I believe no gentleman would
repine to give ten shillings for the carcass of a good fat child, which, as I have

---

* Eds. note — François Rabelais, a sixteenth-century satirical writer.
** Eds. note — Roman Catholics.

said, will make four dishes of excellent nutritive meat, when he hath only some particular friend or his own family to dine with him. Thus the squire will learn to be a good landlord, and grow popular among the tenants; the mother will have eight shillings net profit, and be fit for work till she produces another child.

Those who are more thrifty (as I must confess the times require) may flay   15
the carcass; the skin of which artificially* dressed will make admirable gloves for ladies, and summer boots for fine gentlemen.

As to our city of Dublin, shambles** may be appointed for this purpose in   16
the most convenient parts of it, and butchers we may be assured will not be wanting; although I rather recommend buying the children alive, and dressing them hot from the knife as we do roasting pigs.

A very worthy person, a true lover of his country, and whose virtues I highly   17
esteem, was lately pleased in discoursing on this matter to offer a refinement upon my scheme. He said that many gentlemen of his kingdom, having of late destroyed their deer, he conceived that the want of venison might be well supplied by the bodies of young lads and maidens, not exceeding fourteen years of age nor under twelve, so great a number of both sexes in every county being now ready to starve for want of work and service; and these to be disposed of by their parents, if alive, or otherwise by their nearest relations. But with due deference to so excellent a friend and so deserving a patriot I cannot be altogether in his sentiments; for as to the males, my American acquaintance assured me from frequent experience that their flesh was generally tough and lean, like that of our schoolboys, by continual exercise, and their taste disagreeable; and to fatten them would not answer the charge. Then as to the females, it would, I think with humble submission, be a loss to the public, because they soon would become breeders themselves; and besides, it is not improbable that some scrupulous people might be apt to censure such a practice (although indeed very unjustly) as a little bordering upon cruelty; which, I confess, hath always been with me the strongest objection against any project, how well soever intended.

But in order to justify my friend, he confessed that this expedient was put   18
into his head by the famous Psalmanazar,*** a native of the island Formosa, who came from thence to London above twenty years ago, and in conversation told my friend that in his country when any young person happened to be put to death, the executioner sold the carcass to the persons of quality as a prime dainty; and that in his time the body of a plump girl of fifteen, who was crucified for an attempt to poison the emperor, was sold to the Imperial Majesty's prime minister of state, and other great mandarins of the court, in joints from the gibbet, at four hundred crowns. Neither indeed can I deny that if the same use were made of several plump young girls in this town, who without one

---

* Eds. note — Skillfully.
** Eds. note — A slaughterhouse or meat market.
*** Eds. note — Frenchman who passed himself off as a native of Formosa (present-day Taiwan).

single groat to their fortunes cannot stir abroad without a chair,* and appear at the playhouse and assemblies in foreign fineries which they never will pay for, the kingdom would not be the worse.

Some persons of a desponding spirit are in great concern about the vast   19
number of poor people who are aged, diseased, or maimed, and I have been desired to employ my thoughts what course may be taken to ease the nation of so grievous an encumbrance. But I am not in the least pain upon that matter, because it is very well known that they are every day dying and rotting by cold and famine, and filth and vermin, as fast as can be reasonably expected. And as to the younger laborers, they are now in almost as hopeful a condition. They cannot get work, and consequently pine away for want of nourishment to a degree that if any time they are accidentally hired to common labor, they have not strength to perform it; and thus the country and themselves are happily delivered from the evils to come.

I have too long digressed, and therefore shall return to my subject. I think   20
the advantages by the proposal which I have made are obvious and many, as well as of the highest importance.

For first, as I have already observed, it would greatly lessen the number of   21
Papists, with whom we are yearly overrun, being the principal breeders of the nation as well as our most dangerous enemies; and who stay at home on pur-pose to deliver the kingdom to the Pretender, hoping to take their advantage by the absence of so many good Protestants, who have chosen rather to leave their country than to stay at home and pay tithes against their conscience to an Episcopal curate.

Secondly, the poorer tenants will have something valuable of their own,   22
which by law may be made liable to distress,** and help to pay their landlord's rent, their corn and cattle being already seized and money a thing unknown.

Thirdly, whereas the maintenance of an hundred thousand children, from   23
two years old and upwards, cannot be computed at less than ten shillings a piece per annum, the nation's stock will be thereby increased fifty thousand pounds per annum, besides the profit of a new dish introduced to the tables of all gentlemen of fortune in the kingdom who have any refinement in taste. And the money will circulate among ourselves, the goods being entirely of our own growth and manufacture.

Fourthly, the constant breeders, besides the gain of eight shillings sterling   24
per annum by the sale of their children, will be rid of the charge for maintain-ing them after the first year.

Fifthly, this food would likewise bring great custom to taverns, where the   25
vintners will certainly be so prudent as to procure the best receipts*** for dressing it to perfection, and consequently have their houses frequented by all the fine gentlemen, who justly value themselves upon their knowledge in good

---

* Eds. note — A sedan chair; that is, a portable covered chair designed to seat one person and then to be carried by two men.
** Eds. note — Property could be seized by creditors.
*** Eds. note — Recipes.

eating; and a skillful cook, who understands how to oblige his guests, will contrive to make it as expensive as they please.

Sixthly, this would be a great inducement to marriage, after which all wise   26
nations have either encouraged by rewards or enforced by laws and penalties. It would increase the care and tenderness of mothers toward their children, when they were sure of a settlement for life to the poor babes, provided in some sort by the public, to their annual profit instead of expense. We should see an honest emulation among the married women, which of them could bring the fattest child to the market. Men would become as fond of their wives during the time of pregnancy as they are now of their mares in foal, their cows in calf, or sows when they are ready to farrow; nor offer to beat or kick them (as is too frequent a practice) for fear of miscarriage.

Many other advantages might be enumerated. For instance, the addition   27
of some thousand carcasses in our exportation of barreled beef, the propagation of swine's flesh, and improvements in the art of making good bacon, so much wanted among us by the great destruction of pigs, too frequent at our tables, which are no way comparable in taste or magnificence to a well-grown, fat, yearling child, which roasted whole will make a considerable figure at a lord mayor's feast or other public entertainment. But this and many others I omit, being studious of brevity.

Supposing that one thousand families in this city would be constant cus-   28
tomers for infants' flesh, besides others who might have it at merry meetings, particularly weddings and christenings, I compute that Dublin would take off annually about twenty thousand carcasses, and the rest of the kingdom (where probably they will be sold somewhat cheaper) the remaining eighty thousand.

I can think of no one objection that will possibly be raised against this pro-   29
posal, unless it should be urged that the number of people will be thereby much lessened in the kingdom. This I freely own, and it was indeed one principal design in offering it to the world. I desire the reader will observe; that I calculate my remedy for this one individual kingdom of Ireland and for no other that ever was, is, or I think ever can be upon earth. Therefore, let no man talk to me of other expedients: of taxing our absentees at five shillings a pound: of using neither clothes nor household furniture except what is of our own growth and manufacture: of utterly rejecting the materials and instruments that promote foreign luxury: of curing the expensiveness of pride, vanity, idleness, and gaming in our women: of introducing a vein of parsimony, prudence, and temperance: of learning to love our country, in the want of which we differ even from Lowlanders and the inhabitants of Topinamboo:* of quitting our animosities and factions, nor acting any longer like the Jews,** who were murdering one another at the very moment their city was taken: of being a little cautious not to sell our country and conscience for nothing: of teaching landlords to have at least one degree of mercy toward their tenants: lastly, of putting

---

* Eds. note — A place in the Brazilian jungle.
** Eds. note — In the first century B.C., the Roman general Pompey could conquer Jerusalem in part because the citizenry was divided among rival factions.

a spirit of honesty, industry, and skill into our shopkeepers; who, if a resolution could now be taken to buy only our native goods, would immediately unite to cheat and exact upon us in the price, the measure, and the goodness, nor could ever yet be brought to make one fair proposal of just dealing, though often and earnestly invited to it.

Therefore, I repeat, let no man talk to me of these and the like expedients, till he hath at least some glimpse of hope that there will ever be some hearty and sincere attempt to put them in practice.* 30

But as to myself, having been wearied out for many years with offering vain, idle, visionary thoughts, and at length utterly despairing of success, I fortunately fell upon this proposal, which, as it is wholly new, so it hath something solid and real, of no expense and little trouble, full in our own power, and whereby we can incur no danger in disobliging England. For this kind of commodity will not bear exploration, the flesh being of too tender a consistence to admit a long continuance in salt, although perhaps I could name a country which would be glad to eat up our whole nation without it. 31

After all, I am not so violently bent upon my own opinion as to reject any offer proposed by wise men, which shall be found equally innocent, cheap, easy, and effectual. But before something of that kind shall be advanced in contradiction to my scheme, and offering a better, I desire the author or authors will be pleased maturely to consider two points. First, as things now stand, how they will be able to find food and raiment for an hundred thousand useless mouths and backs. And secondly, there being a round million of creatures in human figure throughout this kingdom, whose sole subsistence put into a common stock would leave them in debt two million of pounds sterling, adding those who are beggars by profession to the bulk of farmers, cottagers, and laborers, with their wives and children who are beggars in effect; I desire those politicians who dislike my overture, and may perhaps be so bold to attempt an answer, that they will first ask the parents of these mortals whether they would not at this day think it a great happiness to have been sold for food at a year old in this manner I prescribe, and thereby have avoided such a perpetual scene of misfortunes as they have since gone through by the oppression of landlords, the impossibility of paying rent without money or trade, the want of common sustenance, with neither house nor clothes to cover them from the inclemencies of the weather, and the most inevitable prospect of entailing the like or greater miseries upon their breed forever. 32

I profess, in the sincerity of my heart, that I have not the least personal interest in endeavoring to promote this necessary work, having no other motive than the public good of my country, by advancing our trade, providing for infants, relieving the poor, and giving some pleasure to the rich. I have no children by which I can propose to get a single penny; the youngest being nine years old, and my wife past childbearing. 33

.   .   .

---

* Eds. note — Note that these measures represent Swift's true proposal.

Comprehension

1. What problem does Swift identify? What general solution does he recommend?
2. What advantages does Swift see in his plan?
3. What does he see as the alternative to his plan?
4. What clues indicate that Swift is not serious about his proposal?
5. In paragraph 29, Swift lists and rejects a number of "other expedients." What are they? Why do you think he presents and rejects these ideas?

Purpose and Audience

1. Swift's target here is the British government, in particular its poor treatment of the Irish. How would you expect British government officials to have responded to his proposal at the time? How would you expect Irish readers to have reacted?
2. What do you think Swift hoped to accomplish in this essay? Do you think his purpose was simply to amuse and shock, or do you think he wanted to change people's minds or even inspire them to take some kind of action? Explain.
3. In paragraphs 6, 14, 23, and elsewhere, Swift presents a series of mathematical calculations. What effect do you think he expected these computations to have on his readers?
4. Explain why each of the following groups might have been offended by this essay: women, Catholics, butchers, the poor.
5. How do you think Swift expected the appeal in his conclusion to affect his audience?

Style and Structure

1. **Vocabulary Project.** In paragraph 6, Swift uses the word *breeders* to refer to fertile women. What connotations does this word have? Why does he use this word rather than a more neutral alternative?
2. What purpose does paragraph 8 serve in the essay? Do the other short paragraphs have the same function? Explain.
3. Swift's remarks are presented as an argument. Where, if anywhere, does Swift anticipate and refute his readers' objections?
4. **Vocabulary Project.** Swift applies to infants many words usually applied to animals who are slaughtered to be eaten — for example, *fore or hind quarter* (10) and *carcass* (15). Identify as many examples of this kind of usage as you can. Why do you think Swift uses such words?
5. Throughout his essay, Swift cites the comments of others — "our merchants" (7), "a very knowing American of my acquaintance" (9), and "an eminent French physician" (13), for example. Find some additional examples. What, if anything, does he accomplish by referring to these people?
6. A **satire** is a piece of writing that uses wit, irony, and ridicule to attack foolishness, incompetence, or evil. How does "A Modest Proposal" fit this definition of satire?

7. Evaluate the strategy Swift uses to introduce each advantage he cites in paragraphs 21 through 26.
8. Swift uses a number of parenthetical comments in his essay — for example, in paragraphs 14, 17, and 26. Identify as many of these parenthetical comments as you can, and consider what they contribute to the essay.
9. Swift begins paragraph 20 with "I have too long digressed, and therefore shall return to my subject." Has he in fact been digressing? Explain.
10. The title of this essay states that Swift's proposal is a "modest" one; elsewhere, he says he proposes his ideas "humbly" (8). Why do you think he chooses these words? Does he really mean to present himself as modest and humble?

Journal Entry

What is your emotional reaction to this essay? Do you find it amusing? Offensive? Why?

Writing Workshop

1. Write a "modest proposal," either straightforward or satirical, for solving a problem in your school or community.
2. Write a "modest proposal" for achieving one of these national goals:
   * Banning assault weapons
   * Eliminating binge drinking on college campuses
   * Promoting sexual abstinence among teenagers
3. **Working with Sources.** Write a letter to an executive of the tobacco industry, a television network, or an industry that threatens the environment. In your letter, set forth a "modest proposal" for making the industry more responsible. Begin by researching industry statements and newspaper editorials on the issue you select. Be sure to cite the sources of all borrowed material and to include a works-cited page. (See Chapter 18 for information on MLA documentation.)

Combining the Patterns

What patterns of development does Swift use in his argument? Annotate the essay to identify each pattern. Use the annotations accompanying "On Dumpster Diving" (page 668) as a guide.

Thematic Connections
* "Soweto" (page 175)
* "The Embalming of Mr. Jones" (page 296)
* "The Irish Famine, 1845–1849" (page 326)
* "I Want a Wife" (page 494)

Writing Assignments for Combining the Patterns

1. Reread Michael Huu Truong's essay at the beginning of this chapter. Responding to the same assignment he was given ("Write an essay about the person and/or place that defined your childhood"), use several different patterns of development to communicate to readers what your own childhood was like.

2. Write an essay about the political, social, or economic events (local, national, or international) that you believe have dominated and defined your life (or a stage of your life). Use cause and effect and any other patterns you think are appropriate to explain and illustrate why these events were important to you and how they affected you.

3. **Working with Sources.** Develop a thesis statement that draws a general conclusion about the nature, quality, or effectiveness of advertising in online media or in print media (in newspapers or magazines or on billboards). Write an essay that supports this thesis statement with specific references to particular ads. Include some of the ads in your essay, and be sure to document all the ads you cite and to include a works-cited page. (See Chapter 18 for information on MLA documentation.)

4. Exactly what do you think it means to be an American? Write a definition essay that answers this question, developing your definition with whatever patterns best serve your purpose.

5. Many of the essays in this text recount the writers' personal experiences. Identify one essay that describes experiences that are either similar to your own or in sharp contrast to your own. Then, write a comparison-and-contrast essay *either* comparing *or* contrasting your experiences with those of the writer. Use several different patterns to develop your essay.

Collaborative Activity for Combining the Patterns

Working in pairs, choose an essay from Chapters 6 through 14 of this text. Then, working individually, identify the various patterns of development used in the essay. When you have finished, compare notes with your classmate. Have both of you identified the same patterns in the essay? If not, try to reach a consensus. Working together, write a paragraph summarizing why each pattern is used and explaining how the various patterns combine to support the essay's thesis.

PART THREE

Working with Sources

Some students see research as a complicated, time-consuming process that seems to have no obvious benefit. They wonder why instructors assign topics that involve research or why they have to spend so much time considering other people's ideas. These are fair questions that deserve straightforward answers.

For one thing, doing research enables you to become part of an academic community — one that attempts to answer some of the most interesting and profound questions being asked today. For example, what steps should be taken to ensure privacy on the Internet? What is the value of a college education, and how should it be paid for? How do we define free speech? How much should the government be involved in people's lives? These and other questions need to be addressed, not just because they are interesting, but also because the future of our society depends on the answers.

In addition, research teaches sound methods of inquiry. By doing research, you learn to ask questions, to design a research plan, to meet deadlines, to collect and analyze information, and to present your ideas in a well-organized essay. Above all, research encourages you to **think critically** — to consider different sources of information, to evaluate conflicting points of view, to understand how the information you discover fits in with your own ideas about your subject, and to reach logical conclusions. Thus, doing research helps you become a more thoughtful writer as well as a more responsible, more informed citizen — one who is capable of sorting through the vast amount of information you encounter each day and of making informed decisions about the important issues that confront us all.

When you use sources in an essay, you follow the same process that guides you when you write any essay. However, in addition to using your own ideas to support your points, you use information that you find in the library and online. Because working with sources presents special challenges, there are certain issues that you should be aware of before you engage in research. The chapters in Part Three identify these issues and give you practical suggestions for dealing with them. Chapter 16 discusses how to find sources and how to determine if those sources are authoritative, accurate, objective, current, and comprehensive. Chapter 17 discusses how to paraphrase, summarize, and quote sources and how to avoid committing plagiarism. Finally, Chapter 18 explains how to use the documentation style recommended by the Modern Language Association (MLA) to acknowledge the source information you use in your papers. (The documentation style recommended by the American Psychological Association [APA] is illustrated in the Appendix.)

Finding and Evaluating Sources

In some essays you write — personal narratives or descriptions, for example — you can use your own ideas and observations to support the points you make. In other essays, however, you will have to supplement your own ideas with **research**, looking for information in magazines, newspapers, journals, and books as well as in the library's electronic databases or on the Internet.

As you do research, keep in mind that the research essay you write should not be just a collection of other people's ideas. It should present an original thesis that you develop with your own insights and opinions as well as with the information you get from your research. In other words, *your* voice, not the voices of your sources, should lead the discussion. Finally, when you do research, make sure that you do not accept information just because it supports your thesis — especially if it comes from a questionable source. Realize that you have an obligation to consider all credible sources, not just information that reinforces your beliefs.

Finding Information in the Library

Although many students turn first to the Internet, the best place to begin your research is in your **college library**, which contains electronic and print resources that you cannot find anywhere else. Your college library houses books, magazines, and journals, and it also gives you access to the various databases to which it subscribes as well as to reference works that contain facts and statistics. The best way to access your college library is to visit its website, which is the gateway to a great deal of information — for example, its *online catalog*, *electronic databases*, and *reference works*.

THE RESOURCES OF THE LIBRARY

The Online Catalog

An **online catalog** enables you to search all the holdings of the library — including print books, print journals, audio books, and more. In addition, by logging in, you can see items you have checked out, examine the status of titles on reserve, renew a book, and put materials on hold.

Electronic Databases

Libraries subscribe to **electronic databases** — for example, *Expanded Academic ASAP* and *LexisNexis Academic Universe*. These electronic databases enable you to access information from hundreds of newspapers, magazines, and academic journals. Some contain lists of bibliographic citations as well as **abstracts** (summaries of articles); many others enable you to retrieve the full texts of articles or books.

Reference Works

Libraries also contain **reference works** — in print and in electronic form — that can give you an overview of your topic as well as key facts, dates, and names. **General encyclopedias** — such as the *New Encyclopaedia Britannica* — include articles on a wide variety of subjects. **Specialized encyclopedias** — such as the *Encyclopedia of Law Enforcement* — contain articles that give you detailed information about a specific field (sociology or criminal justice, for example).

Although general encyclopedias can give you an overview of a topic, they do not usually treat subjects in enough depth to be useful for college-level research. Specialized encyclopedias, however, may be suitable — but be sure to check with your instructor before you use any encyclopedia article as a source.

Sources for Facts and Statistics

Reference works such as *Facts on File*, the *Information Please Almanac*, and the *Statistical Abstract of the United States* can help you locate reliable facts or statistics that you may need to support your points. (These resources are available online as well as in the reference section of your college library.)

Much of the information in library databases — for example, the full text of many scholarly articles — cannot be found on the Internet. In addition, because your college librarians oversee all material coming into the library, the sources you find there are generally more reliable, more focused, and more useful than many you will find on the Internet.

INTERNET	LIBRARY DATABASES
Coverage is general, haphazard	Coverage is focused and often discipline-specific
Sources may not contain bibliographic information	Sources will contain bibliographic information

Web postings are not filtered	Databases are created by librarians and scholars
Material is posted by anyone, regardless of qualifications	Material is checked for accuracy and quality

Many college libraries have a **discovery service** that enables you to carry out a unified, Google-like search of all the physical items held by the library as well as articles, books, ebooks, and other material in the library's electronic databases. When you search the discovery service (or online catalog), you may do either a *keyword search* or a *subject search*.

- **A keyword search**   When you do a keyword search, you enter a word or words associated with your topic into a search box. The more precise your key words, the more specific and useful the information you will retrieve. For example, if you type in a broad term, like *Civil War*, you will literally be overwhelmed with entries that contain these words. If you type in *American Civil War*, you will get fewer, and if you narrow your search even further — for example, to *The Battle of Gettysburg* — you will get even fewer.
- **A subject search**   When you do a subject search, you enter a subject heading into the search box. The holdings of the college library are classified under specific subject headings. Many online catalogs provide lists of subject headings to help you identify the exact words you will need to carry out your search.

Exercise 1

Assume that you are writing a three- to five-page essay on one of the general topics listed below.

Eating disorders	The student-loan bubble
Alternative medicine	Green construction projects
Government health care	Gun control legislation
Hydraulic fracturing	Self-driving cars

Using your college library's online catalog, see how much information you can find. How easy was this system to use? Where did you have difficulty? Did you try asking a librarian for help?

Finding Information on the Internet

Although the Internet (more specifically, the web) gives you access to a vast amount of information, it has its limitations. For one thing, because anyone can publish on the web, you cannot be sure the information found there is trustworthy, timely, or authoritative. There are reliable sources of information on the web, however. For example, the information on your college library's website is usually (but not always) reliable. In addition, Google Scholar provides links to some scholarly sources that are as reliable as those found in a college library's databases. Even so, you have to approach this material with caution; some articles accessed through Google Scholar, for example, are pay-per-view, and others are not current or comprehensive.

A search engine—such as Google or Bing— helps you to locate and view documents, images, and videos on the web. Different types of search engines are suitable for different purposes:

General-purpose search engines General-purpose search engines retrieve information on a great number of topics. They cast the widest possible net and bring in the greatest variety of information. The disadvantage of general-purpose search engines is that you often get a great deal of irrelevant material. Because each search engine has its own unique characteristics, you should try a few of them to see which you prefer. The most popular general-purpose search engines are Google, Bing, Yahoo!, and Ask.com.

Specialized search engines Specialized search engines focus on a specific subject area or a specific type of content—for example, business, government, or health services. The advantage of specialized search engines is that they focus your search, eliminating the need to sort through pages of irrelevant material. These search engines are especially useful when you are looking for in-depth information about a specific topic. (You can find a list of specialized search engines at l-lists.com and at teachthought.com/learning/100-search-engines -for-academic-research/.)

Metasearch engines Because each search engine works differently, results can (and do) vary. So, if you limit yourself to a single search engine, you can miss a great deal of useful information. Metasearch engines solve this problem by taking the results of several search engines and presenting them in a simple, no-nonsense format. The most popular metasearch engines are Dogpile, ixquick, MetaGer, MetaCrawler, and Sputtr.

When using a search engine such as Google or Bing, you have access to millions of online documents. Although that guarantees that you will retrieve a great deal of information, it does not guarantee that you will retrieve a great deal of *useful* information. To make sure you work efficiently, you have to limit your search to information that specifically pertains to your topic. You do so by carrying out a keyword search on your browser the same way you do a keyword search of the library's online catalog (see page 706). Once you enter a keyword into your search engine's search box (or search field), the search engine will retrieve any document in its database that contains this keyword. The more specific your search terms, the more likely you will be to retrieve useful information.

Finding Useful Information

Whenever you carry out an online search, you will get many more results than you need for your essay. Although these results will help you get a broad sense of your topic, they are just a starting point for your research. By skimming the search results, you will be able to get a general sense of the major trends concerning your topic and who the leading experts are.

When you have found a source that seems promising for your research, examine the pages in the works-cited section (if there is one) and click through any links the author may have added to the work. This step will lead you to other material on your topic and could help you with your own search.

Online publications will often contain multiple articles or pages on a single topic. If you find a source that is not quite what you are looking for, go to the home page of the website where you found the source. From there, you can search to see what other material may be available on your topic.

If you find a source that does not address your specific topic or one that does not seem credible, return to your original search results and try again. If you find that many of your results do not fit your topic, try using a different set of keywords or broadening or narrowing your search.

AVOID BACKRACKING

Open promising articles in new tabs or separate windows so that you can easily return to your search results or to your original source. This strategy will allow you to follow leads and to avoid losing track of your sources as you do further research. You can also keep track of your sources by clicking on the History tab at the top of your browser.

ACCESSING WEBSITES: TROUBLESHOOTING

Sometimes you will be unable to connect to the site you want. Before giving up, try these strategies:

- **Check to make sure the URL is correct.** Any error in typing the URL — an extra space or an added letter — will send you to the wrong site or to no site at all.

- **Try using part of the URL.** If the URL is long, try deleting everything after the last slash. If that doesn't work, use just the part of the URL that ends in .com or .gov. If this part of the URL doesn't work, you have an incorrect (or inoperable) URL.

- **Try revisiting the site later.** Sometimes websites experience technical problems that prevent you from accessing them. Wait a while, and then try accessing your site again.

Exercise 2

Carry out an Internet search of the topic you chose for Exercise 1. How much useful information were you able to find? How does this information compare with the information you found when you used the library's online catalog?

Evaluating Sources

Not every source contains trustworthy information. For this reason, after you identify a possible source (either in print or online), you still have to **evaluate** it — that is, determine its suitability. Although a librarian or an instructor has screened many of the print and electronic sources in your college library for general accuracy and trustworthiness, you cannot simply assume that these sources are right for your particular writing project. Before you can proceed, you need to ask two questions: Does this source treat your subject in enough depth? Is this source trustworthy?

The information you find on the Internet demands even closer scrutiny than those accessed through your college library's databases. Although some Internet material (journal articles that are published in both print and digital format, for example) is reliable, other material (such as personal websites and blogs) is questionable and may be unsuitable for your research. On the Internet, almost anything goes — exaggerations, misinformation, errors, and even complete fabrications — so you have to evaluate the material very carefully before you use it. When you encounter a website, be sure to approach it skeptically. In other words, assume that its information is questionable until you establish otherwise. Remember that if you use an untrustworthy source, you undercut your own credibility.

INTERNET SOURCES: ACCEPTABLE AND UNACCEPTABLE

Before you use an Internet source, you should consider if it is acceptable for college-level work. Here are brief guidelines about the types of Internet sources that tend to be acceptable versus unacceptable.

Acceptable Sources

- Websites sponsored by reliable organizations, such as academic institutions, government, and professional organizations
- Websites sponsored by academic journals and reputable magazines and newspapers
- Blogs by recognized experts in their fields
- Research forums

Unacceptable Sources

- Information on anonymous websites
- Information found in chat rooms or on discussion boards
- Personal blogs written by authors whose expertise you cannot verify
- Personal web pages
- Poorly written web pages

To evaluate any source, whether print or digital, ask the following questions.

Is the Source Authoritative?

A source is **authoritative** when it is written by an expert. Given the volume and variety of information online, it is particularly important to determine if it is written by a well-respected scholar or expert in the field. To determine if the author has the expertise to write about a subject, find out what else that author has written on the same subject, and then do a search to see if other authorities recognize the author as an expert.

Trying to determine the legitimacy of information on websites, online publications, and blogs can often be difficult or impossible. Even some print resources, such as unattributed magazine articles without the necessary publication information, can be difficult to verify. Some sites do not list authors, and if they do, they do not always include their credentials. In addition, you may not be able to determine how a website decides what to publish. (Does one person decide, or does an editorial board make decisions?) Finally, you might have difficulty evaluating (or even identifying) the sponsoring organization. If you cannot determine if a website or other source is authoritative, do not use it as a source.

AUTHORITY

You can determine the **authority** of a source by asking the following questions:

What are the author's credentials? Does the source identify the author's academic or professional affiliation? If the author is a recognized expert in the field that he or she is writing about, you can usually rely on the information presented in the source.

What other books or articles on your topic has the author written? If this information is not available, do a web search, using the writer's name as a keyword. If you cannot confirm the author's expertise, do not use the source.

Can you verify the information? Is the information documented? Has the author provided a list of references or works cited? If the source appears on a website, what information do the links reveal? Do they lead to reputable sites or to sites that suggest that the author has a clear bias or a hidden agenda?

Does the source appear in a reputable publication? For example, does the source appear in a book published by a university press or by a high-quality commercial press? In the case of an Internet publication, can you determine if the site is run by a single individual or by an organization? In most cases, you should avoid information that appears on personal websites.

Is the Source Accurate?

A source is **accurate** if its information is factual, correct, detailed, and up-to-date. If a university press or scholarly journal published a book or article, you can be reasonably certain that experts in the field reviewed it to confirm its accuracy. Books published by commercial presses or articles in high-level magazines, such as *The Atlantic* and *The Economist*, may also be suitable for your research — provided experts wrote them. The same is true for newspaper articles. Articles in respected newspapers, such as the *New York Times* or the *Wall Street Journal*, have much more credibility than articles in tabloids, such as the *National Enquirer* or *Globe*.

You can judge the accuracy of a source by comparing specific information it contains to the same information in several other sources. If you find discrepancies, you should assume the source contains other errors as well. You should also check to see if an author includes citations for the information he or she uses. Such documentation can help readers determine the accuracy (and the quality) of the information in the source. Perhaps the best (and safest) course to follow is that if you can't verify the information you find on a website, don't use it.

ACCURACY

You can assess the **accuracy** of the information in a source by asking the following questions.

Does the source contain factual errors? Inaccuracies — especially those that are presented as support for the central point of the source — should immediately disqualify a source as reliable.

Does the source include a list of references or any other type of documentation? Reliable sources indicate where their information comes from. The authors know that people want to be sure that the information they are using is accurate and reliable. If a source provides no documentation, you do not have to reject it, but you should approach it cautiously.

Does the source refer to (or provide links to) other sources? If it does, you can conclude that your source is at least trying to maintain a certain standard of accuracy.

Can you verify information? A good test for accuracy is to try to verify key information in a source. You can do so by checking it in a reliable print source or on a good reference website such as Encyclopedia.com.

Is the Source Objective?

A source is **objective** when it is not unduly influenced by personal opinions or feelings. All sources reflect the **biases** of their authors, regardless of how impartial they may try to be. Some sources — such as those that support one political position over another — make no secret of their biases. In fact, bias does not automatically disqualify a source. At the very least, it should alert you to the fact that you are seeing just one side of an issue and that you have to look elsewhere to get a fuller picture. Bias becomes a problem, however, when it is so extreme that a source distorts an issue or misrepresents opposing points of view.

As a researcher, you should ask yourself if a writer's conclusions are supported by evidence or if they are the result of emotional reactions or preconceived ideas. You can make this determination by looking at the writer's choice of words and seeing if the language is slanted and also by seeing if the writer ignores (or attacks) opposing points of view.

With websites, you should try to determine if the advertising that appears on the site affects the site's objectivity. Also try to determine if the site has a commercial purpose. If it does, the writer may have a conflict of interest. (Commercially motivated content is not easy to recognize, however. For example, critics have charged that companies pay people to write favorable *Wikipedia* articles to promote products.) The same need to assess objectivity exists when a political group or special-interest group sponsors a site. These organizations have agendas, and you should make sure they are not manipulating facts to promote their own goals.

OBJECTIVITY

You can assess the **objectivity** of a site by asking the following questions:

Does the author avoid sweeping statements and overgeneralizations? Are the author's assumptions supported by the facts, or are they simply opinions or preconceived ideas? Does the author use language that suggests bias?

Is the author affiliated with an organization? Does the author's affiliation indicate that the information might be biased? If it does, there is a conflict of interest, and you should be skeptical.

Is the source's purpose just to inform or explain — or is it to persuade or even to sell something? Does that purpose affect its treatment of the issue?

Are there ads on the website on which the source appears? How are these ads connected to the topic being treated? If a commercial company, a political organization, or a special-interest group sponsors a magazine or a website, make sure that the sponsoring organization does not slant content to suit its own purposes.

URL TYPES

A website's URL can give you clues as to the purpose of the site.

.com Commercial site

.edu Educational institution

.gov Government site

.mil Military site

.net Network (a catch-all suffix)

.org Nonprofit organization*

---

*The domain .org is an open domain, so anyone can register for it, even a for-profit business. For this reason, you can't just assume that .org indicates a reputable site.

Is the Source Current?

A source is **current** if the information it contains is up-to-date. It is relatively easy to find out how current a print source is. You can find the publication date of a book on the page that lists its publication information, and you can find the publication date of a periodical on its front cover.

Websites and blogs, however, may present problems. First, check to see when a website was last updated. (Some web pages automatically display the current date, and you should not confuse this date with the date when the site was last updated.) Then, check the dates of individual articles. Even if a site has been updated recently, it may include information that is out-of-date. You should also see if the links on a site are still live. If a number of links are not functioning, you should question the currency of the site.

CURRENCY

You can assess the **currency** of a source by asking the following questions:

Is the source up-to-date? When was it written? If the source is on a website, what is the date on which it was posted or updated? Some websites automatically display the current date, so be careful not to confuse this date with the date on which the page was last updated.

Is the information in the source up-to-date? Does it reflect the most current research? If you are writing about a scientific topic, a current source may be necessary. If you are writing about a historical topic, however, you might not need the latest information.

Are all the links on a website live? If a website is properly maintained, all the links it contains will be live — in other words, a click on a link will take you to other websites. If a site contains a number of links that are not live, you should question its currency.

Is the Source Comprehensive?

A source is **comprehensive** if it covers a subject in sufficient breadth and depth. How comprehensive a source needs to be depends on your purpose and your audience as well as on your assignment. For a short essay, an op-ed from a newspaper or a short article might give you enough information to support your points. A longer essay, however, would call for sources that treat your subject in depth, such as scholarly articles or even whole books.

You can determine the comprehensiveness of a source by seeing if it devotes a great deal of coverage to your subject. Does it discuss your topic in one or two paragraphs, or does it devote much more space to it — say, a chapter in a book or a major section of an article? You should also try to determine the level of the source. Although a source may be perfectly acceptable for high school research, it may not be comprehensive enough for college research.

COMPREHENSIVENESS

You can assess the **comprehensiveness** of a source by asking the following questions:

Does the source simply provide a general overview of your topic, or does it treat it in depth? Are you seeing the complete source or just an excerpt? If you are seeing an excerpt, consult the original source to make sure that what you are seeing is accurate.

Does the source appear in a professional journal or in a popular magazine or general encyclopedia? A professional journal will often treat subjects in great detail, whereas a popular or general-interest magazine may treat topics superficially.

Is the source in a database that focuses on scholarly resources, such as Google Scholar or one of your library's databases? If so, you can assume that the source is suitable for college-level research. Even if that's the case, you should check the information in the source against the information in other sources you have gathered.

Does the source provide information that is not available elsewhere? The sources you use should draw original conclusions, not simply repackage information from other sources.

USING *WIKIPEDIA* AS A SOURCE

Wikipedia — the most popular encyclopedia on the web — has no single editor who checks entries for authority, accuracy, objectivity, currency, and comprehensiveness. In many cases, the users themselves write and edit entries. For this reason, many college instructors do not consider *Wikipedia* to be a credible source of information. It can, however, be a good jumping-off point for your research. Not only can *Wikipedia* articles give you an overview of your topic, but they may also contain bibliographic citations that will enable you to link to trustworthy sources of information.

Exercise 3

Choose one source from the library and one from the Internet. Then, evaluate each source to determine if it is authoritative, accurate, objective, current, and comprehensive.

17

Integrating Sources and Avoiding Plagiarism

After you have gathered and evaluated your sources, it is time to think about how you can use this material in your essay. As you take notes, you should record relevant information in a computer file or in a note-taking application. These notes should be in the form of *paraphrase*, *summary*, and *quotation*. When you actually write your paper, you will **synthesize** this source material, blending it with your own ideas and interpretations — but making sure that your ideas, not those of your sources, dominate your discussion. Finally, you should make certain that you do not inadvertently commit plagiarism.

Paraphrasing

When you **paraphrase**, you use your own words to restate a source's ideas in some detail, presenting the source's main idea, its key supporting points, and possibly an example or two. For this reason, a paraphrase may be only slightly shorter than the original.

You paraphrase when you want to present the information from a source without using its exact words. Paraphrasing is useful when you want to make a difficult discussion easier to understand while still giving readers a sense of the original.

Keep in mind that when you paraphrase, you do not use the exact language or syntax of the original source, and you do not include your own analysis or opinions. The idea is to convey the ideas and emphasis of the source but not to mirror the order of its ideas or reproduce its exact words or sentence structure. If you decide to include a particularly memorable word or phrase from the source, be sure to put it in quotation marks. Finally, remember that because a paraphrase relies on a writer's original ideas, *you must document the source.*

GUIDELINES FOR WRITING A PARAPHRASE

- Read the source you intend to paraphrase until you understand it.
- Jot down the main points of the source.
- As you write, retain the purpose and emphasis of the original.
- Make sure to use your own words and phrases, not the language or syntax of your source.
- Do not include your own analysis or opinions.
- Be sure to provide documentation.

Here is a passage from page 22 of the article "*Wikipedia* and Beyond: Jimmy Wales's Sprawling Vision" by Katherine Mangu-Ward, followed by a paraphrase.

ORIGINAL

An obvious question troubled, and continues to trouble, many people: how could an "encyclopedia that anyone can edit" possibly be reliable? Can truth be reached by a consensus of amateurs? Can a community of volunteers aggregate and assimilate knowledge . . . ?

PARAPHRASE

According to Katherine Mangu-Ward, there are serious questions about the reliability of *Wikipedia*'s articles because any user can add, change, or delete information. There is some doubt about whether *Wikipedia*'s unpaid and nonprofessional writers and editors can work together to create an accurate encyclopedia (22).

Exercise 1

Select one or two paragraphs from any essay in this book, and then paraphrase them. Make sure your paraphrase communicates the main ideas and key supporting points of the passage you selected.

Summarizing

Unlike a paraphrase, which restates the ideas of a source in detail, a **summary** is a brief restatement, in your own words, of a passage's main idea. Because it is so general, a summary is always much shorter than the original.

When you summarize (as when you paraphrase), you use your own words, not the words of your source. Keep in mind that a summary can be one sentence or several sentences in length, depending on the length and complexity of the original passage. Your summary expresses just the main idea of your source, not your own opinions or conclusions. Remember that because a summary expresses a writer's original idea, *you must document your source.*

GUIDELINES FOR WRITING A SUMMARY

- Read the source you intend to summarize until you understand it.
- Jot down the main idea of the source.
- Make sure to use your own words and phrases, not the words and sentence structure of your source.
- Do not include your own analysis or opinions.
- Be sure to provide documentation.

Here is a summary of the passage from the article "*Wikipedia* and Beyond: Jimmy Wales's Sprawling Vision" by Katherine Mangu-Ward.

SUMMARY

According to Katherine Mangu-Ward, *Wikipedia*'s reliability is open to question because anyone can edit its articles (22).

Exercise 2

Write a summary of the material you paraphrased for Exercise 1. How is your summary different from your paraphrase?

Quoting

When you **quote**, you use a writer's exact words as they appear in the source, including all punctuation, capitalization, and spelling. Enclose all words from your source in quotation marks — *followed by appropriate documentation.* Because quotations interrupt the flow of an essay and can distract readers, use them only when you think a writer's exact words will add something to your discussion. In addition, too many quotations will make your paper look like a collection of other people's words. As a rule, unless you have a definite reason to quote a source, you should paraphrase or summarize it instead.

WHEN TO QUOTE SOURCES

1. Quote when the original language is so memorable that paraphrasing would lessen the impact of the writer's ideas.
2. Quote when a paraphrase or summary would change the meaning of the original.
3. Quote when the original language adds authority to your discussion. The exact words of an expert on your topic can help you make your point convincingly.

GUIDELINES FOR QUOTING

- Put all words and phrases that you take from your source in quotation marks.
- Make sure to use the *exact* words of your source.
- Do not include too many quotations.
- Be sure to provide documentation.

Exercise 3

Reread the passage you chose to paraphrase in Exercise 1, and identify one or two quotations you could include in your paraphrase. Which words or phrases did you decide to quote? Why?

Integrating Source Material into Your Writing

When you use source material in your writing, your goal is to integrate this material smoothly into your discussion. To distinguish your own ideas from those of your sources, you should always introduce source material and follow it with appropriate documentation.

Introduce paraphrases, summaries, and quotations with a phrase that identifies the source or its author. You can place this **identifying phrase** (also called a *signal phrase*) at the beginning, in the middle, or at the end of a sentence. Instead of always using the same words to introduce your source material — *says* or *states*, for example — try using different words and phrases — *points out, observes, comments, notes, remarks,* or *concludes.*

IDENTIFYING PHRASE AT THE BEGINNING

According to Jonathan Dee, *Wikipedia* is "either one of the noblest experiments of the Internet age or a nightmare embodiment of relativism and the withering of intellectual standards" (36).

IDENTIFYING PHRASE IN THE MIDDLE

Wikipedia is "either one of the noblest experiments of the Internet age," Jonathan Dee comments, "or a nightmare embodiment of relativism and the withering of intellectual standards" (36).

IDENTIFYING PHRASE AT THE END

Wikipedia is "either one of the noblest experiments of the Internet age or a nightmare embodiment of relativism and the withering of intellectual standards," Jonathan Dee observes (36).

USING IDENTIFYING TAGS

To avoid repeating phrases like *he says* in identifying tags, try using some of the following verbs to introduce your source material. (You can also use *According to . . .* , to introduce a source.)

For Paraphrases and Summaries

[Name of writer]	notes	acknowledges	proposes	that [summary or paraphrase].
The writer	suggests	believes	observes	
The article	explains	comments	warns	
The essay	reports	points out	predicts	
	implies	concludes	states	

For Quotations

As [name of writer]	notes,	acknowledges,	proposes,	"[quotation]."
As the writer	suggests,	believes,	observes,	
As the article	warns,	reports,	points out,	
As the essay	predicts,	implies,	concludes,	
	states,	explains,		

Synthesizing

When you write a **synthesis**, you combine paraphrases, summaries, and quotations with your own ideas. It is important to keep in mind that a synthesis is not simply a collection of your sources' ideas. On the contrary, a synthesis uses source material to support *your* ideas and to help readers see the topic *you* are writing about in a new way. For this reason, when you write a synthesis, it is important to differentiate your ideas from those of your sources and to clearly show which piece of information comes from which source.

GUIDELINES FOR WRITING A SYNTHESIS

1. Identify the key points discussed in each of your sources.
2. Identify the evidence your sources use to support their views.
3. Clearly report what each source says, using summaries, paraphrases, and quotations. (Be sure to document your sources.)
4. Show how the sources are related to one another. For instance, do they agree on everything? Do they show directly opposite views, or do they agree on some points and disagree on others?
5. Decide on your own viewpoint, and show how the sources relate to your viewpoint.

The following synthesis is a paragraph from the model MLA paper that begins on page 743. This paragraph synthesizes several sources to present an overview of *Wikipedia*, focusing on the ease with which its text can be edited. The paragraph begins with the student's own ideas, and the rest of the paragraph includes source material that supports these ideas.

> A wiki allows multiple users to collaborate in creating the content of a website. With a wiki, anyone with a browser can edit, modify, rearrange, or delete content. It is not necessary to know HTML (hypertext mark-up language). The word *wiki* comes from the word *wikiwiki*, which means "quick" or "fast" in Hawaiian. The most popular wiki is *Wikipedia*, a free, Internet-based encyclopedia that relies on the collaboration of those who post and edit entries. Anyone can write a *Wikipedia* article by using the "*Wikipedia* Article Wizard" or edit an entry by clicking on the "Edit" tab. Readers can easily view the revision history of an entry by clicking on "View History" ("Help: Page History"). For its many advocates, *Wikipedia*'s open and collaborative nature makes it a "collectively brilliant creation" (Chozick). This collaboration enables *Wikipedia* to publish a wide variety of entries on timely, unusual, and specialized topics (see fig. 1). According to Casper Grathwohl, President, Dictionaries Division, and Director, Global Business Development at Oxford University Press, it "has become increasingly clear that [*Wikipedia*] functions as a necessary layer in the Internet knowledge system, a layer that was not needed in the analog age." At this time, the site contains 40 million articles in 293 languages ("*Wikipedia*").

Exercise 4

Look at the Model Student Research Paper that begins on page 743. Choose a paragraph (other than the one above) that synthesizes source material. What kind of information (summary, paraphrase, or quotation) is being synthesized?

Avoiding Plagiarism

Plagiarism—whether intentional or unintentional—occurs when a writer passes off the words or ideas of others as his or her own. (Ideas can also be in the form of visuals, such as charts and graphs, or statistics.) Students plagiarize for a number of reasons. Some take the easy way out and buy a paper and submit it as if it were their own. This **intentional plagiarism** compromises a student's education as well as the educational process as a whole. Instructors assign essays for a reason, and if you do not do the work, you miss a valuable opportunity to learn.

For most students, however, plagiarism is unintentional. **Unintentional plagiarism** can be the result of carelessness, poor time management, not knowing the conventions of documentation, laziness, or simply panic. For example, some students do not give themselves enough time to do an assignment, fail to keep track of their sources, inadvertently include the exact words of a source without using quotation marks, forget to include documentation, or cut and paste information from the Internet directly into their essays. In addition, some students have the mistaken belief that if information they find online does not have an identifiable author, it is all right to use it without documentation. Whatever the reason, whenever you present information from a source as if it were your own (either intentionally or unintentionally), you are committing plagiarism — and *plagiarism is theft*.

TIPS FOR AVOIDING PLAGIARISM

You can avoid plagiarism by keeping careful notes and by following these guidelines:

- **Give yourself enough time to do your research and to write your paper.** Do not put yourself in a position where you do not leave enough time to give your assignment the attention it requires.

- **Begin with a research plan.** Make a list of the steps you intend to follow, and estimate how much time they will take.

- **Ask for help.** If you run into trouble, don't panic. Ask your instructor or a reference librarian for help.

- **Do not cut and paste downloaded text directly into your paper.** Summarize and paraphrase this source material first. Boldface or highlight quotation marks so that you will recognize quotations when you are ready to include them in your paper.

- **Set up a system that enables you to keep track of your sources.** Create computer files where you can store downloaded source information. (If you photocopy print sources, maintain a file for this material.) Create another set of files for your notes. Be sure to clearly name and date these files so that you know what is in them and when they were created. You can also use note-taking software tools, such as Zotero, Evernote, or Awesome Note 2, to keep track of your research sources.

- **Include full source information for all paraphrases and summaries as well as for quotations.** As you write, clearly differentiate between your ideas and those of your sources. Do not forget to include documentation. If you try to fill in documentation later, you may not remember where your information came from.

- **Keep a list of all the sources you have downloaded or have taken information from.** Be sure to always have an up-to-date list of the sources you are using.

The easiest way to avoid plagiarism is simple — give credit where credit is due. In other words, document *all* information you borrow from your sources (print or electronic) — not just paraphrases, summaries, and quotations but also statistics, images, and charts and graphs. It is not necessary, however, to document **common knowledge**. Common knowledge includes information that most people are likely to know, information shared by people in a certain discipline or field, and factual information widely available in several reference books. Examples of common knowledge include a writer's date of birth, a scientific fact, and the location of a famous battle. Information widely known by readers in one academic discipline, however, may not be common knowledge outside that field and would, therefore, need documentation. The best and safest course of action is that if you have any doubts, include documentation. (Keep in mind that even though certain information might be common knowledge, you cannot use the exact words of a reference source without quoting the source and providing appropriate documentation.)

WHAT TO DOCUMENT

You Must Document

- All word-for-word quotations from a source
- All summaries and paraphrases of material from a source
- All ideas — opinions, judgments, and insights — that are not your own
- All tables, graphs, charts, statistics, and images you get from a source

You Do Not Need to Document

- Your own ideas
- Common knowledge
- Familiar quotations

Avoiding Common Errors That Lead to Plagiarism

The following paragraph is from page 47 of *The Cult of the Amateur: How Today's Internet Is Killing Our Culture* by Andrew Keen. This paragraph, and the four rules listed after it, will help you understand and avoid the most common causes of plagiarism.

ORIGINAL

The simple ownership of a computer and an Internet connection doesn't transform one into a serious journalist any more than having access to a kitchen makes one into a serious cook. But millions of amateur journalists think that it does. According to a June 2006 study by the Pew Internet and American Life Project, 34 percent of the 12 million bloggers in America consider their online "work" to be a form of journalism. That adds up to millions of unskilled, untrained, unpaid, unknown "journalists" — a thousand-fold growth between 1996 and 2006 — spewing their (mis)information out in the cyberworld.

1. Identify Your Source

PLAGIARISM

One-third of the people who post material on blogs think of themselves as serious journalists.

The writer does not quote Keen directly, but he still must identify Keen as the source of his paraphrased material. He can do so by adding an identifying phrase and parenthetical documentation.

CORRECT

According to Andrew Keen, one-third of the people who post material on Internet blogs think of themselves as serious journalists (47).

2. Place Borrowed Words in Quotation Marks

PLAGIARISM

According to Andrew Keen, the simple ownership of a computer and an Internet connection doesn't transform one into a serious journalist any more than having access to a kitchen makes one into a serious cook (47).

Although the writer cites Keen as his source, the passage incorrectly uses Keen's exact words without putting them in quotation marks. The writer must either place the borrowed words in quotation marks or paraphrase them.

CORRECT (BORROWED WORDS IN QUOTATION MARKS)

According to Andrew Keen, "The simple ownership of a computer and an Internet connection doesn't transform one into a serious journalist any more than having access to a kitchen makes one into a serious cook" (47).

3. Use Your Own Wording

PLAGIARISM

According to Andrew Keen, having a computer that can connect to the Internet does not make someone a real reporter, just as having a kitchen does not make someone a real cook. However, millions of these people think they are real journalists. A Pew Internet and American Life study in June 2006 showed that about 4 million bloggers think they are journalists when they write on their blogs. Thus, millions of people who have no training may be putting erroneous information on the Internet (47).

Even though the writer acknowledges Keen as his source and provides parenthetical documentation, and even though he does not use Keen's exact words, his passage closely follows the order, emphasis, and phrasing of the original.

In the following passage, the writer uses his own wording, quoting one distinctive phrase from his source.

CORRECT

According to Andrew Keen, although millions of American bloggers think of themselves as journalists, they are wrong. As Keen notes, "The simple ownership of a computer and an Internet connection doesn't transform one into a serious journalist any more than having access to a kitchen makes one into a serious cook" (47).

4. Distinguish Your Own Ideas from Your Source's Ideas

PLAGIARISM

The anonymous writers of *Wikipedia* articles are, in some ways, similar to those who put material on personal blogs. Although millions of American bloggers think of themselves as journalists, they are wrong. "The simple ownership of a computer and an Internet connection doesn't transform one into a serious journalist any more than having access to a kitchen makes one into a serious cook" (Keen 47).

In the preceding passage, it appears that only the quotation in the last sentence is borrowed from Keen's book. In fact, the ideas in the second sentence are also Keen's. The writer should use an identifying phrase (such as "According to Keen") to acknowledge the borrowed material in this sentence and to indicate where it begins.

CORRECT

The anonymous writers of *Wikipedia* articles are, in some ways, similar to those who put material on personal blogs. According to Andrew Keen, although millions of American bloggers think of themselves as journalists, they are wrong. As Keen notes, "The simple ownership of a computer and an Internet connection doesn't transform one into a serious journalist any more than having access to a kitchen makes one into a serious cook" (47).

Avoiding Plagiarism with Online Sources

Most students know that using long passages (or entire articles) from a print source without documenting the source is plagiarism. Unfortunately, the Internet presents a particular challenge for students as they try to avoid plagiarism. Committing plagiarism (intentional or unintentional) with electronic sources is easy because it is simple to cut and paste material from online sources into an essay. However, if you insert even a sentence or two from an Internet source (including a blog, an email, or a website) into an essay without including quotation marks and documentation, you are committing plagiarism.

It is also not acceptable to use a visual found on the Internet — a graph, a chart, a table, a photograph, and so on — without acknowledging its source. Finally, even if an Internet source does not identify its author, the words or ideas you find there are not your own original material, so you must identify their source.

USING PLAGIARISM CHECKERS

If you are concerned that you may have accidentally plagiarized material from one of your web sources, there are a number of online tools that can help you identify and correct this problem. These plagiarism checkers, such as the free options available at SmallSEOTools.com or Grammarly.com, allow you to check your work. In addition, your school may subscribe to a commercial plagiarism checker such as Turnitin or PlagiarismSearch, which you can use for this purpose. Once you download the text of your essay into the application, it will highlight and identify content that you should consider documenting. Remember, however, that you cannot simply depend on a computer application to detect possible plagiarism. It is your responsibility to keep track of your sources and to document the information you borrow from your sources.

Exercise 5

Select an essay you have written this semester that refers to a reading selection in this book. Reread both your essay and the selection in the book, and then decide where you could add each of the following:

- A quotation
- A summary of a paragraph
- A paraphrase of a paragraph

Exercise 6

Insert a quotation, a summary, and a paraphrase into the essay you reviewed for Exercise 5. Then, check to make sure you have not committed plagiarism. Finally, consult Chapter 18 to help you document your sources correctly.

18

Documenting Sources: MLA

When you **document**, you tell readers where you have found the information you have used in your essay. The Modern Language Association (MLA) documentation style is commonly used to cite sources in English, the foreign languages, and other disciplines in the humanities.* This format consists *of parenthetical references* in the body of the essay that refer to a *works-cited* list at the end of the essay.

WHY DOCUMENT SOURCES?

- To acknowledge the debt you owe to your sources
- To enable readers to judge the quality of your research
- To avoid plagiarism
- To demonstrate that you are familiar with the conventions of academic discourse
- To make your argument more convincing

Parenthetical References in the Text

A **parenthetical reference** should include enough information to guide readers to a specific entry in your works-cited list.

A typical parenthetical reference consists of the author's last name and the page number: (Mangu-Ward 21). If you use more than one work by the same author, include a shortened form of the title in the parenthetical reference:

---

* For further information, see the eighth edition of the *MLA Handbook* (Modern Language Association, 2016) or the MLA website at mla.org.

(Mangu-Ward, *"Wikipedia and Beyond"* 25). Notice that the parenthetical references do not include a comma after the title or "p." before the page number.

Whenever possible, introduce information with a phrase that includes the author's name. (If you do so, include only the page number in parentheses.)

> According to Andrew Keen, the absence of professional reporters and editors leads
> to erroneous information on *Wikipedia* (4).

Place documentation so that it does not interrupt the flow of your ideas, preferably at the end of a sentence.

The format for parenthetical references departs from these guidelines in the following special situations:

1. Two authors

When you are citing a work by two authors, include both authors' names.

> It is impossible to access all websites by means of a single search engine
> (Sherman and Price 53).

2. Three or more authors

When you are citing a work by three or more authors, include the first author's name followed by *et al.* ("and others").

> *Wikipedia* may be fine for a quick fact, but if you need trustworthy information,
> it often disappoints (Preminger et al. 14).

3. Without a listed author

When you are citing a work without a listed author, include a short version of the title.

> The technology of wikis is important, but many users are not aware of it
> ("7 Things").

4. Indirect source

When you are citing a statement by one author that is quoted in the work of another author, indicate it by including the abbreviation *qtd. in* ("quoted in").

> Marshall Poe notes that information on *Wikipedia* is "not exactly expert knowledge;
> it's common knowledge" (qtd. in Keen 39).

5. Source without page numbers

When you are citing a source without page numbers, cite just the author's name in the text of the essay or in a parenthetical reference. Sources from the Internet or from library databases often do not include page numbers. If the Internet source uses paragraph, section, or screen numbers, use the abbreviation par. or sec., or the full word screen, followed by the corresponding number, in your documentation. (If the citation includes an author's name, place a comma after the name.)

> On its website, *Wikipedia* warns its writers and editors to inspect sources carefully when they make assertions that are not generally held in academic circles (Warnock, sec. 3).

If the electronic source has no page numbers or markers of any kind, include just the name(s) of the author(s). Readers will learn more about the source when they consult the works-cited list.

> A *Wikipedia* entry can be very deceptive, but some users may not realize that its information may not be reliable (McHenry).

GUIDELINES FOR FORMATTING QUOTATIONS

Short Quotations

Quotations shorter than four typed lines are run in with the text. End punctuation comes after the parenthetical reference (which follows the quotation marks).

> According to Andrew Keen, on *Wikipedia*, "the voice of a high school kid has equal value to that of an Ivy League scholar of a trained profession" (42).

Long Quotations

Quotations longer than four lines are set off from the text. Indent a long quotation half an inch from the left-hand margin, and do not enclose the passage in quotation marks. The first line of a long quotation is not indented even if it is the beginning of a paragraph. If a quoted passage has more than one paragraph, indent the first line of each subsequent paragraph one-quarter inch. Introduce a long quotation with a colon, and place the parenthetical reference one space after the end punctuation.

> According to Katherine Mangu-Ward, Wikipedia has changed the world:
> > *Wikipedia* was born as an experiment in aggregating information. But the reason it works isn't that the world was clamoring for a new kind of encyclopedia. It took off because of the robust, self-policing community it created. . . . Despite its critics, it is transforming our everyday lives; as with Amazon, Google, and eBay, it is almost impossible to remember how much more circumscribed our world was before it existed. (21)

NOTE: Ellipses indicate that the writer has deleted some words from the quotation.

The Works-Cited List

The works-cited list includes all the works you cite (refer to) in your essay. Use the following guidelines to help you prepare your list.

- Begin the works-cited list on a new page after the last page of text.
- Number the works-cited page as the next page.
- Center the heading Works Cited one inch from the top of the page; do not underline the heading or put it in quotation marks.
- Double-space the list.
- List entries alphabetically according to the author's last name.
- Alphabetize unsigned articles according to the first major word of the title.
- Begin each entry flush with the left-hand margin.
- Indent second and subsequent lines of each entry one-half inch.
- Follow the author name and title with a period and one space. Follow each element of the publication information with a comma and one space, and end with a period.

CONTAINERS

The MLA recognizes that changing technology and the overwhelming number of sources you may encounter make it impossible to create rules that cover every citation situation. Instead, when you come upon a source for which you do not find a citation model in the guidelines, the MLA suggests using this generic "container" model as a starting point, adapting it as necessary for each new source.

In this model, any larger work that contains the source you are citing might be considered a container. For instance, each of the readings in *Patterns* would have two containers: the first is the reading itself, and the second is the larger book that contains the reading.

> Noah, Trevor. "Soweto." *Patterns for College Writing*, 15th ed., edited by Laurie G. Kirszner and Stephen R. Mandell, Bedford/ St. Martin's, 2021, pp. 175–77.

Below are some generic models for citing sources with only one container (entire books, websites, poems, or films, for example) or for sources with two containers (selections from a book, a single named page on a website, or a film streamed through a repository such as Netflix, for example).

One Container

Author	Title	Title of Container	Publisher/Source

Date	Location/pages

Two Containers

Author	Title	Title of Container 1	volume number if applicable

Date	Location/pages	Title of Container 2	Location

The following sample works-cited entries cover the situations you will encounter most often. Follow the formats exactly as they appear here.

Articles

GUIDELINES FOR MLA ARTICLE CITATIONS

To cite a periodical article in MLA style, follow these guidelines:

1. List the author, last name first.
2. Put the title of the article in quotation marks and italicize the title of the periodical.
3. Include the volume and issue number (when applicable), the year and date of publication, and the pages on which the full article appears (without the abbreviation *p.* or *pp.*).

Journal Articles A journal is a publication aimed at readers who know a lot about a particular subject, such as English, history, or biology.

ARTICLE IN A JOURNAL

Provide the volume number and issue number preceded by vol. and no. List the date of publication and the pages of the article.

> Long, Hoyt, and Richard Jean So. "Turbulent Flow: A Computational Model of World Literature." *Modern Language Quarterly*, vol. 77, no. 3, Sept. 2016, pp. 345–67.

ARTICLE IN A JOURNAL THAT USES ONLY ISSUE NUMBERS

For a journal that uses only issue numbers, cite the issue number, publication date, and page numbers.

> Adelt, Ulrich. "Black, White, and Blue: Racial Politics in B. B. King's Music from the 1960s." *Journal of Popular Culture*, vol. 44, 2011, pp. 195–216.

Magazine Articles A magazine is a publication aimed at general readers. For this reason, it contains articles that are easier to understand than those in journals.

ARTICLE IN A MONTHLY OR BIMONTHLY MAGAZINE

Frequently, an article in a magazine does not appear on consecutive pages; for example, it might begin on page 43, skip to page 47, and continue on page 49. If that is the case, include only the first page followed by a plus sign.

> Edwards, Owen. "Kilroy Was Here." *Smithsonian*, Oct. 2004, pp. 40+.

ARTICLE IN A WEEKLY OR BIWEEKLY MAGAZINE (SIGNED OR UNSIGNED)

> Lansky, Sam. "Science Fiction Knows the Future Is Female." *TIME*, 26 Feb. 2018,
>   pp. 95–97.
> "Real Reform Post-Enron." *Nation*, 4 Mar. 2002, p. 3.

ARTICLE IN A NEWSPAPER

> Murphy, Sean P. "Eighty-Seven, and Left by the Side of the Road by Uber."
>   *The Boston Globe*, 2 Nov. 2018, pp. A1+.

EDITORIAL OR LETTER TO THE EDITOR

> "Cheers to a New University Circle Music Festival." Editorial. *Plain Dealer*
>   [Cleveland], 19 Aug. 2016, p. A5.

REVIEW IN A NEWSPAPER

> Dargis, Manohla. "Adam Sandler's Punch-Drunk Hustle." Review of *Uncut Gems*,
>   directed by Benny Safdie and Josh Safdie. *The New York Times*, 13 Dec.
>   2019, p. C8.

REVIEW IN A WEEKLY OR BIWEEKLY MAGAZINE

> Walton, James. "Noble, Embattled Souls." Review of *The Bone Clocks* and *Slade*
>   *House*, by David Mitchell, *The New York Review of Books*, 3 Dec. 2015,
>   pp. 55–58.

REVIEW IN A MONTHLY MAGAZINE

> Jones, Kent. "The Lay of the Land." Review of *Sunshine State,* directed by John
>   Sayles, *Film Commentary*, May/June 2018, pp. 22–24.

POLITICAL CARTOON OR COMIC STRIP

Include the author and title (if available) of the cartoon or comic strip, followed by a descriptive label and publication information.

> Adams, Scott. "Dilbert." *The Chicago Tribune*, 10 Mar. 2012, p. C9. Comic strip.
> Pett, Joel. *Lexington Herald-Leader*, 30 Apr. 2012, p. A12. Cartoon.

ADVERTISEMENT

Cite the name of the product or company that is advertised, followed by the descriptive label and the publication information.

> Subaru. *Wired*, Aug. 2017, p. 11. Advertisement.

FIGURE IN AN ESSAY

When citing a figure in your essay, include a *label and number*, a *title*, and *full source information*.

- The **label and number** should appear in the text of the paper directly below the actual illustration (see fig. 1, for example). The label name should be capitalized. (Fig. 1, for example.)
- The **title** (or caption) for the visual should appear on the same line as the label and number.
- **Full source information** should follow the title. If the illustration provides complete source information, it is not necessary to include it on the works-cited page.

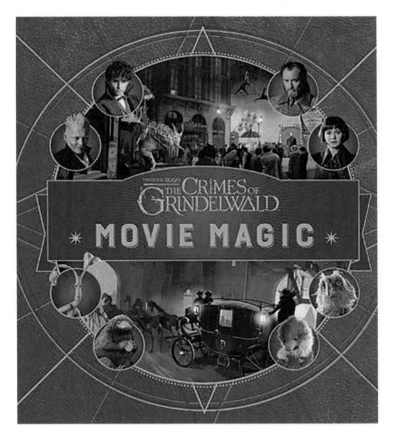

Fig. 1. Book Cover of *Fantastic Beasts: The Crimes of Grindelwald: Movie Magic*; "Fantastic Beasts Companion"; MuggleNet.com, 1 Oct. 2019, www.mugglenet.com/fantastic-beasts/film-companion-books-fantastic -beasts.

Books

GUIDELINES FOR MLA BOOK CITATIONS

To cite a print book in MLA style, follow these guidelines:

1. List the author with last name first.
2. Italicize the title.
3. Include the publisher's name. Use the abbreviation *UP* for *University Press,* as in *Princeton UP* and *U of Chicago P.*
4. Include the year of publication, followed by a period.

The two illustrations that follow show where to find the information you need for your book citations.

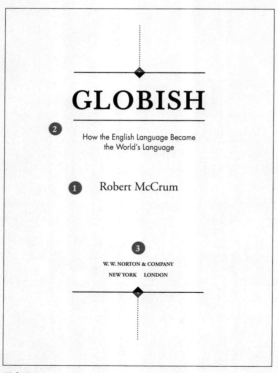

Title Page

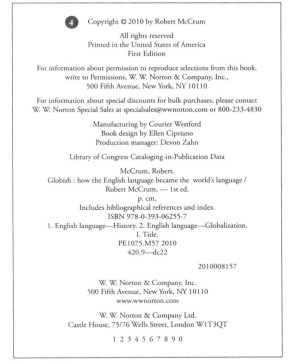

Copyright Page

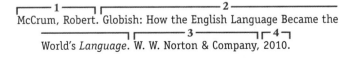

McCrum, Robert. Globish: How the English Language Became the World's *Language*. W. W. Norton & Company, 2010.

BOOK BY ONE AUTHOR

List the author, last name first, followed by the title (italicized). Include the full publisher's name, abbreviated when called for, and end with the date of publication.

Goodwin, Doris Kearns. *Leadership*. Simon & Schuster, 2018.

BOOK BY TWO AUTHORS

List authors in the order in which they are listed on the book's title page. List second and subsequent authors with first names first.

Gardner, Dan, and Philip E. Tetlock. *Super Forecasting: The Art and Science of Prediction*. Penguin Random House, 2015.

BOOK BY THREE OR MORE AUTHORS

List only the first author, followed by the abbreviation *et al.*

Hoffer, Peter Charles, et al. *The Federal Courts: An Essential History*. Oxford UP, 2016.

TWO OR MORE BOOKS BY THE SAME AUTHOR

List two or more books by the same author in alphabetical order according to title. In each entry after the first, use three unspaced hyphens (followed by a period) instead of the author's name.

> García, Cristina. *Dreams of Significant Girls.* Simon and Schuster, 2011.
>
> ---. The Lady Matador's Hotel. Scribner, 2010.

EDITED BOOK

> Horner, Avril, and Anne Rowe, editors. *Living on Paper: Letters from Iris Murdoch.* Princeton UP, 2016.

TRANSLATION

> Ullmann, Regina. *The Country Road: Stories.* Translated by Kurt Beals, New Directions Publishing, 2015.

REVISED EDITION

> Eagleton, Terry. *Literary Theory: An Introduction.* 3rd ed., U of Minnesota P, 2008.

ANTHOLOGY

> Kirszner, Laurie G., and Stephen R. Mandell, editors. *Patterns for College Writing: A Rhetorical Reader and Guide.* 15th ed., Bedford/ St. Martin's, 2021.

ESSAY IN AN ANTHOLOGY

> Gansberg, Martin. "Thirty-Seven Who Saw Murder Didn't Call the Police." *Patterns for College Writing: A Rhetorical Reader and Guide,* 15th ed., edited by Laurie G. Kirszner and Stephen R. Mandell, Bedford/ St. Martin's, 2021, pp. 127–31.

MORE THAN ONE ESSAY IN THE SAME ANTHOLOGY

To avoid repeating the entire entry, list each essay separately with a cross-reference to the entire anthology.

> Gansberg, Martin. "Thirty-Seven Who Saw Murder Didn't Call the Police." Kirszner and Mandell, pp. 127–31.
>
> Kirszner, Laurie G., and Stephen R. Mandell, editors. *Patterns for College Writing: A Rhetorical Reader and Guide.* 15th ed., Bedford/St. Martin's, 2021.
>
> Staples, Brent. "Just Walk On By: A Black Man Ponders His Power to Alter Public Space." Kirszner and Mandell, pp. 231–36.

SECTION OR CHAPTER OF A BOOK

> Rizga, Kristina. "Mr. Hsu." *Mission High: One School, How Experts Tried to Fail It, and the Students and Teachers Who Made It Triumph,* Nation Books, 2015, pp. 89–114.

INTRODUCTION, PREFACE, FOREWORD, OR AFTERWORD

> Dunham, Lena. Foreword. *The Liars' Club*, by Mary Karr, Penguin Classics, 2015,
> pp. xi–xiii.

MULTIVOLUME WORK

> Stark, Freya. *Letters*. Edited by Lucy Moorehead, Compton Press, 1974–82.
> 8 vols.

ARTICLE IN A REFERENCE WORK

A **reference work** is a book (print or electronic) — such as an encyclopedia, a dictionary, a bibliography, an almanac, or a handbook — that contains factual information. If the entries in a reference work are arranged alphabetically, do not include page numbers or volume numbers.

For familiar reference works that publish new editions regularly, include only the edition (if given) and the year of publication.

> "Civil Rights." The World Book Encyclopedia. 2016 ed.

For less familiar reference works, provide a full citation.

> "Ball's in Your Court, The." *The American Heritage Dictionary of Idioms*, 2nd ed.,
> Houghton Mifflin Harcourt, 2013.

Internet Sources

GUIDELINES FOR MLA INTERNET CITATIONS

When citing an Internet source, include the following information:

1. The name of the author or editor of the site
2. The title of the site (italicized)
3. The site's sponsor or publisher
4. The date of electronic publication (if no publication date is available, include the date you accessed the site at the end of the citation instead)
5. The URL of the site (without http:// or https://) or, preferably, the Digital Object Identifier (DOI). (The DOI is a unique code assigned to a digital object, such as a research paper. No matter where on the Internet the paper or other object appears, the DOI is the same.)

ENTIRE INTERNET SITE

> *The Jane Austen Society of North America*. The Jane Austen Society of North
> America, 2020, www.jasna.org.

DOCUMENT WITHIN A WEBSITE

> Clarke, Stewart. "Twitter Hit by Outages around the World." *Variety*, Penske
> Media Corporation, 2 Oct. 2019, www.variety.com/2019/digital/news/
> twitter-global-outage-2-1203355745/.

E-BOOK

Milton, John. *Paradise Lost: Book I. Poetry Foundation*, 2014, www.poetryfoun
    dation.org/poem/174987.

Piketty, Thomas. *Capital in the Twenty-First Century*. Translated by Arthur
    Goldhammer, Harvard UP, 2014. *Google Books*, books.google.com/
    books?isbn=0674369556.

PART OF AN EBOOK

Radford, Dollie. "At Night." *Poems*. London, 1910. *Victorian Women Writers
    Project*, webapp1.dlib.indiana.edu/vwwp/view?docId=VAB7138.xml&chunk
    .id=d1e1027&brand=vwwp&doc.view =0&anchor.id=#VAB7138-022.

ARTICLE IN AN ONLINE JOURNAL

Amao, Olumuyiwa Babatunde, and Ufo Okeke-Uzodike. "Nigeria, Afrocentrism,
    and Conflict Resolution: After Five Decades — How Far, How Well?" *African
    Studies Quarterly*, vol. 15, no. 4, Sept. 2015, pp. 1–23, asq.africa.ufl.edu/
    files/Volume-15-Issue-4-OLUMUYIWA-BABATUNDE-AMAO.pdf.

ARTICLE IN AN ONLINE REFERENCE BOOK OR ENCYCLOPEDIA

Dennis, Geoffrey W. "Demons in Judaism." *Encyclopedia Mythica*, 1 Jan. 2020,
    www.pantheon.org/articles/d/demons_in_judaism.html.

ARTICLE IN AN ONLINE NEWSPAPER

Weinstein, Dave. "Privacy vs. Security: It's a False Dilemma." *Wall Street
    Journal*, 6 Oct. 2019, www.wsj.com/news/opinion.

ONLINE EDITORIAL

"City's Blight Fight Making Difference." *The Columbus Dispatch*, 17 Nov. 2015,
    www.dispatch.com/content/stories/editorials/ 2015/11/17/1-citys-blight
    -fight-making-difference.html. Editorial.

ARTICLE IN AN ONLINE MAGAZINE

Greenstone, Dan. "Down with Classroom Icebreakers." *Salon*, 6 Sept. 2016,
    www.salon.com/2016/09/06/down-with-classroom-icebreakers-can-we-all
    -just-start-teaching-instead/.

REVIEW IN AN ONLINE PERIODICAL

Della Subin, Anna. "It Has Burned My Heart." Review of *The Lives of Muhammad*,
    by Kecia Ali, *London Review of Books*, 22 Oct. 2015, www.lrb.co.uk/v37/
    n20/anna-della-subin-it-has-burned-my-heart.

POSTING TO A DISCUSSION LIST

Yen, Jessica. "Quotations within Parentheses (Study Measures)." *Copyediting-L*, 18 Mar. 2016, list.indiana.edu/sympa/arc/copyediting-l/2016-03/ msg00492.html.

BLOG POST

Goddard, Joanna. "Have a Lovely Weekend." *A Cup of Joe*, 4 Oct. 2019, cupofjo.com.

YOUTUBE VIDEO

Nayar, Vineet. "Employees First, Customers Second." *YouTube*, 9 June 2015, www.youtube.com/watch?v=cCdu67s_C5E.

Other Internet Sources

PAINTING

Clough, Charles. *January Twenty-First*. 1988–89, Joslyn Art Museum, Omaha, www.joslyn.org/collections-and-exhibitions/permanent-collections/modern -and-contemporary/charles-clough-january-twenty-first/.

PHOTOGRAPH

Hura, Sohrab. *Old Man Lighting a Fire*. 2015, *Magnum Photos*, www.magnumphotos .com/C.aspx?VP3=SearchResult&ALID =2K1HRG681B_Q.

CARTOON

Zyglis, Adam. "City of Light." Cartoon. *Buffalo News*, 8 Nov. 2015, adamzyglis .buffalonews.com/2015/11/08/city-of-light/.

MAP OR CHART

"Map of Sudan." *Global Citizen*, Citizens for Global Solutions, 2011, globalsolutions.org/blog/bashir#.VthzNMfi_FI.

SOCIAL MEDIA POST

For posts to social media sites, the content often does not have a specific title. Instead, write out the comment or tweet in its entirety (or use the first line for particularly long comments), and cite the platform as the publisher. Be sure to include the date of the post and a URL.

Bedford English. "Stacey Cochran explores Reflective Writing in the classroom and as a writer: http://ow.ly/YkjVB." *Facebook*, 15 Feb. 2016, www.facebook.com/BedfordEnglish/posts/10153415001259607.

Curiosity Rover. "Can you see me waving? How to spot #Mars in the night sky: https://youtu.be/hv8hVvJlcJQ." *Twitter*, 5 Nov. 2015, twitter.com/marscu riosity/status/672859022911889408.

EMAIL

Thornbrugh, Caitlin. "Coates Lecture." Received by Rita Anderson, 20 Oct. 2020.

MATERIAL FROM A LIBRARY DATABASE

For material retrieved from a library database such as *InfoTrac, LexisNexis, ProQuest,* or *EBSCOhost,* list the publication information for the source, and provide the name of the database (such as *LexisNexis Academic*), italicized, and the URL of the database or the DOI.

Coles, Kimberly Anne. "The Matter of Belief in John Donne's Holy Sonnets." *Renaissance Quarterly*, vol. 68, no. 3, Fall 2015, pp. 899–931. *JSTOR*, doi:10.1086/683855.

Macari, Anne Marie. "Lyric Impulse in a Time of Extinction." *American Poetry Review*, vol. 44, no. 4, July/Aug. 2015, pp. 11–14. *General OneFile*, go .galegroup.com/.

Rosenbaum, Ron. "The Last Renaissance Man." *Smithsonian*, Nov. 2012, pp. 39–44. *OmniFile Full Text Select*, web.b.ebscohost.com .ezproxy.bpl.org/.

Other Nonprint Sources

TELEVISION OR RADIO PROGRAM

"Federal Role in Support of Autism." *Washington Journal*, narrated by Robb Harleston, C-SPAN, 1 Dec. 2012.

FILM, DVD, OR CD

Blige, Mary J. "Don't Mind." *Life II: The Journey Continues (Act 1)*, Geffen, 2011.

The Martian. Directed by Ridley Scott, performances by Matt Damon, Jessica Chastain, Kristen Wiig, and Kate Mara, Twentieth Century Fox, 2015.

PERSONAL INTERVIEW

Huffington, Arianna. Personal interview, 7 May 2020.

Model Student Research Paper in MLA Style

The following research paper, "The Limitations of *Wikipedia*," by Philip Lau, follows MLA format as outlined in the previous pages.

Philip Lau

Professor Carroll

English 101

5 Mar. 2021

The Limitations of *Wikipedia*

Introduction

When students get a research assignment, many immediately go to the Internet to find sources. Searching the web, they may discover a *Wikipedia* article on their topic. But is *Wikipedia* a reliable reference source for a research paper? There is quite a bit of controversy over the use of *Wikipedia* as a source, but the

Thesis statement

consensus seems to be that it is not reliable. Although *Wikipedia* can be a good starting point for general information about a topic, it is not suitable for college-level research.

A wiki allows multiple users to collaborate in creating the content of a website. With a wiki, anyone with a browser can edit, modify, rearrange, or delete content. It is not necessary to know HTML (hypertext mark-up language). The word *wiki* comes from the word *wikiwiki*, which means "quick" or "fast" in Hawaiian. The most popular wiki is *Wikipedia*, a free, Internet-based encyclopedia that relies on the collaboration of those who post and edit entries. Anyone can write a *Wikipedia* article by

Paragraph combines factual information found in more than one source: information and statistics from Wikipedia *articles, quotations from Chozick and Grathwohl*

using the "*Wikipedia* Article Wizard" or edit an entry by clicking on the "Edit" tab. Readers can also view the revision history of an entry by clicking on "View History" ("Help: Page History"). For its many advocates, *Wikipedia*'s open and collaborative nature makes it a "collectively brilliant creation" (Chozick). This collaboration enables *Wikipedia* to publish a wide variety of entries on timely, unusual, and specialized topics (see fig. 1). According to Casper Grathwohl, President, Dictionaries Division, and Director, Global Business Development at Oxford University Press, it "has become increasingly clear that [*Wikipedia*] functions as a necessary layer in the Internet knowledge system, a layer that was not needed in the analog age." At this time, the site contains more than 40 million articles in 301 languages ("*Wikipedia*").

Lau 2

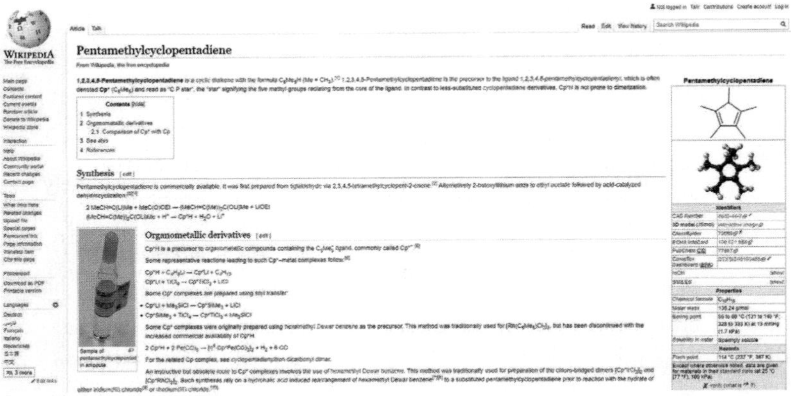

Fig. 1. *Wikipedia* entry for a chemical compound. "Pentamethylcyclopentadiene."
Wikipedia. Wikimedia Foundation, 9 Jan. 2020, en.wikipedia.org/wiki/
Pentamethylcyclopentadiene.

Wikipedia contains two kinds of content. The first kind of
content is factual—that is, information that can be verified
or proved true. Factual material from reliable sources is more
trustworthy than material from other sources. *Wikipedia*'s
own site states, "In general, the most reliable sources are peer-
reviewed journals and books published in university presses;
university-level textbooks; magazines, journals, and books
published by respected publishing houses; and mainstream
newspapers" ("No Original Research"). Most reliable publications
have staff whose job it is to check factual content. However,
because *Wikipedia* relies on a community of contributors to write
articles, no single person or group of people is responsible for
checking facts. The theory is that if enough people work on an

> Paragraph
> combines
> student's
> ideas with
> quotations from
> "No Original
> Research"

Lau 3

article, factual errors will be found and corrected. However, this assumption is not necessarily true.

The second kind of content consists of opinions. Because they are personal beliefs or judgments, opinions — by definition — tend to be one-sided. Because *Wikipedia* entries are supposed to be objective, *Wikipedia's* policy statement stresses the importance of acknowledging various sides of issues and maintaining a sharp distinction between opinions and facts ("Neutral Point of View"). In addition, *Wikipedia* warns users against believing everything they read, including what they read on *Wikipedia*: "Anyone can create a website or pay to have a book published, then claim to be an expert . . ." ("Identifying Reliable Sources"). It also advises readers to examine sources carefully, especially when they make claims that are "contradicted by the prevailing view within the relevant community, or that would significantly alter mainstream assumptions, especially in science, medicine, history, politics, and biographies of living people" ("Verifiability"). However, everything is up to users; no editor at *Wikipedia* checks to make sure that these guidelines are followed.

In spite of its stated policies, *Wikipedia* remains susceptible to certain problems. One problem is the assumption that the knowledge of the community is more valuable than the knowledge of experts in a field. In other words, *Wikipedia* values crowd-sourced information more than the knowledge of an individual specialist. In his book *You Are Not a Gadget,* computer scientist and pioneer of virtual reality Jaron Lanier argues that *Wikipedia's* authors "implicitly celebrate the ideal of intellectual mob rule" (144). According to Lanier, "Wikipedians always act out the ideal that the collective is closer to the truth and the individual voice is dispensable" (144). Adherence to this ideal can have serious consequences for the accuracy of *Wikipedia* entries. For example, historian Timothy Messer-Kruse, an expert on American labor history,

Paragraph combines student's own ideas with quotations from multiple Wikipedia entries

Lau 4

Paragraph combines quotations from two Wikipedia entries and Lanier, as well as a long quotation from Messer-Kruse; it includes student's summary of Messer-Kruse's story and student's own ideas

attempted to edit a *Wikipedia* article to correct a factual error in the entry on the 1886 Chicago Haymarket Riot. Although Messer-Kruse has published extensively on the subject, his correction was rejected. Messer-Kruse's subsequent attempts to correct the entry — which had multiple errors — were dismissed as well. In an article he wrote for *The Chronicle of Higher Education,* Messer-Kruse recounted the experience, including a telling comment from one of the site's editors, with whom he had an online exchange:

> If all historians save one say that the sky was green in 1888, our policies require that we write, "Most historians write that the sky was green, but one says the sky was blue." As individual editors, we're not in the business of weighing claims, just reporting what reliable sources write.

In other words, *Wikipedia*'s policy is to present all views, even incorrect ones, provided they are published in a reliable source ("Neutral Point of View").

Another problem with *Wikipedia* is the ease with which entries can be edited. Because anyone can edit entries, individuals can vandalize content by inserting incorrect information, obscene language, or even nonsense into articles. For example, entries for controversial people, such as President Donald Trump, financier George Soros, or Scientology founder L. Ron Hubbard, or for controversial subjects, such as abortion, are routinely vandalized.

Paragraph contains student's summary of Seigenthaler's story from Torrenzano and Davis's Digital Assassination, as well as paraphrases and quotations from the book

Sometimes the vandalism can be extremely harmful. One notorious case of vandalism involved John Seigenthaler, a journalist and former administrative assistant to Attorney General Robert Kennedy, who was falsely accused in *Wikipedia* of being involved in the assassinations of John F. Kennedy and Robert Kennedy. Ultimately, Seigenthaler contacted *Wikipedia* founder Jimmy Wales, threatened legal action, and even tracked down the writer who had inserted the libelous accusation. If a friend had not alerted Seigenthaler to the vandalized entry, it

Lau 5

would have likely remained in place, with its false claim that
Seigenthaler was "a suspected assassin who had defected to the
Soviet Union for 13 years" (Torrenzano and Davis 60–63).

In addition to misinformation and vandalism, bias is
another problem for *Wikipedia.* Some critics have accused the
site of having a liberal bias. Writing for the web publication
Human Events, Rowan Scarborough notes that observers on the
right have "long complained of *Wikipedia*'s liberal bias that
infects voters with unflattering profiles of their candidates." In
fact, a competitor, *Conservapedia,* lists many examples of this
skewed coverage in *Wikipedia* entries ("Examples of Bias in
Wikipedia"). Other critics have identified different kinds of
biases on the site. For example, a 2010 survey of *Wikipedia*
contributors suggested that "less than 15 percent of its hundreds
of thousands of contributors are women" (Cohen). This imbalance
indicates a significant lack of women's perspectives on the site.
In response, Sue Gardner, the executive director of the Wikimedia
Foundation, "set a goal to raise the share of female contributors
to 25 percent by 2015" (Cohen).[1]

As Gardner indicates, *Wikipedia* has tried to correct some of
the problems that its critics have noted. For example, in
response to criticism of its policy of allowing writers and editors
to remain anonymous, Wales changed this policy. Now, writers
and editors have to provide their user names and thus take
responsibility for the content they contribute. In addition,
Wikipedia has made it possible for administrators to block edits
originating from certain Internet domains and to prevent certain
writers and editors from posting or changing information.
However, authorship is still a problem. Most readers have no
idea who has written an article that they are reading or whether
or not the writer can be trusted. Given *Wikipedia*'s basic
philosophy, it will be difficult to solve this problem.

> **Paragraph contains paraphrase from "Examples of Bias in Wikipedia," quotations from Scarborough and Cohen, and the student's own conclusions**

---

[1] By 2018, almost 17,000 new women's biographies had been added to
Wikipedia. Even today, some critics assert that there are still serious
examples of gender bias in Wikipedia's content.

Lau 6

Of course, even traditional encyclopedias have shortcomings. For example, a 2005 study by the journal Nature found that although *Wikipedia* included errors, the *Encyclopaedia Britannica* also did (Giles). *Britannica* — the oldest English-language encyclopedia still in print at the time — ceased print publication in 2012 after 244 years (Rousseau). However, this venerable source of information persists online because people still value its expertise and trust its credibility. As Jorge Cauz, the president of Encyclopaedia Britannica, Inc., observes, "While *Wikipedia* has become ubiquitous, *Britannica* remains a consistently more reliable source. In other words, *Britannica* brings scholarly knowledge to an editorial process" (qtd. in Rousseau). Although that editorial process is not a 100 percent guarantee of accuracy, *Britannica's* staff of dedicated experts and specialists is more reliable than anonymous *Wikipedia* posters. Moreover, conscientious and knowledgeable editors work to make sure that entries are clear, logical, coherent, and grammatically correct. The same cannot be said for *Wikipedia,* which is known for its inconsistent treatment of subjects and its ungrammatical and awkward prose.

Paragraph contains ideas found in several sources and the student's own ideas

Supporters of *Wikipedia* defend the site against charges of bias and errors, pointing out that even respected peer-reviewed journals have problems. For example, some reviewers of articles submitted for publication in peer-reviewed journals may have conflicts of interest. A reviewer might reject an article that challenges his or her own work, or editors may favor certain authors over others. Also, it may be possible for a reviewer to identify the work of a rival, especially if the number of people working in a field is relatively small, and let bias influence his or her evaluation of an article. Another problem is that it takes a long time for articles in peer-reviewed journals to get into print. Critics point out that by the time an article in a peer-reviewed journal appears, it may be outdated. In short, peer-reviewed journals may not be

Lau 7

either as objective or as up-to-date as many readers think
they are.

Conclusion

Despite their problems, articles that appear in an edited
encyclopedia or journal are more trustworthy than those that
appear in *Wikipedia*. These articles are thoroughly reviewed by
editors or go through a peer-review process (that is, they are
screened by experts in a field), and for this reason, they can be
considered reliable sources of information. *Wikipedia*, however,
is not a reliable research source. The fact that almost anyone
can contribute an article or edit one at any time raises serious
questions about *Wikipedia*'s reliability. In addition, many articles
contain factual errors. Although some errors are found and
corrected immediately, others remain for a long time or go entirely
unnoticed. Finally, articles frequently reflect the biases or political
agendas of contributors and, as a result, present a one-sided or
inaccurate view of a subject. All in all, *Wikipedia*'s open-source
philosophy makes it more prone to errors, inconsistencies, poor
writing, and even vandalism, and for this reason, it should be used
with caution. Perhaps the best that can be said of *Wikipedia* is
that it is a good starting point for research. Although it is a useful
site for getting an overview of a subject before doing in-depth
research, it should not be considered a credible or authoritative
academic source.

Works Cited

Chozick, Amy. "Jimmy Wales Is Not an Internet Billionaire."
The New York Times, 30 June 2013, www.nytimes.com/
2013/06/30/magazine/jimmy-wales-is-not-an-internet
-billionaire.html?_r=0.

Cohen, Noam. "Define Gender Gap? Look Up Wikipedia's
Contributor List." *The New York Times*, 31 Jan. 2011,
pp. A1+.

"Examples of Bias in Wikipedia." *Conservapedia*, 20 Dec. 2019,
www.conservapedia.com/Examples_of_Bias_in_Wikipedia.

"Gender Bias on Wikipedia." *Wikipedia*, Wikimedia Foundation,
6 Oct. 2019, en.wikipedia.org/wiki/Gender_bias_on
_Wikipedia.

Giles, Jim. "Internet Encyclopædias Go Head to Head." *Nature*,
vol. 438, 15 Dec. 2005, pp. 900–901.

Grathwohl, Casper. "Wikipedia Comes of Age." *The Chronicle of
Higher Education*, 7 Jan. 2011, chronicle.com/article/
article-content/125899.

"Help: Page History." *Wikipedia*, Wikimedia Foundation, 29 Aug.
2019, en.wikipedia.org/wiki/Help:Page_history.

"Identifying Reliable Sources." *Wikipedia*, Wikimedia
Foundation, 28 Dec. 2019, en.wikipedia.org/wiki/
Wikipedia:Identifying_reliable_sources.

Lanier, Jaron. *You Are Not a Gadget: A Manifesto*. Allen Lane,
2010.

Messer-Kruse, Timothy. "The 'Undue Weight' of Truth on
Wikipedia." *The Chronicle of Higher Education*, 12 Feb.
2012, chronicle.com/article/The-Undue-Weight-of
-Truth-on/130704.

"Neutral Point of View." *Wikipedia*, Wikimedia Foundation,
3 Sept. 2019, en.wikipedia.org/wiki/Wikipedia:Neutral
_point_of_view.

"No Original Research." *Wikipedia*, Wikimedia Foundation,
1 Oct. 2019, en.wikipedia.org/wiki/Wikipedia:No
_original_research.

Lau 9

Rousseau, Caryn. "Encyclopaedia Britannica to End Print
 Editions." *Yahoo! News,* 13 Mar. 2012, www.yahoo.com/
 news/encyclopaedia-britannica-end-print-editions
 -234637805.html.

Scarborough, Rowan. "Wikipedia Whacks the Right." *Human
 Events,* 27 Sep. 2010, humanevents.com/2010/09/27/
 wikipedia-whacks-the-right/.

Torrenzano, Richard, and Mark Davis. *Digital Assassination:
 Protecting Your Reputation, Brand, or Business against
 Online Attacks.* St. Martin's Press, 2011.

"Verifiability." *Wikipedia,* Wikimedia Foundation, 9 Dec. 2019,
 en.wikipedia.org/wiki/Wikipedia:Verifiability.

"Wikipedia." *Wikipedia,* Wikimedia Foundation, 7 Oct. 2019,
 en.wikipedia.org/wiki/Wikipedia.

APPENDIX

Documenting Sources: APA

The American Psychological Association (APA) format is commonly used to cite sources in the social sciences. Sources are cited to help readers in the social sciences understand new ideas in the context of previous research and show them how current the sources are.*

Using Parenthetical References

In APA style, parenthetical references refer readers to sources in the list of references at the end of the essay. In general, parenthetical references should include the author and year of publication. You may also include page numbers if you are quoting directly from a source. Here are some more specific guidelines:

- Refer to the author's name in the text, or cite it, along with the year of publication, in parentheses: Vang asserted . . . (2004) or (Vang, 2004). Once you have cited a source, you can refer to the author a second time without the publication date as long as it is clear you are referring to the same source: Vang also found . . .
- If no author is identified, use a shortened version of the title: ("Mind," 2007).
- If you are citing multiple works by the same author or authors published in the same year, add a lowercase letter with the year: (Peters, 2004a), (Peters, 2004b), and so on.
- When a work has two authors, cite both names and the year: (Tabor & Garza, 2006). For three or more authors, use the first author followed by et al. and the year.

---

*American Psychological Association, *Publication Manual of the American Psychological Association*, Seventh Edition (2020).

- Omit page numbers or dates if the source does not include them. (Try to find a .pdf version of an online source if it is an option; it will usually include page numbers.)
- When quoting words from a source, include the page number: (Vang, 2004, p. 33). If the work does not have page numbers, use a locator, like a heading, a paragraph number (even if self-counted), or a time stamp.
- If you quote a source found in another source, indicate the original author and the source in which you found it: Psychologist Gary Wells asserted . . . (as cited in Doyle, 2005, p. 122).
- Include in-text references to personal communications and interviews by providing the person's name, the phrase "personal communication," and the date: (J. Smith, personal communication, February 12, 2014). Do not include these sources in your reference list.

Parenthetical citations must be included for all sources that are not common knowledge, whether you are paraphrasing, summarizing, or quoting directly from a source. If a direct quotation is forty words or fewer, include it within quotation marks without separating it from the rest of the text. When quoting a passage that is more than forty words long, indent the entire block of quoted text one-half inch from the left margin, and do not enclose it in quotation marks. It should be double-spaced, like the rest of the essay.

GUIDELINES FOR PREPARING THE REFERENCE LIST

Start your list of references on a separate page at the end of your essay. Center the title References at the top of the page.

- Begin each reference flush with the left margin, and indent subsequent lines one-half inch.
- List your references alphabetically by the author's last name (or by the first major word of the title if no author is identified).
- If the list includes references for two or more sources by the same author, list them in order by the year of publication, starting with the earliest.
- Italicize titles of books and periodicals. Do not italicize article titles or enclose them in quotation marks.
- For titles of books and articles, capitalize the first word of the title and subtitle as well as any proper nouns. Capitalize words in a periodical title as in the original.

When you have completed your reference list, go through your essay and make sure every reference cited is included in the list in the correct order.

Examples of APA Citations

The following are examples of APA citations.

Periodicals

ARTICLE IN A JOURNAL PAGINATED BY VOLUME

Nussbaum, M. C. (2016). Women's progress and women's human rights. *Human Rights Quarterly, 38*, 589–622.

ARTICLE IN A JOURNAL PAGINATED BY ISSUE

Lamb, B., & Keller, H. (2007). Understanding cultural models of parenting: The role of intracultural variation and response style. *Journal of Cross-Cultural Psychology, 38*(1), 50–57.

MAGAZINE ARTICLE

Lasdun, J. (2016, April 11). Alone in the Alps. *The New Yorker*, 34–39.

NEWSPAPER ARTICLE

DeParle, J. (2009, April 19). Struggling to rise in suburbs where failing means fitting in. *The New York Times*, pp. A1, A20–A21.

Books

BOOKS BY ONE AUTHOR

McCrum, R. (2010). *Globish: How the English language became the world's language*. Norton.

BOOKS BY TWO AUTHORS

Cottler, S., Sambrook, R., & Mosdell, N. (2016). *Reporting dangerously: Journalist killings, intimidation, and security*. Palgrave Macmillan.

BOOKS BY THREE TO TWENTY AUTHORS

Lunsford, A., Ruszkiewicz, J., & Walters, K. (2019). *Everything's an argument*. Bedford/St. Martin's.

BOOKS BY TWENTY-ONE OR MORE AUTHORS

Batkie, S., LaScala, M., Wharton, N., Hassenger, J., Lehrman, M., Gilman, K., Lill, J., Morrison, S. B., McKean, K., Stickles, C., Prisco, J., Adams, C., Fitzgibbons, K., Forman, J., Bent, J., Grossman, A., DeLizza, T., Bertino, M., Hart, D., . . . Kuczynski, R. (2019). *The David Bowie principle: His life and music*. SA Press.

EDITED BOOK

> Brummett, B. (Ed.). (2008). *Uncovering hidden rhetorics: Social issues in disguise*. SAGE.

ESSAY IN AN EDITED BOOK

> Alberts, H. C. (2006). The multiple transformations of Miami. In H. Smith & O. J. Furuseth (Eds.), *Latinos in the new south: Transformations of place* (pp. 135–151). Ashgate.

TRANSLATION

> Courville, S. (2008). *Quebec: A historical geography* (R. Howard, Trans.). UBC.

REVISED EDITION

> Johnson, B., & Christensen, L. B. (2008). *Educational research: Quantitative, qualitative, and mixed approaches* (3rd ed.). SAGE.

Internet Sources

Internet webpages and documents are treated like print documents and include a URL at the end the entry.

ENTIRE WEBSITE

> Paris 2015 UN Climate Change Conference COP21 CMP11. (2015). *UN climate change conference*. http://www.cop21.gouv.fr/en/

WEB PAGE WITHIN A WEBSITE

> The great divide: How Westerners and Muslims view each other. (2006, July 6). In *Pew global attitudes project*. http://pewglobal.org/reports/display.php?ReportID=253

UNIVERSITY PROGRAM WEBSITE

> *National Security Archive*. (2009). George Washington University website: http://www.gwu.edu/~nsarchiv/

JOURNAL ARTICLE FOUND ON THE WEB WITH A DOI

Because websites change and disappear without warning, many publishers add a digital object identifier (DOI) to their articles. A DOI is a unique number that can be retrieved no matter where the article ends up on the web.

To locate an article with a known DOI, go to the DOI system website at http://dx.doi.org/, and type in the DOI. When citing an article that has a DOI (usually found on the first page of the article), you do not need to include a URL in your reference or the name of the database in which you may have found the article. The DOI should be formatted at its own type of link that begins with "https://doi.org/" followed by the relevant number.

Geers, A. L., Wellman, J. A., & Lassiter, G. D. (2009). Dispositional optimism and engagement: The moderating influence of goal prioritization. *Journal of Personality and Social Psychology, 94,* 913–932. https://doi.org/10.1037/a0014746

JOURNAL ARTICLE FOUND ON THE WEB WITHOUT A DOI

Bendetto, M. M. (2008). Crisis on the immigration bench: An ethical perspective. *Brooklyn Law Review, 73,* 467–523. http://brooklaw .edu/students/journals/blr.php/

JOURNAL ARTICLE FROM AN ELECTRONIC DATABASE

The name and URL of the database are not required for citations if a DOI is available. If no DOI is available, provide the home page URL of the journal or the book or the report publisher.

Staub, E., & Pearlman, L. A. (2009). Reducing intergroup prejudice and conflict: A commentary. *Journal of Personality and Social Psychology, 11,* 3–23. http://www.apa.org/journals/psp/

ELECTRONIC BOOK

Katz, R. N. (Ed.). (2008). *The tower and the cloud: Higher education in an era of cloud computing.* http://net.educause.edu/ir/library/pdf /PUB7202.pdf

VIDEO BLOG POST

Vlogbrothers. (2016, August 4). *How to vote in every state* [Video file]. https://www.youtube.com/watch?v=bFnI25Pu19k

PRESENTATION SLIDES

Hall, M. E. (2009) *Who moved my job!? A psychology of job-loss "trauma"* [Presentation slides]. http://www.cew.wisc.edu/docs /WMMJ%20PwrPt-Summry2.ppt

Model Student Paper in APA Style

The following research paper follows APA format as outlined in the preceding pages. Note that this paper has the same content as the MLA paper on pages 743–51 but follows APA conventions. For this reason, it includes an abstract, a title page, and internal headings.

Running head: THE LIMITATIONS OF *WIKIPEDIA* 1

The Limitations of *Wikipedia*

Philip Lau

English 101

Professor Carroll

March 5, 2021

THE LIMITATIONS OF *WIKIPEDIA*   2

Abstract

Wikipedia is an online encyclopedia with entries that are created
and updated by users rather than by editors. This essay examines
the benefits and drawbacks associated with *Wikipedia's* open-forum
approach. *Wikipedia* contains information about a great number
of topics and could be a good resource for students who are trying
to narrow the focus of their essays. However, many educators
believe that this information is unreliable and therefore should
not be used for scholarly research. They are concerned that entries
that can be edited by anyone, regardless of their expertise on the
subject, might not be accurate. Although *Wikipedia* strives to be as
accurate as a traditional encyclopedia, there has been at least one
case in which inflammatory and untrue information remained on
the site for months and was disseminated through other outlets
as fact. Because there is no way to determine the expertise of the
authors or the validity of the information on *Wikipedia*, it should
not be considered a reliable source.

The Limitations of *Wikipedia*

Introduction

When students get a research assignment, many immediately go to the internet to find sources. Searching the web, they may discover a *Wikipedia* article on their topic. But is *Wikipedia* a reliable reference source for a research paper? There is quite a bit of controversy over the use of *Wikipedia* as a source, but the

Thesis statement

consensus seems to be that it is not reliable. Although *Wikipedia* can be a good starting point for general information about a topic, it is not suitable for college-level research.

A wiki allows multiple users to collaborate in creating the content of a website. With a wiki, anyone with a browser can edit, modify, rearrange, or delete content. It is not necessary to know HTML (hypertext mark-up language). The word wiki comes from the word wikiwiki, which means "quick" or "fast" in Hawaiian. The most popular wiki is *Wikipedia*, a free, Internet-based encyclopedia that relies on the collaboration of those who post and edit entries.

Paragraph combines factual information found in more than one source: information and statistics from Wikipedia articles, quotations from Chozick and Grathwohl

Anyone can write a *Wikipedia* article by using the "*Wikipedia* Article Wizard" or edit an entry by clicking on the "Edit" tab. Readers can easily view the revision history of an entry by clicking on "View History" ("Help: page history," 2016). For its many advocates, *Wikipedia's* open and collaborative nature makes it a "collectively brilliant creation" (Chozick, 2016). This collaboration enables *Wikipedia* to publish a wide variety of entries on timely, unusual, and specialized topics (see Figure 1). It has certainly altered the way people think about research. Moreover, *Wikipedia* has increasingly become a "necessary layer in the Internet knowledge system, a layer that was not needed in the analog age" (Grathwohl, 2011). At this time, the site contains more than 40 million articles in 301 languages ("*Wikipedia*," 2016).

Wikipedia's Two Kinds of Content

Wikipedia contains two kinds of content. The first kind of content is factual—that is, information that can be verified

THE LIMITATIONS OF *WIKIPEDIA*   4

Figure 1. *Wikipedia* entry for a chemical compound. Pentamethylcyclopentadiene (2020, January 9). *Wikipedia*. Retrieved from http://en.wikipedia.org/wiki/Pentamethylcyclopentadiene

or proved true. Factual material from reliable sources is more trustworthy than material from other sources. *Wikipedia's* own site states, "In general, the most reliable sources are peer-reviewed journals and books published in university presses; university-level textbooks; magazines, journals, and books published by respected publishing houses; and mainstream newspapers" ("No Original Research," 2016). Most reliable publications have staff whose job it is to check factual content. However, because *Wikipedia* relies on a community of contributors to write articles, no single person or group of people is responsible for checking facts. The theory is that if enough people work on an article, factual errors will be

Paragraph combines student's ideas with quotations from "No Original Research"

found and corrected. However, this assumption is not necessarily true.

The second kind of content consists of opinions. Because they are personal beliefs or judgments, opinions — by definition — tend to be one-sided. Because *Wikipedia* entries are supposed to be objective, *Wikipedia's* policy statement stresses the importance of acknowledging various sides of issues and maintaining a sharp distinction between opinions and facts ("Neutral Point of View," 2016). In addition, *Wikipedia* warns users against believing everything they read, including what they read on *Wikipedia*: "Anyone can create a website or pay to have a book published, then claim to be an expert . . ." ("Identifying reliable sources," 2016). It also advises readers to examine sources carefully, especially when they make claims that are "contradicted by the prevailing view within the relevant community, or that would significantly alter mainstream assumptions, especially in science, medicine, history, politics, and biographies of living people" ("Verifiability," 2016). However, everything is up to users; no editor at *Wikipedia* checks to make sure that these guidelines are followed.

Paragraph combines student's own ideas with quotations from multiple Wikipedia entries

Errors and Other Problems with *Wikipedia*

In spite of its stated policies, *Wikipedia* remains susceptible to certain problems. One problem is the assumption that the knowledge of the community is more valuable than the knowledge of acknowledged experts in a field. In other words, *Wikipedia* values crowd-sourced information more than the knowledge of an individual specialist. In his book *You Are Not a Gadget*, Lanier (2010) argues that *Wikipedia's* authors "implicitly celebrate the ideal of intellectual mob rule" (p. 144). According to Lanier, "Wikipedians always act out the ideal that the collective is closer to the truth and the individual voice is dispensable" (p. 144). Adherence to this ideal can have serious consequences for the accuracy of *Wikipedia* entries. For example, historian Timothy Messer-Kruse, an expert on American labor history, attempted to edit a *Wikipedia* article to correct a factual error in the entry on

THE LIMITATIONS OF *WIKIPEDIA*   6

Paragraph combines quotations from two Wikipedia entries and Lanier, as well as a long quotation from Messer-Kruse; it includes student's summary of Messer-Kruse's story and student's own ideas

the 1886 Chicago Haymarket Riot. Although Messer-Kruse has published extensively on the subject, his correction was rejected. Messer-Kruse's subsequent attempts to correct the entry — which had multiple errors — were dismissed as well. In an article he wrote for *The Chronicle of Higher Education*, Messer-Kruse recounted the experience, including a telling comment from one of the site's editors, with whom he had an online exchange:

> If all historians save one say that the sky was green in 1888, our policies require that we write, "Most historians write that the sky was green, but one says the sky was blue." As individual editors, we're not in the business of weighing claims, just reporting what reliable sources write. (Messer-Kruse, 2012)

In other words, *Wikipedia's* policy is to present all views, even incorrect ones, provided they are published in a reliable source ("Neutral Point of View," 2016).

Another problem with *Wikipedia* is the ease with which entries can be edited. Because anyone can edit entries, individuals can vandalize content by inserting incorrect information, obscene language, or even nonsense into articles. For example, entries for controversial people, such as President Donald Trump, financier George Soros, or Scientology founder L. Ron Hubbard, or for controversial subjects, such as abortion, are routinely vandalized. Sometimes the vandalism can be extremely harmful. One notorious case of vandalism involved John Seigenthaler, a journalist and former administrative assistant to Attorney General Robert Kennedy, who was falsely accused in *Wikipedia* of being involved in the assassinations of John F. Kennedy and Robert Kennedy. Ultimately, Seigenthaler contacted *Wikipedia* founder Jimmy Wales, threatened legal action, and even tracked down the writer who had inserted the libelous accusation. If a friend had not alerted Seigenthaler to the vandalized entry, it would have likely remained in place, with its false claim that Seigenthaler was "a suspected assassin who had defected to the Soviet Union for 13 years" (Torrenzano & Davis, 2011, pp. 60–63).

Paragraph contains student's summary of Seigenthaler's story from Torrenzano and Davis's *Digital Assassination,* as well as paraphrases and quotations from the book

THE LIMITATIONS OF *WIKIPEDIA*   7

In addition to misinformation and vandalism, bias is another problem for *Wikipedia*. Some critics have accused the site of having a liberal bias. Writing for the web publication Human Events, Scarborough (2010) noted that observers on the right have "long complained of *Wikipedia*'s liberal bias that infects voters with unflattering profiles of their candidates." In fact, a competitor, *Conservapedia*, lists many examples of this skewed coverage in *Wikipedia* entries ("Examples of Bias in *Wikipedia*," 2016). Other critics have identified different kinds of biases on the site. For example, a 2010 survey of *Wikipedia* contributors suggested that "less than 15 percent of its hundreds of thousands of contributors are women" (Cohen, 2011). This imbalance indicates a significant lack of women's perspectives on the site. In response, Sue Gardner, the executive director of the Wikimedia Foundation, "set a goal to raise the share of female contributors to 25 percent by 2015" (Cohen, 2011).[1]

As Gardner indicates, *Wikipedia* has tried to correct some of the problems that its critics have noted. For example, in response to criticism of its policy of allowing writers and editors to remain anonymous, Wales changed this policy. Now, writers and editors have to provide their user names and thus take responsibility for the content they contribute. In addition, *Wikipedia* has made it possible for administrators to block edits originating from certain Internet domains and to prevent certain writers and editors from posting or changing information. However, authorship is still a problem. Most readers have no idea who has written an article that they are reading or whether or not the writer can be trusted. Given *Wikipedia's* basic philosophy, it will be difficult to solve this problem.

Of course, even traditional encyclopedias have shortcomings. For example, a study by the journal *Nature* found that although

---

[1]By 2018, almost 17,000 new women's biographies had been added to *Wikipedia*. Even today, some critics assert that there are still serious examples of gender bias in *Wikipedia*'s content.

> Paragraph contains para-phrase from "Examples of Bias in Wikipedia," quotations from Scarborough and Cohen, and the student's own conclusions

THE LIMITATIONS OF *WIKIPEDIA*   8

Wikipedia included errors, the *Encyclopædia Britannica* also
did (Giles, 2005). *Britannica* — the oldest English-language
encyclopedia still in print at the time — ceased print publication
in 2012 after 244 years (Rousseau, 2012). However, this venerable
source of information persists online because people still value
its expertise and trust its credibility. As Jorge Cauz, the president
of Encyclopædia Britannica, Inc., observes, "While *Wikipedia* has
become ubiquitous, *Britannica* remains a consistently more reliable
source. In other words, *Britannica* brings scholarly knowledge to
an editorial process" (Rousseau, 2012). Although that editorial
process is not a 100 percent guarantee of accuracy, *Britannica*'s
staff of dedicated experts and specialists is more reliable than
anonymous *Wikipedia* posters. Moreover, conscientious and
knowledgeable editors work to make sure that entries are clear,
logical, coherent, and grammatically correct. The same cannot be
said for *Wikipedia*, which is known for its inconsistent treatment
of subjects and its ungrammatical and awkward prose.

Comparison to Traditional Sources

Supporters of *Wikipedia* defend the site against charges of
bias and errors, pointing out that even respected peer-reviewed
journals have problems. For example, some reviewers of articles
submitted for publication in peer-reviewed journals may have
conflicts of interest. A reviewer might reject an article that
challenges his or her own work, or editors may favor certain
authors over others. Also, it may be possible for a reviewer to
identify the work of a rival, especially if the number of people
working in a field is relatively small, and let bias influence his
or her evaluation of an article. Another problem is that it takes a
long time for articles in peer-reviewed journals to get into print.
Critics point out that by the time an article in a peer-reviewed
journal appears, it may be outdated. In short, peer-reviewed
journals may not be either as objective or as up-to-date as many
readers think they are.

> *Paragraph
> contains ideas
> found in several
> sources and the
> student's own
> ideas*

Conclusion

Conclusion

Despite their problems, articles that appear in an edited encyclopedia or journal are more trustworthy than those that appear in *Wikipedia*. These articles are thoroughly reviewed by editors or go through a peer-review process (that is, they are screened by experts in a field), and for this reason, they can be considered reliable sources of information. *Wikipedia*, however, is not a reliable research source. The fact that almost anyone can contribute an article or edit one at any time raises serious questions about *Wikipedia's* reliability. In addition, many articles contain factual errors. Although some errors are found and corrected immediately, others remain for a long time or go entirely unnoticed. Finally, articles frequently reflect the biases or political agendas of contributors and, as a result, present a one-sided or inaccurate view of a subject. All in all, *Wikipedia's* open-source philosophy makes it more prone to errors, inconsistencies, poor writing, and even vandalism, and for this reason, it should be used with caution. Perhaps the best that can be said of *Wikipedia* is that it is a good starting point for research. Although it is a useful site for getting an overview of a subject before doing in-depth research, it should not be considered a credible or authoritative academic source.

THE LIMITATIONS OF *WIKIPEDIA*   10

References

Chozick, A. (2013, June 30). Jimmy Wales is not an Internet
     billionaire. *The New York Times*. http://nytimes.com/2013/06/30
     /magazine/jimmy-wales-is-not-an-internet-billionaire.html

Cohen, N. (2011, January 31). Define gender gap? Look up
     Wikipedia's contributor list. *The New York Times*, p. A1+.

Examples of bias in *Wikipedia*. (2019, December 20). *Conservapedia*.
     http://www.conservapedia.com/Examples_of_Bias_in_Wikipedia

Gender Bias. (2019, October 6). *Wikipedia*. Retrieved March 12,
     2020, from en.wikipedia.org/wiki/Gender_bias_on_Wikipedia

Giles, J. (2005). Internet encyclopaedias go head to head. *Nature*,
     438, 900–901.

Grathwohl, C. (2011, January 11). *Wikipedia* comes of age.
     Chronicle of Higher Education. http://chronicle.com/article
     /article-content/125899

Help: page history. (2019, August 29). *Wikipedia*. Retrieved March 13,
     2020, from http://en.wikipedia.org/wiki/Help:Page_history

Identifying reliable sources. (2019, December 28). *Wikipedia*.
     Retrieved March 15, 2020, from http://en.wikipedia.org
     /wiki/Wikipedia:Identifying_reliable_sources

Lanier, J. (2010). *You are not a gadget: A manifesto*. Allen Lane.

Messer-Kruse, T. (2012, February 12). The "undue weight" of truth
     on *Wikipedia*. *Chronicle of Higher Education*. http://chronicle
     .com/article/The-Undue-Weight-of-Truth-on/130704

Neutral point of view. (2019, September 3). *Wikipedia*. Retrieved
     March 15, 2020, from http://en.wikipedia.org/wiki
     /Wikipedia:Neutral_point_of_view

No original research. (2019, October 1). *Wikipedia*. Retrieved
     March 15, 2020, from http://en.wikipedia.org/wiki
     /Wikipedia:No_original_research

THE LIMITATIONS OF *WIKIPEDIA*   11

Rousseau, C. (2012, March 13). *Encyclopædia Britannica* to
    end print editions. Yahoo! News. Retrieved from http://
    news.yahoo.com/encyclopaedia-britannica-end-print
    -editions-234637805.html

Scarborough, R. (2010, September 27). *Wikipedia* whacks the right.
    Human Events. http://www.humanevents.com/2010/09/27
    /wikipedia-whacks-the-right

Torrenzano, R., & Davis, M. (2011). *Digital assassination: Protecting
    your reputation, brand, or business against online attacks.*
    St. Martin's Press.

Verifiability. (2019, December 9). *Wikipedia*. Retrieved March 13,
    2020, from http://en.wikipedia.org/wiki/Wikipedia:Verifiability

Wikipedia. (2019, October 7). *Wikipedia*. Retrieved March 15, 2020,
    from http://en.wikipedia.org/wiki/Wikipedia

GLOSSARY

Abstract/Concrete language Abstract language names concepts or qualities that cannot be directly seen or touched: *love, emotion, evil, anguish*. Concrete language denotes objects or qualities that the senses can perceive: *fountain pen, leaky, shouting, rancid*. Abstract words are sometimes needed to express ideas, but they are very vague unless used with concrete supporting details. The abstract phrase, "The speaker was overcome with emotion," could mean almost anything, but the addition of concrete language clarifies the meaning: "He clenched his fist and shook it at the crowd" (anger).

Active reading Approaching a reading with a clear understanding of your purpose and marking or otherwise highlighting the text to help you understand what you are reading.

Allusion A brief reference to literature, history, the Bible, mythology, popular culture, and so on that readers are expected to recognize. An allusion evokes a vivid impression in very few words. "The gardener opened the gate, and suddenly we found ourselves in Eden" suggests in one word (*Eden*) the stunning beauty of the garden.

Analogy A form of comparison that explains an unfamiliar element by comparing it to another that is more familiar. Analogies also enable writers to put abstract or technical information in simpler, more concrete terms: "The effect of pollution on the environment is like that of cancer on the body."

Annotating The technique of recording one's responses to a reading selection by writing notes in the margins of the text. Annotating a text might involve asking questions, suggesting possible parallels with other selections or with the reader's own experience, arguing with the writer's points, commenting on the writer's style, or defining unfamiliar terms or concepts.

Antithesis A viewpoint opposite to one expressed in a *thesis*. In an argumentative essay, the thesis must be debatable. If no antithesis exists, the writer's thesis is not debatable. (See also **Thesis**.)

Argumentation The form of writing that takes a stand on an issue and attempts to convince readers by presenting a logical sequence of points supported by evidence. Unlike *persuasion*, which uses a number of different appeals, argumentation is primarily an appeal to reason. (See Chapter 14.)

Audience The people "listening" to a writer's words. Writers who are sensitive to their audience will carefully choose a tone, examples, and allusions that their readers will understand and respond to. For instance, an effective article attempting to persuade high school students not to drink alcohol would use examples and allusions pertinent to a teenager's life. Different examples would be chosen if the writer were addressing middle-aged members of Alcoholics Anonymous.

Basis for comparison   A fundamental similarity between two or more things that enables a writer to compare them. In a comparison of how two towns react to immigrants, the basis of comparison might be that both towns have a rapidly expanding immigrant population. (If one of the towns did not have any immigrants, this comparison would be illogical.)

Biases   Preferences or prejudices in favor of or against a stance.

Body paragraphs   The paragraphs that develop and support an essay's thesis.

Brainstorming   An invention technique that can be done individually or in a group. When writers brainstorm on their own, they jot down every fact or idea that relates to a particular topic. When they brainstorm in a group, they discuss a topic with others and write down the useful ideas that come up.

Causal chain   A sequence of events when one event causes another event, which in turn causes yet another event.

Cause and effect   The pattern of development that discusses either the reasons for an occurrence or the observed or predicted consequence of an occurrence. Often, both causes and effects are discussed in the same essay. (See Chapter 10.)

Causes   The reasons for an event, situation, or phenomenon. An *immediate cause* is an obvious one; a *remote cause* is less easily perceived. The *main cause* is the most important cause, whether it is immediate or remote. Other, less important causes that nevertheless encourage the effect in some way (for instance, by speeding it up or providing favorable circumstances for it) are called *contributory causes*.

Chronological order   The time sequence of events. Chronological order is often used to organize a narrative; it is also used to structure a process essay.

Claim   In Toulmin logic, the thesis or main point of an essay. Usually the claim is stated directly, but sometimes it is implied. (See also **Toulmin logic**.)

Classification and division   The pattern of development that uses these two related methods of organizing information. *Classification* involves searching for common characteristics among various items and grouping them accordingly, thereby imposing order on randomly organized information. *Division* breaks up an entity into smaller groups or elements. Classification generalizes; division specifies. (See Chapter 12.)

Cliché   An overused expression, such as *beauty is in the eye of the beholder, the good die young,* or *a picture is worth a thousand words.*

Clustering   A method of invention whereby a writer groups ideas visually by listing the main topic in the center of a page, circling it, and surrounding it with words or phrases that identify the major points to be addressed.

The writer then circles these words or phrases, creating new clusters or ideas for each of them.

Coherence The tight relationship between all the parts of an effective piece of writing. Such a relationship ensures that the writing will make sense to readers. For a piece of writing to be coherent, it must be logical and orderly, with effective *transitions* making the movement between sentences and paragraphs clear. Within and between paragraphs, coherence may also be enhanced by the repetition of key words and ideas, by the use of pronouns to refer to nouns mentioned previously, and by the use of parallel sentence structure.

Common knowledge Factual information that is widely available in reference sources, such as the dates of important historical events. Writers do not need to document common knowledge.

Comparison and contrast The pattern of development that focuses on similarities and differences between two or more subjects. In a general sense, *comparison* shows how two or more subjects are alike; *contrast* shows how they are different. (See Chapter 11; see also **Point-by-point comparison**; **Subject-by-subject comparison**.)

Conclusion The group of sentences or paragraphs that brings an essay to a close. To *conclude* means not only "to end" but also "to resolve." Although a conclusion does not review all the issues discussed in an essay, the conclusion is the place to show that those issues have been resolved. An effective conclusion indicates that the writer is committed to what has been expressed, and it is the writer's last chance to leave an impression or idea with readers.

Concrete language See **Abstract/Concrete language**.

Connotation The associations, meanings, or feelings a word suggests beyond its literal meaning. Literally, the word *home* means "one's place of residence," but *home* also connotes warmth and a sense of belonging. (See also **Denotation**.)

Contributory cause See **Causes**.

Deductive reasoning The method of reasoning that moves from a general premise to a specific conclusion. Deductive reasoning is the opposite of *inductive reasoning*. (See also **Syllogism**.)

Definition An explanation of a word's meaning; the pattern of development in which a writer explains what something or someone is. (See Chapter 13; see also **Extended definition**; **Formal definition**.)

Denotation The literal meaning of a word. The denotation of *home* is "one's place of residence." (See also **Connotation**.)

Description The pattern of development that presents a word picture of a thing, a person, a situation, or a series of events. (See Chapter 7; see also **Objective description**; **Subjective description**.)

Digression A remark or series of remarks that wanders from the main point of a discussion. In a personal narrative, a digression may be entertaining because of its irrelevance, but in other kinds of writing, it is likely to distract and confuse readers.

Division See **Classification and division**.

Documentation The formal way of giving credit to the sources a writer borrows words or ideas from. Documentation allows readers to evaluate a writer's sources and to consult them if they wish. Essays written for literature and writing classes use the documentation style recommended by the Modern Language Association (MLA). (See Chapter 18.)

Dominant impression The mood or quality that is central to a piece of writing.

Essay A short work of nonfiction writing on a single topic that usually expresses the author's impressions or opinions. An essay may be organized around one of the patterns of development presented in Chapters 6 through 14 of this book, or it may combine several of these patterns.

Ethos An appeal based on the character reputation of the writer.

Euphemism A polite term for an unpleasant concept. (*Passed away* is a euphemism for *died*.)

Evidence Facts and opinions used to support a statement, position, or idea. *Facts*, which may include statistics, may be drawn from research or personal experience; *opinions* may represent the conclusions of experts or the writer's own ideas.

Example A concrete illustration of a general point.

Exemplification The pattern of development that uses a single extended *example* or a series of shorter examples to support a thesis. (See Chapter 8.)

Extended definition A paragraph-, essay-, or book-length definition developed by means of one or more of the rhetorical strategies discussed in this book.

Fallacy A statement that resembles a logical argument but is actually flawed. Logical fallacies are often persuasive, but they unfairly manipulate readers to win agreement. Fallacies include begging the question, argument from analogy, personal (*ad hominem*) attacks, jumping to a conclusion (hasty or sweeping generalizations), false dilemmas (the either/or fallacy), equivocation, red herrings, you also (*tu quoque*), appeals to doubtful authority, misleading statistics, *post hoc* reasoning, and *non sequiturs*. See the section on "Recognizing Fallacies" (page 532) for explanations and examples.

Figures of speech (also known as *figurative language*) Imaginative language used to suggest a special meaning or create a special effect. Three of the most common figures of speech are *similes*, *metaphors*, and *personification*.

Formal definition A brief explanation of a word's meaning as it appears in the dictionary.

Formal outline A detailed construction that uses headings and subheadings to indicate the order in which key points and supporting details are presented in an essay.

Freewriting A method of invention that involves writing without stopping for a fixed period — perhaps five or ten minutes — without paying attention to spelling, grammar, or punctuation. The goal of freewriting is to let ideas flow and record them.

Grounds In Toulmin logic, the material that a writer uses to support a claim. Grounds may be evidence (facts or expert opinions) or appeals to the emotions or values of an audience. (See also **Toulmin logic**.)

Highlighting A technique used by a reader to record responses to a reading selection by marking the text with symbols. Highlighting a text might involve underlining important ideas, boxing key terms, numbering a series of related points, circling unfamiliar words (or placing question marks next to them), drawing vertical lines next to an interesting or important passage, drawing arrows to connect related points, or placing asterisks next to discussions of the selection's central issues or themes.

Imagery A set of verbal pictures of sensory experiences. These pictures, conveyed through concrete details, make a description vivid and immediate to the reader. Some images are literal ("The cows were so white they almost glowed in the dark"); others are more figurative ("The black-and-white cows looked like maps, with the continents in black and the seas in white"). A pattern of imagery (repeated images of, for example, shadows, forests, or fire) may run through a piece of writing.

Immediate cause See **Causes**.

Implied thesis An essay that conveys its main focus without explicitly stating it.

Inductive reasoning The method of reasoning that moves from specific evidence to a general conclusion based on this evidence. Inductive reasoning is the opposite of *deductive reasoning*.

Informal outline A list of points to be developed in an essay.

Instructions A kind of process essay whose purpose is to enable readers to *perform* a process. Instructions use the present tense and speak directly to readers: "Walk at a moderate pace for twenty minutes."

Introduction An essay's opening. Depending on the length of an essay, the introduction may be one paragraph or several paragraphs. In an introduction, a writer tries to encourage the audience to read the essay that follows. Therefore, the writer must choose tone and diction carefully, indicate what the essay is about, and suggest to readers what direction it will take.

Invention (also known as *prewriting*) The stage of writing when a writer explores the writing assignment, focuses ideas, and ultimately decides on a thesis for an essay. A writer might begin by thinking through the requirements of the assignment — the essay's purpose, length, and audience. Then, using one or more methods of invention — such as *freewriting, questions for probing, brainstorming, clustering*, and *journal writing* — the writer can formulate a tentative thesis and begin to write the essay.

Irony Language that points to a discrepancy between two different levels of meaning. *Verbal irony* is characterized by a gap between what is stated and what is really meant, which often has the opposite meaning—for instance, "his humble abode" (referring to a millionaire's estate). *Situational irony* points to a discrepancy between what actually happens and what readers expect will happen. This kind of irony is present, for instance, when a character, trying to frighten a rival, ends up frightening himself. *Dramatic irony* occurs when the reader understands more about what is happening in a story than the character who is telling the story does. For example, a narrator might tell an anecdote that he intends to illustrate how clever he is, while it is obvious to the reader from the story's events that the narrator has made a fool of himself because of his gullibility. (See also **Sarcasm**.)

Jargon The specialized vocabulary of a profession or academic field. Although the jargon of a particular profession is an efficient means of communication within that field, it may not be clear or meaningful to readers outside that profession.

Journal writing A method of invention that involves recording ideas that emerge from reading or other experiences and then exploring them in writing.

Literacy narrative A personal account focusing on the author's experiences with reading and writing.

Logos An appeal based on logic.

Looping A method of invention that involves isolating one idea from a piece of freewriting and using this idea as a focus for a new piece of freewriting.

Main cause See **Causes**.

Mapping See **Clustering**.

Metaphor A comparison of two dissimilar things that does not use the word *like* or *as* ("The small waves were the same, chucking the rowboat under the chin . . ."—E. B. White).

Narration The pattern of development that tells a story. (See Chapter 6.)

Objective description A detached, factual picture presented in a plain and direct manner. Although pure objectivity is impossible to achieve, writers of science papers, technical reports, and news articles, among others, strive for precise language that is free of value judgments.

Occasion The situation (or situations) that leads someone to write about a topic. For academic writing, it will almost always be a specific assignment from an instructor. The occasion helps a writer determine the purpose, audience, and format of the piece.

Outline See **Formal outline**; **Informal outline**.

Paradox A statement that seems self-contradictory or absurd but is nonetheless true.

Paragraph The basic unit of an essay. A paragraph is composed of related sentences that together express a single idea. This main idea is often stated in a single *topic sentence*. Paragraphs are also graphic symbols on the page, mapping the progress of the ideas in the essay and providing visual breaks for readers.

Parallelism The use of similar grammatical elements within a sentence or sentences. "I like hiking, skiing, and to cook" is not parallel because *hiking* and *skiing* are gerund forms (*-ing*), whereas *to cook* is an infinitive form. Revised for parallelism, the sentence could read either "I like hiking, skiing, and cooking" or "I like to hike, to ski, and to cook." As a stylistic technique, parallelism can provide emphasis through repetition, "Walk groundly, talk profoundly, drink roundly, sleep soundly " (William Hazlitt). Parallelism is also a powerful oratorical technique: "Until justice is blind to color, until education is unaware of race, until opportunity is unconcerned with the color of men's skins, emancipation will be a proclamation but not a fact" (Lyndon B. Johnson). Finally, parallelism can increase *coherence* within a paragraph or an essay.

Paraphrase The restatement of another person's words in one's own words, following the order and emphasis of the original. Paraphrase is frequently used in source-based essays, where the purpose is to use information gathered during research to support the ideas in the essay. For example, Steven Conn's "He was deeply ambivalent about the institution of slavery. As the war began, he believed that saving the Union, not abolishing slavery, was the cause worth fighting for. But as the war ground gruesomely on, he began to see that ending slavery was the only way to save the Union without making a mockery of the nation's founding ideals" (page 421) might be paraphrased as, "Though Lincoln did not explicitly favor slavery at the outset of the Civil War, his priority was preserving the Union; as the war continued, he came to understand that abolishing slavery was necessary to realize that goal."

Pathos An appeal based on emotion.

Personification Describing concepts or objects as if they were human ("the chair slouched"; "the wind sighed outside the window").

Persuasion The method a writer uses to move an audience to adopt a belief or follow a course of action. To persuade an audience, a writer relies on the various appeals — to the emotions, to reason, or to ethics. Persuasion is different from *argumentation*, which appeals primarily to reason.

Plagiarism Presenting the words or ideas of someone else as if they were actually one's own (whether intentionally or unintentionally). Plagiarism should always be avoided.

Point-by-point comparison A comparison in which the writer first makes a point about one subject and then follows it with a comparable point about the other subject. (See also **Subject-by-subject comparison**.)

***Post hoc* reasoning** A logical fallacy that involves looking back at two events that occurred in chronological sequence and wrongly assuming that the first event caused the second. For example, just because a car will not start after a thunderstorm, one cannot automatically assume that the storm caused the problem.

Prewriting See **Invention**.

Principle of classification In a classification-and-division essay, the quality the items have in common. For example, if a writer were classifying automobiles, one principle of classification might be "repair records."

Process The pattern of development that presents a series of steps in a procedure in chronological order and shows how this sequence of steps leads to a particular result. (See Chapter 9.)

Process explanation A kind of process essay whose purpose is to enable readers to understand a process rather than perform it.

Purpose A writer's reason for writing. A writer's purpose may, for example, be to entertain readers with an amusing story, to inform them about a dangerous disease, to move them to action by enraging them with an example of injustice, or to change their perspective by revealing a hidden dimension of a person or situation.

Quotation The exact words of a source, enclosed in quotation marks. A quotation should be used only to present a particularly memorable statement or to avoid a paraphrase that would change the meaning of the original.

Refutation The attempt to counter an opposing argument by revealing its weaknesses. Three of the most common weaknesses are logical flaws in the argument, inadequate evidence, and irrelevance. Refutation greatly strengthens an argument by showing that the writer is aware of the complexity of the issue and has considered opposing viewpoints.

Remote cause See **Causes**.

Rhetorical question A question asked for effect and not meant to be answered.

Rogerian argument A strategy put forth by psychologist Carl Rogers that rejects the adversarial approach that characterizes many arguments. Rather than attacking the opposition, Rogers suggests acknowledging the validity of opposing positions. By finding areas of agreement, a Rogerian argument reduces conflict and increases the chance that the final position will satisfy all parties.

Sarcasm Deliberately insincere and biting irony — for example, "That's okay — I love it when you borrow things and don't return them."

Satire Writing that uses wit, irony, and ridicule to attack foolishness, incompetence, or evil in a person or idea. Satire has a different purpose from comedy, which usually intends simply to entertain. For a classic example of satire, see Jonathan Swift's "A Modest Proposal" (page 693).

Sexist language Language that stereotypes people according to gender. Writers often use plural constructions to avoid sexist language. For example, *the doctors . . . they* can be used instead of *the doctor . . . he*. Words such as *police officer* and *firefighter* can be used instead of *policeman* and *fireman*.

Simile A comparison of two dissimilar things using the word *like* or *as* ("Hills Like White Elephants" — Ernest Hemingway).

Slang Informal words whose meanings vary from locale to locale or change as time passes. Slang is frequently associated with a particular group of people — for example, bikers, musicians, or urban youth. Slang is inappropriate in college writing.

Subject-by-subject comparison A comparison that discusses one subject in full and then goes on to discuss the next subject. (See also **Point-by-point comparison**.)

Subjective description A description that contains value judgments (*a saintly person*, for example). Whereas objective language is distanced from an event or object, *subjective language* is involved. A subjective description focuses on the author's reaction to the event, conveying not just a factual record of details but also their significance. Subjective language may include poetic or colorful words that impart a judgment or an emotional response (*stride, limp, meander, hobble, stroll, plod,* or *shuffle* instead of *walk*). Subjective descriptions often include *figures of speech*.

Summary The ideas of a source as presented in one's own words. Unlike a paraphrase, a summary conveys only a general sense of a passage, without following the order and emphasis of the original.

Support The ideas that explain and expand your thesis or argument. They might include reasons, facts, examples, or statistics. The support helps to convince your readers that your thesis is reasonable.

Syllogism A basic form of deductive reasoning. Every syllogism includes three parts: a major premise that makes a general statement ("Confinement is physically and psychologically damaging"), a minor premise that makes a related but more specific statement ("Zoos confine animals"), and a conclusion drawn from these two premises ("Therefore, zoos are physically and psychologically damaging to animals").

Symbol A person, event, or object that stands for something more than its literal meaning.

Synonym A word with the same basic meaning as another word. A synonym for *loud* is *noisy*. Most words in the English language have several synonyms, but each word has unique nuances or shades of meaning. (See also **Connotation**.)

Synthesize Blending your own ideas and interpretations with those of your source material. It is important to make sure that your own ideas dominate the discussion and that any information from outside sources is cited correctly.

Thesis An essay's main idea; the idea that all the points in the body of the essay support. A thesis may be implied, but it is usually stated explicitly in the form of a *thesis statement*. In addition to conveying the essay's main idea, the thesis statement may indicate the writer's approach to the subject and the writer's purpose. It may also indicate the pattern of development that will structure the essay.

Topic sentence A sentence stating the main idea of a paragraph. Often, but not always, the topic sentence opens the paragraph.

Toulmin logic A method of structuring an argument according to the way arguments occur in everyday life. Developed by philosopher Stephen Toulmin, Toulmin logic divides an argument into three parts: the *claim*, the *grounds*, and the *warrant*.

Transitions Words or expressions that link ideas in a piece of writing. Long essays frequently contain *transitional paragraphs* that connect one part of the essay to another. Writers use a variety of transitional expressions, such as *afterward, because, consequently, for instance, furthermore, however,* and *likewise*. See the list of transitions on page 56.

Unity The desirable attribute of a paragraph in which every sentence relates directly to the paragraph's main idea. This main idea is often stated in a *topic sentence*.

Warrant In Toulmin logic, the inference that connects the claim to the grounds. The warrant can be a belief that is taken for granted or an assumption that underlies the argument. (See also **Toulmin logic**.)

Writing process The sequence of tasks a writer undertakes when writing an essay. During *invention*, or *prewriting*, the writer gathers information and ideas and develops a thesis. During the *arrangement* stage, the writer organizes material into a logical sequence. During *drafting and revision*, the essay is actually written and then rewritten. Finally, during *editing and proofreading*, the writer puts the finishing touches on the essay by correcting misspellings, checking punctuation, searching for grammatical inaccuracies, and so on. These stages occur in no fixed order; many effective writers move back and forth among them. (See Chapters 2–5.)

ACKNOWLEDGMENTS

INDEX

Bedford/St. Martin's puts writers *first*

From day one, our goal has been simple: to provide inspiring resources that are grounded in best practices for teaching reading and writing. For more than 35 years, Bedford/St. Martin's has partnered with the field, listening to teachers, scholars, and students about the support writers need.

Contact your Bedford/St. Martin's sales representative or visit **macmillanlearning.com** to learn more.

. . . .

Looking for digital formats?

- Achieve with *Patterns for College Writing*, Fifteenth Edition, puts writing and revision at the core of your course, with a dedicated composition space that guides students through draft, review, Source Check, reflection, and revision. For details, visit **macmillanlearning.com /college/us/englishdigital**.

- *Popular e-book formats*
  For details about our e-book partners, visit **macmillanlearning.com/ebooks**.

Develop writing skills with patterns that make sense.

Patterns for College Writing, Fifteenth Edition, breaks down the reading, writing, and research processes into manageable, accessible patterns like narration, description, argumentation, and more. For every writing pattern, the text provides instruction, student samples, visual texts, and a variety of classic and contemporary essays—each accompanied by headnotes and discussion questions that leave students better prepared for college writing.

"*Patterns for College Writing* is the most current and comprehensive freshman composition reader available right now. With meaningful rhetorical content and an interesting and diverse array of reading selections, *Patterns* offers the new college student a world of substantive material." —Cheryl Saba, *Cape Fear Community College*

Achieve with *Patterns for College Writing*, Fifteenth Edition, puts writing and revision at the core of your course, with a dedicated composition space that guides students through draft, review, Source Check, reflection, and revision. For details, visit **macmillanlearning.com/college/us/englishdigital**.

Also available as a loose-leaf edition or as an e-book.

Cover image: sbelov / Getty Images

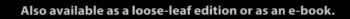

macmillanlearning.com

 bedford/st.martin's
Macmillan Learning

macmillan learning

TDEL-9PG1-L3ZI

AUTHENTIC

ISBN 978-1-319-24379-1

90000

9 781319 243791